Adverse Impact

Implications for Organizational
Staffing and High Stakes Selection

The Organizational Frontiers Series

The Organizational Frontiers Series is sponsored by The Society for Industrial and Organizational Psychology (SIOP). Launched in 1983 to make scientific contributions to the field, the series has attempted to publish books on cutting-edge theory, research, and theory-driven practice in Industrial/Organizational psychology and related organizational science disciplines.

Our overall objective is to inform and to stimulate research for SIOP members (students, practitioners, and researchers) and people in related disciplines including the other subdisciplines of psychology, organizational behavior, human resource management, and labor and industrial relations. The volumes in the Organizational Frontiers Series have the following goals:

- Focus on research and theory in organizational science, and the implications for practice
- Inform readers of significant advances in theory and research in psychology and related disciplines that are relevant to our research and practice
- Challenge the research and practice community to develop and adapt new ideas and to conduct research on these developments
- Promote the use of scientific knowledge in the solution of public policy issues and increased organizational effectiveness

The volumes originated in the hope that they would facilitate continuous learning and a continuing research curiosity about organizational phenomena on the part of both scientists and practitioners.

The Organizational Frontiers Series

SIOP Organizational Frontiers Series

Series Editor

Robert D. Pritchard
University of Central Florida

Outtz: (2009) *Adverse Impact: Implications for Organizational Staffing and High Stakes Selection*

Kozlowski/Salas: (2009) *Learning, Training, and Development in Organizations*

Klein/Becker/Meyer: (2009) *Commitment in Organizations: Accumulated Wisdom and New Directions*

Salas/Goodwin/Burke: (2009) *Team Effectiveness in Complex Organizations: Cross-Disciplinary Perspectives and Approaches*

Kanfer/Chen/Pritchard: (2008) *Work Motivation: Past, Present, and Future*

De Dreu/Gelfand: (2008) *The Psychology of Conflict and Conflict Management in Organizations*

Ostroff/Judge: (2007) *Perspectives on Organizational Fit*

Baum/Frese/Baron: (2007) *The Psychology of Entrepreneurship*

Weekley/Ployhart: (2006) *Situational Judgment Tests: Theory, Measurement, and Application*

Dipboye/Colella: (2005) *Discrimination at Work: The Psychological and Organizational Bases*

Griffin/O'Leary-Kelly: (2004) *The Dark Side of Organizational Behavior*

Hofmann/Tetrick: (2003) *Health and Safety in Organizations*

Jackson/Hitt/DeNisi: (2003) *Managing Knowledge for Sustained Competitive Knowledge*

Barrick/Ryan: (2003) *Personality and Work*

Lord/Klimoski/Kanfer: (2002) *Emotions in the Workplace*

Drasgow/Schmitt: (2002) *Measuring and Analyzing Behavior in Organizations*

Feldman: (2002) *Work Careers*

Zaccaro/Klimoski: (2001) *The Nature of Organizational Leadership*

Rynes/Gerhart: (2000) *Compensation in Organizations*

Klein/Kozlowski: (2000) *Multilevel Theory, Research and Methods in Organizations*

Ilgen/Pulakos: (1999) *The Changing Nature of Performance*

Earley/Erez: (1997) *New Perspectives on International Industrial/ Organizational Psychology*

Murphy: (1996) *Individual Differences and Behavior in Organizations*

Guzzo/Salas: (1995) *Team Effectiveness and Decision Making*

Howard: (1995) *The Changing Nature of Work*

Schmitt/Borman: (1993) *Personnel Selection in Organizations*

Zedeck: (1991) *Work, Families, and Organizations*

Schneider: (1990) *Organizational Culture and Climate*

Goldstein: (1989) *Training and Development in Organizations*

Campbell/Campbell: (1988) *Productivity in Organizations*

Hall: (1987) *Career Development in Organizations*

Adverse Impact

Implications for Organizational Staffing and High Stakes Selection

Edited by
James L. Outtz

Routledge
Taylor & Francis Group
New York London

Routledge
Taylor & Francis Group
270 Madison Avenue
New York, NY 10016

Routledge
Taylor & Francis Group
27 Church Road
Hove, East Sussex BN3 2FA

Printed in the United States of America on acid-free paper
10 9 8 7 6 5 4 3 2 1

International Standard Book Number: 978-0-8058-6374-1 (Hardback)

Library of Congress Cataloging-in-Publication Data

Adverse impact : implications for organizational staffing and high stakes
    selection / edited by James Outtz.
        p. cm. -- (SIOP organizational frontiers series)
    Includes bibliographical references and index.
    ISBN 978-0-8058-6374-1 (alk. paper)
        1. Employee selection. 2. Employment tests. 3. Personnel management.
    4. Psychology, Industrial. I. Outtz, James. II. Society for Industrial and
    Organizational Psychology (U.S.).

    HF5549.5.S38A385 2010
    658.3'112--dc22   2009003530

Visit the Taylor & Francis Web site at
http://www.taylorandfrancis.com

and the Psychology Press Web site at
http://www.psypress.com

Dedicated to C.J. Bartlett, whose mentoring and guidance remain with me.

Contents

Section IV   Facets of the Adverse Impact Problem

Section V   Adverse Impact From an International Perspective

Section VI Methods of Reducing Adverse Impact

Series Foreword

This is the 31st book in the Organizational Frontiers Series of books. The overall purpose of the series volumes is to promote the scientific status of the field. Ray Katzell first edited the series. He was followed by Irwin Goldstein, Sheldon Zedeck, and Neal Schmitt. The topics of the volumes and the volume editors are chosen by the editorial board, or individuals propose volumes to the editorial board. The series editor and the editorial board then work with the volume editor(s) in planning the volume.

The success of the series is evident in the high number of sales (now well over 50,000). Volumes have also received excellent reviews and individual chapters as well as volumes have been cited frequently.

This volume, edited by James Outtz, presents current thinking and research on the topic of adverse impact in organizations. Adverse impact occurs when there is a significant difference in organizational outcomes such as hiring rates, promotion, compensation, or college admissions to the disadvantage of one or more groups defined on the basis of demographic characteristics such as race, ethnicity, gender, or age etc. This phenomenon is important and often misunderstood in our field. A major contribution of this volume is to first to conceptualize this concept and the associated variables around it. However, the most important contribution of the volume is to present a comprehensive assessment of adverse impact that integrates scientific research and practical issues within a conceptual/theoretical framework. In the past, most of the work on this topic has been atheoretical and the conceptual foundation has not always been clear. Practically all of the published research has focused on descriptions of the magnitude of subgroup differences and the measures that produce them. However, there is a conceptual/theoretical position from which adverse impact can be studied and this volume discusses that in detail.

The editors and chapter authors deserve our gratitude for clearly communicating the nature, application, and implications of the theory and research described in this book. Production of a volume such as this involves the hard work and cooperative effort of many individuals. The editors, the chapter authors, and the editorial board all played important roles in this endeavor. As all royalties from the series volumes are used to help support SIOP, none of the editors or authors received any remuneration. The editors and authors deserve our appreciation for engaging in a difficult task for the sole purpose of furthering our understanding of organizational science. We also want to express our gratitude to Anne

Duffy, our editor at Routledge/Psychology Press, who has been a great help in the planning and production of the volume.

Robert D. Pritchard
University of Central Florida
Series Editor

Preface

The purpose of this volume is to present, in a single repository, the current thinking of researchers and practitioners on the issue of subgroup differences in selection and high-stakes assessment. Subgroup differences, or *adverse impact*, present one of the most troublesome problems facing organizations not only in the United States, but also in Europe and other countries. Selection procedures are the gates that determine access to jobs, education, and professional status. If certain subgroups perform less well on these procedures, the outcome has significant social, economic, and legal ramifications. In this volume, scholars in the field of industrial-organizational psychology and related sciences address adverse impact from several perspectives, including what it is, its history, how it is measured, its likely sources, and most important, what we know about reducing it.

The intent of this volume is to harness the expertise of individuals who have researched, written about, and sought to reduce subgroup differences in selection. The hope is that the volume presents a comprehensive, science-based body of knowledge that will be a resource for the business and academic community. Adverse impact is addressed from a practical as well as theoretical perspective that will allow the reader to begin to understand its origins.

Although adverse impact encompasses subgroup differences based on a variety of demographic characteristics, including race, age, religion, and disability, the focus of this volume is on subgroup differences based on race. The primary reason is that reducing racial differences has proved to be an intractable problem, and as a consequence, this topic has drawn substantial social, scientific, and legal scrutiny. Focus on the racial aspect of subgroup differences is not intended to suggest that differences based on other demographic characteristics are in any way less significant.

This is a volume for those who have more than a casual interest in the problem of subgroup differences in selection and high-stakes assessment. Each contributor approaches the subject at a level of detail and scientific rigor that should enhance understanding of the content. The intended audience includes graduate and undergraduate students and faculty in business, psychology, and related disciplines. It also includes human resource managers, practitioners, licensing boards, and college admissions officers. We hope you find the information in this volume relevant, informative, and thought provoking.

This volume is unique in that it attempts to describe adverse impact from different perspectives and offer a theoretical foundation from which to discuss why it occurs. In doing so, a deeper understanding of what is needed to minimize adverse impact and what approaches are likely to be most effective in this regard may be acquired.

Overview of Chapters

In Chapter 1, Zedeck discusses the history and evolution of the concept of adverse impact. He notes that the basic definition comes from the *Uniform Guidelines on Employee Selection Procedures*.[1] He points out that a finding of adverse impact is important because it triggers several requirements. The organization either must demonstrate that the procedure causing the adverse impact is valid or attempt to reduce the adverse impact. Zedeck describes the most common methods of determining whether adverse impact exists and notes that decisions about adverse impact are not based solely on statistical evidence. He discusses the sections of the Uniform Guidelines that directly address adverse impact. Zedeck discusses the evolution of adverse impact in case law and the parallel evolution of scientific research on the topic.

In Chapter 2, Bobko and Roth compare use of the four-fifths rule and statistical significance tests in determining adverse impact. They point out that both methods are mentioned in the Uniform Guidelines. They call attention to the fact, however, that these two methods are based on different premises and logic. They review both methods for utility and potential shortcomings in assessing adverse impact. Bobko and Roth note that the four-fifths rule and statistical significance testing have important uses and limitations. They summarize useful facets and concerns with regard to each approach.

In Chapter 3, Outtz and Newman present a theoretical model of adverse impact. They attempt to integrate the psychological research literature within a social and legal context. Outtz and Newman use models of cognitive ability as well as current discussions regarding the concept of race to propose a theory of adverse impact. They advocate a number of principles and objectives for studying and discussing adverse impact, including (a) focusing on parameters that can be empirically estimated; (b) recognizing that these parameters can take on a range of values between the extremes of 1.0 and 0.0; (c) improving construct validity in high-stakes cognitive testing (which constructs are being measured, what percentage of variance in these constructs can be explained by known antecedents); (d) recognizing the role of the testing industry in making empirical estimates available; (e) recognizing the role of industrial and organizational psychologists in studying the multilevel mechanisms (psychological, sociological, and economic) underlying racial differences in test performance; and (f) viewing race and occupational opportunity in historical context (in contrast to ignoring race, opportunity, and history).

In Chapter 4, Goldstein, Scherbaum, and Yusko revisit the issue of intelligence (defined as g; i.e., general cognitive ability or general mental ability), adverse impact, and personnel selection. They suggest that there should be a broader perspective with regard to intelligence, the way it is defined and measured, and the concept of adverse impact. They explore fundamental questions regarding the intelligence construct in an attempt to understand better the causes of adverse impact and ways to mitigate it. They review the psychological literature with regard to g and note that this literature has led to the acceptance of certain assumptions in the field of personnel selection that, on closer scrutiny, should be questioned. Goldstein, Scherbaum, and Yusko reach this conclusion by examining a number of approaches to conceptualizing and measuring intelligence that show promise in reducing adverse impact.

In Chapter 5, Murphy argues that the univariate models typically used to assess the validity, utility, and impact of psychological tests are either incomplete or misleading. He begins by pointing out that members of demographic groups receive systematically different scores on many of the tests and other assessments used to make high-stakes decisions, such as admission to college or selection for a job. The most common of these tests are tests of cognitive ability. He notes that the cognitive ability tests and assessments in question are often among the best-available predictors based on cost and predictive validity. Murphy points out that continued use of these tests, however, is problematic because test score differences are typically much larger than differences in job performance, academic achievement, and other criteria. He argues, therefore, that the use of cognitive tests results in substantially greater rejection rates for minority applicants than can be justified on the basis of differences in performance.

Murphy suggests that a number of things have to be done to address the problem adequately. First, he suggests that studies of adverse impact inappropriately treat it as a univariate problem in which validity is described in terms of the correlation between a test and overall performance. He argues that this approach is limiting because it treats adverse impact as a consequence of an organization's attempt to achieve a *single* goal, maximizing job performance. He makes the point that organizations attempt to satisfy many goals when making selection decisions, and this fact leads to a different set of conclusions about adverse impact and how to address it. Murphy makes the case that if the success or failure of a selection system is determined on the basis of multiple criteria, then multivariate models (models that define success in terms of multiple dimensions) are needed to evaluate fully that selection system or the effects of different approaches designed to reduce adverse impact.

In Chapter 6, Hattrup and Roberts expand on the discussion of the multidimensionality of performance and present an even broader view of the constructs and issues relevant to conceptualizing the adverse impact and validity problem. They first take issue with the notion that adverse impacts create a dilemma or trade-off between selection quality and diversity. They note that we may not really know with certainty that there is a trade-off. They suggest that to establish that there is a trade-off, we must explore and delineate the criteria that drive decision making in organizations with regard to selection quality, adverse impact, and diversity. Hattrup and Roberts point out that trade-offs require consideration of competing goals, yet the facts that drive the value of these goals to the organization are seldom addressed explicitly. They offer a critical analysis of the so-called validity-diversity dilemma and explore the values that drive what organizations consider important.

There appear to be multiple, concurrent discussions of adverse impact in the academic and legal communities. In Chapter 7, Tippins provides an assessment of adverse impact from the perspective of an organizational consultant. Providing advice to organizations about how to address the adverse impact problem is a daunting task. The consultant must be cognizant of the many goals the organization may have and craft solutions that best meet the organization's needs. Tippins describes the issues confronted by practitioners when dealing with adverse impact in the context of providing advice to employers. She addresses the very specific and pragmatic questions that the practitioner must address. As an example, she addresses the question of which statistics should be used to calculate adverse impact and the pros and cons of each. Another seemingly straightforward, but in fact very difficult, question Tippins addresses regards which data set to use to calculate adverse impact statistics. For example, if applicant data are available, from which time period should the data be drawn? From which geographic locations should applicant data be drawn? Should data be collapsed across regions? Her recommendations provide useful guidance at the ground level and demonstrate the nexus between the scientific literature and current practice.

At the heart of any discussion of adverse impact is performance. Whether defined in terms of academic achievement or job performance, the objective of selection tests is to identify the best performers. It stands to reason then that the possibility of bias in evaluations of performance is a troubling issue. In Chapter 8, Landy revisits the topic of performance rating. Over 30 years ago, he and Jim Farr examined the psychological literature on performance rating and put forth a number of conclusions and propositions. Landy points out that two of those propositions have become somewhat controversial. The first was that a moratorium should be declared on rating scale format. The second was that, from data available at the time, there was little evidence of bias in ratings based on demographic characteristics such as race, gender, or age. Landy notes that the proposition of a lack of bias in performance rating has become increasingly central to arguments of employment discrimination. He notes that plaintiffs often suggest that performance ratings are unduly subjective and thus lend themselves to discriminatory decision making.

Some 30 years later, Landy revisits the issue and presents his conclusions. This time, he examined 10 meta-analyses and 134 individual studies of performance rating. He reports results separately for meta-analyses and individual studies. He points out the methodological flaws in the research designs and factors them into his conclusions. He concludes that (a) it appears there are often significant differences between white and black mean ratings to the disadvantage of black ratees, but all things considered, any Rater × Ratee variance is small; (b) with some possibility for exceptions, women are more likely to receive higher ratings than men, all other things being equal; (c) there is no evidence to suggest that older workers receive significantly lower performance ratings than younger workers; and (d) there are no data available to address the issues of possible bias in performance ratings of disabled workers. He notes that most data related to disability and performance judgments come from laboratory experiments asking students to assume the role of an employer; therefore, these studies are not included in his review.

While Landy focuses on subgroup differences in performance ratings, McKay (Chapter 9) expands the discussion to include moderators of subgroup differences. He discusses black–white and Hispanic–white mean differences as well as differences based on gender. McKay describes the current state of affairs in terms of what we know and do not know about adverse impact in work performance. Consistent with Landy, McKay concludes that research literature shows black–white mean differences in work performance disfavoring blacks. He examines these differences, however, for moderators including measurement method, cognitive loading, job complexity, measurement level, and data source. He incorporates a number of theoretical approaches from disciplines other than industrial and organizational psychology to explain possible moderators of subgroup differences in performance.

In Chapter 10, Cascio, Jacobs, and Silva describe the results of three decades of work in public sector selection. They describe the evolution of a process that broadens the scope of characteristics tested and the effect with regard to validity and adverse impact. They discuss strategies for reducing adverse impact that appear to work well and those that work less well.

Kehoe, in Chapter 11, describes the relationship between adverse impact and various methods for selecting cut scores. He notes that organizations select cut scores for a variety of reasons, only some of which are directly related to adverse impact. Kehoe suggests that cut scores almost always have effects other than adverse impact; thus, a combination of outcomes (e.g., organizational goals with respect to diversity, quality of employees, and legal risks) determines which cut score is most appropriate in a given situation. He argues that the selection system designer's role is to provide accurate information and recommendations, and that the managers or human resource leaders ultimately own the key decisions regarding specific cut scores.

In Chapter 12, Sackett and Shen focus on racial differences on tests in the cognitive domain, including achievement tests, to show that the adverse impact problem reaches far beyond personnel selection. They present data that shows racial group differences in test performance from preschool to application for college. They examine the question of whether there is something specific about the employment context that causes or contributes to subgroup differences.

Hanges and Feinberg (Chapter 13) expand the discussion of adverse impact beyond the boundaries of the United States to the European Union. They argue that adverse impact is a global problem that should be examined from an international, cross-cultural perspective. They make the point that studying adverse impact across nations might change the way we think about its causes.

In Chapter 14, Kriek and Dowdeswell provide a unique international perspective by examining adverse impact in South Africa, a country that has struggled with racial conflict for decades. They note that, after a long history of racial segregation and strife, South Africa has set achieving equality in the workplace as a primary goal. They note, however, that the demand for immediate diversity in the workplace has led to a shift from getting the best people to getting the "right" people in terms of racial makeup. They describe the challenges this presents for organizations that desire to maximize the utility of their selection systems.

The final section of the book is devoted to methods of reducing adverse impact. Aguinis and Smith begin the discussion, in Chapter 15, by focusing on the often-used strategy of lowering the cut score. They argue that simply lowering the cut score to reduce adverse impact ignores the issue of test bias, which often exists unbeknown to the test user. They suggest that this can lead to unexpected performance levels of individuals selected. It can also lead to unexpected levels of applicants selected who perform poorly (false positives) and applicants rejected who would perform well (false negatives). They offer a decision-making model to show why information about test bias should be an explicit component of the decision-making process.

In Chapter 16, Schmitt and Quinn provide a candid assessment of the state of affairs with regard to minimizing adverse impact. They define the problem as one of determining the best way to balance organizational concerns regarding maximization of expected levels of performance against the individual, social, and organizational desire for a diverse workforce/student body and equitable treatment of members of different racial/ethnic groups. They explore various ways researchers have sought to produce valid selection devices and minimize subgroup mean differences.

In all too many instances, the problem of adverse impact is addressed after the fact—that is, after selection decisions have been made. In Chapter 17, Sackett, De Corte, and Lievens describe attempts to estimate, in advance, the likely impact of a given selection system. They make estimates based on factors such as expected magnitude of subgroup differences, interpredictor correlations, and predictor-criteria correlations. They summarize a number of decision aids for adverse impact planning and the advantages of each.

In Chapter 18, Goldstein and Lundquist provide a historical account of a major project, at the Coca-Cola Company, aimed at promoting and fostering equal opportunity in compensation, promotion, and career advancement. This effort, naturally, had to focus on adverse impact or subgroup differences and systemic programs designed to address them. Goldstein and Lundquist provide a brief history of the legal origins of the project and then describe the challenges of trying to implement change in an environment of legal scrutiny. They describe their efforts as part of a task force formed as a result of a settlement agreement entered by the Coca-Cola Company. Their description of this 5-year journey demonstrates the critical role industrial and organizational psychologists can play in addressing organizational and legal problems.

I owe thanks to many people who have provided assistance and encouragement during the planning and writing of this book. First and foremost, I would like to thank each of the contributors who so generously took time to share their thoughts, experiences, and perspectives. Special thanks to Robert D. Pritchard, who provided valuable suggestions during the early planning of the volume. Thanks also to Anne Duffy, senior editor at Routledge/Psychology Press/Taylor & Francis for her seemingly limitless patience during the entire process and to the reviewers commissioned by the publisher.

Finally, I would like to thank my wife, Janice (for putting up with me for some 36 years now); my son, Jabari; and my daughter, Hasina, for their love and support.

Note

1. Equal Employment Opportunity Commission, Civil Service Commission, Department of Labor & Department of Justice. (1978). *Uniform Guidelines on Employee Selection Procedures*. Washington, DC: Author.

Contributors

Herman Aguinis is the Dean's Research Professor in the Department of Management and Entrepreneurship at Indiana University's Kelley School of Business. His programs of research include organizational behavior, human resource management, and research methods and analysis. He is the author of *Performance Management* (2nd edition, 2009), *Applied Psychology in Human Resource Management* (with W. F. Cascio), and *Regression Analysis for Categorical Moderators* (2004). In addition, he has edited *Opening the Black Box of Editorship* (2008, with Y. Baruch, A. M. Konrad, & W. H. Starbuck) and *Test-Score Banding in Human Resource Selection* (2004). Further, he has written about 70 refereed journal articles, 40 book chapters, monographs in edited series, and other publications and delivered more than 150 presentations at professional conferences. Dr. Aguinis is a fellow of the American Psychological Association, the Association for Psychological Science, and the Society for Industrial and Organizational Psychology. He served as editor-in-chief of *Organizational Research Methods* (2005–2007), has also served as chair of the Research Methods Division of the Academy of Management, as program chair of the Iberoamerican Academy of Management, and as an elected member of the Executive Committee of the Human Resources Division. He currently is associate editor of the American Psychological Association's *Handbook of Industrial and Organizational Psychology*, guest co-editor for a special issue of *Journal of Management* on "bridging micro and macro research domains," and serves or has served on the editorial boards of 13 journals.

Philip Bobko is professor of management and psychology at Gettysburg College. His research interests and publications span several topics in methodology, human resources management, and organizational behavior. He has also published a text on correlation and regression analysis (Sage), co-authored several handbook chapters in industrial/organizational psychology, and served as editor of the *Journal of Applied Psychology*. He earned a PhD from Cornell University and a BS from the Massachusetts Institute of Technology.

Wayne F. Cascio received his PhD in industrial and organizational psychology from the University of Rochester. Currently, he holds the Robert Reynolds Chair in Global Leadership at the University of Colorado Denver. He has served as president of the Society for Industrial and Organizational Psychology, as chair of the SHRM Foundation, the Human Resources Division of the Academy of Management, and as a member of the Academy of Management's Board of Governors. He has authored or edited 22 books on human resource management, including *Investing in People* (2008, with John Boudreau), *Managing Human Resources* (8th ed., 2009), and *Applied Psychology in Human Resource Management* (7th ed., with Herman Aguinis, in press). He is a two-time winner of the best-paper award from the Academy of Management Executives for his research on downsizing and responsible restructuring.

In 1999 Dr. Cascio received the Distinguished Career award from the HR Division of the Academy of Management. He received an honorary doctorate from the University of Geneva (Switzerland) in 2004, and in 2008 he was named by the *Journal of Management* as one of the most influential scholars in management in the past 25 years. Dr. Cascio has consulted with more than 150 organizations on six continents and is an elected Fellow of the National Academy of Human Resources, the Academy of Management, and the American Psychological Association. Currently he serves as editor of the *Journal of World Business.*

Wilfried De Corte received a PhD in industrial and organizational psychology from Ghent University, Belgium. After a career as a researcher and professor in the Department of Industrial Psychology, he moved to the Department of Data Analysis at the same university, teaching courses on data analysis and psychometrics. His research interests focus on the estimation and optimization of personnel selection and classification outcomes as well as on the derivation of the small sample properties of these outcomes. He regularly publishes his work in the *Journal of Applied Psychology, Personnel Psychology,* and *International Journal of Selection and Assessment* and in more statistically oriented journals, such as the *British Journal of Mathematical and Statistical Psychology.*

Kim Dowdeswell is a senior research consultant and registered industrial psychologist working for SHL, an international occupational assessment and human resource technology firm. She joined SHL in 2005, and over the years has gained experience in test localization, item trialing and test validation, as well as in culture fairness and equivalence studies. Ms. Dowdeswell holds a master's degree (Cum Laude) in human resource management from the University of Pretoria. In 2006, she received the Achievement Award from the South African Board for Personnel Practice, as the top postgraduate student in the human resources field at the University of Pretoria, and earned academic honorary colors from the university. She is currently working toward her PhD in industrial psychology at the University of Pretoria. She is also a member of the Society for Industrial and Organisational Psychology (SIOPSA), and serves on the executive committee of the People Assessment in Industry (PAI) interest group.

Emily Feinberg is a doctoral student in the organizational psychology program at the University of Maryland. Her research interests are in adverse impact in selection and topics in cross cultural organizational psychology, including the influence of culture on organizational preferences and expatriate management.

Harold W. Goldstein is an associate professor of industrial/organizational psychology at Baruch College, The City University of New York. He received his doctoral degree in industrial/organizational psychology from the University of Maryland. His primary areas of expertise are in the areas of personnel selection, managerial assessment, and leadership development, and his research interests largely focus on how to develop valid selection systems that reduce adverse impact. He co-founded Siena Consulting, a firm that provides a wide variety of human resource management consulting services, and he also serves as an expert for the U.S. Department of Justice on legal issues relating to personnel selection practices.

Irwin Goldstein came to the University of Maryland at College Park in 1966 and served as professor and chair from 1981 to 1991. In 1991, he was selected to be Dean of the College of Behavioral and Social Sciences. In 2001, he was awarded the University of Maryland President's Medal for "extraordinary contributions to the intellectual, cultural and social life of the University." In 2003, he was selected to serve as Vice Chancellor for Academic Affairs for the 13 campuses of the University System of Maryland.

Dr. Goldstein's research career as an industrial-organizational psychologist has focused on issues facing individuals, such as how they are selected and promoted, how they are trained by organizations, and how the climate of the organizations affects human resource practices. He also has a strong interest in understanding and resolving the constraints that affect people in organizations, such as the problems of race and gender discrimination. In these roles, he has served as a consultant to both public and private sector organizations. He has served as an associate editor of the *Journal of Applied Psychology* and the *Human Factors Journal* and as editor of the Frontiers Book Series for the Society of Industrial and Organizational Psychology. In 1992, he received the Distinguished Service Award from the Society of Industrial and Organizational Psychology. In 1995, he received the Swanson award for research excellence from the American Society for Training and Development. Dr. Goldstein has been further honored by being elected to serve as president of the Society for Industrial and Organizational Psychology.

Paul J. Hanges is professor of industrial/organizational psychology and is currently the associate chair/director of graduate studies for the

University of Maryland's Psychology Department. He is also an affiliate of the University of Maryland's R. H. Smith School of Business and the Aston Business School (Birmingham, England). He received his PhD from the University of Akron in 1987. His research focuses on selection, diversity and organizational climate, cross cultural leadership, and computational modeling. He has published 65 articles and book chapters and one book. Dr. Hanges's publications have appeared in such journals as *Advances in Global Leadership, American Psychologist, Applied Psychological Measurement, Applied Psychology: An International Review, Journal of Applied Psychology, Journal of International Business Studies*, and *Psychological Bulletin*. He is on the editorial board of the *Journal of Applied Psychology* and is a fellow of the American Psychological Association, Association for Psychological Sciences, and the Society for Industrial/Organizational Psychology.

Keith Hattrup is professor and associate chair of psychology, and coordinator of the MS Program in Applied Psychology, at San Diego State University. His teaching and research interests include psychological testing and measurement, cross cultural psychology, organizational diversity, adverse impact, personnel selection, job attitudes, and person–environment fit. His research has appeared in the *Journal of Applied Psychology, Applied Psychology: An International Review, Personnel Psychology*, the *Journal of Occupational and Organizational Psychology, Human Performance*, and *Educational and Psychological Measurement*. He currently serves on the editorial boards of the *Journal of Applied Psychology, Human Performance*, and *Applied HRM Research*.

Rick Jacobs is professor of psychology at The Pennsylvania State University and CEO of EB Jacobs, a consulting firm specializing in public sector employee assessment. He has spent the past 30 years in State College, Pennsylvania, teaching, conducting research, and running consulting organizations that provide services nationwide. He is a fellow in the Society for Industrial/Organizational Psychology, American Psychological Association, and Association for Psychological Sciences, and he has won prestigious awards for his research on cost–benefit analysis of human resource programs (James McKeen Cattell, APA Division 14), the measurement of experience (W. A. Owens Scholarly Achievement, SIOP), and understanding performance over time (Yoder-Heneman Personnel Research, SHRM). He consults with private sector organizations and police and fire departments across the country and provides expert testimony on issues of selection and adverse impact.

Jerard F. Kehoe received his doctorate in quantitative psychology in 1975 from the University of Southern California. He joined AT&T in 1982, where he had responsibility for selection programs in manufacturing, customer service, sales, technical, management, and leadership jobs, assuming over-all leadership and direction of that function in 1997. In September 2003, he founded Selection & Assessment Consulting and serves as its president.

Dr. Kehoe has been active professionally with several publications, chapters, and conference presentations on selection and assessment topics including computerized testing, fairness, scoring strategies, cut scores, and test validity. In 2000, he edited the Society of Industrial/Organizational Psychology's (SIOP) Professional Practice Series volume, *Managing Selection in Changing Organizations: Human Resource Strategies*. In 2001–2003 he served on the SIOP subcommittee that revised the *Principles for the Validation and Use of Employment Selection Procedures*.

Hennie J. Kriek is currently president of SHL Americas and Professor Extraordinarius of industrial and organizational psychology at the University of South Africa. He was the founding member and manag-ing director of SHL South Africa for more than 12 years. He received his DLitt et Phil at the University of South Africa in 1988 and was a visiting scholar at Colorado State University from 1989–1990. He is an honorary life member of SIOPSA (Society for Industrial/Organizational Psychology of South Africa) and the Assessment Centre Study Group of South Africa. He has also acted as chair of the Association of Test Publishers (ATP of South Africa) and PAI (People Assessment in Industry), an interest group of SIOPSA. He serves on the editorial board of *Human Performance* (USA), *Industrial and Organizational Psychology: Perspectives on Science and Practice* (USA), *International Journal of Management Reviews* (UK), *Southern African Business Review* (SA), and *Journal of Industrial Psychology* (SA).

Frank Landy is an emeritus professor in the Psychology Department of The Pennsylvania State University, where he served on the faculty for 25 years. He is also a scholar-in-residence and member of the graduate fac-ulty at the Baruch College of the City University of York. In 1980, with his colleague, Jim Farr, Dr. Landy completed an exhaustive review of per-formance rating literature from 1945 through 1979. That literature review guided performance rating research in a move away from format-based investigation and helped to introduce a new cognitive perspective on the performance evaluation process. Frank is also the author of several well-known textbooks in I-O psychology and employment discrimination as well as several dozen scientific publications in leading I-O journals. Frank lives and works in New York City.

Filip Lievens is a professor in the Department of Personnel Management and Work and Organizational Psychology at Ghent University, Belgium. In 1999, he earned his PhD from the same university. He is the author of more than 70 articles in the areas of organizational attractiveness, high-stakes testing, and selection, including assessment centers, situational judgment tests, and Web-based assessment. He has received several awards, including the Distinguished Early Career Award from the Society of Industrial and Organizational Psychology (2006).

Kathleen Kappy Lundquist is a nationally recognized organizational psychologist who testifies frequently as an expert witness in employment discrimination class-action lawsuits for both defendants and plaintiffs. As a result of class-action settlements, she also serves as a court-appointed expert in the design and implementation of legally defensible human resource processes for organizations such as The Coca-Cola Company, Abercrombie & Fitch, Ford Motor Company, Morgan Stanley, the Federal Bureau of Investigation, and the Library of Congress.

Dr. Lundquist is founder and president of APT, a national firm that consults with Fortune® 100 employers on the design and implementation of HR processes. In consulting with clients, she recommends proactive measures to improve the fairness, validity, and legal defensibility of HR processes before they are challenged. Her clients range from multinational corporations in the finance, pharmaceutical, aerospace, telecommunications and technology fields to government and nonprofit employers.

Kathleen Lundquist is a Phi Beta Kappa graduate of Fordham University where she received her PhD in psychology with a specialization in psychometrics. She is a former research associate with the National Academy of Sciences, a fellow in psychometrics with the Psychological Corporation, and a summer research fellow with the Educational Testing Service.

Patrick F. McKay is an associate professor of human resource management in the School of Management and Labor Relations at Rutgers, the State University of New Jersey. Professor McKay received his PhD in industrial-organizational psychology in 1999 from the University of Akron. His primary research interests are racial-ethnic differences on selection test/assessment scores and work outcomes, as well as the influence of organizations' diversity climates on recruitment, job performance, worker attitudes, retention, and organizational-level performance. Dr. McKay's research has been published in prominent publications such as the *Journal of Applied Psychology and Personnel Psychology*. Previously, he worked as a human resource consultant responsible for test development and validation, test administration, performance appraisal system development, training program implementation, job applicant rating, and litigation support. Dr. McKay developed employment tests for nationally known organizations such as Lucent Technologies, Michelin, Sony Magnetic Products, and General Electric.

Kevin Murphy is a professor of psychology and information sciences and technology at The Pennsylvania State University. He earned his PhD from Penn State in 1979, has served on the faculties of Rice University, New York University, and Colorado State University, and has had visiting appointments at the University of California, Berkeley and the University of Limerick. He has also been a Fulbright Scholar at the University of Stockholm and is a fellow of the American Psychological Association, the Society for Industrial and Organizational Psychology, and the American Psychological Society. He is the recipient of the Society for Industrial and Organizational Psychology's 2004 Distinguished Scientific Contribution Award.

Dr. Murphy served as president of the Society for Industrial and Organizational Psychology (1997–1998), and as associate editor, then editor of *Journal of Applied Psychology* (1991–2002), as well as a member of the editorial boards of *Human Performance, Personnel Psychology. Human Resource Management Review, International Journal of Management Reviews, Journal of Industrial Psychology,* and *International Journal of Selection and Assessment.* He is the author of more than 150 articles and book chapters, and author or editor of 11 books, in areas ranging from psychometrics and statistical analysis to individual differences, performance assessment, gender, and honesty in the workplace. Dr. Murphy's main areas of research include personnel selection and placement, performance appraisal, and psychological measurement. His current work focuses on understanding the validation process.

Daniel A. Newman is an assistant professor of social-personality-organizational psychology at the University of Illinois at Urbana-Champaign. He received his PhD in industrial/organizational psychology from The Pennsylvania State University, with minor concentrations in management and research methods. Dr. Newman previously taught at Texas A&M University and the University of Maryland (as a visiting professor). His research focuses on adverse impact (minority recruiting, weighting schemes, personality and ability measurement), research methods (meta-analysis, missing data, multilevel models), and attitude-behavior relationships. His work has been published in the *Academy of Management Journal, American Psychologist, Journal of Applied Psychology,* and *Organizational Research Methods* (he serves on the editorial boards of the latter two). Dr. Newman received the Academy of Management's Human Resources Scholarly Achievement Award, the Sage Publications Research Methods Best Paper Award, Best Student Paper Awards from the HR and Research Methods Divisions, and the Society for Industrial/Oorganizational Psychology's William A. Owens Scholarly Achievement Award.

James L. Outtz earned his PhD in industrial and organizational psychology from the University of Maryland. He is a fellow in the Society for Industrial and Organizational Psychology (SIOP) and the American

Psychological Association. He is president of Outtz and Associates, a consulting firm in Washington, DC, that specializes in personnel selection and human resources management. His professional service in the field of industrial and organizational psychology includes membership on SIOP's Ad Hoc Committee on Revision of the "Principles for the Validation and Use of Personnel Selection Procedures," which addresses best practices in the development and use of such procedures. In addition, he served as consulting editor to the *Journal of Applied Psychology*. He is recognized internationally for his work in the areas of adverse impact and alternative selection procedures, subjects about which he has written extensively. He routinely develops selection procedures for public and private sector employers in complex situations where litigation is, has been or might become a factor. His interests include selection, training, performance management, job analysis and work design, workforce diversity and equal employment opportunity.

Dr. Outtz is highly sought after as an expert for plaintiffs and defendants in major litigation involving the analysis of work, hiring, promotion, performance management, compensation and reductions in force.

Abigail K. Quinn is a doctoral student in the organizational psychology program at Michigan State University. She earned her undergraduate degree in psychology from Scripps College in Claremont, California. Her current research interests include training and development, test validity, decision making, and multicultural competence.

Brandon G. Roberts is earning his master of science degree in industrial/organizational psychology from San Diego State University. He obtained his bachelor's degree in psychology from San Diego State University. His research interests include adverse impact, employee commitment, person-environment fit, and climate strength in multinational contexts. He currently works for Qualcomm Inc., where he is responsible for the development of training programs, analysis of climate surveys, and validation of selection techniques.

Philip L. Roth is professor of management at Clemson University. His research interests include a variety of topics in personnel selection (e.g., interviews, work sample tests, cognitive ability tests) and research methods (e.g., meta-analysis). He is a fellow of the Society for Industrial and Organizational Psychology and past chair of the Research Methods Division of the Academy of Management. He earned his PhD from the University of Houston and his BA from the University of Tennessee.

Paul R. Sackett is the Beverly and Richard Fink Distinguished Professor of Psychology and Liberal Arts at the University of Minnesota. He received his PhD in industrial and organizational psychology at The Ohio State University in 1979. His research interests revolve around various aspects of testing and assessment in workplace and educational settings. He has served as editor of the Society for Industrial and Organizational Psychology's journal *Industrial and Organizational Psychology: Perspectives on Science and Practice*, as editor of *Personnel Psychology*, and as president of SIOP. He has also served as co-chair of the Joint Committee on the Standards for Educational and Psychological Testing, as a member of the National Research Council's Board on Testing and Assessment, as chair of the American Psychological Association's Committee on Psychological Tests and Assessments, and as chair of APA's Board of Scientific Affairs.

Charles A. Scherbaum is an associate professor of psychology at Baruch College in the City University of New York. His research focuses on personnel selection, cognitive ability testing, attitudes toward stigmatized employees, quantitative methods, and applied psychometrics. Publications of his research have appeared in journals such as *Personnel Psychology*, *Organizational Research Methods*, *Educational and Psychological Measurement*, and *Leadership Quarterly*. He received his PhD in industrial and organizational psychology from Ohio University.

Neal Schmitt obtained his PhD in industrial/organizational psychology from Purdue University in 1972 and is currently University Distinguished Professor of Psychology and Management at Michigan State University. He was editor of *Journal of Applied Psychology* from 1988–1994 and has served on 10 editorial boards. He has received the Society for Industrial/ Organizational Psychology's Distinguished Scientific Contributions Award (1999) and its Distinguished Service Contributions Award (1998). He served as SIOP's president in 1989–1990 and president of Division 5 of APA (Measurement, Evaluation, and Statistics-2007–2008). Dr. Schmitt is a fellow of Divisions 5 and 14, the American Psychological Association, and the Association for Psychological Science. He was also awarded the Heneman Career Achievement Award from the Human Resources Division of the Academy of Management and Distinguished Career Award from the Research Methods Division of the Academy of Management. He has co-authored three textbooks, *Staffing Organizations* with Ben Schneider and Rob Ployhart, *Research Methods in Human Resource Management* with Richard Klimoski, *Personnel Selection* with David Chan; co-edited *Personnel Selection in Organizations* with Walter Borman and *Measurement and Data Analysis* with Fritz Drasgow; and published approximately 160 articles. His current research centers on the effectiveness of organizations' selection procedures and the outcomes of these procedures, particularly as they relate to subgroup employment and applicant reactions and behavior.

Winny Shen is a third-year graduate student in industrial-organizational psychology at the University of Minnesota. She is currently serving as the industrial-organizational psychology representative to the American Psychological Association Science Student Council. Her research interests include fairness, bias, and diversity issues in organizational and educational settings, the prediction and measurement of academic and job performance, leadership, and occupational health psychology.

Jay Silva received his PhD in industrial-organizational psychology from The Pennsylvania State University in 1988. Dr. Silva initially conducted research at the U.S. Army Research Institute (ARI) in the areas of personnel selection, classification, retention, promotion systems, psychophysiological predictors of performance under stress, adaptability measures, psychomotor abilities, test fairness, and computerized testing. After ARI, he worked on personnel selection, performance appraisal, and competency modeling projects at Personnel Decisions Research Institutes (PDRI). Over the years, he has published and presented his research on minority selection, fair treatment, and adverse impact to a variety of audiences. Currently, as a senior managing consultant at EB Jacobs, Dr. Silva develops and manages projects, designs and develops Web applications for testing, data collection, and analysis and provides expert analysis guidance.

Marlene A. Smith is an associate professor of quantitative methods in the Business School at the University of Colorado Denver. Her research interests include econometric model selection, statistical issues in human resources management, and evaluation and measurement of business education. Dr. Smith's research articles have appeared in the *Journal of Statistical Computation and Simulation, Communications in Statistics: Computation and Simulation, Journal of Econometrics, Journal of Applied Econometrics, Economic Letters, Personnel Psychology,* the *Decision Sciences Journal of Innovative Education,* and the *Southern Economic Journal,* among others. She has also co-authored a paper describing case-based business statistics courses (*American Statistician,* 1998), co-authored a series of cases designed to be used in business statistics courses (*Practical Data Analysis: Case Studies in Business Statistics,* Irwin/McGraw-Hill, 1999), and has won two teaching awards in the Business School.

Nancy T. Tippins is a senior vice president and managing principal of Valtera Corporation where she is responsible for the development and execution of firm strategies related to employee selection and assessment. She has extensive experience in the development and validation of selection tests and other forms of assessment for all levels of management and hourly employees as well as in designing performance management programs and leadership development programs. Prior to joining Valtera,

Dr. Tippins worked as an internal consultant in large Fortune 100 companies (Exxon, Bell Atlantic, GTE) developing and validating selection and assessment tools. Dr. Tippins is active in professional affairs and is a past president of the Society for Industrial/Organizational Psychology. She is a fellow of SIOP, the American Psychological Association, and the Association for Psychological Science. Dr. Tippins received MS and PhD degrees in industrial and organizational psychology from the Georgia Institute of Technology.

Kenneth P. Yusko is an expert in the design of strategic employee selection, development, and performance management systems. As a co-founder of Siena Consulting, he has worked to help law offices, Fortune 500 companies, small businesses, and government agencies perform more effectively for more than two decades. Dr. Yusko is an associate professor in the School of Business at Marymount University and has lectured and written widely on a variety of human capital management issues. His ground-breaking research on negotiation and conflict management in the legal field was supported by a grant from the National Science Foundation.

Sheldon Zedeck is professor of psychology in the Department of Psychology at the University of California at Berkeley and Vice Provost for Academic Affairs and Faculty Welfare. He has been at Berkeley since 1969, when he completed his PhD in industrial and organizational psychology at Bowling Green State University in Ohio. He served as chair of the Department from 1993–1998 (and as interim chair for the 2003–2004 year); prior to this administrative position, Dr. Zedeck was the director of the campus' Institute of Industrial Relations from 1988–1992.

Dr. Zedeck is co-author of four books on various topics: *Foundations of Behavioral Science Research in Organizations* (1974, with Milton Blood), *Measurement Theory for the Behavioral Sciences* (1981, with Edwin E. Ghiselli and John Campbell), *Performance Measurement and Theory* (1983, with Frank Landy and Jan Cleveland), and *Data Analysis for Research Designs* (1989, with Geoffrey Keppel). In addition, he has edited a volume entitled *Work, Family, and Organizations* (1992), which is part of the Society for Industrial and Organizational Psychology (SIOP) *Frontiers* Series.

Dr. Zedeck has served on the editorial boards of *Journal of Applied Psychology* (editor, 2002–2008), *Contemporary Psychology*, and *Industrial Relations*. He has also served as editor and associate editor of *Human Performance*, a journal that he and Frank Landy founded in 1988, as well as associate editor of *Applied Psychology: An International Review*.

Section I

Background

1

Adverse Impact: History and Evolution

Sheldon Zedeck

Guidelines and Adverse Impact

A major step in employment discrimination legal cases is the establish-ment of adverse impact due to the use of a selection or promotion device. The purpose of this volume is to explore the concept of adverse impact, in particular its measurement, underpinnings, relationship to traditional concepts in selection theory and to particular aspects of selection deci-sions, and the means by which it can be reduced. The purpose of this chapter is to provide some historical basis for the concept, to put it into perspective, and to demonstrate its role in a number of aspects that involve developing and establishing the validity and usefulness of selection and promotion procedures.

The basic definition of *adverse impact* is presented in the *Uniform Guidelines for Employee Selection Procedures* (*UGESP*; Equal Employment Opportunity Commission, Civil Service Commission, Department of Labor, & Department of Justice, 1978). The guidelines are principles designed to provide a framework for determining the proper use of selec-tion/promotion procedures; they are not "legal" guidelines.

A companion document to the *UGESP* (Equal Employment Opportunity Commission et al., 1978) is the *Uniform Employee Selection Guidelines Interpretation and Clarification* (*Questions and Answers*) (*Q&A*, 1979), which were intended to clarify and interpret the *UGESP* but not to modify it. This document also addresses adverse impact. What follows is a discussion of the sections of the *Uniform Guidelines* and the questions and answers that are germane to the purpose of this chapter.

Section 1B: Statement of Purpose.

These guidelines incorporate a single set of principles which are designed to assist employers, labor organizations, employment agen-cies, and licensing and certification boards to comply with require-ments of Federal law prohibiting employment practices which discriminate on grounds of race, color, religion, sex, and national origin. They are designed to provide a framework for determining the proper use of tests and other selection procedures. These guidelines do not require a user to conduct validity studies of selection procedures where no adverse impact results. (EEOC, 1978, Section 1B: Statement of Purpose)

QUESTIONS AND ANSWERS

2. Q. What is the basic principle of the Guidelines?
   A. A selection process which has an adverse impact on the employment opportunities of members of a race, color, religion, sex, or national origin group (referred to as "race, sex, and ethnic group," as defined in Section 16P) and thus disproportionately screens them out is unlawfully discriminatory unless the process or its component procedures have been validated in accord with the Guidelines, or the user otherwise justifies them in accord with Federal law. See Sections 3 and 6. 1 This principle was adopted by the Supreme Court unanimously in Griggs v. Duke Power Co., 401 U.S. 424, and was ratified and endorsed by the Congress when it passed the Equal Employment Opportunity Act of 1972, which amended Title VII of the Civil Rights Act of 1964. (Q&A, 1979)

The establishment of adverse impact suggests the need for (a) demonstration of validity for the procedure; (b) demonstration of test fairness; (c) attempts to identify alternative selection/promotion devices with less but equally valid devices; and (d) attempts to reduce the adverse impact.

Section 3: Discrimination defined: Relationship between use of selection procedures and discrimination.

A. Procedure having adverse impact constitutes discrimination unless justified.

The use of any selection procedure which has an adverse impact on the hiring, promotion, or other employment or membership opportunities of members of any race, sex, or ethnic group will be considered to be discriminatory and inconsistent with these guidelines, unless the procedure has been validated in accordance with these guidelines, or the provisions of section 6 of this part are satisfied.

B. Consideration of suitable alternative selection procedures.

Where two or more selection procedures are available which serve the user's legitimate interest in efficient and trustworthy workmanship, and which are substantially equally valid for a given purpose, the user should use the procedure which has been demonstrated to have the lesser adverse impact. Accordingly, whenever a validity study is called for by these guidelines, the user should include, as a part of the validity study, an investigation of suitable alternative selection procedures and suitable alternative methods of using the selection procedure which have as little adverse impact as possible, to determine the appropriateness of using or validating them in accord with these guidelines. (EEOC, 1978, Section 3)

Adverse impact is operationalized basically in terms of selection ratios and as the "four-fifths rule" or "80% rule." However, and this is a "conditional" in the UGESP, smaller differences or a demonstration of no adverse impact *may* constitute adverse impact if differences between the subgroups are statistically significant. Also, large differences as determined by the four-fifths rule *may* not be considered adverse impact if the differences are based on small numbers or are not statistically significantly different. Thus, although the focus is on the four-fifths rule, sample sizes may need to be considered as well as whether the differences are statistically significant before final determination can be rendered regarding the procedure's adverse impact.

Note that decisions about adverse impact are not solely based on statistical evidence. The UGESP suggests that adverse impact statistics may be interpreted in light of the hiring organization's recruiting practices that encourage or discourage minority applicants, and when sample size is small, the assessment might be supplemented with data from other similar jobs or for the same job across time.

Section 4: Information on impact.

C. Evaluation of selection rates. The "bottom line."

If the information called for by sections 4A and B [dealing with recordkeeping] of this section shows that the total selection process for a job has an adverse impact, the individual components of the selection process should be evaluated for adverse impact. If this information shows that the total selection process does not have an adverse impact, the Federal enforcement agencies, in the exercise of their administrative and prosecutorial discretion, in usual circumstances, will not expect a user to evaluate the individual components for adverse impact, or to validate such individual components, and will not take enforcement action based upon adverse impact of any component of that process, including the separate parts of a multipart selection procedure or any separate procedure that is used as an alternative method of selection. However, in the following circumstances the Federal enforcement agencies will expect a user to evaluate the individual components for adverse impact and may, where appropriate, take enforcement action with respect to the individual components: (1) where the selection procedure is a significant factor in the continuation of patterns of assignments of incumbent employees caused by prior discriminatory employment practices, (2) where the weight of court decisions or administrative interpretations hold that a specific procedure (such as height or weight requirements or no-arrest records) is not job related in the same or similar circumstances. In unusual circumstances, other than those listed in paragraphs (1) and (2) of this section, the Federal enforcement agencies may request a user to evaluate the individual components for adverse impact and may, where appropriate, take enforcement action with respect to the individual component.

D. Adverse impact and the "four-fifths rule."

A selection rate for any race, sex, or ethnic group which is less than four-fifths (4/5) (or eighty percent) of the rate for the group with the highest rate will generally be regarded by the Federal enforcement agencies as evidence of adverse impact, while a greater than four-fifths rate will generally not be regarded by Federal enforcement agencies as evidence of adverse impact. Smaller differences in selection rate may neverthe-less constitute adverse impact, where they are significant in both sta-tistical and practical terms or where a user's actions have discouraged applicants disproportionately on grounds of race, sex, or ethnic group. Greater differences in selection rate may not constitute adverse impact where the differences are based on small numbers and are not statisti-cally significant, or where special recruiting or other programs cause the pool of minority or female candidates to be atypical of the normal pool of applicants from that group. Where the user's evidence concern-ing the impact of a selection procedure indicates adverse impact but is based upon numbers which are too small to be reliable, evidence con-cerning the impact of the procedure over a longer period of time and/or evidence concerning the impact which the selection procedure had when used in the same manner in similar circumstances elsewhere may be considered in determining adverse impact. Where the user has not maintained data on adverse impact as required by the documenta-tion section of applicable guidelines, the Federal enforcement agencies may draw an inference of adverse impact of the selection process from the failure of the user to maintain such data, if the user has an under-utilization of a group in the job category, as compared to the group's representation in the relevant labor market or, in the case of jobs filled from within, the applicable work force. (EEOC, 1978, Section 4)

QUESTIONS AND ANSWERS

10. Q. What is adverse impact?
    A. Under the Guidelines adverse impact is a substantially different rate of selection in hiring, promotion or other employment decision which works to the disadvantage of members of a race, sex or ethnic group. Sections 4D and 16B. See Questions 11 and 12.
11. Q. What is a substantially different rate of selection?
    A. The agencies have adopted a rule of thumb under which they will generally consider a selection rate for any race, sex, or ethnic group

which is less than four-fifths (4/5ths) or eighty percent (80%) of the selection rate for the group with the highest selection rate as a substantially different rate of selection. See Section 4D. This "4/5ths" or "80%" rule of thumb is not intended as a legal definition, but is a practical means of keeping the attention of the enforcement agencies on serious discrepancies in rates of hiring, promotion and other selection decisions.

For example, if the hiring rate for whites other than Hispanics is 60%, for American Indians 45%, for Hispanics 48%, and for Blacks 51%, and each of these groups constitutes more than 2% of the labor force in the relevant labor area (see Question 16), a comparison should be made of the selection rate for each group with that of the highest group (whites). These comparisons show the following impact ratios: American Indians 45/60 or 75%; Hispanics 48/60 or 80%; and Blacks 51/60 or 85%. Applying the 4/5ths or 80% rule of thumb, on the basis of the above information alone, adverse impact is indicated for American Indians but not for Hispanics or Blacks.

12. Q. How is adverse impact determined?
    A. Adverse impact is determined by a four-step process.
    (1) Calculate the rate of selection for each group (divide the number of persons selected from a group by the number of applicants from that group).
    (2) Observe which group has the highest selection rate.
    (3) Calculate the impact ratios, by comparing the selection rate for each group with that of the highest group (divide the selection rate for a group by the selection rate for the highest group).
    (4) Observe whether the selection rate for any group is substantially less (i.e., usually less then 4/5ths or 80%) than the selection rate for the highest group. If it is, adverse impact is indicated in most circumstances. See Section 4D.
    For example:

Applicants	Hires	Selection Rate/Percent Hired
80 White	48	48/80 or 60%
40 Black	12	12/40 or 30%

A comparison of the black selection rate (30%) with the white selection rate (60%) shows that the black rate is 30/60, or one-half (or 50%) of the white rate. Since the one-half (50%) is less than 4/5ths (80%) adverse impact is usually indicated.

The determination of adverse impact is not purely arithmetic however; and other factors may be relevant. See, Section 4D.

18. Q. Is it usually necessary to calculate the statistical significance of differences in selection rates when investigating the existence of adverse impact?
    A. No. Adverse impact is normally indicated when one selection rate is less than 80% of the other. The federal enforcement agencies

normally will use only the 80% (4/5ths) rule of thumb, except where large numbers of selections are made. See Questions 20 and 22.

19. Q. Does the 4/5ths rule of thumb mean that the Guidelines will tolerate up to 20% discrimination?

A. No. The 4/5ths rule of thumb speaks only to the question of adverse impact, and is not intended to resolve the ultimate question of unlawful discrimination. Regardless of the amount of difference in selection rates, unlawful discrimination may be present, and may be demonstrated through appropriate evidence. The 4/5ths rule merely establishes a numerical basis for drawing an initial inference and for requiring additional information. With respect to adverse impact, the Guidelines expressly state (section 4D) that differences in selection rates of less than 20% may still amount to adverse impact where the differences are significant in both statistical and practical terms. See Question 20. In the absence of differences which are large enough to meet the 4/5ths rule of thumb or a test of statistical significance, there is no reason to assume that the differences are reliable, or that they are based upon anything other than chance.

20. Q. Why is the 4/5ths rule called a rule of thumb?

A. Because it is not intended to be controlling in all circumstances. If, for the sake of illustration, we assume that nationwide statistics show that use of an arrest record would disqualify 10% of all Hispanic persons but only 4% of all whites other than Hispanic (hereafter non-Hispanic), the selection rate for that selection procedure is 90% for Hispanics and 96% for non-Hispanics. Therefore, the 4/5 rule of thumb would not indicate the presence of adverse impact (90% is approximately 94% of 96%). But in this example, the information is based upon nationwide statistics, and the sample is large enough to yield statistically significant results, and the difference (Hispanics are 2 1/2 times as likely to be disqualified as non-Hispanics) is large enough to be practically significant. Thus, in this example the enforcement agencies would consider a disqualification based on an arrest record alone as having an adverse impact. Likewise, in Gregory v. Litton Industries, 472 F.2d 631 (9th Cir., 1972), the court held that the employer violated Title VII by disqualifying persons from employment solely on the basis of an arrest record, where that disqualification had an adverse impact on blacks and was not shown to be justified by business necessity.

On the other hand, a difference of more than 20% in rates of selection may not provide a basis for finding adverse impact if the number of persons selected is very small. For example, if the employer selected three males and one female from an applicant pool of 20 males and 10 females, the 4/5ths rule would indicate adverse impact (selection rate for women is 10%; for men 15%; 10/15 or 66 2/3% is less than 80%), yet the number of selections is too small to warrant a determination of adverse impact. In these circumstances, the enforcement agency would not require validity evidence in the absence of additional information (such as selection rates for a longer period of time) indicating adverse impact. For record keeping requirements, see Section 15A(2)(c) and Questions 84 and 85.

21. Q. Is evidence of adverse impact sufficient to warrant a validity study or an enforcement action where the numbers involved are so small that it is more likely than not that the difference could have occurred by chance?

Applicants	Not hired	Hired	Selection rate/ percentage hired
80 White	64	16	20
20 Black	17	3	15

White selection rate = 20
Black selection rate = 15
15 divided by 20 = 75% (which is less than 80%)

A. No. If the numbers of persons and the difference in selection rates are so small that it is likely that the difference could have occurred by chance, the Federal agencies will not assume the existence of adverse impact, in the absence of other evidence. In this example, the difference in selection rates is too small, given the small number of black applicants, to constitute adverse impact in the absence of other information (see Section 4D). If only one more black had been hired instead of a white the selection rate for blacks (20%) would be higher than that for whites (18.7%). Generally, it is inappropriate to require validity evidence or to take enforcement action where the number of persons and the difference in selection rates are so small that the selection of one different person for one job would shift the result from adverse impact against one group to a situation in which that group has a higher selection rate than the other group.

On the other hand, if a lower selection rate continued over a period of time, so as to constitute a pattern, then the lower selection rate would constitute adverse impact, warranting the need for validity evidence.

22. Q. Is it ever necessary to calculate the statistical significance of differences in selection rates to determine whether adverse impact exists?
A. Yes. Where large numbers of selections are made, relatively small differences in selection rates may nevertheless constitute adverse impact if they are both statistically and practically significant. See Section 4D and Question 20. For that reason, if there is a small difference in selection rates (one rate is more than 80% of the other), but large numbers of selections are involved, it would be appropriate to calculate the statistical significance of the difference in selection rates.

23. Q. When the 4/5th rule of thumb shows adverse impact, is there adverse impact under the Guidelines?
A. There usually is adverse impact, except where the number of persons selected and the difference in selection rates are very small. See Section 4D and Questions 20 and 21.

24. Q. Why do the Guidelines rely primarily upon the 4/5ths rule of thumb, rather than tests of statistical significance?
    A. Where the sample of persons selected is not large, even a large real difference between groups is likely not to be confirmed by a test of statistical significance (at the usual .05 level of significance). For this reason, the Guidelines do not rely primarily upon a test of statistical significance, but use the 4/5ths rule of thumb as a practical and easy-to-administer measure of whether differences in selection rates are substantial. Many decisions in day-to-day life are made without reliance upon a test of statistical significance.

Section 14: Technical standards for validity studies.

Once adverse impact is established, the employer has the burden of either eliminating the adverse impact or demonstrating that the selection procedure at issue is valid.

(6) Operational use of selection procedures.

Users should evaluate each selection procedure to assure that it is appropriate for operational use, including establishment of cutoff scores or rank ordering. Generally, if other factors remain the same, the greater the magnitude of the relationship (e.g., correlation coefficient) between performance on a selection procedure and one or more criteria of performance on the job, and the greater the importance and number of aspects of job performance covered by the criteria, the more likely it is that the procedure will be appropriate for use. Reliance upon a selection procedure which is significantly related to a criterion measure, but which is based upon a study involving a large number of subjects and has a low correlation coefficient will be subject to close review if it has a large adverse impact. Sole reliance upon a single selection instrument which is related to only one of many job duties or aspects of job performance will also be subject to close review. The appropriateness of a selection procedure is best evaluated in each particular situation and there are no minimum correlation coefficients applicable to all employment situations. In determining whether a selection procedure is appropriate for operational use the following considerations should also be taken into account: The degree of adverse impact of the procedure, the availability of other selection procedures of greater or substantially equal validity.

(8) Fairness.

(b) Investigation of fairness. Where a selection procedure results in an adverse impact on a race, sex, or ethnic group identified in accordance with the classifications set forth in section 4 of this part and that group is a significant factor in the relevant labor market, the user generally should investigate the possible existence of unfairness for that group if it is technically feasible to do so. The greater the severity of the adverse impact on a group, the greater the need to investigate the possible existence of unfairness. Where the weight of evidence from other studies shows that the selection procedure predicts fairly for the group in question and for the same or similar jobs, such evidence may be relied on in connection with the selection procedure at issue. (EEOC, 1978, Section 14)

Section 15: Documentation of impact and validity evidence.

(2) Information on impact.

(a) Collection of information on impact. Users of selection procedures other than those complying with section 15A(1) of this part should maintain and have available for each job records or other information showing whether the total selection process for that job has an adverse impact on any of the groups for which records are called for by section 4B of this part. Adverse impact determinations should be made at least annually for each such group which constitutes at least 2 percent of the labor force in the relevant labor area or 2 percent of the applicable workforce. Where a total selection process for a job has an adverse impact, the user should maintain and have available records or other information showing which components have an adverse impact. Where the total selection process for a job does not have an adverse impact, information need not be maintained for individual components except in circumstances set forth in subsection 15A(2)(b) of this section. If the determination of adverse impact is made using a procedure other than the "four-fifths rule," as defined in the first sentence of section 4D of this part, a justification, consistent with section 4D of this part, for the procedure used to determine adverse impact should be available. (EEOC, 1978, Section 15)

Section 16: Definitions

The following definitions shall apply throughout these guidelines:

B. Adverse impact. A substantially different rate of selection in hiring, promotion, or other employment decision which works to the disadvantage of members of a race, sex, or ethnic group. See section 4 of these guidelines. (EEOC, 1978, Section 16)

Origin of Guidelines

The material presented gives a view of adverse impact from the perspective of uniform guidelines. One needs to go back to one of the first major test cases of the Civil Rights Act of 1964, *Griggs v. Duke Power* (1971), to find a basis for the need for an adverse impact concept and definition. In this case, the majority (unanimous) opinion wrote that they granted the writ in this case to resolve the question whether an employer is prohibited by the Civil Rights Act of 1964, Title VII, from requiring a high school education or passing of a standardized general intelligence test as a condition of employment in or transfer to jobs when (a) neither standard is shown to be significantly related to successful job performance, (b) both requirements operate to disqualify Negroes at *a substantially higher rate* [emphasis added] than white applicants, and (c) the jobs in question formerly had been filled only by white employees as part of a longstanding practice of giving preference to whites.

The focus on "substantially higher rate" suggested that there needed to be a means to "calculate and determine" what would be considered a substantially higher rate. As a result, strategies were examined by various groups to suggest means for establishing adverse impact, which resulted in its definition as presented in the UGESP (Equal Employment Opportunity Commission et al., 1978).

One additional critical aspect of the *Griggs v. Duke Power* case was the Court's comment that the Equal Employment Opportunity Commission guidelines in existence at the time of the case were to be given "great deference," a position affirmed in a subsequent Supreme Court Case of *Albemarle Paper Company v. Moody* (1975). The point is that guidelines have subsequently been treated with great deference, leading to a focus on how to establish adverse impact.

Summary of Guidelines and Adverse Impact

The essence of the review is to note that

(1) "adverse impact" drives the need for an organization to demonstrate that its selection/promotion system is valid and that its proposed "test" is "fair;"

(2) "adverse impact" considerations drive the need for the organization to consider "suitable alternative selection procedures," a topic that is controversial in its own right;

(3) "adverse impact" is primarily determined by the "four-fifths rule." However, adverse impact can also be established by examining "statistical significance" and "practical significance." Recognized and established analytical strategies are available for testing "statistical significance," though the UGESP (1978) recognizes that small numbers for the groups being compared may influence the interpretation of tests of statistical significance. There is, however, no recognized and established strategy for demonstrating "practical significance." Section 15 (2)(a) also recognizes that there may be "a procedure other than the 'four-fifths rule'" but it does not expound on what this may be.

(4) a statistical test is not a replacement for the "four-fifths rule."

(5) the "four-fifths rule" is a "rule of thumb" that appears to have no theoretical or conceptual basis—it is a "practical means" to identify "serious discrepancies in rates of hiring, promotion and other selection decisions."

(6) the "four-fifths" rule of thumb is "not intended to be controlling" though the UGESP is given "great deference."

(7) the "four-fifths rule" establishes a *prima facie* case and is not proof that the test illegally discriminates against a protected group.

(8) the "four-fifths rule" is framed in terms of selection rates and not rejection rates. A focus on the latter could lead to different conclusions. (Bobko & Roth, 2004)

Other, Prior Guidelines

As noted, there were "guidelines" before the Uniform Guidelines. These prior guidelines were produced by various agencies, foremost among them the federal Equal Employment Opportunity Commission (EEOC). Just after the passage of the Civil Rights Act of 1964, the EEOC produced a set of guidelines (1966), which was effectively a brief primer on selection as practiced in the 1960s. In 1968, the Office of Federal Contract Compliance produced its set of guidelines (1971), which was primarily intended for federal contractors. Each of these agencies produced revised versions as time marched along. In 1969 and 1972, the U.S. Civil Service Commission issued its own regulations. In addition, other agencies, such as the Department of Transportation, Department of Labor, and others, produced their own guidelines. The production of multiple sets of guidelines is bound to yield discrepancies; this fact was recognized in the early 1970s when there began efforts to generate a "uniform" set of guidelines. One such set was produced in 1973 (see Guion, 1998, for a discussion of the generation of the uniform guidelines), but it was not until 1978 that there was finally consensus for the *UGESP* (Equal Employment Opportunity Commission et al., 1978).

Not only were federal agencies involved in establishing guidelines, but also states had their employment enforcement agencies, some of which attempted to generate their set of guidelines. One such critical agency was the California Fair Employment Housing Commission, which created a Technical Advisory Committee on Testing (TACT) in the mid-1960s.

It is the view of many that the four-fifths rule was developed by TACT (see Biddle, 2006, for his account of the rule's origination). (Note that I was active in TACT in 1972, but I do not rely solely on my "reconstruction" of history to present a precise historical account; what follows is my recall with great reliance on Biddle's account.)

As Biddle (2006) recited the history, TACT was interested in developing a statistical tool for determining adverse impact. The committee members who discussed this issue were concerned that the application of statistical significance testing would be too difficult for those responsible for implementing the guidelines, so they argued for an "administrative" guideline. There was a debate between two groups: a 70% versus a 90% rule. I have no recall for the basis of 70% versus 90% except to speculate that 70% represented a C grade for passing examinations in school and 90% represented an A grade in courses. When there are two proposals, one solution is to split the difference, which in the case of 70% versus 90% is 80%. And, that is what resulted.

The TACT 1972 California guidelines consequently defined *adverse effect* as follows:

> Adverse effect refers to a total employment process which results in a significantly higher percentage of a protected group in the candidate population being rejected for employment, placement, or promotion. The difference between the rejection rates for a protected group and the remaining group must be statistically significant at the .05 level. In addition, if the acceptance rate of the protected group is greater than or equal to 80% of the acceptance rate of the remaining group, then adverse effect is said to be not present by definition. (Section 7.1)

Note that the TACT definition calls for the 80% rule *and* significance testing to be considered. This was not the strategy as adopted by those promulgating the *UGESP*, which as noted in the *UGESP Q&A* numbers 11, 12, and 18, rely primarily on the 80% rule. Why the change? Speculation is that it was assumed that it would be difficult for administrators to calculate statistical significance, therefore it was not necessary.

Roth, Bobko, and Switzer (2006) also presented a brief accounting of the "history" of the four-fifths rule. Their account is consistent with that reported by Biddle (2006) and as I recalled. They also noted, based on personal communications with other participants involved in TACT and the *UGESP*, that (a) TACT never expected federal agencies to incorporate the rule into their guidelines and (b) when it was incorporated into the guidelines, there was little focus on how it would behave in different situations.

In summary of the historical account, the four-fifths or 80% rule was generated as a "rule of thumb" or administrative solution to a practical problem. There was no theoretical basis underlying its development or acceptance. (I do recall that one argument put forth for its adoption was that a noted psychometrician believed it was "correct.") As Roth et al. (2006) noted, the rule is an indicator for practitioners of the presence or absence of adverse impact in an organization's use of tests; it is an indicator for potential regulatory intervention, and it represents an image for an organization. These are serious consequences that are generated by a rule of thumb. Its place in history was best described by Barrett (1998), who noted that "the 80% rule has been virtually enshrined as the standard for determining whether or not there is adverse impact" (p. 94). It would be interesting speculation regarding what the employment world would look like today if a different rule of thumb such as 75% had been adopted.

Standards and Principles

Before going further into the evolution of the concept of adverse impact, I want to note two other sources that are relied on by professionals in personnel and human resource management: (a) *Standards for Educational and Psychological Testing* (American Educational Research Association [AERA], 1999) and the *Principles for the Validation and Use of Personnel Selection Procedures* (Society for Industrial and Organizational Psychology [SIOP], 2003). The *Standards* (AERA, 1999) are intended to provide professionals with criteria for the evaluation of tests, testing practices, and the effects of test use. They are intended to provide a frame of reference to ensure that relevant issues in testing are addressed.

The *Principles* (SIOP, 2003) represent established scientific findings and generally accepted practice in the field of employment testing. They are intended to be consistent with the standards (AERA, 1999).

Though the *Standards* (AERA, 1999) and *Principles* (SIOP, 2003) are used together with the *UGESP* (Equal Employment Opportunity Commission et al., 1978) by many professionals involved in employment testing as well as by attorneys representing plaintiffs and defendants, it should be noted that the *Standards* and *Principles* do not directly address issues of adverse impact. My view is that this is appropriate. The adverse impact rules and definitions are used by practitioners to trigger scrutiny of how the selection/promotion procedure was identified, developed, and validated; the *Standards* and *Principles* should be used by practitioners to conduct that scrutiny.

What follows next is how the concept of adverse impact has evolved over time in the courts and literature, with particular emphasis on its meaning and operationalization.

Adverse Impact in the Courts

As noted in the mention of the *Griggs v. Duke Power* (1971) case, the courts have been faced with ruling or determining what is meant by "substantially higher" rates. How large of a disparity should there be to go forward with a case that requires the employer to defend its selection or promotion system? And, how is the difference to be studied: use of the four-fifths rule and/or statistical testing of the significance of the difference between two selection rates?

Two landmark court cases addressed the issues, perhaps in an oblique manner. In *International Brotherhood of Teamsters v. United States* (1977), the court referred to "longlasting and gross disparity," while in *Hazelwood School District v. United States* (1977), the court referred to "gross statistical disparities." But, neither decision gave a precise definition of what disparities were problematic. The *Hazelwood School District* case, however, did produce a comment from the court that the disparity can be examined by "the standard deviation analysis" and suggested that this was a precise method of measuring statistically significant differences. Specifically, the Court stated that "a fluctuation of more than two or three units of standard deviation would undercut the hypothesis that decisions were being made randomly with respect to race." These standard deviation limits are indicative of the p values of .05 and .01, which are the conventional levels of significance used in hypothesis testing.

Esson and Hauenstein (2006) examined the use of the four-fifths rule in the courts and argued that it was dominant at the outset of court cases, but that there has been an increasing reliance on statistical significance tests since the early 1990s. They conducted an extensive review of federal court cases from January 1, 1993, to the end of 2004 and found 36 cases that related to adverse impact at the district court level, and 12 cases at the court of appeals level that were relevant for their analysis. Their findings are as follows:

1. Of 36 district court cases, 14 (39%) used the 80% rule only, 6 (17%) used both the 80% rule and statistical testing, and 16 (44%) used only statistical testing. The reliance on statistical testing occurred during and after 1977. Also, in the six cases that relied on both, statistical tests were used to supplement the 80% rule. The authors tentatively concluded that the use of statistical tests helps to strengthen the case.
2. Of 12 court of appeals cases, 6 (50%) used the 80% rule only, 1 (8%) used both the 80% rule and statistical testing, and 5 (42%) used only statistical testing. The authors similarly concluded that, at this level, statistical testing supplements the 80% rule.

Two relatively more recent cases that were most directly responsible for the increased acceptance of significance testing in the determination of adverse impact were *Bridgeport Guardians v. City of Bridgeport* (1991) and *Waisome v. The Port Authority* (1991). The courts ruled that the detection of a statistically significant difference between majority and minority selection ratios was sufficient to establish prima facie evidence of discrimination. After these two rulings, the use of significance testing to determine adverse impact steadily increased, whereas the use of the four-fifths rule steadily decreased (Esson & Hauenstein, 2006).

Adverse Impact in the Academic Literature

Two basic issues have been explored in the academic literature pertaining to adverse impact. One issue deals with statistics and psychometrics. What statistical properties, if any, influence the four-fifths rule? What statistical tests of significant differences should be used to establish adverse impact? Does the application of both the four-fifths rule and a statistical significance test yield consistent conclusions regarding adverse impact? What psychometric adjustments can influence the adverse impact result? The second issue focuses on a different level of analysis; academics and practitioners have written about the types of tests that yield adverse impact, which tests yield more or less adverse impact, as well as on ways in which adverse impact can be reduced.

A number of chapters in this volume address the issues raised in the preceding paragraph. For the present purposes, I focus on particular references from the literature to illustrate particular aspects of the two issues mentioned.

Use of the Four-Fifths Rule or a Test of Statistical Significance

As noted, a key issue in the litigation arena is whether the plaintiff needs to establish adverse impact by both the 80% rule and statistical significance testing. As I have presented, the *UGESP* (Equal Employment Opportunity Commission et al., 1978), the focus is on the 80% rule, although there are situations for which statistical significance testing *may* be necessary. On the other hand, Esson and Hauenstein (2006) found that, in court cases, there seems to be a reliance on statistical testing. A position that argues for both types of analyses is found in the work of Siskin and Trippi (2005), who argued that statistical significance is a necessary but not a sufficient condition for adverse impact; it is a precursor to the need to establish practical significance, as indicated by the 80% rule. Thus, all positions are represented in the literature. And, this has fostered research that attempts to compare the two strategies.

There are two common ways in which adverse impact has been measured, one of which is derived directly from the definition: the 80% rule. This has been discussed and demonstrated in this chapter. In brief, adverse impact, which is a rule of thumb, stems from subgroup differences (i.e., standardized mean differences between the majority and protected group, or subgroup *d*). Adverse impact is almost completely determined by subgroup differences (*d*), which is why some researchers use the terms subgroup *d* and adverse impact synonymously (or alternatively, refer to subgroup *d* as "adverse impact potential"; Roth et al., 2006). The second approach is more statistical and consistent with hypothesis testing; this analytical strategy involves the determination of whether the two selection rate percentages for the majority and minority groups are statistically significant.

It should be noted that there is some indication that adverse impact can be established by other considerations than strict reliance on the 80% rule or statistical significance testing. Roth et al. (2006) noted that there are variations of the 80% rule such as the "one-person" rule and the "N of 1 rule." Roth et al. described the "one-person" rule as a situation in which the number of minorities selected is different from the number of minorities expected to be selected. The *expected number of minorities* is defined as the overall selection rate multiplied by the number of minority applicants rounded down to the nearest whole number. An organization then compares the actual number of minority hires to the expected number. If the difference is one or more, this "rule" indicates that adverse impact may be occurring, and that analysis should continue on to the determination of validity and test fairness. If the difference is less than one, violations of the four-fifths rule may be attributed to small sample sizes.

Likewise, the N of 1 rule, which is outlined in *Questions and Answers* Number 21 to the *UGESP* (Equal Employment Opportunity Commission et al., 1978), allows one to assume that the organization hired one less majority group member and one more minority group member. Then, if the order of selection ratios is reversed such that the minority selection ratio is now larger than the majority selection ratio, adverse impact is generally not thought to have occurred. From my perspective, these last two rules have received little attention in the literature or practice.

The academic research on the four-fifths rule has examined it from several perspectives. Bobko and Roth (2004) examined the four-fifths rule from arithmetic, intuitive, and logical perspectives. They noted that the adverse impact definition of Section 4(D) of the UGESP (Equal Employment Opportunity Commission et al., 1978) contains both a descriptive (80% rule) and an inferential component (statistical test of differences), although as suggested here, at the outset there was concentration on the 80% rule for practical purposes. They also noted that the 80% rule definition does not invoke statistical assumptions/theory and avoids the fact that statistical significance test results depend on sample sizes.

Sample size and sampling issues pertaining to the four-fifths rule have been explored. Boardman (1979), Greenberg (1979), and Lawshe (1987) demonstrated the problems with the 80% rule and its instability and propensity for inappropriate conclusions. Boardman (1979) and Greenberg (1979) found that the 80% rule did not accurately reflect the true degree of adverse impact and frequently underestimated the extent to which there was adverse impact in the organization. Lawshe (1987) was critical of the 80% rule because it did not take into account sampling error.

Are the statistical problems with the four-fifths rule similar to ones with tests of statistical significance? Before addressing this question, I present a brief discussion of how the literature has explored adverse impact and statistical significance.

In general, tests of the significance of the difference in selection rates (percentages or ratios) have been studied by the use of the z test for the difference between percentages. Other statistics include the chi-square test, binomial, and Fisher's exact test.

As with the four-fifths rule, tests of significance are constrained by sample size—small sample sizes in either subgroup require large differences to yield a conclusion of significant difference. And, since the test of significance is a test of a hypothesis, not only are there problems of statistical power, but also we must be cognizant of the fact that the test of the difference in percentages is based on sampling distributions, which yields the opportunity for Type I and Type II errors in conclusions.

Collins and Morris (2008) compared several alternate test statistics in terms of Type I error rates and power, focusing on situations with small samples. Significance testing was found to be of limited value due to low power for all tests. Among the alternate test statistics, the widely used z test on the difference between two proportions performed reasonably well, except when sample size was extremely small. Use of Fisher's exact test and Yates's continuity-corrected chi-square test was not recommended due to overly conservative Type I error rates and substantially lower power than the z test.

Although the two strategies each have their inherent limitations, it has not prevented researchers from comparing the two strategies to determine if they are consistent in their findings. Unfortunately, in realistic situations, the two calculations produce different results (York, 1995). The reason why the four-fifths rule may yield a different conclusion than the statistical test is because the four-fifths rule is about a ratio of ratios and is not defined by a critical difference in ratios (Bobko & Roth, 2004).

Meier, Sacks, and Zabell (1984) presented an appropriate analysis of the courts' interpretation of tests for differences at the time the article was written. Meier et al. (1984) also contrasted the 80% rule to the binomial test in terms of assumptions and appropriateness for employment situations; they concluded that both types of tests should be used. An important point noted by Meier et al. is that no single measure can capture completely the information one wants when attempting to determine if a test is rejecting a minority group at a different rate than a majority group.

Morris and Lobsenz (2000) highlighted the difference between the two approaches in terms of (a) a practical test versus statistical test of significance; (b) different standards in legal versus scientific fields, such as reliance on the "preponderance of evidence" versus reliance on probability, sampling error, and statistical significance; and (c) reliance on mechanical rules versus a body of evidence. They noted that the comparison of the two types of measures is a function of the size of the individual selection rates; that is, if the two selection rates are 0.15 and 0.20, a difference of 0.05, the adverse impact ratio is 0.75, suggestive of adverse impact. On the other hand the same difference of 0.05 with individual selection rates of 0.50 and 0.55, which yields an adverse impact ratio of 0.91, would show no adverse impact. Morris and Lobsenz (2000) proposed statistics for assessing adverse impact that focused on confidence intervals. My observation is that although their procedure has merit, it has not been widely adopted in the legal arena.

As this discussion illustrates, adverse impact is not uniformly defined; some focus only on the four-fifths rule, others focus on statistically significant differences between selection rates, and yet others apply both operationalizations. A critical issue is whether application of both the four-fifths rule *and* the use of statistical significance tests on the same data set would change conclusions compared to when only one method was used for assessing adverse impact. Roth et al. (2006) conducted such an analysis. They created Monte Carlo simulations representing different situations: (a) no mean score differences between subgroups and (b) standardized mean subgroup differences set at values estimated from the literature. The general purpose of the article was to examine the impact of statistical significance testing if the initial application of the 80% rule suggested adverse impact.

Roth et al. (2006) found that (a) application of the four-fifths rule alone yielded a fairly large number of false-positive readings, influenced by a number of factors, including sample size, selection ratios, and the percentage of minorities in the pool; and (b) adding a statistical test of significance to violations of the 80% rule was associated with markedly fewer false-positive conclusions in moderate size samples (Ns of 200 and 400).

Psychometric Influences on the Conclusion of Adverse Impact

Whereas there is a body of literature that compares the use of statistical tests to the 80% rule, there is also a considerable body of literature that examines the relationship between adverse impact and validity, which tests (predictors) generate the most impact, how to reduce adverse impact, and other topics that are covered in this volume. In this section, I review some of the studies that examined how psychometric adjustments such as different weighting systems, generating different composites of predictors, applying models with different hurdles in use of tests, and other "statistical controls" may influence the conclusion of adverse impact. What is particularly noteworthy in these examinations (and reviews), however, is how adverse impact has been operationalized. A key conclusion from the following presentation is that although there may be a greater reliance on statistical testing of significant differences, the studies cited in this section predominantly relied on operationalizing adverse impact in terms of the 80% rule.

Schmitt, Rogers, Chan, Sheppard, and Jennings (1997) examined the effects of number of predictors, predictor intercorrelations, validity, and level of subgroup difference on a number of outcomes, including adverse impact. This research complemented research by Sackett and his colleagues (Sackett & Ellingson, 1997; Sackett & Roth, 1996; Sackett & Wilk, 1994), which examined impacts of different situations on adverse impact. In each of these research explorations, adverse impact was operationalized in different ways. Schmitt et al. (1997) and Sackett and Wilk (1994) operationalized adverse impact as an "adverse impact ratio," which is the 80% rule. Sackett and Roth (1996) operationalized adverse impact as a situation in which one predictor produced a difference of one standard deviation between subgroups, while another predictor produced a zero standard deviation difference. Sackett and Ellingson (1997) examined standardized differences between minority and majority groups and showed, in one table, the impact based on the 80% rule.

Hattrup, Rock, and Scalia (1997) explored the effects of various strategies of weighting criterion, performance, dimensions on adverse impact. They defined adverse impact in terms of the 80% rule.

De Corte, Lievens, and Sackett (2007) proposed a procedure to determine predictor composites that result in trade-offs between the often-competing goals in personnel selection of quality and adverse impact. They focused on adverse impact ratios.

Newman, Jacobs, and Bartram (2007) assessed the relative accuracy of three techniques—local validity studies, meta-analysis, and Bayesian analysis—for estimating test validity, incremental validity, and adverse impact in a specific selection context. Adverse impact was defined in terms of the 80% rule but operationalized as a mean standardized difference between subgroups.

Aguinis and Smith (2007) proposed an integrative framework for understanding the relationship among test validity, test bias, selection errors, and adverse impact. They defined adverse impact in terms of a ratio of two selection ratios or the 80% rule.

Another body of literature focused on statistical selection strategies designed to reduce adverse impact, including point addition methods, within-group norming, and alternative selection rules (Sackett & Wilk, 1994), and test score banding (Cascio, Outtz, Zedeck, & Goldstein, 1991). However, the effectiveness of these interventions has been limited (Hough, Oswald, & Ployhart, 2001; Ryan, Ployhart, & Friedel, 1998; Sackett et al., 1994), and point addition and within-group norming are considered unlawful under the Civil Rights Act of 1991. In these research articles, the focus again was on the 80% rule outcome.

Personnel psychologists also have devoted considerable effort to identify test and test presentation strategies that reduce adverse impact; however, few strategies have eliminated adverse impact (Hattrup et al., 1997; Murphy, Osten, & Myors, 1995; Pulakos, Schmitt, & Chan, 1996; Ryan et al., 1998; Sackett & Ellingson, 1997; Sackett & Roth, 1996; Sackett & Wilk, 1994; Schmitt et al., 1997). These studies also relied on *d* or adverse impact ratios.

There is also a body of research on the relationship between predictor types and how they influence adverse impact. As early as the 1980s, it was established that cognitive ability tests yield valid prediction of performance for many jobs (Hunter & Hunter, 1984; Schmitt, Gooding, Noe, & Kirsch, 1984). We have also known that the use of cognitive ability tests usually leads to mean differences of approximately one standard deviation between Caucasians and African Americans, which in turn suggests adverse impact. As a consequence, researchers have focused on (a) an alternative to or supplements to cognitive ability tests such that the application of other or additional predictors would result in no or less adverse impact and (b) strategies for forming predictor composites to achieve reduced adverse impact. These research endeavors have been informative and useful. Yet, as in the "psychometric" literature, a critical question in this research domain is how adverse impact is operationalized.

Hough et al. (2001) presented a very thorough review of various selection procedures, such as cognitive ability, personality, and physical ability tests, and their impact on adverse impact, which they defined as "differential hiring rates." Their article presents conclusions in terms of standardized differences between minority and majority test scores. No formal definition was provided to indicate what degree of standardized difference would trigger an examination in terms of the UGESP (Equal Employment Opportunity Commission et al., 1978). When discussing means for reducing adverse impact, they referred to the 80% rule.

Roth et al. (2006) presented a precise summary of the use of the four-fifths rule in the literature, noting that it has been studied in relationship to hiring rates for the use of different types of predictors (e.g., cognitive ability, Schmitt et al., 1997; grade point average, Roth & Bobko, 2000; and structured interviews, Roth, Van Iddekinge, Huffcutt, Eidson, & Bobko, 2002). Chan and Schmitt (1997) found that video-based situational judgment tests resulted in smaller subgroup differences than paper-and-pencil versions of the situational judgment tests.

Berry, Gruys, and Sackett (2006) examined differences in mean level of cognitive ability and adverse impact that can be expected when selecting employees solely on educational attainment as a proxy for cognitive ability versus selecting employees directly on cognitive ability. Adverse impact was operationalized in terms of adverse impact ratios.

Other articles that have relied on the four-fifths rule for determining the presence of adverse impact are those by Bobko, Roth, and Potosky (1999); Reilly and Chao (1982); and Reilly and Warech (1993).

The point of the review here is that the analyses operationalized adverse impact in terms of the four-fifths rule or mean standardized differences. While there are two strategies for analyzing adverse impact, and where statistically significant differences may be the strategy preferred by the courts, academics and others have examined the outcome of psychometric influences in terms of the 80% rule. This is an interesting evaluation of the literature. Whereas early human resource experts were concerned that practitioners would have difficulty with statistical testing of differences, thereby leading to reliance on the 80% rule, the literature from academics showed a greater reliance on the 80% rule when examining its relationship to particular aspects of the personnel process. Why? Perhaps academics are more comfortable translating their analytical strategies into simple language such as the 80% rule, which focuses on ratios that go from 0 to 1 and are intuitive. The courts, however, seem to be more sophisticated in statistics than one would expect and seem to be comfortable with tests of statistical significance.

Roth et al. (2006) presented an accurate summary of the literature when they stated:

> ... the 4/5ths rule often plays an important role in the measurement and understanding of adverse impact in a variety of settings. The academic literature heavily relies on the 4/5ths rule to analyze the relationship between majority and minority hiring rates. Examples include the use of the 4/5ths rule to understand hiring rates for cognitive ability tests (e.g., Olian & Guthrie, 1987; Schmitt et al., 1997), grade point averages (e.g., Roth & Bobko, 2000), and structured interviews (e.g., Roth, Van Iddekinge, Huffcutt, Eidson, & Bobko, 2002) as well as adding predictors such as personality to a measure of cognitive ability (e.g., Ryan et al., 1998), substituting alternative predictors for a measure of cognitive ability (e.g., Pulakos & Schmitt, 1996), and composites of predictors (Bobko et al., 1999; Schmitt et al., 1997). The state of the 4/5ths rule in the applied psychology literature is summarized by Barrett (1998), who noted that "the 80% rule has been virtually enshrined as the standard for determining whether or not there is adverse impact (p. 94)." (p. 509)

Roth et al. (2006) concluded with the point with which I totally concur. That is, one way to indicate the importance of the four-fifths rule in the applied psychology literature is to consider how often an alternative approach such as significance testing is used to compare hiring rates. In this regard, Roth et al. found it quite difficult to locate instances in the academic literature of researchers testing differences in hiring rates using statistical significance tests. Thus, although we have explored comparisons between the four-fifths rule and statistical tests, when we have attempted to manipulate/adjust the adverse impact, we have focused on impacting the four-fifths rule, which as already established does not always lead to the same conclusion as when significance tests are undertaken. For the purposes of this chapter, the particular findings of the research endeavors noted in this section of the chapter are not critical, but the point to be made is that the implications for the impact on adverse impact are generally confined to adverse impact as defined by the four-fifths rule or standard deviation differences; there is no research of impact on adverse impact as measured by statistically significant differences.

Conclusion

This introductory chapter on adverse impact has attempted to highlight the definition, measurement, and history of the concept. Although there is a reasonable amount of research on the different means for measuring and defining adverse impact, the bottom line is that adverse impact

1. is a practical rule of thumb and not a legal definition
2. is predominantly focused on selection rates and the four-fifths rule
3. is an initial signal that more information is required
4. based on the four-fifths rule, is not controlling, and statistical significance *may* be considered depending on the sample sizes of the groups and the degree of difference in selection ratios and selection rates

These are the messages taken away by the practitioner from the guidelines and the research on adverse impact.

References

Aguinis, H., & Smith, M. A. (2007). Understanding the impact of test validity and bias on selection errors and adverse impact in human resource selection. *Personnel Psychology, 60*, 165–199.

Albemarle Paper Company v. Moody, 422 U.S. 405 (1975).

American Educational Research Association. (1999). *Standards for educational and psychological testing*. Washington, DC: Author.

Barrett, R. S. (1998). *Challenging the myths of fair employment practices*. Westport, CT: Quorum.

Berry, C. M., Gruys, M. L., & Sackett, P. R. (2006). Educational attainment as a proxy for cognitive ability in selection: Effects on levels of cognitive ability and adverse impact. *Journal of Applied Psychology, 91*, 696–705.

Biddle, D. (2006) *Adverse impact and test validation: A practitioner's guide to valid and defensible employment testing* (2nd ed.). Aldershot, U.K.: Gower.

Boardman, A. E. (1979). Another analysis of the EEOC "four-fifths" rule. *Management Science, 25*, 770–776.

Bobko, P., & Roth, P. (2004). The four-fifths rule for assessing adverse impact: An arithmetic, intuitive, and logical analysis of the rule and implications for future research and practice. In J. J. Martocchio (Ed.), *Research in personnel and human resources management* (pp. 177–198). Amsterdam: Elsevier.

Bobko, P., Roth, P., & Potosky, D. (1999). Deviation and implications of a meta-analytic matrix incorporating cognitive ability, alternative predictors, and job performance. *Personnel Psychology, 52*, 561–589.

Bridgeport Guardians v. City of Bridgeport, 933 F. 2d 1140. (1991).

Cascio, W. F., Outtz, J., Zedeck, S., & Goldstein, I. L. (1991). Statistical implications of six methods of test score use in personnel selection. *Human Performance, 4*, 233–264.

Chan, D., & Schmitt, N. (1997). Video-based versus paper-and-pencil method of assessment in situational judgment tests: Subgroup differences in test performance and face validity perceptions. *Journal of Applied Psychology, 82*, 143–159.

Collins, M. W., & Morris, S. B. (2008). Testing for adverse impact when sample size is small. *Journal of Applied Psychology, 93*, 463–471.

De Corte, W., Lievens, F., & Sackett, P. R. (2007). Combining predictors to achieve optimal trade-offs between selection quality and adverse impact. *Journal of Applied Psychology, 92*, 1380–1393.

Equal Employment Opportunity Commission. (1966). *Guidelines on employment testing procedures*. Washington, DC: Author.

Equal Employment Opportunity Commission, Civil Service Commission, Department of Labor, & Department of Justice. (1978) *Uniform guidelines on employee selection procedures*. 29 C.F.R. 1607.

Esson, P. L. & Hauenstein, N. M. (2006). *Exploring the use of the four-fifths rule and significance tests in adverse impact court case rulings*. Paper presented at the 21st Annual Conference of the Society for Industrial and Organizational Psychology, Dallas, TX.

Greenberg, I. (1979). An analysis of the EEOC "four-fifths" rule. *Management Science, 25*, 762–769.

Gregory v. Litton Systems, Inc., 472 F. 2d 631 (9th Cir. 1972).

Griggs v. Duke Power Company, 401 U.S. 424 (1971).

Guion, R. M. (1998). *Assessment, measurement, and prediction for personnel decisions*. Mahwah, NJ: Erlbaum.

Hattrup, K., Rock, J., & Scalia, C. (1997). The effects of varying conceptualizations of job performance on adverse impact, minority hiring, and predicted performance. *Journal of Applied Psychology, 82,* 656–664.

Hazelwood School District v. United States, 433 U.S., 299 (1977).

Hough, L. M., Oswald, F. L., & Ployhart, R. E. (2001). Determinants, detection and amelioration of adverse impact in personnel selection procedures: Issues, evidence and lessons learned. *International Journal of Selection and Assessment, 9,* 152–194.

Hunter, J. E., & Hunter, R. F. (1984). Validity and utility of alternative predictors of job performance. *Psychological Bulletin, 96,* 72–98.

International Brotherhood of Teamsters v. United States, 431 U. S. 324, at 339–40 (1977).

Lawshe, C. H. (1987). Adverse impact: Is it a viable concept? *Professional Psychology: Research and Practice, 18,* 492–497.

Meier, P., Sacks, J., & Zabell, S. L. (1984). What happened in Hazelwood: Statistics, employment discrimination, and the 80% rule. *American Bar Foundation Research Journal, 9,* 139–186.

Morris, S. B., & Lobsenz, R. E. (2000). Significance tests and confidence intervals for the adverse impact ratio. *Personnel Psychology, 53,* 89–111.

Murphy, K. R., Osten, K., & Myors, B. (1995). Modeling the effects of banding in personnel selection. *Personnel Psychology, 48,* 61–84.

Newman, D. A., Jacobs, R. R., & Bartram, D. (2007). Choosing the best method for local validity estimation: Relative accuracy of meta-analysis versus a local study versus Bayes-analysis. *Journal of Applied Psychology, 92,* 1394–1413.

Office of Federal Contract Compliance. Employee testing and other selection procedures. 36 Fed. Reg. (192), 19307–19310 (1971).

Olian, J. D., & Guthrie, J. P. (1987). Cognitive ability tests in employment: Ethical perspectives of employers and society. *Research in Corporate Social Performance and Policy, 9,* 185–213.

Pulakos, E. P., & Schmitt, N. (1996). An evaluation of two strategies for reducing adverse impact and their effects on criterion related validity. *Human Performance, 9,* 241–258.

Pulakos, E. P., Schmitt, N., & Chan, D. (1996). Models of job performance ratings: An examination of ratee race, ratee gender, and rater level effects. *Human Performance, 9,* 103–119.

Questions and Answers to Clarify and Provide a Common Interpretation of the Uniform Guidelines on Employee Selection Procedures, 44 Fed. Reg. 43 (March 2, 1979).

Reilly, R. R., & Chao, G. T. (1982). Validity and fairness of some alternative employee selection procedures. *Personnel Psychology, 35,* 1–62.

Reilly, R. R., & Warech, M. A. (1993). The validity and fairness of alternatives to cognitive tests. In L. C. Wing & B. R. Gifford (Eds.), *Evaluation in education and human services: Vol. 35. Policy issues in employment testing* (pp. 131–224). Norwell, MA: Kluwer Academic.

Roth, P. L., & Bobko, P. (2000). College grades as employment selection mechanisms: Ethnic group differences and adverse impact. *Journal of Applied Psychology, 85,* 399–406.

Roth, P. L., Bobko, P., & Switzer, F. S., III. (2006). Modeling the behavior of the 4/5ths rule for determining adverse impact: Reasons for caution. *Journal of Applied Psychology, 91*, 507–522.

Roth, P. L., Van Iddekinge, C. H., Huffcutt, A. I., Eidson, C. E., Jr., & Bobko, P. (2002). Corrections for range restriction in structured interviews: The values may be larger than researchers thought. *Journal of Applied Psychology, 87*, 369–376.

Ryan, A. M., Ployhart, R. E., & Friedel, L. A. (1998). Using personality testing to reduce adverse impact: A cautionary note. *Journal of Applied Psychology, 83*, 298–307.

Sackett, P. R., & Ellingson, J. E. (1997). The effects of forming multi-predictor composites on group differences and adverse impact. *Personnel Psychology, 50*, 707–721.

Sackett, P. R., & Roth, L. (1996). Multi-stage selection strategies: A Monte Carlo investigation of effects on performance and minority hiring. *Personnel Psychology, 49*, 549–572.

Sackett, P. R., & Wilk, S. L. (1994). Within-group norming and other forms of score adjustment in preemployment testing. *American Psychologist, 49*, 929–954.

Schmitt, N., Gooding, R. Z., Noe, R. A., & Kirsch, M. P. (1984). Meta-analyses of validity studies published between 1964 and 1982 and the investigation of study characteristics. *Personnel Psychology, 37*, 407–422.

Schmitt, N., Rogers, W., Chan, D., Sheppard, L., & Jennings, D. (1997). Adverse impact and predictive efficiency of various predictor combinations. *Journal of Applied Psychology, 82*, 719–730.

Siskin, B. R., & Trippi, J. (2005). Statistical issues in litigation. In F. Landy (Ed.), *Employment discrimination litigation: Behavioral, quantitative, and legal perspectives* (pp. 132–166). San Francisco: Jossey-Bass.

Society for Industrial and Organizational Psychology. (2003). *Principles for the validation and use of personnel selection procedures* (4th ed.). Bowling Green, OH: Author.

Technical Advisory Committee on Testing. (1972). *Guidelines on employee selection procedures.* Sacramento, CA: Fair Employment Practice Commission.

Uniform employee selection guidelines interpretation and clarification (questions and answers). Equal Employment Opportunity Commission (29 CFR 1607), Office of Personnel Management (5 CFR 300), U.S. Department of Justice (28 CFR, Ch. 1, Part 50), U.S. Treasury Department (31 CFR, Ch. 1, Part 51), and the Office of Federal Contract Compliance Programs (41 CFR, Ch. 60, Part 68–3). Supplemental questions and answers (No. 91 through 93) became effective as of May 2, 1980 (45 F.R. 29350).

Waisome v. Port Authority, 758 F. Supp. 171 (1991).

York, K. M. (1995). Disparate results in adverse impact tests. The four-fifths rule versus chi-square. *Proceedings of the Association of Management Conference, Human Resource Management Group, 13*, 128–141.

2

An Analysis of Two Methods for Assessing and Indexing Adverse Impact: A Disconnect Between the Academic Literature and Some Practice

Philip Bobko and Philip L. Roth

Introduction

Applied psychologists have made substantial efforts toward analyzing the validity and adverse impact of various predictors of job performance (e.g., Bobko, Roth, & Potosky, 1999; Hough, Oswald, & Ployhart, 2001; Reilly & Warech, 1993; Roth, Bobko, & McFarland, 2005; Ryan, Ployhart, & Friedel, 1998). When assessing adverse impact, there is a strong emphasis on the use of the four-fifths rule from the Uniform Guidelines on Employee Selection Procedures (U.S. Equal Opportunity Employment Commission, U.S. Civil Service Commission, U.S. Department of Labor, & U.S. Department of Justice, 1978) (e.g., Hoffman & Thornton, 1997; Schmitt, Rogers, Chan, Sheppard, & Jennings, 1997). At the same time, previous work has shown that the four-fifths rule is subject to a relatively high rate of false positives (e.g., Boardman, 1979; Roth, Bobko, & Switzer, 2006). For example, Roth et al. demonstrated that the four-fifths rule signaled adverse impact approximately 20% or more of the time at selection ratios of 0.1 and 0.3 (in samples of $n = 200$ and 400) when there were no mean ethnic group differences between the "majority" and "minority" groups.

The purpose of this chapter is to investigate the reliance of the applied psychology research literature on the four-fifths rule for determining adverse impact and to remind researchers and practitioners that this approach, as well as statistical significance testing, has important uses and limitations.

The Uniform Guidelines and Two Perspectives on Adverse Impact

The Uniform Guidelines on Employee Selection Procedures (U.S. Equal Opportunity Employment Commission et al., 1978), or Uniform Guidelines, were a joint effort of several government agencies. These guidelines were "designed to provide a framework for determining the proper use of tests and other selection procedures" (Section 1607.1B) in regard to prohibiting discriminatory employment practices. Those guidelines define *adverse impact* as follows:

> A selection rate for any race, sex, or ethnic group which is less than four-fifths (4/5) (or eighty percent) of the rate for the group with the highest rate will generally be regarded by the Federal enforcement agencies as evidence of adverse impact, while a greater than four-fifths rate will generally not be regarded by Federal enforcement agencies as evidence of adverse impact. Smaller differences in selection rate may nevertheless constitute adverse impact, where they are significant in both statistical and practical terms. ... Greater differences in selection rate may not constitute adverse impact where the differences are based on small numbers and are not statistically significant. ... (Section 1607.3D).

Note that, as discussed at length by Bobko and Roth (2004), the first sentence in the definition of the four-fifths rule is based on an algebraic, *descriptive* definition in which one selection rate is arithmetically compared to four fifths of another selection rate. This has come to be known as the *four-fifths (or 80%) rule*. In contrast, note that the second and third sentences indicate that selection rates that do meet the four-fifths rule may nonetheless constitute adverse impact—as a function of *statistical* and practical significance. Bobko and Roth pointed out that this change in focus (from descriptive to inferential) mirrors how most basic statistical texts are organized, that is, the first half of the text is descriptive and the second half inferential.

It is important to realize that two somewhat different approaches to adverse impact are implied in the Uniform Guidelines (U.S. Equal Opportunity Employment Commission et al., 1978). Both approaches consider selection rates for two subgroups. However, the four-fifths rule focuses on a ratio of rates, while the inferential approach focuses on the statistical significance of the difference in rates. Thus, it could be that two organizations have the same ratio of selection rates (e.g., 0.10 to 0.05 = 2:1 and 0.80 to 0.40 = 2:1), yet the differences in rates are themselves different (e.g., 0.10 − 0.05 = 0.05 is different from 0.80 − 0.40 = 0.40). The converse is also possible (same difference in selection rates within organizations but different ratios across organizations). In addition, note that the outcome of the application of one approach (statistical significance) is directly dependent on sample size; all else equal, larger n leads to greater likelihood of significance. In contrast, although there is sampling variation around the adverse impact ratio (ratio of two selection rates), the outcome of the application of the four-fifths rule is not directly dependent on sample size.

Based on the work of Bobko and Roth (2004), we briefly summarize some useful facets, and concerns, about each of these two approaches. We then conduct an analysis of the frequency of use of these two approaches in the academic literature, and we report a somewhat surprising finding. We then discuss this finding and try to interweave some implications for future efforts.

The Four-Fifths (80%) Rule

As noted, the four-fifths rule from the Uniform Guidelines (U.S. Equal Opportunity Employment Commission et al., 1978) arithmetically compares the selection ratio of the group with the highest selection ratio (often thought of as the majority) to the selection ratio of other groups (e.g., blacks, Hispanics, women). Adverse impact is signaled if the selection ratio of the other group is less than four-fifths of the selection rate of the group with the highest selection ratio. The Uniform Guidelines also state that a predictor with adverse impact that has not been validated according to the guidelines can be considered discriminatory (see Section 1607.3A).

The four-fifths rule (or 80% rule) is a particularly important indicator of adverse impact according to many researchers, especially those in the academic literature. Some stated that "the 80% rule has been virtually enshrined as the standard for determining whether or not there is adverse impact" in the academic literature (Barrett, 1998, p. 94) or "despite problems ... the 4/5ths rule remains the usual definition of adverse impact" (Guion, 1998, p. 172). Yet others (Outtz & Hanges, 2006) have referred to it as the golden rule. Further, the literature is replete with examples of its use (e.g., Olian & Guthrie, 1987; Pulakos & Schmitt, 1996; Ryan et al., 1998; Schmitt et al., 1997). Finally, some researchers have suggested that the four-fifths rule is the most frequently used indicator for determining adverse impact in employment discrimination cases (Morris & Lobsenz, 2000).

Development of the Four-Fifths Rule

The development of the four-fifths rule was in part a reaction to significance tests. Developers of the four-fifths rule were concerned about two related issues. First, they were worried that significance tests required relatively large sample sizes (Bill Burns, personal communication, May 27, 2004). That is, at least some of the developers believed that the need for a large sample size was a "fatal flaw." For example, researchers could find two organizations with the same adverse impact ratios, but results would be different based on sample size (e.g., samples of 500 and 75) and associated statistical power. In addition, large sample sizes would make even trivial differences significant (for related sample size issues, see also Morris, 2001).

Second, developers of the four-fifths rule were concerned that most individuals charged with enforcement of equal employment opportunity would find it difficult to conduct and interpret results of significance tests (see Biddle, 2005, or Meier, Sacks, & Zabell, 1984). The alternative was a simpler rule of thumb that compared the selection ratio of the group with the highest hiring rate to the selection ratio of other "protected" groups.

Also, as noted in the Uniform Guidelines (U.S. Equal Opportunity Employment Commission et al., 1978), this rule was adopted as a rule of thumb. It was not originally intended as a legal definition of discrimination but as a "practical device to keep the attention of enforcement agencies on serious discrepancies in hire or promotion rates or other employment decisions" (Supplementary Information, Section II). If disparity in selection rates is evidenced, then a prima facie case of disparate impact can be alleged.

Some Positive and Negative Facets of the Four-Fifths Rule

Sample Size

When comparing two subgroups, researchers have noted that a key issue is the number of individuals in the smaller of the two subgroups (Bobko & Roth, 2004; Lawshe, 1987; Morris, 2001; Tversky & Kahneman, 1971). In the case of the four-fifths rule, the smaller of the two groups could have a substantial influence on the results. For example, hiring 1 of 10 members of a minority group and 15 of 80 of a majority group would lead to a signal of adverse impact. However, hiring just one more minority group member would lead to a signal of no adverse impact. This issue has been noted in the Questions and Answers (Q&As) following the Uniform Guidelines (U.S. Equal Opportunity Employment Commission et al., 1978; e.g., see

Q&A 21). Overall, small differences in hiring within the minority group can have substantial influences on signals from the four-fifths rule.

On the other hand, the four-fifths rule is not directly dependent on sample size. As noted in this chapter, tests of statistical significance can make even minuscule differences in selection rates be "statistically significant" if the sample size (n) is very large.

Practical Significance

Note also that the extensive quotation mentioned from the Uniform Guidelines places the concept of "practical significance" in the same sentence with the concept of statistical significance (e.g., "Smaller differences in selection rate may nevertheless constitute adverse impact, where they are significant in both statistical and practical terms"). It is our experience that individuals sometimes use a test of statistical significance to signal adverse impact—even though the four-fifths rule is not violated. This is ironic because, as also noted above, the Uniform Guidelines offer the four-fifths rule as a "practical device," and thus the rule is presumably meant to offer some level of practicality to the significance test.

Influence of Selectivity

It has also been noted that the level of organizational selectivity can influence the outcome of the four-fifths rule. For example, following Bobko and Roth (2004), assume that the highest selection rate in an organization is for the majority group (rate is 0.70). The four-fifths rule implies that any minority selection rate below a value of $0.80 \times 0.70 = 0.56$ might be interpreted as evidence of adverse impact. Thus, the minority rate might drop $0.70 - 0.56 = 0.14$ percentage points below the majority rate before adverse impact is claimed. In contrast, if another organization is more selective in its hiring (e.g., majority selection rate of 0.20), then minority rates need to differ only by 0.04 (i.e., $0.20 - 0.16$) to be interpreted as evidence of adverse impact. The second organization is, all else equal, more susceptible to claims of adverse impact.

Framing

As another issue, Bobko and Roth (2004) noted that the Uniform Guidelines frame the notion of adverse impact in terms of *selection* rate (positive frame) rather than rejection rate (negative frame). This is important because the four-fifths rule is about ratios of rates (which depend on framing) and not differences in rates (which are the same if one uses selection rates or rejection rates).

For example, as noted by those Bobko and Roth (2004), two rates of 0.10 and 0.15 are not within 80% of one another, yet the rates of 0..85 and 0..90

are within 80% of one another even though the difference in selection rates (a comparison typically used in significance testing) is the same. The converse possibility is also possible. Suppose further that the two *selection* rates for an organization are 0.85 and 0.90. Even though the two rates meet the four-fifths rule, some might be tempted to compute the two associated *rejection* rates of 0.10 and 0.15 and claim the four-fifths rule is violated. This does not appear to be the intent in the Uniform Guidelines as the four-fifths rule refers to selection, not rejection, rates.

Simpson's Paradox

Bobko and Roth (2004) also discussed the fact that because the four-fifths rule (as well as the statistical test of the difference between selection ratios) is based on use of percentages/proportions, analyses are subject to a phenomenon in mathematics often labeled *Simpson's paradox*. In essence, the level of the organization at which one computes percentages can make a substantial difference. For example, Bobko and Roth reported an example in which the majority selection rate was higher than the female selection rate across an entire organization, yet in virtually all departments within the organization the majority selection rate was lower than the minority rate (see that work or Blank, Dabady, & Citro, 2004, for more detail).

Research Evaluating the Four-Fifths Rule

To our knowledge, only a few articles have focused directly on the false-positive error rates in the determination of adverse impact using the four-fifths rule. Two management scientists used a derivational approach (Boardman, 1979; Greenberg, 1979) to study single-hurdle selection systems. They both showed that the four-fifths rule could indicate adverse impact when no differences actually existed (i.e., Type I errors or false positives), and Greenberg also demonstrated the existence of Type II errors. Unfortunately, the conclusions from this research were limited by a number of factors, including not properly representing the proportions of various groups in the United States, assuming sampling with replacement in some instances (see Roth et al., 2006).

A pair of researchers in industrial relations demonstrated that the four-fifths rule is more demanding in terms of the number of minority hires needed when sample sizes are small (e.g., *n* of 20 through 100), whereas a significance test was more demanding as sample sizes were large and the proportion of minority applicants was small (Sobol & Ellard, 1988). Many of their conclusions might be readily explained by small sample sizes (of minority subgroups) and consequent low statistical power.

Roth et al.'s (2006) simulation also showed relatively frequent false-positive signals from the four-fifths rule. Consistent with prior work, their single-hurdle and multiple-hurdle Monte Carlo analysis showed that false positives were fairly likely (e.g., often 20% of the time) when sample sizes were moderate (e.g., $n = 200$ or 400) and when selection ratios were in the range of 0.1 to 0.3. The percentage of false positives declined markedly, to roughly chance levels, when a test of statistical significance was added as a second step to any signal of adverse impact from the four-fifths rule. The authors found this somewhat ironic given that the four-fifths rule was designed at least partially because of the perceived difficulties of statistical significance tests.

Statistical Significance Testing

Some individuals familiar with the assessment of adverse impact in legal environments suggested that courts do not rely solely on the four-fifths rule when assessing adverse impact (e.g., Barrett, 1995; Biddle, 1993). These individuals suggested that statistical significance tests are often used either in conjunction with the four-fifths rule or in place of it in court proceedings (e.g., Barrett, 1998; Biddle, 2005; Siskin & Trippi, 2005). In their analysis of court cases, Esson and Hauenstein (2007) concluded that there is an increased reliance on significance testing in assessing adverse impact. Also, the statistical significance testing approach mirrors part of the second and third sentences in the quotation from the Uniform Guidelines in the beginning of this chapter (although this approach does not necessarily mirror the issue of practical significance).

Some Positive and Negative Facets of the Statistical Significance Approach

The scientific literature and many methodological textbooks are replete with discussion about the use, benefits, and concerns about statistical significance testing. Significance testing has a strong presence in many social science disciplines, although some of its negatives have on occasion led to calls for its abandonment (Schmidt, 1996). Rather than review this extensive literature, we point out a few issues that are directly related to detecting differences in two selection rates (i.e., differences in two proportions) in the adverse impact arena. Once again, see Bobko and Roth (2004) for a more extended discussion of these particular application issues. See also the work of Meier et al. (1984) for a discussion of the use of significance testing in adverse impact cases as well as the possibility that gross statistical disparities alone could constitute prima facie proof of disparate impact.[1]

Error Rates and Sample Size

It was noted that the four-fifths rule can be subject to both Type I and Type II errors. By design, statistical significance testing controls for Type I error rate by setting that probability a priori. For example, the so-called level of significance is often set at 0.05 or sometimes 0.01 (see also U.S. Equal Opportunity Employment Commission et al., 1978, Uniform Guidelines, Section 1607.145, for mention of the 0.05, or 1 in 20, value). It is our experience that in court proceedings the use of 0.05 and 0.01 (and their associated critical values of 1.96 and 2.58 standard deviations in normal distributions) has led to lawyer-based terminology of the "two or three standard deviation test" (a Supreme Court decision that is often cited in this domain is *Hazelwood School District v. United States*, 1977).

However, when sample sizes are small, Type II errors (failing to "find" a difference when one exists) can occur, and their probability is not controlled in significance testing. In fact, the Uniform Guidelines (U.S. Equal Opportunity Employment Commission et al., 1978, Supplementary Information, General Principles, Section 6) recognize that many employers do not hire enough individuals for primary reliance on a significance testing approach.

The converse (large sample sizes) is also an area of concern for significance testing—because as most students know, almost any nonzero difference (e.g., nonzero difference in selection rates) can result in a "statistically significant" difference if the sample size (n) is large enough. Assume that there is a nonzero difference in selection rates for two subgroups—and that the same difference in rates occurs for two organizations. An implication of the opening sentence of this paragraph is that the larger of the two organizations is more likely to be associated with statistical adverse impact solely because it has more employees (see Bobko & Roth, 2004, for a hypothetical example in which a difference in selection rates would be significant in one organization, but the same rates would not be statistically different in another organization that was one fifth the size).

Comparison Group

Another issue in the determination of adverse impact is the fact that the comparison group is nominally the group with the highest rate and not necessarily the majority group (see the initial quotation from the Uniform Guidelines, U.S. Equal Opportunity Employment Commission et al., 1978). In our experience, the comparison group generally is taken to be the majority group, but it does not have to be if the Uniform Guidelines are taken literally. So, for example, if the highest selection rate was for the minority subgroup of Hispanics, then adverse impact ratios for blacks might be computed against the Hispanic rate rather than the white rate.

The process of waiting to see the data and then deciding what the comparison group is (i.e., which subgroup had the highest rate) deserves further study as a method because it appears to violate standard statistical procedure by which groups are identified a priori. That is, post hoc use of the highest rate might require different distribution theory about maximum values (such as in the Tukey honestly significant difference test in experimental design).

Experimentwise Error

A related issue is that, in our experience, the white (or highest) rate is "tested" against several subgroups (e.g., black, Hispanic, etc.) separately, resulting in multiple significance tests, each at the 0.05 level of significance. However, as also noted in Bobko and Roth (2004), this increases the overall experimentwise error rate. We are unaware of any statistical testing procedure used in adverse impact analyses that considers this issue.

An Analysis of the Degree of Reliance of the Applied Psychological Literature on the Four-Fifths Rule and Statistical Significance

We examined recent journal articles in applied psychology to understand better which method of measurement is used to determine adverse impact in the published academic literature. We searched the database of PsycINFO from 1990 to present (May 2007) for "adverse impact" in the area of applied psychology (classification code 3600). We focused on four journals likely to publish articles on personnel selection: *Journal of Applied Psychology, Personnel Psychology, Human Performance,* and the *International Journal of Selection and Assessment.*

We limited our search to empirical articles with analyses of primary data sets or analyses based on meta-analytic values (e.g., empirically based meta-analytic matrices) and samples of job applicants or incumbents. So, for example, we did not include work by Morris and Lobsenz (2000) and Roth et al. (2006). These articles were either simulations or discussions and algebraic analyses of adverse impact, and they did not focus on primary or meta-analytic data to discuss the presence or degree of adverse impact. However, these works are important, and we discuss them in the section on hybrid approaches. We found 24 empirical articles that matched our selection criteria.

Results

The results in Table 2.1 suggest there are two ways that authors have explicitly addressed the overall empirical issue of adverse impact in the applied psychology academic literature. The first way is calculation of the standardized ethnic or gender group difference (i.e., *d*). In our sample, six articles used this as the primary approach to indexing possible levels of adverse impact (e.g., Bobko, Roth, & Buster, 2005; Ones & Viswesvaran, 1998). Use of the standardized *d* statistic is helpful in understanding how various ethnic or gender groups perform on an exam even when no hiring has yet taken place based on the exam.

The second way that researchers have addressed adverse impact is to compare hiring or passing rates of various subgroups. There were 18 such articles in our sample. In 16 instances, the four-fifths rule was used. In 2 instances, authors reported the adverse impact ratio (i.e., the selection rate of a minority group divided by the selection rate of a majority group) but did not formally invoke the four-fifths rule.

Interestingly, as shown in Table 2.1, there was *no* use of statistical significance testing to assess adverse impact in the studies using empirical data (primary or meta-analytic). Overall, it appears that the four-fifths rule is the dominant approach to assessing adverse impact in selection in the applied psychology academic literature.

The heavy reliance on the four-fifths rule is interesting as it is prevalent across more than 15 years of articles, and it was used in both primary studies and meta-analytic efforts. Note also that use of the four-fifths rule is pervasive across a variety of predictor types and study emphases. The four-fifths rule was used to assess adverse impact in tests of cognitive ability (e.g., Bobko et al., 1999), assessment centers (Hoffman & Thornton, 1997), college grades (Roth & Bobko, 2000), and interviews (Roth, Van Iddekinge, Huffcutt, Eidson, & Schmit, 2005). Further, the four-fifths rule was used to analyze adverse impact in terms of combinations of predictors or types of criteria (e.g., Hattrup, Rock, & Scalia, 1997), how to weight predictors (Doverspike, Winter, Healy, & Barrett, 1996; Ryan et al., 1998), and even how to score exams (McKinney & Collins, 1991). The rule has also been used in Europe as well as the United States (Higuera, 2001).

Although our analysis was focused on the published academic literature, the same result occurs in other academic domains. For example, the human resources text by Gomez-Mejia, Balkin, and Cardy (2007) prominently defined the four-fifths rule and provided a numerical example, but there was no mention of significance testing; a similar summary applies to Pulakos's (2005) book on selection assessment methods. The staffing text by Heneman and Judge (2006) discussed the assessment of adverse impact by using the four-fifths rule; that text only mentioned statistical significance testing as an "exception" (p. 466) to the use of the four-fifths rule. Or, in the

TABLE 2.1

Use of Approaches to Detect Adverse Impact (AI), Presented Reverse Chronologically

Article	Method used	Study type	Comments
Aguinis and Smith (2007)	Four-fifths rule	Meta-analytic values used	Authors focus on AI ratio
DeCorte, Leivens, and Sackett (2006)	Four-fifths rule	Meta-analytic matrix	Authors examined trade-offs between AI and quality of hires
Potosky, Bobko, and Roth (2005)	Four-fifths rule	Meta-analytic matrix	Authors tested the validity increase and AI reduction from adding alternative predictors to measures of mental ability
Buster, Roth, and Bobko (2005)	AI ratio[a]	Primary study	Authors compared AI of two types of minimum qualifications
Bobko, Roth, and Buster (2004)	Neither	Primary study	Authors compared subgroup *d*s
Klinger and Schuler (2004)	Neither	Primary study	Authors focused on subgroup differences and did not compute formal AI analyses
Stark, Charnyshenko, and Drasgow (2004)	Some use of four-fifths rule	Primary study	Authors examined differential item test functioning and used four-fifths rule as a benchmark for index development
DeCorte and Lievens (2003)	Four-fifths rule	Meta-analytic matrix	Four-fifths rule used to constrain selection systems to have no adverse impact (or minimize AI)
Thornton, Murphy, Everest, and Hoffman (2000)	Four-fifths rule	Meta-analytic values	Meta-analytically based values used for utility analyses and AI analysis
Roth and Bobko (2000)	Four-fifths rule	Primary study	Authors examined *d*s on grades and computed AI
Bobko, Roth, and Potosky (1999)	Four-fifths rule	Meta-analytic matrix	Authors compared validity and AI of predictor composites

Continued

TABLE 2.1 (*Continued*)

Use of Approaches to Detect Adverse Impact (AI), Presented Reverse Chronologically

Article	Method used	Study type	Comments
DeCorte (1999)	Four-fifths rule	Meta-analytic matrix	Four-fifths rule used to constrain selection systems to have no adverse impact
Ryan et al. (1998)	AI ratio and four-fifths rule	Primary study	Authors used two samples to examine adding measures of personality to measures of cognitive ability and weighting approaches
Olson-Buchanan et al. (1998)	Neither	Primary study	Authors reported group means and standard deviations
Ones and Viswesvaran (1998)	Neither	Primary study	Authors focused on subgroup ds
Hattrup, Rock, and Scalia (1997)	Four-fifths rule	Meta-analytic matrix	Authors examined the roles of task and contextual performance on validity and AI
Hoffman and Thornton (1997)	Four-fifths rule	Primary study	Authors examined use of assessment centers and cognitive ability tests
Levine, Maye, Ulm, and Gordon (1997)	AI ratio	Primary study	Ratio used to determine AI for 14 jobs using minimum qualifications
Schmitt, Rogers, Chan, Sheppard, and Jennings (1997)	Four-fifths rule	Meta-analytic matrix	Authors compared validity and AI of predictor composites
Weekley and Jones (1997)	Neither	Primary study	Authors focused on subgroup ds
Doverspike Winter, Healy, and Barrett (1996)	Four-fifths rule	Meta-analytic matrix	The authors used a meta-analytic matrix to predict hiring rates for a future exam and to compare weighting approaches.
Pulakos and Schmitt (1996)	Four-fifths rule	Primary study	The authors examined ds for subgroups and assessed AI with the four-fifths rule

TABLE 2.1 (*Continued*)

Use of Approaches to Detect Adverse Impact (AI), Presented Reverse Chronologically

Article	Method used	Study type	Comments
Barrett (1995)	Neither	Primary study	The author examined ds for subgroups
Cascio, Outtz, Zedeck, and Goldstein (1991, 1995)	Four-fifths rule	Primary study	Authors examined methods of referral (e.g., banding) on hiring rates

[a] The AI ratio is the adverse impact ratio that is typically operationalized with the group with the highest hiring rate in the denominator (e.g., whites) and the group with a lower selection rate in the numerator (e.g., blacks).

recent *Encyclopedia of Industrial and Organizational Psychology* (Rogelberg, 2007), Ellingson's definition of "adverse (disparate) impact" mentioned three forms (the four-fifths rule, evidence of a restricted policy, and workforce utilization analysis), but there is no mention of significance testing.

Discussion

As noted, there are two distinct methods of assessing adverse impact that are implied by the Uniform Guidelines (U.S. Equal Opportunity Employment Commission et al., 1978). Some individuals suggest, and routinely use, the four-fifths rule to index the presence of adverse impact. The related adverse impact ratio (ratio of selection rates) is then used to index the level of the adverse impact. Others have suggested that significance tests are the more appropriate and more often used approach for assessment of adverse impact. Again, the Uniform Guidelines explicitly mention both of these assessment procedures, yet the assessments are based on somewhat different premises and logic.

We also briefly reviewed some positive and negative facets of these two approaches. For example, the adverse impact ratio (and the related four-fifths rule approach) is susceptible to choices of framing and the level of selection selectivity in each organization. Or, for example, the statistical significance approach is substantially influenced by sample size and is focused on the difference in rates rather than their ratio.

Use by Academicians

Our analysis in Table 2.1 might lead applied psychologists to believe that the empirical, academic literature endorses the use of the four-fifths rule as the benchmark for assessing adverse impact. Or, as noted, Barrett (1998) stated that the four-fifths rule has been "enshrined" (p. 94) as the method of assessing adverse impact.

On the other hand, although this chapter is not intended as a review of court cases, others have noted that the courts often use statistical significance testing to assess adverse impact (e.g., Biddle, 2005; Biddle, 1993; Bobko & Roth, 2004; Siskin & Trippi, 2005). In fact, in contrast to the analysis in Table 2.1, Jeanneret (2005, p. 81) said that the four-fifths rule "has no standing in the scientific literature."[2]

Thus, it appears that there is an important disconnect in the assessment of adverse impact. The academic literature appears to use the four-fifths rule almost exclusively, while many practitioners and the courts might also consider statistical significance testing.

Possible Reasons for a Disconnect

It is interesting to speculate on the reasons for this disconnect and apparent bifurcation:

Perhaps academics are looking for an index of the degree to which adverse impact occurs (or might occur). Thus, academics choose statistics that have a continuum of values (*d* or adverse impact ratio, which leads to natural use of the four-fifths rule). In contrast, statistical significance is not used because its outcome is simply dichotomous (significant or not).

Perhaps academics who use meta-analytic matrices do not have fixed sample sizes in mind and desire an analysis that is not dependent on *n* (i.e., an effect size such as *d* or the adverse impact ratio).

Perhaps the backlash against statistical significance testing is stronger than thought (although significance testing certainly occurs in the literature in other social science subdisciplines).

Perhaps authors can more readily explain the four-fifths rule in textbooks. This may be particularly true at the undergraduate level or in texts that might be used before a graduate student is more statistically proficient.

In any event, the existence of the two approaches in the Uniform Guidelines (U.S. Equal Opportunity Employment Commission et al., 1978), and their use by different sets of individuals, leads to possible combinations of the two procedures. We next consider some of these combinations.

Hybrid Approaches

As noted, there are a few other academic articles that consider the assessment of adverse impact—articles of a more theoretical nature that do not incorporate primary or meta-analytic data. For example, the work by Morris and Lobsenz (2000) developed statistical theory around a combination of the four-fifths rule and statistical significance testing. In particular, based on earlier work by Fleiss (1994), these authors provided formulas for standard errors of the adverse impact ratio (i.e., a standard error for the ratio of selection rates rather than the difference between the rates). As such, one could perform a statistical significance test on the ratio that is used in the four-fifths rule (e.g., compare the ratio to a baseline value of 0.80 or 1.0). This approach is therefore a "hybrid" approach across the two perspectives discussed, although the outcome is still a function of sample size. Interestingly, although we have seen this hybrid approach used in practice, it did not seem to appear in any of the academic literature within 7 years after its publication.

Another hybrid approach was implied in the Roth et al. (2006) article mentioned. To repeat, those authors found that the relatively high percentage of false positives associated with the four-fifths rule declined markedly, to roughly chance levels, when a test of statistical significance was added as a second step. Thus, the hybrid approach of contingent use of statistical significance testing (contingent on the four-fifths rule being violated) is implied. Interestingly, this matches the procedure noted by the U.S. Department of Labor's *Federal Contract Compliance Manual* (2007). Section 7E06(a) of that manual indicates that adverse impact is to be measured by first invoking the four-fifths rule and then conducting a test of statistical significance if one selection rate is less than 80% of the other rate.

It might be that other hybrid approaches have merit. For example, as noted, sample size can influence the result of a statistical significance test. Low sample sizes are associated with low power and possible inability to demonstrate that two rates are different, while very large sample sizes lead to labeling even trivial differences as "statistically different." Thus, very small and very large sample sizes can be problematic for significance testing. Thus, it might be interesting to study a hybrid approach that uses the four-fifths rule when sample sizes are either very small or very large and uses statistical significance testing when sample sizes are "moderate" (to be defined). We also note that the use of the four-fifths rule when sample sizes are very small might have to accommodate the notion that one or two hires might influence the result (see Q&A 21 of the Uniform Guidelines, U.S. Equal Opportunity Employment Commission et al., 1978). In any event, studying these types of hybrid approaches might also help our field's understanding of the two different perspectives denoted in the current Uniform Guidelines.

Finally, we also suggest efforts that consider the use of additional terms and constructs to describe more clearly various analyses. We have used and suggest the term *adverse impact potential* for analyses and interpretations of the *d* statistic. When used in conjunction with estimates of selection ratios (cf. Sackett & Ellingson, 1997), this standardized statistic helps index potential degrees of adverse impact even when no hiring has yet occurred, its standardized nature makes comparability clearer, and the statistic is not dependent on sample size.

We also suggest the need for increased meta-analytic work on adverse impact. There has been substantial work on generalization of validities—suggesting that certain types of tests are valid across a wide variety of jobs (Rothstein, Schmidt, Erwin, Owens, & Sparks, 1990; Schmidt, Gast-Rosenberg, & Hunter, 1980; Schmidt, Hunter, & Caplan, 1981). That level of research could also be directed toward adverse impact to study how it relates to the adverse impact potential of various predictors of job performance and which moderators might appear to influence such relationships (see, e.g., Roth, Huffcutt, & Bobko, 2003).

Research or modeling by scientists or practitioners also needs to address predictor intercorrelations (Bobko et al., 1999; Schmidt & Hunter, 1998) because predictor intercorrelations influence the size of standardized group differences in selection composites (Sackett & Ellingson, 1997). All told, there is relatively little empirical work on how predictors intercorrelate (Hunter & Hunter, 1984). There are exceptions, such as the meta-analytic work of McDaniel, Hartman, Whetzel, and Grubb (2007), which addresses the relationships of situational judgment tests with both cognitive ability and personality, or work by Salgado and Moscoso (2002), which addresses the relationships of interviews with both personality and cognitive ability. More primary and meta-analytic work is needed in areas such as situational judgment tests, biodata, and so on.

Researchers might also examine how decision makers react to different assessments of adverse impact. One approach might be to see if there are differences in court decisions based on the type of information used to assess adverse impact (e.g., four-fifths rule vs. significance testing). Other research might survey judges, attorneys, and those in regulatory agencies to assess their views. In light of our findings in Table 2.1, managerial decision makers may also be surprised at how lawyers and courts look at evidence of adverse impact based on what applied psychologists relate to them.

In sum, the academic literature is replete with nearly exclusive use of the four-fifths rule for assessing adverse impact in empirically based articles. We have discussed pros and cons of this approach (and statistical significance testing) and suggested that future work and guidelines may need to think beyond these approaches. We look forward to the understanding that all of the research mentioned will bring to bear on this important topic.

Notes

1. We reprint an admonition from Bobko and Roth (2004) that "the statistically significant result might be used as a way to determine adverse impact, but as in the case of the four-fifths rule, the evidence is just prima facie. There could be a variety of reasons for the significant relationship (or the fact that one rate is not arithmetically within 80% of the other rate). For example, the selection system might be discriminatory, or the selection system might be associated with group differences that are related to group differences in job performance (i.e., the test is valid and 'fair'), or the group differences in selection rate might be related to group differences in test scores which are related to group applicant differences in prior job (or educational) experience, or there may have been differential recruiting efforts such that the two applicant pools are not of equal quality, and so forth" (pp. 182–183).
2. Jeanneret criticized the four-fifths rule as highly influenced by sample size, yet as noted here, this criticism may apply more appropriately to significance tests.

References

Aguinis, H., & Smith, M. (2007). Understanding the impact of test validity and bias in selection errors and adverse impact in human resource selection. *Personnel Psychology, 50*, 165–199.

Barrett, R. (1995). Employee selection with the performance priority survey. *Personnel Psychology, 48*, 653–662.

Barrett, R. (1998). *Challenging the myths of fair employment practices.* Westport, CT: Quorum.

Biddle, D. (2005). *Adverse impact and test validation: A practitioner's guide to valid and defensible employment testing.* Burlington, VT: Gower.

Biddle, R. (1993). How to set cutoff scores for knowledge tests used in promotion, training, certification, and licensing. *Public Personnel Management, 22*, 63–79.

Blank, R., Dabady, M., & Citro, C. (2004). *Measuring racial discrimination.* Washington, DC: National Academies Press.

Bobko, P., & Roth, P. (2004). The four-fifths rule for assessing adverse impact: An arithmetic, intuitive, and logical analysis of the rule and implications for future research. In J. Martocchio (Ed.), *Research in personnel and human resources management* (Vol. 23, pp. 177–197). New York: Elsevier.

Bobko, P., Roth, P., & Buster, M. (2005). Work sample selection tests and expected reduction in adverse impact: A cautionary note. *International Journal of Selection and Assessment, 13*, 1–10.

Bobko, P., Roth, P., & Potosky, D. (1999). Derivation and implications of a meta-analytic matrix incorporating cognitive ability, alternative predictors and job performance. *Personnel Psychology, 52*, 561–589.

Boardman, A. (1979). Another analysis of the EEOC Four-Fifths Rule. *Management Science, 8,* 770–776.

Buster, M., Roth, P., & Bobko, P. (2005). A process for content validation education and experienced-based minimum qualifications: An approach resulting in federal court approval. *Personnel Psychology, 58,* 771–799.

Cascio, W., Outtz, J., Zedeck, S., & Goldstein, I. (1991). Statistical implications of six methods of test score use in personnel selection. *Human Performance, 4,* 233–264.

Cascio, W., Outtz, J., Zedeck, S., & Goldstein, I. (1995). Statistical implications of six methods of test score use in personnel selection. *Human Performance, 8*(3), 133–164.

DeCorte, W. (1999). Weighing job performance predictors to both maximize the quality of the selected workforce and control the level of adverse impact. *Journal of Applied Psychology, 84,* 695–702.

DeCorte, W., & Lievens, F. (2003). A practical procedure to estimate the quality and the adverse impact of single-stage selection decisions. *International Journal of Selection and Assessment, 11,* 89–97.

DeCorte, W., Leivens, F., & Sackett, P. (2006). Predicting adverse impact and mean criterion performance in multistage selection. *Journal of Applied Psychology, 91,* 523–537.

Doverspike, D., Winter, J., Healy, M., & Barrett, G. (1996). Simulations as a method of illustrating the impact of differential weights on personnel selection outcomes. *Human Performance, 9,* 259–273.

Esson, P., & Hauenstein, N. (2007, April). *Exploring the use of the four-fifths rule and significance tests in adverse impact court case rulings.* Paper presented at the annual meetings of the Society for Industrial and Organizational Psychology, New York.

Fleiss, J. (1994). Measures of effect size for categorical data. In H. Cooper & L. Hedges (Eds.), *The handbook of research synthesis* (pp. 245–260). New York: Russell Sage Foundation.

Gomez-Mejia, L., Balkin, D., & Cardy, R. (2007). *Managing human resources* (5th ed.). Upper Saddle River, NJ: Pearson/Prentice Hall.

Greenberg, I. (1979). An analysis of the EEOC Four-Fifths Rule. *Management Science, 8,* 762–769.

Guion, R. (1998). *Assessment, measurement, and prediction for personnel decisions.* Mahwah, NJ: Erlbaum.

Hattrup, K., Rock, J., & Scalia, C. (1997). The effects of varying conceptualizations of job performance on adverse impact, minority hiring, and predicted performance. *Journal of Applied Psychology, 82,* 656–664.

Hazelwood School District v. United States, 433 U.S. 299 (1977).

Heneman, H., & Judge, T. (2006). *Staffing organizations* (5th ed.). Boston: McGraw-Hill Irwin.

Higuera, L. (2001). Adverse impact in personnel selection: The legal framework and test bias. *European Psychologist, 6,* 103–111.

Hoffman, C., & Thornton, G. (1997). Examining selection utility where competing predictors differ in adverse impact. *Personnel Psychology, 50,* 455–470.

Hough, L., Oswald, F. L., & Ployhart, R. E. (2001). Determination, detection, and amelioration of adverse impact in personnel selection procedures: Issues, evidence and lessons learned. *International Journal of Selection and Assessment, 9*(1&2), 152–194.

Hunter, J., & Hunter, R. (1984). Validity and utility of alternative predictors of job performance. *Psychological Bulletin, 96*, 72–98.

Jeanneret, R. (2005). Professional and technical authorities and guidelines. In F. Landy (Ed.), *Employment discrimination litigation: Behavioral, quantitative, and legal perspectives* (pp. 47–100). San Francisco: Jossey-Bass.

Klinger, Y., & Schuler H. (2004). Improving participants' evaluations while maintaining validity by a work sample-intelligence test hybrid. *International Journal of Selection and Assessment, 12*(1/2), 120–134.

Lawshe, C. (1987). Adverse impact: Is it a viable concept? *Professional Psychology: Research and Practice, 18*, 492–497.

Levine, E., Maye, D., Ulm, R., & Gordon, T. (1997). A methodology for developing and validating minimum qualifications (MQs). *Personnel Psychology, 50*, 1009–1023.

McDaniel, M., Hartman, N., Whetzel, D., & Grubb, W. (2007). Situational judgment tests, response instructions, and validity: A meta-analysis. *Personnel Psychology, 60*, 63–91.

McKinney, W., & Collins, J. (1991). The impact on utility, race, and gender using three standard methods of scoring selection examinations. *Public Personnel Management, 20*, 145–169.

Meier, P., Sacks, J., & Zabell, S. (1984). What happened in Hazelwood: Statistics, employment, discrimination and the 80% rule. *American Bar Foundation Research Journal, 83*, 139–187.

Morris, S. (2001). Sample size required for adverse impact analysis. *Applied HRM Research, 1*, 13–32.

Morris, S., & Lobsenz, R. (2000). Significance tests and confidence intervals for the adverse impact ratio. *Personnel Psychology, 53*, 89–111.

Olian, J., & Guthrie, J. (1987). Cognitive ability tests in employment: Ethical perspectives of employers and society. *Research in Corporate Social Performance and Policy, 9*, 185–213.

Olson-Buchanan, J., Drasgow, F., Moberg, P., Mead, A., Keenan, P., & Donovan, M. (1998). Interactive video assessment of conflict resolution skills. *Personnel Psychology, 51*, 1–24.

Ones, D., & Viswesvaran C. (1998). Gender, age, and race differences on overt integrity tests: Results across four large-scale job applicant data sets. *Journal of Applied Psychology, 83*, 35–42.

Outtz, J., & Hanges, P. (2006). *Recent practical, methodological, and statistical advances in the detection of adverse impact and test bias.* Workshop presented at the 21st annual meeting of the Society for Industrial and Organizational Psychology, May 2006, Dallas, TX.

Potosky, D., Bobko, P., & Roth, P. (2005). Forming composites of cognitive ability and alternative measures to predict job performance and reduce adverse impact: Corrected estimates and realistic expectations. *International Journal of Selection and Assessment, 13*, 304–315.

Pulakos, E. (2005). *Selection assessment methods.* Alexandria, VA: Society for Human Resource Management (SHRM) Foundation.

Pulakos, E., & Schmitt, N. (1996). An evaluation of two strategies for reducing adverse impact and their effects on criterion related validity. *Human Performance, 9,* 241–258.

Reilly, R., & Warech, M. (1993). The validity and fairness of alternatives to cognitive ability tests. In L. Wing and B. Gifford (Eds.), *Policy issues in employment testing.* Boston: Kluwer.

Rogelberg, S. (Ed.). (2007). *Encyclopedia of industrial and organizational psychology.* Thousand Oaks, CA: Sage.

Roth, P., & Bobko, P. (2000). College grades as employment selection mechanisms: Ethnic group differences and adverse impact. *Journal of Applied Psychology, 85,* 399–406.

Roth, P., Bobko, P., & McFarland, L. (2005). A meta-analysis of work sample test validity: Updating and integrating some classic literature. *Personnel Psychology, 58,* 1009–1037.

Roth, P., Bobko, P., & Switzer, F. (2006). Modeling the behavior of the 4/5ths rule for determining adverse impact: Reasons for caution. *Journal of Applied Psychology, 91,* 507–522.

Roth, P., Huffcutt, A., & Bobko, P. (2003). Ethnic group differences in measures of job performance: A new meta-analysis. *Journal of Applied Psychology, 88,* 694–706.

Roth, P., Van Iddekinge, C., Huffcutt, A., Eidson, C., & Schmit, M. (2005). Construct research in structured interviews: The case of personality saturation. *International Journal of Selection and Assessment, 13,* 261–273.

Rothstein, H., Schmidt, F., Erwin, F., Owens, W., & Sparks, C. (1990). Biographical data in employment selection; Can validities be made generalizable? *Journal of Applied Psychology, 75,* 175–184.

Ryan, A., Ployhart, R., & Friedel, L. (1998). Using personality testing to reduce adverse impact: A cautionary note. *Journal of Applied Psychology, 83,* 298–307.

Sackett, P. R., & Ellingson, J. E. (1997). The effects of forming multi-predictor composites on group differences and adverse impact. *Personnel Psychology, 50,* 707–721.

Salgado, J., & Moscoso, S. (2002). Comprehensive meta-analysis of the construct validity of the employment interview. *European Journal of Work and Organizational Psychology, 11,* 299–324.

Schmidt, F. (1996). Statistical significance testing and cumulative knowledge in psychology; implications for training of researchers. *Psychological Methods, 1,* 115–129.

Schmidt, F., Gast-Rosenberg, I., & Hunter, J. (1980). Validity generalization results for computer programmers. *Journal of Applied Psychology, 65,* 643–661.

Schmidt, F., & Hunter, J. (1998). The validity of selection methods in personnel psychology: Practical and theoretical implications of 85 years of research findings. *Psychological Bulletin, 124,* 262–274.

Schmidt, F., Hunter, J., & Caplan, J. (1981). Validity generalization results for two job groups in the petroleum industry. *Journal of Applied Psychology, 66,* 261–273.

Schmitt, N., Rogers, W., Chan, D., Sheppard, L., & Jennings, D. (1997). Adverse impact and predictive efficiency of various predictor combinations. *Journal of Applied Psychology, 82,* 719–730.

Siskin, B., & Trippi, J. (2005). Statistical issues in litigation. In F. Landy (Ed.), *Employment discrimination litigation: Behavioral, quantitative, and legal perspectives* (pp. 132–167). San Francisco: Jossey-Bass.

Sobol, M., & Ellard, C. (1988). Measures of employment discrimination: A statistical alternative to the four-fifths rule. *Industrial Relations Law Journal, 10,* 381–399.

Stark, S., Chernyshenko, O., & Drasgow, F. (2004). Examining the effects of differential item (functioning and differential) test functioning on selection decisions: When are statistically significant effects practically important? *Journal of Applied Psychology, 89,* 497–508.

Thornton, G., Murphy, K., Everest, T. & Hoffman, C. (2000). Higher cost, lower validity and higher utility: Comparing the utilities of two tests that differ in validity, costs and selectivity. *International Journal of Selection and Assessment, 8*(2), 61–75.

Tversky, A., & Kahneman, D. (1971). Belief in the law of small numbers. *Psychological Bulletin, 67,* 105–110.

U.S. Department of Labor (2007). *Federal contract compliance manual.* Employment Standards Administration, Office of Federal Contract Compliance Programs. Retrieved May 18, 2007, from www.dol.gov/esa/regs/compliance/ofccp/fccm/fccmanul

U.S. Equal Opportunity Employment Commission, U.S. Civil Service Commission, U.S. Department of Labor, & U.S. Department of Justice. (1978). Uniform Guidelines on Employee Selection Procedures. *Federal Register, 43,* 38295–38309.

Weekley, J., & Jones, C. (1997). Video-based situational testing. *Personnel Psychology, 50,* 25–49.

Section II

Theoretical Perspectives

3

A Theory of Adverse Impact

James L. Outtz and Daniel A. Newman

Introduction

Subgroup differences in mental ability have been the subject of research and debate in the United States for almost nine decades (Brigham, 1923). Differences between African Americans and Caucasians with regard to mental ability have been of particular interest (Garth, 1931; Shuey, 1958). Within the field of industrial and organizational (I/O) psychology, subgroup differences and related issues (social, legal, and technical) are embodied in the concept of adverse impact. Broadly speaking, *adverse impact* has been defined as subgroup differences in selection rates (e.g., hiring, licensure and certification, college admissions) that disadvantage subgroups protected under Title VII of the 1964 Civil Rights Act. Protected subgroups are defined on the basis of a number of demographics, including race, sex, age, religion, and national origin (Uniform Guidelines, 1978). Most of the I/O psychology literature addressing adverse impact has focused on documenting the magnitude of subgroup differences on specific assessment devices.

Unfortunately, progress in psychological research on the social and legal problem of adverse impact has been limited due to lack of theory. In this chapter, we first explore models of cognitive ability as well as current discussions regarding the concept of race and then propose an initial theory of adverse impact. Specifically, we build on the Cattell-Horn-Carroll (CHC) model to enumerate the latent constructs measured by tests of "cognitive ability." Cognitive tests are shown to measure multiple facets that—while correlated—are not always best explained by a unitary underlying factor g. Further, several facets measured by cognitive tests appear unambiguously to capture learned material, rather than stable, immutable traits. In this chapter, we also examine the concept of race: what race is, potential reasons why race correlates differentially with different facets of cognitive tests, and the key problem: that using cognitive tests for hiring (or high-stakes selection) purposes results in substantial reduction in the number of individuals hired/selected from underrepresented racial groups, for reasons that have nothing to do with actual job performance.

The purpose of this chapter is to integrate these literatures by proposing an initial theory of why adverse impact occurs. We do not argue that this theory is the final word on the antecedents of adverse impact. Rather, we hope that it can be a meaningful beginning of a theory. Our theory focuses on black–white racial subgroup differences. We do this because race has been the most frequently studied demographic regarding adverse impact, and black–white differences have proven to be a key problem in organizational staffing and high-stakes selection contexts.

We generally advocate the following principles, objectives, and recognitions for studying (and discussing) adverse impact: (a) focusing on parameters that can be empirically estimated; (b) recognizing that these parameters can take on a range of values between the extrema of 1.0 and 0.0; (c) improving construct validity in high-stakes cognitive testing (which constructs are measured, what percentage of variance in these constructs can be explained by known antecedents); (d) recognizing the role of the testing industry in making empirical estimates available; (e) recognizing the role of industrial psychologists in studying the multilevel mechanisms (psychological, sociological, and economic) underlying racial differences in test performance; and (f) viewing race and occupational opportunity in historical context (in contrast to ignoring race, opportunity, and history).

Focusing on Performance-Irrelevant Race-Related Test Variance

Cognitive tests predict certain aspects of job performance far better, on average, than any other currently available psychometric instruments (Hunter & Hunter, 1984; Schmidt & Hunter, 1998). Using cognitive tests for hiring purposes therefore promises to improve greatly individual-level productivity and to decrease some of the error associated with other hiring methods (e.g., unstructured interviews; Huffcutt & Arthur, 1994). On the other hand, cognitive tests measure many constructs associated with social status and privilege (i.e., scholastic knowledge and skills), giving rise to sizable mean black–white race differences on these tests (Roth, Bevier, Bobko, Switzer, & Tyler, 2001). Indeed, racial subgroup differences on cognitive tests are so large that they will create substantial reductions in the number of black applicants hired, to an extent that far exceeds the performance advantages of these tests.

We believe that the central problem of adverse impact in cognitive ability tests is attributable to race differences in *criterion-irrelevant test variance*. More specifically, we present the following expression for the critical parameter that drives our current framing of the central problem of adverse impact (see related work by Cole, 1973; Darlington, 1971; Hanges & Gettman, 2004; Hunter & Schmidt, 1976):

$$r_{PIRV} = r_{race,(test \cdot performance)} = \frac{r_{race,test} - r_{race,performance} r_{test,performance}}{\sqrt{1 - r^2_{test,performance}}} \tag{3.1}$$

where *PIRV* is an acronym for performance-irrelevant race-related variance in scores on preemployment or admissions tests. Performance-irrelevant race-related test variance is a function of the correlation between race and test scores $r_{race,test}$, the correlation between race and job performance $r_{race,performance}$, and the correlation between test scores and job performance $r_{test,performance}$. When r_{PIRV} is large, it means that using the test for hiring or admissions will exclude the lower-scoring demographic group based on factors *unrelated to job performance*.

The meta-analytic semipartial correlation between race and cognitive test scores, after *holding job performance constant*, is a whopping 0.42 (Newman, Hanges, & Outtz, 2007). As discussed in that article, "using cognitive tests for hiring purposes will result, on average, in a substantial reduction in Black hires, *for reasons having nothing to do with job performance*" (p. 1083). Figure 3.1 shows how variance in scores on a selection test can be partitioned into four parts: variance uniquely attributable to race (unrelated to job performance) (Component a), variance uniquely related to job performance (unrelated to race) (Component b), variance related to both job performance and race (Component c), and variance unrelated to job performance and race (Component d). In the case of cognitive ability tests, meta-analytic estimates for these variance components (corrected for criterion unreliability [Hunter & Hunter, 1984; Roth, Huffcutt, & Bobko, 2003] and range restriction [Hunter & Hunter, 1984]) are as follows (see additional detail in Newman, Hanges, et al., 2007): Component a = 13%, b = 22%, c = 6%, and d = 59%. The parameter r_{PIRV} (squared) is equal to $0.42^2 = 18\%$. That is, 18% of the variance in cognitive tests, *independent of job performance*, corresponds to black–white race differences.

So, the core problem of adverse impact from our perspective is not the variance related to both job performance and race (Component c in Figure 3.1) but rather variance uniquely attributable to race but unrelated to job performance (Component a in Figure 3.1). In other words, our

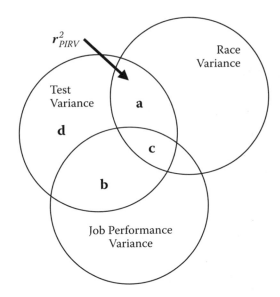

FIGURE 3.1
Performance-irrelevant race-related variance in test scores.

primary concern is that cognitive tests capture race differences that *do not* correspond to true differences in job performance (Component a = 13% of the variance in test scores).

An alternative way of presenting this empirical result is in terms of odds ratios. Lipsey and Wilson (2001, pp. 199, 202) provided an approximation formula that can be used to convert r_{PIRV} into an odds ratio (where $\pi = 3.14$):

$$Odds_{PIRV} = e^{\frac{r_{PIRV}(\pi)}{\sqrt{3(1-r_{PIRV}^2)(p(1-p))}}} \tag{3.2a}$$

A more general approximation of this odds ratio (which is sensitive to the selection ratio) is

$$Odds_{PIRV} = \frac{\left(\sqrt{e^{(x_{cut}+d_{PIRV})^2}}\right)\left(1.64(x_{cut}+d_{PIRV})+\sqrt{.76(x_{cut}+d_{PIRV})^2+4}\right)-1}{\left(\sqrt{e^{x_{cut}^2}}\right)\left(1.64x_{cut}+\sqrt{.76x_{cut}^2+4}\right)-1} \tag{3.2b}$$

where

$$x_{cut} = z_{cut}\sqrt{1+d_{PIRV}^2[p(1-p)]} - d_{PIRV}p$$

$$d_{PIRV} = r_{PIRV} \Big/ \sqrt{(1 - r_{PIRV}^2)(p(1-p))}$$

p is the proportion of applicants from the protected racial subgroup, and z_{cut} is the standard normal cut score across all applicants (a transformation of the overall selection ratio). To illustrate the consequences of race differences in nonjob performance-related components of cognitive ability tests, we plugged in the meta-analytic estimate of $r_{PIRV} = 0.42$ (Newman, Hanges, et al., 2007) and the corresponding proportion of black applicants $= 0.264$ (from Roth et al., 2003) into Formula 2b. Assuming a selection ratio of 20%, $Odds_{PIRV} = 7.40$. In other words, if one considers two job applicants (one black and one white) who would actually display *exactly equal job performance* if hired, the use of a cognitive ability test to base hiring recommendations will result in the *white applicant being 7.40 times more likely to be hired than the black applicant* (note that the odds ratio becomes even larger as either the selection ratio or the proportion of black applicants decreases).

Basic Concepts

What Is Race?

An important step toward the development of a theory of adverse impact is to define key terms clearly. The definition of race, for example, is not clear-cut by any means. Is race determined biologically? Zyphur (2006) suggested that studies using statistical clustering technology to assess genetic information on race show that the amount of genetic variation within subgroups is larger than variation between them. Genetic differences within the human race are not large enough to support racial grouping (Graves & Rose, 2006). An alternative to the biological approach is to define race as a social construct rooted in historical and anthropological context (Smedley & Smedley, 2005; Sternberg, Grigorenko, & Kidd, 2005). Social constructionists explain that the very meaning of race can change across situations as well as across perceivers. One version of this approach involves seeing race as a sociopolitical construct that functions to justify societal oppression (Feagin, 2006; i.e., race as a "complex of contested social meanings," Omi & Winant, 1986, p. 68). The social constructivist perspective can be seen in various discussions of adverse impact. For example, Helms, Jernigan, and Mascher (2005) used the social constructivist perspective to recommend that race be dismissed altogether as an explanatory construct.

While we agree with the premise that race is a social construct, we believe that race can still be considered a meaningful explanatory construct. Our reasoning is based on our belief that race-related constructs can be simultaneously conceptualized at multiple levels of analysis

(Newman, Hanges, et al., 2007). In the models we present, race is conceptualized to include group-level *shared* perceptions/meanings, resulting
from common societal experiences, as well as individual-level constructs
(e.g., unique personal meanings drawn from the common experience).
We define race generically as a social category consisting of persons who
share biological characteristics that society considers socially significant
(Macionis, 1999). We also agree that in some respects race is a concept
used within a society to symbolize or signify social conflicts, such as conflicting interests, by referring to different phenotypic characteristics (Omi
& Winant, 2001). The psychological content of racial category membership reflects experiences, culture, and identity (Phinney, 1996), although
we posit that these contents tend to be shared within groups. As with
any group-level psychological construct (see Schneider, 1990), race-related
psychological constructs (i.e., shared meanings) can be empirically justified through within-group agreement and intraclass correlation (Bliese,
2000). These group constructs are likewise subject to the ecological fallacy
or overgeneralization from the group to the individual (Thorndike, 1939).

What Is Cognitive Ability?

A second critical issue in any discussion of adverse impact is defining
cognitive ability. Identifying a common definition in the psychological
literature has proven extremely difficult. Ability testing typically refers
to standardized measures of intelligence, aptitude, or achievement. The
history of the problem of defining cognitive ability (and cognitive ability
tests) is exemplified by the following quotation from Goslin (1963):

> We have included in our definition tests that purport to measure
> abilities which for the most part reflect learning, as well as those des-
> ignated as general intelligence and aptitude tests, because it is becom-
> ing increasingly difficult to decide where to draw the line between
> the innate and acquired components of measured abilities. It is clear
> that all tests must measure developed abilities, and many psychome-
> tricians have given up the terms "intelligence" and "IQ" with their
> connotation of innate ability, in favor of words such as "scholastic
> aptitude" that call attention to the contribution of the individual's
> environment as well as the purpose of the test.

It is important to note that this chapter focuses on adverse impact within
the context of organizational staffing and high-stakes assessment (or selection). The selection devices most often used in this context are standardized tests designed to measure developed abilities that are influenced, to
no small degree, by environmental factors such as formal education. As
an example, the Wonderlic Personnel Test, recognized as a traditional test
of cognitive ability, consists of items that measure vocabulary, reading

comprehension, and math. The cognitive requirements for answering such items are developed, at least in part, in formal educational settings. The Watson Glaser Critical Thinking Appraisal, another recognized ability test used frequently in employment settings, contains items that rely heavily on reading comprehension and vocabulary. Finally, the Armed Forces Vocational Aptitude Battery (discussed elsewhere in this chapter) consists of subtests that measure educational achievement, including word knowledge and arithmetic reasoning. We define *cognitive ability* as a person's "entire repertoire of acquired skills, knowledge, learning sets, and generalization tendencies considered intellectual in nature that [is] available at any one period of time" (Humphreys, 1984, p. 243; see Dragsow, 2003, p. 117).

What Do Cognitive Tests Measure?

An empirically grounded construct model for cognitive tests that has achieved recent ascendance is the CHC model (McGrew, 1997, 2008; Roid, 2003; Woodcock, McGrew, & Mather, 2001; cf. Johnson & Bouchard, 2005). The CHC model is a hybrid of Carroll's (1993) three-stratum model with Cattell's (1971) and Horn's (1991) earlier models of fluid intelligence (*Gf*) and crystallized intelligence (*Gc*). The CHC model is depicted in Figure 3.2 (see Flanagan, McGrew, & Ortiz, 2000). Before proceeding, we should note that an important difference between the two predecessor models (i.e., the Cattell-Horn *Gf-Gc* model vs. Carroll's three-stratum theory) is that Cattell and Horn proposed that the most viable psychometric model did *not* include an overall cognitive ability factor (*g*; Spearman, 1904), whereas Carroll's model did specify a higher-order *g* factor (*g* stands for general mental ability). As seen in Figure 3.2, the combined CHC model of cognitive tests comprises 8 to 10 distinct but correlated factors. These factors that underlie cognitive tests are defined in Table 3.1.

An Empirical Example

Most of the validity data demonstrating the strong connection between cognitive test scores and job performance come from two specific cognitive tests: the Armed Services Vocational Aptitude Battery (ASVAB) and the General Aptitude Test Battery (GATB; see Hunter, 1983, 1986; Hunter, Crosson, & Friedman, 1985; Schmidt, Hunter, Outerbridge, & Goff, 1988). But, what do these tests actually measure? To illustrate some of the complexities in answering this question, we conducted a confirmatory factor analysis on a large database of cognitive subtest scores, including the ASVAB ($N = 10,963$; Alderton, Wolfe, & Larson, 1997; estimates corrected for range restriction). This database comprises 16 cognitive subtests, labeled in Table 3.2. For the confirmatory factor analysis of these subtests,

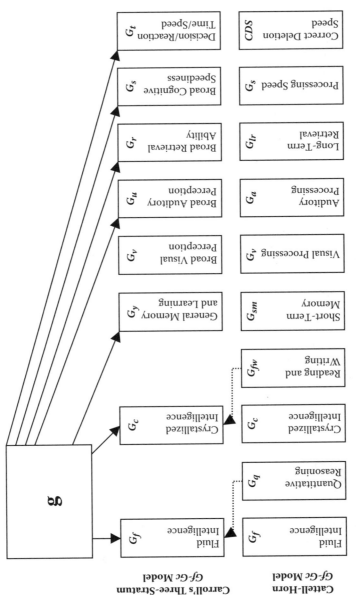

The Broad and General Strata of the Cattell-Horn and Carroll *Gf-Gc* Models

FIGURE 3.2

Combining Cattell-Horn and Carroll models of intelligence. From *The Wechsler Intelligence Scales and Gf-Gc theory: A contemporary interpretive approach,* by D. P. Flanagan, K. S. McGrew, & S. O. Ortiz, 2000, Boston: Allyn and Bacon.

TABLE 3.1

Factors Underlying Cognitive Test Scores (Cattell-Horn-Carroll Model)

Factor name	Definition
Fluid Intelligence (*Gf*)	Mental operations for novel tasks that cannot be performed automatically; forming and recognizing concepts, drawing inferences, comprehending implications, problem solving, extrapolation. Inductive and deductive reasoning
Quantitative Knowledge (*Gq*)	Store of acquired mathematical declarative and procedural knowledge
Crystallized Intelligence (*Gc*)	Breadth and depth of acquired knowledge of a culture and the application of this knowledge; primarily verbal and language-based knowledge developed through investment of other abilities during educational and life experiences
Reading/Writing Ability (*Grw*)	Acquired store of knowledge that includes basic reading and writing skills required for the comprehension of written language and the expression of thought in writing
Short-Term Memory (*Gsm*)	Ability to apprehend and hold information in immediate awareness and then use it within a few seconds; related to working memory
Visual Processing (*Gv*)	Ability to generate, perceive, analyze, synthesize, store, retrieve, transform, and think with visual patterns and stimuli; mental reversal and rotation of objects in space
Auditory Processing (*Ga*)	Ability to perceive, analyze, and synthesize patterns among auditory stimuli and discriminate nuances in patterns of music and speech
Long-Term Storage and Retrieval (*Glr*)	Ability to store and fluently retrieve acquired information (concepts, ideas, names) from long-term memory
Cognitive Processing Speed (*Gs*)	Ability to perform cognitive tasks fluently and automatically, especially when under pressure to maintain focused attention and concentration
Decision Reaction Time or Speed (*Gt*)	Reaction time and decision speed

Source: Adapted from *The Wechsler Intelligence Scales and Gf-Gc Theory: A Contemporary Interpretive Approach,* by D. P. Flanagan, K. S. McGrew, & S. O. Ortiz, 2000, Boston: Allyn and Bacon, pp. 30 to 45.

TABLE 3.2

Fit Indices for Cognitive Test Factor Models (ASVAB and ECAT)

Model	χ^2	*df*	RMSEA	TLI	CFI	SRMR	PGFI
One-factor model (*g*)	39,571.8	104	0.186	0.886	0.901	0.095	0.527
Three-factor model (*Gf* & *Gs*, *Gc* & TK, Nonverbal)	20,910.8	101	0.137	0.932	0.942	0.076	0.600
Four-factor model (*Gf*, *Gc* & TK, *Gs*, Nonverbal)	15,890.0	98	0.121	0.946	0.956	0.066	0.610
Five-factor model[a] (*Gf*, *Gc*, TK, *Gs*, Nonverbal)	9,652.8	94	0.096	0.962	0.970	0.058	0.623
Higher-order model							
Five factor plus higher order (*g*)	13,411.2	99	0.111	0.953	0.961	0.070	0.631
Omitting cognitive speed (*Gs*)							
Four-factor model (*Gf*, *Gc*, TK, Nonverbal)	14,557.7	72	0.135	0.916	0.933	0.177	0.576
Four factor plus higher order (*g*)	15,370.6	74	0.137	0.915	0.931	0.179	0.587

[a] Best-fitting model.

our a priori factor model was created by combining the exploratory factor solutions of Roberts et al. (2000) and McHenry, Hough, Toquam, Hanson, and Ashworth (1990) to propose a five-factor model of these cognitive subtests. The five factors were: F1, Mathematics/Fluid Intelligence; F2, Verbal/ Crystallized Intelligence; F3, Noverbal Reasoning/Spatial Intelligence; F4, Technical Knowledge; and F5, Cognitive Speed.

We empirically compared the fit of our a priori five-factor model against several, more parsimonious models. Results of this series of nested model comparisons are shown in Table 3.2. As seen in Table 3.2, the five-factor model of cognitive subtests fits the data better than any of the alternative models, including four-, three-, and one-factor models (note that the one-factor model is the popular *g* model). Indeed, the five-factor model is the only one that comes close to exhibiting adequate fit (root mean square error of approximation [RMSEA] = 0.096; Hu & Bentler, 1999). It should also be noted that the parsimony goodness-of-fit index (PGFI) shows greater fit for the five-factor model than for the more parsimonious models with fewer factors, indicating fit improves for the five-factor model beyond the parsimony penalty.

In deference to the theoretically dominant single-factor model (the general mental ability or *g* model), we also estimated a multifactor model in which the five factors reflected a single, higher-order factor (Table 3.2). Again, the fit of this model (RMSEA = 0.111) was inferior to the model with five separate-but-oblique factors (RMSEA = 0.096).

Next, noting that as of 2002 the cognitive speed (*Gs*) factor has been dropped from the ASVAB battery, we reestimated the five-factor model and its corresponding higher-order (*g*) model, with cognitive speed subtests omitted from analysis. Again, these models displayed empirically worse fit (RMSEA = 0.135, 0.137, respectively) than the model with five oblique factors. In sum, the simple concept that cognitive subtests are all highly correlated because they reflect a single underlying factor of general mental ability (*g*) is not a particularly good theoretical model of the cognitive test analyzed here.

We must confess that these findings were somewhat surprising to us given the supremacy the single-factor (*g*) model has achieved in many academic explanations for the construct validity of cognitive ability tests. According to Drasgow (2003, p. 111), Spearman might have explained away empirical results like ours (which appear to support a multidimensional model of cognitive ability) by using the concept of "swollen specifics" or the idea that "including two measures of a single skill (e.g., Arithmetic Reasoning and Math Knowledge) in a test battery causes the quantitative specific factor falsely to appear." But, this criticism—the idea that any factor analytic solution can be conditioned by simply adding more subtests of a particular type to an instrument—can also be applied to the entire concept of *g* itself. That is, one viewpoint on Spearman's *g* is that if we simply measure the same sorts of things in the same sorts of ways, of course we will see a general factor. Such developments are the natural result of imposing high standards of convergent validity (Campbell & Fiske, 1959), by which a new test is only considered to measure cognitive ability if it correlates highly with existing measures of cognitive ability. Although convergent validity is a cornerstone of scientific psychology, it contributes to what we call *homometric reproduction* of cognitive tests— perpetuation of status quo validity inferences and instrumentation. So, *g* itself could be considered a "swollen specific" in the context of the universe of psychological measures. Regardless of the social/political aspects of factor analysis, Table 3.2 supports a five-factor—not a one-factor—model for cognitive ability.

Next, we wondered whether the pattern of racial subgroup differences on the five underlying cognitive factors (from Table 3.3) would be consistent with the idea that there are strong racial differences on an underlying unitary cognitive ability construct (*g*; Spearman, 1904). If race differences on the unitary construct *g* drive the observed race differences on cognitive subtests, then we would expect to see similar subgroup difference estimates across subtests to the extent that these subtests reflect *g* (also known as *Spearman's hypothesis*). Figure 3.3 shows the average racial subgroup differences across subtests corresponding to each of the five cognitive factors identified in Table 3.3. As shown in Figure 3.3, black–white differences in cognitive subtest scores are strongest for technical knowledge (Auto

TABLE 3.3

Factor Loadings for ASVAG and ECAT Cognitive Subtests (Best-Fitting Model)

Cognitive subtests	Gf	Gc	Nv	TK	Gs
1. Paragraph Comprehension (15-item reading comprehension test)		0.78			
2. Word Knowledge (35-item vocabulary test)		0.87			
3. General Science (25-item knowledge test of physical and biological science)		0.84			
4. Arithmetic Reasoning (30-item arithmetic world-problem test)	0.88				
5. Math Knowledge (25-item test of algebra, geometry, fractions, decimals, and exponents)	0.80				
6. Mechanical Comprehension (25-item test of mechanical and physical principles)				0.84	
7. Auto and Shop Information (25-item knowledge test of automobiles, shop practice, tools, and tool use)				0.74	
8. Electronics Information (20-item test about electronics, radio, electrical principles, and information)				0.80	
9. Numerical Operations (50-item speeded addition, subtraction, multiplication, and division test using one- and two-digit numbers)					0.87
10. Coding Speed (84-item speeded test of recognition of number strings arbitrarily associated with words in a table)					0.74
11. Mental Counters (40-item working memory test, figural content)			0.74		
12. Sequential Memory (35-item working memory test, numerical content)			0.68		
13. Figural Reasoning (35-item series extrapolation test, figural content)			0.77		
14. Integrating Details (40-item spatial problem-solving test)			0.78		
15. Assembling Objects (32-item spatial and semimechanical test)			0.77		
16. Spatial Orientation (24-item spatial apperception or rotation test)			0.72		
Factor intercorrelations (φ)					
Fluid Intelligence (Gf)	1.00				
Crystallized Intelligence (Gc)	0.795	1.00			
Nonverbal Reasoning (Nv)	0.837	0.671	1.00		
Technical Knowledge (TK)	0.686	0.784	0.698	1.00	
Cognitive Speed (Gs)	0.645	0.465	0.464	0.236	1.00

Note: $N = 10,963$; estimates based on range-corrected correlation.

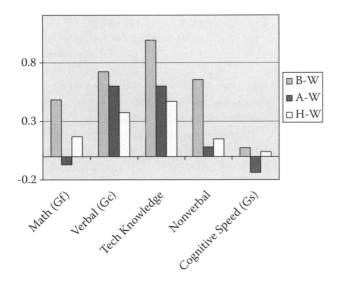

FIGURE 3.3
Racial subgroup differences (*d*) for cognitive subtest facets.

and Shop Information, Mechanical Comprehension, and Electronics Information), followed by Verbal/Crystallized Intelligence (General Science, Vocabulary Tests, and Paragraph Comprehension), followed by Nonverbal/Spatial tests, then Math/Fluid Intelligence, and finally Cognitive Speed. Interestingly, the same pattern obtains for Asian–white differences and Hispanic–white differences (Figure 3.3).

To test Spearman's hypothesis, we calculated the correlation across cognitive subfacets between (a) facet black–white *d* and (b) the loading of each facet on the higher-order *g* factor ($r = 0.41$; $N = 5$ subfacets). This correlation is far from unity. For example, the black–white *d* for Fluid Intelligence/ Mathematics is $d = 0.48$, which is less than half the black–white *d* for technical knowledge ($d = 0.98$)—and Fluid Intelligence/Mathematics has the highest *g* loading of 0.86. In other words, racial subgroup differences on specific cognitive subtests (e.g., Technical Knowledge tests) are much too large to be explained by subgroup differences on latent *g* alone.

So, in explaining racial differences on cognitive subtests, we must explain more than just the differences on a single, underlying *g* factor (general mental ability). We must also explain why racial differences in cognitive subtests vary across the subtest content domains (see Figure 3.3). Why are the greatest racial differences found for Auto and Shop Information and Mechanics, followed by General Science and Vocabulary? Why are racial differences much smaller with regard to Numerical Operations, Coding Speed, Sequential Memory, and Figural Reasoning?

In attempting to answer these important questions, we note that scientists and practitioners hoping to forward any hypotheses or hunches about race differences should ensure that these hypotheses are driven by theories of how members of ascribed racial groups differ on actual psychological variables (experience, efficacy) rather than relying on race itself as a lone explanatory variable. Indeed, while race may covary with several psychological variables owing to racial socialization experiences, race is hardly an individual difference construct, and impoverished explanations that identify racial differences without advancing theoretical mediators of these differences are conceptually bankrupt (Helms et al., 2005).

On the other hand, racial categories serve an important function. The notion of adverse impact is explicitly defined with regard to racial categories. As such, we believe it is premature to do away with racial categories in psychological research altogether (cf. Helms et al., 2005). Our reasoning is simple: If we do not conduct investigations that treat race/racial categories as a meaningful variable, then we lose some ability to identify racially exploitative practices (see American Sociological Association, 2003; Newman, Hanges et al., 2007). In short, adverse impact researchers must still measure race and consider race an important variable in itself, although it is helpful if one also acknowledges the system within which racial meanings are ascribed as well as the psychological mediators of race/racial socialization effects. What sets adverse impact research apart from the general sociological study of race is its focus on intervening in specific human resource practices that increase or decrease racial gaps in occupational attainment.

From a psychological perspective, adverse impact research should attempt to explain why racial groups might differ with regard to cognitive test scores, organizational attraction, performance motivation, turnover intentions, and so on. This research should invoke well-developed theories of social exchange, stereotype and stigmatization, individual differences, and job performance. Just as important, this research should identify and estimate experiential constructs that capture racial socialization. In this vein, we present an initial model of the adverse impact process to advance the dialogue about how racial disparities come about and to highlight why race differences in cognitive test scores are far larger than corresponding differences in actual job performance.

Models of Adverse Impact

In the previous sections, we (a) defined adverse impact, race, and cognitive ability; (b) pinpointed our concern with performance-irrelevant variance

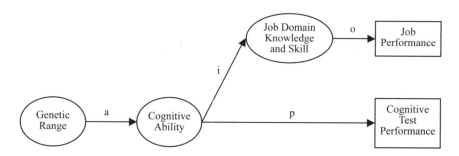

FIGURE 3.4
First-generation model of adverse impact (no theory of race).

on psychological tests; (c) presented the CHC model of cognitive ability subfacets; and (d) offered an empirical demonstration that a popular cognitive test (the ASVAB) is multidimensional, with different magnitudes of racial subgroup differences across the cognitive subdimensions. Next, we forward a theoretical model of the origins of cognitive ability test scores, offering a framework to better explain racial subgroup differences in cognitive test scores.

First-Generation Adverse Impact Model

The first model we present is the first-generation adverse impact model and reflects much of the classic (and some current) thinking and research in the field of personnel selection. This model has been extremely helpful in advancing hiring practices that produce high economic utility and is depicted in Figure 3.4. The first-generation model incorporates no explicit theory of race. That is, race is only incidentally correlated with cognitive ability, largely due to individual differences in genetic endowments, according to the model. More important, perhaps, is the philosophical notion that personnel selection can be carried out in a color-blind fashion or that the basic psychological validity model is value neutral and reflects an attempt to "treat everyone the same" or to "hire the most qualified applicants, considering ability to perform the job" (for problems with color-blind ideology, see American Psychological Association, 1997, and Neville, Lilly, Duran, Lee, & Browne, 2000).

The elements of the first-generation model are as follows: First, there is no widely recognized antecedent to cognitive ability other than an individual's genetic range (Path a in Figure 3.4). The heritability of intelligence has been estimated at around 50% (Bouchard & McGue, 1981; Chipuer, Rovine, & Plomin, 1990). Second, cognitive tests are proposed to be very good indicators of latent cognitive ability (i.e., Path p in Figure 3.4 is presumed to approach 1.0). Third, the connection between cognitive ability and job performance is mediated by the acquisition of job knowledge and skills (Paths i and o in Figure 3.4; Schmidt, Hunter, & Outerbridge, 1986). A great deal of empirical evidence has been amassed to support the correlation between cognitive test scores and job performance measures (Hunter & Hunter, 1984; Kuncel, Hezlett, & Ones, 2004; Le, Oh, Shaffer, & Schmidt, 2007).

Second-Generation Adverse Impact Model

Next, we present a model that we label the second-generation adverse impact model (Figure 3.5). This model is overlain on the first-generation model as it incorporates the same conceptual relationships plus several additional propositions.

Environmental Effects on Cognitive Ability

The second-generation model begins by noting that cognitive ability is not entirely stable and develops gradually over the life course. During the first 16 years of life, the retest stability of observed cognitive test scores varies from $r = 0.4$ to 0.8 (for a 1- to 5-year lag) and from $r = 0.3$ to 0.6 (for a 7- to 14-year lag), with higher stabilities observed at older ages (Petrill et al., 2004). Among adults, some large-sample estimates for the stability of latent cognitive ability across an 18-year lag are $r = 0.85, 0.79,$ and 0.82 for general mental ability, arithmetic, and verbal ability, respectively (Larsen, Hartmann, & Nyborg, 2008) (note that due to statistical corrections, these values may overestimate the observed retest correlations among cognitive test scores—and it is the observed/uncorrected scores that serve as the basis for personnel selection). Further, verbal score mean levels increased 0.41 standard deviations over time among adults, while arithmetic/math score means remained almost constant (Larsen et al., 2008). These empirical results suggest that cognitive ability is relatively—but far from perfectly—stable, and that it tends to stabilize from childhood into adulthood.

One important point in our noting the less-than-perfect rank-order stability of cognitive test scores (especially in childhood, for which observed stability is often below $r = 0.5$) is that these stability estimates imply a potentially large role for *environment* in the development of cognitive ability (particularly in childhood). (Indeed, stability estimates themselves do not suggest a genetic basis for cognitive ability—they merely put an upper limit on the genetic basis because environmental factors can also be stable over time.) The fact that cognitive test scores develop over time begs the question: Which environmental factors contribute to this development? Before we discuss these environmental factors (both what is known and speculative), refer to Path b in Figure 3.5. Note that when Path b exceeds zero, it suggests the genetic aspect of intellectual ability is matched with environmental factors, such that individuals with greater genetic

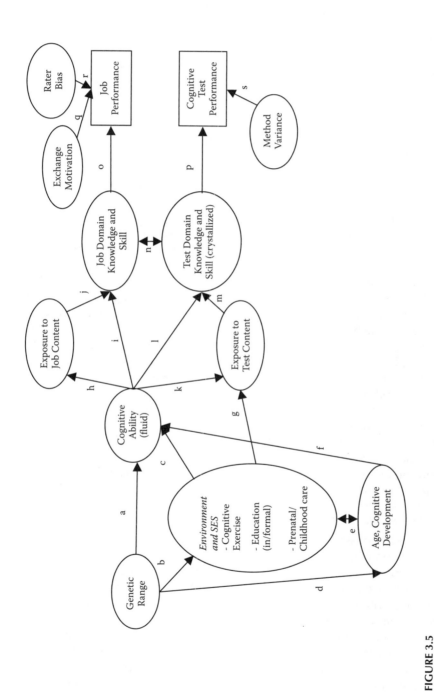

FIGURE 3.5

Second-generation model of adverse impact (without theory of race).

advantages are gravitated into situations with heightened environmental advantages (see review by Dickens & Flynn, 2001, 2002). If we had chosen to arbitrarily constrain Path b to zero (forcing genetics and environment to be orthogonal), then Path a (from genetics to cognitive ability) would be overestimated (see Figure 3.5). This is the case with the first-generation model of adverse impact—the specification to omit Path b (see Figure 3.4) will invariably overestimate the genetic basis of cognitive ability.

Social Status Effects

Our theoretical model of adverse impact incorporates socioeconomic status (SES) as an environmental variable. From the time a human being is conceived, social class plays a critical role in cognitive development. As an example, class affects prenatal development via the prenatal care received. After birth, social class affects significant environmental factors such as preschool learning, nutrition, and early (family) socialization. What follows is a discussion of the link between social class and mediating factors that lead to subgroup differences on measures used in employment selection and high-stakes assessment.

We begin with a definition of social class and how it is determined. In a broad sense, class refers to an individual's social standing within a given society. Social scientists have used multiple methods to measure class (Lindsey & Beach, 2000). Some methods are subjective and ask individuals simply to self-report the class to which they think they belong (or alternatively to place themselves into one of several discrete classes ranging from upper-upper to lower-lower). These methods are imprecise because persons may (a) have different definitions of class structure and (b) overestimate or underestimate their actual placement within the class structure.

A more useful/objective method of measuring social class defines class on the basis of SES. SES is determined using three indicators: income, occupation, and education (Lindsey & Beach, 2000). In our model, SES is a mediating factor that transmits some of the effects of race to prenatal care and formal education (see Table 3.4).

Prenatal/Childhood Care

SES has been found to correlate with a number of factors that affect cognitive development, not the least of which is health, both prenatal and postbirth. Brooks-Gunn and Duncan (1997) found, for example, that only 37% of poor children were reported to be in excellent health compared to 55% of children who were not poor. Research also indicates that children of low socioeconomic families are more likely to experience growth retardation (poor-to-nonpoor prevalence ratio = 2.0); lead poisoning (ratio = 3.5); learning disability (ratio = 1.4); school grade repetition (ratio = 2.0) and dropout (ratio = 2.2); food insufficiency/hunger in past year (ratio = 9.9); and child abuse and neglect (ratio = 6.8; Brooks-Gunn & Duncan, 1997; for review, see

TABLE 3.4

Race and Socioeconomic Status

	Black	White	White/black
Educational attainment			
Below high school	19%	15%	78%
High school graduate	36%	31%	87%
Some college	21%	19%	92%
Associate's degree	8%	8%	104%
Bachelor's degree	12%	18%	153%
Graduate degree	5%	9%	187%
Income level			
Median family income	38,269	61,280	160%

Note: Educational attainment data from 2007 (Current Population Survey, 2007; U.S. Census Bureau; black N = 25,991; white N = 181,414); income data from 2006 (Economic Report of the President, 2008). Final column may differ slightly from the quotient of the second and third columns due to rounding.

Bradley & Corwyn, 2002). In addition, black children are more likely than white children to suffer preterm birth (ratio = 1.7) and low birth weight (ratio = 2.0; U.S. Department of Health and Human Services, 2000).

Premature and low-birth-weight infants suffer from a number of problems related to cognitive development. Gross et al. (2001) found full-term children were 3.4 times more likely than premature children to achieve appropriate grade level without additional classroom assistance. Preterm children tend to perform less well in school, although family environment plays a significant role. A substantial amount of research has been devoted to exploring the cognitive effects of low birth weight. Kohlhauser et al. (2000) found that only 58% of low-birth-weight infants were cognitively normal. The rate of cognitive normalcy remained at about the same level at age 2. Dezoete, MacArthur, and Tuck (2003) administered the Bayley Scales of Infant Development and the Stanford Binet Intelligence Scale to a population of 334 children at both 18 months and 4 years who had birth weights of 1,500 g or less. They found that longer gestation (≥ 28 weeks) was associated with higher scores on cognitive measures ($d = 0.36$). Dezoete et al. (2003) also found that higher birth weight (≥ 1,000 g) was associated with higher scores on cognitive measures ($d = 0.32$) . Anderson and Doyle (2003) compared children who were extremely low birth weight or very preterm with normal birth weight cohorts on several measures of cognitive development. The results indicated that the extremely low-birth-weight and preterm children scored significantly below their cohorts in terms of full-scale IQ ($d = 0.62$) and indices of verbal comprehension ($d = 0.46$), perceptual organization ($d = 0.65$), freedom from distractibility ($d =$

0.56), processing speed ($d = 0.45$), and reading ($d = 0.43$). Similar findings were reported by Achenbach, Howell, Aoki, and Rauh (1993), Weisglas-Kuperus, Baerts, Smrkovsky, and Sauer (1993), and Saigal et al. (1991).

Just as interesting as the research findings indicating harmful effects of prenatal factors on cognitive development are findings that indicate specific interventions may be useful in ameliorating the disadvantages of low birth weight and poor prenatal care. Ramey and Ramey (1998) assessed the effects of controlled early interventions on the social competence and cognitive development of poor and low-birth-weight infants. Randomly assigned intervention groups received an early childhood education program within the context of a specially developed child care center. Multiple measures of cognitive development, including the Bayley Mental Development Indices and the Stanford-Binet, showed that the intervention groups consistently outperformed the control groups at age 36 months ($d = 0.80$ and $d = 1.1$ for the two intervention studies). Thus, some research showed that environmental interventions can reduce the effects of poor prenatal care and low birth weight.

A considerable amount of research has been devoted to the role of poverty with regard to cognitive stimulation in the home, parenting style, physical environment of the home, and poor child health (Guo & Harris, 2000). Guo and Harris used factor analysis to identify three factors associated with poverty that influence cognitive development. Their analysis was based on data from the National Longitudinal Survey of Youth (NLSY). The original study included a total of 12,686 youths aged 14 to 21 as of January 1979. Scales measuring mediating factors were constructed from the preschool version of the Home Observation for Measurement of the Environment (Caldwell & Bradley, 1984). The following four measures of cognitive development were used:

1. The Reading Recognition Assessment of the Peabody Individual Achievement Test (measures word recognition and pronunciation)
2. The Reading Comprehension Assessment of the Peabody Individual Achievement Test (measures the ability to derive meaning from reading sentences silently)
3. The Mathematics Assessment of the Peabody Individual Assessment Test (measures a child's achievement in mathematics as commonly taught in American schools)
4. The Peabody Picture Vocabulary Test–Revised (measures an individual's hearing vocabulary and verbal ability)

Guo and Harris (2000) derived three mediating factors (as defined by the items shown) via exploratory factor analysis of the items in the NLSY preschool home (see Table 3.5). Their results (based on a structural

TABLE 3.5

Environmental Factors of Cognitive Development

Cognitive stimulation	Parenting style	Physical environment
How often mother reads to child	Mother conversed with child twice or more	Home interior is reasonably clean
Number of books child has	Mother answered child's questions verbally	Home interior is minimally cluttered
Child has record/tape player	Mother's voice showed positive feelings toward child	Play environment appears safe
How often child is taken to museum per year	Mother hugged and kissed child	Home interior is not dark or monotonous
Number of magazines family receives		

equation model) confirmed two proposed mediators of poverty's effect on intellectual development: Living in poverty is associated with cognitive stimulation (standardized path coefficient $\beta = -0.18$), parenting style ($\beta = -0.11$), and physical setting ($\beta = -0.25$), while both cognitive stimulation ($\beta = 0.34$) and parenting style ($\beta = 0.10$) in turn had significant effects on intellectual development.

The relationships among SES, childhood care, and early achievement (particularly in basic areas such as reading skills) are more complex than one might assume. Aikens and Barbarin (2008) made use of the Early Childhood Longitudinal Study to track the 1998–1999 kindergarten cohort across 5 years, modeling both initial reading (intercepts) and changes in reading (slopes). They examined the degree to which three categories of variables (family, neighborhood, and school) accounted for the impact of SES on children's early reading (Table 3.6).

Data in each category were collected from several sources (parents, teachers, school administrators, and field staff) via multiple methods, including observation, interview, and questionnaire. Results of the study showed significant differences in reading intercepts and slopes by SES (11-point gap between the highest- and lowest-SES quintiles in kindergarten, which grew to 17 points by third grade). A third major finding of the study was that family variables accounted for 16% of SES differences in children's initial reading scores but did not help account for SES differences in reading slopes. The SES effect on reading growth rates was barely explained by neighborhood characteristics (1%; beyond demographic and family characteristics), while school characteristics accounted for a larger portion of the SES gap in reading slopes (13%; beyond demographic and family characteristics).

To summarize, it is clear from the research evidence that prenatal care affects the level of cognitive development at birth, and family environment

TABLE 3.6

Categories of Variables That Connect SES With Reading

Variable category		
Family variables	**Neighborhood variables**	**School variables**
Home literacy environment Frequency of potential involvement with child in joint book reading Frequency with which children read books outside school Frequency with which household members visited the library with the child	Home neighborhood safety	School poverty status At least 50% of the student body is poor Percentage of students in the school eligible for free or reduced lunch
Involvement in child's school Attending parent-teacher conference Attending a PTA meeting Attending an open house Volunteering/participating in fund-raising Attending a school event	Home neighborhood problems Garbage/litter in the streets Individuals selling or using drugs in the street Burglary or robbery in the area Violent crime in the area Vacant homes in the area	Peers reading below grade
Parental role strain The degree of difficulty and strain experienced in functioning as a parent	Community support for the school that served the community	Participation of students in literacy-related activities (e.g., working on learning the names of letters, practicing reading aloud and silently, reading a variety of texts, engaging in writing activities and working on phonics)

affects continued cognitive development, particularly in terms of readiness for school. The combination of family environment and initial schooling can significantly influence early achievement. Not surprisingly, school factors appear to influence the rate of growth rather than initial achievement at the time of entry into school.

Educational Opportunity

The rate of growth in early educational achievement sets the foundation for subsequent educational opportunity. One of the reasons for this may be that early on students are typically grouped, either formally or informally, on the basis of ability or achievement. Therefore, any achievement gap that exists initially often continues or even increases. Studies of ability grouping typically focus on a specific aspect of grouping (Kulik & Kulik, 1982). The various forms of grouping range from assigning students to groups within a given class, to systems in which students are assigned to different schools on the basis of test scores. Beyond systems of assigned grouping, there is voluntary grouping in the form of parental choice, including the choice of public versus private schooling. Regardless of the specific form, grouping typically involves separating students into categories that differ in average ability level, with ability level measured by either a cognitive ability test or an achievement test. Although research results are mixed regarding the effects of grouping, one clear finding is that the greatest effects occur when high-ability students receive enriched instruction such as honors classes (Kulik & Kulik, 1982). Another finding is that grouping may perpetuate, if not increase, initial differences in achievement ($d = 0.10$). The net effect of perpetuating initial differences between students is to produce subsequent differences in formal education between poor minority groups and Caucasians (see Table 3.4). In addition to disparities in the number of years of formal education, the *quality* of available education may vary across children of different races. Thirty-two percent of African American students attend high-poverty schools compared with only 4% of Caucasian students (U.S. Department of Education, 2008). *High-poverty schools* are defined as public schools with more than 75% of students eligible for free or reduced priced lunch. We speculate that measures of educational quality—such as teachers' standardized test scores—would also tend to favor white children. Research has further shown that the differences described can be compounded by teachers' differential expectations in school, as described next.

Teacher Attitudes and Expectations

Teacher expectations toward or interactions with students can have an impact on student outcomes in significant ways. Smith (1980) conducted a meta-analysis to study the effects of teacher expectations on a number of teacher behaviors, including providing advice and support, sustaining feedback, reinforcement, and providing learning opportunities. Results showed teachers tended to ignore students for whom they had low expectations ($d = 0.52$) and provided fewer learning opportunities to students for whom they had lower expectations ($d = 1.0$) compared with students for whom they had high expectations. Harris and Rosenthal (1985) provided a comprehensive meta-analytic review of mediators of interpersonal expectancy effects.

Dusek and Joseph (1983) conducted a meta-analysis of factors that determine teacher expectations. Among the types of information teachers use in forming expectations for students' academic potential were physical attractiveness, gender, cumulative folder information (such as fictitious information about student behavior), estimates of academic achievement, grades, IQ, psychological characteristics, family background information, and diagnostic label (e.g., learning disabled, educable mentally retarded). The data showed that teacher expectations were related to student attractiveness ($d = 0.30$), cumulative folder information ($d = 0.85$), black–white race ($d = 0.11$), and social class ($d = 0.47$). Overall, the results indicated teachers expect different levels of performance from students based on information that is, at least in part, stereotypic (e.g., race, social class, and student attractiveness).

Many individual studies on the relationships between students' characteristics and teacher expectations have been conducted. As an example, McIntyre and Pernell (1985) found that teachers were more likely to recommend students for special education placement who were racially dissimilar from themselves. Oates (2003), using data from the U.S. Department of Labor's Educational Longitudinal Study of 1988, studied whether racial similarity between student and teacher affected teacher perception of student performance. Results showed that the effects of teacher perceptions on student test performance were more pronounced when the teacher and student were dissimilar with regard to race (white teacher, black student: $\beta = -0.06$). Having examined the literature that exists today on the achievement gap between minority and nonminority students, some educators argue that stereotyping plays a major role in teacher behavior, which in turn contributes significantly to differential achievement rates (White-Clark, 2005). Given the substantial differences between African Americans and Caucasians in terms of educational opportunity (including school poverty, teacher knowledge and qualifications, teacher expectations and attitudes, and student grouping), it is little wonder that a gap exists between these groups in terms of achievement (see Chapter 12, this volume).

Exposure to Test Content

As an extension of SES and environmental factors, another area in which the first-generation and second-generation adverse impact models diverge is in the inclusion of the construct Exposure to Test Content (see Figure 3.5). By ignoring this construct, the first-generation model essentially constrains Paths k and m to zero. Doing so enables selection practitioners to view cognitive ability as a unidimensional, undifferentiated concept, implying that Path i in Figure 3.4 can be effectively treated as 1.0. That is, the first-generation model does not distinguish fluid reasoning/ intelligence from crystallized/acquired intelligence. The common treatment of the cognitive ability construct as unidimensional by I/O psychologists has the effect of directing research attention away from the unstable and learned facets of cognitive test scores (see the definitions in Table 3.1, denoting the *learned* or *acquired* aspects of many cognitive ability facets that underlie cognitive test scores; also see Fagan & Holland, 2002; 2007) and disregards empirical findings suggesting the multidimensionality of common cognitive tests (see Tables 3.2 and 3.3).

To put the issue a bit differently, we would say that the question of whether cognitive ability can be acquired through formal and informal educational experiences has tended to be ignored by I/O psychologists. When the issue of exposure to test content has been addressed, it has often been done with coarse and unreliable measures of exposure, such as years of education and parental income (i.e., ignoring education quality, teacher knowledge and skill, parental vocabulary, etc.).

Finally, we note that the question of exposure to test content is not an issue of the psychometric validity of cognitive tests. We believe that many cognitive tests provide excellent measures of vocabulary, reading comprehension, arithmetic skill, etc. The problems are that these components of cognitive ability differ greatly between races and most of these differences do not correspond to differences in job performance (see Figure 3.1).

Job Performance, Rater Bias, and Exchange Motivation

Job performance rating is not an objective process but reflects political and motivated behavior (Murphy, Cleveland, Skattebo, & Kinney, 2004). One issue that has prompted great concern and considerable misunderstanding in research and popular conceptions of adverse impact is *racial bias* in performance ratings. The existing data suggest that (a) white raters give much higher ratings to white ratees as opposed to black ratees ($d = 0.3$), and (b) black raters give only slightly higher ratings to white as opposed to black ratees ($d < 0.05$; Stauffer & Buckley, 2005). Unfortunately, these data do not enable one to determine whether the differences in performance ratings are due to negative racial bias by white raters against black ratees (assuming zero true race differences in actual performance) versus an alternative interpretation of positive racial bias by black raters in favor of black ratees (assuming true race differences in actual performance at around $d = 0.3$). On this point, meta-analytic evidence by Roth et al. (2003) has shown average race differences around $d = 0.3$ for a variety of job performance measures (confirmed by McKay and McDaniel's 2006 meta-analysis), and that *objective measures* of job performance show black–white race differences nearly as large as subjective performance measures (cf. McKay & McDaniel, 2006, p. 544, which showed race differences for objective performance measures were four fifths as large as for subjective performance ratings, $d = 0.22$ vs. $d = 0.28$). Altogether, it would appear that black–white differences in job performance ratings are attributable, on average, to actual differences in job performance rather than to rater bias.

Closer examination of the research in this area, however, produces a different picture. One difficulty is that the "objective" measures include a potpourri of performance criteria with different measurement formats that may influence subgroup differences (Outtz, 1998). As an example, objective performance measures include paper-and-pencil multiple-choice tests, work samples with varying degrees of fidelity to actual job performance, or highly structured in-basket exercises in which all responses must be submitted in writing. It is reasonable to ask whether such performance measures may vary in the degree of subgroup differences they produce largely by virtue of variations in format. Campbell, Crooks, Mahoney, and Rock (1973), for example, studied black–white differences on subjective and objective criterion measures, including supervisor ratings, paper-and-pencil job knowledge tests, work sample (job simulation tasks), and an in-basket exercise. Their data showed increasingly larger subgroup differences as the performance measure less resembled actual job performance (i.e., mean black–white effect size for supervisor ratings was 0.12; for work sample simulation was 0.36; for paper-and-pencil [job knowledge] tests was 0.43; and for written response in-basket exercise was 0.55).

In trying to explain the modest objective job performance difference between races (aside from cognitive ability explanations posed in the first-generation model; see Figure 3.3), the second-generation model of adverse impact adds another possible reason: social exchange. That is, one mechanism by which black and white employees may come to display different levels of job performance is that they are rewarded differently (see Table 3.4). If this is the case, then theories of organizational justice (see review by Colquitt, Greenberg, & Zapata-Phelan, 2005) would support race differences in performance motivation. Consistent with this interpretation is a set of findings by Avery, McKay, and colleagues (Avery, McKay, Wilson, & Tonidandel, 2007; McKay et al., 2007) showing that negative diversity climates increase employee withdrawal (both absenteeism and turnover intentions), with stronger effects for black employees.

Phenotype, Categorization, and Self-Identity

Finally, we incorporate race into the second-generation model of adverse impact (Figure 3.6). *Phenotype* refers to the outward physical manifestations of a person's biological makeup. *Genotype*, on the other hand, refers to the internally coded inheritable information passed from one generation to the next. An individual's phenotype serves as a basis for social categorization. Categorization is simply classification of a person as a member of a social group (Whitley & Kite, 2006). We tend to classify others into three basic categories: sex, race, and age. When we first encounter someone, the initial categorization is race, followed by gender (Ito & Urland, 2003). However, all three categories are considered by the time the process is complete. Research indicates that social categorization occurs frequently in daily social interactions, and it is used habitually in almost all social situations (Stangor, Lynch, Duan, & Glass, 1992).

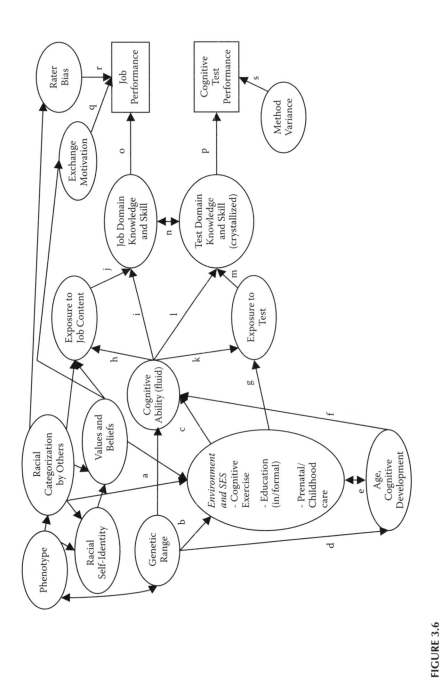

FIGURE 3.6
Second-generation model of adverse impact (full model).

Social scientists believe the primary purpose of categorization is to simplify and streamline how we perceive others (Macrae & Bodenhausen, 2000). However, a person can be categorized as a member of a stereotyped group. That is, the person takes on the characteristics of the group into which he or she has been categorized. Categorization sets the stage for stereotype activation. When an otherwise-dormant stereotype is activated, it is capable of influencing thoughts about and behavior toward the stereotyped group. Whitley and Kite (2006) summarized that although stereotype activation is usually automatic, it can be influenced by three factors: prototypicality, context, and prejudice. *Prototypicality* is the degree to which the person being categorized possesses the features considered typical of the stereotyped group. The context in which the target person is seen can also influence the degree to which stereotypes are activated. As an example, observing a young African American male standing on a street corner might produce a different perception than observing that same individual leaving a church service. A third factor that can influence stereotype activation is prejudice. For example, there is a positive correlation between level of prejudice and the tendency to ascribe stereotypes to particular groups (see, e.g., Kawakami, Dion, & Dovidio, 1998; Lepore & Brown, 1999; Wittenbrink, Judd, & Park, 1997.)

Self-Identity

Categorization and subsequent stereotyping can affect an individual's self-concept, ethnic identity, and academic achievement (Hughes et al., 2006). Social science research indicated that children are taught about their racial and ethnic heritage by their parents (Hughes et al., 2006). Parents may engage in practices that promote cultural customs and traditions as well as racial and ethnic pride. Groups such as African Americans, Hispanic Americans, and American Indians gradually increase their racial-ethnic identity exploration during adolescence (Quintana, 2007). Racial identity has come to be viewed as a multidimensional construct made up of a number of components that include ethnic awareness, sociopolitical attitudes, and cultural or in-group/out-group preferences (Chavous et al., 2003; Sellers, Smith, Shelton, Rowley, & Chavous, 1998). Chavous et al. studied the relationships between three aspects of the multidimensional racial identity model and academic attainment. They focused on *racial centrality*, defined as the importance of race to an individual's definition of self; *private regard*, an individual's affective beliefs about their group (e.g., the extent to which African Americans feel good about being an African American); and *public regard*, which is an individual's perception of societal beliefs about their group or whether others view the group (African Americans) positively or negatively. The primary purpose of the Chavous et al. study was to assess ways in which African American youths' beliefs about themselves, their race, and society influenced their academic beliefs and behaviors (e.g., dropout). Chavous et al. found a cluster of students who (a) felt their race was important to them, (b) felt positive about being African American, and (c) reported negative public regard for their group; were less likely to drop out of high school (ratio of dropout rates = 0.46) and more likely to attend college (ratio of college rates = 1.54) compared with other clusters of students who exhibited different racial identity profiles.

Finn and Rock (1997) classified 1,803 low-income minority students (Hispanic and African American) into three categories based on grades, test scores, and persistence from 8th through 12th grade. The classifications were "resilient students," those who were academically successful and completed high school; "nonresilient completers," students who completed high school, but with poor academic records; and "dropouts." The three categories of students were compared in terms of school engagement, defined in terms of a student's compliance or noncompliance with school and classroom requirements, as well as the degree to which they took initiative to engage in school-related behaviors outside the classroom (e.g., completing homework and participation in academic or sports-related extracurricular activities). Not surprisingly, Finn and Rock found that resilient students tended to work harder ($d = 0.82$), to attend class more regularly ($d = 0.76$), and to be more engaged in learning activities ($d = 0.84$). Doing more homework tended to differentiate between resilient students and nonresilient completers but not between the latter and dropouts. Extracurricular activities such as sports, band, or academic clubs did not differentiate among any of the three groups.

The variables or models that have been discussed all affect adverse impact because they influence cognitive development and academic achievement or educational opportunity. Experiences in formal educational settings can influence adverse impact by contributing to subgroup differences in exposure to test content and crystallized intelligence.

Test Methods and Formats: Convergent Versus Divergent Thinking

Performance in formal educational settings is typically measured with paper-and-pencil multiple-choice tests. As a consequence, the better a student's formal education, the more likely it is that the student gains practice at taking such tests and, more important, engaging in the convergent thinking these tests reinforce. We speculate that this practice behavior with regard to convergent thinking may be key (along with formal knowledge) in contributing to adverse impact. The reason is that most of the employment and high-stakes selection devices that produce the greatest adverse impact rely on a convergent thinking (e.g., multiple-choice) format.

Convergent thinking involves producing a single best (or correct) answer to a clearly defined problem (Cropley, 2006). Divergent thinking, on the other hand, is the ability to generate multiple solutions to a question or problem (Guilford, 1950). Divergent thinking may also involve the ability to arrive at a solution to a problem via different strategies. The significance of convergent and divergent thinking to the phenomenon of adverse impact is that tests that rely on convergent thinking almost always produce adverse impact, whereas tests that are based on divergent thinking may not. The adverse impact of cognitive ability tests with a convergent thinking response format, for example, is well documented. However, there is direct evidence of the possibility that tests based on divergent thinking do not create adverse impact. Price-Williams and Ramirez (1977), for example, compared the performance of Mexican American, African American, and Caucasian fourth-grade children on the Peabody Picture Vocabulary Test and the Test of Fluency and Flexibility of Ideas. While the Caucasian children scored higher than African American and Mexican American children on the Peabody test, the reverse was true for the Test of Fluency and Flexibility of Ideas.

Torrance (1971) reported the results of several studies showing that there was either no difference or a difference in favor of African American children on the Torrance Test of Creative Thinking. A significant component of creativity is ideational fluency or divergent thinking. Torrance also reported research evidence that showed that divergent thinking is not correlated with SES. Iscoe and Pierce-Jones (1964) obtained scores on ideational fluency and flexibility for 267 Caucasian and African American children in Texas to demonstrate that divergent thinking scores were significantly higher for the African American children.

More recent research with adult samples also supported the proposition that a divergent thinking format can reduce the adverse impact of a selection device. Outtz, Goldstein, and Ferreter (2006) used a divergent thinking and convergent thinking response mode on a video-based situational judgment test and compared the degree of adverse impact produced by each. Their results suggested that the African American sample performed better than the Caucasian sample when the response mode required divergent thinking, but the reverse was true when convergent thinking was required.

It may be that many aspects of job performance do not require convergent thinking, but rather divergent thinking. If this is the case, limiting selection devices to a convergent thinking (multiple-choice) response mode may produce subgroup differences that are unrelated to criterion performance. As mentioned at the start of this chapter, the key desideratum in improving test use for adverse impact reduction is to try to minimize r_{PIRV}. To accomplish this, not only must we demonstrate reductions in black–white differences on a proposed alternative test, but also the test must continue to predict a performance criterion effectively (e.g., Edwards & Arthur, 2007). At a minimum, more research is needed in this area.

What Can Be Done About Adverse Impact? Long-, Medium-, and Short-Term Strategies

Adverse impact is a major social problem and is directly linked to psychometrics, the sociology of race, and the psychology of individual differences. Adverse impact systematically excludes African Americans from many occupations. To make things worse, a huge majority of this exclusion is completely unjustified by the corresponding improvement in job performance (Figure 3.1; Newman, Hanges et al., 2007). But, what can be done, in light of our theoretical model, to redress this problem? We next attempt to answer this question, summarizing long-term, medium-term, and short-term strategies.

Long-Term Strategies

A brief inspection of the second-generation model of adverse impact suggests several major areas that could be the targets of intervention. These include the structures of quality control and opportunity creation within the education system, child care and prenatal health services, issues of poverty, and the entire system of socially and politically constructed racial meanings (with their attached stereotypes, prejudices, identities, and values). Attempting to influence these features of the adverse impact problem is an admirable (and ambitious) goal. Attempting to study these factors will be a good next step. Changing these features of the adverse impact problem, however, will likely require resources and skills (e.g., legal, political, and financial influence) that are not the traditional strengths of I/O psychologists. As such, we do not recommend that these aspects of the model be chosen as the first points of intervention and focus for I/O psychology.

Even further, we would warn I/O psychologists against focusing exclusively on the educational system, poverty, and racism per se when attempting to reduce adverse impact. Although these factors are critical in a descriptive sense, they are prescriptively inefficient. Inefficiencies come from both the expense related to changing these factors directly and the tendency for gap-closing interventions to increase gaps by helping members of the advantaged group even more than they help the disadvantaged group members (Ceci & Papierno, 2005).

In a prescriptive sense, noting that the adverse impact problem originates in the educational system, class stratification, and so on is tantamount to "passing the buck." It is far better for I/O psychology researchers and practitioners to focus on those aspects of the problem for which we are personally responsible and in control.

Medium-Term Strategies

One part of the adverse impact problem over which I/O psychologists have direct and pervasive influence is in the creation and usage of tests for personnel selection. On this front, we recommend that researchers focus on the parameter r_{PIRV}. Only 6% of the variance in cognitive tests is related to race *and to job performance*; while a full 13% of cognitive test variance is related to race *but unrelated to job performance* (see Figure 3.1). It is the latter (and much larger) portion of variance in cognitive tests that should become our immediate focus. The goal here is to reduce performance-irrelevant race-related variance to a smaller amount than the current $r_{PIRV}^2 = 18\%$. Yes, many strategies for shrinking racial variance in cognitive tests have been attempted with only limited success (Sackett, Schmitt, Ellingson, & Kabin, 2001; cf. Brown & Day, 2006). But, we must acknowledge that $r_{PIRV}^2 = 18\%$ is not the best we can do.

Note that in our proposed focus on r_{PIRV} there are two popular arguments related to race and test fairness that we are specifically *not* making. First, we are not saying that job performance is unimportant compared with diversity. We are fully acknowledging the critical importance of maximizing job performance and organizational effectiveness by using highly predictive tests. However, the core problem of adverse impact is not created by the fact that cognitive tests predict job performance; it is created by the fact that they predict race far better than they predict performance (r_{PIRV}). Second, our proposed framework for addressing adverse impact does *not* operate by claiming that *we do not know what intelligence is* or by claiming that *we do not know what race is* (Sternberg et al., 2005). Although there is a limited respect in which this criticism is applicable to all psychological constructs, some cognitive ability tests are among the most psychometrically sound and theoretically valid instruments in all of psychology (noting validation is a never-ending and value-laden process; Messick, 1995). Instead, we are focusing on a specific problem pertaining to the use of cognitive tests for personnel selection: the r_{PIRV} parameter. That is, regardless of the psychometric reliability of cognitive tests, they are measuring a lot of superfluous constructs that (a) do not predict job performance and (b) are strongly correlated with race. We need to take another look at cognitive ability tests from this framework. It is not that selection tests should be expected to exhibit zero subgroup differences—after all, there are many realistic disadvantages that distinguish racial subgroups, and these disadvantages logically have some implications for job performance. The problem is that the subgroup differences on cognitive ability tests are far larger than subgroup differences on actual job performance, so using the current cognitive tests will strongly exclude black applicants for reasons that have nothing to do with job performance—and that is grossly unfair (see Equation 3.2).

We need better tests that are more exclusively tied to the construct of job performance. Specifically, the goal is not to develop better, less-biased tests of the latent construct of cognitive ability. Instead, the goal is to develop better, less-biased tests that predict future job performance.

Short-Term Strategies

Ployhart and Holtz (2008) have provided a useful summary of short-term strategies for dealing with adverse impact. We incorporate and extend the strategies these authors deemed consistently effective; we propose three broad categories of approaches to adverse impact reduction: (a) predictor weighting schemes (whether to include and how to combine different measurement methods [test, interview, work sample, biodata], different constructs [personality, ability, social skill], and different facets [narrow facets vs. broad composites]); (b) criterion-weighting schemes (whether to include and how to combine different elements of work performance); and (c) recruiting.

For predictor weights, an extremely useful advancement is De Corte, Lievens, and Sackett's (2007) routine for showing how alternative predictor-weighting schemes correspond to a set of Pareto-optimal trade-off points between job performance and adverse impact. This approach can be used to devise weighting schemes that produce large improvements in the adverse impact ratio at optimally small costs in terms of productivity. A related development is Newman, Jacobs, and Bartram's (2007) Bayesian procedure for estimating whether adverse impact will occur in a particular selection setting. Newman, Jacobs, et al. demonstrated that meta-analytic data can be combined with a local validity study to determine very accurately what levels of adverse impact and productivity can be expected in a local selection scenario (including selection scenarios with multiple cognitive and noncognitive predictors). In the future, Newman, Jacobs, et al.'s approach can be integrated with De Corte et al.'s approach to yield the most accurate set of a priori predictor weights for achieving a particular, optimal diversity-performance outcome in a local selection setting.

On the topic of criterion weighting, Hattrup, Rock, and Scalia (1997) suggested incorporating aspects of contextual performance into the criterion to reduce adverse impact. The utility of this technique will depend on the company's relative financial valuation of contextual performance (Orr, Sackett, & Mercer, 1989). Both criterion-weighting schemes and predictor-weighting schemes can influence r_{PIRV}.

A third and final strategy for adverse impact reduction involves targeted recruiting. Traditional research in the area of minority recruiting has focused almost exclusively on getting more applicants from underrepresented groups to apply (Avery & McKay, 2006). An article by Newman and Lyon (2009) introduced a formal model of recruiting effects on adverse impact, to show the relative *unimportance* of simply increasing the number of minority applicants, contrasted with the critical importance of considering job-related attributes (cognitive ability and conscientious personality) simultaneously with race. Analytic and empirical results confirmed that adverse impact reduction and job performance improvement could both be achieved simultaneously, especially if the recruiting intervention produces a three-way interaction (i.e., race × conscientiousness × job ad), to create racial subgroup differences in the correlation between job-related qualifications (conscientiousness) and the probability of applying for (or accepting) a job (Newman & Lyon, 2009). Future research on recruiting and adverse impact may also benefit from consideration of black–white differences in vocational interests (Armstrong, Hubert, & Rounds, 2003; Fouad, 2002).

Conclusions

Adverse impact is a major social problem connected to a set of psychological phenomena (subgroup differences), but often without a theoretical explanation. The current chapter proposed an initial theoretical model that included factors of SES, exposure to test content, and exchange motivation. This was only a first attempt to specify a theory of adverse impact, with the goals of pushing for more thoughtful, psychologically oriented research and moving the field away from simply documenting the magnitude of adverse impact. Although various links specified in the model seem to be justified in the empirical literature, a big question is whether all the links will continue to be supported once the full model is tested. Past research results on zero-order effect sizes might be biased because important variables were left out of those studies. Now that we have specified the variables, it is time to ask whether those zero-order relationships will still be significant in a multivariate test of the causal model.

In addition to the theoretical model, we also attempted to reparameterize the adverse impact problem in terms of performance-irrelevant race-related variance in test scores (called r_{PIRV}). The magnitude of this variance for cognitive tests was empirically demonstrated. We then showed racial subgroup differences to be nonuniform across cognitive subtests, with crystallized intelligence subtests showing much larger race differences than fluid intelligence subtests. We concluded by proposing one medium-term (test development) and three short-term (predictor-weighting, criterion-weighting, and recruiting) strategies for addressing adverse impact in practice.

Acknowledgment

We would like to thank Paul Hanges for his helpful comments on this chapter.

References

Achenbach, T. M., Howell, C. T., Aoki, M. F., & Rauh, V. A. (1993). Nine-year outcome of the Vermont Intervention Program for Low Birth Weight Infants. *Pediatrics, 91*, 45–55.

Aikens, N. L., & Barbarin, O. (2008). Socioeconomic differences in reading trajectories: The contribution of family, neighborhood, and school contexts. *Journal of Educational Psychology, 100*, 235–251.

Alderton, D. L., Wolfe, J. H., & Larson, G. E. (1997). The ECAT battery. *Military Psychology, 9*, 5–37.

American Psychological Association. (1997). *Can—or should—America be color-blind? Psychological research reveals fallacies in a color-blind response to racism* [Pamphlet]. Washington, DC: Author.

American Sociological Association. (2003). *The importance of collecting data and doing social scientific research on race.* Washington, DC: Author.

Anderson, P., & Doyle, L. W. (2003). Neurobehavioral outcomes of school-age children born extremely low birth weight or very preterm in the 1990s. *JAMA, 289*, 3264–3272.

Armstrong, P. I., Hubert, L., & Rounds, J. (2003). Circular unidimensional scaling: A new look at group differences in interest structure. *Journal of Counseling Psychology, 50*, 297–308.

Avery, D. R., & McKay, P. F. (2006). Target practice: An organizational impression management approach to attracting minority and female job applicants. *Personnel Psychology, 59*, 157–187.

Avery, D. R., McKay, P. F., Wilson, D. C., & Tonidandel, S. (2007). Unequal attendance: The relationships between race, organizational diversity cues, and absenteeism. *Personnel Psychology, 60*, 875–902.

Bliese, P. D. (2000). Within-group agreement, non-independence, and reliability: Implications for data aggregation and analysis. In K. J. Klein & S. W. J. Kozlowski (Eds.), *Multilevel theory, research, and methods in organizations* (pp. 349–381). San Francisco: Jossey-Bass.

Bouchard, J. T., Jr., & McGue, M. (1981). Familial studies of intelligence: A review. *Science, 212*, 1055–1059.

Bradley, R. H., & Corwyn, R. F. (2002). Socioeconomic Status and Child Development. *Annual Review of Psychology, 53*, 372–399.

Brigham, C. C. (1923). *A study of American intelligence.* London: Princeton University Press.

Brooks-Gunn, J., & Duncan, G. J. (1997). The Effects of poverty on children. *The Future of Children, 7*, 55–71.

Brown, R. P., & Day, E. A. (2006). The difference isn't black and white: Stereotype threat and the race gap on Raven's Advanced Progressive Matrices. *Journal of Applied Psychology, 91*, 979–985.

Caldwell, B. M., & Bradley, R. H. (1984). *Home observation for measurement of the environment.* Little Rock: University of Arkansas at Little Rock.

Campbell, D. T., & Fiske, D. W. (1959). Convergent and discriminant validation by the multitrait-multimethod matrix. *Psychological Bulletin, 56*, 81–105.

Campbell, J. T., Crooks, L. A., Mahoney, M. H., & Rock, D. A. (1973). *An investigation of sources of bias in the prediction of job performance: A six-year study.* Princeton, NJ: Educational Testing Service.

Carroll, J. B. (1993). *Human cognitive abilities: A survey of factor-analytic studies.* New York: Cambridge University Press.

Cattell, R. B. (1971). *Abilities: Their structure, growth, and action.* Boston: Houghton Mifflin.

Ceci, S. J., & Papierno, P. B. (2005). The rhetoric and reality of gap closing: When the "have-nots" gain but the "haves" gain even more. *American Psychologist, 60*, 149–160.

Chavous, T. M., Bernat, D. H., Schmeelk-Cone, K., Caldwell, C. H., Kohn-Wood, L., & Zimmerman, M. A. (2003). Racial identity and academic attainment among African American adolescents. *Child Development, 74*, 1076–1090.

Chipuer, H. M., Rovine, M. J., & Plomin, R. (1990). LISREL modeling: Genetic and environmental influences on IQ revisited. *Intelligence, 14*, 11–29.

Cole, N. S. (1973). Bias in selection. *Journal of Educational Measurement, 10*, 237–255.

Colquitt, J. A., Greenberg, J., & Zapata-Phelan, C. P. (2005). What is organizational justice? An historical overview. In J. Greenberg and J. A. Colquitt (Eds.), *Handbook of organizational justice* (pp. 3–56). Mahwah, NJ: Erlbaum.

Cropley, A. (2006). In praise of convergent thinking. *Creativity Research Journal, 18*, 391–404.

Darlington, R. B. (1971). Another look at "culture fairness." *Journal of Educational Measurement, 8*, 71–82.

De Corte, W., Lievens, F., & Sackett, P. R. (2007). Combining predictors to achieve optimal trade-offs between selection quality and adverse impact. *Journal of Applied Psychology, 92*, 1380–1393.

Dezoete, J. A., MacArthur, B. A., & Tuck, B. (2003). Prediction of Bayley and Stanford-Binet scores with a group of very low birthweight children. *Child: Care, Health and Development, 29,* 367–372.

Dickens, W. T., & Flynn, J. R. (2001). Heritability estimates versus large environmental effects: The IQ paradox resolved. *Psychological Review, 108,* 346–369.

Dickens, W. T., & Flynn, J. R. (2002). The IQ paradox is still resolved: Reply to Loehlin (2002) and Rowe and Rodgers (2002). *Psychological Review, 109,* 764–771.

Drasgow, Fritz. (2003). Intelligence and the workplace. In W. C. Borman, D. R. Ilgen, and R. J. Klimoski (Eds.), *Handbook of psychology: Industrial and organizational psychology* (Vol. 12, pp. 107–130). Hoboken, NJ: Wiley.

Dusek, J. B., & Joseph, G. (1983). The bases of teacher expectancies: A meta-analysis. *Journal of Educational Psychology, 75,* 327–346.

Edwards, B. D., & Arthur, W. (2007). An examination of factors contributing to a reduction in subgroup differences on a constructed-response paper-and-pencil test of scholastic achievement. *Journal of Applied Psychology, 92,* 794–801.

Equal Employment Opportunity Commission. (1978). *Uniform Guidelines on Employee Selection Procedures.* Washington, DC.

Executive Office of the President. (2008, February). *Economic Report of the President.* Washington, DC: U.S. Government Printing Office.

Fagan, J. F., & Holland, C. R. (2002). Equal opportunity and racial differences in IQ. *Intelligence, 30,* 361–387.

Fagan, J. F., & Holland, C. R. (2007). Racial equality in intelligence: Predictions from a theory of intelligence as processing. *Intelligence, 35,* 319–334.

Feagin, J. R. (2006). *Systemic racism: A theory of oppression.* New York: Routledge.

Finn, J. D., & Rock, D. A. (1997). Academic success among students at risk for school failure. *Journal of Applied Psychology, 82,* 221–234.

Flanagan, D. P., McGrew, K. S., & Ortiz, S. O. (2000). *The Wechsler Intelligence Scales and Gf-Gc theory: A contemporary interpretive approach.* Boston: Allyn and Bacon.

Fouad, N. A. (2002). Cross-cultural differences in vocational interests: Between-groups differences in the Strong Interest Inventory. *Journal of Counseling Psychology, 49,* 283–289.

Garth, T. R. (1931). *Race psychology: A study of racial mental differences.* New York: McGraw-Hill Book Company, Inc.

Goslin, D. A. (1963). *The search for ability: Standardized testing in social perspective.* New York: Russell Sage Foundation.

Graves, J. L., Jr., & Rose, M. R. (2006). Against racial medicine. *Patterns of Prejudice, 40,* 481–493.

Gross, S. J., Mettelman, B. B., Dye, T. D., & Slagle, T. A. (2001). Impact of family structure and stability on academic outcome in preterm children at 10 years of age. *Journal of Pediatrics, 138,* 169–175.

Guilford, J. P. (1950). Creativity. *American Psychologist, 5,* 444–454.

Guo, G., & Harris, K. M. (2000). The mechanisms mediating the effects of poverty on children's intellectual development. *Demography, 37,* 431–447.

Hanges, P. J., & Gettman, H. (2004). A comparison of test-focused and criterion-focused banding methods: Back to the future? In H. Aguinis (Ed.), *Test score banding in human resource selection: Legal, technical, and societal issues* (pp. 29–48). Westport, CT: Praeger.

Harris, M. J., & Rosenthal, R. (1985). Mediation of interpersonal expectancy effects: 31 Meta-analyses. *Psychological Bulletin, 97,* 363–386.

Hattrup, K., Rock, J., & Scalia, C. (1997). The effects of varying conceptualizations of job performance on adverse impact, minority hiring, and predicted performance. *Journal of Applied Psychology, 82,* 656–664.

Helms, J. E., Jernigan, M., & Mascher, J. (2005). The meaning of race in psychology and how to change it: A methodological perspective. *American Psychologist, 60,* 27–36.

Horn, J. L. (1991). Measurement of intellectual capabilities: A review of theory. In K. S. McGrew, J. K. Werder, & R. W. Woodcock (Eds.), *Woodcock-Johnson technical manual* (pp. 197–232). Chicago: Riverside.

Hu, L. T. & Bentler, P. M. (1999). Cutoff criteria for fit indexes in covariance structure analysis: Conventional criteria versus new alternatives. *Structural Equation Modeling, 6,* 1–55.

Huffcutt, A. I., & Arthur, W., Jr. (1994). Hunter and Hunter (1984) revisited: Interview validity for entry-level jobs. *Journal of Applied Psychology, 79,* 184–190.

Hughes, D., Rodriguez, J., Smith, E. P., Johnson, D. J., Stevenson, H. C., & Spicer, P. (2006). Parents' ethnic-racial socializations practices: A review of research and directions for future study. *Developmental Psychology, 42,* 747–770.

Humphreys, L. G. (1984). General intelligence. In C. R. Reynolds & R. T. Brown (Eds.), *Perspectives on bias in mental testing* (pp. 221–247). New York: Plenum.

Hunter, J. E. (1983). *The dimensionality of the General Aptitude Test Battery (GATB) and the dominance of general factors over specific factors in the prediction of job performance for the U.S. Employment Services* (Report No. USES-TRR-44). Detroit: Michigan State Department of Labor. (ERIC Document Reproduction Service No. ED236166)

Hunter, J. E. (1986). Cognitive ability, cognitive aptitudes, job knowledge, and job performance. *Journal of Vocational Behavior, 29,* 340–362.

Hunter, J. E., Crosson, I. J., & Friedman, D. H. (1985). *The Validity of the Armed Services Vocational Aptitude Battery for civilian and military job performance.* Rockville, MD: Research Applications.

Hunter, J. E., & Hunter, R. F. (1984). Validity and utility of alternative predictors of job performance. *Psychological Bulletin, 96,* 72–98.

Hunter, J. E., & Schmidt, F. L. (1976). Critical analysis of the statistical and ethical implications of various definitions of test bias. *Psychological Bulletin, 83,* 1053–1071.

Iscoe, I., & Pierce-Jones, J. (1964). Divergent thinking, age, and intelligence in white and Negro Children. *Child Development, 35,* 785–797.

Ito, T. A., & Urland, G. R. (2003). Race and gender on the brain: Electrocortical measures of attention to the race and gender of multiply categorizable individuals. *Journal of Personality and Social Psychology, 85,* 616–626.

Johnson, W., & Bouchard, T. J., Jr. (2005). The structure of human intelligence: It is verbal, perceptual, and image rotation (VPR), not fluid and crystallized. *Intelligence, 33,* 393–416

Kawakami, K., Dion, D. L., & Dovidio, J. F. (1998). Racial prejudice and stereotype activation. *Personality and Social Psychology Bulletin, 24,* 407–416.

Kohlhauser, C., Fuiko, R., Panagl, A., Zadra, C., Haschke, N., Brandstetter, S., et al. (2000). Outcome of very-low-birth-weight-infants at 1 and 2 years of age: The importance of early identification of neurodevelopment deficits. *Clinical Pediatrics, 39*(8), 441–449. doi:10.1177/000992280003900801.

Kulik, C. C., & Kulik, J. A. (1982). Effects of ability grouping on secondary school students: A meta-analysis of evaluation findings. *American Educational Research Journal, 19,* 415–428.

Kuncel, N. R., Hezlett, S. A., & Ones, D. S. (2004). Academic performance, career potential, creativity, and job performance: Can one construct predict them all? *Journal of Personality and Social Psychology, 86,* 148–161.

Larsen, L., Hartmann, P., & Nyborg, H. (2008). The stability of general intelligence from early adulthood to middle-age. *Intelligence, 36,* 29–34.

Le, H., Oh, I. S., Shaffer, J., & Schmidt, F. (2007). Implications of methodological advances for the practice of personnel selection: How practitioners benefit from meta-analysis. *Academy of Management Perspectives, 21,* 6–15.

Lepore, L., & Brown, R. (1999). Exploring automatic stereotype activation: A challenge to the inevitability of prejudice. In D. Abrams & M. A. Hogg (Eds.), *Social identity and social cognition* (pp. 141–163). Malden, MA: Blackwell.

Lindsey, L. L., & Beach, S. (2000). *Sociology: Social life and social issues.* Upper Saddle River, NJ: Prentice Hall.

Lipsey, M. W., & Wilson, D. B. (2001). *Practical meta-analysis.* Thousand Oaks, CA: Sage.

Macionis, J. J. (1999). *Sociology: Student media version.* Upper Saddle River, NJ: Prentice Hall.

Macrae, C., & Bodenhausen, G. (2000). Social cognition: Thinking categorically about others. *Annual Review of Psychology, 51,* 93–120.

McGrew, K. S. (1997). Analysis of major intelligence batteries according to a proposed comprehensive Gf-Gc framework. In D. P. Flanagan, J. L. Genshaft, & P. L. Harrison (Eds.), *Contemporary intellectual assessment: Theories, tests, and issues* (pp. 151–180). New York: Guilford.

McGrew, K. S. (2008). CHC theory and the human cognitive abilities project: Standing on the shoulders of the giants of psychometric intelligence research. *Intelligence, 37*(1), 1–10. doi: 10.1016/j.intell.2008.08.004.

McHenry, J. J., Hough, L. M., Toquam, J. L., Hanson, M. A., & Ashworth, S. (1990). Project A validity results: The relationship between predictor and criterion domains. *Personnel Psychology, 43,* 335–354.

McIntyre, L. D., & Pernell, E. (1985). The impact of race on teacher recommendations for special education placement. *Journal of Multicultural Counseling and Development, 13,* 112–120.

McKay, P. F., & McDaniel, M. A. (2006). A reexamination of black-white mean differences in work performance: More data, more moderators. *Journal of Applied Psychology, 91,* 538–554.

McKay, P. F., Avery, D. R., Tonidandel, S., Morris, M. A., Hernandez, M., & Hebl, M. R. (2007). Racial differences in employee retention: Are diversity climate perceptions the key? *Personnel Psychology, 60*, 35–62.

Messick, S. (1995). Validity of psychological assessment: Validation of inferences from persons' responses and performances as scientific inquiry into score meaning. *American Psychologist, 50*, 741–749.

Murphy, K. R., Cleveland, J. N., Skattebo, A. L., & Kinney, T. B. (2004). Raters who pursue different goals give different ratings. *Journal of Applied Psychology, 89*, 158–164.

Neville, H. A., Lilly, R. L., Duran, G., Lee, R. M., & Browne, L. (2000). Construction and initial validation of the Color-Blind Racial Attitudes Scale (CoBRAS). *Journal of Counseling Psychology, 47*, 59–70.

Newman, D. A., Hanges, P. J., & Outtz, J. L. (2007). Racial groups and test fairness: Considering history and construct validity. *American Psychologist, 62*, 1082–1083.

Newman, D. A., Jacobs, R. R., & Bartram, D. (2007). Choosing the best method for local validity estimation: Relative accuracy of meta-analysis vs. a local study vs. Bayes-analysis. *Journal of Applied Psychology, 92*, 1394–1413.

Newman, D. A., & Lyon, J. S. (2009). Recruitment efforts to reduce adverse impact: Targeted recruiting for personality, cognitive ability, and diversity. *Journal of Applied Psychology, 94*(2), 298–317.

Oates, G. L. St. C. (2003). Teacher-student racial congruence, teacher perceptions, and test performance. *Social Science Quarterly, 84*, 508–525.

Omi, M., & Winant, H. (1986). *Racial formation in the United States: From the 1960s to the 1980s*. New York: Routledge and Kegan Paul.

Omi, M., & Winant, H. (2001). Racial formation. In M. Anderson, K. Logio, & H. Taylor (Eds.), *Understanding society* (pp. 243–249). Belmont, CA: Wadsworth.

Orr, J. M., Sackett, P. R., & Mercer, M. (1989). The role of prescribed and nonprescribed behaviors in estimating the dollar value of performance. *Journal of Applied Psychology, 74*, 34–40.

Outtz, J. (1998). Testing medium, validity and test performance. In M. Hakel (Ed.), *Beyond multiple choice: Evaluating alternatives to traditional testing for selection* (pp. 41–57). Hillsdale, NJ: Erlbaum.

Outtz, J., Goldstein, H., & Ferreter J. (2006, April). *Testing divergent and convergent thinking: Test response format and adverse impact*. Paper presented at the 20th Annual Conference of the Society for Industrial and Organizational Psychology, Los Angeles.

Petrill, S. A., Lipton, P. A., Hewitt, J. K., Plomin, R., Cherny, S. S., Corley, R., et al. (2004). Genetic and environmental contributions to general cognitive ability through the first 16 years of life. *Developmental Psychology, 40*, 805–812.

Phinney, J. S. (1996). When we talk about American ethnic groups, what do we mean? *American Psychologist, 51*, 918–927.

Ployhart, R. E., & Holtz, B. C. (2008). The diversity-validity dilemma: Strategies for reducing racioethnic and sex subgroup differences and adverse impact in selection. *Personnel Psychology, 61*, 153–172.

Price-Williams, D. R., & Ramirez M. (1977). Divergent thinking, cultural differences, and bilingualism. *The Journal of Social Psychology, 103*, 3–11.

Quintana, S. M. (2007). Racial and ethnic identity: Developmental perspectives and research. *Journal of Counseling Psychology, 54,* 259–270.

Ramey, C. T., & Ramey, S. L. (1998). Prevention of intellectual disabilities: Early interventions to improve cognitive development. *Preventive Medicine, 27,* 224–232.

Roberts, R. D., Goff, G. N., Anjoul, F., Kyllonen, P. C., Pallier, G., & Stankov, L. (2000). The Armed Services Vocational Aptitude Battery (ASVAB): Little more than acculturated learning (Gc)!? *Learning and Individual Differences, 12,* 81–103.

Roid, G. H. (2003). *Stanford-Binet Intelligence Scale* (5th ed.). Itasca, IL: Riverside.

Roth, P. L., Bevier, C. A., Bobko, P., Switzer, F. S., III, & Tyler, P. (2001). Ethnic group differences in cognitive ability in employment and educational settings: A meta-analysis. *Personnel Psychology, 54,* 297–330.

Roth, P. L., Huffcutt, A. I., & Bobko, P. (2003). Ethnic group differences in measures of job performance: A new meta-analysis. *Journal of Applied Psychology, 88,* 694–706.

Sackett, P. R., Schmitt, N., Ellingson, J. E., & Kabin, M. B. (2001). High-stakes testing in employment, credentialing, and higher education: Prospects in a post-affirmative action world. *American Psychologist, 56,* 302–318.

Saigal, S., Szatmari, P., Rosenbaum, P., Campbell, D., & King, S. (1991). Cognitive abilities and school performance of extremely low birth weight children and matched term control children at age 8 years: A regional study. *Journal of Pediatrics, 118,* 751–760.

Schmidt, F. L., & Hunter, J. (1998). The validity and utility of selection methods in personnel psychology: Practical and theoretical implications of 85 years of research findings. *Psychological Bulletin, 124,* 262–274.

Schmidt, F. L., Hunter, J. E., & Outerbridge, A. N. (1986). Impact of job experience and ability on job knowledge, work sample performance, and supervisory ratings of job performance. *Journal of Applied Psychology, 71,* 432–439.

Schmidt, F. L., Hunter, J. E., Outerbridge, A. N., & Goff, S. (1988). Joint relation of experience and ability with job performance: Test of three hypotheses. *Journal of Applied Psychology, 73,* 46–57.

Schneider, B. (1990). *Organizational climate and culture.* San Francisco: Jossey-Bass.

Sellers, R. M., Smith, M. A., Shelton, J. N., Rowley, S. A. J., & Chavous, T. M. (1998). Multidimensional model of racial identity: A reconceptualization of African American racial identity. *Personality and Social Psychology Review, 2,* 18–39.

Shuey, A. M. (1958). *The testing of Negro intelligence.* Lynchburg: VA: Bell.

Smedley, A., & Smedley, B. D. (2005). Race as biology is fiction, racism as a social problem is real: Anthropological and historical perspectives on the social construction of race. *American Psychologist, 60,* 16–26.

Smith, M. L. (1980). Teacher expectations. *Evaluation in Education, 4,* 53–55.

Spearman, C. (1904). "General intelligence," objectively determined and measured. *American Journal of Psychology, 15,* 201–293.

Stangor, S., Lynch, L., Duan, C., & Glass, B. (1992). Categorization of individuals on the basis of multiple social features. *Journal of Personality and Social Psychology, 62,* 207–218.

Stauffer, J. M., & Buckley, M. R. (2005). The existence and nature of racial bias in supervisory ratings. *Journal of Applied Psychology, 90,* 586–591.

Sternberg, R. J., Grigorenko, E. L., & Kidd, K. K. (2005). Intelligence, race, and genetics. *American Psychologist, 60,* 46–59.

Thorndike, E. L. (1939). On the fallacy of imputing the correlations found for groups to the individuals or smaller groups composing them. *American Journal of Psychology, 52,* 122–124.

Torrance, E. P. (1971). Are the Torrance tests of creative thinking biased against or in favor of "disadvantaged" groups? *The Gifted Child Quarterly, 15,* 75–80.

U.S. Bureau of Labor Statistics, & U.S. Census Bureau. (2007). *Current population survey.* Washington, DC: Author.

U.S. Department of Education, National Center for Education Statistics. (2008). *The Condition of Education 2008.* Washington, DC: Author.

U.S. Department of Health and Human Services. (2000). *Healthy People 2010* (2nd ed., Vol. 1). Washington, DC: U.S. Government Printing Office.

Weisglas-Kuperus, N., Baerts, W., Smrkovsky, M., & Sauer, P. J. (1993). Effects of biological and social factors on the cognitive development of very low birth weight children. *Pediatrics, 92,* 658–665.

White-Clark, R. (2005). Training teachers to succeed in a multicultural climate. *Principal, 2,* 40–44.

Whitley, B. E., & Kite, M. E. (2006). *The psychology of prejudice and discrimination.* Belmont, CA: Thomson Higher Education.

Wittenbrink, B., Judd, C. M., & Park, B. (1997). Evidence for racial prejudice at the implicit level and its relation to questionnaire measures. *Journal of Personality and Social Psychology, 72,* 262–274.

Woodcock, R. W., McGrew, K. S., & Mather, N. (2001). *Woodcock-Johnson Psychoeducational Battery Third Edition (WJ-3).* Chicago: Riverside.

Zyphur, M. J. (2006). On the complexity of race. *American Psychologist, 61,* 179–180.

4

Revisiting g: Intelligence, Adverse Impact, and Personnel Selection

Harold W. Goldstein, Charles A. Scherbaum, and Kenneth P. Yusko

Introduction

Consider the following:

- We know the most important quality one should possess for success at work (and in life, for that matter).
- We know this quality exists, and we understand its nature.
- We know how to measure this quality.
- We know this quality is mostly attributable to genetics and heredity.
- We know we can do little to increase this quality in people.
- We know that minorities (e.g., African Americans) have significantly less of this quality.

The quality referred to is known as g (i.e., intelligence, general cognitive ability, general mental ability), and these statements reflect a particular perspective within the study of intelligence known as the *psychometric approach* (Jensen 1998, 2000) that many within the field of industrial and organizational (I/O) psychology have seemingly adopted (Murphy, Cronin, & Tam, 2003; Schmidt & Hunter, 1998; Viswesvaran & Ones, 2002). Most specifically, the impact can be observed in the area of personnel selection, in which intelligence tests are often viewed as the single best predictor of job performance (Schmidt & Hunter, 1998) and their use is expected to result in adverse impact against certain minority groups

(Hough, Oswald, & Ployhart, 2001). These outcomes of using intelligence tests for staffing are seen as a foregone conclusion, and as a result the field has generally shifted to focus on the development of alternative predictors (e.g., structured interviews, biodata) and strategies for implementation (e.g., cutoff scores, banding).

The purpose of this chapter is to point out that a great opportunity is being missed by the field of I/O psychology with regard to the role of intelligence in personnel selection. By allowing one perspective on intelligence, the psychometric approach, to dominate the thinking of the field of I/O psychology, we are limiting our exploration of this topic. A particular problem of the psychometric approach is its notion that most critical questions regarding intelligence that are pertinent to personnel selection have been answered, as reflected in the absolutist nature of the statements listed at the beginning of the chapter. Such beliefs of the psychometric approach, especially with regard to the statement that racial differences are inherent in the construct of intelligence, have deterred the field of I/O psychology from conducting further research in personnel selection on intelligence and from attempting to develop measures of intelligence that do not produce racial differences. This chapter focuses on examining other perspectives and research from the field of intelligence that do not agree with these fundamental statements of the psychometric approach in hopes of stimulating thinking within the field of I/O psychology on intelligence, adverse impact, and personnel selection.

In this chapter, we explore some fundamental questions regarding the intelligence construct and its measurement in an attempt to understand better the causes of as well as how to mitigate adverse impact. While many in our field consider such central questions to be resolved, we reexamine the intelligence literature that calls into question these assumptions regarding the intelligence construct that have been adopted as truths by many in personnel selection. We begin by providing a brief overview of the central tenets of the psychometric perspective. Next, we take an in-depth look at the type of psychometric-based statements listed that are assumed to be true by many in our field and discuss how the intelligence literature has evolved on these issues. Based on findings from this review of the literature, we conclude the chapter by discussing future directions and briefly describing some current initiatives for measuring intelligence in a valid manner that simultaneously reduces adverse impact against particular minority groups. Thus, despite claims to the contrary and the "case-closed" mentality demonstrated by many in the field (e.g., Gottfredson, 1998; Schmidt, 2002), this chapter shows that there are still numerous questions that need to be investigated when it comes to measuring intelligence, adverse impact, and personnel selection.

Overview of a Psychometric Perspective on Intelligence: The *g* Factor

The roots of this particular psychometric approach to intelligence can be found in the seminal work of Charles Spearman, who first published a paper in 1904 that focused on the existence of a general factor of intelligence that reportedly underlies "all branches of intellectual activity" (1927, p. 284). Spearman described this *g* factor as an "amount of general mental energy" (1927, p. 137) and mathematically derived it from the "shared variance that saturates batteries of cognitive/intelligence tests" (Wasserman & Tulsky, 2005, p. 16). This notion of a general factor of intelligence contrasts with the idea of separate factors of intelligence posited by other researchers (e.g., Cattell, 1963; Horn, 1976; Thurstone, 1938), which includes distinct facets such as memory, verbal comprehension, and numerical facility. While the concept of *g* has been greatly debated from the beginning (Wasserman & Tulsky, 2005), it is a concept that has demonstrated resiliency and remains a part of a number of major models of intelligence that have evolved over the century. Even many hardened critics of the *g* factor rarely have dismissed the possibility that it exists, although what role it plays, its characteristics, and its centrality in various models of intellectual ability have greatly varied (e.g., Carroll, 1993; Thurstone, 1947).

Arthur Jensen has served as one of the strongest proponents of the notion of a *g* factor and has argued vehemently for its existence and for its prominent role in models of intelligence. Jensen (1980, 1998) has also popularized the notion of key characteristics of intelligence like the statements listed to start this chapter. While not necessarily the originator of all these statements, some can be traced back to Spearman as well as others, he has worked tirelessly to promote and support them as factual and has served as a driving force of the *g*-oriented psychometric perspective (Gottfredson, 1998; Neisser et al., 1996; Rushton, 1998) that has seemingly been embraced by many in I/O psychology and personnel selection (Murphy et al., 2003; Schmidt & Hunter, 1998).

There are a number of focal points to this perspective, as reflected in the statements listed at the beginning of this chapter. The first is that *g* exists; that is, intelligence is a single entity or factor. This is the notion that there is a general factor or capability that underlies intellectual functioning rather than separate group factors of intelligence. The general factor approach emphasizes what the facets of intellectual functioning have in common (Neisser et al., 1996). Those who subscribe to the *g* factor propose that it is the latent trait underlying all mental abilities, including activities such as learning, memory, grasping concepts, reasoning, problem solving, and more (Jensen, 2000).

To a great extent, support for the existence of a general factor of intelligence has been fundamentally based on one main phenomenon: positive manifold. *Positive manifold* refers to the idea that tests of different mental abilities positively correlate (Spearman, 1904, 1927). This implies that people who score well on one cognitive test are likely to score well on other cognitive tests. With few exceptions, research has shown that indeed tests of cognitive ability tend to be positively intercorrelated, although to varying degrees (Horn & Blankson, 2005; Neisser et al., 1996). Some researchers have taken this empirical phenomenon of positive manifold as proof that there is an underlying factor of general intelligence (Carroll, 1993; Gottfredson, 1998; Jensen, 1998; Spearman, 1927). As asserted by Spearman (1927), the positive correlation between tests of mental ability indicates that some portion of variance in the scores is mathematically attributed to this general factor. That is, the measures of cognitive ability positively correlate because of g (Jensen, 1998, 2000), or put another way, "g simply summarizes the positive relationship between mental tests" (Detterman, 2002, p. 225).

A related finding, which some feel provides further support for the existence of a general factor of intelligence, is the outcome of factor analytic research on intelligence (McGrew, 2005). Factor analysis is a statistical technique that can be used to examine the structure of correlations among variables. Some assume that the structure of intelligence can be discovered by examining the interrelationship of scores on mental ability tests using factor analytic techniques (Davidson & Downing, 2000). Carroll's (1993) *Human Cognitive Abilities: A Survey of Factor Analytic Studies* provides a summary of what many consider to be the most extensive factor analytic research carried out on intelligence to date. Carroll conducted factor analysis on 460 sets of data from the relevant literature to examine the question of how many factors or latent traits are indicated by the set of correlations between tests of mental ability. He concluded that his analyses produced a dominant first-order general factor that many label as psychometric g. That is, g is frequently represented as the highest factor of a hierarchical factor analysis of a battery of cognitive ability tests (Ree & Carretta, 2002). The positive manifold or the fact that tests generally positively correlate leads to this large first factor derived by factor analysis and referred to as g. "In this view, g is a summary measure or index of the positive manifold" (van der Maas et al., 2006, p. 842). This empirical phenomenon is cited by the psychometric perspective as clear evidence for the existence of a general factor of intelligence.

Another focal point of the psychometric perspective on intelligence is that g can be readily measured. Attempts to assess intelligence can be traced back centuries, although most credit Francis Galton (1865) as the first individual who focused on designing objective techniques for measuring intelligence. While many of these initial tests of Galton and his disciples (e.g., James McKeen Cattell) tended to measure sensory and motor functioning (e.g., reaction time, sensory thresholds), Alfred Binet, whom many consider the founder of modern intelligence testing, began to focus on measuring various aspects of intellectual processing, such as knowledge of language and visual and auditory processing, as well as learning and memory (Binet & Henri, 1895; Binet & Simon, 1905/1916). Building off and adapting from this initial work, numerous measures of intelligence have been developed over the past century. While these intelligence tests have taken many different forms, the most familiar include a range of item types that involve performing different mental tasks such as defining words, identifying the relationship between concepts, solving quantitative and logical problems, and pattern identification. Some intelligence tests have just one type of item, but many consist of an array of different types of verbal and nonverbal items (Neisser et al., 1996). Examples of well-known established tests of intelligence include the Stanford-Binet, the Wechsler intelligence scales (e.g., Wechsler Intelligence Scale for Children [WISC], the Wechsler Adult Intelligence Scale [WAIS]), the Wonderlic, and the Raven's Progressive Matrices.

According to the psychometric perspective, g can be measured by creating a composite score from a set of diverse but purportedly highly g-loaded tests of intellectual functioning (Jensen, 1998). Rooting back to the definition of g as the shared variance that saturates batteries of cognitive/intelligence tests, the idea is that an estimate of this variance that represents intelligence can be captured by averaging performance across a wide array of these tests. As described by Jensen (1998), "the greater the number of such diverse (but g-loaded) tests that enter into the composite score, the more the unwanted sources of variance are averaged out and the more accurately the composite scores indicate individual differences in g level" (p. 309). This approach to measuring g relies also on the phenomenon of positive manifold in that, because tests of cognitive ability tend to correlate positively, there is the notion that the shared variance that drives this intercorrelation reflects the latent intelligence construct. Thus, by capturing this shared variance by deriving a composite across an array of cognitive tests, one can obtain a measure of g. As a result, those subscribing to the psychometric perspective state that "given enough tests, the simple sum of the test scores will produce an acceptable estimate of g..." (Ree & Carretta, 2002, pp. 5–6).

Building on this approach to measuring g, the psychometric perspective argues that the type of measure used as well as the content of the device are not necessarily important. This principle, first developed by Spearman (1923), is referred to as the notion of "indifference of the indicator." This means that when creating tests of intelligence, the content and form of the test do not matter as long as the test takers perceive it the same way (Jensen, 1998; Ree & Carretta, 2002). Based on this principle, the psychometric perspective notes that these tests are merely vehicles for measuring g, and that many different vehicles can accomplish this in an acceptable manner.

In addition, the psychometric perspective asserts that measurement of g occurs in an unbiased manner. While it is acknowledged that subgroup means often significantly differ on tests of general cognitive ability (e.g., whites outperform blacks by approximately 1 standard deviation [*SD*]), the psychometric claim is largely based on a model of fairness that focuses instead on the concept of differential validity and predictive fairness for subgroups (Schmidt & Hunter, 1998). With regard to differential validity, the research generally shows that the validity of intelligence tests for predicting performance outcomes (e.g., academic achievement, job performance) does not differ significantly for different subgroups. Further, with regard to the notion of predictive bias, research provides evidence that similar scores on an intelligence test link similarly to future performance outcomes regardless of subgroup (Jensen, 1980; Wigdor & Garner, 1982). Thus, the psychometric perspective concludes that g not only exists but also can be measured and in a fair manner.

An additional central point of the psychometric perspective is that g is the most important quality that determines success of all types, including at work. Research on g provides support for a strong positive relationship between intelligence and outcomes that include academic success, social status, and income as well as a strong negative relationship with socially undesirable outcomes such as crime and juvenile delinquency (Herrnstein & Murray, 1994; Neisser et al., 1996). In addition and of particular importance to this chapter given its focus on g and personnel selection, research shows support for a significant relationship between intelligence and work performance outcomes (Schmidt & Hunter, 1998). For instance, findings from meta-analytic studies (Hunter, 1980; Hunter & Hunter, 1984) are quoted by the psychometric perspective as demonstrating that measures of intelligence strongly predict training and job performance (validities of 0.56 and 0.51, respectively). Furthermore, this research is interpreted as indicating that the validity of intelligence tests generalizes across a wide range of jobs (e.g., the Hunter and Hunter study included 515 widely diverse civilian jobs) that vary in complexity (although it was noted that intelligence tests predict more strongly for highly complex jobs [0.58] in comparison to jobs that require less skill [0.23]). Given these findings of validity and generalizability as well as how they compare to other types of selection devices, those representing the psychometric perspective argue that tests of g should have a special status in the field of personnel selection and should be considered the primary tool for making selection decisions in work organizations (Schmidt & Hunter, 1998).

A final focal point of the psychometric perspective to be examined in this chapter, and arguably the most controversial, involves the statement regarding racial differences on *g*. On the issue of race and intelligence, the psychometric perspective subscribes to what Jensen (1985) labeled the *Spearman hypothesis*. The Spearman hypothesis as formulated by Jensen generally predicts that racial differences in test performance will increase as the *g* loading of the test increases. Spearman (1927) was the first to note that tests with higher *g* saturation seemed to be associated with larger racial subgroup differences. Thus, arguably highly *g*-loaded tests such as those that tap verbal comprehension and spatial ability tend to show larger racial differences, while arguably lowly *g*-loaded tests such as those that measure perceptual speed and memory tend to show smaller racial differences (Jensen, 1985; Loehlin, 2000; Reeve & Hakel, 2002). Across 149 tests of this hypothesis, Jensen (1998) reported an average correlation of 0.60 between the extent of *g* load and the resulting racial subgroup differences. He concluded that, based on these strong empirical findings as well as the lack of evidence for alternative explanations, the Spearman hypothesis should be accepted as factual.

While the Spearman hypothesis has been looked at with regard to a wide array of racial and ethnic groups, it is the finding with regard to blacks and whites that has spurred the most controversy and has arguably fueled the debate on intelligence over the past century. Generally, a difference of 1 *SD* favoring whites over blacks has been reported for intelligence tests; however, the size of the difference varies depending on which test of intelligence is referenced (Naglieri, 2005; Wasserman & Becker, 2000). According to the Spearman hypothesis, the better the test is at measuring intelligence (i.e., the higher the *g* load), the greater the resulting differences will be in terms of whites outscoring blacks. Because tests of intelligence often serve as gateways to education and employment, this hypothesis would result in disparate outcomes for blacks when it comes to entrance into schools and access to jobs in work organizations. As noted, some in personnel selection have argued vehemently that tests of intelligence should serve as the primary device for making hiring decisions in work organizations. If this path is followed and the Spearman hypothesis is true, the use of intelligence tests for making staffing decisions will by necessity result in lower employment rates for blacks.

Two additional tenets of the psychometric perspective on intelligence that are outside the scope of this chapter and are not discussed further involve the causal factors that determine intelligence. These tenets reflect the nature-versus-nurture debate that has been discussed in the scientific literature for longer than the century-old debate on intelligence. The first involves heredity, on which the psychometric perspective states that genetics is the primary determinant of an individual's intelligence (Bouchard, 1997; Jensen, 1998). The second involves environment, on which the psychometric perspective argues that environmental interventions can do little to change or enhance an individual's intelligence (Herrnstein & Murray, 1994; Jensen, 1998). The psychometric perspective generally asserts the dominance of genetic causal factors over that of the environment when it comes to the development of intelligence as well as when explaining the presence of subgroup differences on intelligence. Research on these points has taken many interesting forms (e.g., twin and adoption studies; evaluation of education intervention programs such as Head Start); other writings more fully delve into these issues (e.g., Jensen, 1998; Sternberg & Grigorenko, 1997). Thus, besides noting that the psychometric perspective poses these as answered questions (i.e., intelligence is primarily due to genetics, and little can be done to change it), this chapter does not look more closely at this issue.

In summary, a review of the focal points of the psychometric perspective on intelligence results in the following assumptions that have pervaded the field of personnel selection: (a) We know intelligence exists and understand its nature, (b) we know how to measure intelligence, (c), we know intelligence is the most important predictor of job performance, and (d) we know that whites possess more intelligence than a number of minority groups (e.g., blacks, Hispanics). One can certainly see why such a stance could be considered controversial, depending on one's sociopolitical point of view. However, from a scientific standpoint, the key question is whether these assumptions, which have seemingly been adopted by many in our field, are true. A review of the intelligence literature raises many questions regarding these issues that should signal the need to pause and proceed with caution when it comes to embracing such assumptions as fact.

Evolving Perspectives and Continuing Debates

A review of the literature on intelligence clearly reveals that the assumptions of the psychometric perspective are not held as undisputed truths but instead merely represent one point of view of the field. The research on intelligence shows evidence both in support and against this psychometric approach as well as information and data that substantiate other views and perspectives. Certainly, what is clear from the literature is that there is vigorous debate on all critical tenets of the psychometric perspective, and that this is a debate that is just as relevant today as it was when it started over a century ago (McGrew, 2005; Tulsky, Saklofske, & Ricker, 2003). As noted in the Neisser et al. (1996) article, which was written by a committee representing the American Psychological Association to highlight the known and unknown regarding intelligence in the wake of the public debate spurred by the publishing of Herrnstein and Murray's *The Bell Curve* (1994), the issues regarding intelligence "remain complex and in many cases still unresolved" (p. 77). In the light of this continuing research and ever-evolving debate on intelligence, the key focal points of the psychometric perspective are now explored.

The Existence and Nature of Intelligence

Does intelligence exist as described by the psychometric perspective? That is, is there a clearly defined singular latent variable (i.e., g) that underlies cognitive functioning? Perhaps a reasonable starting point for the discussion of the existence and nature of any construct is to examine whether it can in fact be defined. An agreed-on definition allows for clear conceptualization of the construct, which would be a strong advantage when it comes to developing measures of the construct domain and using them to predict important outcomes as is done in personnel selection (Schmidt & Hunter, 1998). However, without a clear definition, it is difficult to create theories of prediction of performance with any level of depth or develop construct-valid measures. What becomes readily apparent in examining the intelligence literature is that there is great debate with regard to both the definition of intelligence and whether intelligence is singular in nature. In other words, there is a lack of agreement on whether "g" exists as described by the psychometric approach.

Despite vehement claims to the contrary by many who subscribe to this psychometric perspective (Gottfredson, 1994, 2002; Herrnstein & Murray, 1994; Schmidt & Hunter, 1998), an agreed-on definition for intelligence at this time simply does not exist. While one has been actively sought since the beginning of the study of intelligence, it continues to elude the field. The large divergence found when defining intelligence is a point that has been recognized by numerous researchers over the century. This is seen as far back as 1921, when the publishers of the *Journal of Educational Psychology* asked 17 leading scientists (e.g., Thorndike, Thurstone, Terman) to define the intelligence construct, and the views expressed varied in many more ways than they were similar (Wechsler, 1975). Basically, for every researcher asked to define the intelligence construct, a different definition emerged. This is still the case today, as noted by Sternberg and Detterman (1986), who described how two dozen prominent theorists were asked to define intelligence and gave two dozen different definitions. In truth, we are currently no closer to reaching consensus on how to define the construct of intelligence than we were a century ago (Neisser et al., 1996; Wasserman & Tulsky, 2005).

In many ways, the nature of the definition espoused depends on numerous factors. For instance, one's field of study and specialization has an impact on what is focused on and emphasized when defining intelligence

(Wasserman & Tulsky, 2005). Thus, those representing various fields, such as anthropology, sociology, and psychology, may construct very different definitions of intelligence (Wechsler, 1975). Wechsler provided the example that an anthropologist is more likely to develop a definition of intelligence that focuses on the ability to adapt to the environment while an educator may emphasize learning. Even within a field of study, divergence is often found with regard to a definition. For instance, whether one is a learning, developmental, cognitive, or clinical psychologist is likely to have an impact on the nature of the definition crafted. Perhaps those from a learning perspective emphasize the ability to acquire and apply concepts, while those from a clinical perspective emphasize the ability to think in a logical and rational manner. Even within the same perspective, different definitions of intelligence often emerge. For example, those representing a psychometric perspective have defined intelligence in a variety of ways, including as the ability to learn (Schmidt, 2002), a general capability for processing complex information (Gottfredson, 2002), and the ability to infer and apply relationships (Spearman, 1927).

In examining different conceptualizations of intelligence as reflected in the diverse definitions, they do not vary only in surface-level aspects but also in fundamental ways that truly alter the nature of the construct. For example, some of the definitions and accompanying models of intelligence include prior knowledge, such as expertise in language and vocabulary (e.g., Binet & Simon, 1905/1916). Other models remove such knowledge and instead focus solely on the processing of information (e.g., Fagan, 1992, 2000; Fagan & Holland, 2007). Even these conceptualizations vary in that some define processing based more on *quality*, such as the accurate identification of trends and patterns (Fagan, 2000), while others place more of an emphasis on *speed* (e.g., neural speed as posited by Spearman, 1927) by assessing outcomes such as reaction and inspection time (Jensen, 2006).

When reviewing the conceptualization of intelligence over time, one can identify different trends in what has been emphasized. For example, a major focus initially was on an organism's ability to adapt to the environment (Binet & Simon, 1911/1916; Spenser, 1855/1885; Stern, 1912/1914). Using what could be labeled almost a Darwinian perspective, numerous researchers concentrated on the ability to adjust one's thinking to new requirements of the environment or adapt "to new problems and conditions of life" (Stern, 1912/1914, p. 41). While some retained this adaptation foundation (e.g., Sternberg and Salter defined intelligence as "goal directed adaptive behavior," 1982), other trends emerged over time. For instance, at the turn of the century Binet, one of the first scientists to study and find ways to measure intelligence, actually avoided creating an official definition, yet in his description of the construct emphasized judgment and the ability to make sound decisions. Binet and Simon noted that "a person may be a moron or an imbecile if he is lacking in judgment; but with good judgment he can never be either" (1905, pp. 42–43).

Recent trends have attempted to pinpoint more basic mental functions that may be *g*. For example, Kyllonen (1996) and his colleagues theorized about working memory as the essence of general intelligence, while Horn and Blankson (2005) as well as others (e.g., Ericsson & Kintsch, 1995) examined the application of memory as a form of expertise that serves as a central foundation for defining intelligence (e.g., expert memory or expertise wide-span memory). It should be further noted that some have chosen to define intelligence much more broadly, such as Howard Gardner's multiple intelligence (MI) theory, which includes factors such as bodily-kinesthetic intelligence, interpersonal intelligence, and even musical intelligence (Gardner, 1983, 1999). For the purposes of this chapter, intelligence is conceptualized more traditionally in terms of what are thought of as mainstream cognitive processes. However, what should be realized is that even within this more traditional and narrow cognitive view, there is great disagreement regarding the nature of intelligence and a wide variety of divergent definitions for this construct.

As one can see just from these limited examples (see Bartholomew, 2004; Sternberg & Detterman, 1986; or Sternberg, 2000, for more extensive reviews on defining intelligence), intelligence can be a very different entity depending on how one defines it. As noted by Bartholomew, "almost everyone uses the word intelligence but it is one of those Humpty Dumpty words whose meaning is so elastic that it can cover virtually anything we choose" (2004, p. 1). He goes on to state that this "lack of clarity does not make for rational discussion" (p. 1). That is, the lack of a clear agreed-on definition for the construct makes it difficult to discuss the existence of intelligence. The question becomes, "Does *what* exist?" Without a common conceptualization of what the intelligence construct is, it is difficult to delineate the domain and what it encompasses and to ask further questions about its origin, nature, and characteristics. For instance, we need to know what intelligence is before we discuss whether there are racial differences. We need to know what intelligence is before we can speak to how it predicts performance. The problem is that when statements are made regarding the qualities and characteristics of intelligence, inevitably the answer is that it depends on how you define intelligence (Mackintosh, 1998).

A second major issue is whether intelligence is singular in structure. That is, is there a single factor of general mental functioning that underlies intelligence? A review of the literature revealed that this is also a topic of great contention. As noted, the main evidence relied on by the psychometric perspective to support this notion is positive manifold (i.e., the general empirical finding of a positive intercorrelation across most tests of cognitive ability). Those subscribing to the psychometric perspective feel that this finding indicates the existence of intelligence as a single latent variable that they labeled g (Carroll, 1993; Jensen, 1998; Spearman, 1927). However, others stated that while one would expect to find a positive correlation across cognitive tests if g did exist, this finding does not prove that it does indeed exist (van der Maas et al., 2006).

Bartholomew noted in describing the empirical phenomena of g as reflected by positive manifold that "if a set of test scores tends to be positively correlated among themselves there is a *prima facie* case for believing that those correlations are induced by a common dependence on a latent variable" (2004, p. 62). However, he went on to state that while positive manifold is "what we would have expected if an underlying variable, called g, did exist ... [that this type of evidence] leaves open the possibility that some other mechanism could have produced the correlation" (p. 73). The fact is that analysis of correlations provides insufficient proof for the existence of g (Bartholomew, 2004; Borsboom, Mellenbergh, & van Heerden, 2004; Horn & Blankson, 2005; van der Mass et al., 2006). As expressed by Horn and Blankson, "Many variables are positively correlated, but that fact does not indicate one cause, or only one influence operating or only one common factor" (p. 52).

From very early, it was recognized that there are many explanations for positive manifold that do not rely on one common causal factor (Thomson, 1916; Thurstone, 1947). For example, sampling theory posits that cognitive functioning is dependent on many uncorrelated lower-level neural processes (i.e., bonds), some of which appear to overlap when measured, thus resulting in positive manifold (Thomson, 1951; Thorndike, 1927). In this theory, positive manifold is a result of measurement error due to the difficulty in independently tapping these various lower-level processes. Others have posited that positive manifold is caused by contaminating factors of measures designed to tap a narrow conceptualization of intelligence. For instance, Chen and Gardner (2005) stated that most measures aim predominantly at logical-mathematical and linguistic aspects of intelligence and do so using paper-and-pencil techniques. They noted that this is a possible explanation for the positive manifold observed, and that when a wider range of intellectual capabilities is tapped using a variety of techniques that the correlations among these abilities will not be as high (Gardner & Walters, 1993; Walters & Gardner, 1986).

A more recent alternative explanation for positive manifold is a developmental model called *mutualism theory* (van der Maas et al., 2006). Mutualism is a mathematically formulated model that focuses on the positive beneficial relationships between cognitive processes. A key notion of this theory is that cognitive processes have mutually beneficial or facilitating relations, and thus each process supports the growth of other processes. Thus, from a dynamical systems perspective (Wagner, 1999), there are direct and indirect reciprocal causal relationships between independent cognitive factors that facilitate their growth and development, and thus the positive manifold observed is merely a reflection of this interactive growth. These alternative explanations as well as others must be addressed before one can conclude that positive manifold is proof of the existence of a single latent variable of intelligence. That is, analysis of correlations is not sufficient evidence of a single factor (Bartholomew, 2004; Borsboom et al., 2004; Horn & Blankson, 2005; van der Maas et al., 2006).

In fact, Spearman (1927) recognized this from the beginning, noting that not only do tests of *g* need to correlate positively but also they need to represent comprehensively the spectrum of capabilities regarded as human intelligence and to correlate with the common factor alone. That is, the correlations must show that one and only one common factor accounts for the intercorrelations between variables that represent the wide domain of intelligence. According to Horn and Blankson (2005), the factor analytic research (e.g., Carroll, 1993; Gustafsson, 1984) on this correlational data shows a lack of support for the existence of a single underlying factor. While Carroll (1993, 2005) disagreed, Horn noted that the findings do not reveal one and only one factor underlying intellectual functioning (McGrew, 2005). Similarly, Bartholomew stated that it is "clear that variation in one dimension was not sufficient to explain individual differences in test performance" (2004, p. 75). Instead, Bartholomew concluded that factor analysis showed that several dimensions rather than one (e.g., *g*) are needed to fit the data reasonably and determine an "individual's position in the space of mental ability" (p. 145).

This multiple-factor approach has been subscribed to by many within the field of intelligence (e.g., Cattell, 1963; Horn, 1976; Sternberg, 1985; Thurstone, 1938). While those from the psychometric approach argue for a single factor, others have built multiple-dimensional models of intelligence, such as Horn and Cattell's fluid-crystallized model (Cattell, 1971; Horn, 1994) and Sternberg's triarchic approach, which focuses on analytical, creative, and practical abilities (Sternberg, 1985, 1997, 1999). Other perspectives and disciplines have generated multidimensional models as well, such as cognitive science which developed the PASS theory, which describes intelligence as reflecting the planning, attention, simultaneous, and successive functioning of the brain (Naglieri & Das, 1997).

Even scientists who examined the factor analytic work by Carroll (1993), which he claimed supports the one-factor solution, have generated multiple-factor models that they interpreted as a better fit for the data (Bartholomew, 2004; Horn & Blankson, 2005). One such current model that is gaining widespread acceptance is known as the Cattell-Horn-Carroll (CHC) theory of cognitive abilities, which combines Carroll's factor analytic empirical "map" of cognitive abilities with the strongly supported Cattell-Horn theoretically based notion of fluid and crystallized intelligence (Daniel, 1997, 2000; McGrew, 2005; Sternberg & Kaufman, 1998). This model leaves the notion of singular g as unresolved and instead focuses on the multidimensional nature of intelligence that includes the following factors: fluid intelligence, crystallized intelligence, general memory and learning, visual processing, auditory processing, retrieval ability, processing speed, decision speed, and quantitative knowledge. Strong support has been found over the past decade for the validity of the CHC model and its multiple dimensions (McGrew & Evans, 2004). The fact that a comprehensive and current model such as CHC leaves the question of the existence of g unsettled should be a clear indicator to those working in the field of I/O psychology that despite claims to the contrary by the psychometric perspective, the issue of the existence of singular g is far from an accepted truth and is instead a question of extensive and ongoing debate.

Furthermore, others have noted that intelligence does not behave like a singular variable, and that this has been demonstrated across a wide range of research, including work on psychological development, neurological functioning, education, and genetic structure (Horn & Masunaga, 2000; McGrew, 2005). That is, factors of intelligence such as those reflected in the CHC model have "differential relationships with (1) different outcome criteria (e.g., in the area of academic achievement ...); (2) developmental growth curves; (3) neurological functions; and (4) degree of heritability" (McGrew, 2005, p. 162). Horn and Blankson (2005) provided the example from a developmental perspective that different aspects of intelligence develop and decline at varying speeds and rates as people age, which is not indicative of a single latent entity. As summarized by Horn and Masunaga (2000), "The many relationships defining the construct validities of the different broad factors [of intelligence] do not indicate a single unitary principle" (p. 139).

Perhaps in an attempt to resolve these definitional and structural problems, Jensen decided to circumvent the issue by defining intelligence as the psychometric phenomena of g. That is, Jensen defined intelligence as "the highest-order common factor in a hierarchical factor analysis of a large number of highly diverse mental tests or tasks" (2000, p. 124). In this way, Jensen defined g as the shared variance across cognitive tests that is observed due to positive manifold (i.e., that all tests of mental ability positively correlate to some degree). Thus, Jensen recommended defining the psychological construct of intelligence by the psychometric phenomenon that reflects positive manifold. This is obviously a problem given the questions raised regarding what positive manifold means or reflects. While the phenomenon of positive manifold has been clearly observed, there is truly a lack of understanding regarding why it exists and what it represents (Borsboom & Dolan, 2006). Thus, establishing a psychometric phenomenon of g does not mean that a psychological construct exists (van der Maas et al., 2006).

Jensen (2000) acknowledged that defining intelligence in such a manner is unsatisfying and inadequate, yet he rationalized that intelligence is just too complex a scientific construct to convey with a simple definition.

Jensen perhaps was merely demonstrating his frustration with these core issues regarding intelligence, which results in his circular and inappropriate definition of the construct. At other points in time, Jensen (1998) even recommended dropping the ill-fated word *intelligence* from our scientific vocabulary. In some ways, this frustration with trying to conceptualize intelligence was mirrored by Carroll (1998) when he attempted to describe the *g* factor that purportedly emerged from his factor analytic work by noting in a vague manner that "we can infer that *something* is there" (p. 11), but he was unable to be more specific in his assessment. Such vague descriptions of the construct leave much to be desired and certainly call for continued scientific research and investigation.

And, this is really a central point of this chapter. That is, rather than claiming that our understanding of intelligence is complete and comprehensive in the manner that characterizes many of the writings by proponents of the psychometric approach (e.g., Jensen, 2000), perhaps the proper tact is to continue developing sound theoretical models of the intelligence domain and conducting further empirical investigations of this complex construct. It is important to acknowledge the problems present in defining intelligence as well as the only circumstantial nature of the evidence presented for its existence. In addition, we must recognize that these types of fundamental problems lead us to other concerns, such as if we cannot define what it is we wish to measure, how can we create a valid measure?

The Measurement of Intelligence

The *Standards of Educational and Psychological Testing* (American Educational Research Association [AERA], American Psychological Association [APA], & National Council on Measurement in Education [NCME], 1999) provided a structure for conceptualizing the validity of test measures. In the latest version of the standards, notions of validity were updated to reflect current thinking on the topic, which views validity as the extent to which multiple forms of evidence exist that support the notion that the test measures the construct of interest. In other words, validity is the degree to which evidence supports that the test score reflects the construct that the test is purported to measure. The following sources of evidence for validity were recognized by the standards: (a) test content, (b) response processes, (c) internal structure, (d) relations to other variables, and (e) consequences of testing. While some of these are similar to earlier notions of different types of validity (e.g., the test content dimension is comparable to what was previously referred to as content validity), others are relatively new evaluative standards for assessing the validity of a measure (e.g., response processes). In reviewing this latest version of the standards as well as other expansive writings on the topic of validity (e.g., Guion, 1980, 1998; Messick, 1988, 1989), one can see that the evaluative criteria for designing a construct-valid test have appropriately become more rigorous and complex.

This notion of meticulousness and precision does not characterize the picture painted by the psychometric perspective when it comes to designing valid measures of intelligence. Based on the psychometric perspective's notion that intelligence is the shared variance that saturates batteries of cognitive/intelligence tests, Jensen (1998) noted that it can be measured by creating a composite score from a set of diverse but purportedly highly g-loaded tests of intellectual functioning that test takers perceive in the same way. Jensen went on to state that the greater the number of diverse but g-loaded tests used in the composite, the more that unwanted variance is averaged out, thus resulting in a composite score that more accurately reflects individual differences in intelligence.

While there are numerous problems and concerns regarding the scientific precision of this approach that are discussed next, it is important for those in personnel selection who subscribe to this psychometric approach to realize that a certain level of rigor is still required when creating intelligence tests for work organizations. These requirements often seem to be ignored by those working in personnel selection. For instance, the psychometric approach requires a wide range of diverse tests of intellectual functioning to be used and that these tests are similarly interpreted by those taking them. These requirements often would not be met for selection batteries purporting to measure intelligence using a narrow range of tests (e.g., a basic reading and math test) that may not be perceived in a similar way by all candidates (e.g., some applicants may have previous knowledge of topics presented on the test).

Similar criticisms could be levied against many developers of intelligence tests in general over the years. As noted by Chen and Gardner (2005) as well as Alfonso, Flanagan, and Radwan (2005), conventional psychological tests tend to measure narrow aspects of the construct (e.g., linguistic, quantitative) using limited formats (e.g., written form, multiple choice). These tests also often measure only narrow parts of the areas of the construct that they target (e.g., for a linguistic area, the test may focus to a large extent solely on vocabulary, while for a quantitative area the test may focus solely on certain mathematical functions). Thus, these tests may not even broadly tap the areas of intelligence that they intend to measure. Such tests do not necessarily reflect the requirement of the psychometric approach to use a diverse array of highly g-loaded tests when creating a composite score for intelligence. In addition, researchers have noted the lack of consideration in test design for whether the test takers are similarly situated (i.e., have similar exposure to the material). For example, Fagan (1992, 2000) pointed out that test takers often have unequal exposure to language and other knowledge required to perform on the intelligence tests. From another perspective, Sternberg (1981) discussed the negative implications of having what he referred to as "entrenched" tasks on intelligence tests, which are test items with which test takers are familiar. Given that test takers may differ in their familiarity and past experience with certain types of test items, this could result in a lack of similar exposure to the material that would arguably violate this requirement of the psychometric approach. In summary, even if trying to design a measure of intelligence using the psychometric approach, it must be recognized that there are still rigorous principles that must be followed when attempting to develop an acceptable test of intelligence using this approach. The lack of urgency sometimes shown regarding this need for rigor, particularly by those designing tests of intelligence in personnel selection, is troublesome and cause for concern.

Even if one does properly adhere to the requirements of the psychometric approach for designing a measure of intelligence, there are still numerous potential problems with this approach that have been discussed and debated in the intelligence literature. As pointed out, a great deal of rigor is required by the evaluative criteria outlined in the standards (AERA, APA, & NCME, 1999) to establish validity, and when examined in this light, the psychometric approach for creating a valid measure of intelligence is highly questionable. As discussed, the psychometric method focuses on measuring intelligence by creating a composite from the shared common variance that emerges across a diverse set of g-loaded tests. In terms of validity, the question is whether the composite based on this shared variance reflects the intelligence construct as conceptualized by the psychometric perspective. That is, to what extent are measures developed in this manner construct relevant and to what extent are they contaminated or deficient.

One issue that potentially concerns both contamination and deficiency is that positive manifold, which is reflected in the shared common variance and labeled g by the psychometric perspective, is not necessarily an indicator of intelligence. In terms of contamination, as discussed, there are multiple alternative explanations for positive manifold (e.g., sampling theory, mutualism theory) that make the case that the shared variance reflects constructs other than intelligence (e.g., multiple skills acquired at the same time; the ability to complete written test formats; knowledge of language). With regard to deficiency, while the common variance associated with positive manifold may represent part of the intelligence domain, this does not mean it comprehensively samples the wide and complex space associated with the intelligence construct. For instance, the positive manifold may tap narrow aspects of the domain (e.g., linguistic and quantitative abilities) while not measuring higher-level intellectual processes (e.g., logical thinking, judgment).

Deficiency concerns such as these have been expressed for a century when it comes to tests of intelligence (Chen & Gardner, 2005; Neisser et al., 1996). From the beginning, Binet and Henri (1895) worried about the lack of attention paid to measuring superior processes of intellectual functioning in the tests. After years of attempting to tap the domain, Binet concluded that certain aspects of intelligence could not be readily and independently measured (Binet & Simon, 1905/1916). Given that Binet's tests were a prototype for a large number of mainstream intelligence tests (e.g., Army Alpha, Otis's Group Intelligence Scale, Terman's Group Test of Mental Ability, and even the College Board's Scholastic Aptitude Test [SAT]), there is a concern that these higher-level aspects of the intelligence domain are not properly measured. In reviewing the literature, Braden and Niebling (2005) noted that tests of intelligence are typically criticized more for failing to assess their intended construct than for other psychometric characteristics, such as reliability and norms. One probable reason for this deficiency is that the lack of consensus on the definition of intelligence discussed in the section above on the existence and nature of intelligence hinders the design of appropriate measures to tap the construct. As noted by Bartholomew (2004), "If we cannot define what it is that we wish to measure with precision, how can we expect to find an agreed upon measure" (p. 1). In other words, it is difficult to know if one has tapped the construct and properly sampled the test content domain if one is uncertain regarding what the construct is. Thus, people's different conceptualization of intelligence has negative implications for the construct validity of the measures.

Furthermore, until recently, most tests designed to measure intelligence had little theoretical foundation on which they were developed (Kaufman, 2000). It was not until the 1980s that researchers began to build intelligence tests that reflected psychological theory on the nature of the construct (e.g., Kaufman & Kaufman, 1983; Thorndike, Hagen, & Sattler, 1986; Woodcock & Johnson, 1989). Prior to this, various subtests were compiled to generate a composite as described by the psychometric approach without much thought given to creating a battery of subtests that comprehensively reflected the diverse areas of the intelligence domain. Without a sound theory to guide the design, this is a haphazard approach to measuring the domain and likely to result in deficiency given that critical parts of the intelligence construct may not be represented by a subtest. It should also be noted that this atheoretical approach will likely lead to contamination as well given that subtests may be included or overemphasized that do not reflect the intelligence construct.

As noted by Kamphaus, Winsor, Rowe, and Kim (2005), the history of intelligence testing "has been characterized by a disjuncture between the design of tests and inferences made from those tests. A test, after all, should be designed a priori with a strong theoretical foundation, and supported by considerable validity evidence in order to measure a particular construct or set of constructs (and *only* those constructs)" (p. 31). On a promising note, a number of tests have been revised (e.g., WAIS, version 3), and new tests have been developed (e.g., Cognitive Assessment System) that reflect more current theories of intelligence. Such measures supposedly focus on developing subtests that tap the critical aspects of intelligence pinpointed by their respective theory (e.g., the key group factors of CHC theory). However, realize that this work has only just begun, and that it will take time to reach the proper results. For instance, Alfonso et al. (2005) reviewed test batteries published prior to 1998, which included updated versions of the WAIS, WISC, Woodcock-Johnson, and Stanford-Binet, and found that such tests did not reflect diversity of measurement when it came to the key factors of intelligence identified by Carroll (1993). The study concluded that most of these more modern measures only tapped two or three broad dimensions of intelligence. Thus, most of the research on intelligence referred to from the last century was completed using measures that were not theoretically based and thus were possibly deficient when it came to containing subtests that properly tap the key areas of the intelligence construct domain (Kaufman, 1979, 2000). This would seem to indicate that caution should be used when drawing conclusions from such research.

Instead of caution, the psychometric response toward much of this deficiency argument is centered predominantly on the indifference of the indicator principle. This is the notion that the type of measure used as well as the content of the device are not necessarily important when it comes to measuring intelligence (Jensen, 1998; Ree & Carretta, 2002; Spearman, 1923). However, while the psychometric approach states that as long as a diverse set of tests is used the emerging shared variance reflected in the composite will accurately measure intelligence, others state that the different tests used to form the composite result in very different outcomes. Daniel (2000) showed support for this point by demonstrating that different intelligence test batteries correlate with each other to a wide and varying degree (e.g., he reported that the percentage of reliable variance shared on composite scores across seven mainstream intelligence batteries ranged from 50% to 86%). Daniel noted that:

> It is an observable fact that not all overall composite scores measure the same construct. The way in which a test author conceptualized general ability will affect how the overall composite is designed and will significantly influence how it may be interpreted. Therefore, they should not all be interpreted in the same way. (p. 480)

Thus, the tests of intelligence are not interchangeable, and the way one forms a composite will have an impact on the resulting scores. In terms of how this should be done, Thorndike (1994) made the point that the set of subtests used to form the composite must be sampled sufficiently broadly and uniformly. Building off prior points, this should be undertaken using a well-developed theory regarding intelligence and which factors should be included in its domain (Daniel, 2000; Kamphaus et al., 2005).

Contamination is also a very real problem discussed in the literature when it comes to measures of intelligence. One possibility that again roots back to positive manifold is that part of the intercorrelation observed across tests of intelligence is caused by the tests having similar contaminating factors. As described by Chen and Gardner (2005), "Given that conventional psychological tests measure primarily two intelligences, sample a narrow range of knowledge and skills for each intelligence, and rely on the same means of measurement, it is not surprising the scores on these tests are correlated" (p. 80). Based on this thinking, it could be the use of the same means of measurement and test formats (e.g., written, multiple choice) across the tests that leads to intercorrelation across measures. That is, the common underlying factor that at least partially drives the observed intercorrelation could be these contaminating characteristics rather than a latent intelligence construct. Thus, rather than positive manifold being proof of the existence of intelligence and the resulting g being an index of intelligence, it could be that positive manifold is at least partially an indication of contamination, and g is an index of the level of contamination.

In addition to the possible contaminants noted by Chen and Gardner (2005), there are numerous others than could have a negative impact on the construct validity of intelligence tests. One factor noted by Horn and Blankson (2005) as a potential contaminant is the speeded nature of most measures of intelligence. Another possible contaminant identified by Fagan (2000) is reliance on language in intelligence testing. While some nonverbal measures exist, most measures of intelligence utilize language. Fagan noted that tests that require familiarity with language as well as other knowledge could be considered contaminated. Sternberg (1981) raised the point that using entrenched tasks (i.e., tasks with which test takers have previous familiarity) could be another contaminant. By using entrenched tasks, one could be introducing a form of testwiseness as a contaminant of the resulting test scores.

What is important to recognize with regard to these and other potential contaminants is that the extent to which any are contaminants depends a great deal on one's definition of the intelligence construct. For instance, if one's conceptualization of intelligence includes knowledge of language, then including language in a test may not necessarily be contamination. However, if one's conceptualization of intelligence does not include knowledge of language, then its presence on the test could be a form of contamination. The lack of clarity described regarding the definition of the intelligence construct makes it all the more difficult to pinpoint what is construct relevant and what is construct contamination. Thus, again, the lack of a clear and agreed-on definition and theoretical foundation for intelligence makes it difficult to create a proper and valid measure.

Given the concerns presented regarding the extent to which the variance measured by tests of intelligence is relevant, deficient, or contaminated, one could make the case that great attention should be paid to investigating the validity of an intelligence test. As noted, the *standards* (AERA, APA, & NCME, 1999) outlined multiple and rigorous evaluative criteria that should be considered when determining support for the validity of a measure. Braden and Niebling (2005) scrutinized a set of modern tests of intelligence on these criteria to determine the extent to which evidence supported the validity of the instruments. They presented mixed findings with regard to validity and further noted that some types of validity evidence were more thoroughly collected than others. They found that test developers tended to provide validity evidence regarding the internal structure of the instrument as well as information regarding its relationship to other variables, while they did not tend to provide much evidence regarding response processes and test consequences. They concluded the need to collect further validity data regarding these tests.

Furthermore, because some of the evaluative criteria of the standards (AERA, APA, & NCME, 1999) were not even in place when many well-known tests of intelligence were developed, it may be even more important to revisit the validity of these devices and gather in a rigorous manner multiple forms of validity evidence. In fact, Braden and Niebling (2005) noted that the validity evidence provided for the modern tests that they reviewed was "a substantial improvement over earlier versions of intelligence tests, which often failed to provide any meaningful validity evidence" (p. 628). Given these findings, one could argue that caution is needed, and a great deal of work is required regarding the construct validity of measures of intelligence.

In summary, while the psychometric approach states that intelligence can be readily measured and often does not convey much urgency when it comes to the level of rigor and precision required to attempt to do so, other approaches to intelligence disagree, noting the difficulty of creating sound measures of such a complex construct. They state that ignoring the basics of how to build a construct-valid instrument as discussed in the standards (AERA, APA, & NCME, 1999) is problematic, and that rigor and scientific precision is required to measure intelligence in a proper and comprehensive manner. It is only when we carefully develop valid measures of the construct that we can examine how useful they are in predicting important outcomes.

Intelligence as a Predictor of Job Performance

Many would say that the strongest (and nearly only) contribution made by the field of I/O psychology to the study of intelligence has centered on exploring the use of intelligence tests to predict job performance.

Research in personnel selection has shown support for a significant relationship between intelligence test scores and work performance outcomes (Schmidt & Hunter, 1998). The central findings referred to by the intelligence literature are from meta-analytic studies conducted by Hunter and his colleagues (Hunter, 1980; Hunter & Hunter, 1984) that demonstrated a strong relationship between general cognitive ability test scores and indicators of training and job performance (validities are reported for 0.56 and 0.51, respectively). They further noted that the validity for intelligence tests generalizes across a wide range of jobs (i.e., validity generalization) that vary in complexity (although it was noted that they predicted more strongly for high-complexity jobs [0.58] in comparison to low-complexity jobs [0.23]). These results were referenced by those subscribing to the psychometric approach (e.g., Herrnstein & Murray, 1994) as supporting the important and fundamental contributions that intelligence makes to critical outcomes.

Schmidt and Hunter (1998) stated that, based on these results, intelligence tests are the single best predictor of job performance and thus should be afforded special status in the area of personnel selection. While individuals in the field of I/O psychology are likely well versed in the literature that focuses on the use of intelligence tests for staffing, the main purpose of the current chapter is to examine views from the intelligence field on such a topic. While those from the psychometric perspective often tend to recite the findings from Hunter and his colleagues, others in the field of intelligence tend to see these results as exaggerated. One of the central issues raised in the intelligence literature focuses on the impact of the statistical corrections (e.g., for reliability of the measures) advocated by Schmidt and Hunter (1998) that result in inflated correlations in the 0.50s. Many from the intelligence literature noted the need for caution in using these corrections (e.g., Kaufman & Lichtenberger, 2005; Linn, 1986) and subsequently presented substantially lower numbers as a more accurate estimate of the strength of the relationship. For example, Ghiselli (1966, 1973) placed the average correlations between intelligence tests and job performance in the 0.20s. Neisser et al. (1996) stated that the correlations between intelligence tests and work-related outcomes lie between 0.30 and 0.50 and only trend toward the upper part of this range when corrected for unreliability. Interestingly, even an earlier analysis by Jensen (1980) of some of the same data used by Hunter offered a more tempered view of the relationship between intelligence tests and job performance. For instance, Hunter and Hunter (1984) stated that intelligence tests predict performance at 0.58 for complex jobs, while Jensen (1980) concluded that the values for highly complex jobs fall in a lower range of 0.35 to 0.47. Similarly, Jensen's (1980) analyses placed the average correlation between intelligence tests and success in training programs at 0.50, which is significantly below the 0.60 reported by Hunter and his colleagues. Thus, while those from the intelligence literature viewed the validity findings for intelligence tests as quite respectable and useful, they generally did not state the findings to be as strong as reported in the field of personnel selection.

In assessing these findings, Kaufman and Lichtenberger (2005) concluded that the data analyses by Hunter and Jensen provided support for intelligence "as reasonably valid in its role as a predictor of job success, although the claims made by Hunter may be exaggerated by his incautious and, perhaps, overzealous correction of obtained coefficients" (p. 18). This view as well as other similar statements found in the intelligence literature reflect a more conservative approach when it comes to the strength of the intelligence test to job performance relationship. For instance, Neisser et al. (1996) characterized intelligence scores as at least weakly related to job performance in most settings and went on to note that "such tests predict considerably less than half the variance of job-related measures" (p. 83). They were also careful to point out that other individual characteristics (e.g., interpersonal skills, aspects of personality) are probably of equal or greater importance for predicting job performance. In fact, using these more conservative numbers places intelligence tests more on the level of what has been found in terms of the predictive validity of alternative tests (e.g., structured interviews, work samples), thus perhaps arguing against anointing any type of "special status" on tests of intelligence. Sternberg, Wagner, Williams, and Horvath (1995) stated that with intelligence tests explaining at best about 25% of the variance in performance (and if one relies on more conservative estimates, as low as 4% of the variance; Ghiselli, 1966, 1973; Wigdor & Garner, 1982), it leaves a great deal of variance unexplained. As Kaufman and Lichtenberger (2005) concluded, although intelligence "seems to be a valid predictor of job performance, the general findings from this line of research indicate that a relatively small amount of variance in job performance is accounted for [by these tests]" (p. 18).

Whether one subscribes to the higher or lower estimates of the strength of the relationship between intelligence and job performance, many in personnel selection tend to view tests of intelligence as an important predictor for staffing purposes. However, it is important to realize that while some have greatly praised the predictive power of intelligence tests (e.g., Schmidt & Hunter, 1998), others in the field of I/O psychology have raised criticisms and potential problems with these tests, such as concerns regarding the impact of common method variance, the role of bias in the criterion measures, and the possible influence of motivational issues (e.g., stereotype threat). More in-depth discussion of these factors can be found in the literature (e.g., Goldstein, Zedeck, & Goldstein, 2002; Murphy, 1996; Sackett, Borneman, & Connelly, 2008; Steele, Spencer, & Aronson, 2002), but for the purposes of this chapter, it is just important to realize that these concerns exist and are discussed and debated by the field.

One further concern regarding intelligence tests as predictors of job performance that is more central to the current chapter is that many in personnel selection have seemingly interpreted these findings to mean that any test that targets the cognitive domain is a valid predictor of job performance for any job. That is, some in the field seek to apply the validity and validity generalization evidence (Hunter & Hunter, 1984; Schmidt & Hunter, 1998) for intelligence tests to any reading comprehension, vocabulary, or basic math test used in personnel selection. This latitude regarding what constitutes a test of intelligence is not at all supported by the intelligence literature or even for that matter by the basic tenets of the psychometric perspective, which discuss the need for using a wide array of cognitive tests perceived in a similar manner by the test takers.

In summary, a review of the intelligence literature revealed a more sober view of the extent to which intelligence tests predict pertinent job performance outcomes than the one presented by the psychometric perspective, which tends to rely strongly on some of the work that has emerged in I/O psychology (e.g., Hunter & Hunter, 1984). In general, there is a sense that while tests of intelligence are valid predictors of job performance, the amount of variance accounted for is moderate, and other predictors may be of equal or greater importance (Kaufman & Lichtenberger, 2005; Neisser et al., 1996). In addition, from the perspective of personnel selection, it is important to realize that just because a test purportedly measures aspects of the cognitive domain does not make it an intelligence test (i.e., a test of general cognitive ability) and thus does not mean it should be viewed in terms of the validity and validity generalization evidence that exists with regard to such tests. In general, perhaps it is best to be conservative in our conclusions, which is an example that has not been set by the absolutism that characterizes the psychometric point of view. It is interesting to note that this same absolutism has also been conveyed by the psychometric approach when it comes to the point that tests of intelligence must produce racial differences, a point that perhaps also needs further exploration in light of the ever-evolving intelligence literature.

Racial Differences in Intelligence

The most controversial tenet of the psychometric perspective is the so-called Spearman hypothesis formulated by Jensen (1985, 1998) that focuses on racial differences in intelligence. Such differences were noted as far back as Spearman's work (1927) and have been studied in more depth by researchers such as Jensen (1998). In particular, the black–white differences that emerge on tests of intelligence that show whites significantly outperforming blacks have served to fuel the controversy. This controversy stems from the fact that the psychometric perspective interprets these findings as reflecting reality rather than representing bias or measurement problems;

thus, those subscribing to this perspective conclude that whites actually possess greater intelligence than blacks.

The Spearman hypothesis generally predicts that racial differences in test performance increase as the g loading of a test increases. Since the psychometric approach equates intelligence with g, this means that the better the test is at measuring intelligence (i.e., higher g load), the greater the differences that will be observed between races. However, as discussed in this chapter, some researchers have a different perspective on what g signifies (e.g., Chen & Gardner, 2005; Thomson, 1916; van der Maas et al., 2006). As noted by Borsboom and Dolan (2006), while the psychometric phenomena of g representing positive manifold can clearly be observed, we lack a true understanding of what it represents. Thus, while there is the psychometric view of g, there are also alternative theories regarding what g represents (e.g., sampling theory, mutualism theory) that do not consider it to be an index of intelligence. Within the framework of these theories, since g does not represent intelligence, racial differences in g would not translate into racial differences in intelligence.

From a slightly different perspective, some researchers (e.g., Chen & Gardner, 2005) argued that instead of g representing the construct of intelligence, it could equate with the amount of deficiency or contamination in the measures. For example, if tests of intelligence are narrow in scope and focus on a limited part of the construct domain (e.g., linguistic and quantitative), then they would highly intercorrelate yielding g because they are similarly deficient rather than as an indicator of construct relevance. Also, if tests of intelligence have common forms of contamination (e.g., multiple-choice written formats, reliance on language, use of tasks with which test takers have previous experience), then they would highly intercorrelate yielding g because they are similarly contaminated rather than as an indicator of construct relevance. If any of these alternatives is the case, then it is possible that g at least partially represents deficiency or contamination, and that these errors lead to the observed racial differences rather than greater construct relevance driving racial differences.

In terms of possible sources of contamination, one conceptualization of g is that it is representative of culture rather than intelligence (Flanagan, McGrew, & Ortiz, 2000; Flanagan & Ortiz, 2001; Flanagan, Ortiz, & Alfonso, 2007; Helms-Lorenz, Van de Vijver, & Poortinga, 2003; Ortiz & Ochoa, 2005). Thus, the extent to which a test is g loaded does not indicate the extent to which it measures intelligence but instead represents the extent to which it is biased by culture. From this vantage point, the g load indicates the amount that the measure is contaminated by culture, and it is this contamination that contributes to the racial differences observed. Helms-Lorenz et al. (2003) completed a compelling study in which a factor analysis of intelligence test batteries resulted in two nearly unrelated factors representing cognitive (g) and cultural complexity (c). The results of the study provided some initial support for the idea that majority and minority performance differences are better predicted by c than by g. The point made is that cognitive and cultural load are often confounded in the first factor extracted by factor analysis, and that when they are disentangled the racial differences observed are better explained by cultural load than by cognitive load. Given the findings, further research of this nature is certainly warranted to explore the impact of culture on racial differences for intelligence tests.

Another related possible source of contamination is the linguistic demands of the test (Fagan & Holland, 2007; Freedle, 2003; Ortiz & Ochoa, 2005). Ortiz and Ochoa made the point that the linguistic load of the intelligence test could render the results invalid for those that are linguistically diverse (e.g., culturally diverse groups). They noted that language issues are often only dealt with at a surface level (e.g., use of an interpreter, test translation) at best. Test designers must consider which language test takers must know and how well they must know that language for the test format to be appropriate. In addition, when designing a test, the extent to which knowledge of language has an impact on multiple parts of an intelligence test and not just a subtest designed to tap this knowledge must be taken into account (e.g., the extent that knowledge of language used in the instructions for a mathematical portion of the test has an impact on performance). Researchers in the field noted that these types of linguistic issues run deep in terms of impact, and that such issues are rarely appropriately addressed (Flanagan et al., 2000; Ortiz & Flanagan, 1998). As described by Helms-Lorenz et al. (2003), who viewed the language issue as embedded within the cultural one, "differential mastery of the testing language by cultural groups creates a spurious correlation between g and intergroup performance differences, if complex tests require more linguistic skills than do simple tests" (p. 13). Thus, as one can see, cultural and linguistic demands are complex issues on intelligence tests that could have an impact on observed racial differences.

In some ways, the extent to which one views these cultural and linguistic demands of intelligence tests as problematic depends again on how one defines intelligence. That is, if one defines intelligence as including knowledge of language and other specific information, then designing a test with linguistic demands and particular knowledge requirements may be appropriate. For instance, Carroll stated that "a human being becomes a 'member of society' only by acquiring aspects of special knowledge" (McGrew, 2005, p. 163), and that testing for these taps the general factor of intelligence. (As an aside, one may question who determines what knowledge is needed to be a "member of society" and perhaps wonder if this varies by culture, thus yielding culturally biased intelligence tests.) However, if one does not define intelligence as involving particular knowledge, then including it as part of the test could be seen as inappropriate and a form of contamination. One of the best examples of this is the groundbreaking work of Fagan.

Fagan (2000) defined intelligence as the ability to process information rather than defining it based on how much knowledge one has (e.g., knowledge of language, knowledge of certain facts). He pointed out and demonstrated that people from different cultures often have been unequally exposed to knowledge used on typical tests of intelligence, such as the vocabulary and language contained on such tests (Fagan & Holland, 2002). Given this, Fagan asserted that racial group differences observed on such tests are due to differences in access to this type of information rather than differences in the ability to process such information, which was his definition of intelligence. Based on this line of thinking, Fagan and Holland (2002, 2007) completed a series of studies that demonstrated that when whites and blacks had similar exposure to the words and language used as test stimuli, there was no difference in the ability of the races to process the information and thus no difference in intelligence. In summary, Fagan and his colleagues viewed whites and blacks (as well as other racial groups) as differentially exposed to certain information (e.g., language and other facts) but not different in terms of their level of intelligence. These findings may be particularly important when viewed within the requirement of the psychometric perspective that test takers perceive the test in the same way. That is, if the tests are not perceived the same way because they contain words and facts to which cultures are differentially exposed (as demonstrated by Fagan & Holland, 2002), then such tests violate this requirement and arguably are invalid for properly assessing intelligence for these particular groups.

Other interesting work that has focused on culture and language and its impact on racial differences on intelligence tests has been conducted by Freedle and his colleagues (Freedle, 2003, 2006; Freedle & Kostin, 1988, 1990, 1992, 1997). In studying performance on the SAT, Freedle and colleagues discussed how differential racial interpretation of language results in underrepresentation of black verbal ability on intelligence tests. Freedle and his colleagues demonstrated how this results in item difficulty on such verbal intelligence tests being related to race in an unexpected manner; that is, they found, as did others (e.g., Scherbaum & Goldstein, 2008), that the easier the test question, the greater the black–white difference. They explained this nonintuitive finding by stating that more difficult items require more precision of language and thus are not easily interpreted in different ways by different cultures, while easier items have looser precision with regard to language, thus opening them up to different cultural translation. Such unexpected findings require more research to gain a clearer understanding of the phenomenon.

The work of Sternberg (1981) on nonentrenched tasks represents another approach to understanding determinants of racial differences on tests of intelligence. Sternberg defined *nonentrenched tasks* as those test items that require a test taker to solve problems in an atypical manner to which they are not accustomed. Thus, these novel problems did not allow test takers to rely on prior experience or knowledge of how to solve the problem. Because there may be racial differences in this prior experience or knowledge, Sternberg posited that fewer racial differences would be observed when using nonentrenched tasks to measure intelligence. Results from his study provided support for this hypothesis and led Sternberg to state that intelligence is best understood using novel and unentrenched tasks.

Thus, while these types of findings from the current intelligence literature called into question the veracity of the Spearman hypothesis and showed the promise of designing tests of intelligence that do not demonstrate racial differences (Naglieri, 2005; Ortiz & Ochoa, 2005; Sternberg, 2006), the psychometric perspective dwells on quoting the failure of dated attempts to build such tests (e.g., the so-called BITCH or Black Intelligence Test of Cultural Homogeneity developed by Williams [1975]) and stand by the notion that it absolutely cannot be done (e.g., Jensen, 2000). What is important for the field of I/O psychology and personnel selection to know is that the intelligence literature continues to develop on this topic, and attempts to build intelligence tests of high validity and low racial differences are currently ongoing. Perhaps some of the best work in this area is being done in the area of education and clinical psychology, for which it is paramount to assess culturally and linguistically diverse individuals accurately so that one can properly assist these individuals in learning or in obtaining appropriate clinical treatment. Such fields may feel more urgency from an ethical standpoint to assess such individuals accurately and thus, in good conscience, cannot as easily ignore false negatives in the manner that seems to be perceived as more acceptable in personnel selection. If we did not do this in personnel selection, we might actually look at the results of common intelligence tests that label approximately one of every six minorities (e.g., blacks, Hispanics) as mentally disabled and realize given the ludicrous nature of these results that the tests are not accurate for such groups (Mackintosh, 1998).

For the purposes of educational and clinical assessment, Ortiz and Ochoa (2005) made a case for assessing tests based on various dimensions to determine if they are appropriate for the target population. On a two-dimensional grid, they assessed the degree of linguistic demand by the degree of cultural loading. They demonstrated how this can be done by placing subtests of the WISC onto this grid. Given the discussion regarding the possible causes of racial differences in intelligence test scores, it may be useful to add other dimensions to the grid, such as the extent to which the tasks of the test are familiar (i.e., entrenched). This type of approach for identifying appropriate tests of intelligence could be used in personnel selection. As noted, it is important to consider this even from a psychometric perspective because should there be cultural, linguistic, or task familiarity differences across test takers, in many ways this violates the psychometric rule that test takers are similarly situated (i.e., that test takers see the test in the same way) and thus threatens the validity of the tests for certain groups. In other words, without taking into account what is a proper test for a given group, we will not accurately assess the intelligence of these groups. While I/O psychology and personnel selection do not typically seem overly concerned with false negatives, this may not be the case when the false negatives are unequally distributed across racial groups. As those who work in personnel selection know, such a finding could involve adverse impact against protected groups, which is unlawful according to the Uniform Guidelines on Employee Selection Procedures (Equal Employment Opportunity Commission, Civil Service Commission, Department of Labor, & Department of Justice, 1978).

In summary, a case can be made that the racial differences observed on intelligence tests are not inherent in the construct as argued by the psychometric perspective (i.e., Spearman hypothesis) but instead are produced by aspects of the measures of the construct. In some ways, this can be observed in the fact that the size of racial differences observed varies depending on which measures of intelligence are used. For instance, in a review of race differences for most of the major established intelligence tests (e.g., Stanford-Binet Intelligence Scale, Fourth Edition; WISC-III) conducted initially by Wasserman and Becker (2000) and later updated and expanded by Naglieri (2005), differences between mean scores for blacks and whites varied considerably, ranging from 0.25- to 0.75-SD difference. Interestingly, not only do these tests fluctuate widely in the size of the black–white difference observed but also they all fall below the 1-SD difference typically referred to by the psychometric approach (Herrnstein & Murray, 1994; Hunter & Hunter, 1984; Jensen, 1980). The psychometric perspective would argue that the fluctuation just reflects how well the measure taps intelligence, with the instruments exhibiting larger racial differences better measures of the construct. However, the opposite could be true. That is, an alternative explanation is that those instruments exhibiting larger differences are not better instruments but instead instruments that are less construct valid. In other words, measures of intelligence that produce larger racial differences could be more deficient or contaminated by factors such as those described here (e.g., culture/linguistic load) or others (e.g., stereotype threat, testwiseness). Thus, the racial differences for intelligence could be reflective of construct validity problems in the measure rather than inherent in the construct itself. If this is the case, it would certainly be possible to attempt to design construct-valid tests of intelligence that have reduced racial differences.

New Directions: Building Valid Intelligence Tests With Reduced Racial Differences

The tautology of the psychometric perspective on intelligence generally states that a general factor of intelligence exists that underlies all intellectual activity, that it is singular in nature, that it is the most important predictor of job performance outcomes, and that whites possess significantly more of it than certain minorities (e.g., blacks, Hispanics). Despite the fact that the psychometric perspective represents only one of the numerous approaches that exist regarding intelligence, many within the field of I/O psychology and practice of personnel selection have seemingly embraced it and accepted its assumptions as fundamental truths. Arguably, this has been greatly encouraged by many proponents of the psychometric perspective who vehemently present its tenets in an uncompromising case-closed manner (e.g., Jensen, 2000).

For reasons presented (e.g., Fagan & Holland, 2007; Helms-Lorenz et al., 2003; Sternberg, 1981), many researchers do not agree with the conclusions of the psychometric perspective and therefore have undertaken efforts to develop valid tests of intelligence with reduced racial differences. In general, what has been found is that "more process-oriented tests, and those containing more novel stimuli and communicative requirements, tend to yield less discriminatory estimates of functioning or ability" (Ortiz & Ochoa, 2005, p. 243). As Sternberg (1981) demonstrated, tests that limit task familiarity by using novel nonentrenched stimuli tend to show reduced racial differences. Research by others showed how controlling for cultural and linguistic factors could also reduce the racial differences observed (e.g., Fagan & Holland, 2002, 2007; Helms-Lorenz et al., 2003; Ortiz & Ochoa, 2005). The case has also been made that more theoretically based tests such as those that focus on measuring key factors of intelligence (e.g., fluid reasoning, general memory and learning) as delineated by the factor analytic work of Carroll (1993) could demonstrate lower racial differences (as well as greater validity). The thinking is that tests developed based on sound theory could result in reducing deficiency- and contamination-related factors that might contribute to the racial differences observed. In fact, Wasserman and Becker (2000) reported racial differences below the 1 SD typically reported for some mainstream tests (e.g., black–white SD differences for the Woodcock-Johnson III (WJ III), Stanford-Binet 5 (SB5), WISC-IV ranged from 0.54 to 0.73) that have been revised to better fit the dimensions of Carroll's theoretical framework. In addition, even the way one defines intelligence could have an impact on the extent to which racial differences emerge, such as the reduction reported when defining intelligence as processing (Fagan, 2000) or as adaptability (Mackintosh, 1998).

Approaches from other perspectives on intelligence have also shown promise in terms of creating valid tests of intelligence with reduced subgroup differences. For example, the Cognitive Assessment System (CAS) was recently developed from the cognitive perspective of psychology. The CAS was designed based on the PASS theory, which is a cognitive model of intelligence created by Naglieri and Das (1997). They conceptualized the key processes of intelligence using the neuropsychological research of Luria (1980, 1982) as a foundation. The cognitive processes emphasized by the model focus on performance and delineate four main factors as the cognitive building blocks of human intellectual functioning (Naglieri, 2005). For a more in-depth description of this theoretical model, refer to the works by Naglieri and Das (1997, 2005) and Naglieri (2005).

The CAS is an individually administered test designed for children and adolescents; it consists of 12 subtests organized into the four scales that represent the planning, attention, simultaneous, and successive dimensions of the model. A number of the subtests focus on having test takers make decisions when facing novel tasks, and other subtests aim at measuring very specific cognitive functions, such as closely examining the features of stimuli and making decisions based on what is observed, performing tasks involving speech, and using memory when examining various geometric objects. A key distinction of the CAS compared to traditional tests is that it does not contain the typical verbal subtest. It instead uses a number of novel tasks to focus on specific cognitive functions, such as decision making, attention, memory, and processing of information.

While research on the CAS is still in the beginning stages, results thus far have shown predictive validity for achievement in school settings that is similar to traditional tests of intelligence (Naglieri, 2005). In addition, the CAS shows much lower racial differences than found with other traditional tests of intelligence. For instance, Naglieri (2005) reported a black–white difference of only 0.26 *SD*. Thus, the CAS shows solid initial promise as an alternative test of intelligence. While it may not currently be appropriate for personnel selection because it is for children and adolescents, its structure and design could possibly be leveraged to create tests that are appropriate for a work setting. In particular, tests could be designed that more specifically target the dimensions of intelligence pinpointed by cognitive theory. Similar to the CAS, such tests may show strong validity and reduced racial differences.

With regard to high-stakes testing, a high-profile initiative for developing intelligence tests with increased validity and reduced racial differences is Sternberg's Rainbow Project. Sternberg (2006) is currently in the middle of a large-scale project with the College Board focused on designing additional tests of intelligence to augment the Scholastic Aptitude Test (SAT). He noted that while the current SAT predicts academic performance in college, there is room for improvement in terms of the variance explained. Sternberg uses his triarchic theory of successful intelligence as a guide for designing supplementary assessments of analytical, practical, and creative thinking. This supplemental battery requires test takers to (a) address familiar types of problems by making abstract judgments (i.e., analytical); (b) apply practical ideas in a real-world context (i.e., practical); and (c) handle problems in a creative manner that are novel in nature (i.e., creative). In particular, the creative intelligence tests focus on handling novel unentrenched stimuli and situations, a format that Sternberg (1981) previously showed would reduce racial differences. The tests also make use of a number of novel methodologies and formats when it comes to both stimuli and response (e.g., video-based stimuli, oral responses recorded by computer). These new tests sharply contrast with the current format of the SAT, which is more traditional in nature.

Research has been conducted on these various subtests across a wide range of demographics, and the data have been collected across a diverse set of universities to enhance the generalizability of the results. While only initial phases of this large-scale project have been completed, the data thus far support construct validity according to the triarchic model of the newly designed measures of intelligence. In addition, Sternberg (2006) reported that the new measures "enhanced predictive validity for college GPA relative to high school grade point average (GPA) and the SAT and also reduced ethnic group differences" (p. 321). In summary, the types of measures designed for the Rainbow Project show promise in academic settings and should encourage those who would attempt to design similar measures for personnel selection.

In terms of personnel selection, the Siena Reasoning Test (SRT) represents a new test of general cognitive ability that could potentially show strong validity while reducing racial differences (Yusko & Goldstein, 2008a). The SRT was designed based on the findings of Fagan and his associates (Fagan, 2000; Fagan & Holland, 2002, 2007) regarding limiting previous exposure of test takers to test stimuli as well as the work of Sternberg (1981, 2006) that focused on using tasks that were novel and unfamiliar to test takers. The SRT specifically aimed at having test takers process information in novel ways in which they could not rely on past experience and knowledge. Items were designed with reduced verbal/linguistic requirements by using nonsense words as well as graphical figures. The test items focused on having test takers perform basic functions of intelligence, including processing and manipulating information, drawing inferences, reasoning, making decisions, and integrating knowledge. The test was designed to be group administered and relatively brief (approximately 25 to 30 minutes in length) to enhance the utility of the device for a work setting.

Initial research with the device in real-world settings again painted a promising picture of what may be achieved when designing intelligence tests (Ferreter, Goldstein, Scherbaum, Yusko, & Jun, 2008; Yusko & Goldstein, 2008b). Across six studies conducted thus far, the SRT yielded significant uncorrected correlations with performance that ranged from 0.27 to 0.49. These studies were conducted across diverse positions that included entry-level firefighter, deputy sheriff/corrections officer, production operator, and academic student. These studies were a mixture of concurrent and predictive designs and involved a range of different criteria, including both on-the-job performance and learning criteria such as training academy grades and school grade point average. For each study, a traditional cognitive test of varying type (e.g., Wonderlic; written mechanical ability test, reading comprehension test) was also administered for comparison purposes. In general, the SRT performed equal to or better than such tests in terms of predictive validity. In terms of racial differences, the SRT consistently outperformed these standardized tests, yielding, for example, black–white mean differences that ranged from approximately 0.00 to 0.40 *SD*s. These initial findings provided further support for the concept that tests of intelligence can be developed that are valid and show reduced racial differences.

Conclusion

In examining the current state of intelligence testing in personnel selection, the field seems to be standing still. A review of the evolving literature revealed intelligence to be an extremely complex construct that involves multifaceted and intricate issues that are concurrently being examined in a host of fields and disciplines (e.g., cognitive science, neurology, sociology, psychology). Thus, there is an exciting and dynamic exploration of the notion of intelligence happening in science that is not reflected in the static perspective embraced by the field of I/O psychology or displayed in the practice of personnel selection. We have made the case in this chapter that this is generally a result of the impact of the psychometric perspective of intelligence that many in our field have strongly embraced. Given the expected outcomes according to this psychometric perspective of high validity but also large-scale racial differences, the field of I/O psychology has apparently shifted to pursuing alternative predictors (e.g., structured interview, work samples) or means of implementation (e.g., cut scores, banding) rather than engaging in cutting-edge research on the topic of intelligence and personnel selection. However, while we have remained stagnant, the field of intelligence has continued to evolve theoretically and conduct empirical research on central issues involving the nature of the construct, the measurement of the construct, the predictive capabilities of the construct, and the racial differences reflected in the construct. We believe that it is time for the field of I/O psychology to revisit intelligence, update and reacquaint itself with the current state of the field on this important construct, and reengage in conducting research on the possible role of modern conceptualizations of intelligence in personnel selection.

___

References

Alfonso, V. C., Flanagan, D. P., & Radwan, S. (2005). The impact of the Cattell-Horn-Carroll theory on test development and interpretation of cognitive and academic performance. In D. P. Flanagan & P. L. Harrison (Eds.), *Contemporary intellectual assessment: Theories, tests, and issues* (2nd ed., pp. 185–202). New York: Guilford Press.

American Educational Research Association, American Psychological Association, & National Council on Measurement in Education. (1999). *Standards for educational and psychological testing.* Washington, DC: American Educational Research Association.

Bartholomew, D. J. (2004). *Measuring intelligence: Facts and fallacies.* New York: Cambridge University Press.

Binet, A., & Henri, V. (1895). La psychologie individuelle. *L'Annee Psychologique, 2,* 411–465.

Binet, A., & Simon, T. (1916). New methods for diagnosis of the intellectual level of subnormals. In *The development of intelligence children* (E. S. Kite, Trans.) Baltimore: Williams & Wilkins. (Original work published 1905)

Binet, A., & Simon, T. (1916). New investigation upon the measure of the intellectual level among school children. In *The development of intelligence in children* (E. S. Kite, Trans.). Baltimore: Williams & Wilkins. (Original work published 1911)

Borsboom, D., & Dolan, C. V. (2006). Why g is not an adaptation: A comment on Kanazawa. *Psychological Review, 113,* 433–437.

Borsboom, D., Mellenbergh, G. J., & van Heerden, J. (2004). The concept of validity. *Psychological Review, 111,* 1061–1071.

Bouchard, T. J. (1997). IQ similarity in twins reared apart: Findings and responses to critics. In R. Sternberg & E. Grigorenko (Eds.), *Intelligence, heredity and environment* (pp. 126–160). New York: Cambridge University Press.

Braden, J. P., & Niebling, B. C. (2005). Using the joint test standards to evaluate the validity evidence for intelligence tests. In D. P. Flanagan & P. L. Harrison (Eds.), *Contemporary intellectual assessment: Theories, tests, and issues* (2nd ed., pp. 615–630). New York: Guilford Press.

Carroll, J. B. (1993). *Human cognitive abilities: A survey of factor analytic studies.* New York: Cambridge University Press.

Carroll, J. B. (1998). Human cognitive abilities: A critique. In J. J. McArdle & R. W. Woodcock (Eds.), *Human cognitive abilities in theory and practice* (pp. 5–24). Mahwah, NJ: Erlbaum.

Carroll, J. B. (2005). The three-stratum theory of cognitive abilities. In D. P. Flanagan & P. L. Harrison (Eds.), *Contemporary intellectual assessment: Theories, tests, and issues* (2nd ed., pp. 69–76). New York: Guilford Press.

Cattell, R. B. (1963). Theory of fluid and crystallized intelligence: A critical experiment. *Journal of Educational Psychology, 54,* 1–22.

Cattell, R. B. (1971). *Abilities: Their structure, growth, and action.* Boston: Houghton-Mifflin.

Chen, J., & Gardner, H. (2005). Assessment based on multiple-intelligence theory. In D. P. Flanagan & P. L. Harrison (Eds.), *Contemporary intellectual assessment: Theories, tests, and issues* (2nd ed., pp. 77–102). New York: Guilford Press.

Daniel, M. H. (1997). Intelligence testing: Status and trends. *American Psychologist, 52,* 1038–1045.

Daniel, M. H. (2000). Interpretation of intelligence test scores. In R. J. Sternberg (Ed.), *Handbook of intelligence* (pp. 477–491). New York: Cambridge University Press.

Davidson, J. E., & Downing, C. L. (2000). Contemporary models of intelligence. In R. Sternberg (Ed.), *Handbook of intelligence* (pp. 34–52). New York: Cambridge University Press.

Detterman, D. K. (2002). General intelligence: Cognitive and biological explanations. In R. J. Sternberg & E. L. Grigorenko (Eds.), *The general factor of intelligence* (pp. 223–243). Mahwah, NJ: Erlbaum.

Ericsson, K. A., & Kintsch, W. (1995). Long-term working memory. *Psychological Review, 105,* 211–245.

Fagan, J. F. (1992). Intelligence: A theoretical viewpoint. *Current Directions in Psychological Science, 1,* 82–86.

Fagan, J. F. (2000). A theory of intelligence as processing: Implications for society. *Psychology, Public Policy, and Law, 6,* 168–179.

Fagan, J. F., & Holland, C. R. (2002). Equal opportunity and racial differences in IQ. *Intelligence, 30,* 361–387.

Fagan, J. F., & Holland, C. R. (2007). Racial equality in intelligence: Predictions from a theory of intelligence as processing. *Intelligence, 35,* 319–334.

Ferreter, J., Goldstein, H., Scherbaum, C., Yusko, K., & Jun, H. (2008, April). *Reducing adverse impact using a nontraditional cognitive ability assessment.* Poster presented at the Society for Industrial and Organizational Psychology, San Francisco.

Flanagan, D. P., McGrew, K. S., & Ortiz, S. O. (2000). *The Wechsler intelligence scales and Gf-Gc theory: A contemporary approach to interpretation.* Boston: Allyn and Bacon.

Flanagan, D. P., & Ortiz, S. O. (2001). *Essentials of cross-battery assessment.* New York: Wiley.

Flanagan, D. P., Ortiz, S. O., & Alfonso, V. C. (2007). *Essentials of cross-battery assessment* (2nd ed.). New York: Wiley.

Freedle, R. O. (2003). Correcting the SAT's ethnic and social-class bias: A method for reestimating SAT scores. *Harvard Educational Review, 73,* 1–42.

Freedle, R. O. (2006). How and why standardized tests systematically underestimate African-Americans' true verbal ability and what to do about it: Towards the promotion of two new theories with practical applications. *St. John's Law Review,* 1–23.

Freedle, R. O., & Kostin, I. (1988). *Relationship between item characteristics and an index of Differential Item Functioning (DIF) for the four GRE verbal item types* (Research Report RR-88-29). Princeton, NJ: Educational Testing Service.

Freedle, R. O., & Kostin, I. (1990). Item difficulty of four verbal item types and an index of differential item functioning for black and white examinees. *Journal of Educational Measurement, 27,* 329–343.

Freedle, R. O., & Kostin, I. (1992). *The prediction of GRE reading comprehension item difficulty for expository prose passages for each of three item types: Main ideas, inferences and explicit statements* (GRE Board Professional Report 87-10P; ETS RR-91-59). Princeton, NJ: Educational Testing Service.

Freedle, R. O., & Kostin, I. (1997). Predicting black and white differential item functioning in verbal analogy performance. *Intelligence, 24,* 417–444.

Galton, F. (1865). Hereditary talent and character. *Macmillan's Magazine, 12,* 157–166, 318–327.

Gardner, H. (1983). *Frames of mind: The theory of multiple intelligences.* New York: Basic Books.

Gardner, H. (1999). *Intelligence reframed: Multiple intelligences for the 21st century.* New York: Basic Books.

Gardner, H., & Walters, J. M. (1993). A rounded version. In H. Gardner (Ed.), *Multiple intelligences: The theory in practice* (pp. 13–34). New York: Basic Books.

Ghiselli, E. E. (1966). *The validity of occupational aptitude tests.* New York: Wiley.

Ghiselli, E. E. (1973). The validity of aptitude tests in personnel selection. *Personal Psychology, 26,* 461–477.

Goldstein, H. W., Zedeck, S., & Goldstein, I. L. (2002). *g:* Is this your final answer? *Human Performance, 15,* 123–142.

Gottfredson, L. S. (1994, December 13). Mainstream science on intelligence. *The Wall Street Journal,* p. A18.

Gottfredson, L. S. (1998). Jensen, Jensenism, and the sociology of intelligence. *Intelligence, 26,* 291–299.

Gottfredson, L. S. (2002). Where and why *g* matters: Not a mystery. *Human Performance, 15*(1/2), 25–46.

Guion, R. M. (1980). On trinitarian doctrines of validity. *Professional Psychology, 11,* 385–398.

Guion, R. M. (1998). *Assessment, measurement, and prediction for personnel decisions.* Mahway, NJ: Erlbaum.

Gustafsson, J. P. (1984). A unifying model for the structure of intellectual abilities. *Intelligence, 8,* 179–203.

Helms-Lorenz, M., Van de Vijver, F. J. R., & Poortinga, Y. H. (2003). Cross-cultural differences in cognitive performance and Spearman's hypothesis: *g* or *c*? *Intelligence, 31,* 9–29.

Herrnstein, R. J., & Murray, C. (1994). *The bell curve: Intelligence and class structure in American life.* New York: Free Press.

Horn, J. L. (1976). Human abilities: A review of research and theory in the early 1970s. *Annual Review of Psychology, 27,* 437–485.

Horn, J. L. (1994). The theory of fluid and crystallized intelligence. In R. J. Sternberg (Ed.), *The encyclopedia of human intelligence* (pp. 443–451). New York: Macmillan.

Horn, J. L., & Blankson, N. (2005). Foundations for better understanding of cognitive abilities. In D. P. Flanagan & P. L. Harrison (Eds.), *Contemporary intellectual assessment: Theories, tests, and issues* (2nd ed., pp. 41–68). New York: Guilford Press.

Horn, J. L., & Masunaga, H. (2000). New directions for research into aging and intelligence: The development of expertise. In T. J. Perfect & E. A. Maylor (Eds.), *Models of cognitive aging* (pp. 125–159). Oxford: Oxford University Press.

Hough, L., Oswald, F., & Ployhart, R. (2001). Determinants, detection and amelioration of adverse impact in personnel selection procedures: Issues, evidence and lessons learned. *International Journal of Selection and Assessment, 9,* 152–194.

Hunter, J. E. (1980). *Test validation for 12,000 jobs: An application of synthetic validity and validity generalization to the General Aptitude Test Battery (GATB).* Washington, DC: U.S. Employment Service.

Hunter, J. E., & Hunter, R. F. (1984). Validity and utility of alternative predictors of job performance. *Psychological Bulletin, 96,* 72–98.

Jensen, A. R. (1980). *Bias in mental testing.* New York: Free Press.

Jensen, A. R. (1985). The nature of the black-white difference on various psychometric tests: Spearman's hypothesis. *Behavioral and Brain Sciences, 8,* 193–263.

Jensen, A. R. (1998). *The g factor: The science of mental ability.* Westport, CT: Praeger.

Jensen, A. R. (2000). Testing: The dilemma of group differences. *Psychology, Public Policy, and Law, 6,* 121–128.

Jensen, A. R. (2006). *Clocking the mind: Mental chronometry and individual differences.* New York: Elsevier Science.

Kamphaus, R. W., Winsor, A. P., Rowe, E. W., & Kim, S. (2005). A history of intelligence test interpretation. In D. P. Flanagan & P. L. Harrison (Eds.), *Contemporary intellectual assessment: Theories, tests, and issues* (2nd ed., pp. 23–38). New York: Guilford Press.

Kaufman, A. S. (1979). *Intelligence testing with the WISC-R.* New York: Wiley-Interscience.

Kaufman, A. S. (2000). Tests of intelligence. In R. J. Sternberg (Ed.), *Handbook of intelligence* (pp. 445–476). New York: Cambridge University Press.

Kaufman, A. S., & Kaufman, N. L. (1983). *Kaufman Assessment Battery for Children.* Circle Pines, MN: American Guidance Service.

Kaufman, A. S., & Lichtenberger, E. O. (2005). *Assessing adolescent and adult intelligence* (3rd ed.). San Francisco: Wiley.

Kyllonen, P. C. (1996). Is working memory capacity Spearman's *g*? In I. Dennis & P. Tapsfield (Eds.), *Human abilities: Their nature and measurement* (pp. 49–76). Mahwah, NJ: Erlbaum.

Linn, R. L. (1986). Educational testing and assessment: Research needs and policy issues. *American Psychologist, 41,* 1153–1160.

Loehlin, J. C. (2000). Group differences in intelligence. In R. J. Sternberg (Ed.), *Handbook of intelligence* (pp. 176–196). New York: Cambridge University Press.

Luria, A. R. (1980). *Higher cortical functions in man* (2nd ed.). New York: Basic Books.

Luria, A. R. (1982). *Language and cognition.* New York: Wiley.

Mackintosh, N. J. (1998). *IQ and human intelligence.* New York: Oxford University Press.

McGrew, K. S. (2005). The Cattell-Horn-Carroll theory of cognitive abilities: Past, present, and future. In D. P. Flanagan & P. L. Harrison (Eds.), *Contemporary intellectual assessment: Theories, tests, and issues* (2nd ed., pp. 136–182). New York: Guilford Press.

McGrew, K. S., & Evans, J. (2004). *Carroll Human Cognitive Abilities Project: Research Report No. 2. Internal and external factorial extensions to the Cattell-Horn-Carroll (CHC) theory of cognitive abilities: A review of factor analytic research since Carroll's seminal 1993 treatise.* St. Cloud, MN: Institutes of Applied Psychometrics.

Messick, S. (1988). The once and future issues of validity: Assessing the meaning and consequences of measurement. In H. Wainer & H. I. Braun (Eds.), *Test validity* (pp. 33–46). Hillsdale, NJ: Erlbaum.

Messick, S. (1989). Validity. In R. L. Linn (Ed.), *Educational measurement* (3rd ed., pp. 13–104). New York: American Council on Education and Macmillan.

Murphy, K. R. (1996). Individual differences and behavior in organizations: Much more than *g*. In K. R. Murphy (Ed.), *Individual differences and behavior in organizations* (pp. 3–30). San Francisco: Jossey-Bass.

Murphy, K., Cronin, B., & Tam, A. (2003). Controversy and consensus regarding the use of cognitive ability testing in organizations. *Journal of Applied Psychology, 88,* 660–671.

Naglieri, J. A. (2005). The cognitive assessment system. In D. P. Flanagan & P. L. Harrison (Eds.), *Contemporary intellectual assessment: Theories, tests, and issues* (2nd ed., pp. 441–460). New York: Guilford Press.

Naglieri, J. A., & Das, J. P. (1997). Intelligence revised. In R. Dillon (Ed.), *Handbook on testing* (pp. 136–163). Westport, CT: Greenwood Press.

Naglieri, J. A., & Das, J. P. (2005). Planning, attention, simultaneous, successive (PASS) theory: A revision of the concept of intelligence. In D. P. Flanagan & P. L. Harrison (Eds.), *Contemporary intellectual assessment: Theories, tests, and issues* (2nd ed., pp. 120–135). New York: Guilford Press.

Neisser, U., Boodoo, G., Bouchard, T. J., Boykin, A. W., Brody, N., Ceci, S. J., et al. (1996). Intelligence: Knowns and unknowns. *American Psychologist, 51,* 77–101.

Ortiz, S. O, & Flanagan, D. P. (1998). Gf-Gc cross-battery interpretation and selective cross-battery assessment: Referral concerns and the needs of culturally and linguistically diverse populations. In K. S. McGrew & D. P. Flanagan (Eds.), *The intelligence test desk reference (ITDR): Gf-Gc cross-battery assessment* (pp. 401–444). Boston: Allyn and Bacon.

Ortiz, S. O., & Ochoa, S. H. (2005). Advances in cognitive assessment of culturally and linguistically diverse individuals. In D. P. Flanagan & P. L. Harrison (Eds.), *Contemporary intellectual assessment: Theories, tests, and issues* (2nd ed., pp. 234–250). New York: Guilford Press.

Ree, M. J., & Carretta, T. R. (2002). *g*2K. *Human Performance, 15*(1/2), 3–24.

Reeve, C. L., & Hakel, M. D. (2002). Asking the right questions about g. *Human Performance, 15*(1/2), 47–74.

Rushton, J. (1998). The Jensen effect and the Spearman-Jensen hypothesis of black-white IQ differences. *Intelligence, 26,* 217.

Sackett, P. R., Borneman, M. J., & Connelly, B. S. (2008). High stakes testing in higher education and employment: Appraising the evidence for validity and fairness. *American Psychologist, 63,* 215–227.

Scherbaum, C. S., & Goldstein, H. W. (2008). Examining the relationship between differential item functioning and item difficulty. *Educational and Psychological Measurement, 68*, 537–553.

Schmidt, F. (2002). The role of general cognitive ability and job performance: Why there cannot be a debate. *Human Performance, 15*(1–2), 187–210.

Schmidt, F. L., & Hunter, J. E. (1998). The validity and utility of selection methods in personnel psychology: Practical and theoretical implications of 85 years of research findings. *Psychological Bulletin, 124*, 262–274.

Spearman, C. E. (1904). "General intelligence" objectively determined and measured. *American Journal of Psychology, 15*, 201–293.

Spearman, C. E. (1923). *The nature of intelligence and the principles of cognition.* London: Macmillan.

Spearman, C. E. (1927). *The abilities of man, their nature and measurement.* New York: Macmillan.

Spenser, J. (1885). *The principles of psychology.* New York: Appelton. (Original work published 1855)

Steele, C. M., Spencer, S. J., & Aronson, J. (2002). Contending with group image: The psychology of stereotype and social identity threat. In M. P. Zanna (Ed.), *Advances experimental social psychology* (Vol. 34, pp. 379–440). San Diego, CA: Academic Press.

Stern, W. (1914). *The psychological methods of testing intelligence* (Educational Psychology Monographs No. 13; G. M. Whipple, Trans.). Baltimore: Warwick and York. (Original work published 1912)

Sternberg, R. J. (1981). Intelligence and non-entrenchment. *Journal of Educational Psychology, 73*, 1–16.

Sternberg, R. J. (1985). *Beyond IQ: A triarchic theory of human intelligence.* New York: Cambridge University Press.

Sternberg, R. J. (1997). *Successful intelligence.* New York: Plume.

Sternberg, R. J. (1999). The theory of successful intelligence. *Review of General Psychology, 3*, 292–316.

Sternberg, R. J. (Ed.). (2000). *Handbook of intelligence.* New York: Cambridge University Press.

Sternberg, R. J. (2006). The Rainbow Project: Enhancing the SAT through assessments of analytical, practical, and creative skills. *Intelligence, 34*, 321–350.

Sternberg, R. J., & Detterman, D. K. (1986). *What is intelligence?: Contemporary viewpoints on its nature and definition.* Norwood, NJ: Ablex.

Sternberg, R. J., & Grigorenko, E. (Eds.). (1997). *Intelligence, heredity and environment.* New York: Cambridge University Press.

Sternberg, R. J., & Kaufman, J. C. (1998). Human abilities. *Annual Review of Psychology, 49*, 1134–1139.

Sternberg, R. J., & Salter, W. (1982). *Handbook of human intelligence.* New York: Cambridge University Press.

Sternberg, R. J., Wagner, R. K., Williams, W. M., & Horvath, J. A. (1995). Testing common sense. *American Psychologist, 50*, 912–927.

Thomson, G. A. (1916). A hierarchy without a general factor. *British Journal of Psychology, 8*, 271–281.

Thomson, G. A. (1951). *The factorial analysis of human ability* (5th ed.). London: University of London Press.

Thorndike, R. L. (1927). *The measurement of intelligence.* New York: Teachers College.

Thorndike, R. L. (1994). *g. Intelligence, 19,* 145–155.

Thorndike, R. L., Hagen, E. P., & Sattler, J. M. (1986). *The Stanford-Binet Intelligence Scale: Fourth edition. Guide for administering and scoring.* Chicago: Riverside.

Thurstone, L. L. (1938). *Primary mental abilities.* Chicago: University of Chicago Press.

Thurstone, L. L. (1947). *Multiple factor analysis.* Chicago: University of Chicago Press.

Tulsky, D. S., Saklofske, D. H., & Ricker, J. H. (2003). Historical overview of intelligence and memory: Factors influencing the Wechsler scales. In D. S. Tulsky et al. (Eds.), *Clinical interpretations of the WAIS-III and WMS-III* (pp. 7–41). San Diego, CA: Academic Press.

Uniform Guidelines on Employee Selection Procedures. (1978). 43 Fed. Reg. 38, 290–38, 315.

van der Maas, H., Dolan, C., Grasman, R., Wicherts, J., Huizenga, H., & Raijmakers, M. (2006). A dynamical model of general intelligence: The positive manifold of intelligence by mutualism. *Psychological Review, 113,* 842.

Viswesvaran, C., & Ones, D. (2002). Agreements and disagreements on the role of general mental ability (GMA) in industrial, work, and organizational psychology. *Human Performance, 15,* 212–231.

Wagner, A. (1999). Causality in complex systems. *Biology and Philosophy, 14,* 83–101.

Walters, J. M., & Gardner, H. (1986). The theory of multiple intelligences: Some issues and answers. In R. Sternberg & R. Wagner (Eds.), *Practical intelligences* (pp. 163–183). New York: Cambridge University Press.

Wasserman, J. D., & Becker, K. A. (2000, August). Racial and ethnic group mean score differences on intelligence tests. In J. A. Naglieri (Chair), *Making assessment more fair: Taking verbal and achievement out of ability tests.* Paper presented at the annual convention of the American Psychological Association, Washington, DC.

Wasserman, J. D., & Tulsky, D. S. (2005). A history of intelligence assessment. In D. P. Flanagan & P. L. Harrison (Eds.), *Contemporary intellectual assessment: Theories, tests, and issues* (2nd ed., pp. 3–22). New York: Guilford Press.

Wechsler, D. (1975). Intelligence defined and undefined: A relativistic appraisal. *American Psychologist, 30,* 135–139.

Wigdor, A. K., & Garner, W. R. (Eds.). (1982). *Ability testing: Uses, consequences, and controversies. Part 1: Report of the committee.* Washington, DC: National Academy Press.

Williams, R. L. (1975). The BITCH—A culture specific test. *Journal of Afro-American Issues, 3,* 103–116.

Woodcock, R. W., & Johnson, M. B. (1989). *Woodcock-Johnson Psycho-Educational Battery Revised Tests of Achievement: Standard and supplemental batteries.* Itasca, IL: Riverside.

Yusko, K. P., & Goldstein, H. W. (2008a). *Siena Reasoning Test.* Princeton, NJ: Siena Consulting.

Yusko, K. P., & Goldstein, H. W. (2008b, June). *Testing for cognitive ability with reduced adverse impact.* Paper presented at the International Public Management Association and Assessment Council, Oakland, CA.

Section III

Adverse Impact and Traditional Selection Theory

5

How a Broader Definition of the Criterion Domain Changes Our Thinking About Adverse Impact

Kevin R. Murphy

Introduction

Members of several demographic groups receive systematically different scores on many of the tests and other assessments used to make high-stakes decisions, such as admission to college or graduate school or selection into a job or an organization. Research on the impact of such tests on the opportunities of members of lower-scoring groups has focused for several reasons largely on standardized tests of cognitive ability. First, these tests are widely recognized as valid predictors of performance in an extraordinarily wide range of settings (Gottfredson, 1986, 1988; Hartigan & Wigdor, 1989; Jensen, 1980; Neisser et al., 1996; Ree & Earles, 1991, 1992; Ree, Earles, & Teachout, 1994; Schmidt & Hunter, 1981, 1999) and are often among the best-available predictors when considered in terms of the trade-off between their cost and their predictive validity. As a result, there is often a strong argument for using these tests as an important part of making decisions about applicants. On the other hand, the use of these tests will result in substantial adverse impact against members of lower-scoring groups (Gottfredson, 1986; Herrnstein & Murray, 1994; Jensen, 1980; Scarr, 1981). For example, because of the relatively large differences in the mean scores obtained by white, Hispanic, and black examinees on standardized tests of cognitive ability, the use of these tests in contexts for which there are a large number of applicants for a small number of positions (e.g., medical school) will virtually eliminate black and Hispanic applicants from consideration. The continued use of these tests in academic admissions and personnel selection is almost certain to contribute to the racial and ethnic segregation of many jobs and institutions.

The adverse impact of cognitive tests is particularly egregious because test score differences are known to be substantially larger than differences in job performance, academic achievement, and other criteria typically used to evaluate the success of selection decisions. For example, black–white differences in mean test scores are typically two to three times as large as differences in job performance (Hattrup, Rock, & Scalia, 1997; Murphy, 2002; Roth, Huffcutt, & Bobko, 2003; Waldman & Avolio, 1991). In other words, these tests not only have an adverse impact on the opportunities open to members of lower-scoring groups, they also have a *disproportionately* adverse effect on black and Hispanic applicants. The use of these tests tends to screen out many more black and Hispanic applicants than would be screened out if there were better predictors of performance available (however, there often are no reasonable alternatives).

Suppose a battery of tests was developed that perfectly predicted performance in school or on the job. The use of such a test battery as a means of making selection decisions would result in reduced selection rates for black and Hispanic applicants relative to their representation in the applicant population, but these differences in selection outcomes might arguably be justified on the basis of real differences in job performance, academic achievement, and so on. The use of cognitive tests in selection results in a much more substantial culling of minority applicants than can be justified on the basis of differences in the performance of black, Hispanic, and white applicants. Because of the widespread use of cognitive tests and because of the frequent lack of reasonable alternatives to these tests, it is unlikely that adverse impact in personnel selection will disappear in the foreseeable future. It is therefore critically important to understand the dynamics of adverse impact personnel selection.

This chapter makes the case for a multivariate model of the relationships between test scores and the broad range of criteria organizations care about. Virtually every study of adverse impact has treated it as a univariate problem in which the only real basis for describing the validity of tests is in terms of each test's correlation with overall job performance. This perspective is limiting in a number of ways, but most fundamentally, it is limiting because it treats adverse impact as an afterthought or as an unfortunate consequence of the organization's attempt to attain a single goal of maximizing job performance. If we think more broadly and more realistically about the criteria organizations are interested in satisfying when making hiring decisions, we are likely to come to quite different conclusions about adverse impact and about methods of dealing with the adverse impact of selection tests.

The Need for a Broader Approach to the Criterion Domain

There is substantial research literature dealing with methods for reducing the adverse impact of cognitive ability tests (Sackett & Ellingson, 1997; Sackett & Wilk, 1994). These studies have made a number of worthwhile contributions, but their potential contribution to understanding the dynamics of adverse impact and the methods that might be used to reduce adverse impact is substantially limited by the reliance on univariate models for addressing what is fundamentally a multivariate problem. Most real-world selection decisions are influenced by a number of tests and assessments. Thus, college admissions decisions not only are influenced by scores on standardized tests, such as the SAT (Scholastic Aptitude Test) but also are affected by high school grades, the type of courses taken in high school, outside activities, and so on. Similarly, test scores affect decisions made about job applicants, but these decisions are also affected by interviews, background and qualifications, and more. More to the point, the evaluation of the success or failure of any particular system for making high-stakes decisions about individuals often requires the consideration of several different criteria. Our current models for evaluating adverse impact simply do not reflect the complexity of the phenomenon.

In this chapter, I argue that univariate models typically used to assess the validity, utility, and impact of psychological tests often lead to results that are either incomplete or misleading. Virtually all important decisions that are made about applicants can and should be evaluated in terms of several different criteria, and models that are based on any single criterion variable, considered in isolation, will not allow us to develop complete understanding of the impact of tests, or of strategies designed to reduce the adverse impact of tests, on the range of criteria that define the success or failure of a selection system.

I also argue that univariate models for thinking about validity lead to an unfortunate and indeed mistaken tendency to treat adverse impact as an afterthought. That is, most selection research starts with the goal of developing a valid selection system (in which *valid* is defined in terms of success in predicting performance). Once the system is designed and adverse impact is detected, there might or might not be some programmatic efforts to reduce adverse impact, but the likelihood of creating adverse impact is rarely thought of as an integral part of the criterion domain. If organizations truly care about reducing adverse impact, this aspect of tests should be considered as part of an overall evaluation of their value and validity.

Virtually all existing studies and models of adverse impact in personnel selection start with the assumptions that (1) the goal of personnel selection is to maximize the job performance of those selected, (2) job performance can be treated as a unidimensional variable that is measured reasonably well (albeit with some amount of random measurement error), and (3) it is therefore reasonable to analyze selection systems and the consequences of various interventions designed to reduce adverse impact in terms of univariate models (e.g., evaluating the bivariate correlation between test scores and performance measures, the changes in predicted performance levels as selection policies change) or in terms of models that include multiple predictors and a univariate criterion (e.g., evaluating the multiple correlation between a weighted selection battery and some performance measure). There are good questions regarding all three assumptions.

Organizations Pursue Multiple Goals

First, the assumption that the one and only goal of a personnel selection system is to maximize expected performance of the set of applicants selected is rarely if ever true. Organizations are indeed interested in maximizing performance or effectiveness, but they often must consider a broader set of goals and metrics in determining whether a selection system is successful. For example, organizations might value both selecting a group of applicants who are likely to perform well and selecting a group of applicants who broadly reflect the diverse nature of the communities in which the organization exists. They might value a wide range of related goals, including building a more positive image in the community and among potential customers, avoiding lawsuits, hiring employees who are least likely to engage in counterproductive behaviors, and more.

If organizations pursue multiple goals, a system for evaluating the success of personnel selection, or the effects of different adjustments to selection system (e.g., changes in the composition or use of a test battery to reduce adverse impact), must also be evaluated with reference to multiple criteria for success. It is very possible that the selection battery that maximizes expected job performance is *not* the best battery for maximizing the entire set of goals pursued by the organization.

Adverse impact has traditionally been treated as an unfortunate but unavoidable effect of the decision to maximize predicted job performance. It is not. Adverse impact is one of several aspects of a selection system that should be part of the overall evaluation of that system. Adverse impact is bad for organizations; it can lead not only to substantial legal costs but also to opportunity costs (e.g., failing to hire individuals who could contribute to the organization). Adverse impact is bad for job applicants, at least for those in lower-scoring groups. Adverse impact is bad for communities because it leads to a disproportionate tendency to deny employment opportunities to members of several racial and ethnic minority groups. Organizations may place more value on outcomes of performance (e.g., maximizing task performance) than on reducing adverse impact, but it is hard to imagine any organization that would, if properly informed, be indifferent to the possibility that their selection system will have adverse impact. It is therefore useful to include adverse impact in the criterion domain organizations are hoping to affect with their choice of selection methods.

Performance Is Multidimensional

Several studies have examined the dimension of job performance (e.g., Campbell, 1990; Campbell, McCloy, Oppler, & Sager, 1993; Conway, 1996; Murphy, 1989), and there is considerable consensus that the domain of job performance can be broken down into at least two broad categories: (a) individual task performance and (b) behaviors that create and maintain the social and organizational context that allows others to carry out their individual tasks. Individual task performance involves learning the task and the context in which it is performed as well as being able to and motivated to perform the task when it is needed. Many validity studies appear to equate individual task performance with overall job performance (Hunter, 1986; Murphy, 1989, 1996).

In addition to the specific tasks that are included in most job descriptions, the domain of job performance includes a wide range of behaviors, such as teamwork, customer service, and organizational citizenship, that are not always necessary to accomplish the specific tasks in an individual's job but are necessary for the smooth functioning of teams and organizations (Borman & Motowidlo, 1993; Brief & Motowidlo, 1986; Campbell, 1990; Campbell et al., 1993; J. E. Edwards & Morrison, 1994; McIntyre & Salas, 1995; Murphy, 1989; Organ, 1988; Smith, Organ, & Near, 1983). Labels such as "contextual performance," "organizational citizenship," and "prosocial behaviors" have been applied to this facet of the performance domain, and while these three terms are not interchangeable, they all capture aspects of effective job performance that are not always directly linked to accomplishing specific individual tasks.

Individual task performance and contextual performance are not likely to be orthogonal, but there are good reasons to believe that these two aspects of job performance are not highly correlated, and that they may have both different antecedents and different consequences (Murphy & Shiarella, 1997). As a result, validity studies that use "overall performance" as the principal criterion measure might do a poor job of capturing the complex process by which individual differences in abilities, personality, interests, and so on are translated into good or poor performance on the job.

Although assessments of job performance usually reflect both individual task performance and contextual performance, it is unlikely that the precise mix of these two facets is the same in all settings. Some organizational or national cultures may lead to more emphasis on individual task performance, whereas others may more strongly emphasize contextual performance. Thus, even if job descriptions, technologies, organizational structures, and so on are identical, the definition of what "performance" actually means in a particular job could vary substantially across organizations or across settings. If one organization defines good performance in terms of a very individualistic definition and another pays more attention to group-oriented contextual performance, the antecedents of performance and the consequences of various interventions aimed at increasing performance may vary substantially across organizations (Murphy & Shiarella, 1997).

Univariate Models Misrepresent Selection Systems

If the success or failure of a selection system is defined in terms of multiple criteria, it follows that multivariate models are needed to evaluate fully the validity of that system or the effects of different interventions designed to reduce adverse impact. Murphy and Shiarella (1997) presented a multivariate model for evaluating the validity and utility of selection tests; this model allows researchers and practitioners to assess the validity of selection tests and the effects of selection strategies on multiple criteria that might be of interest to organizations. These authors considered the use of test batteries that included both cognitive ability and personality measures and evaluated the validity of these batteries for a composite performance criterion that was made up of a weighted combination of individual task performance and contextual performance. Their analysis showed that very different conclusions about validity would be reached, depending on (a) the weight given to cognitive ability versus personality in the test battery, (b) the weight given to individual task performance versus contextual performance in defining the overall performance construct, and (c) the compatibility between the definition of a high-scoring applicant (i.e., the relative weight given to ability vs. personality) and the definition of good performance (i.e., the relative weight given to individual task performance vs. contextual performance). In other words, the success of a selection test battery as a predictor of future performance depends on how the battery is assembled (i.e., what sorts of tests are included and how much weight is given to each one) and how performance is defined (i.e., how much weight is given to each of the facets of performance).

Suppose decision makers in an organization identify two criteria for defining the success of a selection system: (1) it should do the best job possible identifying individuals who are likely to perform well on the job, and (2) it should lead to the selection of a workforce that, to the greatest extent possible, reflects the demographic composition of the applicant pool or the surrounding community. Several articles have examined the question of developing selection systems that are evaluated in terms of both their predictive validity and their level of adverse impact (De Corte, Lievens,

& Sackett, 2006; Schmitt, Rogers, Chan, Sheppard, & Jennings, 1997), but none of these models presents a clear method for evaluating the trade-off between these two criteria. Murphy (2002) suggested that the multiattribute utility assessment methods (Edwards & Newman, 1982) might be applied to evaluate the effects of different selection systems on multiple criteria but did not provide a concrete example of exactly how this could be done. The purpose of this chapter is to identify a general approach for evaluating the success of personnel selection systems when success is defined in terms of multiple dimensions that might be orthogonal or even negatively correlated and to use this model to evaluate the effects of various interventions aimed at reducing adverse impact.

A General Multivariate Approach for Evaluating Selection Systems

Murphy and Shiarella (1997) developed a multivariate validation model that can be applied to a wide range of situations in which the criterion for the success of a selection system is not limited to measures of job performance but rather might include a mix of dimensions that reflect both performance dimensions and social outcomes of selection. This approach provides an integrated system for determining the effects of various decisions made in the design and administration of a selection system (e.g., how many tests and what kinds, how should tests be weighted) on the overall success of a selection system.

Multivariate validity models start by noting that when multiple predictors are used to make selection decision and there are multiple criterion dimensions, the overall score on this selection test battery **SB** can be defined as a weighted linear combination of scores on each of several selection tests, and the overall score on a criterion composite **CC** can be similarly defined as a weighted linear combination of scores on several aspects of performance, social outcomes of tests, and so on. It is also possible to develop multivariate models in which multiple-hurdle methods are used and in which the "score" an individual receives is a function of the number of hurdles he or she passes, but in the present chapter, I limit my analyses to compensatory selection systems in which the scores on each of the tests in a battery are part of the overall score received by each applicant.

The validity of the selection battery can then be expressed as the correlation between **SB** and **CC**. The main challenges in operationalizing this model involve scaling the predictors and the criteria in such a way that meaningful composites can be formed and in determining the weights that should be applied to each of the aspects of the criterion domain.

As will be discussed here, organizational decision makers may face some daunting challenges in defining the relative weight they give to different criteria in defining the success of a selection system. In laying out a multivariate model for evaluating the relationship between scores on various selection composites and a composite criterion that reflects a combination of these multiple-criterion facets, I will assume that these decisions can be made, and that the weights assigned to each of the criterion dimensions can be specified. I return to a discussion of how these weights might be determined.

This multivariate validity model can be used to answer two key questions: What is the validity of any particular test battery for predicting this composite success criterion? What is the optimal test battery for predicting this same composite criterion? In answering these questions, we can use well-known matrix equations for the correlations between composites (Nunnally, 1978). Following Murphy and Shiarella (1997), let

nx = number of tests in a selection battery

ny = number of criterion dimensions

N = number of applicants

$\mathbf{w_y}$ = $1 \times ny$ vector of weights that reflect the relative importance of each of these dimensions in defining the overall success of a selection system

$\mathbf{Y}$ = $N \times ny$ matrix of measures of ny specific criterion facets for each of N applicants

$\mathbf{w_x}$ = $1 \times nx$ vector of weights that reflect the relative weight assigned to each test in the selection battery

$\mathbf{X}$ = $N \times nx$ matrix of scores on nx selection tests for each of N applicants

We can define the criterion composite **CC** and the composite score on the selection battery **SB** as

$$\mathbf{CC} = \mathbf{w_y Y}$$

and

$$\mathbf{SB} = \mathbf{w_x X}$$

In other words, the criterion composite **CC** is formed by multiplying the individual's score on each facet of the criterion domain by a weight that reflects its relative importance. Similarly, the score on the selection test battery **SB** is formed by multiplying the individual's score on each test by a weight that reflects its relative importance.

Next, define the following:

Cx = variance-covariance matrix ($nx \times nx$) among the X variables (i.e., selection tests)

Cy = variance-covariance matrix ($ny \times ny$) among the Y variables (i.e., criterion dimensions)

Cxy = $nx \times ny$ matrix of covariances between X variables and Y variables

The covariance between the two composites and the variance of each is given by

$$\text{Cov}_{\text{SB,CC}} = w_x C_{xy} w'_y \tag{5.1}$$

The variance of each composite is given by

$$\text{Var}_{\text{SB}} = w_x C_x w'_x \quad (\text{Var}_{\text{SB}} \text{ is the variance of } \mathbf{SB}) \tag{5.2}$$

$$\text{Var}_{\text{CC}} = w_y C_y w'_y \quad (\text{Var}_{\text{CC}} \text{ is the variance of } \mathbf{CC}) \tag{5.3}$$

which means that the correlation between a selection composite and a performance composite is given by

$$r_{\text{SB,CC}} = \text{Cov}_{\text{SB,CC}} / \left(\sqrt{\text{Var}_{\text{SB}}} * \sqrt{/\text{Var}_{\text{CC}}} \right) \tag{5.4}$$

An equivalent formulation that does not use matrix algebra starts with the correlations among all X and Y variables. Compute

$$a = \Sigma(wx_i^2) + 2 * \Sigma\Sigma\, ((wx_i * wx_j) * \text{Correlation between } x_i \text{ and } x_j) \tag{5.5}$$

$$b = \Sigma(wy_i^2) + 2 * \Sigma\Sigma\, ((wy_i * wy_j) * \text{Correlation between } y_i \text{ and } y_j) \tag{5.6}$$

$$c = \Sigma\Sigma((wy_i * wy_j) * \text{Correlation between } x_i \text{ and } y_j) \tag{5.7}$$

Here, single summation Σ designates summing the squared weights in X or Y, while double summation $\Sigma\Sigma$ indicates summing products of weights of variables i and j multiplied by the correlations between the two variables, taken over all pairs of variables.

The correlation between a selection composite and a criterion composite is given by

$$r_{SB,CC} = c / \left(\sqrt{a} * \sqrt{b} \right) \tag{5.8}$$

Formulas 5.4 and 5.8 are equivalent.

Sturman and Judge (1995) noted that once w_y is defined, it is possible to solve for the optimal w_x using a matrix equation that is equivalent to

$$\text{Optimal } w_x = (Rx^{-1}R_{xy}\, w_y) / \sqrt{w'_y R_{yy} w_y} \tag{5.9}$$

where Rx, Ry, and Rxy represent the matrices of correlations among the variables in X, the variables in Y, and the correlations between variables in X and variables in Y, respectively. This optimal w_x represents the set of weights that can be applied to test scores to maximize the correlation between the selection test battery **SB** and the criterion composite **CC**.

Applying the Multivariate Model

To illustrate the application of this model for evaluating validity, consider an organization that used both cognitive ability tests and personality inventories that measure conscientiousness to predict performance in an organization. The organization values both task performance and contextual performance and values selecting applicants who most closely reflect the distribution of white and black applicants in the applicant pool. Application of the multivariate model described here requires an estimate of the relationships among ability, personality, performance, and adverse impact. A number of recent studies and meta-analyses (De Corte et al., 2006; Murphy & Shiarella, 1997; Bobko, Roth, & Potosky, 1999) provided a good basis for estimating all of the relationships in question. Table 5.1 presents estimates of the correlations among the predictor and criterion dimensions relevant to this organization.

A traditional, univariate validation study would probably concentrate on task performance as the primary criterion, which would suggest that cognitive ability is the obvious choice as a predictor or perhaps would note that somewhat different conclusions might be reached depending on whether the criterion was task performance or contextual performance. A slightly more sophisticated study might combine task performance and contextual performance into a composite variable, giving equal weights to both facets of performance. The validity of cognitive ability and

TABLE 5.1

Estimated Correlations Among Predictor Tests and
Criterion Dimensions

	1	2	3	4	5
Cognitive ability					
Conscientiousness	0.10				
Task performance	0.50	0.30			
Contextual performance	0.20	0.35	0.20		
Adverse impact	0.45	0.05	0.25	0.10	

conscientiousness measures for predicting this unit-weighted composite
would be approximately 0.45 and 0.19, respectively.[1]

Murphy and Shiarella (1997) noted that the validity of different selection test batteries would depend on the relative weight of task performance and contextual performance in defining the meaning of *overall performance* in an organization. Table 5.2 shows the estimated univariate validities and the estimated battery validity for a unit-weighted selection test battery in four different organizations that define performance in different ways. This table suggests several interesting conclusions. First, the validity of the same tests or of the same test battery is not likely to be the same across organizations. It is important that this variation in validities is *not* the same thing as "situational specificity" as defined in the validity generalization literature. That is, variation in the validity of this test battery is not the result of random error. Rather, Table 5.2 suggests that the organization's definition of performance is a systematic moderator of the validity of these tests and of this test battery. Organizations that define performance in different ways will and should reach different conclusions about the validity of particular selection tests and test batteries. As a result, the conclusions an organization reaches about which test is most useful might depend on exactly how performance is defined. Organizations that define performance in context-heavy terms might find a measure of conscientiousness more useful than a measure of cognitive ability.

TABLE 5.2

Estimated Validities as a Function of the Definition of Performance[a]

Performance definition	Cognitive ability	Conscientiousness	Unit-weighted battery
Task heavy (0.9, 0.1)	0.50	0.32	0.56
Equal (0.5, 0.5)	0.45	0.42	0.58
Contextual heavy (0.1, 0.9)	0.24	0.37	0.42

[a] Relative weights assigned to task performance and contextual performance, respectively, are shown in parentheses.

The results presented in Table 5.2 mirror those presented in Murphy and Shiarella (1997), suggesting that the definition of performance does indeed have some bearing on the validity of selection tests. However, if you are using a composite of the two tests to predict performance (the last column in Table 5.2), the effects of varying the definition of performance are not large. In Table 5.2, the estimated battery validities vary from 0.42 to 0.58. If differential weighting of selection tests is used, the estimated validities vary a bit more (Murphy & Shiarella, 1997), but these validity estimates are in the moderate-to-high range for a wide array of performance definitions.

Expanding the Criterion Space

The true importance of taking a multivariate perspective becomes clearer when the criteria organizations use to evaluate the success of their selection systems are broadened to include both performance and social goals. It is reasonable to believe that many organizations care about task performance, contextual performance, *and* reducing adverse impact, and the potential conflict between these different definitions of success poses distinct challenges for organizations (Murphy, 2002). Unlike the two traditional performance facets (i.e., task performance and contextual performance), adverse impact is likely to be negatively valued by organizations, and this mix of positively and negatively valued outcomes makes it difficult for organizations to create a single selection system that will accomplish all of its goals. As Table 5.1 suggests, the tests that do the best job predicting job performance (i.e., cognitive tests) also create the most adverse impact, and if the goal is to increase performance *and* decrease adverse impact, there will be real barriers to accomplishing this goal.

The algebra of linear combinations suggests that the weights assigned to various tests or performance facets tend not to matter much *except when these weights differ in sign* (Wainer, 1976). This is certainly the case for adverse impact. Some organizations might choose to ignore adverse impact (i.e., give it a weight of zero), but it is unlikely that any organization will assign a positive value to the likelihood that a particular test will contribute to adverse impact. Except in the rare case when the weight assigned to this aspect of testing is exactly zero, it is likely that most organizations will define a successful test battery in terms of a mix of criterion dimensions, some of which receive positive weights (performance dimensions) and some of which receive negative weights (social impact dimensions). Under these conditions, the weights assigned to different criterion dimensions *do* matter, and difference across organizations in the specific way their three criterion dimensions are combined to yield an overall assessment of the selection tests can have a substantial effect on the conclusions reached about the validity and value of a test battery.

TABLE 5.3

Estimated Validities for Combination of Performance and Social Outcomes

Performance definition	Cognitive ability	Conscientiousness	Unit-weighted battery	Optimal battery	Optimal weights[a]
Task heavy and social light (0.9, 0.1, 0.1)[b]	0.50	0.33	0.54	0.54	0.72, 0.29
Task heavy and social heavy (0.9, 0.1, 0.9)	0.06	0.23	0.19	0.24	0.04, 0.26
Equal and social light (0.5, 0.5, 0.1)	0.40	0.42	0.55	0.55	0.28, 0.29
Equal and social heavy (0.5, 0.5, 0.9)	−0.05	0.27	0.14	0.28	−0.08, 0.29
Contextual heavy and social light (0.1, 0.9, 0.1)	0.20	0.37	0.38	0.40	0.15, 0.32
Contextual heavy and social heavy (0.1, 0.9, 0.9)	−0.14	0.25	0.07	0.32	−0.20, 0.32

[a] Relative weights assigned to cognitive ability and conscientiousness, respectively.
[b] Relative weights assigned to task performance, contextual performance, and adverse impact are shown in parentheses.

Table 5.3 illustrates different values that six hypothetical organizations assign to the two traditional performance dimensions (i.e., task performance and contextual performance) and in the negative weight they assign to adverse impact. When organizations give social goals a small weight (e.g., a weight of −0.1 vs. −0.9), the results shown in Table 5.3 are quite similar to those shown in Table 5.2. That is, including social goals but giving them a relatively small weight has some impact on the evaluation of different tests or test batteries, but the effect is not all that dramatic. However, when social goals are given a large weight, the conclusions reached about the extent to which different tests or test batteries meet the needs of the organization can be substantially affected.

For example, suppose an organization values task performance highly and assigns low values to contextual performance and to adverse impact reduction in defining a successful test battery. Table 5.3 suggests that it will be possible to achieve a high overall level of validity ($r = 0.54$), and that the optimal test battery will give much more weight to ability than to personality (relative weights of 0.72 and 0.29, respectively). Another organization that defines job performance in the same way (i.e., places high emphasis on task performance) but gives a large weight to reducing adverse impact faces a much tougher prospect. The optimal test battery (one that gives substantially more weight to personality than to ability) will achieve a validity of only 0.24.

Organizations that place equal value on task performance and contextual performance will likely place less emphasis on cognitive ability in hiring and may even choose to give it a negative weight, depending on the relative importance of avoiding adverse impact. Organizations that value contextual performance more highly than task performance will give personality consistently greater weight than ability in developing optimal hiring composites and may even (if they place a high value on avoiding adverse impact) give substantial negative weight to cognitive ability.

Table 5.3 leads to a number of conclusions, the most important being (a) the validity of a test battery depends strongly on the goals of the organization, (b) very different batteries will be best for organizations that pursue different goals, and (c) it is difficult to achieve a high level of validity when the criterion domain places strong emphasis on both maximizing performance and avoiding adverse impact.

The most surprising aspect of Table 5.3 is that the best test battery is sometimes one that assigns a *negative* weight to cognitive ability. Nearly a century of validation research leads to the conclusion that cognitive ability is among the best predictors of performance (Schmidt & Hunter, 1999). However, cognitive ability tests are also one of the most important sources of adverse impact. If an organization values avoiding adverse impact as much as it values maximizing task performance, it might be perfectly sensible to give ability tests a negative weight. From the perspective of an organization that is attempting to attain this set of values, it might be very reasonable to conclude that ability tests cause more problems than they solve.

Values Affect Validity

The statement "This is a valid test" is impossible to interpret without first answering "Valid for what?" Cognitive tests are excellent predictors of future performance, but they are one of the chief culprits in causing adverse impact. The question of whether a particular test battery is a good one or a poor one depends strongly on the outcomes the organization values. Organizations that care a lot about minimizing adverse impact will come to very different conclusions about validity than organizations that care a little about this aspect of their selection systems.

Messick (1995) introduced the controversial notion of "consequential validity," that is, the idea that the validity of a test depends in part on the consequences of the decisions that are made on the basis of test scores. This idea has been strongly criticized (*Educational Measurement: Issues and Practice*, Vol. 16, No. 2, Summer, 1997), in part on the grounds that consequential validity depends on subjective value judgments. This criticism is shortsighted because value decisions are an inescapable part of organizational life. Organizations that choose to employ cognitive tests are making at least an implicit value judgment that the social consequences of testing are less important than the performance-related consequences. Organizations that decide not to use these tests are making a judgment that it is worthwhile forgoing the performance increments associated with cognitive tests to avoid the social consequences of these tests. Organizations are probably better off understanding the value judgments they must make in personnel selections and making these decisions in a thoughtful and deliberate way (Murphy, 2002; Murphy & Cleveland, 1995).

The best answer to "Valid for what?" is that tests should be valid for predicting outcomes that are important to the organization. Thus, the first step in developing a validation strategy should be to understand what organizations are trying to accomplish when they develop and administer selection tests. The goal of selection tests usually includes a mix of performance-related outcomes and social outcomes (Murphy, 2002), and these outcomes can be combined into sensible composites, even when the various outcomes of testing are negatively correlated. They key is to develop a weighting scheme that corresponds to the values pursued by the organization.

Different Test Batteries Are Best for Organizations That Pursue Different Goals

The conventional wisdom in personnel psychology is that cognitive ability tests are the best predictors of performance and should be routinely included in selection test batteries (Schmidt & Hunter, 1981, 1999). Table 5.3 suggests that when social goals are important (i.e., when adverse impact receives a weight of −0.9 rather than a weight of −0.1), cognitive tests do not contribute to the validity of a system, and they may in fact hurt more than they help. If an organization cares about task performance *and* social goals, the advantages and disadvantages of cognitive tests virtually cancel each other out (the univariate validity of cognitive tests for predicting a criterion domain that gives strong emphasis to both individual task performance and social outcomes is 0.06), and the optimal selection test battery will be one that gives only a low weight to cognitive ability.

If an organization cares about both task and contextual performance *and* gives a strong weight to social goals in defining a successful selection system, the validity of cognitive tests is actually negative, and the optimal test battery is one that gives a negative weight to cognitive tests. Finally, if an organization cares most about contextual performance and social goals, the best selection test battery is one that gives a fairly substantial negative weight to cognitive tests.

It Is Hard to Maximize Competing Objectives

The third general lesson of Table 5.3 is that organizations that value both high levels of performance (especially individual task performance) and low levels of adverse impact will find it difficult to create a highly successful test battery. It is easy to predict performance—simply give a large positive weight to cognitive tests. It is also easy to avoid adverse impact—simply give a low weight or even a negative weight to cognitive ability. However, the relatively small validity coefficients achieved when organizations value both performance and social outcomes suggest that it is very difficult to accomplish both goals with the same selection test battery. For example, if an organization values both individual task performance and avoiding adverse impact, the best possible combination of cognitive and conscientiousness measures will not do a very good job predicting the composite criterion (the optimal test battery has a validity of only 0.24 for predicting this composite criterion).

Articulating the Goals of a Selection System

Managers and executives who are responsible for making decisions about personnel selection systems might find it quite difficult to answer the question, "How important is it that the selection system minimizes adverse impact?" It might be even more difficult to answer the question, "What is the value of a 10% reduction in adverse impact?" The fact that these are hard questions to answer does not mean that we can ignore them. A manager who chooses a selection system with a relatively strong track record of validity and a relatively high level of adverse impact over an alternative that has less-impressive validation data and lower adverse impact has already made an implicit statement of values (Murphy, 2002).

There are a number of methods for structuring and simplifying these judgments (Edwards & Newman, 1982). A common first step is to identify the set of important outcomes. For example, suppose an organization now uses unstructured interviews to select salespeople and is considering changing to a battery of written tests that measure both cognitive ability and the personality dimensions of emotional stability and agreeableness. This change might lead to several outcomes, including:

- Task performance will probably improve (in comparison to the outcomes expected if you do not use a systematic strategy for selecting among applicants).
- Contextual performance will probably improve.
- There will almost certainly be more adverse impact and a greater risk for lawsuits.

- Some applicants will find the personality tests objectionable and may be less likely to apply or join the organization.
- It will be easier to make decisions about applicants in a quick and consistent manner.
- It will be easier to maintain a paper trail to document decisions and the reasons why some people are or are not hired.

Multiattribute utility theory suggests that the decision about whether to choose this selection test battery depends on two things: the value assigned to each outcome and the likelihood that each outcome will actually happen given this choice. The likelihoods can be estimated on the basis of existing research and theory (e.g., validity studies will allow you to estimate the correlation between the test and various performance dimensions), but the values cannot. Different stakeholders may value different outcomes, and the relative emphasis given to each outcome is likely to vary across decision makers and across organizations.

The simplest way of assessing values starts with a list like the one given, laying out the outcomes that are likely if the organization makes this choice. Stakeholders in the organization (e.g., human resource managers, legal department, union officials, executives) are given this list and are asked to make several decisions, ranging from trimming the list of outcomes to ranking and rating their importance.

From Outcomes to Values

The process of moving from a set of outcomes like the one given to a statement of values is easiest if it is broken down into a series of steps. At each step, it is important to check for consistency and agreement and, if different stakeholders disagree, to negotiate an acceptable agreement about which outcomes to rank, how much value to assign to each, and so on.

Trimming the List of Outcomes

The first step is to isolate outcomes that decision makers really value. For example, it is possible that the stakeholders involved in this decision do not really care whether their potential applicants will find the proposed tests objectionable on the theory that these applicants would not fit in the company. A useful first step in assigning values to outcomes is to determine which outcomes are worth considering.

A concrete way of determining whether a specific outcome is important enough to keep or sufficiently marginal to drop from the list of valued outcomes is to think through the implications of that outcome and to ask whether that outcome could reasonably affect your final decision. For example, if stakeholders agreed that their final choice about whether to adopt the new tests will be the same regardless of whether some applicants find these tests objectionable, this outcome should be dropped from the list. The first decision, then, is whether stakeholders care enough about particular outcomes even to include them in a list of possible reasons to choose or to reject this set of tests.

Ranking the Remaining Outcomes

Once a list of outcomes that are sufficiently important to treat as valued outcomes that might affect organizational decisions is created, the next step is to rank order these outcomes in importance. These ranks can in many cases be translated directly into statements of relative value. For example, suppose a set of decision makers has determined that all six of the outcomes described here are important. The next task is to have the group rank order the six. These ranks can easily be translated into a variety of measures of the estimated importance or value assigned to each outcome. Table 5.4 lists these outcomes in a hypothetical rank order and illustrates the process of translating these ranks into a normalized metric that might provide a measure of the relative importance of or value assigned to each outcome.

In Table 5.4, the six outcomes are ranked in terms of their overall importance in making a decision, not in terms of whether they are good or bad things. Therefore, it is important to keep in mind that some signs might need to be reversed (e.g., a system that leads to more adverse impact is probably negatively valued). An alternative is to phrase all outcomes in terms that will lead them to be scaled in the same direction. For example, you might rephrase, "There will almost certainly be more adverse impact and a greater risk for lawsuits," in terms such as, "There will almost certainly be less adverse impact and a lower risk for lawsuits." This makes the process of assigning values simpler, but in this case, it will be important to remember to reverse signs when incorporating information about the

TABLE 5.4

Six Likely Outcomes of Adopting a Test, Presented in Ranked Order of Importance

Outcome	Rank	Reciprocal rank	Normalized rank
Task performance improves	1	6	0.285
More adverse impact	2	5	0.238
Contextual performance improves	3	4	0.190
Easier to maintain a paper trail	4	3	0.142
Easier to make decisions	5	2	0.095
Some applicants find tests objectionable	6	1	0.047
Sum	21	21	0.997

likelihood that the system in mind will produce adverse impact because the outcome being assessed is the *reduction* impact.

In Table 5.4, we illustrate the process of translating ranks into normalized reciprocal ranks. Normalized reciprocal ranks have two desirable properties: higher values are assigned to more important or more valued outcomes, and the ranks sum to approximately 1.0, allowing you to interpret these as relative weights. To produce normalized reciprocal ranks, first reverse the normal ranking system (in which the most important or most valued outcome is ranked 1, the second most important is ranked 2, and so on), so that the least-important outcome is ranked 1, and ranks increase as importance increases. Next, sum the reciprocal ranks (the sum of the ranks of these six outcomes is 21; because reciprocal ranking is a simple score reversal, the sum of the reciprocal ranks is also 21). Finally, divide each reciprocal rank by the sum of the ranks. Thus, in Table 5.4, the outcome task performance improves is ranked first in importance. In other words, this is the outcome that is seen as having the largest impact on your decision about whether to adopt these tests. The reciprocal rank for this outcome is therefore 6. Divide this reciprocal rank by the sum of the ranks, and you will obtain a value of 0.285 (i.e., $6/21 = 0.285$), which represents an estimate of the relative importance of this outcome.

Check for Reasonableness

Table 5.4 suggests that the outcome *task performance improves* is slightly more important than *more adverse impact* in influencing decisions and is about twice as important as *easier to maintain a paper trail*. Does this make sense to stakeholders? It is important to determine whether the normalized reciprocal ranks do a good job or a poor job of capturing the relative differences in importance or value for each of these six outcomes. If the outcomes are pretty evenly spread over a continuum of importance or value, they should match fairly well with these normalized reciprocal ranks. On the other hand, if there are large differences in the relative importance of some adjacent pairs of outcomes (e.g., adverse impact is seen by stakeholders as much more important than contextual performance, while making it easier to maintain a paper trail and making it easier to make decisions about applicants are seen as very similar in importance), these normalized ranks will not adequately capture the relative importance or value of different outcomes.

When the number of outcomes is reasonably small, one easy method of checking the adequacy if these normalized reciprocal ranks is with a pair comparison task. You might ask each decision maker a series of questions, such as, "Is the difference in importance between task performance (0.285) and adverse impact (0.238) about the same as the difference in importance between adverse impact (0.238) and contextual performance (0.190)?"

If normalized reciprocal ranks do a pretty good job of capturing the relative importance or value of these six outcomes, the difference in importance among each adjacent set of outcomes (1 vs. 2 as compared with 2 vs. 3) should be roughly similar. On the other hand, decision makers may see large gaps in importance (e.g., seeing task performance, adverse impact, and contextual performance as all much more important than maintaining a good paper trail. The pair comparison method allows you to determine where there are gaps between the importance implied by normalized reciprocal ranks and the perceived importance of different outcomes. Sometimes, the existence of large gaps may lead decision makers to trim the list of relevant outcomes further (e.g., they may decide after completing this step that outcomes ranked lower than contextual performance just are not important enough to make a real difference). However, it is also possible that large gaps in the importance assigned to the set of outcomes will imply that there may be other outcomes that have not been considered and that would fill these gaps.

From Values to Multivariate Validity Estimates

The multivariate validity model described requires both a correlation matrix depicting the relationship between the tests being considered and each of the outcomes in the criterion domain and a set of weights for each of the elements in the criterion domain. I described a set of procedures that can be used to obtain the values or importance weights. It is not always obvious, however, how to estimate all of the components of the correlation matrix.

Relationships between selection constructs and the major components of job performance can be estimated on the basis of existing theory and research (e.g., Table 5.1 was produced on the basis of meta-analyses). However, there will probably be a limited body of research on the relationships between some of the outcomes shown in Table 5.4 (e.g., the ease of creating a paper trail to justify decisions) and selection tests or performance dimensions. One solution is to use well-established conventions to describe these correlations. For example, in the behavioral and social sciences, relationships that are described as small, medium, and large commonly translate into correlations of 0.10, 0.30, and 0.50, respectively (Murphy & Myors, 2003). Thus, if I thought there was a strong link between using paper-and-pencil tests and ease in creating a paper trail, this would translate into estimated correlations between this outcome and each of the tests in the proposed selection battery of 0.50. If I thought that ease in making decisions about applicants and ease in creating a paper trail were essentially interchangeable, I might represent the correlation between these two variables as very high, say $r = 0.85$. It would not be wise to use a perfect correlation of $r = 1.00$, even if you think outcomes are essentially interchangeable because there is error and uncertainty in any outcome, so perfect correlations probably overestimate true relationships.

Once the values and the intercorrelations among tests and outcomes are estimated, it is easy to combine them to form an overall estimate of the extent to which a particular test battery is related to the set of outcomes that are valued by the organization. This is a validity coefficient in the same sense as the traditional correlation between tests and performance measures, but when the criterion set is expanded to go beyond performance measures, it now assesses the extent to which the proposed selection system is likely to lead to end states that are valued by the organization.

Interpreting Multivariate Validities

The formal interpretation of a multivariate validity coefficient is that it is the correlation between a weighted set of predictors and a weighted set of criteria. On the predictor side, weights reflect the organization's policy for using test information. On the criterion side, the weights reflect the relative value or importance of each of the outcomes in the criterion set.

By itself, the multivariate validity coefficient is valuable and useful, but its greatest value is probably when it is used as a basis for comparing among various options available to the organization. For example, the equations presented here allow the organization to answer two questions that are likely to be of interest: How are the outcomes of testing affected if different choices are made about the relative emphasis given to different tests? Given the outcomes and values identified here, what is the optimal method of using tests in selection? The first question can be answered by trying out different methods of using tests to make decisions (e.g., equal weighting, giving ability more weight relative to personality). The second question can be answered by solving for the predictor weights given the weights chosen for the criterion dimensions. Similarly, this framework allows you to answer questions like, "How would things change if I thought differently about specific criterion dimensions?" This can be thought of as a type of sensitivity analysis in which you try out different sets of criterion weights to determine whether different ways of thinking about task performance, contextual performance, adverse impact, and so on would make a meaningful difference in the conclusions you draw about the validity and value of your predictors.

Putting Adverse Impact Front and Center

The greatest advantage of the methods proposed here is that they allow you, indeed force you, to think about all of the criteria that matter to an organization in defining the validity of selection tests and in deciding how to use these tests. Traditionally, personnel psychologists have worked to design valid selection systems (in which *valid* is defined solely in terms of test-performance correlations) and then have looked into ways of reducing the adverse impact that these systems often produce. Viewed in this light, adverse impact is largely an afterthought, that is, a problem to be solved, to the extent possible, once a valid selection system has been designed. The multivariate perspective requires users to think about the entire set of relevant criteria as a group and to make hard decisions about the relative importance of different criterion dimensions. By forcing users to think simultaneously about traditional criteria (e.g., performance measures) and nontraditional criteria (e.g., adverse impact), the multivariate approach gives adverse impact its due. If reducing adverse impact is truly important to an organization's decision makers, it will receive a large weight. If it is truly less important, it will receive a smaller weight. Either way, there is little chance that decision makers will make choices about personnel selection systems without first thinking long and hard about the likelihood those systems will produce adverse impact and the importance of adverse impact in their organization.

Note

1. These values are obtained by applying Equations 5.5–5.8, using weights of 1, 1, and 0 for the three criterion dimensions and weights of 0 and 1 for the two predictors.

References

Bobko, P., Roth, P. K., & Potosky, D. (1999). Derivation and implications of a meta-analytic matrix incorporating cognitive ability, alternative predictors and job performance. *Personnel Psychology, 52*, 561–590.

Borman, W. C., & Motowidlo, S. J. (1993). Expanding the criterion domain to include elements of contextual performance. In N. Schmitt & W. C. Borman (Eds.), *Personnel selection in organizations* (pp. 71–98). San Francisco: Jossey-Bass.

Brief, A. P., & Motowidlo, S. J. (1986). Prosocial organizational behaviors. *Academy of Management Review, 10*, 710–725.

Campbell, J. P. (1990). Modeling the performance prediction problem in industrial and organizational psychology. In M. D. Dunnette & L. M. Hough (Eds.), *Handbook of industrial and organizational psychology* (Vol. 1, pp. 687–732). Palo Alto, CA: Consulting Psychologists Press.

Campbell, J. P., McCloy, R. A., Oppler, S. H., & Sager, C. E. (1993). A theory of performance. In N. Schmitt and W. Borman (Eds.), *Personnel selection in organizations* (pp. 35–70). San Francisco: Jossey Bass.

Conway, J. M. (1996). Additional evidence for the task-contextual performance distinction. *Human Performance, 9*, 309–330.

Crocker, L. (Ed.). (1997). The great validity debate. *Educational Measurement: Issues and Practice, 16*(2).

De Corte, W., Lievens, F., & Sackett, P. R. (2006). Predicting adverse impact and mean criterion performance in multistage selection. *Journal of Applied Psychology, 91,* 523–537.

Edwards, J. E., and Morrison, R. F. (1994). Selecting and classifying future naval officers: The paradox of greater specialization in broader arenas. In M. Rumsey, C. Walker, & J. Harris (Eds.), *Personnel selection and classification* (pp. 69–84). Hillsdale, NJ: Sage.

Edwards, W., & Newman, J. R. (1982). *Multiattribute evaluation.* Beverly Hills, CA: Sage.

Gottfredson, L. S. (1986). Societal consequences of the g factor in employment. *Journal of Vocational Behavior, 29,* 379–410.

Gottfredson, L. S. (1988). Reconsidering fairness: A matter of social and ethical priorities. *Journal of Vocational Behavior, 33,* 293–319.

Hartigan, J. A., & Wigdor, A. K. (1989). *Fairness in employment testing: Validity generalization, minority issues, and the General Aptitude Test Battery.* Washington, DC: National Academy Press.

Hattrup, K., Rock, J., & Scalia, C. (1997). The effects of varying conceptualizations of job performance on adverse impact, minority hiring, and predicted performance. *Journal of Applied Psychology, 82,* 656–664.

Herrnstein, R. J., & Murray, C. (1994). *The bell curve: Intelligence and class structure in American life.* New York: Free Press.

Hunter, J. E. (1986). Cognitive ability, cognitive aptitudes, job knowledge, and job performance. *Journal of Vocational Behavior, 29,* 340–362.

Jensen, A. R. (1980). *Bias in mental testing.* New York: Free Press.

McIntyre, R. M., & Salas, E. (1995). Measuring and managing for team performance: Emerging principles from complex environments. In R. Guzzo and E Salas (Eds.), *Team effectiveness and decision making in organizations* (pp. 9–45). San Francisco: Jossey-Bass.

Messick, S. (1995). Validity of psychological assessment: Validation of inferences from persons' responses and performances as scientific inquiry into score meaning. *American Psychologist, 50,* 741–749.

Murphy, K. R. (1989). Dimensions of job performance. In R. Dillon & J. Pelligrino (Eds.), *Testing: Applied and theoretical perspectives* (pp. 218–247). New York: Praeger.

Murphy, K. R. (1996). Individual differences and behavior in organizations: Much more than g. In K. Murphy (Ed.), *Individual differences and behavior in organizations* (pp. 3–30). San Francisco: Jossey-Bass.

Murphy, K. (2002). Can conflicting perspectives on the role of "g" in personnel selection be resolved? *Human Performance, 15,* 173–186.

Murphy, K. R., & Cleveland, J. N. (1995). *Understanding performance appraisal: Social, organizational and goal-based perspectives.* Thousand Hills, CA: Sage.

Murphy, K., & Myors, B. (2003). *Statistical power analysis: A simple and general model for traditional and modern hypothesis tests* (2nd ed.). Mahwah, NJ: Erlbaum.

Murphy, K., & Shiarella, A. (1997). Implications of the multidimensional nature of job performance for the validity of selection tests: Multivariate frameworks for studying test validity. *Personnel Psychology, 50,* 823–854.

Neisser, U., Boodoo, G., Bouchard, T. J., Boykin, A. W., Brody, N., Ceci, S., et al. (1996). Intelligence: Knowns and unknowns. *American Psychologist, 51,* 77–101.

Nunnally, J. C. (1978). *Psychometric theory.* New York: McGraw-Hill.

Organ, D. W. (1988). *Organizational citizenship behavior: The good soldier syndrome.* Lexington, MA: Lexington Books.

Ree, M. J., & Earles, J. A. (1991). Predicting training success: Not much more than g. *Personnel Psychology, 44,* 321–332.

Ree, M. J., & Earles, J. A. (1992). Intelligence is the best predictor of job performance. *Current Directions in Psychological Science, 1,* 86–89.

Ree, M. J., Earles, J. A., & Teachout, M. S. (1994). Predicting job performance: Not much more than g. *Journal of Applied Psychology, 79,* 518–524.

Roth, P. L., Huffcutt, A. I., & Bobko, P. (2003). Ethnic group differences in measures of job performance: A new meta-analysis. *Journal of Applied Psychology, 88,* 694–706.

Sackett, P. R., & Ellingson, J. E. (1997). The effects of forming multi-predictor composites on group differences and adverse impact. *Personnel Psychology, 50,* 707–721.

Sackett, P. R., & Wilk, S. L. (1994). Within-group norming and other forms of score adjustment in preemployment testing. *American Psychologist, 49,* 929–954.

Scarr, S. (1981). *Race, social class, and individual differences in I.Q.* Hillsdale, NJ: Erlbaum.

Schmidt, F. L., & Hunter, J. E. (1981). Employment testing: Old theories and new research findings. *American Psychologist, 36,* 1128–1137.

Schmidt, F. L., & Hunter, J. E. (1999). The validity and utility of selection methods in personnel psychology: Practical and theoretical implications of 85 years of research findings. *Psychological Bulletin, 124,* 262–274.

Schmitt, N., Rogers, W., Chan, D., Sheppard, L., & Jennings, D. (1997). Adverse impact and predictive efficiency of various predictor combinations. *Journal of Applied Psychology, 82,* 719–730.

Smith, C. A., Organ, D. W., & Near, J. P. (1983). Organizational citizenship behavior: Its nature and antecedents. *Journal of Applied Psychology, 68,* 653–663.

Sturman, M., & Judge, T. (1995). *Utility analysis for multiple selection devices and multiple outcomes.* Ithaca, NY: Cornell University: Center for Advanced Human Resources Studies.

Wainer, H. (1976). Estimating coefficients in linear models: It don't make no never mind. *Psychological Bulletin, 83,* 213–217.

Waldman, D. A., & Avolio, B. J. (1991). Race effects in performance evaluations: Controlling for ability, education, and experience. *Journal of Applied Psychology, 76,* 897–901.

6

What Are the Criteria for Adverse Impact?

Keith Hattrup and Brandon G. Roberts

Introduction

Adverse impact (AI) has very often been presented as a *dilemma* (e.g., Arthur & Edwards, 2002; Campion et al., 2001; De Corte, 1999; De Corte & Lievens, 2003; Huffcut & Roth, 1998; Kehoe, 2002; Ployhart & Holts, 2008; Pyburn, Ployhart, & Kravitz, 2008; Sackett, Schmitt, Ellingson, & Kabin, 2001), a *trade-off* (e.g., Bobko, Roth, & Potosky, 1999; De Corte & Lievens, 2003; Roth & Bobko, 2000; Ryan, Ployhart, & Friedel, 1998; Sackett & Roth, 1996; Schmitt, Rogers, Chan, Sheppard, & Jennings, 1997), or a "perplexing problem" to solve (Campion et al., 2001, p. 150). For example, a study by De Corte, Lievens, and Sackett (2007) attempted to address a "selection quality-adverse impact problem" (p. 150), and a series of recent articles sought to describe a "diversity-validity dilemma" (Pyburn et al., 2008, p. 143). Indeed, according to Sackett et al. (2001), "this dilemma is well-known" (p. 303).

But, is there really a trade-off or a dilemma? If there is, what is the true nature and magnitude of this trade-off? The perspective taken in this chapter is that we just do not know with any certainty. Not only do we lack much insight about the trade-off, we also have not studied it in much depth. So, when it comes to AI versus validity, it is less a dilemma and more a question that has not been answered or perhaps a question that has not even been asked. Thus, the goal of the present chapter is to present a broad view of the constructs and issues relevant to conceptualizing the AI-validity problem.

In particular, this chapter explores and delineates the criteria that drive decision making in organizations relevant to selection quality, AI, and diversity. Trade-offs, or compromises, require consideration of competing goals, outcomes, or values. Yet, these criteria and the values that drive their importance in organizational contexts have seldom been addressed explicitly. Thus, the present chapter discusses the criteria that lie at the heart of the so-called diversity-validity dilemma, including criteria that represent individual job performance and criteria relevant to organizational diversity. A critical analysis of the diversity-validity dilemma is offered, followed by discussions of competing criteria at the individual and aggregate levels of analysis. Values that drive our notions about what is important in organizations are explored in an effort to contextualize the nature of the so-called dilemma. The chapter concludes with some suggestions for integrating what we know about hiring decisions that result in AI with what we know about managing diversity in organizations.

The Adverse Impact–Validity "Dilemma"

At the core of the so-called AI-validity dilemma is the consistent finding that some of the most valid predictors of individual job performance show large and persistent distributional differences between different racio-ethnic groups (e.g., Hough, Oswald, & Ployhart, 2001). Most troubling is evidence of mean test score differences between African Americans and whites (or "white European Americans") on tests of cognitive ability (Hough et al., 2001; Sackett et al., 2001). The difference in mean test scores is substantial, averaging roughly three fourths to one standard deviation and appears largest on those tests that best measure the general factor in intelligence, or g (Neisser et al., 1996). At the same time, tests of intelligence show very substantial, cross-situationally generalizable, robust, and linear relationships with individual job performance criteria (e.g., Murphy, Cronin, & Tam, 2003; Neisser et al., 1996; Schmidt & Hunter, 1998). Whereas top-down, within-group hiring was a common practice in the 1980s, federal law now prohibits adjustments to test scores or the use of bonus points or different standards for different demographic groups when making hiring decisions. Therefore, top-down selection typically results in considerable differences in the hiring ratios for different demographic groups, or AI, when overall selection ratios are low and cognitive ability is the basis for hiring decisions.

A wide variety of approaches has been explored for reducing AI while maintaining validity in the prediction of individual job performance (Hough et al., 2001; Ployhart & Holtz, 2008; Sackett et al., 2001). These have included the use of alternative predictor constructs or test methods, variations in the weights assigned to predictor tests, the use of test orientation or coaching, predictor banding, and elimination of biased test items (see Ployhart & Holtz, 2008; Sackett et al., 2001, for reviews). This has resulted in the overall conclusion that AI is a very stubborn problem, at least as it has been understood in our literature. An important finding relevant to the AI-validity trade-off is that the consequences for validity, or individual job performance, of hiring practices that alter AI depend fundamentally on how performance is defined (Hattrup, 2005; Hattrup & Rock, 2002; Hattrup, Rock, & Scalia, 1997; Sackett et al., 2001). Recent research has attempted to grapple with this problem, in part, by developing methods that require organizational decision makers to deal explicitly with the relative values that are placed on dimensions of individual job performance on the one hand and diversity on the other (e.g., De Corte et al., 2007).

However, there are several basic conceptual complications when characterizing AI and validity as a dilemma or trade-off. First, AI and validity are outcomes that exist at different levels of analysis (Ployhart, 2004; Ployhart & Schneider, 2002). In particular, *validity*, in the context of research on AI, refers to the prediction of individual job performance criteria. Although these individual performance criteria may be conceptualized broadly and inclusively to incorporate traditional task-related performance outcomes as well as contextual and citizenship performance, the criteria represent behaviors (e.g., Borman & Motowidlo, 1993; Campbell, Gasser, & Oswald, 1996) exhibited by individuals (Ployhart, 2004; Ployhart & Schneider, 2002). In contrast, AI, diversity, and compliance with the "four-fifths rule," are outcomes that exist at an aggregate level of analysis (Ployhart, 2004; Ployhart & Schneider, 2002; van Knippenberg & Schippers, 2007). Thus, direct comparisons between individual performance outcomes on the one hand and diversity on the other are exceedingly difficult to do given our current state of knowledge.

The difficulty of comparing diversity and individual job performance is exacerbated by our lack of understanding of how individual behavior translates into group or organizational performance (Ployhart, 2004; Ployhart & Schneider, 2002; Schneider, Smith, & Sipe, 2000). Indeed, in most of the research on techniques for ameliorating AI, it is either explicitly or implicitly assumed that individual job performance translates directly into organizational-level performance (e.g., De Corte et al., 2007). For example, a number of studies have explored the effects of various methods for using predictors to make hiring decisions on both job performance outcomes and AI without explicitly considering whether or how aggregate individual job performance affects outcomes at the organizational level of analysis (e.g., De Corte, 1999; De Corte et al., 2007; Hattrup & Rock, 2002; Hattrup et al., 1997; Hunter, Schmidt, & Rauschenberger, 1977; Ledvinka, Markos, & Ladd, 1982; Ones, Viswesvaran, & Schmidt, 1993; Sackett & Roth, 1996; Schmitt et al., 1997). Ployhart and Schneider (2002; Ployhart, 2004) attempted to explicate some of the linkages among these outcomes at different levels of analysis; however, as they noted, much is still to be learned. Indeed, our knowledge of the linkages between individual job performance and organizational effectiveness is nascent at best. Therefore, it is virtually impossible to ascertain, given our current state of knowledge, the true magnitude and nature of the trade-off between validity and diversity.

A second complication relevant to the validity-diversity dilemma is that in competitive hiring situations that involve low selection ratios on the individual predictors that have occupied the most attention in our literature, the individuals who are hired are likely to have similar knowledge, skill, ability, and other characterstics (KSAOs) (cf. Ostroff, 2002). Attraction, selection, and attrition (ASA) processes (Schneider, 1987) lead to an increase in homogeneity within the organization on deep-level characteristics, such as values, attitudes, beliefs, and even life experiences. In other words, traditional standardized hiring practices, even those that are designed to increase demographic diversity, combine with ASA processes to decrease diversity on deep-level characteristics. Yet, as described in more detail in this chapter, it is this deep-level diversity, and not necessarily demographic diversity, that is assumed to contribute to better decision making and performance in organizations (e.g., Lawrence, 1997; Lorbiecki & Jack, 2000; Mannix & Neale, 2005; van Knippenberg, De Dreu, & Homan, 2004; van Knippenberg & Schippers, 2007). Therefore, the meaning of diversity and its consequences for organizational performance have not been fully explicated in research that has examined the trade-offs between individual job performance and AI.

Furthermore, most of the research on AI takes a very narrow view of diversity, focusing on hiring outcomes for a few specific racioethnic groups, age, and biological gender (e.g., Hough et al., 2001). The diversity literature, by contrast, casts diversity in very broad terms, focusing in an inclusive sense on all kinds of differences and similarities among people at work and on myriad issues in the understanding and management of diversity in organizational contexts (e.g., Harrison & Klein, 2007; Mannix & Neale, 2005; van Knippenberg & Schippers, 2007). Little has been written about the ways in which hiring practices connect with diversity management in organizations (Ostroff, 2002). Indeed, as Ostroff noted, "It is sets of mutually reinforcing practices that result in higher performance" (p. 151). Or, as Davis (1995) noted, "Everything relates to everything else in organizations" (p. 112). Although increasing diversity is often touted as a mechanism for increasing organizational performance (e.g., Ployhart & Schneider, 2002), these connections have not been fully explicated in the literature on AI. If anything, diversity has mixed effects on group and organizational performance, as the evidence has shown (e.g., Mannix & Neale, 2005; van Knippenberg & Schippers, 2007), meaning that the effects of diversity on organization performance depend on various moderators. As discussed in more detail in this chapter, one of the most powerful moderators of the effects of diversity is the organizational context, including the set of policies, practices, and climate perceptions that contribute to improving interpersonal interactions among diverse individuals at work (Lorbiecki & Jack, 2000; Mannix & Neale, 2005; van Knippenberg & Schippers, 2007; van Knippenberg, van Ginkel, Homan, & Kooij-de Bode, 2005). Therefore, whether there is a large, small, or nonexistent trade-off between diversity and validity depends on whether diversity is effectively managed in an organization.

Finally, trade-offs or compromises, by their nature, require careful consideration of competing values. In other words, deciding how to trade off one outcome for another requires deciding which outcome is more valued. Indeed, in recent research, attempts have been made to clarify how organizational decision makers can consider these value trade-offs explicitly when deciding how to increase diversity and individual job performance simultaneously (De Corte et al., 2007). Of course, the meaning of individual and aggregate job performance itself is also, by its nature, dependent on values (Hattrup, 2005). What is rewarded or punished at work, who gets hired and promoted, and how an organization defines itself depend fundamentally on decisions about what is important and what outcomes matter the most (Hattrup, 2005). Of course, values, by their nature, are social and cultural constructions (e.g., Hofstede, 1980), meaning that what constitutes effectiveness at the individual and organizational levels of analysis is at least in part social constructions (Hattrup, 2005). As Parekh (1992) noted, "What constitutes merit is a social decision and a matter of social policy" (p. 276). At the extreme, some might assert that what is valued in terms of individual merit or performance are those qualities that maintain the status quo by rewarding those already in power (Parekh, 1992). Whether the values that drive organizational decision are fair minded, inclusive, and supportive of the organization's "bottom line," or whether they are defined narrowly or implicitly to maintain the status quo and to support a "tyranny of the majority," they lie at the heart of organizational decision making. Therefore, no determination of the nature and magnitude of a validity-diversity trade-off can be made unless the origin and validity of the values that define the trade-off are considered.

Hence, a full understanding of the AI-validity dilemma requires consideration of the dimensions of individual job performance that are valued and the connection between valued outcomes at the organizational level, including diversity. In the following sections, individual job performance criteria are outlined, followed by a discussion of the role of values in determining their importance in any particular organization. The relationships between individual performance and organizational performance are then explored, as are the connections between aggregate-level outcomes such as diversity and organizational performance.

Individual Job Performance Criteria

As noted, job performance represents one side of the diversity-validity trade-off or dilemma. And, as noted, whether hiring practices that increase diversity require a large or a small trade-off in individual job performance depends on how performance is defined and valued (Hattrup & Rock, 2002; Sackett et al., 2001). Fundamental to this conclusion is the fact that job performance is multidimensional, meaning that there are a variety of ways in which an individual's behavior at work may be valued and rewarded or discouraged or unappreciated (Borman & Motowidlo, 1993; Campbell et al., 1996; Hattrup & Jackson, 1996; Hattrup et al., 1997). And, just as fundamentally, different dimensions or classes of behavior are predicted by different trait and situational constructs (e.g., Hattrup & Jackson, 1996; Hattrup et al., 1997; Murphy & Shiarella, 1997; Wittmann, 1988). Thus, validity in the prediction of individual job performance is maximized through multivariate symmetry (Wittmann, 1988) by which predictors are identified that best match criterion dimensions in terms of specificity/ generality and predictive efficiency (Hattrup, 2005; Murphy & Shiarella, 1997). AI varies as a function of the way performance is defined because not all trait predictors of valued job performance dimensions demonstrate the same mean differences across demographic groups. In particular, because many noncognitive predictors show small-to-nonexistent mean differences between racioethnic groups (Hough et al., 2001), valuing criterion dimensions that are best predicted by noncognitive measures has the effect of increasing racioethnic diversity in the organization (Hattrup et al., 1997). It also follows that hiring practices that increase diversity by weighing noncognitive predictors more than cognitively loaded predictors result in variations in the magnitude of the trade-offs that need to be made in terms of aggregated individual job performance (Hattrup & Rock, 2002). Thus, the role of individual performance criteria in the context of AI, and the validity-diversity trade-off, requires careful consideration.

A number of taxonomic models of the dimensions underlying individual job performance variability have appeared in the literature. Models have been developed to summarize the performance of entry-level service workers (Hunt, 1996), managers (Borman & Brush, 1993; Conway, 1999), and military occupations (Campbell, McHenry, & Wise, 1990). Campbell and colleagues (Campbell, McCloy, Oppler, & Sager, 1993; Campbell et al., 1996) developed a taxonomy consisting of eight performance dimensions to account for the latent structure of individual performance in all jobs. Not all of the dimensions are relevant to all jobs, however. Moreover, some authors have identified broader dimensions that have greater bandwidth (e.g., Borman & Motowidlo, 1993), whereas others have argued for narrower performance dimensions that have higher fidelity (e.g., Tett,

Guterman, Bleier, & Murphy, 2000), which, following multivariate symmetry, has direct consequences for the breadth or narrowness of the predictors to use in making hiring decisions. The consequences of defining individual job performance broadly or narrowly for AI and diversity have not been investigated; however, it is likely that the explication of specific job performance dimensions will lead to the identification and valuing of dimensions that result in increases in organizational diversity. Presently, much of the attention in the literature has focused on task versus contextual performance and a few other unique dimensions.

Task Versus Contextual Performance

Borman and Motowidlo (1993; Motowidlo, Borman, & Schmidt, 1997) suggested that at the most general level of analysis, job performance can be summarized parsimoniously with two broad factors that are relevant to all jobs, namely, task performance and contextual performance. *Task performance* represents behaviors that contribute either to transforming raw materials into goods and services or to maintaining the organization's technical core. *Contextual performance*, in contrast, includes behaviors that do not necessarily support the organization's technical core as much as they support the organization's climate and culture. Although contextual performance may be a prescribed part of many jobs, it includes helping, prosocial, and citizenship behaviors that are usually more affective in tone. Borman and Motowidlo (1993) listed five categories of contextual performance behaviors: (a) volunteering for extra work, (b) persisting with enthusiasm, (c) helping and cooperating with others, (d) following rules and procedures even when they are inconvenient, and (e) endorsing, supporting, or defending the organizational objectives.

Both task and contextual performance are important in organizations (Motowidlo & Schmit, 1999; Murphy & Shiarella, 1997). Supervisory ratings of overall job performance are influenced by behaviors falling in each category (Borman, White, & Dorsey, 1995; Motowidlo & Van Scotter, 1994; Van Scotter & Motowidlo, 1996), and both dimensions have been related to indices of organizational effectiveness (Motowidlo & Schmit, 1999; Podsakoff & MacKenzie, 1997). Because task performance is strongly correlated with cognitively loaded predictor measures, whereas contextual performance is better predicted by noncognitive measures, such as personality or temperament, AI is reduced and the validity trade-off is minimized as the relative value of contextual performance in the organization increases (De Corte, 1999; De Corte et al., 2007; Hattrup et al., 1997). The same could probably be said about a handful of additional job performance dimensions that have recently been identified, including counterproductive behavior, adaptability, and effectiveness in multicultural environments.

Counterproductive Behavior

Whereas task and contextual performance represent classes of behavior that are positive and desirable, a variety of behaviors exist that represent negative or dysfunctional organizational behaviors (Motowidlo, 2003), including antisocial behavior (Robinson & O'Leary-Kelly, 1998), incivility (Andersson & Pearson, 1999), withholding effort (Kidwell & Bennett, 1993), deviant workplace behavior (Robinson & Bennett, 1995), and counterproductive behavior (Sackett, 2002). Counterproductive behavior is the higher-order construct that subsumes the other negative performance dimensions and broadly represents "any intentional behavior on the part of the organizational member viewed by the organization as contrary to its legitimate interest" (Sackett, 2002, p. 5). These behaviors include theft, destruction of property, misuse of information, misuse of time and resources, unsafe behavior, poor attendance, poor-quality work, alcohol or drug use, and inappropriate verbal or physical acts. Although counterproductive behavior bears a close conceptual resemblance to low levels of contextual performance (Motowidlo, 2003) and demonstrates moderately negative correlations with contextual performance (Sackett, 2002), it appears conceptually distinct in important ways. As Motowidlo (2003) noted, it represents low levels of both task and contextual performance, and as Sackett (2002) argued, high levels of counterproductive behavior are different from low levels of contextual performance, as illustrated by the example of a worker who performs tasks effectively and seems to contribute to the organizational context but secretly embezzles from the organization.

In a policy-capturing study, Rotundo and Sackett (2002) observed that counterproductive behavior was just as important to supervisor's ratings of job performance as was task and contextual performance. Research has linked counterproductive behavior to a variety of noncognitive predictors of job performance (Martinko, Gundlach, & Douglas, 2002), including locus of control (Storms & Spector, 1987), core self-evaluations (Martinko et al., 2002), integrity (Martinko et al., 2002), and negative affectivity (Martinko et al., 2002). Yet, its role in context of the diversity-validity trade-off has not been explored. Given that counterproductive behaviors are linked with noncognitive predictors more than they are to cognitive constructs, its value within the context of individual job performance is a potential determinant of AI. As with contextual performance, the higher the value an organization places on counterproductive behavior, the higher the weight given to noncognitive predictors of counterproductive behavior and the lower the AI for some groups. Likewise, hiring strategies that increase diversity for certain groups by relying on noncognitive predictor constructs lead to smaller individual performance trade-offs when counterproductive behaviors are valued more.

Adaptive Performance

It has become widely recognized that rapid changes in technology (Thach & Woodman, 1994), organizational structures (Ilgen, 1999; Kinicki & Latack, 1990), demographic and cultural diversity (Jackson, 1992; Triandis, Kurowski, & Gelfand, 1994), and international business and commerce (Black, Mendenhall, & Oddou, 1991) have placed new demands on workers to be increasingly tolerant, flexible, and adaptable (e.g., Ilgen & Pulakos, 1999; London & Mone, 1999; Mol, Born, & van der Molen, 2005; Murphy & Jackson, 1999; Pulakos et al., 2002). Indeed, adaptability is an important construct that exists at multiple levels of analysis, including the individual, group, and organization levels (Pulakos et al., 2002). Pulakos and colleagues (Pulakos, Arad, Donovan, & Plamondon, 2000; Pulakos et al., 2002) have sought to identify and empirically evaluate dimensions on adaptable behavior at the individual level of analysis and in the process have identified eight subdimensions: creative problem solving, dealing with uncertain or unpredictable work situations, learning new things, demonstrating interpersonal adaptability, demonstrating cultural adaptability, demonstrating physically oriented adaptability, handling work stress, and handling crises or emergency situations. Although little empirical evidence has been reported that evaluates the relationships between adaptability and task and contextual performance (Pulakos et al., 2002), adaptable behaviors would appear to cut across both dimensions. According to Pulakos et al. (2002), adaptability can be separated empirically from task and contextual performance and has unique predictors (Hesketh, Allworth, & Considine, 1996).

Pulakos et al. (2002) observed a number of significant relationships between adaptable behaviors at work and stable individual difference constructs. In particular, cognitive ability, achievement motivation, and openness to experience demonstrated significant incremental associations with a composite measure of adaptable performance, as did several measures of a worker's prior experience with learning new things and being interpersonally adaptable. Thus, like counterproductive behavior at work, adaptability may represent an additional performance dimension that is at roughly the same level of specificity/generality as task and contextual performance yet is predicted by somewhat unique predictor measures. Although cognitive ability appears to play an important role in predicting adaptability, adaptability also appears related to noncognitive constructs, such as openness, achievement motivation, and previous relevant experience. Thus, to the degree adaptability is valued as a dimension of individual job performance and predictors are weighed accordingly when making hiring decisions, AI for some groups may be reduced. Clearly, there is a need for additional research that examines when and why adaptability at work is valued and how it fits in the context of multivariate job performance prediction.

Performance in Diverse Multicultural Contexts: Expatriate Performance

As noted, organizations are becoming increasingly diverse as a result of changes in population demography and as a result of the values that organizations often place on increasing and managing their workforce diversity (Mannix & Neale, 2005). Moreover, rapid globalization has created additional demands and opportunities for employees who engage in work activities abroad and for those whose work involves staying in their local setting but requires interacting with individuals from other nations and cultures. Behaviors relevant to individual performance in multicultural contexts have clearly increased in their relevance and importance in most modern firms. This has been well recognized in the literature on the performance of expatriate employees (Mol et al., 2005), and in this context, a number of additional specific performance dimensions have been identified (Mol et al., 2005; Shaffer, Harrison, Gregersen, Black, & Ferzandi, 2006; Vulpe, Kealey, Protheroe, & MacDonald, 2001).

Much of the focus in the expatriate performance literature has been on adaptability (Mol et al., 2005), or adjustment, including cultural adjustment, interpersonal adjustment, and work adjustment (Shaffer et al., 2006). Shaffer et al. (2006) observed considerable independence of measures of adjustment relative to task and contextual performance and withdrawal cognitions, which they argued are all relevant to effective individual performance of expatriate workers. Mol et al. (2005), in contrast, argued for a broader and more inclusive set of expatriate performance dimensions and in particular suggested that Vulpe et al.'s (2001) *Profile of the Interculturally Effective Person* may serve as a useful model for understanding the dimensions of performance that are important for working effectively in a multicultural context. These dimensions include adaptability, an attitude of modesty and respect, an understanding of the concept of culture, knowledge of the host country and culture, relationship building, self-knowledge, intercultural communication, organizational skills, and personal and professional commitment.

Thus, given the increasingly international and multicultural nature of work in modern firms, performance dimensions like those explicated in Vulpe et al.'s (2001) *Profile of the Interculturally Effective Person* would seem to have increased relevance and importance. Moreover, to the degree that diversity is valued as an outcome in organizations, it would seem that performance management, including the definition of what it means to be an effective performer, must include individual behaviors that are consistent with effectiveness in multicultural contexts. Hiring decisions would also reflect these values, and in this context, Shaffer et al. (2006) demonstrated significant unique empirical associations between various aspects of expatriate performance and individual differences in noncognitive constructs, such as emotional stability, extraversion, agreeableness, and openness to experience. Conscientiousness was not consistently correlated with expatriate performance, but ethnocentrism and interpersonal orientation were important correlates of effectiveness in expatriate assignments (Shaffer et al., 2006). Therefore, in organizations that value diversity and multicultural inclusiveness, behaviors that support these goals take on added importance. Because some of the most important predictors of these performance constructs are noncognitive in nature, valuing diversity has the effect of increasing diversity, in this case not because the organization necessarily hires on the basis of group membership (which is prohibited by federal law) but because the organization hires on the basis of constructs that are distributed in similar ways across different demographic groups. Similarly, hiring practices that decrease AI result in smaller performance trade-offs at the individual level of analysis when behaviors that support effectiveness in multicultural and diverse contexts are valued.

Valuing Individual Job Performance Criteria

As noted, variations in the values that an organization attaches to various dimensions of job performance influence the weights assigned to job performance predictors, which influences AI in competitive hiring contexts (De Corte, 1999; De Corte et al., 2007; Hattrup et al., 1997). Likewise, whether an organization needs to make a large or a small trade-off between the values of diversity and low AI on the one hand and individual job performance on the other depends on which job performance dimensions are most valued in the organization (Hattrup & Rock, 2002). As the value of job performance dimensions that are predicted by noncognitive measures increases, diversity is also increased, at least for some demographic groups. Thus, a critical need for practical and scientific knowledge are the sources and dynamics that lead to the values that underlie the importance placed on various dimensions of behavior at work. Indeed, these values form the basis of a definition of what it means for an individual to be effective or meritorious and as such represent social and cultural constructions (Hattrup, 2005; Parekh, 1992). Unfortunately, we know very little about the factors that influence the values placed on different dimensions of performance in modern firms, and this severely constrains our ability to evaluate in any meaningful way the true nature and magnitude of the validity-diversity dilemma.

The Origins of Values About Individual Work Behavior

Of course, research demonstrates that organizational members often value different behaviors or value the same behaviors differently. For example, empirical research has demonstrated that supervisors differ in the importance that they place on task, contextual, and counterproductive behaviors when rating an incumbent's overall job performance (e.g., Johnson, 2001; Rotundo & Sackett, 2002). One implication is that decisions about human resources management, including hiring decisions, performance evaluations, and promotions or other rewards, depend on the relative values that decision makers have for different kinds of behaviors at work. Thus, a key element of human resource policy is the explication of a set of core values and goals of the organization and the individual behaviors that contribute to the accomplishment of those goals (Schuler, 1992; Schuler & Jackson, 1987). Pragmatically, values about the relative importance of job behaviors find their clearest expression in the context of a thorough job and organization analysis (e.g., Harvey, 1991). Indeed, well-conducted job analyses almost always include an explication of the importance of specific job-relevant behaviors or KSAOs, and they form the basis of hiring, promotion, evaluation, and compensation programs.

Obviously, the collection of data within an organization about the importance of job tasks, behaviors, and KSAOs involves perceptual and subjective processes (Morgeson & Campion, 1997). As a consequence, descriptions of the importance or value of different behaviors are likely to vary among individuals, groups, and organizations as has been consistently demonstrated in empirical research (Ferris, Fedor, Rowland, & Porac, 1985; Landy & Vasey, 1991; Mullins & Kimbrough, 1988; Schmitt & Cohen, 1989). Although variability in perceptions of the importance of job dimensions has important implications throughout the organization, most of the research on these value differences has been atheoretical and piecemeal in nature (Harvey, 1991; Schmitt & Chan, 1998). Although numerous studies have observed a small number of weak effects associated with rater experience, sex, race, or other variables, there is little understanding of the underlying theoretical processes that explain these differences. Morgeson and Campion (1997) offered a conceptual model that included 16 possible social and cognitive sources of variance in job importance ratings and a number of method and source variables that might influence ratings of job tasks and behaviors.

Another theoretical model identified a series of variables at the individual, group, organization, and cultural levels of analysis that might influence the relative values that organization members place on task and contextual performance (Hattrup, 2005). At the individual level, differences in age, experience, gender, national origin, racioethnicity, job attitudes, reinforcement histories, and job roles were hypothesized to lead to differences in the perceived importance of behaviors related to task and contextual performance. For example, given differences in socialization experiences and normative expectations (Cross & Madson, 1997), women may place greater value than men on affiliative and interpersonal behaviors that contribute to contextual performance, whereas men may display greater value for task performance. Similarly, it has been suggested that African Americans, Asian Americans, and Hispanic Americans develop values that are more collectivist than white Americans, who are higher in individualism (Allen, Dawson, & Brown, 1989; Marin & Triandis, 1985). This might translate into differences in the way members of these groups value task and contextual performance because of differences in the way the two dimensions relate to individualistic and collectivistic goals, respectively. Likewise, an individual's nation of origin would be predicted to have similar effects due to the correlation between national boundaries and individualism/collectivism (Hofstede, 1980). Age and experience might explain variation in perceptions of the importance of task and contextual performance through their effects on learning and job role changes (e.g., Befort & Hattrup, 2003).

At the group and organization levels of analysis, norms, social influence processes, and climate perceptions should operate to influence the perceived value of different dimensions of individual behavior at work. Organizational strategies and structures might also influence the values placed on dimensions of individual work behavior. For example, Motowidlo and Schmit (1999) suggested that an increased reliance on teams in modern firms increases the need for effective contextual performance among team members and managers. Moreover, as individual worker autonomy increases as a result of larger spans of control, the need for effective contextual performance also increases due to an increased need for cooperation and creative problem solving (Motowidlo & Schmit, 1999; Murphy & Jackson, 1999). Of course, job and industry differences are also potentially relevant sources of value differences in that contextual performance may be more or less required in jobs that differ in their focus on individual work, teamwork, and customer service.

Thus, although a number of potential sources of variability in the values placed on different dimensions of individual behavior have been identified, empirical research on the sources and dynamics leading to values about the importance of different work behaviors remains scant. If effective human resources management requires identifying and communicating a coherent set of values and expectations, research is clearly needed that tackles the questions of how values develop, how they become shared, and how they are communicated within organizations. If not made explicit and used formally to guide organizational decision making, they will influence decisions in unknown and idiosyncratic ways. For example, Norton, Sommers, Vandello, and Darley (2006) observed that decision makers appeared to vary the importance they placed on different dimensions of performance in an effort to formulate academic admissions decisions that allowed them to select the specific kinds of persons they wanted to admit (see also Posthuma, Morgeson, & Campion, 2002). And, as noted, some have suggested that the values that guide organizational and social policy are those that maintain the status quo and reward those in power (Parekh, 1992). From a practical point of view, what is needed is a serious, inclusive, and thorough discussion of the value of different kinds of behavior within the organization prior to the formulation of human resource policy. Without knowing the origins and validity of the values that guide policies and practices in organizations, it is impossible to ascertain the meaning and magnitude of the validity-AI trade-off. Some clarity about these processes is needed, both for research and for practice.

Organizational Criteria

Although individual job performance is presumed to occupy one side of the AI-selection quality trade-off, its comparison with AI, or diversity, is inherently complicated due to the fact that the constructs exist at different levels of analysis (Ostroff, 2002; Ployhart, 2004; Ployhart & Schneider, 2002). Whereas individual job performance represents an individual-level construct, AI and diversity are characteristics of groups or organizations (Harrison & Klein, 2007; van Knippenberg & Schippers, 2007). Thus, as Ployhart noted, "The 'diversity vs. prediction' problem cannot be answered at the individual level" of analysis (p. 155). Any meaningful comparisons between performance or "selection quality" or "validity" on the one hand and diversity on the other would require a clear understanding and valid operationalization of the constructs at comparable levels of analysis and in a comparable metrics. Given our current state of knowledge, this would seem particularly challenging.

One key problem in developing any certainty about the diversity-performance comparison is that we lack much understanding of the cross-level relationships among hiring practices, individual job performance, unit performance, and organizational-level effectiveness (Ostroff, 2002; Ployhart, 2004; Ployhart & Schneider, 2002; Schneider et al., 2000). The vast majority of our knowledge is of relationships between individual predictors and individual job performance (Schmidt & Hunter, 1998) or between firm-level human resources practices and firm performance (Huselid, 1995; Huselid, Jackson, & Schuler, 1997; Lepak & Snell, 2002; Terpstra & Rozell, 1993). We simply lack much understanding of how hiring decisions influence organizational-level outcomes through their mediating effects on individual and unit-level constructs. Indeed, the constructs that predict performance at the individual level of analysis may not be the same, or may not predict performance outcomes the same way, at the group and organization levels of analysis (Ostroff, 2002; Ployhart, 2004; Ployhart & Schneider, 2002; Schneider et al., 2000). Moreover, effectiveness at the group or organization levels of analysis may depend more on configurations of variation on individual attributes than on overall mean levels of specific individual difference constructs, such as cognitive ability or personality (Ostroff, 2002). As Ployhart (2004) and Ployhart and Schneider (2002) argued, what is needed is research that examines these cross-level and multilevel effects.

Ployhart (2004) in particular drew on theoretical developments in research on cross-level and multilevel phenomena (Kozlowski & Klein, 2000) in identifying a set of features to consider when understanding relationships that cross levels of analysis in the context of personnel selection. First, the concept of *bond strength* implies that relationships between constructs become weaker as the levels of analysis at which the constructs are measured become more distant (Kozlowski & Klein, 2000). For example, relationships between predictor constructs measured at the individual level of analysis and individual-level behavior will be stronger than relationships between individual-level predictors and organizational-level outcomes (Ployhart, 2004). Second, levels of analysis differ in *temporal scale* in that phenomena and cause-effect relationships unfold at different rates in different levels. Changes occur more rapidly at the individual level of analysis in organizations than they occur at the subunit or organization levels (Simon, 1973). Finally, the concept of *near decomposability* is used to describe the difficulty of isolating phenomena within a given level due to influences operating at other levels of analysis (Kozlowski & Klein, 2000; Ployhart, 2004). Thus, any meaningful understanding of the selection quality-AI trade-off requires a thorough understanding of the cross-level relationships that mediate between individual-level hiring outcomes and aggregate subunit or organizational performance. Of course, in this context, diversity and aggregate unit or organizational performance become outcomes that are compared against a variety of other organizational-level criteria that might be valued by various stakeholders.

This presents a second major challenge in ascertaining the magnitude of the trade-off between diversity and performance in that we lack much understanding of the role of these constructs within the context of overall organizational performance, including the relative value, or importance, of these outcomes compared to other measures of organizational effectiveness (Ployhart, 2004). Indeed, much like performance at the individual level of analysis, organizational performance is also a multidimensional construct consisting of a variety of dimensions that may or may not show much correlation (Campbell, 1977; Meyer & Gupta, 1994; Rogers & Wright,

1998). Little consensus has emerged about the dimensions of organizational performance that matter the most, and in many cases, alternative organizational performance outcomes are measured in different metrics, making their comparisons even more complicated (Meyer & Gupta, 1994; Rogers & Wright, 1998). Dyer and Reeves (1995), for example, identified four major categories of organizational-level performance measures, including outcomes relevant to human resources (turnover, absenteeism, job satisfaction); organizational outcomes (productivity, quality, customer service); financial outcomes (return on assets, profitability); and market outcomes (stock price, returns, shareholder value). As Meyer and Gupta (1994) argued, organizational performance measures have a tendency to proliferate, and a very wide assortment of measures has been developed. What is important to consider, they argued, is the way in which organizational outcomes are identified and become valued. In this context, Rogers and Wright (1998) suggested that specific organizational outcomes are pursued to satisfy a variety of stakeholders that fall roughly into four categories, or markets, namely, the financial market, the labor market, the consumer (product) market, and the political (social) market. The meaning and assessment of organizational performance require comparing organizational outcome measures with goals or purposes, where goals and purposes are driven by the values of the various stakeholders. Thus, much like the explication and valuing of dimensions of individual job performance, organizational performance is a social and cultural construction that reflects the values of the stakeholders who define it (Lewin & Minton, 1986; Rogers & Wright, 1998).

Organizational diversity (or low levels of AI, specifically), therefore, represents one of a variety of organizational-level outcomes that might be valued by stakeholders, along with a host of other outcomes, such as productivity, quality, shareholder value, growth, customer satisfaction, profitability, and corporate image. Indeed, there is little doubt that diversity is a highly valued outcome in many organizations. This is partly because it is often assumed to enhance individual, subunit, and organizational performance (e.g., Ostroff, 2002; Ployhart & Schneider, 2002). Diversity is presumed to contribute to better problem solving, enhanced marketing success, higher creativity and innovation, and improved flexibility (Cox & Blake, 1991; Robinson & Dechant, 1997). To some, effective diversity management is seen as "a product of enlightened corporate self-interest" (Yakura, 1996, p. 25). Thus, diversity is often highly valued not only for its own sake, but also because it is thought to lead to tangible improvements in other dimensions of organizational performance, such as those representing financial or market-based interests. However, the empirical evidence hardly supports the optimistic view that diversity is good for teams or organizations (Mannix & Neale, 2005). Indeed, in a more general sense, comparisons between diversity and organizational performance as potentially valued outcomes require a good theoretical understanding of the constructs and an awareness of their interdependencies.

What Is Diversity?

Although research in the area of AI casts diversity and AI in narrow terms, focusing primarily on only a handful of specific racioethnic groups, recent research on team diversity and diversity management has conceptualized the construct of diversity broadly, focusing on a wide range of differences among people in demographic characteristics, functional roles, backgrounds, personalities, values, and so on (Harrison & Klein, 2007; Jackson, May, & Whitney, 1995; Mannix & Neale, 2005; van Knippenberg & Schippers, 2007). A number of taxonomic models have been developed to organize the types of differences among employees that are thought to be important (Harrison & Klein, 2007; Mannix & Neale, 2005; van Knippenberg & Schippers, 2007). One well-known approach, for example, differentiates between surface-level and deep-level diversity (Harrison, Price, & Bell, 1998). Whereas social category differences, such as differences in racioethnicity, age, gender, or sexual orientation, represent surface-level characteristics, their effects on individual and group outcomes are presumed to operate through differences in deep-level characteristics, such as attitudes, values, beliefs, or behavior (Harrison et al., 1998; Lawrence, 1997). Empirical research has largely failed to support the hypothesized relationships between characteristics representing surface- and deep-level diversity, however (Mannix & Neale, 2005; van Knippenberg & Schippers, 2007). Still another approach distinguishes between diversity that is job related, such as differences in education or functional area, versus non-job-related diversity, such as differences in demographic characteristics, values, attitudes, and personality (Jehn, Northcraft, & Neale, 1999; Pelled, Eisenhardt, & Xin, 1999).

In more recent work, *diversity* has been defined very broadly as "any attribute people use to tell themselves that another person is different" (Mannix & Neale, 2005, p. 39; Williams & O'Reilly, 1998, p. 81). A broad definition of diversity does not imply that all identifiable differences have the same effects as social groups and their members vary in a number of important ways in their histories and experiences (e.g., Clair, Beatty, & MacLean, 2005; Lorbiecki & Jack, 2000), legal rights (e.g., Dietch, Butz, & Brief, 2003; Ragins, 2004), and needs and goals. An inclusive perspective on diversity also recognizes that individuals fall into multiple social categories simultaneously and differ along a variety of dimensions, which vary in their relevance, salience, and significance across situations (Harrison & Klein, 2007;

Lorbiecki & Jack, 2000). Ultimately, context is everything when it comes to creating and defining "differences" among people (Mannix & Neale, 2005). Whether a person is a "minority" or majority group member, unique or normative, salient or unnoticed, depends on the other people in the context (e.g., Mannix & Neale, 2005; Stroessner, 1996). Table 6.1 presents a summary of kinds of diversity that have been discussed in the literature and shows the wide variety of ways in which diversity has been approached in the scientific literature. Of particular significance in the present context is the breadth and inclusiveness with which diversity has been cast in most modern research on work group performance, as compared to the narrow definition of diversity considered in research on hiring practices and AI.

Does Diversity Contribute to Group or Organizational Performance?

Although diversity is often presumed to contribute to better organizational performance through its effects on enhanced creativity, better problem solving, improved marketing, and higher customer satisfaction, little empirical evidence exists to support these optimistic predictions. Two competing theoretical perspectives have been used to explain and guide the majority of empirical research on the effects of work group diversity, with each predicting very different outcomes resulting from work group diversity (Williams & O'Reilly, 1998). The *social categorization/ similarity-attraction* perspective predicts negative effects of diversity on group functioning due to the formation of ingroup/outgroup biases that cut along salient dimensions of group diversity (Jackson, 1992; Tajfel & Turner, 1986; van Knippenberg & Schippers, 2007; Williams & O'Reilly, 1998). Consistent with this view are studies reporting higher cohesiveness, lower turnover, and higher performance in groups that are more homogeneous (e.g., Murnighan & Conlon, 1991; O'Reilly, Caldwell, & Barnett, 1989; Wagner, Pfeffer, & O'Reilly, 1984). Similarly, Tsui, Egan, and O'Reilly (1992) reported lower psychological attachment, higher turnover intentions, and higher absenteeism among individuals who differed more from their work groups compared to individuals who had a greater resemblance with their work groups in terms of demographic characteristics.

By contrast, the *information/decision-making* perspective proposes that diversity leads to improved performance because of the greater elaboration of task-relevant information that takes place in diverse groups (Mannix & Neale, 2005; van Knippenberg et al., 2004; van Kippenberg & Schippers, 2007; Williams & O'Reilly, 1998). A central component of this theory is the notion that as diversity increases in a group, the variety and quality of

TABLE 6.1

Categories and Types of Differences of Interest in Diversity Research

Social category variables
Race
Ethnicity
Gender
Age
Religion
Social class
National origin
Sexual orientation
Transgender identity
Physical abilities
Knowledge, skills, and abilities
Education
Functional knowledge
Information or expertise
Training
Experience
Abilities
Personality
Cognitive style
Affective disposition
Motivational factors
Values and beliefs
Cultural background
Ideological beliefs
Behaviors
Dress
Speech
Organizational or social status
Tenure and length of service
Title
Position
Pay
Differences in social network ties
Work-related ties
Friendship ties
Community ties
In-group memberships

Source: Adapted (with permission) from Mannix, E., & Neale, M. A. (2005). "What Differences Make a Difference? The Promise and Reality of Diverse Teams in Organizations," in E. Mannix and M. A. Neale, 2005, *Psychological Science in the Public Interest*, 6, p. 36. Wiley-Blackwell.

information, knowledge, and perspectives increase, leading to more thorough consideration, analysis, and elaboration of task-relevant information (van Knippenberg et al., 2004). For example, Earley and Mosakowski (2000) found that a measure of team communication mediated the effects of group diversity on performance, and Dahlin, Weingart, and Hinds (2005) reported that diversity was associated with greater information use. Moreover, higher levels of diversity are also presumed to stimulate enhanced reflection on and consideration of team functioning, or *team reflexivity* (Schippers, Den Hartog, Koopman, & Wienk, 2003). Schippers, Den Hartog, and Koopman (2007), for example, reported that team reflexivity mediated the effects of group diversity on team performance, commitment, and satisfaction. Others have suggested that the positive effects of work group diversity operate through higher levels of task conflict (Jehn et al., 1999), although meta-analytic evidence does not support a positive relationship between task conflict and team performance (De Dreu & Weingart, 2003).

Overall, the cumulative body of empirical research on the effects of diversity fails to reveal any consistently positive or consistently negative effects of diversity on group outcomes (Bowers, Pharmer, & Salas, 2000; Mannix & Neale, 2005; van Knippenberg & Schippers, 2007; Webber & Donahue, 2001). Although diversity may lead to positive group performance due to increases in the elaboration of task-relevant information and internal group functioning, social categorization and similarity-attraction may operate to create social divisions among work group members that lead to negative ingroup-outgroup biases (van Knippenberg & Schippers, 2007, p. 528). As Mannix and Neale (2005) pointed out, "Unless diverse teams are able to overcome the disruptive effects of their differences or avoid the tendency to drive out distinctiveness and move toward similarity, they will be unable to engage in effective and creative problem solving" (p. 43). Thus, research has moved to the identification of moderators of the effects of diversity on group performance and in the process has identified a number of variables that have the potential to enhance our understanding of how to best manage a diverse organization and reap the potential benefits of diversity in the workplace (Mannix & Neale, 2005; van Knippenberg et al., 2004; van Knippenberg & Schippers, 2007).

Managing Organizational Diversity: Reaping the Benefits of a Diverse Workforce

Although the particular type of diversity, the specific and salient difference between people, does not appear to moderate in any reliable way the positive and negative effects of diversity on work group performance (Bowers et al., 2000; van Knippenberg & Schippers, 2007; Webber & Donahue, 2001), a number of situational variables have been identified in theoretical models of the effects of work group diversity on group performance (Mannix & Neale, 2005; van Knippenberg et al., 2004; van Knippenberg & Schippers, 2007). These include task and organizational design variables, time, the diversity context, and work group and organization climate variables. Thorough understanding and management of these contextual variables may improve an organization's ability to benefit from a diverse workforce and thereby minimize any potential trade-offs between "selection quality" and organizational diversity.

Task and Organizational Design Variables

A number of authors have suggested that the benefits of diversity for group performance are more likely to occur when the group task requires higher levels of creativity, innovation, and information processing (van Knippenberg et al., 2004; van Knippenberg & Schippers, 2007). Bowers et al.'s (2000) meta-analysis, for example, found that diversity was positively related to group performance when task complexity was high but was negatively related to group performance for simple tasks. Similarly, Jehn et al. (1999) reported that informational diversity was more strongly related to positive group performance when tasks were novel as compared to tasks that were more routine. Presumably, diversity leads to improved group effectiveness through its mediating effects on the elaboration of task-relevant information for those tasks that especially require thorough elaboration of information (van Knippenberg et al., 2004). As van Knippenberg et al. (2004) noted, these effects presume that group members possess sufficient task-relevant ability and motivation to engage in the thorough elaboration and analysis of information that takes place within the team.

Another relevant task design variable that has been discussed is the degree of interdependence and cooperation required among group members (Mannix & Neale, 2005; van Knippenberg et al., 2004). Presumably, cooperative interdependence, and the identification and sharing of a super-ordinate group goal, stimulates group members to focus more on a common group identity and less on their individual uniquenesses (Gaertner & Dovidio, 2000; Mannix & Neale, 2005). Moreover, interdependence increases contact among group members, which leads to a decrease in the salience and usefulness of task-irrelevant differences (Pettigrew, 1998; van Knippenberg & Schippers, 2007). Schippers et al. (2003), for example, reported that diversity was positively related to group performance, reflexivity, and satisfaction when outcome interdependence was high but showed negative relationships with group outcomes when interdependence was low. Jehn et al. (1999) also showed that diversity was more positively related to group member satisfaction and commitment when task interdependence was higher, and van der Vegt and Janssen (2003) reported that diversity contributed to improved group performance only when task and outcome interdependence were high.

Yet another perspective argues that the positive effects of diversity are more likely to be realized when diversity-related criteria are incorporated in the evaluation of team and management performance (e.g., Holvino, Ferdman, & Merrill-Sands, 2004; Mannix & Neale, 2005). For example, specific criteria can be established that focus on diversity-related outcomes, such as goals for increasing inclusion of traditionally underrepresented groups (Mannix & Neale, 2005), measures of learning from and adapting to diversity (Holvino et al., 2004), and attitudes about diversity in the workplace (Gagnon & Cornelius, 2000). Thus, a variety of variables related to the design of tasks and task interdependencies might contribute to enhancing the organizational benefits of having a diverse workforce.

Time

Several authors have emphasized the importance of time and team tenure when considering the consequences of diversity on group outcomes (e.g., Harrison et al., 1998; Harrison, Price, Gavin, & Florey, 2002; Sacco & Schmitt, 2005; van Knippenberg et al., 2004; van Knippenberg & Schippers, 2007). With increased time, group members may learn to focus less on surface-level, task-irrelevant differences (Harrison et al., 1998), partly because contact with diverse others requires increased processing of individuating information that may undermine stereotypes (Pettigrew, 1998; van Knippenberg & Schippers, 2007). Consistent with this view are several studies demonstrating that the negative effects of surface-level diversity on team outcomes decreased over time (e.g., Chatman & Flynn, 2001; Harrison et al., 1998, 2002). The effects of deeper-level diversity may become increasingly negative over time, however (Harrison et al., 1998, 2002), and in other research, time failed to improve the effects of demographic diversity on team performance (Watson, Johnson, & Merritt, 1998). As van Knippenberg and Schippers (2007) noted, the evidence clearly indicates a need to consider time as an important moderator of the effects of diversity on work group performance. As they noted, the positive effects of various kinds of diversity may take various amounts of time to emerge. Of course, this underscores the importance of carefully managing a diverse workplace and not just assuming it will yield immediate benefits to the organization's bottom line (Mannix & Neale, 2005).

The Diversity Context

Diversity depends on context because the "differences" that are considered salient or relevant depend on the characteristics of the people in the situation (Mannix & Neale, 2005; Williams & O'Reilly, 1998). In diverse organizations and groups, differences among individuals are more common and therefore less salient and therefore have weaker negative effects on group outcomes (e.g., Martins, Milliken, Wiesenfeld, & Salgado, 2003). As Earley and Mosakowski (2000) demonstrated, social categorization occurs more readily in teams consisting of fewer social divisions compared to teams that consist of a wide diversity of members (Lau & Murnighan, 1998). As noted, social categorization phenomena are at the core of negative group processes that result from diversity, leading to ingroup-outgroup biases that undermine group performance unless the group finds ways to overcome their differences. According to self-categorization theory, the salience of social divisions is a function of three variables: comparative fit, normative fit, and cognitive accessibility (Oakes, Haslam, & Turner, 1994; van Knippenberg et al., 2004).

Comparative fit refers to the extent to which a social categorization accurately reflects the perceived similarities and differences among people. *Normative fit*, in contrast, refers to the extent to which interpersonal differences are considered by perceivers to be meaningful or relevant (Oakes et al., 1994; van Knippenberg & Schippers, 2007). Individuals who harbor racial prejudices, for example, are more likely to categorize others on the basis of racioethnicity than individuals who are less prejudiced (e.g., Stangor, Lynch, Duan, & Glass, 1992). Van Knippenberg, Haslam, and Platow (2003) argued, however, that a critical factor that determines which differences are considered salient and relevant is their perceived relevance to the task at hand. Thus, methods that reduce the degree to which perceivers believe that social category membership is relevant to task performance should help to minimize negative social categorization processes in diverse groups. A focus on superordinate goals (Gaertner & Dovidio, 2000; Mannix & Neale, 2005), and certain training initiatives, are representative examples of these kinds of initiatives.

Finally, social categorization also depends on the *cognitive accessibility* of social divisions and categories (Oakes et al., 1994; van Knippenberg & Schippers, 2007). For example, well-learned or chronically accessible categories, such as gender and racioethnicity, are more likely to be used than less-obvious categorizations, such as consumer preferences or value structures (Stangor et al., 1992). Contextual cues in the workplace, such as the frequency and type of comments made about interpersonal differences, also contribute to the cognitive accessibility of social categories (van Knippenberg & Schippers, 2007). Thus, one clear conclusion that emerges from research on the role of diversity context as a moderator of the effects of diversity on group performance is that the greater the organizational diversity, the less apt organizational members are to engage in social categorization processes that lead to ingroup-outgroup biases and therefore the more apt the group is to reap the benefits of the diversity of its members.

Work Group and Organizational Climate

Without question, work group and organizational climate variables may be powerful influences on the degree to which diversity leads to increases or decreases in group performance (Mannix & Neale, 2005; van Knippenberg et al., 2004; van Knippenberg & Schippers, 2007). Chatman and Spataro (2005), for example, observed higher cooperativeness among demographically diverse individuals when their groups emphasized collectivist values as compared to individualist values. Similar results were reported by Van der Vegt and Bunderson (2005). Others have emphasized the value of encouraging a superordinate group or organization identity (Huo, 2003).

Van Knippenberg et al. (2005) coined the term *diversity mind-sets* to refer to the set of shared cognitions about the meaning, relevance, and value of workplace diversity. To the degree that organizational members have favorable beliefs about the inherent value of diversity, are committed to learning from and benefiting from diversity, and understand how to reap the benefits of diversity, positive outcomes resulting from workplace diversity are more likely to occur (Chen & Eastman, 1997; Ely & Thomas, 2001; Holvino et al., 2004; Lorbiecki & Jack, 2000; Mannix & Neale, 2005). Ely and Thomas, for example, found that racioethnic diversity was more positively related to performance of bank branches that believed in the value of learning from diversity. Moreover, as Mannix and Neale pointed out, those who are considered members of traditionally underrepresented or stigmatized groups and those with unique perspectives may be reluctant to pay the perceived social costs of sharing their viewpoints at work unless there is a climate that welcomes and affirms all persons regardless of their background or social category and promotes values of human dignity and freedom (Gagnon & Cornelius, 2000).

Valuing Diversity: (When) Is Diversity a Valued Outcome?

Without careful management of task-related and contextual variables, work group diversity is unlikely to contribute in any straightforward way to the ability of a group to accomplish its goals. There is simply little direct empirical evidence that diversity is "good" for work groups. Of course, it is worth reiterating a point. To support the inference that diversity contributes to organizational effectiveness requires either demonstrating a direct effect at the organization level of analysis (e.g., Richard, Murthi, & Ismail, 2007), which has seldom been investigated, or finding evidence to support the mediating linkages between work group diversity, work group performance, and effectiveness at the organization level of analysis (Ployhart, 2004; Ployhart & Schneider, 2002; Schneider et al., 2000). At a minimum, the benefits of an increasingly diverse workforce are more likely to be realized in organizations that manage a variety of task-relevant and organizational context variables, including task interdependencies, time, the diversity context, and organizational climate and culture.

Of course, the value of diversity to an organization can be separated from its value as a direct causal determinant of performance outcomes, including group and organization effectiveness, marketing success, or customer satisfaction. Indeed, traditionally, justifications for the value of diversity have fallen into three identifiable categories: the discrimination/fairness, access-and-legitimacy, and integration-and-learning perspectives (Ely & Thomas, 2001; Lorbiecki & Jack, 2000; Mannix & Neale, 2005; Thomas & Ely, 1996). The discrimination/fairness perspective emphasizes the importance of increasing diversity to comply with federal and state equal employment legislation and to avoid charges of unfair discrimination in employment decision making. It emphasizes the importance of ensuring equality of opportunities in hiring and promotion, and the suppression of bias and unfair discrimination, and may see cultural diversity in the workplace as a "moral imperative" (Ely & Thomas, 2001, p. 245). According to this view, cultural diversity is an end in itself; hence, progress in enhancing organizational diversity is measured according to how well the organization meets its hiring and retention goals (Ely & Thomas, 2001).

The access-and-legitimacy perspective, in contrast, emphasizes the value of diversity in improving an organization's ability to reflect the diversity of its markets and gain access to and legitimacy in a wider range of markets (Cox & Blake, 1991; Ely & Thomas, 2001; Thomas & Ely, 1996). According to this view, progress in managing diversity is measured by the degree to which the composition of the organization resembles and is perceived as legitimate in its markets and the degree to which the organization has succeeded in expanding its market penetration. The integration and learning perspective, on the other hand, emphasizes the value of diversity in increasing opportunities for organizational learning and growth (Ely & Thomas, 2001; Lorbiecki & Jack, 2000; Mannix & Neale, 2005; Thomas & Ely, 1996) and sees diversity as a resource for adaptive change. The integration and learning perspective encourages a welcoming and affirming environment in which organizational members perceive inherent value in the unique perspectives of all of its members (Chen & Eastman, 1997; Gagnon & Cornelius, 2000; Holvino et al., 2004). Successful management of diversity, according to this view, is measured by the degree to which newly represented groups have access to power and play a central role in shaping the organization's strategy, its definitions of success, its management and operating systems, and it core values and norms (Ely & Thomas, 2001; Holvino et al., 2004; Thomas & Ely, 1996). As Ely and

Thomas (2001) demonstrated, a climate and culture that emphasizes integration and learning is more likely to facilitate positive outcomes resulting from workforce diversity than either of the other two perspectives. Of the three perspectives, the discrimination/fairness viewpoint seems to have dominated much of the current thinking about AI and individual job performance. This may be partly why AI and performance are seen as a trade-off or dilemma.

Conclusions

The goal of this chapter has been to present a broad and integrative view of the relationships among AI in hiring, workforce diversity, and performance in an effort to expand our thinking about the so-called diversity-validity dilemma that has so often dominated our literature and our apparent understanding about AI in personnel selection. In doing so, the present approach drew on recent work relevant to the conceptualization and valuing of individual job performance, the meaning and consequences of workplace diversity, and the role of workplace diversity as a valued criterion of organizational effectiveness in conceptualizing the nature of the diversity-validity dilemma in broad terms. A number of conclusions follow from this perspective.

First, although previous research that has sought to examine the AI-selection quality trade-off has contributed substantially to our understanding of various hiring practices, the present approach emphasizes a need to consider the trade-off much more broadly than has been the case in the past if the goal is to provide meaningful information about the costs and benefits of altering personnel selection practices to decrease AI. Inferences about the meaning and magnitude of the so-called validity-diversity dilemma require consideration of several important questions: (a) What are the dimensions of individual job performance that are valued, and how are they increased through hiring practices? (b) How does performance (behavior) at the individual level of analysis translate into group-level and organization-level performance? (c) What are the valued dimensions of organizational performance, and to what degree is diversity among the outcomes valued by the organization? (d) What are the moderating variables that influence the likelihood that workforce diversity will contribute positively or negatively to organizational functioning?

Second, a broader view of the validity-diversity trade-off encourages an integrative view of organizational policies and practices and the degree to which they operate in mutually supportive ways. A narrow focus on hiring practices that alter AI outcomes for various subgroups is not enough.

As Mannix and Neale (2005) asserted, "to implement policies and practices that increase diversity of the workforce without understanding how diverse individuals can come together to form effective teams is irresponsible" (p. 32). Effective organizational management requires acknowledging and managing the interdependencies among practices and outcomes at various levels of analysis.

Third, we need to take seriously the socially constructed nature of performance at the individual and aggregate levels of analysis. The goals pursued by organizations, and by their individual members, are driven by underlying values that are seldom made explicit (Argyris & Schön, 1978; Dawis, 1991; Hattrup, Mueller, & Aguirre, 2007). Values determine the individual behaviors that are desired, appreciated, and rewarded, and values determine what kinds of organizational outcomes are considered most appropriate, desirable, or important. Thus, a thorough analysis of whether an organization has achieved its goals, whether in terms of workforce diversity or in terms of some aggregate measure of organizational performance, should include an analysis of how the goals were identified in the first place.

Finally, we need to think carefully about what we mean by diversity and why it is being valued. Research on AI treats diversity far too narrowly, particularly given the fact that federal equal employment protections are not guaranteed for all identified subgroups in the United States. Diversity is a broad and inclusive construct, representing differences along multiple dimensions with flexible and changing boundaries. Social categorization is a social and cultural construction process and is therefore subject to reconsideration and reconceptualization. Whether the distinctions that are made between people help to identify unique talents and perspectives and acknowledge and address the unique historical and cultural experiences of identifiable groups or whether they distract people from their commonalities and their shared fates depends substantially on the organizational and cultural context. Without effective understanding of the meaning and management of diversity in the workplace, the comparison between AI in hiring and organizational performance will continue to be a "perplexing problem."

References

Allen, R. L., Dawson, M C., & Brown, R. E. (1989). A schema based approach to modeling an African American racial belief system. *American Political Science Review, 83,* 421–442.

Andersson, L. M., & Pearson, C. M. (1999). Tit for tat? The spiraling effect of incivility in the workplace. *Academy of Management Review, 24,* 452–471.

Argyris, C., & Schön, D. A. (1978). *Organizational learning: A theory of action perspective.* Reading, MA: Addison-Wesley.

Arthur, W., Jr., & Edwards, B. D. (2002). Multiple-choice and constructed response tests of ability: Race-based subgroup performance differences on alternative paper-and-pencil test formats. *Personnel Psychology, 55,* 985–1008.

Befort, N., & Hattrup, K. (2003). Valuing task and contextual performance: Experience, job roles, and ratings of the importance of job behaviors. *Applied HRM Research, 8,* 17–32.

Black, J. S., Mendenhall, M., & Oddou, G. (1991). Toward a comprehensive model of international adjustment: An integration of multiple theoretical perspectives. *Academy of Management Review, 16,* 291–317.

Bobko, P., Roth, P. L., & Potosky, D. (1999). Derivation and implications of a meta-analytic matrix incorporating cognitive ability, alternative predictors, and job performance. *Personnel Psychology, 52,* 561–590.

Borman, W. C., & Brush, D. H. (1993). More progress towards a taxonomy of managerial performance requirements. *Human Performance, 6,* 1–21.

Borman, W. C., & Motowidlo, S. J. (1993). Expanding the criterion domain to include elements of contextual performance. In N. Schmitt & W. C. Borman (Eds.), *Personnel selection in organizations* (pp. 71–98). San Francisco: Jossey-Bass.

Borman, W. C., White, L. A., & Dorsey, D. W. (1995). Effects of ratee task performance and interpersonal factors on supervisor and peer performance ratings. *Journal of Applied Psychology, 80,* 168–177.

Bowers, C. A., Pharmer, J. A., & Salas, E. (2000). When member homogeneity is needed in work teams: A meta analysis. *Small Group Research, 31,* 305–327.

Campbell, J. P. (1977). On the nature of organizational effectiveness. In P. S. Goodman & J. M. Pennings (Eds.), *New perspectives on organizational effectiveness* (pp. 13–55). San Francisco: Jossey-Bass.

Campbell, J. P., Gasser, M. B., & Oswald, F. L. (1996). The substantive nature of job performance variability. In K. R. Murphy (Ed.), *Individual differences and behavior in organizations* (pp. 258–299). San Francisco: Jossey-Bass.

Campbell, J. P., McCloy, R. A., Oppler, S. H., & Sager, C. E. (1993). A theory of performance. In N. Schmitt and W. C. Borman (Eds.), *Personnel selection in organizations* (pp. 35–70). San Francisco, CA: Jossey-Bass.

Campbell, J. P., McHenry, J. J., & Wise, L. L. (1990). Modeling job performance in a population of jobs. *Personnel Psychology, 43,* 313–333.

Campion, M. A., Outtz, J. L., Zedeck, S., Schmidt, F. L., Kehoe, J. F., Murphy, K. R., et al. (2001). The controversy over score banding in personnel selection: Answers to 10 key questions. *Personnel Psychology, 54,* 149–185.

Chatman, J. A., & Flynn, F. J. (2001). The influence of demographic heterogeneity on the emergence and consequences of cooperative norms in work teams. *Academy of Management Journal, 44,* 956–974.

Chatman, J. A., & Spataro, S. E. (2005). Using self-categorization theory to understand relational demography-based variations in people's responsiveness to organizational culture. *Academy of Management Journal, 48,* 321–331.

Chen, C. C., & Eastman, W. (1997). Toward a civic culture for multicultural organizations. *Journal of Applied Behavioral Science, 33,* 454–470.

Clair, J. A., Beatty, J. E., & MacLean, T. L. (2005). Out of sight but not out of mind: Managing invisible social identities in the workplace. *Academy of Management Review, 30,* 1, 78–95.

Conway, J. M. (1999). Distinguishing contextual performance from task performance for managerial jobs. *Journal of Applied Psychology, 84,* 3–13.

Cox, T. H., & Blake, S. (1991) Managing cultural diversity: Implications for organizational competitiveness. *Executive, 5,* 45–50.

Cross, S. E., & Madson, L. (1997) Models of the self: Self-construals and gender. *Psychological Bulletin, 122,* 5–38.

Dahlin, K. B., Weingart, L. R., & Hinds, P. J. (2005). Team diversity and information use. *Academy of Management Journal, 48,* 1107–1123.

Davis, D. D. (1995). Form, function, and strategy in boundaryless organizations. In A. Howard (Ed.), *The changing nature of work* (pp. 112–138). San Francisco, CA: Jossey-Bass.

Dawis, R. V. (1991). Vocational interests, values, and preferences. In M. D. Dunnette & L. M. Hough (Eds.), *Handbook of industrial and organizational psychology* (2nd Ed., Vol. 2, pp. 833–872). Palo Alto, CA: Consulting Psychologists Press.

De Corte, W. (1999). Weighting job performance predictors to both maximize the quality of the selected workforce and control the level of adverse impact. *Journal of Applied Psychology, 84,* 695–702.

De Corte, W., & Lievens, F. (2003). A practical procedure to estimate the quality and adverse impact of single-stage selection decisions. *International Journal of Selection and Assessment, 11,* 89–97.

De Corte, W., Lievens, F., & Sackett, P. R. (2007). Combining predictors to achieve optimal trade-offs between selection quality and adverse impact. *Journal of Applied Psychology, 92,* 1380–1393.

De Dreu, C. K. W., & Weingart, L. R. (2003). Task and relationship conflict, team performance, and team member satisfaction: A meta-analysis. *Journal of Applied Psychology, 88,* 741–749.

Dietch, E., Butz, R., & Brief, A. (2003). Out of the closet and out of a job? The nature, import, and causes of sexual orientation discrimination in the workplace. In R. Griffin and A. O'Leary-Kelly (Eds.), *The dark side of organizational behavior* (pp. 187–231). San Francisco: Jossey-Bass.

Dyer, L., & Reeves, T. (1995). Human resource strategies and firm performance: What do we know and where do we need to go? *International Journal of Human Resource Management, 6,* 656–670.

Earley, P. C., & Mosakowski, E. (2000). Creating hybrid team cultures: An empirical test of transnational functioning. *Academy of Management Journal, 43,* 26–49.

Ely, R. J., & Thomas, D. A. (2001). Cultural diversity at work: The effects of diversity perspectives on work group processes and outcomes. *Administrative Science Quarterly, 46,* 229–273.

Ferris, H. S., Fedor, D. B., Rowland, R. M., & Porac, J. F. (1985). Social influence and sex effects on task performance and task perceptions. *Organizational Behavior and Human Decision Processes, 36,* 66–78.

Gaertner, S. L., & Dovidio, J. F. (2000). *Reducing intergroup bias: The common ingroup identity mode.* Philadelphia: Psychological Press.

Gagnon, S., & Cornelius, N. (2000). Re-examining workplace equality: The capabilities approach. *Human Resource Management, 10,* 68–87.

Harrison, D. A., & Klein, K. J. (2007). What's the difference? Diversity constructs as separation, variety, or disparity in organizations. *Academy of Management Review, 32,* 1199–1228.

Harrison, D. A., Price, K. H., & Bell, M. P. (1998). Beyond relational demography: Time and the effects of surface- and deep-level diversity on work group cohesion. *Academy of Management Journal, 41,* 96–107.

Harrison, D. A., Price, K. H., Gavin, J. H., & Florey, A. T. (2002). Time, teams, and task performance: Changing effects of surface- and deep-level diversity on group functioning. *Academy of Management Journal, 45,* 1029–1045.

Harvey, R. J. (1991). Job analysis. In M. D. Dunnette & L. M. Hough (Eds.), *Handbook of industrial and organizational psychology* (2nd ed., Vol. 2, pp. 71–164). Palo Alto, CA: Consulting Psychologists Press.

Hattrup, K. (2005). Multivariate symmetry and organizational policy: Where values and statistical realities intersect. In A. Beauducel et al. (Eds.), *Multivariate research strategies* (pp. 39–62). Aachen, Germany: Shaker Verlag GmbH.

Hattrup, K., & Jackson, S. E. (1996). Learning about individual differences by taking situations seriously. In K. R. Murphy (Ed.), *Individual differences and behavior in organizations* (pp. 507–541). San Francisco: Jossey-Bass.

Hattrup, K., Mueller, K., & Aguirre, P. (2007). Operationalizing value importance in cross-cultural research: Comparing direct and indirect measures. *Journal of Occupational and Organizational Psychology, 80,* 499–513.

Hattrup, K., & Rock, J. (2002). A comparison of predictor-based and criterion-based methods for weighing predictors to reduce adverse impact. *Applied HRM Research, 7,* 22–38.

Hattrup, K., Rock, J., & Scalia, C. (1997). The effects of varying conceptualizations of job performance on adverse impact, minority hiring, and predicted performance. *Journal of Applied Psychology, 82,* 656–664.

Hesketh, B., Allworth, E., & Considine, G. (1996). *Preliminary report on phase 1 of the selection project for Hilton Hotel.* Unpublished manuscript, MacQuarie University, Sydney, Australia.

Hofstede, G. (1980). *Culture's consequences.* Beverly Hills, CA: Sage.

Holvino, E., Ferdman, B. M., & Merrill-Sands, D. (2004). Creating and sustaining diversity and inclusion in organizations: Strategies and approaches. In M. S. Stockdale & F. J. Crosby (Eds.), *The psychology and management of workplace diversity* (pp. 245–276). Malden, MA: Blackwell.

Hough, L. M., Oswald, F. L., & Ployhart, R. E. (2001). Determinants, detection and amelioration of adverse impact in personnel selection procedures: Issues, evidence and lessons learned. *International Journal of Selection and Assessment, 9,* 152–195.

Huffcut, A. I., & Roth, P. L. (1998). Racial group differences in employment interview evaluations. *Journal of Applied Psychology, 83,* 179–189.

Hunt, S. T. (1996). Generic work behavior: An investigation into the dimensions of entry-level hourly job performance. *Personnel Psychology, 49,* 51–83.

Hunter, J. E., Schmidt, F. L., & Rauschenberger, J. M. (1977). Fairness of psychological tests: Implications of four definitions for selection utility and minority hiring. *Journal of Applied Psychology, 62,* 245–260.

Huo, Y. (2003). Procedural justice and social regulation across group boundaries: Does subgroup identification undermine relationship-based governance? *Personality and Social Psychology Bulletin, 29,* 336–348.

Huselid, M. A. (1995). The impact of human resource management practices on turnover, productivity, and corporate financial performance. *Academy of Management Journal, 38,* 635–672.

Huselid, M. A., Jackson, S. E., & Schuler, R. S. (1997). Organizational characteristics as predictors of personnel characteristics. *Personnel Psychology, 42,* 727–786.

Ilgen, D. R. (1999). Teams embedded in organizations: Some implications. *American Psychologist, 54,* 129–139.

Ilgen, D. R., & Pulakos, E. D. (1999). Employee performance in today's organizations. In D. R. Ilgen & E. D. Pulakos (Eds.), *The changing nature of work performance: Implications for staffing, motivation, and development* (pp. 1–18). San Francisco: Jossey-Bass.

Jackson, S. E. (1992). Team composition in organizational settings: Issues in managing an increasingly diverse workforce. In S. Worchel, W. Wood, & J. A. Simpson (Eds.), *Group process and productivity* (pp. 136–180). Newbury Park, CA: Sage.

Jackson, S. E., May, E., & Whitney, K. (1995). Understanding the dynamic of diversity in decision-making teams. In R. Guzzo & E. Salas (Eds.), *Team decision making effectiveness in organizations* (pp. 204–261). San Francisco: Jossey-Bass.

Jehn, K. A., Northcraft, G. B., & Neale, M. A. (1999). Why differences make a difference: A field study of diversity, conflict, and performance in workgroups. *Administrative Science Quarterly, 44,* 741–763.

Johnson, J. W. (2001). The relative importance of task and contextual performance dimensions to supervisor judgments of overall performance. *Journal of Applied Psychology, 86,* 984–996.

Kehoe, J. (2002). General mental ability and selection in private sector organizations: A commentary. *Human Performance, 15,* 97–106.

Kidwell, R. E., & Bennett, N. B. (1993). Employee propensity to withhold effort: A conceptual model to intersect three avenues of research. *Academy of Management Review, 18,* 429–456.

Kinicki, A. J., & Latack, J. C. (1990). Explication of the construct of coping with involuntary job loss. *Journal of Vocational Behavior, 36,* 339–360.

Kozlowski, S. W. J., & Klein, K. J. (2000). A multilevel approach to theory and research in organizations: Contextual, temporal, and emergent processes. In K. J. Klein & S. W. J. Kozlowski (Eds.), *Multilevel theory, research, and methods in organizations: Foundations, extensions, and new directions* (pp. 3–90). San Francisco: Jossey-Bass.

Landy, F. J., & Vasey, J. (1991). Job analysis: The composition of SME samples. *Personnel Psychology, 44,* 27–50.

Lau, D. C., & Murnighan, J. K. (1998). Demographic diversity and faultlines: The compositional dynamics of organizational groups. *Academy of Management Review, 23,* 325–340.

Lawrence, B. (1997). The black box of organizational demography. *Organizational Science, 8,* 1–22.

Ledvinka, J., Markos, V. H., & Ladd, R. T. (1982). Long-range impact of "fair selection" standards on minority employment. *Journal of Applied Psychology, 67,* 18–36.

Lepak, D. P., & Snell, S. A. (2002). Examining the human resource architecture: Toward a theory of human capital allocation and development. *Academy of Management Review, 24,* 34–48.

Lewin, A. Y., & Minton, J. W. (1986). Determining organizational effectiveness: Another look, and an agenda for research. *Management Science, 32,* 514–538.

London, M., & Mone, E. M. (1999). Continuous learning. In D. R. Ilgen & E. D. Pulakos (Eds.), *The changing nature of performance: Implications for staffing, motivation, and development* (pp. 119–153). San Francisco: Jossey-Bass.

Lorbiecki, A., & Jack, G. (2000). Critical turns in the evolution of diversity management. *British Journal of Management, 11,* 17–31.

Mannix, E., & Neale, M. A. (2005). What differences make a difference? The promise and reality of diverse teams in organizations. *Psychological Science in the Public Interest, 6,* 31–55.

Marin, G., & Triandis, H. C. (1985). Allocentrism as an important characteristic of the behavior of Latin Americans and Hispanics. In R. Diaz-Guerrero (Ed.), *Cross-cultural and national studies in social psychology* (pp. 69–80). Amsterdam: North-Holland.

Martinko, M. J., Gundlach, M. J., & Douglas, S. C. (2002). Toward an integrative theory of counterproductive workplace behavior: A causal reasoning perspective. *International Journal of Selection and Assessment, 10,* 36–50.

Martins, L. L., Milliken, F. J., Wiesenfeld, B. M., & Salgado, S. R. (2003). Racioethnic diversity and group members' experiences: The role of racioethnic diversity of the organizational context. *Group and Organization Management, 28,* 75–106.

Meyer, M. W., & Gupta, V. (1994). The performance paradox. In B. M. Staw & L. L. Cummings (Eds.), *Research in organizational behavior* (Vol. 16, pp. 309–369). Greenwich, CT: JAI Press.

Mol, S. T., Born, M. P., & van der Molen, H. T. (2005). Developing criteria for expatriate effectiveness: Time to jump off the adjustment bandwagon. *International Journal of Intercultural Relations, 29,* 339–353.

Morgeson, F. P., & Campion, M. A. (1997). Social and cognitive sources of potential inaccuracy in job analysis. *Journal of Applied Psychology, 82,* 627–655.

Motowidlo, S. J. (2003). Job performance. In W. C Borman, D. R. Ilgen, & R. J. Klimoski (Eds.), *Handbook of psychology: Industrial and organizational psychology* (pp. 39–53). Hoboken, NJ: Wiley.

Motowidlo, S. J., Borman, W. C., & Schmidt, M. J. (1997). A theory of individual differences in task and contextual performance. *Human Performance, 10,* 71–84.

Motowidlo, S. J., & Schmit, M. J. (1999). Performance assessment in unique jobs. In D. R. Ilgen & E. D. Pulakos (Eds.), *The changing nature of performance* (pp. 56–86). San Francisco: Jossey-Bass.

Motowidlo, S. J., & Van Scotter, J. R. (1994). Evidence that task performance should be distinguished from contextual performance. *Journal of Applied Psychology, 79,* 475–480.

Mullins, W. C., & Kimbrough, W. W. (1988). Group composition as a determinant of job analysis outcomes. *Journal of Applied Psychology, 73,* 657–664.

Murnighan, J. K., & Conlon, D. E. (1991). The dynamics of intense work groups: A study of British string quartets. *Administrative Science Quarterly, 36,* 165–186.

Murphy, K. R., Cronin, B. E., & Tam, A. P. (2003). Controversy and consensus regarding the use of cognitive ability testing in organizations. *Journal of Applied Psychology, 88*, 4, 660–671.

Murphy, K. R., & Shiarella, A. H. (1997). Implications of the multidimensional nature of job performance for the validity of selection tests: Multivariate frameworks for studying test validity. *Personnel Psychology, 50*, 823–854.

Murphy, P. R., & Jackson, S. E. (1999). Managing work role performance: Challenges for twenty-first-century organizations and their employees. In D. R. Ilgen & E. D. Pulakos (Eds.), *The changing nature of performance: Implications for staffing, motivation, and development* (pp. 325–365). San Francisco: Jossey-Bass.

Neisser, U., Boodoo, G., Bouchard, T. J., Jr., Boykin, A. W., Brody, N., Ceci, S. J., et al. (1996). Intelligence: Knowns and unknowns. *American Psychologist, 51*, 77–101.

Norton, M. I., Sommers, S. R., Vandello, J. A., & Darley, J. M. (2006). Mixed motives and racial bias: The impact of legitimate and illegitimate criteria on decision making. *Psychology, Public Policy, and Law, 12*, 36–55.

Oakes, P. J., Haslam, S. A., & Turner, J. C. (1994). *Stereotyping and social reality.* Malden, MA: Blackwell.

Ones, D. S., Viswesvaran, C., & Schmidt, F. L. (1993). Comprehensive meta-analysis of integrity test validities: Findings and implications for personnel selection and theories of job performance. *Journal of Applied Psychology, 78*, 579–603.

O'Reilly, C. A., Caldwell, D. F., & Barnett, W. P. (1989). Work group demography, social integration, and turnover. *Administrative Science Quarterly, 34*, 21–37.

Ostroff, C. (2002). Leveling the selection field. In F. J. Yammarino & F. Dansereau (Eds.), *Research in multilevel issues, Vol. 1: The many faces of multi-level issues* (pp. 141–154.) London: Elsevier.

Parekh, B. (1992). A case for positive discrimination. In B. Hepple & E. M. Szyszczak (Eds.), *Discrimination: The limits of the law* (pp. 261–280). London: Mansell.

Pelled, L. H., Eisenhardt, K. M., & Xin, K. R. (1999). Exploring the black box: An analysis of work group diversity, conflict, and performance. *Administrative Science Quarterly, 44*, 1–28.

Pettigrew, T. F. (1998). Intergroup contact theory. *Annual Review of Psychology, 49*, 65–85.

Ployhart, R. E. (2004). Organizational staffing: A multilevel review, synthesis, and model. In J. J. Martocchio (Ed.), *Research in personnel and human resources management* (Vol. 23, pp. 121–176). Oxford, UK: Elsevier.

Ployhart, R. E., & Holtz, B. C. (2008). The diversity-validity dilemma: Strategies for reducing racioethnic and sex subgroup differences and adverse impact in selection. *Personnel Psychology, 61*, 153–172.

Ployhart, R. E., & Schneider, B. (2002). A multilevel perspective on personnel selection research and practice: Implications for selection system design, assessment, and construct validation. In F. J. Yammarino & F. Dansereau (Eds.), *Research in multilevel issues, Vol. 1: The many faces of multi-level issues* (pp. 95–140.) London: Elsevier.

Podsakoff, P. M., & MacKenzie, S. B. (1997). Impact of organizational citizenship behavior on organizational performance: A review and suggestions for future research. *Human Performance, 10*, 133–151.

Posthuma, R. A., Morgeson, F. P., & Campion, M. A. (2002). Beyond employment interview validity: A comprehensive narrative review of recent research and trends over time. *Personnel Psychology, 55,* 1–81.

Pulakos, E. D., Arad, S., Donovan, M. A., & Plamondon, K. E. (2000). Adaptability in the work place: Development of a taxonomy of adaptive performance. *Journal of Applied Psychology, 85,* 612–624.

Pulakos, E. D., Schmitt, N., Dorsey, D. W., Arad, S., Hedge, J. W., & Borman, W. C. (2002). Predicting adaptive performance: Further tests of a model of adaptability. *Human Performance, 15,* 299–323.

Pyburn, K. M., Jr., Ployhart, R. E., & Kravitz, D. A. (2008). The diversity-validity dilemma: Overview and legal context. *Personnel Psychology, 61,* 143–151.

Ragins, B. R. (2004). Sexual orientation in the workplace: The unique work and career experiences of gay, lesbian, and bisexual workers. In J. J. Martocchio (Ed.), *Research in personnel and human resources management* (Vol. 23, pp. 35–129). New York: Elsevier.

Richard, O. C., Murthi, B. P. S., & Ismail, K. (2007). The impact of racial diversity on intermediate and long-term performance: The moderating role of environmental context. *Strategic Management Journal, 28,* 1213–1233.

Robinson, G., & Dechant, K. (1997). Building a business case for diversity. *Academy of Management Executive, 11,* 21–31.

Robinson, S. L., & Bennett, R. J. (1995). A typology of deviant workplace behaviors: A multidimensional scaling study. *Academy of Management Journal, 38,* 555–572.

Robinson, S. L., & O'Leary-Kelly, A. M. (1998). Monkey see, monkey do: The influence of work groups on antisocial behavior of employees. *Academy of Management Journal, 41,* 658–672.

Rogers, E. W., & Wright, P. M. (1998). Measuring organizational performance in strategic human resource management: Problems, prospects, and performance markets. *Human Resource Management Review, 8,* 311–331.

Roth, P. L., & Bobko, P. (2000). College grade point average as a personnel selection device: Ethnic group differences and potential adverse impact. *Journal of Applied Psychology, 85,* 399–406.

Rotundo, M., & Sackett, P. R. (2002). The relative importance of task, citizenship, and counterproductive performance to global ratings of job performance: A policy capturing approach. *Journal of Applied Psychology, 87,* 66–80.

Ryan, A. M., Ployhart, R. E., & Friedel, L. (1998). Using personality tests to reduce adverse impact: A cautionary note. *Journal of Applied Psychology, 83,* 298–307.

Sacco, J. M., & Schmitt, N. (2005). A dynamic multilevel model of demographic diversity and misfit effects. *Journal of Applied Psychology, 90,* 203–231.

Sackett, P. R. (2002). The structure of counterproductive work behaviors: Dimensionality and relationships with facets of job performance. *International Journal of Selection and Assessment, 10,* 5–11.

Sackett, P. R., & Roth, L. (1996). Multi-stage selection strategies: A Monte Carlo investigation of effects on performance and minority hiring. *Personnel Psychology, 49,* 549–572.

Sackett, P. R., Schmitt, N., Ellingson, J. E., & Kabin, M. B. (2001). High-stakes testing in employment, credentialing, and higher education: Prospects in a post-affirmative action world. *American Psychologist, 56,* 302–318.

Schippers, M. C., Den Hartog, D. N., & Koopman, P. L. (2007). Reflexivity in teams: A measure and correlates. *Applied Psychology: An International Review, 56,* 189–211.

Schippers, M. C., Den Hartog, D. N., Koopman, P. L., & Wienk, J. A. (2003). Diversity and team outcomes: The moderating effects of outcome interdependence and group longevity and the mediating effect of reflexivity. *Journal of Organizational Behavior, 24,* 779–802.

Schmidt, F. L., & Hunter, J. E. (1998). The validity and utility of selection methods in personnel psychology: Practical and theoretical implications of 85 years of research findings. *Psychological Bulletin, 124,* 262–274.

Schmitt, N., & Chan, D. (1998). *Personnel selection: A theoretical approach.* Thousand Oaks, CA: Sage.

Schmitt, N., & Cohen, S. A. (1989). Internal analyses of task ratings by job incumbents. *Journal of Applied Psychology, 74,* 96–104.

Schmitt, N., Rogers, W., Chan, D., Sheppard, L., & Jennings, D. (1997). Adverse impact and predictive efficiency of various predictor combinations. *Journal of Applied Psychology, 82,* 5, 719–730.

Schneider, B. (1987). The people make the place. *Personnel Psychology, 40,* 437–453.

Schneider, B., Smith, D. B., & Sipe, W. P. (2000). Personnel selection psychology: Multilevel considerations. In K. J. Klein & S. W. J. Kozlowski (Eds.), *Multilevel theory, research, and methods in organizations: Foundations, extensions, and new directions* (pp. 91–120). San Francisco: Jossey-Bass.

Schuler, R. S. (1992). Strategic human resources management: Linking the people with the strategic needs of the business. *Organizational Dynamics, 21,* 18–32.

Schuler, R. S., & Jackson, S. E. (1987, August). Linking human resource strategies with competitive strategies. *Academy of Management Executive,* 207–219.

Shaffer, M. A., Harrison, D. A., Gregersen, H., Black, J. S., & Ferzandi, L. A. (2006). You can't take it with you: Individual differences and expatriate effectiveness. *Journal of Applied Psychology, 91,* 109–125.

Simon, H. A. (1973). The organization of complex systems. In H. H. Pattee (Ed.), *Hierarchy theory* (pp. 1–27). New York: Braziller.

Stangor, C., Lynch, L., Duan, C., & Glass, B. (1992). Categorization of individuals on the basis of multiple social features. *Journal of Personality and Social Psychology, 62,* 207–218.

Storms, P. L., & Spector, P. E. (1987). Relationships of organizational frustration with reported behavioral reactions: The moderating effects of locus of control. *Journal of Occupational and Organizational Psychology, 60,* 635–637.

Stroessner, S. (1996). Social categorization by race or sex: Effects of perceived non-normalcy on response times. *Social Cognition, 14,* 274–276.

Tajfel, H., & Turner, J. (1986). The social identity of intergroup behavior. In S. Worchel & W. Austin (Eds.), *Psychology and intergroup relations* (pp. 7–24). Chicago: Nelson-Hall.

Terpstra, D. E., & Rozell, E. J. (1993). The relationship of staffing practices to organizational level measures of performance. *Personnel Psychology, 46,* 27–48.

Tett, R. P., Guterman, H. A., Bleier, A., & Murphy, P. J. (2000). Development and content validation of a "hyperdimensional" taxonomy of managerial competence. *Human Performance, 13,* 205–251.

Thach, L., & Woodman, R. W. (1994). Organizational change and information technology: Managing on the edge of cyberspace. *Organizational Dynamics, 23,* 30–46.

Thomas, D. A., & Ely, R. J. (1996, September–October). Making differences matter: A new paradigm for managing diversity. *Harvard Business Review, 74,* 79–90.

Triandis, H. C., Kurowski, L. L., & Gelfand, M. J. (1994). Workplace diversity. In M. D. Dunnette & L. M. Hough (Eds.), *Handbook of industrial and organizational psychology* (2nd ed., Vol. 4, pp. 769–827). Palo Alto, CA: Consulting Psychologists Press.

Tsui, A. S., Egan, T. D., & O'Reilly, C. A. (1992). Being different: Relational demography and organizational attachment. *Administrative Science Quarterly, 37,* 549–579.

Van der Vegt, G. S., & Bunderson, J. S. (2005). Learning and performance in multi-disciplinary teams: The importance of collective team identification. *Academy of Management Journal, 48,* 532–547.

Van der Vegt, G. S., & Janssen, O. (2003). Joint impact of interdependence and group diversity on innovation. *Journal of Management, 29,* 29–51.

Van Knippenberg, D., De Dreu, C. K. W., & Homan, A. C. (2004). Work group diversity and group performance: An integrative model and research agenda. *Journal of Applied Psychology, 89,* 1008–1022.

Van Knippenberg, D., Haslam, S. A., & Platow, M. J. (2003, May). *Work group diversity and work group identification: Diversity as an aspect of group identity.* Paper presented at the 11th European Congress for Work and Organizational Psychology, Lisbon.

Van Knippenberg, D., & Schippers, M. C. (2007). Work group diversity. *Annual Review of Psychology, 58,* 515–541.

Van Knippenberg, D., van Ginkel, W. P., Homan, A. C., Kooij-de Bode, & H. J. M. (2005, May). *Diversity mind sets: A new focus in diversity research.* Paper presented at the 12th European Congress for Work and Organizational Psychology, Istanbul.

Van Scotter, J. R., & Motowidlo, S. J. (1996). Interpersonal facilitation and job dedication as separate facets of contextual performance. *Journal of Applied Psychology, 81,* 525–531.

Vulpe, T., Kealey, D. J., Protheroe, D. R., & MacDonald, D. (2001). *A profile of the interculturally effective person.* Edmonton, Canada: Centre for Intercultural Learning: Canadian Foreign Service Institute.

Wagner, G. W., Pfeffer, J., & O'Reilly, C. A. (1984). Organizational demography and turnover. *Administrative Science Quarterly, 29,* 74–92.

Watson, W., Johnson, L., & Merritt, D. (1998). Team orientation, self-orientation, and diversity in task groups: Their connection to team performance over time. *Group and Organization Management, 23,* 161–188.

Webber, S. S., & Donahue, L. M. (2001). Impact of highly and less job-related diversity on work group cohesion and performance: A meta analysis. *Journal of Management, 27,* 141–162.

Williams, K. Y., & O'Reilly, C. A. III. (1998). Demography and diversity in organizations: A review of 40 years of research. *Research in Organizational Behavior, 20,* 77–140.

Wittmann, W. W. (1988). Multivariate reliability theory: Principles of symmetry and successful validation strategies. In J. R. Nesselroade & R. B. Cattell (Eds.), *Handbook of multivariate experimental psychology* (pp. 505–560). New York: Plenum Press.

Yakura, E. K. (1996). EEO law and managing diversity. In E. E. Kossek & S. A. Lobel (Eds.), *Managing diversity: Human resource strategies for transforming the workplace* (pp. 25–50). Cambridge, U.K.: Blackwell.

Section IV

Facets of the Adverse Impact Problem

7

Adverse Impact in Employee Selection Procedures From the Perspective of an Organizational Consultant

Nancy T. Tippins

Introduction

Adverse impact is a legal term that refers to a substantially different rate of selection for one group relative to another. In the context of equal employment opportunity (EEO) laws, one group is protected; the other is a majority group. The Uniform Guidelines on Employee Selection Procedures (Equal Employment Opportunity Commission, 1978) define adverse impact as follows:

> A selection rate for any race, sex, or ethnic group which is less than four-fifths (or 80 percent) of the rate for the group with the highest rate will generally be regarded by Federal Enforcement Agencies as evidence of adverse impact, while a greater than four-fifths rate will generally not be regarded by Federal enforcement agencies as evidence of adverse impact. (Section 4D).

Many human resources (HR) professionals believe that adverse impact is illegal (or that it should be illegal), and the use of any selection instrument that is found to have adverse impact at any time on any group of people should be discontinued. In fact, a finding of adverse impact does not necessarily indicate bias in a selection procedure or unfair treatment and is not a conclusive indicator that the use of a test should be discontinued.

Title VII of the Civil Rights Act of 1964 (42 U.S.C. 2000e-5) states clearly that an employment practice that results in adverse impact is unlawful only when the employer fails to show the employment practice is job relevant and consistent with business practice:

> An unlawful employment practice based on disparate impact is established under this subchapter only if- (i) a complaining party demonstrates that a respondent uses a particular employment practice that causes a disparate impact on the basis of race, color, religion, sex, or national origin and the respondent fails to demonstrate that the challenged practice is job related for the position in question and consistent with business necessity. (Title VII as amended by the Civil Rights Act of 1991, 42 U.S.C. § 2000e-2(k)(1)(a))

Virtually all employers seek to avoid or minimize adverse impact, and some demand that their employee selection procedures produce no adverse impact at all. Many employers are fully committed to a diverse employee body who can meet the needs of a diverse customer group, and substantial adverse impact can inhibit achievement of that goal. Some employers probably want to avoid the problems attendant to a selection procedure with adverse impact against a protected group (e.g., the costs of a potential legal defense to show the selection procedure is job relevant and consistent with business necessity). And, a few simply do not understand the law, believing they cannot use selection procedures that have adverse impact. Regardless of where an employer stands on the topic of adverse impact, it must be measured.

The purpose of this chapter is to highlight the issues confronted by practitioners when dealing with adverse impact in the context of evaluating employee selection procedures. The first section of the chapter addresses the questions that arise when evaluating adverse impact in employee selection procedures. The latter portion of the chapter discusses the organizational implications of adverse impact and the actions that might ameliorate adverse impact.

Establishing Adverse Impact

Industrial and organizational (I/O) psychologists and other professionals who are responsible for selection programs generally understand their obligation to monitor the adverse impact of employee selection systems. Yet, that understanding does not always translate into confidence about the appropriate way to proceed with those analyses. Fundamental questions about what statistics should be calculated to evaluate adverse impact, who should be included in the groups being analyzed, and what time frames to use have no clear answers.

What Statistic Should Be Used to Calculate Adverse Impact?

Virtually all I/O psychologists know how to calculate adverse impact using the four-fifths rule or the 80% rule, and many are familiar with other approaches to assessing adverse impact such as z tests, chi square tests, and Fisher's exact probability tests. However, there are other more complex statistics that are sometimes useful, and there are corrections to some statistics for certain conditions. The essential problem facing the practitioner charged with evaluating adverse impact is understanding differences in statistics and their underlying assumptions and choosing the appropriate statistics to use. A detailed statistical discussion is beyond the scope of this chapter; instead, a brief review of the more common approaches is provided.

80% Rule

As defined by the Uniform Guidelines (Equal Employment Opportunity Commission, 1978), the 80% rule (or four-fifths rule) compares the selection rate of the group with a lower selection rate to that of the group with a higher selection rate. In practice, however, the 80% rule generally compares the pass rate of the protected subgroup of interest (e.g., women, African Americans) to the pass rate of the majority group (e.g., males, whites). As a rule of thumb, a ratio of 0.80 or greater indicates that there is no adverse impact. This test is the most commonly used method of evaluating adverse impact, but it is not appropriate for small sample sizes. Another drawback is the lack of a commonly accepted method to determine which ratios are statistically significant.

z Test

The z test is used to compare the difference between the pass rate proportions of the majority group and protected group of interest by calculating the z statistic. The two proportions are considered statistically equivalent ($p < 0.05$) when the z statistic is less than or equal to 1.96. A z value greater than 1.96 (or less than –1.96) indicates that the proportion passing for one subgroup is significantly greater than that of another. This test is not appropriate for small sample sizes, often defined as fewer than 30; however, the definition of *small* is not consistent.

There are two common forms of z test approximations; one is based on the binomial distribution and the other on the hypergeometric distribution. The z test based on the binomial distribution assumes sampling with replacement; in other words, any number of people can pass. The z test based on the hypergeometric distribution assumes sampling without replacement; only a limited number of people can pass (which is rarely the case when evaluating test scores but is characteristic of hiring/not hiring decisions). This z test is often corrected because the statistic assumes a normal distribution, and the categorization of test scores into pass or fail results in discrete values.

Paetzold and Willborn (1994) indicated that the choice of binomial or hypergeometric distribution is dependent on the model assumptions. The hypergeometric model assumes that selections are made from a finite pool without replacement. Although this assumption may have little relevance to evaluating the adverse impact of a test on which any number of people may pass or fail, it is particularly relevant to "batch-hiring" decisions in which a fixed number of people are tested and a fixed number of people are selected for hire. In contrast, the binomial distribution assumes that either replacements are made or selections are made from an infinite pool, so an individual's chance of selection does not change as selections are made. Thus, the binomial distribution may be more appropriate in situations in which "continuous" hiring occurs. In other words, people are tested every day, and some are selected; then more people are tested and selected on subsequent days. Regardless of the distribution used, operationally both often have similar results.

There is no clear consensus that one statistic is superior to the other. The binomial distribution tends to yield slightly higher estimates of the z value and is thus more likely to indicate differences. The binomial distribution was used to compare the number of minority group members in a job to their number in the population and accepted in *Hazelwood School District v. United States* (1977), suggesting some court acceptance of this statistic.

Fisher's Exact Probability Test

Fisher's exact probability statistical test is used to compare the frequencies of passing and failing individuals in each subgroup when the sample in at least one subgroup is small (≤ 5) or numbers in each subgroup are unbalanced. Fisher's exact test is appropriate when the population from which selections are made is finite such that after a selection, the population is reduced by one. Pass rates are considered different if the probability of an error is less than or equal to 0.05. A debated question is whether to use one- or two-tailed tests of significance. Unless the protected class always passes at a lower rate, the two-tailed test seems more appropriate.

Chi Square

The chi square statistical test is used to compare differences in proportions for two or more groups. Generally, each cell must have more than five observations. The test is appropriate for moderate-to-large samples and approximates the Fisher's exact test and the two-sample binomial test. Like all nonparametric statistics, a chi square test is less likely to reject the null hypothesis when it is false. Thus, parametric statistics are preferred.

The Yates correction is used with the chi square test to improve the approximation to the theoretical distribution when one or more cells have fewer than five observations. The Yates correction is conservative, making it more difficult to find statistical significance. Some statisticians feel the Yates correction is too conservative. When the results are close to the level of significance, the Fisher's exact test is preferred.

The Cochran-Mantel-Haenszel procedure is used for analyzing decisions that have been aggregated across strata such as job level or time periods. This statistic assumes any differences will be in one direction only. If differences are expected in both directions, the analysis will cancel positive and negative disparities.

A fundamental question for practitioners is when to use which test. Often, the answer is to calculate adverse impact in many different ways to determine if there is any way an argument of adverse impact can be made. Unfortunately, this approach often produces conflicting results and creates new questions regarding which results are more reliable and which results should be reported. Consider the following example that illustrates the problem in Table 7.1 and Table 7.2. The numbers in these tables reflect the number of test takers who passed or failed a test. Each observation is independent. One person's passing score in no way limits another's opportunity.

TABLE 7.1

Percentage Pass and Fail by Sex Subgroups (Test Scores)

	Total		Males		Females	
	N	% pass	N	% pass	N	% pass
Pass	825	96	796	96	29	97
Fail	36	4	35	4	1	3
Total	861		831		30	
	80% rule ratio			100.9%		
	z test: binomial distribution			.236		
	z test: hypergeometric distribution			.236		
	z test: hypergeometric distribution (corrected)			0.000		
	Fisher's exact (*p* value)			1.000		
	Chi square (*p* value)			.813		
	Chi square with Yates correction (*p* value)			.820		

TABLE 7.2

Percentage Pass and Fail by Race Subgroups (Test Scores)

	Total		White		African American		Hispanic		Asian		Native American	
	N	% pass	N	% pass	N	% pass	N	% pass	N	% pass	N	% pass
Pass	810	96%	489	99	220	92	86	91	12	86	3	100
Fail	36	4%	5	1	20	8	9	9	2	14	0	0
Total	846		494		240		95		14		3	
80% rule ratio					92.6%		91.5%		86.6%		101.0%	
z test: binomial distribution					−5.130[a]		−4.958[a]		−4.201[a]		0.175	
z test: hypergeometric distribution					−5.126[a]		−4.954[a]		−4.197[a]		0.175	
z test: hypergeometric distribution(corrected)					−4.910[a]		−4.587[a]		−3.036		0.000	
Fisher's exact (p value)					0.000[a]		0.000[a]		0.014[a]		1.000	
Chi square (p value)					0.000[a]		0.000[a]		0.000[a]		0.861	
Chi square with Yates correction (p value)					0.000[a]		0.000[a]		0.002[a]		0.006[a]	

[a] Indicates that the test shows a difference between the minority and majority subgroups.

In Table 7.1, the percentage of females passing exceeds the percentage of males passing, and the adverse impact ratio is 101%. Using the four-fifths rule, there is no adverse impact against females. Similarly, the z test comparing the differences in pass rates for males and females and the Fisher's test are not significant. The Fisher's test takes into account the discrepant population of females in this study. Thus, Table 7.1 shows a consistent pattern for sex differences. The rate at which males and females pass is not statistically different by any measure. In fact, the pass rate for females is slightly higher than that of males.

Table 7.2 tells a different story for the protected racial subgroups. Although the adverse impact ratios for each minority group exceed 80%, the z test based on the binomial distribution is significant for all racial subgroups except Native Americans. Because the z test is not appropriate for small samples, the z test results for the Native American group (n = 3) can probably be discounted due to unreliability. Depending on your point of view, the z test results of Asians (n = 14) might also be interpreted cautiously due to small sample size; however, the results for the African Americans (n = 240) and Hispanics (n = 95) cannot be questioned on the basis of sample size. The Fisher's test, appropriate for small samples, shows results similar to the z test based on the binomial distribution. There are significant differences for all groups except Native Americans.

Most psychologists would probably agree that in the set of data in Table 7.1 there is no adverse impact against females. But, the conclusions in Table 7.2 are not so clear with racial subgroups. If we consider only the 80% rule, there is no evidence of adverse impact. However, all the other statistical tests indicate significant differences between the white subgroup and the African American, the Hispanic, and Asian subgroups. Looking at the results of the z tests and the Fisher's exact probability test, we find evidence that African Americans, Hispanics, and Asians are selected at a disproportionately lower rate when compared to whites. According to the Fisher's test, there is no adverse impact against the very small Native American group. Although no other test indicates a difference in selection rates for Native Americans, the corrected chi square test does. Consequently, the psychologist who stops at the four-fifths rule will get a different answer about the adverse impact for all racial subgroups from the psychologist who calculates additional statistics.

With respect to these results, two questions remain: (1) What additional efforts (if any) should be made to ameliorate the adverse impact? (2) What results should be reported? Of course, the answer to the first question depends on the organization's particular goals and circumstances. An organization seeking to eliminate all adverse impact in its testing programs may well look for alternative measures or take some of the steps discussed in the latter half of this chapter. Another organization may accept the current levels of adverse impact on selection instruments and address recruiting strategies to ensure a diverse employee body. The second part of this chapter looks at a number of options for redressing adverse impact.

The answer to the question of what results to report may be more a political issue than a scientific one. On one hand, reporting all the statistics may assist someone in a challenge to the selection procedure. On the other, anyone challenging the selection procedure is very likely to calculate the same statistics quickly. Although the Uniform Guidelines (Equal Employment Opportunity Commission, 1978) are clear on the reporting requirement, they do not specify the statistics to use or report.

> Users of selection procedures other than those users complying with section 15A(1) of this section should maintain and have available for each job information on adverse impact of the selection process for that job and, where it is determined a selection process has an adverse impact, evidence of validity as set forth below. (Section 15.A)

However, the Uniform Guidelines do address statistics other than the four-fifths rule.

> If the determination of adverse impact is made using a procedure other than the "four-fifths rule," as defined in the first sentence of section 4D of this part, a justification, consistent with section 4D of this part, for the procedure used to determine adverse impact should be available. (Section 15.A.2.b)

On Which Set of Data Should Adverse Impact Statistics Be Calculated?

Legal guidelines are clear on an employer's responsibility to keep accurate records and monitor adverse impact. However, another dilemma for the psychologist or HR professional is defining the appropriate sample on which to calculate adverse impact. A number of questions arise:

- If data from a concurrent criterion-related validity study are available, does it make sense to calculate adverse impact statistics in the absence of applicant data?
- If applicant data are available, from what time period should the data be drawn?
- From what geographic locations should the applicant data be drawn? Should data be collapsed across regions?

Many calculate adverse impact statistics on the sample of employees who participated in the concurrent validity study that justifies the use of the selection procedure because at the time of implementation those are the only data available. Yet, these calculations raise some significant concerns.

Consider a hypothetical example derived from Table 7.1. Assume the sex data came from an incumbent sample tested in the context of a concurrent validity study. The test measured a construct such as "upper body strength" that typically has adverse impact against females. If the 30 females tested in the concurrent sample represent females who successfully completed training and were performing well enough on the job to be retained, they may represent a small subset of the female applicant population who would pass the test. In contrast, in an applicant sample, we might find 90% of the males passing the strength test but only 10% of females—a clear case of adverse impact—as determined by almost any statistic. In this case, reporting adverse impact statistics based on incumbents may lead to a false conclusion that adverse impact will not result from the test.

Even determining the appropriate applicant pools on which to base adverse impact calculations can pose important questions. If you are calculating hire statistics, then the stated desires of the applicant may influence who is aggregated into which groups. For example, applicants who apply for a job in one city may not be an applicant for the same job in another city. In addition, the applicants for a job in one city may not be similar to applicants for the same job in another city. Similarly, an applicant who applies for one job may not be considered for another job that requires the same test if there are no openings for the second job. The psychologist must decide whether it is appropriate to aggregate data across locations or jobs.

The evaluation of test scores, however, poses a slightly different problem. The point is to evaluate the adverse impact of the test—not the bottom line decision to hire or not hire. Consequently, it is not a foregone conclusion that the applicant sample should be broken into subsamples based on location or job. A more appropriate evaluation of the test may be to aggregate the data of all the people who took the test for a particular job with the same cutoff score into one group regardless of location.

Caution is advised when evaluating the adverse impact of a test that is used for two jobs that have different skill expectations despite the same cutoff score on the same test. For example, consider a cognitive ability test with a single cutoff score that is used for all exempt positions, including executive hires. Because of other job requirements (e.g., successful work experience), the applicant pool for executive jobs may be more highly educated or trained than the applicant pool for entry-level professional jobs. Moreover, there are likely to be many more positions and applicants for the lower-level positions. Consider the data for sex subgroups in Table 7.3. Alone, neither group reflects adverse impact; however, the

TABLE 7.3

Percentage Pass and Fail by Sex Subgroups

Executive Group

	Total		Males		Females	
	N	% pass	N	% pass	N	% pass
Pass	45	45	30	40	15	60
Fail	55	55	45	60	10	40
Total	100		75		25	
80% rule ratio					1.500	
z test: binomial distribution					1.741	
z test: hypergeometric distribution					1.732	
z test: hypergeometric distribution (corrected)					1.501	
Fisher's exact (*p* value)					0.105	
Chi square (*p* value)					0.082	
Chi square with Yates correction (*p* value)					0.131	

Entry-Level Professional

	Total		Males		Females	
	N	% pass	N	% pass	N	% pass
Pass	185	16.8	20	20	165	16.5
Fail	915	83.2	80	80	835	83.5
Total	1100		100		1000	
80% rule ratio					0.825	
z test: binomial distribution					−0.892	
z test: hypergeometric distribution					−0.892	
z test: hypergeometric distribution (corrected)					−0.752	
Fisher's exact (*p* value)					0.400	
Chi square (*p* value)					0.372	
Chi square with Yates correction (*p* value)					0.452	

Combined Executive and Entry-Level Professional

	Total		Males		Females	
	N	% pass	N	% pass	N	% pass
Pass	230	19.2	55	31.4	175	17.1
Fail	970	80.8	120	68.6	850	82.9
Total	1200		175		1025	

TABLE 7.3 (*Continued*)

Percentage Pass and Fail by Sex Subgroups

80% rule ratio	0.543
z test: binomial distribution	−4.459[a]
z test: hypergeometric distribution	−4.457[a]
z test: hypergeometric distribution (corrected)	−4.353[a]
Fisher's exact (*p* value)	0.000[a]
Chi square (*p* value)	0.000[a]
Chi square with Yates correction (*p* value)	0.000[a]

[a] Indicates that the test shows a difference between the minority and majority subgroups.

combined groups do show adverse impact on all measures because of the distribution of men and women in each group.

Similar questions arise with respect to the appropriate time frames used to define a sample. Certainly, fundamental changes in the applicant pool would indicate that time frames should be adjusted. For example, if all candidates for a job are current employees seeking a promotion until some point in time when the company changes its policies and also seeks external candidates, the calculation of adverse impact should take the change in policy into account. Similarly, changes in economic conditions may lead to distinct changes in the size and composition of the applicant pool.

The federal government's changes in the definition of race subgroups confuse the issue of which data should be used to calculate adverse impact. The EEO-1 Report, formally called the Employer Information Report, requires certain employers[1] to provide a count of their employees by job category and then by ethnicity, race, and gender to both the Equal Employment Opportunity Commission (EEOC) and the Office of Federal Contract Compliance Programs (OFCCP). On January 27, 2006, the EEOC promulgated revisions to EEO-1 reporting that took effect in 2007. Among other things, the new EEO-1 reporting requirements changed the racial categories used in the report. Specifically, the new EEO-1 reporting:

- Added a new category, "Two or More Races"
- Divided "Asian or Pacific Islander" into two separate categories: "Asian" and "Native Hawaiian or other Pacific Islander"
- Renamed "African American" as "Black or African American"
- Renamed "Hispanic" as "Hispanic or Latino"
- Strongly endorsed self-identification of race and ethnic categories as opposed to visual identification by employers

Section 3.4B of the Uniform Guidelines (Equal Employment Opportunity Commission, 1978), which defines the race categories and links them to the EEO-1 reporting, states:

B. Applicable race, sex, and ethnic groups for record keeping.

The records called for by this section are to be maintained by sex, and the following races and ethnic groups: African Americans (Negroes), American Indians (including Alaskan Natives), Asians (including Pacific Islanders), Hispanic (including persons of Mexican, Puerto Rican, Cuban, Central or South American, or other Spanish origin or culture regardless of race), whites (Caucasians) other than Hispanic, and totals. The race, sex, and ethnic classifications called for by this section are consistent with the Equal Employment Opportunity Standard Form 100, Employer Information Report EEO-1 series of reports. The user should adopt safeguards to insure that the records required by this paragraph are used for appropriate purposes such as determining adverse impact, or (where required) for developing and monitoring affirmative action programs, and that such records are not used improperly.

The implications of these changes, particularly the new category of Two or More Races, for adverse impact analyses are not clear. Employers may well need to add another race category, "multiracial," to their adverse impact calculations. However, the degree to which a multiracial group composed of white Asians is comparable to a multiracial group of African American Hispanics also is not clear.

How Can Adverse Impact Be Minimized?

Many practitioners working with large organizations must answer the question of what to do when adverse impact is found. Most employers are striving to minimize the adverse impact in their testing programs for myriad reasons: desire for a diverse workforce, reduction of the likelihood of legal challenges, avoidance of validation work, need to attract candidates from diverse backgrounds, and so on. Three review articles (Hough, Oswald, & Ployhart, 2001; Ployhart & Holtz, 2008; Sackett, Schmitt, Ellingson, & Kabin, 2001) evaluated strategies for reducing mean subgroup differences. Although subgroup differences do not automatically result in adverse impact depending on selection rates and cutoff scores, they provide information about potential adverse impact. Together, these articles offer numerous ways in which the employer can respond to a finding of adverse impact; however, their effectiveness is often limited or the implications for the capability of the future workforce can be significant. Some of the more commonly used approaches are discussed next.

Do Nothing

Because adverse impact in test results is not unlawful, one option is to do nothing—provided the employer can demonstrate the job related-ness and business necessity of the selection procedure through a strong, carefully documented validity study. This strategy clearly does not lessen the level of adverse impact or achieve any of the related diversity goals; however, it is listed here as a possible response to a finding of adverse impact.

Eliminate Testing

In contrast to simply accepting adverse impact and preparing to defend the test, another approach is to discontinue testing. However, this approach raises serious questions about the capabilities of the workforce and the extent to which an informal selection process would comply with legal and professional guidelines. In addition, amelioration of adverse impact by substituting informal selection practices for more formal ones is not a given.

Investigate Alternatives and Replace Selection Procedures

One choice is to investigate alternative selection procedures and replace procedures with high adverse impact and low validity with those that have lower adverse impact and equal or greater validity. The Uniform Guidelines (Equal Employment Opportunity Commission, 1978) specifi-cally call for the employer to seek alternative selection procedures that minimize adverse impact while achieving equal or greater validity:

> **B. Consideration of suitable alternative selection procedures.**
>
> Where two or more selection procedures are available which serve the user's legitimate interest in efficient and trustworthy workmanship, and which are substantially equally valid for a given purpose, the user should use the procedure which has been demonstrated to have the lesser adverse impact. Accordingly, whenever a validity study is called for by these guidelines, the user should include, as a part of the validity study, an investigation of suitable alternative selection pro-cedures and suitable alternative methods of using the selection pro-cedure which have as little adverse impact as possible, to determine the appropriateness of using or validating them in accord with these guidelines. If a user has made a reasonable effort to become aware of such alternative procedures and validity has been demonstrated in accord with these guidelines, the use of the test or other selection procedure may continue until such time as it should reasonably be reviewed for currency. (Section 3B)

Most psychologists actively investigate alternative selection procedures in a variety of ways. Common approaches to alternative selection procedures include the following:

- Different tools using similar methods to measure the same construct (e.g., two different paper-and-pencil tests that measure the ability to work math word problems). Although two different multiple-choice tests measuring the same construct are likely to have similar levels of adverse impact, occasionally a change in instructions or item content can reduce adverse impact. For example, a mechanical comprehension test that uses more common examples from everyday life may have less adverse impact against women than one that uses examples involving machines with which women may be less familiar. The format of the test is arguably the same.

- Different tools using different methods to measure the same construct (e.g., a paper-and-pencil test that measures the ability to work math word problems and a work sample that has math word problems embedded in it).

- Different tools using similar methods to measure different constructs (e.g., one paper-and-pencil test measuring verbal reasoning and one paper-and-pencil test measuring quantitative reasoning). The degree of difference between measures of two different constructs undoubtedly depends on the constructs measured. The difference between levels of adverse impact in measures of verbal reasoning and quantitative reasoning may be relatively small; the differences in measures of conscientiousness and mathematical knowledge may be large.

- Different tools using different methods to measure different constructs (e.g., a paper-and-pencil test measuring reading and interpretation skills and a structured oral interview measuring communication skills).

- Different methods of weighting a battery of tests.

- Different cutoff scores.

- Different models for the use of the test score (e.g., rank order, cutoff scores, fixed bands, sliding bands).

- Different orders of selection components in a multiple-hurdles selection process.

Although the process of investigating different alternatives can be challenging, time consuming, and expensive, the more difficult question facing psychologists is how to balance adverse impact and validity. There is no legal requirement to trade lower validity for lower adverse impact. Nevertheless, a finding of adverse impact may raise questions of the thoroughness of the search for alternative selection procedures.

Use Only Tests That Have No Adverse Impact

Although there is no legal requirement to eliminate adverse impact, an employer working with an external consultant will occasionally state that the selection procedure that is proposed or developed must have no adverse impact. This goal seems to ignore the Uniform Guidelines (Equal Employment Opportunity Commission, 1978) requirement to look for solutions that minimize adverse impact while achieving similar levels of validity and is at least theoretically, if not always, practically possible if the employer is willing to accept limited coverage of the knowledge, skills, abilities, and other characteristics required by the job. However, the problem comes when the client also wants a selection procedure that is at the same time highly predictive. As a profession, I/O psychology has had little success meeting both goals, elimination or at least minimization of adverse impact and maximization of prediction, when predicting task performance; however, when predicting contextual performance, the likelihood of reducing adverse impact and maintaining validity is more likely. If meeting both goals is not possible, then someone must choose which goal is more important.

Anecdotally at least, there appears to be an increase in the number of employers who require that a selection procedure have no adverse impact for the life of the tool. Figure 7.1 contains an edited example of such a requirement from a recent request for proposal (RFP). Statements such as these reflect the employer's interest in creating or maintaining a diverse employee body and avoiding adverse impact in hiring. But, they also reflect impractical business relationships and unattainable ideals. No I/O psychologist without control over the client organization's applicant population and recruiting methods can ethically commit to solving adverse impact problems indefinitely. That I/O psychologist also cannot feasibly

---

Supplier will develop and validate the test according to legal standards. The test developed by Supplier will not be accepted if it shows any adverse impact, and the Supplier will be expected to revise the test so that it has no adverse impact. If adverse impact results from the use of this test, the Supplier will be asked to demonstrate that the assessment predicts job success and there is no other test that can be substituted. Supplier will be asked to define/identify alternative assessment tools/tests with lesser or no adverse impact.

FIGURE 7.1
Example of RFP requirement for no adverse impact.

engage in an infinite search for the ideal and compare all other tests in the world to the one he or she developed or recommended.

Avoid Tests of Cognitive Ability

One specific way to use tests that have no adverse impact is to avoid tests of cognitive ability. Cognitive ability tests are known to have significant amounts of adverse impact (Hunter & Hunter, 1984) and to be predictive of job performance in a wide range of jobs (Hunter, 1986; Schmidt, Ones, & Hunter, 1992). The dilemma the employer is sometimes left with is whether to minimize the adverse impact at the expense of prediction or vice versa. Of course, measures of noncognitive knowledge, skills, abilities, and other characteristics (KSAOs) have some validity; the question is one of *maximizing validity.*

Substitute Educational Achievement for Tests of Cognitive Ability

Educational attainment is dependent on cognitive ability as well as other job-relevant KSAOs such as conscientiousness and personal motivation; however, the reduction in adverse impact is modest when educational credentials are substituted for cognitive ability and is often accompanied by decreases in validity (Berry, Gruys, & Sackett, 2006; Roth & Bobko, 2000).

Assess KSAOs and Combine Tests

Another approach is to assess the full range of KSAOs and combine tests with high adverse impact with tests of lower adverse impact. Some researchers (Hough, Eaton, Dunnette, Kamp, & McCloy, 1990) have recommended adding tests with lower adverse impact to those with higher adverse impact. Measures of some constructs like cognitive ability are known to have significant levels of adverse impact for some subgroups; yet, many jobs require other KSAOs in addition to cognitive ability, and many of these KSAOs have less adverse impact than cognitive ability.

Several researchers have found a consistent pattern of increasing validity and decreasing group differences when cognitive ability tests are combined with alternative measures, although the size of the changes in validity and group differences vary from study to study (Bobko, Roth, & Potosky, 1999; Pulakos & Schmitt, 1996; Ryan, Ployhart, & Friedel, 1998). However, the value of the decrease in group differences when cognitive ability is removed relative to the loss of validity remains in question.

It is important to note that combining tests with high adverse impact with those of lower adverse impact into a test battery does not always result in lower overall adverse impact for the battery (Sackett & Ellingson, 1997). The degree to which adverse impact is lowered depends on several factors, including the applicant pool characteristics, the degree of adverse impact, the selection ratio, correlations between tests, and weighting of the tests (Bobko et al., 1999; Cascio, Outtz, Zedeck, & Goldstein, 1991; Murphy, Osten, & Myors, 1995; Sackett & Ellingson, 1997; Sackett & Roth, 1996; Schmitt, Rogers, Chan, Sheppard, & Jennings, 1997). Moreover, the assumption that a compensatory model for combining tests is an effective method of selection may not be true for all jobs. Some jobs may require minimum amounts of KSAOs like cognitive ability that typically are associated with large subgroup differences.

Adjust the Weighting of Predictors

An approach to lessening adverse impact that is similar to adding non-cognitive measures is weighting predictors with less adverse impact more heavily; however, this approach may lower validity (De Corte, 1999; De Corte & Lievens, 2003; Ryan, Ployhart, & Friedel, 1998).

Change the Format of the Test

Many researchers (e.g., Hough et al., 2001; Schmitt, Clause, & Pulakos, 1996) have noted that some formats of testing have less adverse impact than other formats. A number of differing test formats have been investigated, including video-based test stimuli (e.g., video-based situational judgment tests [SJTs]), work samples, assessment centers, portfolios, and accomplishment records. While there are some differences in subgroup performance on such measures, the differences are not always attributable to the format alone. Explanations of the differences in subgroup performance range from the measurement of multiple cognitive and noncognitive KSAOs in the alternative formats to the minimization of cognitively loaded items and instructions. Pulakos and Schmitt (1996) compared different testing modalities and found that visual stimulus reduced subgroup differences, although the traditional paper-and-pencil testing had the highest validity. Chan and Schmitt (1997) compared written and video-based SJTs and found decreases in d for the video-based SJT. Sackett et al. (2001) pointed out in their review that several factors influenced the changes in d when comparing various testing modalities: similarity of the construct being measured and the reliability of each testing modality. In addition, tests such as work samples are often based on work tasks that have fewer subgroup differences. However, when the same construct is measured in both modalities, the reduction in subgroup differences has not always been established.

A promising test format is the use of constructed response options in which the candidate constructs a response rather than selects from a set of already-constructed responses. Arthur and his colleagues have demonstrated that group differences between African Americans and whites declined while scores of African Americans increased when using a constructed response format (Arthur, Edwards, & Barrett, 2002; Edwards & Arthur, 2004). They demonstrated that these effects were partly due to differences in the reading load of the test and applicant perceptions of the predictors.

Although the financial impact of a test is often not considered in evaluating alternatives, it must be noted that some test formats have significant costs associated with administration and scoring. Hoffman and Thornton (1997) compared a paper-and-pencil test to an assessment center and found that although the assessment center had slightly lower validity than the aptitude tests, it had much less adverse impact. However, the cost of the assessment center was approximately 10 times greater per candidate.

There may also be intangible costs. On the positive side, some applicants may perceive assessment tools that evaluate their performance of work tasks as particularly fair and equitable in contrast to a paper-and-pencil test that appears abstract and potentially unrelated. On the negative side, the demand some of these formats place on applicants who must assemble information may cause some to withdraw from the selection process (Ryan, Ployhart, Greguras, & Schmit, 1998; Schmit & Ryan, 1997)

Broaden the Conceptualization of the Job

Some research has suggested that emphasizing contextual performance as well as task performance in definitions of the job and the subsequent criterion measures leads to broader KSAO requirements that deemphasize cognitive ability and emphasize other KSAOs that typically have less adverse impact (Hattrup, Rock, & Scalia, 1997). However, criterion weighting will affect the validity of the selection procedures, and reductions in subgroup differences are not always large. Nevertheless, the size of the reduction need not be large to warrant consideration of this approach.

Minimize the Cognitive Demands in the Instructions and Items That Do Not Measure Cognitive Ability

Some research has investigated the effect of cognitive demands in instructions on test performance and in items that do not measure cognitive ability and found that removal of the cognitively loaded materials can affect group differences. For example, Chan and Schmitt (1997) compared video and written SJTs and found substantial reductions in d between whites and blacks. Although removal of the cognitive demands from instructions and items that measure another construct may lessen adverse impact, it should be noted that cognitive ability is still relevant for many, if not most, jobs.

Avoid Culturally Specific Item Content

One theory behind adverse impact and group differences is that test items contain unfamiliar content for some cultures. By eliminating the culturally specific test content, the test would have less adverse impact. Good testing practice would suggest that irrelevant cultural references be removed. Research comparing "culture-fair" tests to those with verbal content that is presumably culturally specific does not show substantial reductions in subgroup differences (Hausdorf, LeBlanc, & Chawla, 2003).

In their summary of the value of differential item functioning (DIF) analysis, Sackett et al. (2001) concluded that the magnitude of DIF effects is small; no consistent pattern of items favoring one group or another emerges from the research; results do not indicate that removal of items will affect the overall score; and little is known about DIF item removal on test validity.

Adjust the Cutoff Score

A common consideration in setting a cutoff score is the level of adverse impact at various possible cutoff scores. Some researchers (e.g., De Corte, 1999) have found that the costs of removing adverse impact in terms of the quality of applicants may be quite substantial. However, there are also situations in which lowering the cutoff score reduces adverse impact without substantially reducing the quality of applicants subsequently hired. Banding procedures group test scores of individuals and treat individuals within a band the same; however, banding does not always increase the selection of members of the lower-scoring group (Sackett & Wilk, 1994). Again, the psychologist must balance reduction of adverse impact with the required level of performance, placing a value on each.

Target Recruiting

One approach to reducing adverse impact is to increase the likelihood that the protected subgroups have the necessary KSAOs by targeting recruiting efforts. For example, if a quantitative reasoning test has adverse impact against women in the general population, one strategy is to recruit women who are likely to have higher quantitative reasoning skills (e.g., engineering graduates).

Set Minimum Qualifications

Another way to increase the likelihood that protected group members have the KSAOs needed is to set minimum qualifications. For example, requiring that candidates for an engineering position have two years of relevant college-level education may increase the pass rate of women on the test of quantitative reasoning. It merits noting, however, that the adverse impact problem may simply be transferred to the minimum qualifications.

Retesting

Investigations of the effects of retesting found little reduction of adverse impact (Sin, Farr, Murphy, & Hausknecht, 2004). Although scores of applicants who retook a test increased, group differences remained.

Provide Test-Taking Training

Some psychologists advocate teaching applicants how to take tests and recommend practice tests (Bartram, 1995). Such courses probably do help when an applicant is not familiar with certain item types, the computer software on which some tests are administered, or effective strategies for taking timed tests. However, the research on test preparation programs seems to show a positive effect for all attendees and little reduction of d (Sackett, Burris, & Ryan, 1989; Sackett et al., 2001). Nevertheless, these types of programs are well received by applicants. Moreover, when an "absolute cutoff score" (i.e., one that is independent of the group being tested) is used, improving all test takers' scores will result in more members of protected classes passing.

Increase Test-Taking Motivation

If protected subgroups are less motivated to take a test, then taking measures to increase their motivation might increase their test scores. Chan, Schmitt, DeShon, Clause, and Delbridge (1997) demonstrated the relationship between race and test performance was partially mediated by the motivation of the test taker.

The research on stereotype threat (Steele & Aronson, 1995) suggests that certain "threatening" conditions embedded in the testing instructions may inhibit the performance of minority groups. However, this research has not been replicated in employment settings in which all test takers experience somewhat threatening instructions as they know the test is being administered for employment purposes (Cullen, Hardison, & Sackett, 2004; Sackett, 2003; Sackett, Hardison, & Cullen, 2004).

Increase Time Limits

One explanation for subgroup differences is attitudes toward speeded tests according to race and ethnicity. Research in educational settings suggests that increasing time limits has little effect on *d*s and may in fact increase them (Evans & Reilly, 1973; Wild, Durso, & Rubin, 1982).

In summary, there are a number of activities to mitigate adverse impact that have varying levels of effectiveness. Some of these activities do not work well with respect to mitigating adverse impact (e.g., using test preparation training to reduce group differences); some are a component of good testing practice (e.g., avoiding culturally specific item content); and some are not always feasible (e.g., target recruiting). Some of these activities work but have severe consequences for the capability of the workforce. Although there are few, if any, actions that will completely eliminate adverse impact while maintaining high levels of validity, some of them reduce adverse impact to some degree without affecting validity substantially. Thus, an important question for the psychologist is the value placed on small reductions of adverse impact when validity remains substantially the same.

Conclusion

In conclusion, there are three criteria for a useful action to minimize adverse impact:

First, the action should work. Many of the activities suggested do not have the intended outcome—reduction of adverse impact. For example, reducing subgroup differences through DIF analysis does not consistently reduce adverse impact, and its effect on validity is not clear. However, some actions do reduce adverse impact to varying degrees. For example, targeted recruiting can reduce the level of adverse impact. When the action does succeed in reducing adverse impact, even to a limited extent, the action should be weighed against other criteria, including the effect on validity, and feasibility.

Second, the action should not limit the capability of the workforce extensively. Several actions will lower adverse impact but may limit the capability of the workforce. For example, avoiding cognitive predictors and using only noncognitive predictors will reduce adverse impact against some protected subgroups and validity if task performance is being predicted. An important issue for psychologists and their clients is determining what an acceptably capable workforce is.

Third, the action must be feasible. Most employers are concerned about the costs of adverse impact mitigation techniques, particularly when they will also suffer the costs associated with a lower-ability group of employees. The question of how much effort to reduce adverse impact is sufficient is unanswered. From the employer's point of view, the answer probably varies according to factors ranging from the financial stability of the organization to the job for which the selection procedure is being used. From a legal perspective, the question is also unanswered. Experts in testing litigation (Gutman, 2005) see these issues, such as the financial obligations of employer to identify alternative selection procedures, evolving.

Employers must also be concerned about the practicality of certain actions. The best test of all may be a job tryout with significant training and coaching; however, this strategy is neither practical nor cost-effective. It is not feasible for a company of any size to take on the task of training large numbers of people in the applicant pool when there is no guarantee the trainees will improve their skills, accept the company's job offer, and stay on the job long enough for the employer to recoup its investment.

There are no easy answers to the questions of adverse impact. There is no checklist for calculating and reporting adverse impact or easy solutions to mitigating it. The I/O practitioner is well advised to stay up to date on litigation involving testing and the evolving research literature.

Note

1. Employers with federal contracts of $50,000 or more and 50 employees or more or employers without federal contracts who have 100 or more employees must file EEO-1 reports.

References

Arthur, W., Edwards, B. D., & Barrett, G. V. (2002). Multiple-choice and constructed response tests of ability: Race-based subgroup performance differences on alternative paper-and-pencil test formats. *Personnel Psychology, 55,* 985–1008.

Bartram, D. (1995). Predicting adverse impact in selection testing. *International Journal of Selection and Assessment, 3,* 52–61.

Berry, C., Gruys, M., & Sackett, P. R. (2006). Educational attainment as a proxy for cognitive ability in selection: Effects on levels of cognitive ability and adverse impact. *Journal of Applied Psychology, 91*, 696–705.

Bobko, P., Roth, P. L., & Potosky, D. (1999). Derivation and implications of a meta-analysis matrix incorporating cognitive ability, alternative predictors, and job performance. *Personnel Psychology, 52*, 561–589.

Cascio, W. F., Outtz, J., Zedeck, S., & Goldstein, I. L. (1991). Statistical implications of six methods of test score use in personnel selection. *Human Performance, 4*, 233–264.

Chan, D., & Schmitt, N. (1997). Video-based versus paper-and-pencil method of assessment in situational judgment tests: Subgroup differences in test performance and face validity perceptions. *Journal of Applied Psychology, 82*, 143–159.

Chan, D., Schmitt, N., DeShon, R. P., Clause, C. C., & Delbridge, K. (1997). Reactions to cognitive ability tests: The relationships between race, test performance, face validity perceptions, and test-taking motivation. *Journal of Applied Psychology, 82*, 300–310.

Cullen, M, J., Hardison, C. M., & Sackett, P. R. (2004). Using SAT-grade and ability-job performance relationships to test predictions derived from stereotype threat theory. *Journal of Applied Psychology, 89*, 220–230.

De Corte, W. (1999). Weighting job performance predictors to both maximize the quality of the selected workforce and control the level of adverse impact. *Journal of Applied Psychology, 84*, 695–702.

De Corte, W. & Lievens, F. (2003). A practical procedure to estimate the quality and adverse impact of single-stage selection decisions. *International Journal of Selection and Assessment, 11*, 89–97.

Edwards, B. D., & Arthur, W. (2004, April). *Race-based subgroup differences on a constructed response paper-and-pencil test.* Poster session presented at the 19th Annual Conference of the Society for Industrial and Organizational Psychology, Chicago.

Evans, F. R., & Reilly, R. R. (1973). A study of test speededness as a potential source of bias in the quantitative score of the admission test for graduate study in business. *Research in Higher Education, 1*, 173–183.

Gutman, A. (2005). Adverse impact: Judicial, regulatory, and statutory authority. In F. Landy (Ed.), *Employment discrimination litigation* (pp. 20–46). New York: Wiley.

Hattrup, K., Rock, J., & Scalia, C. (1997). The effects of varying conceptualizations of job performance on adverse impact, minority hiring, and predicted performance. *Journal of Applied Psychology, 82*, 656–664.

Hausdorf, P. A., LeBlanc, M. M., and Chawla, A. (2003). Cognitive ability testing and employment selection: Does test content relate to adverse impact? *Applied HRM Research, 7*, 41–48.

Hazelwood School District v. United States, 433 U.S. 299 (1977).

Hoffman, C. C., & Thornton, G. C., III. (1997). Examining selection utility where competing predictors differ in adverse impact. *Personnel Psychology, 50*, 455–470.

Hough, L. M., Eaton, N. K., Dunnette, M. D., Kamp, J. D., & McCloy, R. A. (1990). Criterion-related validities of personality constructs and the effect of response distortion on those validities. *Journal of Applied Psychology, 75*, 581–595.

Hough, L. M., Oswald, F. L., & Ployhart, R. E. (2001). Determinants, detection, and amelioration of adverse impact in personnel selection procedures: Issues, evidence, and lessons learned. *International Journal of Selection and Assessment, 9*, 152–194.

Hunter, J. E. (1986). Cognitive ability, cognitive aptitudes, job knowledge, and job performance. *Journal of Vocational Behavior, 29*, 340–362.

Hunter, J. E., & Hunter, R. (1984). Validity and utility of alternative predictors. *Psychological Bulletin, 96*, 72–98.

Murphy, K. R., Osten, K., & Myors, B. (1995). Modeling the effects of banding in personnel selection. *Personnel Psychology, 48*, 61–84.

Paetzold, R. L., and Wilborn, S. L. (1994). *The statistics of discrimination: Using statistical evidence in discrimination cases.* New York: West.

Ployhart, R. E., and Holtz, B. C. (2008). The diversity-validity dilemma: Strategies for reducing racioethnic and sex subgroup differences and adverse impact in selection. *Personnel Psychology, 61*, 153–172.

Pulakos, E. E., & Schmitt, N. (1996). An evaluation of two strategies for reducing adverse impact and their effects on criterion-related validity. *Human Performance, 9*, 241–258.

Roth, P. L., & Bobko, P. (2000). College grade point average as a personnel selection device: Ethnic group differences and potential adverse impact. *Journal of Applied Psychology, 85*, 399–406.

Ryan, A. M, Ployhart, R. E., & Friedel, L. (1998). Using personality tests to reduce adverse impact: A cautionary note. *Journal of Applied Psychology, 83*, 298–307.

Ryan, A. M., Ployhart, R. E., Greguras, G. J., and Schmit, M. J. (1998). Test preparation programs in selection contexts: Self-selection and program effectiveness. *Personnel Psychology, 51*, 599–621.

Sackett, P. R. (2003). Stereotype threat in applied selection settings: A commentary. *Human Performance, 16*, 295–309.

Sackett, P. R., Burris, L. R., & Ryan, A. M. (1989). Coaching and practice effects in personnel selection. In C. L. Cooper & I. Robertson (Eds.), *International review of industrial and organizational psychology* (Vol. 4, pp 145–183). London: Wiley.

Sackett, P. R., & Ellingson, J. E. (1997). The effects of forming multi-predictor composites on group differences and adverse impact. *Personnel Psychology, 50*, 707–721.

Sackett, P. R., Hardison, C. M., & Cullen, M. J. (2004). On interpreting stereotype threat as accounting for African American-White differences on cognitive tests. *American Psychologist, 59*, 7–13.

Sackett, P. R., & Roth, L. (1996). Multi-stage selection strategies: A Monte Carlo investigation of effects on performance and minority hiring. *Personnel Psychology, 49*, 549–572.

Sackett, P. R., Schmitt, N., Ellingson, J. E., & Kabin, M. B. (2001). High-stakes testing in employment, credentialing, and higher education: Prospects in a post-affirmative action world. *American Psychologist, 56*, 302–318.

Sackett, P. R., & Wilk, S. L. (1994). Within-group norming and other forms of score adjustment in preemployment testing. *American Psychologist, 49*, 929–954.

Schmidt, F. L., Ones, D. S., & Hunter, J. E. (1992). Personnel selection. *Annual Review of Psychology, 43*, 627–670.

Schmit, M. J., & Ryan, A. M. (1997). Applicant withdrawal: The role of test-taking attitudes and racial differences. *Personnel Psychology, 50, 955–876.*

Schmitt, N., Clause, C. S., & Pulakos, E. D. (1996). In C.R. Cooper & I.T. Robertson (Eds.), Subgroup differences associated with different measures of some common job-relevant constructs. *International review of industrial and organizational psychology* (Vol. 11, pp. 115–139). New York: Wiley.

Schmitt, N., Rogers, W., Chan, D., Sheppard, L., & Jennings, D. (1997). Adverse impact and predictive efficiency of various predictor combinations. *Journal of Applied Psychology, 82, 719–730.*

Sin, H. P., Farr, J. L., Murphy, K. R., & Hausknecht, J. P. (2004, August). *An investigation of Black-White differences in self-selection and performance in repeated testing.* Paper presented at the 64th annual meeting of the Academy of Management, New Orleans.

Steele, C. M., & Aronson, J. (1995). Stereotype threat and the intellectual test performance of African Americans. *Journal of Personality and Social Psychology, 69, 797–811.*

Uniform guidelines on employee selection procedures. 29 C.F.R. § 1607 *et seq.* (1978).

Wild, C. L., Durso, R., & Rubin, D. B. (1982). Effects of increased test-taking time on test scores by ethnic group, years out of school, and sex. *Journal of Educational Measurement, 55*, 177–185.

8

Performance Ratings: Then and Now

Frank Landy

Introduction

Over 30 years ago, Jim Farr and I finished one of the last large-scale manual literature reviews and narrative analyses of a central topic in industrial and organizational (I/O) psychology: performance rating (Landy & Farr, 1980). We considered hundreds of empirical and theoretical articles that appeared over the 30 years preceding our article. Since the appearance of that article, it has been cited over 500 times, so it clearly did and still does address a topic of interest to I/O psychologists. We drew a number of conclusions in that article. Some of the conclusions remain as true today as they were then and are hardly controversial. For example, we argued that performance rating was much more complicated than it might appear. We suggested a process model that included some of the complicating factors. Although that model can and has been improved, no one has suggested that rating is any *simpler* than we suggested. Even that preliminary model was likened by Jim Naylor to the plumbing in an old Scottish castle. We also suggested that cogni tive operations of raters deserved serious consideration. Although t' may have been a novel proposition for I/O psychologists, it was ha earthshaking for the rest of the psychological research community cognitive revolution was well under way in most areas *other* th psychology. Again, this proposition was embraced and, along v work of Feldman (1981), could be seen as a valuable point of d for later research.

Two other propositions, while apparently accepted at the become more "controversial." The first was that a moratoriu declared on rating scale format. Since the beginning of this millenium, this proposition has been increasingly questioned. New technologies, new deconstructions of the performance domain, and new forms of work have led researchers to suggest that the moratorium should be lifted. As an example, Borman's introduction of computer-adaptive rating scales (CARSs; Borman et al., 2001; Schneider et al., 2003) shows great promise with respect to both the accuracy and the validity of ratings as well as the effectiveness of a new process for gathering information. I cannot speak for Jim Farr, but I am delighted with this line of research and willingly hereby officially lift the moratorium (as if it mattered). The second proposition that can be found in that article (Landy & Farr, 1980) dealt with the effect of demographic rater and rate characteristics, particularly race, gender, and age, on ratings. Simply put, Jim and I suggested that, from data available at the time, there was little clear evidence of bias on ratings based on demographic characteristics. For example, we said

- Rater and ratee demographic characteristics (ignoring possible moderator variables such as cognitive complexity or ratee familiarity) have little systematic effect on ratings.
- Rater and ratee demographic characteristics do not appear to interact to produce biased ratings.

These conclusions have been repeated many times and are often cited for the proposition that ratings are not biased against women, ethnic minorities, or older employees. This proposition of a lack of bias has become increasingly central to arguments of employment discrimination. Plaintiffs often suggest that performance ratings are unduly subjective and themselves to discriminatory decision making by managers and They suggest underlying dynamics such as negative stereo- licit attitudes.

s since Jim Farr and I completed our literature review 80), substantial data have appeared on the topic of atings. Better yet, many of the research designs realistic work settings and powerful analytic that provide a form of statistical control not Finally, the nature of the performance data ample, performance data are increas- nance, Organizational Citizenship erformance, and even adaptive and t, Jim Outtz asked me to revisit this would be the same today as they were 30 excellent idea, and it forms the substance

8

Performance Ratings: Then and Now

Frank Landy

Introduction

Over 30 years ago, Jim Farr and I finished one of the last large-scale manual literature reviews and narrative analyses of a central topic in industrial and organizational (I/O) psychology: performance rating (Landy & Farr, 1980). We considered hundreds of empirical and theoretical articles that appeared over the 30 years preceding our article. Since the appearance of that article, it has been cited over 500 times, so it clearly did and still does address a topic of interest to I/O psychologists. We drew a number of conclusions in that article. Some of the conclusions remain as true today as they were then and are hardly controversial. For example, we argued that performance rating was much more complicated than it might appear. We suggested a process model that included some of the complicating factors. Although that model can and has been improved, no one has suggested that rating is any *simpler* than we suggested. Even that preliminary model was likened by Jim Naylor to the plumbing in an old Scottish castle. We also suggested that cognitive operations of raters deserved serious consideration. Although this may have been a novel proposition for I/O psychologists, it was hardly earthshaking for the rest of the psychological research community. The cognitive revolution was well under way in most areas *other* than I/O psychology. Again, this proposition was embraced and, along with the work of Feldman (1981), could be seen as a valuable point of departure for later research.

Two other propositions, while apparently accepted at the time, have become more "controversial." The first was that a moratorium should be declared on rating scale format. Since the beginning of this millenium, this proposition has been increasingly questioned. New technologies, new deconstructions of the performance domain, and new forms of work have led researchers to suggest that the moratorium should be lifted. As an example, Borman's introduction of computer-adaptive rating scales (CARSs; Borman et al., 2001; Schneider et al., 2003) shows great promise with respect to both the accuracy and the validity of ratings as well as the effectiveness of a new process for gathering information. I cannot speak for Jim Farr, but I am delighted with this line of research and willingly hereby officially lift the moratorium (as if it mattered). The second proposition that can be found in that article (Landy & Farr, 1980) dealt with the effect of demographic rater and rate characteristics, particularly race, gender, and age, on ratings. Simply put, Jim and I suggested that, from data available at the time, there was little clear evidence of bias on ratings based on demographic characteristics. For example, we said

- Rater and ratee demographic characteristics (ignoring possible moderator variables such as cognitive complexity or ratee familiarity) have little systematic effect on ratings.
- Rater and ratee demographic characteristics do not appear to interact to produce biased ratings.

These conclusions have been repeated many times and are often cited for the proposition that ratings are not biased against women, ethnic minorities, or older employees. This proposition of a lack of bias has become increasingly central to arguments of employment discrimination. Plaintiffs often suggest that performance ratings are unduly subjective and lend themselves to discriminatory decision making by managers and employers. They suggest underlying dynamics such as negative stereotypes or implicit attitudes.

In the 30 years since Jim Farr and I completed our literature review (Landy & Farr, 1980), substantial data have appeared on the topic of biased performance ratings. Better yet, many of the research designs have included both more realistic work settings and powerful analytic tools, such as meta-analysis, that provide a form of statistical control not widely available 30 years ago. Finally, the nature of the performance data is becoming more specific. For example, performance data are increasingly parsed into technical performance, Organizational Citizenship Behavior (OCB), counterproductive performance, and even adaptive and proactive performance. As a result, Jim Outtz asked me to revisit this arena and see if my conclusions would be the same today as they were 30 years ago. I think this was an excellent idea, and it forms the substance of my chapter.

The Literature Search and Review

The search for literature began with 1979 (the first year after the completion of the Landy and Farr article) and carried on to 2007. It was accomplished through PsychINFO (http://www.apa.org/psycinfo/), the American Psychological Association electronic database using the following key words: *performance appraisal, performance rating and race, gender, age, disability, bias; gender bias, age bias, race bias, disability bias.* Google Scholar (http://scholar.google.com/) was also searched using the same key words. Finally, a Social Sciences Citation Index (http://thomsonreuters.com/products_services/scientific/Social_Sciences_Citation_Index) search was completed using the Landy and Farr (1980) article as the search key. The search produced 230 empirical and theoretical articles. It is important to point out that these articles can be thought of as often "nested." Various meta-analyses often included the individual databases in their analytic scheme. Thus, one can consider the results of individual studies, the results of meta-analyses, or both. In my consideration, I do both. Nevertheless, it is instructive to know that of the 134 individual studies, 5 or 6.7% were also included in a meta-analysis. Naturally, a meta-analysis provides greater confidence of inference since it not only can control for statistical artifacts but also often tests possible moderator variables. That is not to say that the individual studies provide no unique insight on the phenomenon of interest (particularly when they include contextual variables that do not lend themselves to large-scale moderator subanalyses in meta-analyses), just that they are vulnerable to artifactual influences.

Table 8.1 presents the descriptive results of the literature search. As shown, some topics were of much greater interest to researchers than others. For example, gender variables produced the greatest number of empirical articles, while disability variables appear to be of less interest. Age and race fall somewhere in between. Similarly, meta-analyses have been completed on race and age, but less commonly gender and never disability. In part, this is an issue related to the coding of data in original studies. An analysis of gender, race, age, or disability can only be done if that variable is recorded at the individual rating level. In the subsequent

TABLE 8.1

Number of Studies 1997–2007

	Meta-analyses	Individual studies
Age	4	22
Gender	2	68
Race	4	40
Disability	0	14

sections of this chapter, I first consider meta-analyses and what one might conclude from them regarding bias in performance ratings. Next, I provide a sample of intriguing findings in individual studies. Finally, I address the larger issue of whether we know more now about potential rating bias than we did in 1980 and, of equal importance, whether there are forces at work that will limit the half-life of what we know today.

Performance Ratings and Race

Meta-Analyses

There have been three meta-analyses directly on point with respect to racial differences (commonly black–white differences) in performance ratings. Unfortunately, they each share a common flaw: The design was a between-subject design rather than a within-subject or repeated-measures design. The gold standard would be a meta-analysis of studies that used a repeated-measures design. This would mean that the stimulus objects (the employees) would be constant across raters. In the concrete, an example of this design would be black and white raters each rating the same black and white ratees. That way, we could be sure that any substantial Rater × Ratee race interaction was not due to simple cohort differences in which employees were rated. This design also allows us to identify main effects for both rater race and ratee race.

Thus, in considering the three meta-analyses on point, I found the following:

1. Kraiger and Ford, 1985: This meta-analysis dealt with the issues of performance ratings. All but 1 of the 88 studies included in the meta-analysis were between-subject designs and not able to address Rater × Ratee race effects that are critical for inferences about racial bias in ratings. In addition, although Kraiger and Ford examined some moderator variables (e.g., training, rating scale format, research setting), the small number of studies in which there were black raters (14 of 78) made it impossible to examine these moderators for black raters.

2. Ford, Kraiger, and Schectmann, 1986: This meta-analysis dealt with a comparison of race effects in performance ratings versus objective indices of performance. Again, the critical design flaw was the use of a between-subject design. The contaminating effect in ratings is the same as noted: There could have been real differences in performance rather than biased ratings. With

respect to objective indices, the contaminating effect was more subtle. If there was not a direct comparison on objective indices for blacks and whites at least *holding the same job title*, we are again unable to distinguish between true performance differences and differences biased by race of the subject.

3. Kraiger and Ford, 1990: In this meta-analysis, Kraiger and Ford used an indirect approach to study the question of possible bias on ratings: They examined the strength of the relationship between two different measures of job performance (objective indices and scores on job knowledge tests) and supervisory ratings for black and white employees. As was true in the earlier studies, the rating variable was a between-subject variable, and there was no way of ensuring that the differences in ratings between black and white raters were not the result of true performance differences. In other words, there was no way of estimating the Rater × Ratee race interaction effect—the gold standard for tests of bias.

Individual Studies

Even though meta-analyses of race differences in ratings are scarce (and all use a flawed design), there are some individual studies that have been done with more appropriate designs. I consider several of those studies and their findings. For none of the single studies I consider, whether for race or other demographic characteristics, will I consider studies that were done with student participants or with hypothetical employees. I have argued in other places that these studies are largely irrelevant for the purpose of drawing inferences about workplace decision making (Landy, 2005, 2008). They employ a stranger-to-stranger paradigm that suppresses the effect of individuating information. It is exactly this individuating information that characterizes the nature of workplace performance evaluations. I also do not deal with studies of assessment centers or employee development since they address other issues (and virtually all are between-subject designs).

There have been many individual studies of the main effects of race on performance evaluations. Most of those have used a between-subject design so are generally uninformative about the specific issue of narrowly construed "bias" in ratings. By narrowly construed, I mean the hypothesis that ethnic minorities receive unfairly low performance ratings. To test this proposition, it would be necessary to show that when exactly the same ratees are involved, there is a Ratee × Rater race interaction that works to the disadvantage of ethnic minorities. Note that even in these appropriate designs, it would be useful to know if majority ratings are unduly positive, minority ratings are unduly negative, or both. To date, even those studies that have uncovered a Rater × Ratee race effect cannot answer that question. For all practical purposes, however, that is largely irrelevant to the extent to which minority employees may be deprived of scarce resources. If I am an ethnic minority, it hardly matters that whether I am unduly hammered in an appraisal or a majority member is unduly favored if I do not get a promotion or a pay raise.

To begin with individual studies that used only a between-subject design, there are some consistent findings, and they are consistent with the initial meta-analysis of Kraiger and Ford (1985). Generally, blacks received lower ratings than whites when race of rater was not crossed with race of ratee (Elvira & Zatick, 2002; Greenhaus & Parasuraman, 1993; Greenhaus, Parasuraman, & Wormley, 1990; Lefkowitz & Battista, 1995; Ostroff, Atwater, & Feinberg, 2004). The effect sizes were remarkably consistent at about 0.2 standard deviation (*SD*). Note that this consistency mirrors the consistency of differences in black–white differences in general mental ability (i.e., we consistently find differences of this magnitude), but it is a good deal lower in terms of effect size than the common finding of 1-*SD* difference in test scores. Another finding to emerge from these individual studies is that peer ratings showed larger race main effects than supervisory ratings (e.g., Pulakos, Oppler, White, & Borman, 1989). This might be argued as evidence that rater training (provided more often to supervisors than peers) and supervisory responsibility act as a check and balance against discrimination.

There have been several individual studies that have been completed using a repeated-measures design. Although this falls short of the power of a meta-analysis, most of these studies have been done with very large samples from both public sector and private sector employment covering many job titles and work contexts. As a result, we can place greater confidence in these findings than if they were from a small sample with one context and one job title. To be fair, it is not clear if there will ever be sufficient studies with appropriate information to do a meta-analysis to test for Rater × Ratee race effects. Such data are scarce in the field both because race of rater is not always coded and because the opportunities for having the same employees rated by both a minority and a majority supervisor are few and far between. Thus, the best we can hope for are large data sets.

As I described here, Kraiger and Ford (1985) were early meta-analytic investigators of possible race effects in ratings. After the appearance of their 1985 results, Pulakos, Oppler et al. (1989) conducted an analysis of military data from Project A. Pulakos et al. calculated point biserial correlations between race and ratings while controlling for the Rater × Ratee race interaction. They concluded that the "effect" of that interaction was much smaller (accounting for less than 1% of the rating variance) than the one found in the between-subject design of Kraiger and Ford.[1] A follow-on study (Oppler, Campbell, Pulakos, & Borman, 1992) examined the effect of objective indices of performance as a way of determining if any main effects were due to favoring majority applicants, disfavoring minority applicants, or both. Generally, they found that minority–majority rating differences were mirrored by minority–majority objective criterion differences, rendering a bias interpretation less tenable. In addition, they concluded that supervisory ratings were more performance relevant than peer ratings. Finally, they raised an issue that had been largely ignored to that point: Maximal measures of performance (i.e., in this case objective performance indicators) demonstrated greater race effects than typical measures of performance (i.e., supervisory ratings).

Sackett and DuBois (1991) also questioned the Kraiger and Ford (1985) results from the perspective of experimental design. Sackett and DuBois correctly stated that a repeated-measures design was more helpful in teasing out any racial animus in ratings than a between-subject design. As a result, Sackett and DuBois analyzed both a large civilian and a large military database using, in part, a repeated-measures design. In addition, they reanalyzed the Kraiger and Ford data. Sackett and DuBois came to the following conclusions:

1. There was no statistical evidence of a Rater × Ratee race effect when employing a repeated-measures design; this was true both in the private sector and the military data. The earlier large-scale military analysis of Pulakos et al. (1989) had cautioned that the finding with military samples needed to be replicated with private sector data. Sackett and DuBois filled that private sector "hole."

2. When the Kraiger and Ford (1985) data were deconstructed to examine (a) the status of the raters (supervisors vs. peers), (b) the setting for the research (laboratory vs. field), and (c) the year in which the study was conducted (pre- vs. post-1970), the effect sizes became vanishingly small and in fact favored minority ratees slightly. Sackett and DuBois also controlled for peer versus supervisor ratings in their military data set.

Sackett and DuBois concluded that, when appropriately analyzed, rating data provided no evidence of a bias against minority ratees or evidence to suggest that raters provided higher ratings to ratees of their own race.

Waldman and Avolio (1991) analyzed a large data set derived from a U.S. Employment Service database covering many job titles and contexts. Although they could not do a true repeated-measures analysis, they did use a common criterion definition (supervisory ratings) as well as rater-ratee pairings by race. From their analysis, they concluded that the ratee differences reported by Kraiger and Ford (1985) were much larger than those found in their study. They attributed these smaller differences to controls they applied for ability, education, and job experience. In addition, they found much smaller Ratee × Rater race interactions (similar to the findings of Pulakos et al., 1989 and Oppler et al., 1992). In essence, they concluded that when controls that might signal true score differences in the performance of whites and blacks were applied, differences in rating diminished to de minimis levels.

Rotundo and Sackett (1999) analyzed a large U.S. Employment Service performance-rating database with varied job titles and contexts. They had a slightly different focus in this study than the simple difference between black and white ratings. Instead, they sought to determine if bias ratings in a criterion could artificially influence validity coefficients involving cognitive ability tests. They were able to conduct both within- (repeated-measures) and between-subject analyses of these data. They found a very small combined effect size (0.07) between matched rater-ratee race data points and, based on hierarchical regression analyses, concluded that there was no evidence of bias on ratings; thus, it was unlikely that observed validity coefficients involving cognitive ability tests were artificially inflated by biased criterion scores.

Dewberry (2001) considered the potential presence of racial discrimination in the evaluation of written examination answers provided by white and black trainees in a legal education program. The wrinkle in this study was that the answers were graded in both a blind (to race) and nonblind condition by the same raters. Although Dewberry found small ratee effects (suggesting that black trainees performed more poorly than white trainees on the written examinations), there was no evidence of bias on the part of the raters (answer evaluators) since their black performance ratings were largely identical regardless of whether the ratings were blind or nonblind. It is axiomatic that blind ratings are unlikely to lend themselves to bias. Nevertheless, there were some common confounds in this study: It was not a repeated-measures design with respect to raters; plus, there was no study of rater race in either the blind or nonblind condition.

Stauffer and Buckley (2005) reanalyzed the Sackett and DuBois (1991) data set and concluded that Sackett and Du Bois were mistaken in their conclusions. Stauffer and Buckley showed that there were significant Rater × Ratee race effects that were both statistically (and they argued, practically) significant. Although there has been no formal response to this article by Sackett and DuBois (or others), there are some points than can be made in response.[2] As I have said here, when I consider the term *bias* in the context of performance ratings, I generally consider the narrow construction that addresses whether underrepresented groups (women, ethnic minorities, older employees, disabled employees) *suffer* as a result of biased ratings. More broadly and literally construed, bias can be seen as *any* differences between protected and nonprotected groups, even when the protected groups fare more favorably than the nonprotected groups. Stauffer and Buckley assumed the latter construction and argued that there are interaction effects but conceded that these effects do not necessarily favor majority employees. Stauffer and Buckley noted that they do not know if any interaction is the result of more (unfair) favorable black ratings by black supervisors, less (unfair) favorable black ratings by white raters, or both. Stauffer and Buckley further argued that if the ratings disadvantage black employees, if the ratings determine who is considered "successful," and if the rating level necessary to be considered successful places more black employees below that level, then up to 12% of those employees could be inappropriately classified as "unsuccessful" with the possibility of palpable practical consequences. But, these hypotheticals do not deal with the complementary possibility that these black employees may actually be unfairly advantaged by higher-than-deserved ratings from black supervisors. Stauffer and Buckley concluded that there should be continued and vigorous research on the topic of race bias in performance ratings. As I argue in a concluding section of this chapter, there is every reason to agree with their plea, although not necessarily for the reasons they suggest.

Summary of Recent Literature on Race Bias in Performance Ratings

After reviewing recent meta-analyses on the possible bias of same-race raters on ratee performance evaluation, it appears that there are often significant differences between white and black mean ratings, to the disadvantage of the black ratees. Nevertheless, when we consider the results of within-subject designs and eliminate the effect of peer ratings and laboratory (student) ratings, any remaining Rater × Ratee race variance is small. Further, research that does not employ a within-subject design yet controls for attributes such as ability, education, and experience similarly points to small main effect black–white differences. Performance evaluations do not seem to be the type of egregiously subjective instruments that plaintiff lawyers allege. This does not mean that performance evaluations cannot be used as a pretext for unfair discrimination in a given instance. It does, however, suggest that there is nothing fundamental in the performance evaluation process that unleashes invidious negative race-based stereotypes

It would be valuable to see studies that examine Hispanic, Asian, and other ethnic minority subgroups to complete the picture.

Performance Ratings and Gender

Before addressing the research on performance ratings and gender, I make the following observation. Unlike race research, gender research has centered on the dual issues of leadership and "male" and "female" jobs. These two movements are not independent. The reason for concentrating on leadership issues is likely the recognition that women are underrepresented in leadership and management positions—particularly senior leadership and management positions—and the assumption that this must be the result of invidious discrimination, most often laid at the feet of negative stereotypes of women as managers or leaders. Although this is certainly a noble and fruitful line of research, important issues related to performance ratings have been sidestepped, so we know a great deal less about the "observables" in the gender-related performance-rating research than we do about the possible consequences if there is a disadvantage that accrues to female workers in employment settings.

In addition, the gender performance evaluation research has largely been conducted in tightly controlled laboratory settings and to a lesser extent in field settings. Thus, students are asked to provide evaluations of hypothetical employees as seen in video or paper descriptions of their "work." As is true of demographic research to follow in this chapter (age and disability), there is little recognition in the gender research of the value of repeated-measures designs, which may tightly control at least the characteristics of the employee, or designs that control for experience, education, or abilities. This is unfortunate because we learn a lot from such designs, even though they are difficult to achieve in field settings. Nevertheless, it would appear that in the broad area of gender-related performance-rating research, it is probably easier to conduct a repeated-measures analysis than it is for race or certainly disability. Leaving aside the interest in leadership or senior management titles, there are plenty of female workers below those levels who could be (and often are) rated by both male and female supervisors. This was certainly true in the Pulakos et al. (1989) military study, and there is no reason to believe it could not be achieved in a counterpart private sector study. It is not my role to deconstruct *why* gender research has become centered on leadership issues, just to note that the empirical research is skewed toward those issues. And, one is left to wonder why race research did not follow a similar track since it is arguably true that a glass ceiling or a glass wall is just as pernicious for ethnic minorities as it is for women.

Meta-Analyses

Bowen, Swim, and Jacobs published a meta-analysis of gender-based performance-rating research in 2000. In that publication, they identified previous meta-analyses and reviewed them in some detail. I do not reprise the Chieh-Chen et al. review of other meta-analyses, but I summarize some of the salient points that they made regarding those other meta-analyses since it clearly sets the limits for what I cover in my review of both meta-analyses and individual studies.

1. Meta-analyses conducted by Swim, Borgida, Muruyama, and Myers (1989); Eagly, Makhijani, and Klonsky (1992); Olian, Schwab, and Hammerfield (1988); and Davison and Burke (2000) analyzed only laboratory studies.

2. With the exception of the Olian et al. (1988) meta-analysis, all considered the sex stereotype of the job in question (in the studies included in the meta-analysis) as a control variable, a manipulated variable, or a moderator variable.

3. With the exception of the Olian et al. (1988) meta-analysis, all found slight advantages to women in ratings.

4. In several of the meta-analyses (Davison & Burke, 2000; Eagly et al., 1992; Swim et al., 1989), women fared better in masculine-stereotyped jobs and when rated by males. This is puzzling from the perspective of negative female stereotypes since females should have been rated more harshly in male-stereotyped jobs and by male raters if the proposed stereotypes were operating as proposed.

Eagly, Karau, and Makhijani published a meta-analysis of mixed field and laboratory studies of leader effectiveness in 1995. The dependent variables that were examined were the rated satisfaction with or the performance of leaders. Necessarily, the performance dimensions dealt with leader-related behaviors rather than broader issues related to technical performance, citizenship behavior (at least directly), counterproductive behavior, or adaptive behavior (Landy & Conte, 2004, 2007). Laboratory studies included both Goldberg paradigm designs (presentation of resumes) or ad hoc group interactions. Since both of these scenarios involve stranger-to-stranger paradigms, I concentrate on the field studies rather than the laboratory studies because the field studies more directly address the point of this chapter. The studies in the meta-analysis included 10 military samples. Since the Pulakos et al. (1989) study described in the race section of this section and elsewhere in this section was not included in the meta-analysis, I presume it was because Pulakos et al. did not address leadership directly. Nevertheless, as we shall see, Pulakos et al. found little gender effect in performance ratings.

Of the 74 studies that were classified as "organization," 22 were classified as "business," 21 as "educational," 7 as governmental or social service, 10 as military, and 14 as miscellaneous. For the sake of this review, I accept the organizational category as the appropriate level (although I comment, as do Eagly et al. (1995), on the apparent uniqueness of the

military sample). The results of the meta-analysis with respect to organizational studies showed little of the effect that had been found in the
meta-analysis of race by Kraiger and Ford (1985), at least with respect to
leadership ratings. There were some modest effect sizes (e.g., $d = 0.05$) suggesting lower ratings for female leaders, but when these were further dis-
aggregated into organizational versus other, there were small advantages
for women leaders in ratings in all categories (ranging from $d = 0.05$ to $d = 0.15$), except military settings, for which there was a pronounced advantage for male leaders ($d = 0.42$).

The conclusions to be drawn from the Eagly et al. (1995) meta-analysis
are best stated by the authors themselves:

> When all of the studies in our sample were aggregated, female and
> male leaders did not differ in effectiveness. [This] suggests that
> despite barriers and possible handicaps in functioning as leaders, the
> women who actually serve as leaders and managers are in general
> succeeding as well as their male counterparts. (p. 137)

So, with respect to the purposes of this chapter, we may conclude that in
the limited (but important) world of leader behavior, women seem not to
be disadvantaged in performance ratings. Although there were military
data to suggest that women leaders are rated lower than male counterparts, I reserve discussion of this point for a reconsideration of the Pulakos
et al. (1989) study of female soldiers.

Chieh-Chen et al. (2000) conducted a meta-analysis of the broader topic
of gender effects on performance ratings in field studies. They did not further confine the study to leadership ratings. Like other meta-analyses (of
race and gender), there were no analyses that compared between-subject
designs with repeated-measures designs. This means that it was not possible to control for ratee characteristics by matching rater gender with
ratee gender directly. Nevertheless, the authors did consider controls for
organizational level, experience, and education, although not for ability as
had been done in some earlier research on race. Chieh-Chen et al. specifically targeted field studies for their meta-analysis. Using various selection
rules, 32 study samples were analyzed in the meta-analysis. As had been
found by Eagly et al. (1995), there were only small effect sizes for ratee gender, and they slightly favored female ratees. Further, no significant effect
sizes were discovered for masculine- versus feminine-typed jobs or for
the relative proportion of male ratees in a work group (a significant effect
for group composition is often interpreted as evidence for "tokenism" in
performance ratings). Rater training and individuating information both
tended to decrease any bias in the ratings (although the effect of training
appeared to *decrease* pro-female bias). Although the stereotypicality of the
job (male or female) influenced ratings, it appeared to simply *decrease* the

female rate advantage. This has been an argument of many proponents of stereotyping processes. They argue that perhaps women *should have an advantage* when certain performance domains (e.g., citizenship, interpersonal skills) are considered. This simply further amplifies the need for repeated-measures designs in deconstructing the effect of gender on performance ratings.

Chieh-Chen et al. concluded that "there is little systematic evidence of overall gender bias in performance evaluations in actual work settings" (p. 2205). Nevertheless, they did caution that when the stereotypicality of the performance measure is taken into account and the gender composition of the raters is taken into account, there does seem to be some evidence of lower ratings for women. The absence of the repeated-measures design element renders this caution less dramatic than it might seem. The authors did, however, reasonably ask that if we take the results of performance appraisals at face value, then we may question why there is not a similar advantage to women when applying for promotions in an organization, but this is the meat for another time and another chapter.

Individual Studies

In the section on race, I described the large-scale study conducted by Pulakos et al. (1989) as part of the Project A effort. I do not repeat that description. In addition to race, Pulakos et al. studied gender, using both a between- and a within-subject (repeated measure) design. Unlike the Eagly et al. (1995) meta-analysis, the Pulakos et al. analysis did not address leadership issues but instead analyzed ratings of technical skill and job effort, personal discipline, and military bearing. The technical skill and job effort dimension did include a consideration of "demonstrating leadership and support toward peers." Unlike the race analyses performed, which included large and equal numbers of blacks and whites, the gender analyses included many fewer females as raters and ratees as compared to males. In the repeated-measures analysis of supervisory ratings, there was neither a significant main effect for gender nor a significant Rater × Ratee gender interaction effect.

Although the repeated-measures design remains the gold standard for examining demographic effects on performance ratings, it is useful to consider studies of main effects as well. When considering field studies, and eliminating those studies included in the Chieh-Chen et al. (2000) and Eagly et al. (1995) meta-analyses, the results of single studies are interesting. These studies did not appear in the meta-analyses either because they appeared after the meta-analysis was completed or because they did not have the accompanying information sought by the meta-analysts. Nevertheless, they largely confirmed the results of those meta-analyses.

One subset of these studies showed no main effect for ratee gender or no Rater × Ratee gender interactions. These include work by Lefkowitz and Battista (1995); Shore and Thornton (1986); Shore, Tashchian, and Adams (1997); and Sinangil and Ones (2003). A larger subset of these individual studies reported main effects favoring female ratees. These include studies by Furnham and Stringfield, 2001; Lewis, 1997; Ostroff et al., 2004; and Shore, 1992. In a related study, Guetal, Luciano, and Michaels (1995) examined the extent to which pregnancy might uniquely stigmatize and unfavorably influence female performance ratings. They discovered that performance ratings actually increased during pregnancy when compared to prepregnancy ratings for the same employees and when compared to control groups of nonpregnant women who held matched job titles and who were evaluated at the same time as the pregnant women.

There were two other individual studies that were not so simple to categorize. Sackett, DuBois, and Wiggins Noe (1991) examined the possible role of tokenism in ratings of both blacks and women. The results were nuanced. No tokenism effects were found for blacks; that is, the racial composition of the work group played no role in ratings. But, for gender, when women made up 20% or fewer of the work group in question, they were rated about 0.5 *SD* lower than men. In contrast, when women represented more than 50% of the work group, they were actually rated *higher* than their male counterparts. The authors explained the nuanced effects of token status by invoking the possibility that certain "jobs" (i.e., those with fewer than 20% female incumbents) may be more "masculine" in type than the jobs in which females predominate. If that is the case, tokenism is less likely the explanation than gender typing of jobs, as has been suggested by Eagly, Heilman, and others. Further, Sackett et al., using regression analysis, found that when controls were put in place for education, ability, and firm experience, gender composition accounted for an additional 4% of the variation in performance ratings. So, we are left with an intriguing individual study that raised more questions than it answered.

A second study that bears attention was conducted by Lyness and Heilman (2006). In this study, the variable of interest was the fit between gender and the line versus staff nature of a position. Line positions were considered stereotypically male, while staff positions were considered stereotypically female. A follow-on analysis examined the promotional history of women in line and staff positions and their performance ratings. The results were interesting. According to the authors, "Women in managerial line jobs received lower ratings than women in managerial staff jobs or men in either managerial line or staff jobs but promoted women had received higher performance ratings than promoted men." The research design included neither a repeated-measures aspect, which would permit a Rater × Ratee gender interaction analysis, nor controls for ability or experience (although they did control for organizational tenure and age). Thus, as the authors correctly noted, one cannot rule out true performance differences between the female line managers and the comparator groups. The most appropriate summary of the study results might be that there are some special circumstances (upper level, female, line managers) in which bias may occur even though in aggregate there is no evidence of gender bias in ratings.

Summary of Recent Literature on Gender Bias in Performance Ratings

If, as I suggested, we narrowly construe the notion of bias to mean that women are disfavored in performance ratings, the available evidence suggests that this is not true, and in fact women are more likely to receive higher ratings than men, all other things being equal. This is different from race, for which we could conclude that there were no *disadvantages* to ethnic minority status in terms of ratings. Nevertheless, there are three equivocal possibilities for exception. I use the word *equivocal* because there are several potential explanations other than gender for the results. The three possibilities are (a) upper-level female managers are viewed differently from lower-level female managers; (b) female line managers are viewed differently from female staff managers; and (c) when women make up less than 20% of a work group, they may occupy a special stigmatized position.

But in general, my conclusion based on 30 years of research on the question is similar to the conclusion that Jim Farr and I drew in 1980: The evidence of any systemic discrimination in the ratings of working women is scarce and possibly localized.

Performance Ratings and Age

Unlike gender or race, age is (unfortunately) not an immutable demographic characteristic. Those who were young will eventually become old (barring untimely death). This means that research designs have the additional option of longitudinal and time-lagged cohort analyses that are not available in the study of race or gender. Although longitudinal analyses of ratings for gender and race could be completed, they would inevitably be confounded by age. One does not become more female or more Hispanic over time, but one does become older. As was the case in the study of race and gender, repeated-measures designs are just as valuable and just as informative for age as they are for other demographic characteristics. Unfortunately, age researchers seem as constrained to conventional between-subject designs as race and gender researchers.

Meta-Analyses

There have been four meta-analyses of the relationship between age and performance ratings since the late 1980s. I review these studies next.

Waldman and Avolio (1986) analyzed 40 samples of relationship of age to performance data. Using correlational analysis, the authors reported that age accounts for approximately 2% of the rating variance, and that older workers generally receive lower ratings. When positions classified as professional are distinguished from those classified as nonprofessional, the percentage of variance in professional ratings associated with age drops to near zero, while the percentage of variance associated with age for nonprofessionals remains at approximately 2%. The authors were not able to rule out the possibility that even these modest associations were not true performance differences.

In 1989, McEvoy and Cascio conducted a meta-analysis of 96 independent studies (including some of the same studies included in the Waldman & Avolio, 1986, analysis described in the preceding paragraph). McEvoy and Casio found a very small correlation between age and performance, accounting for less than 1% of the rating variance. Unlike the Waldman and Avolio results, McEvoy and Cascio found no effect for professional versus nonprofessional status.

The third meta-analysis was conducted by Finkelstein, Burke, and Raju (1995) and, like the meta-analysis of gender by Davison and Burke (2000), only considered laboratory experiments rather than field studies. As a result, I do not review this meta-analysis in any detail. I note that when individuating information was provided to experimental subjects, bias was drastically reduced, a common finding in stereotyping research.

The fourth meta-analysis was conducted by Gordon and Arvey in 2004. An analysis of 52 samples (including both laboratory and field studies, and including many of the studies that appeared in earlier meta-analyses) revealed an overall effect size of $d = 0.11$. This is considered small. Using publication date as a moderator variable, they found that there was less evidence of age bias in more recent than in more distant studies. In a comparison of laboratory versus field studies, the researchers found considerably more evidence of bias in laboratory studies using student raters. Gordon and Arvey concluded that when raters are supervisors, when there is ample information about the ratees, and when the data were collected recently, there was little evidence of age bias in ratings.

Individual Studies

I was able to identify only two individual studies that were either not laboratory studies or not included in the meta-analyses described. The first (Vecchio, 1993) examined the situation of (teacher) subordinates who were older than their (principal) supervisors. He found that there was a non-significant association between teacher age and principal's evaluations of the teacher performance. More specifically, in examining the scenario of older subordinates and younger supervisors, he found no evidence of age bias against those older subordinates. In the second study, a related study of age similarity/dissimilarity between supervisors and subordinates, Ferris, Judge, Chachere, and Liden (1991) found no evidence of same-age bias; instead, ratings were more favorable when there was a *dissimilarity* in the age of supervisors and subordinates.

Summary of Recent Literature on Age Bias in Performance Ratings

As we have seen in race and gender analyses, there is no evidence to suggest that older workers receive significantly lower performance ratings than younger workers. In fact, when these older workers have younger supervisors, it appears that these older workers may actually receive higher ratings. The bad news is that the research designs used to study age influences on ratings are either inappropriate (i.e., cross sectional rather than longitudinal or cohort based) or lack control (of experience, ability, education, etc.). The good news is that there is no age-related variance to partial out of associations.

Performance Ratings and Disability

Disability is a relatively new focus of work-related research. The Americans With Disabilities Act (ADA) was passed in 1990, thus it is the "new" statute on the block compared those for to race, gender, and age, which have longer-standing statutory protections. As a result, the research database is embarrassingly sparse. There have been no meta-analyses and few empirical field studies of ratings of the disabled. Without research, one must concede that disability has a special status in America and many nations. Assumptions regarding capabilities seem so likely that the ADA even incorporates a protection and a claim of action for the "perception" of a disability by an employer. Thus, I think that we might assume a priori that disabled workers will receive lower performance evaluations than their more able counterparts. But as scientists, we deal with empirical confirmations of hypotheses, not impassioned speculation. Most data related to disability and performance judgments come from laboratory experiments asking students to assume the role of an employer. These studies hold no value for the present review. Other publications are largely descriptive, cataloguing the indignities suffered by disabled workers. There are a few studies that surveyed employers about their concerns regarding the hiring of disabled workers. As one might expect, potential and actual employers were concerned about ineffective performance (e.g., Johnson, Greenwood, & Shriner, 1988; Smith, Webber, Graffam, & Wilson, 2004; Tse, 1994). Nevertheless, sad to say, there are simply no data available to address the issues of possible bias in performance ratings of disabled workers.

General Summary and Conclusions

Thirty years ago, Jim Farr and I suggested that with the data available to us, we saw no substantial evidence of bias in performance ratings related to demographic characteristics of ratees or raters. Based on a review of hundreds of studies, meta-analyses, regression analyses controlling variously for ability, education, experience, and organizational level and job type, and designs incorporating repeated measures as a control for true performance levels, I find no reason to change that conclusion.

Nevertheless, this is not a call for a moratorium on anything—I have learned that lesson at least. If for no other reason, the parsing of the performance domain into technical, citizenship, counterproductive, and adaptable facets of performance signals a need for new analyses or reanalyses of these noneffects (including fresh meta-analyses of old data that permit such a parsing) to see if they remain noneffects. Further, the changing nature of work (larger spans of control, more team-oriented work, etc.) suggests additional moderator variables to examine. I encourage such research. Further, the intriguing findings related to gender-job stereotypes and work group gender composition require continued investigation. But, I would still argue that these more complex analyses should be accompanied by more basic analyses of Ratee × Rater gender interaction effects using repeated measures and control variables in the conduct of the research.

This fresh view of the performance-rating literature provides little foundation for a broad claim in the litigation context that performance ratings are inherently unfair to protected groups. That is not to say that, in a given instance, a performance rating was not used as a pretext for invidious discrimination. But, it is to say that there is no undue cause for alarm when performance ratings are assigned to protected groups—at least those defined by race, gender, or age.

Acknowledgments

I gratefully acknowledge the assistance of Jacob Seybert, Barbara Nett, and Kylie Harper in article search and production. Kylie Harper also assisted in editing drafts of this chapter. Kevin Murphy, Paul Sackett, Rick Jacobs, Jeff Conte, and Jim Farr provided thoughtful reviews of a draft of the chapter.

Notes

1. In a conversation with Elaine Pulakos, she expressed a reservation about her work and, more importantly, about other "field or operational" studies. I have made the point that an important distinction is between laboratory and field studies in part because laboratory studies have little of the accountability factor that field operational studies have. She was concerned that many field studies are carried out in the context of research studies, and participants are promised anonymity and that their ratings will not "count" even though they represent real and intact supervisor-subordinate dyads. Thus, she suggested, that the actual Rater × Ratee interaction might be higher than she estimated in her earlier studies and in later studies (e.g., Sackett & Dubois, 1991). This suggests that a new meta-analysis moderator should be examined that distinguishes between the truly operational (these "count") and the "research operational" (these do not count) to see if estimates of psychometric bias area are affected by this contextual issue.
2. I acknowledge the thoughts of Paul Sackett on the Stauffer and Buckley article (2005) in a recent personal communication to me.

References

Americans With Disabilities Act of 1990, 42 U.S.C.A. § 12101 et seq. (West 1993).

Borman, W. C., Buck, D. E., Hanson, M. A., Motowidlo, S. J., Stark, S., & Drasgow, F. (2001). An examination of the comparative reliability, validity, and accuracy of performance ratings made using computerized adaptive rating scales. *Journal of Applied Psychology, 86,* 965–973.

Bowen, C., Swim, J. K., & Jacobs, R. R. (2000). Evaluating gender biases on actual job performance of real people: A meta-analysis. *Journal of Applied Social Psychology, 30*(10), 2194–2215.

Davison, H. K., & Burke, M. J. (2000). Sex discrimination in simulated employment contexts: A meta-analytic investigation. *Journal of Vocational Behavior, 56,* 225–248.

Dewberry, C. (2001). Performance disparities between whites and ethnic minorities: Real difference or assessment bias? *Journal of Occupational and Organization Psychology, 74,* 659–673.

Eagly, A. H., Karau, S. J., & Makhijani, M. G (1995). Gender and the effectiveness of leaders: A meta-analysis. *Psychological Bulletin, 117,* 125–145.

Eagly, A. H., Makhijani, M. G., & Klonsky, B. G. (1992). Gender and the evaluation of leaders: A meta-analysis. *Psychological Bulletin, 111,* 3–22.

Elvira, M. M., & Zatick, C. D. (2002). Who's displaced first? The role of race in lay-off decisions. *Industrial Relations, 41,* 329–361.

Feldman, J. M. (1981). Beyond attribution theory: Cognitive process in performance appraisal. *Journal of Applied Psychology, 66,* 127–148.

Ferris, G. R., Judge, T. A., Chachere, J. G., & Liden, R. C. (1991). The age context of performance-evaluation decisions. *Psychology and Aging, 6,* 616–622.

Finkelstein, L. M., Burke, M. J., & Raju, N. S. (1995). Age discrimination in simulated employment contexts: An integrative analysis. *Journal of Applied Psychology, 80,* 652–663.

Ford, J. K., Kraiger, K., & Schechtmann, S. L. (1986). Study of race effects in objective indices and subjective evaluations of performance: A meta analysis of performance criteria. *Psychological Bulletin, 99,* 330–337.

Furnham, A., & Stringfield, P. (2001). Gender differences in rating reports: Female managers are harsher raters, particularly of males. *Journal of Managerial Psychology, 16,* 281–288.

Gordon, R. A., & Arvey, R. D. (2004). Age bias in laboratory field settings: A meta-analytic investigation. *Journal of Applied Social Psychology, 34,* 468–492.

Greenhaus, J. H., & Parasuraman, S. (1993). Job performance attributions and career advancement prospects: An examination of gender and race effects. *Organizational Behavior and Human Decision Processes, 55,* 273–297.

Greenhaus, J. H., Parasuraman, S., & Wormley, W. M. (1990). Effects of race on organizational experiences, job performance evaluations, and career outcomes. *Academy of Management Journal, 33,* 64–86.

Guetal, H. G., Luciano, J., & Michaels, C. A. (1995). Pregnancy in the workplace: Does pregnancy affect performance appraisal ratings? *Journal of Business and Psychology, 10,* 155–167.

Johnson, V. A., Greenwood, R., & Shriner, K. (1988). Work performance and work personality: Employer concerns about workers with disabilities. *Rehabilitation Counseling Bulletin, 32,* 40–57.

Kraiger, K., & Ford, J. K. (1985). A meta-analysis of ratee race effects in performance ratings. *Journal of Applied Psychology, 70,* 56–65.

Kraiger, K., & Ford, J. K. (1990). The relation of job knowledge, job performance and supervisory ratings as a function of ratee race. *Human Performance, 3,* 269–279.

Landy, F. J. (2005). *Employment discrimination litigation: Behavioral, quantitative, and legal perspectives.* San Francisco: Jossey-Bass.

Landy, F. J. (2008). The tenuous bridge between research and reality: The importance of research design in inferences regarding work behavior. In E. Borgida and S. T. Fiske (Eds.), *Beyond common sense: Psychological science in the courtroom* (pp. 341–352). Malden, MA: Blackwell.

Landy, F. J., & Farr, J. L. (1980). Performance rating. *Psychological Bulletin, 87,* 72–107.

Lefkowitz, J., & Battista, M. (1995). Potential sources of criterion bias in supervisor ratings used for test validation. *Journal of Business and Psychology, 9,* 389–414.

Lewis, G. B. (1997). Race, sex, and performance ratings in the federal service. *Public Administration Review, 57,* 479–489.

Lyness, K. S., & Heilman, M. E. (2006). When fit is fundamental: Performance evaluations and promotions of upper-level female and male managers. *Journal of Applied Psychology, 91,* 777–785.

McEvoy, G. M., & Cascio, W. F. (1989). Cumulative evidence of the relationship between employee age and job performance. *Journal of Applied Psychology, 74,* 11–17.

Olian, J. D., Schwab, D. P., & Hammerfield, Y. (1988). The impact of applicant gender compared to qualifications on hiring recommendations: A meta-analysis of experimental studies. *Organizational Behavior and Human Decision Processes, 41,* 180–195.

Oppler, S. H., Campbell, J. P., Pulakos E. D., & Borman, W. C. (1992). Three approaches to the investigation of subgroup bias in performance measurement: Review, results, and conclusions. *Journal of Applied Psychology, 77,* 201–217.

Ostroff, C., Atwater, L. E., & Feinberg, B. J. (2004). Understanding self-other agreement: A look at rater and ratee characteristics, context and outcomes. *Personnel Psychology, 57,* 333–375.

Pulakos, E. D., Oppler, S. H., White, L. A., & Borman, W. C. (1989). Examination of race and sex effects on performance ratings. *Journal of Applied Psychology, 74,* 770–780.

Rotundo, M., & Sackett, P. (1999). Effect of rater race on conclusions regarding differential prediction on cognitive ability tests. *Journal of Applied Psychology, 84,* 815–822.

Sackett, P. R., & Dubois, C. L. Z. (1991). Rater-ratee race effects on performance evaluation—challenging meta-analytic conclusions. *Journal of Applied Psychology, 76,* 873–877.

Sackett, P. R., Dubois, C. L. Z., & Wiggins Noe, A. (1991). Tokenism in performance evaluation: The effects of work group representation on male-female and white-black differences in performance ratings. *Journal of Applied Psychology, 76,* 263–267.

Schneider, R. J., Goff, M., Anderson, S., & Borman, W. C. (2003). Computerized adaptive rating scales for measuring managerial performance. *International Journal of Selection and Assessment, 11,* 2–3, 237–246.

Shore, T. H. (1992). Subtle gender bias in the assessment of managerial potential. *Sex Roles, 27*(9–10), 499–515.

Shore, T. H., Tashchian, A., & Adams, J. S. (1997). The role of gender in a developmental assessment center. *Journal of Social Behavior and Personality, 12,* 191–203.

Shore, L. M., & Thornton, G. C. (1986). Effects of gender on self-ratings and supervisory ratings. *Academy of Management Journal, 29,* 115–129.

Sinangil, H. K., & Ones, D. S. (2003). Gender differences in expatriate job performance. *Applied Psychology: An International Review, 52,* 461–475.

Smith, K., Webber, L., Graffam, J., & Wilson, C. (2004). Employer satisfaction with employees with a disability: Comparisons with other employees. *Journal of Vocational Rehabilitation, 21,* 61–69.

Stauffer, J. M., & Buckley, M. R. (2005). The existence and nature of racial bias in supervisory ratings. *Journal of Applied Psychology, 90,* 586–591.

Swim, J. K., Borgida, E., Muruyama, G., & Myers, D. G. (1989). Joan McKay versus John McKay: Do gender stereotypes bias evaluations? *Psychological Bulletin, 105,* 409–429.

Tse, J. (1994). Employers' expectations and evaluation of the job performance of employees with intellectual disability. *Australia and New Zealand Journal of Developmental Disabilities, 19,* 139–147.

Vecchio, R. P. (1993). The impact of differences in subordinate and supervisor age on attitudes and performance. *Psychology and Aging, 8,* 112–119.

Waldman, D. A., & Avolio, B. J. (1986). A meta-analysis of age differences in job performance. *Journal of Applied Psychology, 71,* 33–38.

Waldman, D. A., & Avolio, B. J. (1991). Race effects in performance evaluations—controlling for ability, education, and experience. *Journal of Applied Psychology, 76,* 897–901.

9

Perspectives on Adverse Impact in Work Performance: What We Know and What We Could Learn More About

Patrick F. McKay

Introduction

For decades, industrial-organizational psychologists have studied the relative magnitudes of racial-ethnic and sex mean differences in work performance (Kraiger & Ford, 1985; Pulakos, White, Oppler, & Borman, 1989). Members of groups judged to perform poorly, relative to their peers, may forgo advancement opportunities and pay raises and, perhaps, be dismissed from their jobs. A number of perspectives have been advanced regarding the origins of observed performance differences, the chief of which have been ratings bias (Ford, Kraiger, & Schechtman, 1986; Kraiger & Ford, 1985; Stauffer & Buckley, 2005) and racial differences in cognitive ability (McKay & McDaniel, 2006; Roth, Huffcutt, & Bobko, 2003; Waldman & Avolio, 1991). Some additional perspectives on group differences that have been offered include (a) the nature of the performance criterion (McKay & McDaniel, 2006; Roth et al., 2003); (b) cognitive loading (McKay & McDaniel, 2006); (c) job complexity (Roth et al., 2003); (d) measurement level (i.e., single-item vs. multiple-item scales; McKay & McDaniel, 2006); and (e) data source (McKay & McDaniel, 2006). Still other views on the topic that have garnered less attention in the personnel literature include human capital disparities (Sackett, DuBois, & Noe, 1991; Waldman & Avolio, 1991) and the racial/gender context of firms (Avery, McKay, Wilson, & Tonidandel, 2007; Joshi, Liao, & Jackson, 2006; McKay, Avery, & Morris, 2008).

The goal of the present chapter is to present an overview of the current wisdom on adverse impact in work performance. In addition, I expound on both established and prospective determinants of adverse impact in performance. Consequently, there appear to be myriad reasons why differences exist, and increased understanding of possible causes may aid researchers and practitioners alike in ameliorating disparities in work performance between groups. The subsequent sections of this chapter are organized as follows: First, I review what we know about adverse impact on performance criteria, discussing racial-ethnic mean differences in work performance and highlighting previous explanations for the obtained disparities. I conclude coverage of racial-ethnic mean disparities by presenting recent research findings that uncover some additional moderators of differences in performance. The same general procedure ensues for the presentation of mean sex differences in work performance, although this work is less voluminous than that directed toward racial-ethnic disparities in performance. Finally, several theoretical perspectives are described in an attempt to spur research and expand thinking directed toward future investigations of racial-ethnic and sex disparities in work performance.

Readers should recognize that I do not attempt to provide an exhaustive review of racial-ethnic and sex differences in job performance but discuss general trends in the area based, primarily, on meta-analytic research. Meta-analyses provide a more solid platform than single primary studies for discussing the cumulative findings of research on racial-ethnic and sex mean differences in work performance. Select primary studies are discussed, however, to elaborate on reported meta-analytic trends or areas yet to be studied meta-analytically. In addition, the research reviewed here is limited to that involving actual work employees as opposed to studies involving student participants, ratings of videotaped performance, or laboratory contexts. Finally, any discussion of performance ratings refers to supervisory ratings, the most common form of subjective criteria (Murphy & Cleveland, 1995).

Mean Racial–Ethnic Differences in Work Performance

What We Know

The bulk of research on mean racial–ethnic differences in work performance compared black and white workers; however, Roth et al. (2003) considered disparities in performance between Hispanics and whites, while little to no work has contrasted majority-minority differences involving

Asians and Native Americans. Therefore, the research presented here focuses mainly on black–white and Hispanic–white mean differences.

Black–white Mean Differences in Work Performance

Consistently, black–white mean differences in work performance, disfavoring the former group, have been reported across various meta-analytic studies (Chung-Yan & Cronshaw, 2002; Ford et al., 1986; Hauenstein, Sinclair, Robson, Quintella, & Donovan, 2003; Kraiger & Ford, 1985; McKay & McDaniel, 2006; Roth et al., 2003). The magnitude of differences, reported in standard deviation units (Cohen's d), ranged from 0.24 (Chung-Yan & Cronshaw, 2002) to 0.39 (Kraiger & Ford, 1985). Although the seminal Kraiger and Ford (1985) meta-analysis focused on examination of disparities in overall performance, which collapsed ratings across various performance dimensions, later studies assessed disparities on various types of criteria considered separately (e.g., Ford et al., 1986; Hauenstein et al., 2003; McKay & McDaniel, 2006; Roth et al., 2003). Researchers have investigated a series of proposed moderators of observed performance disparities. Kraiger and Ford (1985) studied rater-ratee race effects on performance ratings. Rater-ratee race effects posit raters of job performance provide higher or more desirable ratings to ratees who are members of the same racial-ethnic group as the rater. Kraiger and Ford (1985) reported an overall effect size, in standard deviation units (Cohen's d), of 0.39 ($k = 64$, $N = 16,149$) for field studies disfavoring blacks relative to their white peers. Although blacks were judged as less-effective performers than whites, this finding was qualified by observed rater-ratee race effects. Effect size comparisons disparaged black ratees among white raters ($d = 0.37, k = 74$, $N = 17,159$) and white ratees when ratings were provided by black raters ($d = -0.45, k = 14, N = 2,428$), suggesting ratings bias.

On this basis, Ford et al. (1986) examined the influence of measurement method (whether performance is rated subjectively involving human judgment or mechanically/objectively scored using some mechanical or electronic apparatus, such as supermarket scanners, thereby presumably precluding rating bias) on black–white disparities in job performance. The authors studied measurement method effects across a series of criterion types or the nature of the performance measure, including performance indicators (e.g., units produced, accidents, and customer complaints), cognitive criteria (e.g., training and job knowledge), and absenteeism (e.g., absenteeism and tardiness). Ford et al. did not find a clear pattern of measurement method moderation since similar effect size estimates were obtained for objective ($d = 0.21, k = 53, N = 10,222$) and subjective ($d = 0.20$, $k = 53, N = 9,443$) criteria. Moreover, slightly larger mean racial disparities were reported for subjective performance indicators (e.g., units produced and complaints; $d = 0.22, k = 20, N = 4,130$) than objective measures of these criteria (d = 0.16, k = 20, N = 4,287). Measurement method moderated mean differences on cognitive criteria such as training and job knowledge, with larger effect sizes found for objective measures (d = 0.34, k = 16, N = 3,389) than subjective criteria (d = 0.23, k = 16, N = 2,782). Racial mean differences for absenteeism criteria varied just slightly when measured subjectively (d = 0.15, k = 13, N = 2,221) versus objectively (d = 0.11, k = 13, N = 2,151).

Three additional meta-analytic studies assessed measurement method moderation of black–white mean differences, with each failing to obtain a consistent pattern of results. Supporting Kraiger and Ford's (1985) reasoning, Chung-Yan and Cronshaw (2002) found larger mean racial differences for subjective (d = 0.30, k = 57, N not reported) versus objective criteria (d = 0.12, k = 30, N not reported). Roth et al. (2003), in contrast, reported larger black–white mean differences for objective measures of work quantity (d = 0.32, k = 3, N = 774), job knowledge (d = 0.55, k = 10, N = 2,027), and absenteeism (d = 0.23, k = 8, N = 1,413) than subjective measures of these criteria (quantity d = 0.09, k = 5, N = 495; job knowledge d = 0.15, k = 4, N = 1,231; absenteeism d = 0.13, k = 4, N = 642). Effect sizes for work quality criteria did not vary by measurement method (objective d = 0.24, k = 8, N = 2,538; subjective d = 0.20, k = 10, N = 1,811). McKay and McDaniel (2006) reported similar magnitude effect sizes for subjective (d = 0.28, k = 510, N = 94,555) and objective (d = 0.22, k = 62, N = 15,419) criteria overall. For some criteria, such as work samples, effect sizes were larger in magnitude for single-item subjective (d = 0.52, k = 3, N = 576) versus objective (d = 0.39, k = 4, N = 767) measures. These effects did not follow for scale-level (i.e., multiple-item) work sample measures (subjective d = 0.43, k = 8, N = 2,744; objective d = 0.39, k = 8, N = 2,470). Comparably, single-item task measures showed very little difference in effect sizes when moving from subjective (d = 0.18, k = 48, N = 8,263) to objective measurement (d = 0.20, k = 8, N = 1,723). Finally, absenteeism/lost time criteria, measured at the single-item level, exhibited larger magnitude effects for objective (d = 0.11, k = 12, N = 2,340) than for subjective (d = −.01, k = 6, N = 1,245) measures of performance. Correlated vectors analyses, which estimate the strengths of several proposed moderators simultaneously, revealed a multiple correlation of 0.10 (k = 572) between measurement method and black–white mean performance effect sizes (i.e., measurement method accounted for 1% of the variance in effect sizes).

Although not a meta-analytic study, Stauffer and Buckley (2005) investigated the extent of racial bias in performance ratings by reanalyzing data from the U.S. military utilized in the work of Sackett and DuBois (1991). The authors employed a repeated-measures design to determine if the magnitude and direction of black–white mean disparities in work performance varied for personnel rated by both white and black raters. In the absence of bias, a zero-order mean disparity should be observed, which means that black and white raters rate the same single employee identically.

Findings suggested clear racial bias in that white raters assigned slightly higher ratings than black raters to white civilian ratees ($d = 0.03$, $N = 286$); however, white raters provided markedly lower ratings than their black counterparts when rating black civilian personnel ($d = -0.27$, $N = 331$). For military personnel, black raters rated white ($d = -0.03$, $N = 1,259$) and black subordinates ($d = -0.29$, $N = 561$) higher than white raters, yet the rating difference was much larger for black ratees. It appears that there were systematic differences in the way black and white raters viewed the same employee performance.

Collectively, however, meta-analytic studies of measurement method moderator effects on the magnitude of black–white mean differences in work performance have been nil. To some extent, this conclusion has resulted from the confounding of measurement method with criterion type. Some criteria, such as contextual performance or nonrequired behaviors aimed at helping individuals or organizations (Borman & Motowidlo, 1993), are only measured subjectively, while others (e.g., job knowledge) can be measured both subjectively and objectively. As a consequence, it is difficult to provide a full test of measurement method effects on disparities in performance. Thus, criterion type has been raised as a focal moderator variable.

Criterion type is an important consideration because it refers to differences between performance measures in the requirements for effective job performance. According to Borman and Motowidlo (1993), task performance, which addresses the core requirements of jobs, is dependent primarily on general mental ability. Contextual performance, in contrast, is a function of employee personality or temperament. Furthermore, Campbell, McCloy, Oppler, and Sager (1993) proposed that effective work sample performance requires declarative knowledge (DK; knowledge about facts and things) and procedural knowledge (PK; knowing what to do). The acquisition of DK is largely a function of general mental ability (Ackerman, 1988). Cognitive ability is the strongest single predictor of job performance (Schmidt & Hunter, 1998), mostly through its impact on the acquisition of job knowledge (Hunter, 1986). High-ability individuals tend to master job requirements more quickly than their low-ability counterparts, with facilitative effects on subsequent job performance. Personnel research also showed large black–white mean differences in cognitive ability among job incumbents ($d = 0.90$, $k = 13$, $N = 50,799$; Roth, BeVier, Bobko, Switzer, & Tyler, 2001), disfavoring the former, while disparities in personality were negligible ($d = 0.09$, $k = 6$, $N = 801$; Schmitt, Clause, & Pulakos, 1996). Based on theory and research evidence, it follows that criteria that are highly dependent on cognitive ability will exhibit larger black–white mean disparities than those more contingent on personality.

A number of the studies reviewed in this chapter provide corroboration for this reasoning. For instance, Ford et al. (1986) reported larger racial mean effect sizes for objective versus subjective cognitive criteria than on absenteeism and performance indicators, which differed little based on measurement method. Given the types of measures categorized as cognitive criteria (i.e., job knowledge and training performance), effective performance was more conditional on cognitive ability than the last two criteria. Moreover, Roth et al. (2003) found effect sizes were largest for work samples ($d = 0.52$, $k = 10$, $N = 3,651$), followed by job knowledge ($d = 0.48$, $k = 12$, $N = 2,460$); promotion ($d = 0.31$, $k = 0.7$, $N = 1,404$); ratings of quality ($d = 0.21$, $k = 15$, $N = 3,613$) and quantity ($d = 0.21$, $k = 8$, $N = 1,268$); absenteeism ($d = 0.19$, $k = 11$, $N = 2,376$); and on-the-job training ($d = 0.14$, $k = 2$, $N = 132$). In support of Borman and Motowidlo's (1993) reasoning, Hauenstein et al. (2003) obtained larger mean racial differences for task ($d = 0.37$, $k = 10$, $N = 18,481$) versus contextual performance measures ($d = 0.27$, $k = 10$, $N = 1,634$). Similarly, in a large-scale, non-meta-analytic military study, Pulakos et al. (1989) showed that white soldiers received significantly higher technical skill and job effort ratings (i.e., performance of core technical task for job specialties, a cognitive criterion) than blacks. Black enlistees, in contrast, earned significantly higher military bearing ratings (i.e., physical fitness and military appearance, a noncognitive criterion) than white personnel. In correlated vector analyses, McKay and McDaniel (2006) demonstrated that criterion type was the strongest moderator of black–white mean differences in work performance ($R = 0.40$, $k = 572$), accounting for 16% of the variance in effect sizes. The largest effect sizes were obtained for job knowledge tests ($d = 0.53$, $k = 9$, $N = 2,216$) and work sample tests ($d = 0.42$, $k = 23$, $N = 6,557$), followed in order by overall job performance ($d = 0.35$, $k = 302$, $N = 58,808$); task performance ($d = 0.21$, $k = 93$, $N = 15,868$); promotions ($d = 0.18$, $k = 7$, $N = 1,422$); salary ($d = 0.14$, $k = 5$, $N = 1,233$); contextual performance ($d = 0.13$, $k = 31$, $N = 3,333$); absenteeism/lost time ($d = 0.09$, $k = 20$, $N = 3,779$); personality-applied social skills ($d = 0.07$, $k = 60$, $N = 10,648$); on-the-job training ($d = 0.05$, $k = 7$, $N = 1,510$); commendations-reprimands ($d = 0.02$, $k = 9$, $N = 2,229$); and accidents ($d = -0.06$, $k = 6$, $N = 2,371$).

This pattern of criterion type results implies that the degree performance indicators are dependent on cognitive ability or personality (which tend not to correlate; Bobko, Roth, & Potosky, 1999) should influence black–white mean differences in job performance. In the first formal test of this notion, McKay and McDaniel examined the moderating effects of cognitive loading, or the degree to which a criterion measure correlated with cognitive ability, and personality loading, the extent performance measures related with personality. Correlated vectors analyses showed a correlation of 0.34 ($k = 291$) between cognitive loading and the size of mean racial effect sizes. Furthermore, McKay and McDaniel (2006) uncovered a similar pattern of findings as reviewed in regard to criterion type, with large effect sizes evident for criteria more strongly correlated with cognitive ability (e.g., job knowledge tests and work samples) than criteria weakly related to ability (e.g., personality-applied social skills and contextual performance). Accordingly, the authors showed that the criterion type and cognitive loading vectors were correlated strongly ($r = 0.60$, when weighted by the number of effect sizes estimated). By implication, this suggests criterion-type moderation relates to differences between criteria in cognitive loading. In addition, these authors reported negative relations between the personality dimensions of conscientiousness (i.e., dependable, reliable; $r = -0.23$, $k = 138$); emotional stability (i.e., calm, relaxed; $r = -0.46$, $k = 90$); agreeableness (i.e., warm, friendly; $r = -0.06$, $k = 135$); ambition ($r = -0.17$, $k = 90$); openness (i.e., curious, imaginative; $r = -0.11$, $k = 96$); and school success (e.g., achievement; $r = -0.17$, $k = 96$) and racial mean effect sizes. These correlations indicate smaller effect sizes for highly personality-loaded performance measures.

Roth et al. (2003) examined the moderating role of job complexity on black–white mean differences in work performance. Job complexity moderates the validity of cognitive ability tests in predicting job performance (Hunter & Hunter, 1984); however, Roth et al. (2001) found lower racial-ethnic mean disparities in cognitive ability test scores for personnel in high-complexity jobs. Accordingly, Roth and colleagues (2003) proposed job complexity as a possible influence on racial mean effect sizes for work performance. Meaningful differences in effect size magnitudes did not emerge across jobs of low complexity (e.g., mail sorter; $d = 0.32$, $k = 5$, $N = 994$); low-medium complexity (e.g., truck driver; $d = 0.27$, $k = 20$, $N = 11,916$); medium complexity (skilled crafts; $d = 0.32$, $k = 6$, $N = 11,375$); and medium complexity with large N size studies removed ($d = 0.31$, $k = 5$, $N = 942$).

Two moderators assessed by McKay and McDaniel (2006) are measurement level and data source. *Measurement level* refers to whether performance criteria are measured using a single-item or multiple-item scales. Single-item indicators tend to be more unreliable than multiple-item scales (Hunter & Schmidt, 2004), with implications for the magnitudes of racial effects on job performance. *Data source* represents the medium through which meta-analytic data were collected, such as from published journal articles and books or less-accessible means, including conference papers or dissertations/theses and consultants' internal technical reports. The presumption here involves the undesirable circumstances that could result from companies openly providing data which exhibit significant mean racial differences, such as legal challenges, negative publicity, and marred company image. As a result, the effect sizes available in published sources may differ markedly from those available in unpublished ones, a tendency termed *publication bias* (Rothstein, 2003). Findings showed significant measurement level moderation, with larger black–white mean differences observed for scale ($d = 0.33$, $k = 385$, $N = 73,035$) versus single-item criteria ($d = 0.15$, $k = 187$, $N = 36,939$). Consequently, correlated vector analyses revealed a sizable multiple correlation ($R = 0.28$, $k = 572$) between measurement level and effect size magnitudes, accounting for 8% of effect size variance. Data source results showed smaller black–white mean differences in performance for data extracted from books ($d = -0.01$, $k = 8$, $N = 1,681$); dissertations ($d = 0.12$, $k = 36$, $N = 6,291$); and journals ($d = 0.17$, $k = 118$, $N = 32,026$), while larger racial effects were obtained from technical reports ($d = 0.34$, $k = 394$, $N = 67,646$) and conference papers ($d = 0.38$, $k = 16$, $N = 2,330$). Interestingly, the effect size estimate for journals was one half smaller than that derived for technical reports, a finding suggestive of publication bias. Correlated vector analyses indicated a 0.30 multiple correlation between the data source vector and effect sizes, capturing 9% of the variance.

To summarize, we know that prior meta-analytic studies reported consistent black–white mean differences in work performance disfavoring blacks. Examination of a series of moderators demonstrated strong effects for criterion type and cognitive loading, intermediate-level effects for measurement level and data source, and weak effects of measurement method. The findings suggest larger racial effect sizes result with cognitively loaded criteria, scale-level criteria, and data from unpublished sources.

Hispanic–White Mean Differences in Work Performance

Substantially less is known about the magnitude of Hispanic–white mean differences in work performance. The one study that meta-analyzed these disparities (Roth et al., 2003) showed a slight performance advantage for white personnel ($d = 0.04$, $k = 11$, $N = 46,530$). Further analyses of these findings, by criterion type, showed sizable differences for job knowledge ($d = 0.47$, $k = 3$, $N = 977$) and work sample criteria ($d = 0.45$, $k = 4$, $N = 1,197$). Theory reviewed earlier and results indicating large Hispanic–white mean differences in cognitive ability among job incumbents, disfavoring the former ($d = 0.83$, $k = 14$, $N = 313,635$), may account for these derived effects. For job knowledge measures, some evidence of measurement method moderation was obtained, such that effect sizes appreciably were larger for objective ($d = 0.67$, $k = 2$, $N = 698$) than subjective measures ($d = 0.04$, $k = 2$, $N = 621$). Job complexity moderation was observed such that racial-ethnic effect sizes were smaller for jobs of low-medium ($d = 0.07$, $k = 6$, $N = 7,499$) than medium complexity ($d = 0.16$, $k = 3$, $N = 10,213$). Readers should exercise caution in interpreting these results considering they were based on few effect size estimates. Tentatively, we can conclude minimal Hispanic–white mean differences in work performance overall, yet some slight indication of moderation by criterion type as sizable differences occurred for criteria known to be strongly cognitively loaded. Moreover, larger effect sizes were observed for jobs of medium complexity than low-medium complexity.

What We Could Learn More About

Meta-analytic studies have examined a limited number of variables as moderators of black–white mean differences in work performance. It seems that most of these variables were convenient to code in meta-analytic investigations, with less-than-optimal theoretical consideration of others. There are a number of possible candidates in this regard, including additional human capital variables (e.g., work experience, education) and the racial environment of work contexts.

Human Capital

Human capital theory (Becker, 1993) states that individuals should accrue advantages for making higher human capital investments in the form of greater educational attainment, work experience, and training. These investments improve an employee's potential contributions to employers. Several advantages enjoyed by high human capital individuals include increased job opportunities, pay, work performance, advancement opportunities, and overall career success (Judge, Cable, Boudreau, & Bretz, 1995; Schmidt & Hunter, 1998).

Regarding black–white mean differences in work performance, human capital disparities exist disfavoring the former group in terms of educational attainment and work experience (Avery et al., 2007; U.S. Census Bureau, 2004). Suggestive in terms of human capital moderation, Waldman and Avolio (1991) examined black–white mean disparities in overall job performance for data from the General Aptitude Test Battery (GATB) validation study conducted by the U.S. Employment Service. The authors found racial effects on job performance were due in part to lower cognitive ability, work experience, and education among black personnel. Sackett et al. (1991) examined the effects of the proportions of minorities and women (i.e., tokenism) on racial and sex effects on job performance, also using the GATB database. Focusing on black–white mean disparities, Sackett et al. also found cognitive ability and firm experience (but not education) to predict racial mean performance effect sizes. Surprisingly, the moderating roles of work experience and education have not been considered in meta-analyses. Consequently, the possibility exists of confounded conclusions due to comparing groups of employees with differing qualifications without proper statistical controls.

Racial Environment of Work Contexts

Little work has examined the moderating influence of the racial environment of work contexts on minority–majority mean differences in work performance. This tendency is apparent in spite of voluminous organizational behavior research that chronicles the barriers faced by minority workers, such as racial discrimination (Avery, McKay, & Wilson, 2008; Deitch et al., 2003); reduced access to influential social networks (Ibarra, 1995); lower returns on human capital investments (Dreher & Cox, 2000); less social acceptance and work discretion (Greenhaus, Parasuraman, & Wormley, 1990); and reports of less-satisfactory relationships with white supervisors (who form the majority of managers in firms; Jeanquart-Barone, 1996) than their white counterparts. Pulakos and colleagues' (1989) large-scale study of racial and sex effects on performance ratings did broach the subject of black and sex representation on subgroup mean disparities in performance. Thinking in regard to group representation effects on job performance follows from Kanter's (1977) seminal work on workplace demography. According to this author, negative outcomes result from token status, in which a person is a single member of his or her group (e.g., race) in a work setting. In particular, tokens experience higher salience due to their low proportionality, thereby increasing performance pressures. In addition, negative stereotyping may result from an inference of inability since only a single member of the individual's group is present in the work context, leading to biased performance evaluations. Accordingly, Pulakos et al. (1989) expected larger black–white differences in performance ratings in contexts in which few blacks were present; however, this hypothesis was not supported.

Work in the area of minority representation suggests a reduction in voluntary turnover results among minorities in settings where they predominate (Zatzick, Elvira, & Cohen, 2003). In addition, nonlinear effects of minority representation were observed, such that the influence of representation was stronger for minority groups who were few in number. The authors explained these effects in terms of the similarity-attraction paradigm (Byrne, 1971), social contact theories (Blau, 1977), and social identity theory (SIT; Tajfel & Turner, 1986). According to the similar-attraction paradigm, increased minority representation should reduce turnover among minorities because this suggests a greater preponderance of similar individuals in the work setting. Perceived similarity fosters cohesion and a sense of shared history between individuals, leading to more positive affect. Social contact theories suggest less discrimination and negative stereotyping should occur as minorities have greater contact with majority group members. SIT argues that people exhibit ingroup bias toward members of their own salient social group (e.g., race and sex) because of a perception of shared fate between members of the same group. These three theories imply more positive attitudes amid minorities in work contexts in which they were highly represented, thereby reducing turnover.

A series of studies examined the role of diversity climate, measured at the individual and business unit levels, on performance outcomes (Avery et al., 2007; McKay et al., 2008). *Diversity climate* refers to perceptions of the degree that a firm uses fair personnel practices and socially integrates underrepresented employees into the workplace (Mor Barak, Cherin, & Berkman, 1998). Cox (1994) developed the interactional model of cultural diversity (IMCD) to distill the effects of diversity climate on individual- and organizational-level outcomes. According to the model, diversity climate is manifested in terms of individual-level factors (e.g., social identity, prejudice, stereotyping); group/intergroup factors (e.g., intergroup conflict); and organizational-level factors (e.g., integration of underrepresented groups at various levels of the organizational hierarchy, institutional bias in human resource systems). These factors, collectively, influence employee perceptions of the degree to which group membership plays a role in work outcomes. Furthermore, diversity climate directly relates to both affective outcomes (e.g., job satisfaction) and achievement outcomes (e.g., job performance ratings), which in turn affect organizational outcomes such as labor turnover, work productivity, and service quality.

Avery et al. (2007) investigated the moderating effects of organizational diversity cues on mean racial-ethnic differences in absenteeism. The authors postulated greater effects of individual-level diversity climate perceptions on absenteeism among blacks and Hispanics than whites. In line with SIT, they reasoned that minority workers should more greatly appreciate organizational efforts to maintain pro-diversity work climates as means to mitigate identity threats such as racial discrimination. In addition, minorities would perceive pro-diversity work climates as a form of organizational support of their best interests. From a social exchange perspective, this should engender a felt obligation on the parts of these employees to reciprocate such organizational goodwill through improved work attitudes and reduced withdrawal (Blau, 1964; Rhoades & Eisenberger, 2002). Furthermore, viewing same-race supervisors as symbols of organizational value for diversity, minority employees were expected to respond more favorably to same-race supervisors but only when value for diversity expectations were met (i.e., the climate was viewed as supportive of diversity). In a national probability sample of working adults, Avery et al. (2007) found support for these notions among black personnel. Specifically, these workers were less absent in work contexts perceived as highly pro-diversity; moreover, they were absent to a greater extent in less pro-diversity contexts when they worked for black supervisors.

McKay et al. (2008) studied the moderating effect of diversity climate, measured at the business unit level, on racial-ethnic mean differences in sales performance. The authors used SIT to predict greater influence of diversity climate on sales among black and Hispanic than white personnel, with greater facilitative effects on sales per hour (measured objectively via electronic cash register). Their rationale was the expectation of greater identification with the organization among black and Hispanic sales associates when store units were perceived as more pro-diversity.

Consequently, these salespersons should expend greater efforts to sell products on behalf of the organization, with beneficial influence on sales performance. Following from this reasoning, larger black–white and Hispanic–white mean differences in sales performance were predicted for stores with less pro-diversity work climates, and smaller disparities were expected in more pro-diversity store units. Analyzing data from a sample of sales associates from a national retail organization, McKay et al. found support for these hypotheses. Black–white mean differences in sales per hour ($8.90), favoring whites, were larger in less pro-diversity climates. In contrast, the direction of racial disparity reversed within more pro-diversity climates, advantaging black sales associates ($7.41), representing a nearly $20.00 facilitative effect of pro-diversity work climates on blacks' average sales performance. Stronger moderating effects occurred for Hispanic–white mean disparities, disparaging the former group, which were quite large in less pro-diversity store units ($23.40) and negligible in more pro-diversity units ($1.21). Moving from less to more pro-diversity work contexts resulted in an approximately $26.00 enhancement in sales, on average, among Hispanic sales associates.

In summary, work has suggested that the racial environment in work contexts is a moderator of racial-ethnic mean differences in work performance. It appears that minorities are less likely to turn over in firms in which they predominate (Zatzick et al., 2003). Moreover, Avery et al. (2007) showed that organizational diversity cues such as individual-level pro-diversity climate perceptions and same-race minority supervisors influence turnover among black personnel. Finally, McKay et al. (2008) found diversity climate, aggregated to the unit level, moderated black–white and Hispanic–white mean differences in sales performance. In light of these preliminary results, racial environmental variables such as minority representation and diversity climate should be included as moderators, when available, in future meta-analytic studies of racial-ethnic mean differences in work performance.

Mean Sex Differences in Work Performance

What We Know

Large primary studies tend to report small and inconsistent mean sex differences in work performance. Pulakos et al. (1989) reported mean effect sizes of −0.02 and 0.07 as assigned by male and female superiors, respectively. Positive effect size values indicate higher ratings assigned to men, while negative ones connote the reverse. Referring to individual performance criteria, effect sizes ranged from −0.02 for military bearing (rated by female supervisors) to 0.10 for technical skill and job effort (rated by male supervisors). Similarly, Sackett et al. (1991), using the GATB database, found a small mean sex difference in overall work performance favoring women ($d = -0.07$, $k = 486$, N at least 4,860, but not actually reported). More recently, Bowen, Swim, and Jacobs (2000) meta-analyzed sex differences in work performance, reporting a mean effect size of −0.05 ($k = 22$, N not reported) for observer ratings.

Few moderators of mean sex differences in work performance have been considered. Sackett et al. (1991) examined the effects of sex composition of the workplace indicative of the gender context of work settings. Negative effects of token status were expected to accentuate sex effects on job performance, as supported by subsequent findings. A positive relationship was obtained between the proportion of women in work groups and sex differences in work performance, favoring females ($\beta = 0.21$, $p < 0.01$). In other words, performance disparities against women were larger in predominantly male work groups, while the reverse was true in largely female work groups. Joshi et al. (2006) considered the cross-level, interactive effects of Ethnicity (Sex) × Proportion of minority (female) coworkers and Ethnicity (Sex) × Proportion of minority (female) managers in sales units on sales performance and pay. The reasoning behind this investigation was that members of stigmatized groups (i.e., minorities and women) benefit from greater representation of their groups in a work context, in line with ingroup advantages described by SIT. This applies to the management process as well since subordinates from a manager's in-group might enjoy advantages not available to outgroup subordinates. Only results for sex are reviewed since minority group employees were collapsed due to small sample sizes. Using data from sales employees of a large information-processing company, findings revealed significant Sex × Proportion of female managers in sales unit interactions on annual salary and annual sales goal achievement. Female sales associates in sales units with higher proportions of female managers earned $2,976 greater annual salaries and achieved 14% higher percentage of their sales targets (108% and 94%, respectively) than those in sales units with a low proportion of women in management. In contrast, the proportion of male managers in sales units had little effect on pay or sales performance among male sales personnel given their social status advantage (Chattopadhyay, Tluchowska, & George, 2004).

Bowen et al. (2000) also assessed, yet failed to find support for, a gender stereotypicality of job influence on effect sizes. The resulting d values for masculine, gender-neutral, and feminine jobs were −0.03, −0.27, and −0.07, respectively, all favoring females ($ks = 16$, 3, and 3, respectively). In addition, these authors considered rater's gender, rater training (i.e., low, medium, and high), and familiarity with the ratee (i.e., low, medium, and high) and found each to be significant moderators. Rater gender effects indicated a pro-male slant in all male work groups ($d = 0.32$, $k = 5$, N not reported), while females were judged to perform better than males when ratings were provided by male and female raters combined ($d = -0.17$, $k = 15$, N not reported). The rater training trend comprised a female performance advantage when ratings were provided by raters with low training ($d = -0.15$, $k = 14$, N not reported), males obtained higher ratings from moderately trained raters ($d = 0.29$, $k = 2$, N not reported), while near-zero sex differences resulted with highly trained raters ($d = 0.03$, $k = 5$, N not reported). Rater familiarity results indicated pro-female differences in ratings among raters with moderate familiarity with ratees ($d = -0.19$, $k = 11$, N not reported) and little mean difference for raters with higher ratee familiarity ($d = 0.04$, $k = 9$, N not reported). The results of Bowen et al. should be interpreted cautiously since they were based on relatively few effect sizes.

In summary, mean sex differences in work performance were evaluated as inconsistent and relatively small in magnitude. Tentatively, there is evidence of moderation of sex effects by sex representation (in work groups and management; Joshi et al., 2006; Sackett et al., 1991), rater gender, extent of rater training, and (ratee) familiarity. Females earned higher performance ratings than males in largely female work contexts, from male and female raters combined, raters with low training, and raters with medium ratee familiarity.

What We Could Learn More About

Generally, there is a need for an updated, comprehensive, meta-analytic study of sex mean disparities in work performance. In literature searches, I only found one published meta-analysis of sex effects that included data from the overall literature (Bowen et al., 2000), as opposed to those limited to estimation of effects from the GATB database (Sackett et al., 1991) or Project A Army data (Pulakos et al., 1989). The Bowen et al. (2000) study, although recently published, is rather dated because it only included effect sizes from two studies from 1990 or later (i.e., Cannings & Montmarquette, 1991; Radhakrishna, 1990). Given the influx of women into the workforce (Fullerton & Toossi, 2001), the topic of mean sex differences in work performance deserves greater attention. Furthermore, voluminous studies are available for meta-analyses of mean sex differences in performance, making this a ripe area for future research.

Continued work on the moderating effects of sex contexts of work environments on male-female differences in performance would be informative, particularly in the vein of the Joshi et al. (2006) investigation. Possibly, sex bias may become more problematic in response to changing sex demography in the workforce. Relational demography research has shown men to respond negatively to increased female representation (Tsui, Egan, &

O'Reilly, 1992), and most management personnel are male (Ragins, 1997). According to the visibility discrimination hypothesis (VDH; Blalock, 1956), members of high-status groups tend to perceive increased threat to their economic and social well-being as minority group proportions rise in a context, with an increase in discriminatory behavior. Although initially applied to blacks, the VDH could apply to women, as recent work by Ostroff and Atwater (2003) reported adverse pay consequences for managers who supervised predominantly female (and minority) subordinates. It would be useful to conduct additional study of diversity climate moderation of sex disparities in work performance. McKay et al. (2008) addressed this issue initially, reporting significant mean sex differences in sales per hour disfavoring females; however, diversity climate failed to moderate the observed differences.

Theoretical Perspectives of Racial-Ethnic and Sex Mean Differences in Work Performance

Most work on racial-ethnic mean differences in work performance has been based on what Nkomo (1992) called the "deficit hypothesis." This hypothesis assumes that disparities against members of lower-status groups result from inherent limitations in members of these groups. By implication, the notion follows that something in the minority group member needs to be "fixed" to ameliorate racial-ethnic effects on work performance. While clearly plausible as a rationale for observed mean differences, the deficit hypothesis does not preclude examination of antecedents of differences that lie outside the minority group members, such as the stereotyping (and resulting bias) and dyadic feedback processes that could disparage minorities and women as well. In the following sections, I summarize briefly three theoretical approaches (status characteristics, stigma, and aversive racism) potentially useful in explaining racial-ethnic (and sex) mean differences in work performance.

Status Characteristics Theory

Status characteristics theory (SCT; Berger, Rosenholtz, & Zelditch, 1980; Ridgeway, 1991) proposes that groups in society are arranged into a status hierarchy based on power and prestige. In the United States, whites and men are perceived as higher in status, on average, than minorities and women. According to the theory, group membership is a diffuse characteristic used to form expectations of a person's behavior, competence, morality, or other personal qualities. In a performance context, members of high-status social groups will be expected to make greater contributions than members of low-status social groups. Internalization of these expectations by both high-status and low-status social group members suggests a scripted form of interaction in which high-status persons will more readily contribute to work activities, while low-status individuals may be less inclined (due to reduced confidence). Through this cycle, the status hierarchy is maintained through a self-fulfilling prophecy as the actors in the group context play their socially constructed (and expected) "parts."

Applied to racial-ethnic and sex mean differences in work performance, SCT suggests minorities and women may not receive equal opportunities to perform challenging tasks, relative to whites and men, with negative implications for work performance, employee development, and advancement prospects (Greenhaus et al., 1990; Kanter, 1977). Subtle stereotypical treatment of minority and female employees by supervisors could perpetuate performance deficits and in turn accentuate racial-ethnic and sex mean differences in work performance. Additional research that examines the work performance ramifications of SCT would be a useful addition to the subgroup differences in performance literature.

Stigma Theory and Aversive Racism Theory

Stigmatization refers to adverse, oppressive treatment suffered typically by members of certain social groups (Crocker & Major, 1989). In the United States, minorities and women can be considered stigmatized groups, often encountering discriminatory treatment based on race-ethnicity or gender (Avery et al., 2008; Deitch et al., 2003; Lim & Cortina, 2005). Remarkably, research has shown that in spite of daily slights encountered by members of stigmatized groups, they are able to maintain high self-esteem (Crocker & Major, 1989). Originally, it was thought that stigmatized people maintained esteem in the face of negative outcomes by attributing them to prejudice; however, subsequent studies suggested that minorities and women suffer attributional ambiguity (Blaine, Crocker, & Major, 1995; Crocker, Voelkl, Testa, & Major, 1991). The concept reflects uncertainty on the part of stigmatized persons to accept negative feedback because it is attributed to prejudice. Furthermore, positive feedback or treatment might be explained away as a form of sympathy due to the person's relatively low social status. This reasoning was supported for women and minorities (Blaine et al., 1995; Crocker et al., 1991).

Aversive racism theory (Dovidio, Gaertner, Kawakami, & Hodson, 2002) proposes some whites hold simultaneously egalitarian beliefs in opposition to racial-ethnic prejudice and an implicit aversion to minorities. The egalitarian aspect of aversive racism is explicit (or verbal), while the implicit portion is expressed nonverbally through excessive blinking, backward body lean, and maintaining poor eye contact during interactions with minorities. Perpetrators of aversively racist behavior during social interactions typically are unaware of their conduct, whereas targets are quite perceptive of these behaviors. Findings suggest minorities are more attuned to aversively racist acts than whites (Dovidio, Kawakami, Johnson, Johnson, & Howard, 1997).

The outcome of such interactions is the development of cultural mistrust. Dovidio, Kawakami, and Gaertner (2002) examined videotaped social interactions between blacks and whites. Participants in these interactions were asked to report their impressions of the encounter. In addition, trained confederates and a group of outside observers were asked to rate the interactions in both verbal and nonverbal behavioral terms. Results showed that in interactions with white participants, black confederates' evaluations of participants' friendliness were more strongly correlated with observers' ratings of participants' nonverbal than verbal behaviors. In contrast, participants' self-evaluations of friendliness were more strongly related to outsiders' ratings of their verbal than nonverbal behaviors.

In combination, stigma and aversive racism theories suggest potential challenges to performance appraisal in organizations, with relevance for subgroup differences in work performance. As part of the feedback function of performance appraisals, subordinates are informed of the quality of their performance in the aim of employee development. Because white men are represented disproportionately in management positions (Ragins, 1997), minority (and perhaps female) personnel could be subjected to aversively racist (or sexist) behavior during interactions with white male supervisors. As a consequence of cultural (or gender) mistrust, these employees are likely to discount negative feedback regarding their performance, denying them the performance benefits of potentially constructive feedback. Even supervisor praise, under such social conditions, may be discounted with potentially negative effects on work attitudes (Jeanquart-Barone, 1996; Tsui & O'Reilly, 1989). Future research based on insights from stigma and aversive racism theories, within the supervisor-subordinate dyad, would be an intriguing contribution to the literature on subgroup differences in performance.

Conclusions

Black–white mean differences in work performance persist, although recent meta-analyses have demonstrated a reduction in effect sizes (McKay & McDaniel, 2006; Roth et al., 2003). These effects are moderated by a number of factors, including criterion type/cognitive loading of criteria, measurement level, and data source. Small-magnitude mean disparities are evident for Hispanics, although some moderation by criterion type and job complexity was evident (Roth et al., 2003). Some intriguing new moderators of racial-ethnic effects on performance have emerged from primary studies, the most pivotal of which appear to be diversity climate and minority representation in the work setting. Sex effects on work performance are inconsistent and small in magnitude; it appears that adverse impact on work performance against women is less problematic than that suffered by blacks. Despite this general conclusion, primary research investigations seem to implicate sex representation strongly in work groups (and in management) as a moderator of sex mean disparities in work performance. A new, comprehensive meta-analytic study of sex effects on performance would be a useful addition to the field on subgroup differences in performance. The one meta-analysis on the topic (Bowen et al., 2000) included studies from primarily 16 or more years ago.

In closing, I wish to encourage additional research that investigates the racial-ethnic and sex contexts of work environments and how these moderate subgroup differences in work performance. The deficit hypothesis, while an initial driver of work in this area, is unnecessarily limiting and, according to recent research, does not fully account for observed racial-ethnic and sex mean differences in work performance. Ameliorating these differences, by implication, would be advantageous to the organizational bottom line monetarily and perhaps legally.

References

Ackerman, P. L. (1988). Determinants of individual differences during skill acquisition: Cognitive abilities and information processing. *Journal of Experimental Psychology: General, 117,* 288–318.

Avery, D. R., McKay, P. F., & Wilson, D. C. (2008). What are the odds: How demographic similarity affects the likelihood of experiencing employment discrimination. *Journal of Applied Psychology, 93,* 235–249.

Avery, D. R., McKay, P. F., Wilson, D. C, & Tonidandel, S. (2007). Unequal attendance: The relationships between race, organizational diversity cues, and absenteeism. *Personnel Psychology, 60,* 875–902.

Becker, G. S. (1993). *Human capital: A theoretical and empirical analysis with special reference to education.* Chicago: University of Chicago Press.

Berger, J., Rosenholtz, S. J., & Zelditch, M. (1980). Status organizing processes. *Annual Review of Sociology, 6,* 479–508.

Blaine, B., Crocker, J., & Major, B. (1995). The unintended consequences of sympathy for the stigmatized. *Journal of Applied Social Psychology, 25,* 889–905.

Blalock, H. M. (1956). Economic discrimination and Negro increase. *American Sociological Review, 21,* 584–588.

Blau, P. M. (1964). *Exchange and power in social life*. New York: Wiley.

Blau, P. M. (1977). *Inequality and heterogeneity*. New York: Free Press.

Bobko, P., Roth, P. L., & Potosky, D. (1999). Derivation and implications of a meta-analytic matrix incorporating cognitive ability, alternative predictors, and job performance. *Personnel Psychology, 52,* 561–589.

Borman, W. C., & Motowidlo, S .J. (1993). Expanding the criterion domain to include elements of contextual performance. In N. Schmitt & W. C. Borman (Eds.), *Personnel selection in organizations* (pp. 71–98). San Francisco: Jossey-Bass.

Bowen, C. C., Swim, J. K., & Jacobs, R. R. (2000). Evaluating gender biases on actual job performance of real people: A meta-analysis. *Journal of Applied Social Psychology, 30,* 2194–2215.

Byrne, D. (1971). *The attraction paradigm*. New York: Academic Press.

Campbell, J. P., McCloy, R. A., Oppler, S. H., & Sager, C. E. (1993). A theory of performance. In N. Schmitt & W. C. Borman (Eds.), *Personnel selection in organizations* (pp. 35–70). San Francisco: Jossey-Bass.

Cannings, K., & Montmarquette, C. (1991). Managerial momentum: A simultaneous model of the career progress of male and female managers. *Industrial and Labor Relations, 44,* 212–228.

Chattopadhyay, P., Tluchowska, M., & George, E. (2004). Identifying the ingroup: A closer look at the influence of demographic dissimilarity on employee social identity. *Academy of Management Review, 29,* 180–202.

Chung-Yan, G. A., & Cronshaw, S. F. (2002). A critical re-examination and analysis of cognitive ability tests using the Thorndike model of fairness. *Journal of Occupational and Organizational Psychology, 75,* 489–509.

Cox, T. H., Jr. (1994). *Cultural diversity in organizations: Theory, research, and practice*. San Francisco: Berrett-Koehler.

Crocker, J., & Major, B. (1989). Social stigma and self-esteem: The self-protective properties of stigma. *Psychological Bulletin, 96,* 608–630.

Crocker, J., Voekl, K., Testa, M., & Major, B. (1991). Social stigma: The affective consequences of attributional ambiguity. *Journal of Personality and Social Psychology, 60,* 218–228.

Deitch, E. A., Barsky, A., Butz, R. M., Chan, S., Brief, A. P., & Bradley, J. C. (2003). Subtle yet significant: The existence and impact of everyday racial discrimination in the workplace. *Human Relations, 56,* 1299–1324.

Dovidio, J. F., Gaertner, S. L., Kawakami, K., & Hodson, G. (2002). Why can't we just get along? Interpersonal biases and interracial distrust. *Cultural Diversity and Ethnic Minority Psychology, 8,* 88–102.

Dovidio, J. F., Kawakami, K., & Gaertner, S. L. (2002). Implicit and explicit prejudice and interracial interaction. *Journal of Personality and Social Psychology, 82,* 62–68.

Dovidio, J. F., Kawakami, K., Johnson, C., Johnson, B., & Howard, A. (1997). The nature of prejudice: Automatic and controlled processes. *Journal of Experimental Social Psychology, 33,* 510–540.

Dreher, G. F., & Cox, Jr., T. H. (2000). Labor market mobility and cash compensation: The moderating effects of race and gender. *Academy of Management Journal, 43,* 890–900.

Ford, J. K., Kraiger, K., Schechtman, S. L. (1986). Study of race effects in objective indices and subjective evaluations of performance: A meta-analysis of performance criteria. *Psychological Bulletin, 99,* 330–337.

Fullerton, H. N., Jr., & Toossi, M. (2001). Labor force projections to 2010: Steady growth and changing composition. *Monthly Labor Review, 124,* 21–38.

Greenhaus, J. H., Parasuraman, S., & Wormley, W. M. (1990). Effects of race on organizational experiences, job performance evaluations, and career outcomes. *Academy of Management Journal, 33,* 64–86.

Hauenstein, N. M. A., Sinclair, A. L., Robson, V., Quintella, Y., & Donovan, J. J. (2003, April). *Performance dimensionality and the occurrence of ratee race effects.* Paper presented at the 18th Annual Conference of the Society for Industrial-Organizational Psychology, Orlando, FL.

Hunter, J. E. (1986). Cognitive ability, cognitive aptitudes, job knowledge, and job performance. *Journal of Vocational Behavior, 29,* 340–362.

Hunter, J. E., & Hunter, R. F. (1984). Validity and utility of alternative predictors of job performance. *Psychological Bulletin, 96,* 72–98.

Hunter, J. E., & Schmidt, F. L. (2004). *Methods of meta-analysis: Correcting error and bias in research findings* (2nd ed.). Newbury Park, CA: Sage.

Ibarra, H. (1995). Race, opportunity, and diversity of social circles in managerial networks. *Academy of Management Journal, 38,* 673–703.

Jeanquart-Barone, S. (1996). Implications of racial diversity in the supervisor-subordinate relationship. *Journal of Applied Social Psychology, 26,* 935–944.

Joshi, A., Liao, H., & Jackson, S. E. (2006). Cross-level effects of workplace diversity on sales performance and pay. *Academy of Management Journal, 49,* 459–481.

Judge, T. A., Cable, D. M., Boudreau, J. W., & Bretz, R. D., Jr. (1995). An empirical investigation of the predictors of executive career success. *Personnel Psychology, 48,* 485–519.

Kanter, R. M. (1977). *Men and women of the corporation.* New York: Basic Books.

Kraiger, K., & Ford, J. K. (1985). A meta-analysis of ratee race effects in performance ratings. *Journal of Applied Psychology, 70,* 56–65.

Lim, S., & Cortina, L. M. (2005). Interpersonal mistreatment in the workplace: The interface and impact of general incivility and sexual harassment. *Journal of Applied Psychology, 90,* 483–496.

McKay, P. F., Avery, D. R., & Morris, M. A. (2008). Mean racial differences in employee sales performance: The moderating role of diversity climate. *Personnel Psychology, 61,* 349–374.

McKay, P. F., & McDaniel, M. A. (2006). A reexamination of black-white mean differences in work performance: More data, more moderators. *Journal of Applied Psychology, 91,* 538–554.

Mor Barak, M. E., Cherin, D. A., & Berkman, S. (1998). Organizational and personal dimensions in diversity climate: Ethnic and gender differences in employee perceptions. *Journal of Applied Behavioral Science, 34,* 82–104.

Murphy, K. R., & Cleveland, J. N. (1995). *Understanding performance appraisal: Social, organizational, and goal-based perspectives.* Thousand Oaks, CA: Sage.

Nkomo, S. M. (1992). The emperor has no clothes: Rewriting "race in organizations." *Academy of Management Review, 17,* 487–513.

Ostroff, C., & Atwater, L. E. (2003). Does whom you work with matter? Effects of referent group gender and age composition on managers' compensation. *Journal of Applied Psychology, 88,* 725–740.

Pulakos, E. D., White, L. A., Oppler, S. H., & Borman, W. C. (1989). Examination of race and sex effects on performance ratings. *Journal of Applied Psychology, 74,* 770–780.

Radhakrishna, R. B. (1990). *Time management and job performance of county extension directors.* Unpublished doctoral dissertation, Pennsylvania State University, University Park.

Ragins, B. R. (1997). Diversified mentoring relationships in organizations: A power perspective. *Academy of Management Review, 22,* 482–521.

Rhoades, L., & Eisenberger, R. (2002). Perceived organizational support: A review of the literature. *Journal of Applied Psychology, 87,* 698–714.

Ridgeway, C. (1991). The social construction of status value: Gender and other nominal characteristics. *Social Forces, 70,* 367–386.

Roth, P. L., BeVier, C. A., Bobko, P., Switzer, F. S., III, & Tyler, P. (2001). Ethnic group differences in cognitive ability in employment and educational settings: A meta-analysis. *Personnel Psychology, 54,* 297–330.

Roth, P. L., Huffcutt, A. I., & Bobko, P. (2003). Ethnic group differences in measures of job performance: A new meta-analysis. *Journal of Applied Psychology, 88,* 694–706.

Rothstein, H. R. (2003). Progress is our most important product: Contributions of validity generalization and meta-analysis to the development and communication of knowledge in I/O psychology. In K. R. Murphy (Ed.), *Validity generalization: A critical review* (pp. 115–154). Mahwah, NJ: Erlbaum.

Sackett, P. R., & DuBois, C. L. Z. (1991). Rater-ratee effects on performance evaluation: Challenging meta-analytic conclusions. *Journal of Applied Psychology, 76,* 873–877.

Sackett, P. R., DuBois, C. L. Z., & Noe, A. W. (1991). Tokenism in performance evaluation: The effects of work group representation on male-female and White-Black differences in performance ratings. *Journal of Applied Psychology, 76,* 263–267.

Schmidt, F. L., & Hunter, J. E. (1998). The validity and utility of selection methods in personnel psychology: Practical and theoretical implications of 85 years of research findings. *Psychological Bulletin, 124,* 262–274.

Schmitt, N., Clause, C. S., & Pulakos, E. D. (1996). Subgroup differences associated with different measures of some common job-relevant constructs. In C. L. Cooper & I. T. Robertson (Eds.), *International review of industrial and organizational psychology* (Vol. 11, pp. 115–139). New York: Wiley.

Stauffer, J. M., & Buckley, M. R. (2005). The existence and nature of racial bias in supervisory ratings. *Journal of Applied Psychology, 90,* 586–591.

Tajfel, H., & Turner, J. C. (1986). The social identity theory of intergroup behavior. In S. Worchel & W. G. Austin (Eds.), *Psychology of intergroup relations* (2nd ed., pp. 7–24). Chicago: Nelson-Hall.

Tsui, A. S., Egan, T. D., & O'Reilly, C. A., III (1992). Being different: Relational demography and organizational attachment. *Administrative Science Quarterly, 37,* 549–579.

Tsui, A. S., & O'Reilly, C. A. (1989). Beyond simple demographic effects: The importance of relational demography in supervisor-subordinate relationships. *Academy of Management Journal, 32,* 402–423.

U.S. Census Bureau. (2004). *Current population survey*. Washington, DC: U.S. Department of Commerce.

Waldman, D. A., & Avolio, B. J. (1991). Race effects in performance evaluations: Controlling for ability, education, and experience. *Journal of Applied Psychology, 76,* 897–901.

Zatzick, C. D., Elvira, M. M., & Cohen, L. M. (2003). When more is better? The effects of racial composition on voluntary turnover. *Organization Science, 14,* 483–496.

10

Validity, Utility, and Adverse Impact: Practical Implications From 30 Years of Data

Wayne F. Cascio, Rick Jacobs, and Jay Silva

Introduction

The business case for building a diverse workforce includes at least five arguments (Cascio, 2006): (a) the shift from a manufacturing to a service economy, (b) the globalization of markets, (c) new business strategies that require more teamwork, (d) mergers and alliances that require different corporate cultures to work together, and (e) the changing labor market. Diversity includes characteristics that one can see (gender, race, ethnicity, age) as well as those that one cannot (e.g., functional expertise, previous experience and training, personality). In this chapter, we focus on the former because that is the focus of the legal system as well as much scientific research (Pyburn, Ployhart, & Kravitz, 2008).

To have a diverse workforce, it is necessary to hire and promote individuals who reflect heterogeneity in gender, race, ethnic group, and age, among other characteristics. As Pyburn et al. (2008) noted, the ability of organizations simultaneously to identify high-quality candidates and to establish a diverse workforce can be hindered because many of the more predictive selection procedures have a negative influence on the pass rates of non-whites and women. They termed this state of affairs the *diversity-validity dilemma*.

A diverse workforce is the ultimate objective, but the means to achieve that objective, namely, selection and promotion systems, often get in the way

271

because they produce adverse impact. The Uniform Guidelines on Employee Selection Procedures (Equal Employment Opportunity Commission, Civil Service Commission Department of Labor, & Department of Justice, 1978) defines *adverse impact* as "a substantially different rate of selection in hiring, promotion, or other employment decision that works to the disadvantage of a race, sex, or ethnic group." Adverse impact (unintentional) discrimination occurs when identical standards or procedures are applied to everyone despite the fact that they lead to a substantial difference in employment outcomes (e.g., selection, promotion, layoffs) for the members of a particular group, *and* they are unrelated to success on a job.

The reduction or elimination of adverse impact is an ongoing process that requires a variety of considerations. We have been working on large-scale public-sector testing programs for three decades. The good news is that we see some progress in creating valid tests that result in a diverse workforce. We also see trends in results, of which some are very positive, while others are less so. Our data come from a variety of public-sector selection programs for which considerations of validity and diversity of the selected group are the most important objectives of participating organizations.

The data we discuss in this chapter come from two samples, one that includes a large group of incumbent police officers (our validation sample of 1,108) and the other an even larger pool of applicants (our applicant database of 14,858). We drew conclusions regarding how to maintain validity and utility while minimizing adverse impact against protected groups. Our data showed the profound influence of cognitive ability testing on adverse impact. These data also provided insight into methods for reducing this influence with the addition of other valid predictors. After years of investigating the public-sector selection paradigm, we offer the following information regarding what we consider the 10 commandments of testing and adverse impact.

Broadening the Scope of Characteristics Tested Improves Validity and Reduces Adverse Impact

In our specific area of inquiry, there is a long and rich history of testing. For decades, civil service and other public-sector organizations found that testing large pools of candidates for a variety of positions was done best by assessing knowledge or cognitive abilities via written, multiple-choice tests. In some of these applications, the tests were simply broad, fact-based devices tapping everything from geography to current events. Others took a more ability-based approach and measured math, vocabulary, and reasoning. Whatever the underlying factors measured, to the extent that the predictors focused on cognitive abilities or, more specifically, verbal abilities, one outcome was highly likely: White candidates significantly outperformed African American candidates. As these tests became more and more tailored to specific job characteristics, the difference between the two groups began to shrink, but the difference remained large, and any selection process based solely on test scores that were predominantly the result of assessing cognitive abilities would certainly lead to adverse impact.

Since the 1980s, many agencies have adopted a much broader definition of jobs, and the corresponding areas identified for selection testing have expanded. In police officer selection, it is no longer the accepted practice to assess only cognitive abilities. First, it is widely recognized (and many job analyses have demonstrated) that other abilities, experiences, and personal characteristics are important for success in that profession. Clearly, successful police officers must have the ability to listen to others, to provide oral communications to a wide-ranging audience of individuals, and to act empathetically toward the public they serve. Simply measuring their thinking skills does not tap into the broad range of underlying skills and abilities that are required for the successful performance of their jobs.

Consistent with this perspective, more recent testing programs to identify new police officers have incorporated a variety of assessment tools, including cognitive abilities, biographical data, and personality scales. Our data indicate that by increasing the scope of abilities that the tests measure, and therefore the breadth of the relevant criterion space, there are corresponding improvements in validity and reductions in adverse impact. Figure 10.1 reflects data from one project that we conducted. What can be seen on the left side is how the correlation (validity) between supervisory assessments of performance and test scores increases as we move from a single test of cognitive ability to a series of tests, including scales from biographical data (biodata) and personality measures (work styles). We also find that as the test battery increases in scope, levels of adverse impact against African American candidates (defined as the ratio of the selection rate of African American candidates to that of white candidates) show large-scale improvements for every selection ratio. These data highlight the advantages of broadening the scope of the assessment program.

Validity Improves When Job-Relevant Personality Characteristics and Biodata Are Part of the Total Score

Our data clearly document a critical fact regarding the relationship between personality and biodata predictors on the one hand and measures of performance on the other. These potential predictors have demonstrated

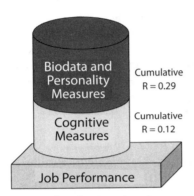

Cumulative
R = 0.29

Cumulative
R = 0.12

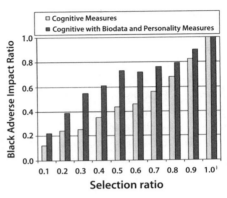

N = 1,108 based on *incumbents* from seven law-enforcement agencies. Biodata and personality measures included: achieving, motivation, intuitive, conscientious, emotionally controlled, and careful/detail conscious.

N = 15,003. Based on *candidates* from five law-enforcement agencies. First adverse impact was first computed within each of the five agencies and then equally weighted across the five agencies.

FIGURE 10.1
Assessing personal characteristics in addition to cognitive ability improves validity and decreases adverse impact at all selection ratios.

meaningful, significant, and consistent relationships with performance. We see this in our total validation sample and in the individual police departments that contributed to the data set. Whether we collapsed across samples or analyzed our seven departments independently, we found that personality variables and biodata scales forecast job performance in a way that boosts validity above and beyond measures of cognitive abilities alone (Figure 10.1). Table 10.1 and Table 10.2 elaborate these relationships. Table 10.1 shows the correlations between and among performance measures and predictor measures. Table 10.2 shows the correlations between performance measures and predictor measures after partialing out the effect of cognitive ability from the performance measures. A description of the personality and biodata scales we used is presented next.

Scale	Type	Definition
Carefulness/Detail Conscious	Biodata/Personality	Items refer to candidates' previous work- and driving-related instances in which carefulness/attentiveness played a role in performance. Focuses on detail, likes to be methodical and organized.
Motivation	Biodata	Items ask candidates to report grade-point averages, involvement in organizations, and other means by which motivation to succeed are manifested.

Scale	Type	Definition
Achieving	Personality	Ambitious and career-centered, likes to set demanding goals and targets.
Intuitive	Personality	Avoids being overly analytical.
Conscientious	Personality	Likes to get things finished on time, persists until the job is done.
Emotionally Controlled	Personality	Avoids displaying emotion.

Deemphasizing Cognitive Ability Tests Reduces Adverse Impact

An important feature of the data presented is the fact that when we added more scales into the test battery, we simultaneously reduced the weighting of cognitive ability on the final test score. When cognitive ability is the only test used, it makes up 100% of the final score. When more tests are included, however, and when these tests are clearly linked to important requirements of the job, we find that we improve validity due to the larger sampling of the criterion space. This is consistent with the latest perspective on staffing strategy (Cascio & Aguinis, 2008). The same strategy serves to reduce adverse impact largely because the other measures that contribute to the final score show much smaller or no differences between majority and minority group test takers (see Figure 10.2). Expressed another way, we are replacing a test with a weight of 1.0 that traditionally generates large subgroup differences with a new way of defining the total test score that may assign a much lower weight, say, 0.33, to the test component that generates the largest subgroup difference. We then distribute the remainder of the 0.67 weight to test scores that generate smaller or no subgroup differences. We have replicated these findings for multiple police agencies. It is important to emphasize, however, that the predictor weights should reflect the relative importance of each of the characteristics measured by the predictors in the overall performance of the job.

Eliminating Cognitive Ability Testing Is an Ineffective Strategy in Terms of Validity and Selection System Utility

If one believes that the end (a diverse workforce) justifies the means (the selection or promotion systems used), then a logical extension of the

TABLE 10.1

Correlations Between and Among Performance Measures and Predictor Measures

Performance/predictor measure	1	2	3	4	5	6	7	8	9	10
1: Performance: Core	1.00	0.74**	0.97**	0.12**	0.19**	−0.01	0.01	0.15**	0.17**	0.24**
2: Performance: Interactive		1.00	0.87**	0.09**	0.13**	0.06*	0.11**	0.06	0.14**	0.18**
3: Performance: Overall			1.00	0.12**	0.18**	0.01	0.05	0.12**	0.17**	0.24**
4: Predictor: Cognitive				1.00	0.10**	−0.16**	0.06	0.13**	0.05	0.12**
5: Predictor: Achieve					1.00	−0.39**	0.15**	0.49**	0.55**	0.43**
6: Predictor: Intuitive						1.00	−0.09**	−0.45**	−0.35**	−0.25**
7: Predictor: Emotionally Controlled							1.00	0.19**	0.23**	0.07*
8: Predictor: Careful/Detail Conscious								1.00	0.60**	0.32**
9: Predictor: Conscientious									1.00	0.31**
10: Predictor: Motivated										1.00

Notes: $N = 1,108$. *$p < 0.05$. **$p < 0.01$.

TABLE 10.2

Correlations Between Performance Measures and Predictor Measures After Partialing the Effect of Cognitive Ability From the Performance Measures

Performance measure	Achieve	Intuitive	Emotionally controlled	Careful/detail conscious	Conscientious	Motivated
Performance: Core	0.18**	0.01	0.00	0.13**	0.17**	0.23**
Performance: Interactive	0.12**	0.08**	0.11**	0.05	0.13**	0.17**
Performance: Overall	0.17**	0.03	0.04	0.11**	0.17**	0.23**

Notes: $N = 1,108$. *$p < 0.05$. **$p < 0.01$.

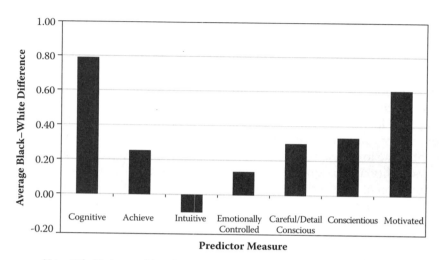

Notes: N for blacks ranged from 3,420 to 3,426. N for whites ranged from 8,896 to 8,912.
Positive average black–white differences indicate higher average scores for whites.

FIGURE 10.2
Measures of personality and biodata show smaller black–white differences than do measures of cognitive ability.

previous discussion might be simply to remove cognitive ability assessment from the selection process. In the terminology we used, we could assign this test component a weight of 0.00. This might be attractive from the standpoint of adverse impact reduction given the consistent demonstration of large subgroup differences (Ployhart & Holz, 2008), but it will certainly lead to a precipitous drop in validity. This is so because the test battery would not include a component that is demonstrably job related. *Validity*, the degree to which evidence and theory support the interpretation of test scores (American Educational Research Association, 1999), is related to workforce productivity (Schmidt & Hunter, 1998). A highly productive workforce, in turn, is critical to organizational success, so unless decision makers are willing to tolerate lower levels of service to the public (public-sector organizations) or less innovation, less productivity, and lower sales (private-sector firms), such a strategy makes no sense. There is little doubt that measures of cognitive abilities predict job performance for a large and varied group of jobs (Schmidt & Hunter, 1998). This has been documented repeatedly, and the evidence is clear that cognitive ability assessment has a place in most selection programs.

Noncognitive Predictors Help Reduce Adverse Impact, but They Are Not as Effective as Originally Proposed

In our analysis of personality, biodata, performance, and race, we have also uncovered some interesting findings that explain why we cannot improve levels of adverse impact as much as originally expected. We see one major underlying reason and then a surprising set of associations that contribute to the lack of progress on adverse impact reduction. First, while personality and biographical data often yield smaller or no differences as a function of race and almost always yield much smaller differences than measures of cognitive abilities, consistent differences do appear between African American and white applicants, largely due to how they respond to questions about their background and personality characteristics. In most cases, whites generate more favorable scores. In some cases, the level of subgroup differences is enough to reduce the effectiveness of a given predictor in terms of its ability to reduce adverse impact. Figure 10.2 summarizes findings regarding these types of variables and the standardized group differences for each in our police officer-applicant sample. What is important to note is that these are the same variables listed as demonstrating stable relationships with job performance.

In addition to demonstrating subgroup differences and being the variables that correlate most consistently with job performance, these same personality variables and biodata measures consistently yielded modest positive

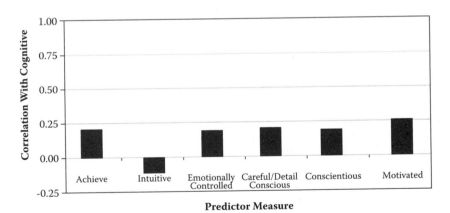

Notes: All correlations are statistically significant ($p < 0.01$) N ranged from 15,005 to 15,008.
The regression of five of these predictors on Cognitive yielded a multiple R of 0.30 ($p < .01$).
Only the Conscientiousness predictor did not significantly ($p > 0.05$) contribute to the prediction of Cognitive.

FIGURE 10.3
Correlations of measures of personality and biodata with cognitive ability.

correlations (except for "intuitive," which yielded a modest negative correlation) with assessments of cognitive ability (see Figure 10.3). We believe that the better candidates for the job of police officer not only demonstrated higher levels of cognitive abilities, but they also had higher levels of the performance-relevant characteristics measured by the alternative predictor measures. This helps to explain why, despite including personality and biodata measures in our predictor composite, adverse impact persisted.

The clear problem we seem to be facing with respect to predicting the performance of police officers, and to reducing adverse impact among police candidates, is that the best noncognitive predictors also generate subgroup differences as a function of race, perhaps through their relationship with cognitive ability. We cannot say, however, that the same relationships hold for other types of workers.

Trade-Offs Between Validity and Adverse Impact Reduction Produce Nonlinear Losses in Utility and Show a Decelerating Curve

Given the multiplicity of predictors that can be used with our data, it is possible to investigate the use of various combinations of them and various predictor-weighting strategies to examine their effects on validity and adverse impact. We can alternate between the candidate database and the concurrent validity data to identify predictors that generate smaller subgroup differences in the sample of candidates and then evaluate those predictors of performance in the sample of incumbents. We sometimes develop selection models by changing predictors and by changing the weights attached to each. When we do this, we find that it is possible to reduce adverse impact or to eliminate it completely.

We began by looking at the validation sample and attempting to maximize validity via regression analysis. Then, we looked at the candidate database and input the maximum validity model, specified a selection ratio, and then evaluated adverse impact. When we did this, we found several consistent results. Increasing the selection ratio (by using a lower cutoff score so that more candidates "pass") reduced adverse impact (see the right side of Figure 10.4). When we changed the weights of the prediction model to increase the importance of predictors that generated smaller subgroup differences (thereby reducing the weight for those predictors that generated higher subgroup differences), we saw systematic decreases both in adverse impact and in validity. When we removed predictors that generated large subgroup differences and replaced them

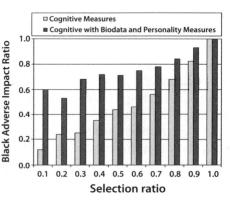

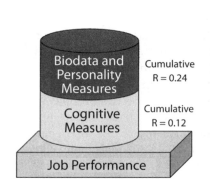

N = 1,108 based on *incumbents* from seven law-enforcement agencies. Biodata and personality measures included: motivation, achieving, intuitive, conscientious, emotionally controlled, and careful/detail conscious.

N = 15,003. Based on *candidates* from five law-enforcement agencies. First adverse impact was first computed within each of the five agencies and then equally weighted across the five agencies.

FIGURE 10.4

Increasing the selection ratio decreases adverse impact, as does dropping the biodata/personality predictor that generated the largest subgroup difference (motivation). The latter strategy, however, also decreases validity.

with predictors that showed smaller subgroup differences, we got the same result, namely, lower adverse impact and lower validity. To appreciate this fact, see the left side of Figure 10.4 and compare the validity to that shown in Figure 10.1. Our data suggest that adverse impact and validity are related to each other positively. Further, at certain points in this analysis, decreases in validity increased at a faster rate than did improvements in adverse impact.

Researchers have developed procedures to examine the validity–adverse impact tradeoff more systematically. Thus, De Corte, Lievens, and Sackett (2007) provided a computer program that shows the set of predictor weights that yields the lowest possible degree of subgroup difference at any given degree of reduction in validity. In other words, the procedure estimates the reduction in subgroup differences that would be attainable should the decision maker be willing to accept, say, a 1%, a 5%, or a 10% reduction in validity. Thus, it makes the validity-diversity tradeoff explicit. In a related study, Aguinis and Smith (2007) offered a computer program that examines the effect of the choice of selection ratio on mean criterion performance and adverse impact. These are helpful adjuncts to important decisions about possible trade-offs between validity and adverse impact.

Test-Score Banding, Which Is Legal, Offers No Guidelines on What Constitutes a Useful Tiebreaker Within Bands

Much has been made of test-score banding and its impact on reductions in adverse impact. Journals have dedicated issues to the topic, different types of banding techniques have been created (e.g., fixed vs. sliding bands), and some courts have even mandated banding in an effort to reduce or eliminate adverse impact (Aguinis, 2004). Cascio, Outtz, Zedeck, and Goldstein (1991) proposed the sliding-band method as a way to incorporate both utility and adverse impact considerations into the staffing process. It is an attempt to reconcile economic and social objectives within the framework of generally accepted procedures for testing hypotheses about differences in individual test scores. The sliding-band model is one of a class of approaches to test use (banding) in which individuals within a specific score range, or band, are regarded as having equivalent scores. It does not correct for very real differences in test scores that may be observed among groups. It only allows for flexibility in decision making.

Several conclusions have emerged as banding has been used since the 1990s. First, banding only makes a difference within the last band reached. In many selection situations, organizations move to Band 5 or Band 8. When this happens, the banded solution does nothing to change relative levels of adverse impact in the first four or seven bands, respectively. Second, banding only allows organizations to use a predictor other than test scores to break ties within bands, and it is clear, according to the law and professional practice, that using the race of the candidate to break ties within a band is generally prohibited (*Chicago Firefighters Local 2 v. City of Chicago*, 2001). Finally, what predictor should be used to select candidates within a band? If the variable is reliable and valid, why is it not part of the overall selection model?

Sackett and Lievens (2008) noted that, although banding is not advocated only as a device for reducing adverse impact, the reduction of adverse impact is a key reason for the interest in this method. A clearer picture is emerging of the circumstances under which banding does or does not affect minority hiring rates, with key features including the width of the band and the basis for selection within a band. Clearly, banding may work in some situations but is not appropriate in all circumstances. While it has demonstrated a generally minor but positive impact on adverse impact reduction with relatively no cost in terms of validity or utility, it is not a general solution.

The Method Known as Within-Group Percentiles, Dual Lists, or "Race Norming" Simultaneously Maximizes Validity and Reduces Adverse Impact (Except That It Is Not Legal)

Our data consistently showed that the single best way to maximize validity and utility simultaneously, while minimizing adverse impact, is to use what is known in the profession as dual (or multiple) lists. In its simplest form, candidates from different groups, for example, African American and white candidates, are placed on separate lists, and individuals are selected from each list in proportion to their application rate. When this is done strictly based on application rate, adverse impact is eliminated. Our data showed that while there are decrements in validity and utility relative to a traditional single-list approach, the drop in validity is far less than that seen using any other strategy. The technical solution seems clear, with the exception that it is not legal under the 1991 Civil Rights Act since it is clearly an example of race norming. Figure 10.5 shows the results of a Monte Carlo simulation using a sample size of 5,000 candidates. The figure shows the average standardized score on a measure of job performance across four different selection ratios for four different methods of test use: top-down and dual-list selection (each with an assumed validity of 0.30) and two methods with assumed lower validities (0.25 and 0.20,

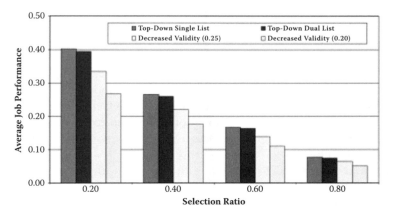

Notes: Results were simulated with Monte Carlo techniques using a sample size of 5,000 candidates (for stability). We made the following assumptions: (1) Predictor composite is normally distributed for blacks and whites; (2) blacks comprised 20% of the candidates; (3) the average predictor-composite difference between blacks and whites was 0.50; and (4), the validity of the predictor composite for the single-list and dual-list methods was 0.30. The validity for the other two methods represent estimated lower validities, as predictors with large black–white differences are removed from the predictor composite.

FIGURE 10.5
Results of Monte Carlo simulation of the effects of four different methods of test use on a standardized measure of job performance.

respectively) as predictors with large black–white differences are removed from the predictor composite.

Across all four selection ratios, the loss of productivity (average standardized job performance score) was minimal for top-down selection from dual lists versus top-down selection from a single list. The productivity loss was systematically lower across all selection ratios, regardless of whether single or dual lists were used, when predictors with large black–white differences were removed from the predictor composite. The loss was greatest when that method was used with dual lists.

Selection Rates Have a Major Impact on Utility and Adverse Impact

The 80% rule is usually the first, and is certainly the simplest, means of determining the presence or absence of adverse impact. All that is required is the calculation of the passing rates for the majority and minority groups and then computation of a ratio of one relative to the other. It is simple, but it turns out that the 80% threshold is possible to achieve when there are very large differences in test scores between the two groups, that is, there appears to be no adverse impact, but very large differences in test scores of African American and White candidates. The opposite is also true; we can have small differences in test performance but high levels of adverse impact as measured by the 80% rule. The problem is that the 80% rule is insensitive to another very important variable in any selection situation: the percentage of applicants selected (selection ratio).

When the selection ratio is very large (approaching 1.0), indicating many open positions relative to applicants to fill them, achieving the 80% threshold is easier than when the selection ratio is very small (approaching 0.05 or smaller). Under conditions of enhanced competition, for which employers have the opportunity to reject 19 of every 20 applicants, even very small differences in test scores can create high levels of adverse impact. Figure 10.6 shows this effect graphically for a very low selection ratio, 0.05.

In fact, adverse impact increases dramatically as selection ratios get smaller and as the average standardized predictor-score difference between blacks and whites increases. The point here is that there should be more to the analysis of adverse impact than test-score differences and selection ratios between groups. Like the Taylor-Russell (1939) tables taught us, there is complexity in determining the effectiveness of a selection program, and we must include other variables in our understanding of adverse impact. Clearly, the inclusion of the selectivity level of a

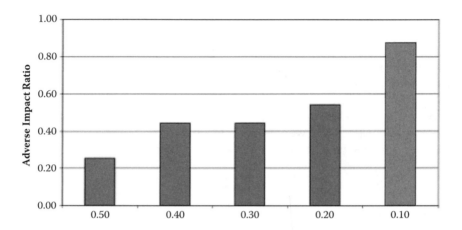

Notes: Results were simulated with Monte Carlo techniques using a sample size of 500 candidates. For many occupations, a candidate pool of 500 would be large. We made the following assumptions: (1) Predictor composite is normally distributed for blacks and whites; (2) blacks comprised 20% of the candidates; and (3), the average standardized predictor-score difference between blacks and whites varied between 0.10 and 0.50, in favor of whites.

FIGURE 10.6
Adverse impact ratios at a given selection ratio (0.05) as the average standardized predictor-score difference between blacks and whites varied between 0.10 and 0.50, in favor of whites.

selection program, as indicated by the selection ratio, is warranted if we are to understand the complexities of adverse impact. The 80% rule and other legal standards that focus solely on group differences do not reflect the intricacies of selection.

In Selection Paradigms, Selecting Beyond the Base Rate of Any Group (Oversampling) Will Result in Large Decreases in Utility

Unfortunately, in many early court cases a decision was made to mandate the selection of members of a specific group to make up for past inequities. When this is done, it comes at a cost. If differences in test scores are related to differences in job performance, and if we are forced to sample more exhaustively from members of the lower-performing group, there will certainly be decreases in the overall performance of the group selected. This will, of necessity, yield a decrease in validity, and since validity is linearly related to utility (Brogden, 1949), it will reduce the ultimate utility of the selection process. The only way to mitigate this result is to create a system that allows for past inequities to be addressed, but over a longer period of time, so that new candidates can be brought into the process. Figure 10.7 illustrates this clearly.

Figure 10.7 shows both the incremental loss and the cumulative loss in job performance (in standard score units). When 50% of the blacks are hired (i.e., equal representation), then the performance difference is −.50. As minority representation increases beyond this point, the performance loss exceeds the black–white difference in the candidate pool (presumably also in the broader population). That then gives people in the workplace the idea that performance between blacks and whites is even worse than it is (i.e., because it was manipulated through higher-than-representation minority hiring). Also note that the incremental job-performance cost of hiring additional minorities decreased for every unit until some later point (in this case, when we increased black hiring from 0.14 to 0.15).

Conclusions and Implications for Future Research

Based on large data sets of police officer-incumbents and police officer-candidates, we found the following results: (a) Broadening the scope of job-related characteristics tested beyond cognitive ability improved validity and decreased adverse impact; (b) validity improved incrementally when job-related measures of personality and biographical data were added to a test battery; (c) reducing the weight of cognitive ability scores in a test battery reduced adverse impact, but (d) reducing its weight to zero significantly reduced the overall validity and utility of a test battery that seeks to forecast job performance that requires, in part, cognitive ability; (e) measures of personality and biodata characteristics also yielded consistent differences between African American and white test takers, thereby reducing the overall effectiveness of these measures in lessening adverse impact; (f) validity–adverse impact trade-offs produced non-linear losses in utility; (g) test-score banding, which is legal and which has produced modest reductions in adverse impact with relatively no cost in validity or utility, is not a general solution to the problem of reducing adverse impact; (h) the use of within-group percentiles (race norming) produces the optimal technical solution in terms of maximizing validity and minimizing adverse impact, but it is not legal; (i) selection rates, which legal standards like the 80% rule do not address, have a major impact on utility and adverse impact; and (j) selecting beyond the base rate of any group (oversampling) resulted in very large decreases in utility.

While research since the 1980s has revealed very useful, practical findings with respect to the validity–adverse impact trade-off, there remains much that we do not know. For example, there are no legal or scientific

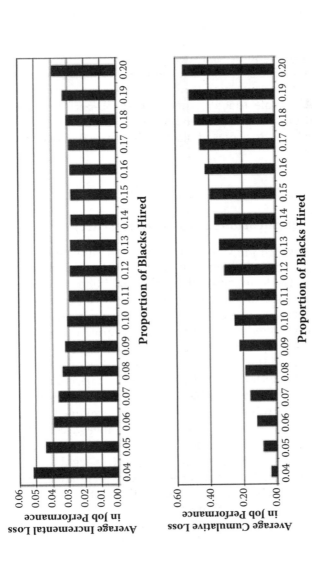

FIGURE 10.7

Average incremental loss and average cumulative loss in job performance as the proportion of blacks hired varied from 0.04 to 0.20.

Notes: We made the following assumptions: (1) Predictor composite is normally distributed for blacks and whites; (2) blacks comprised 20% of the candidates; (3) the average job-performance difference between blacks and whites was 0.25; (4) the validity of the predictor composite was 0.30; and (5), the selection ratio was 0.50.

guidelines to help employers identify how much of a loss in validity or utility is warranted in their attempts to reduce adverse impact. Further, the legal standard for determining adverse impact, the 80% rule, is blind to considerations of sample size and selection ratios. As a result, it can lead to conclusions that are not warranted based on those variables. Social scientists have much to contribute to the debate on issues such as these, and we fully expect that they will do so in the years to come.

References

Aguinis, H. (Ed.). (2004). *Test-score banding in human resource selection: Legal, technical, and societal issues.* Westport, CT: Quorum.

Aguinis, H., & Smith, M. A. (2007). Understanding the impact of test validity and bias on selection errors and adverse impact in human resource selection. *Personnel Psychology, 60,* 165–199.

American Educational Research Association, American Psychological Association, & National Council on Measurement in Education. (1999). *Standards for educational and psychological testing.* Washington, DC: American Educational Research Association.

Brogden, H. E. (1949). When testing pays off. *Personnel Psychology, 2,* 171–183.

Cascio, W. F. (2006). *Managing human resources: Productivity, quality of work life, profits* (7th ed.). Burr Ridge, IL: McGraw-Hill/Irwin.

Cascio, W. F., & Aguinis, H. (2008). Staffing 21st-century organizations. *Academy of Management Annals, 2*(1), 133–165.

Cascio, W. F., Outtz, J. L., Zedeck, S., & Goldstein, I. L. (1991). Statistical implications of six methods of test-score use in personnel selection. *Human Performance, 4,* 233–264.

De Corte, W., Lievens, F., & Sackett, P. R. (2007). Combining predictors to achieve optimal trade-offs between selection quality and adverse impact. *Journal of Applied Psychology, 92,* 1380–1393.

Equal Employment Opportunity Commission, Civil Service Commission, Department of Labor, & Department of Justice. (1978). Uniform guidelines on employee selection procedures. *Federal Register, 43,* 382990–38315.

Chicago Firefighters Local 2 v. City of Chicago, 249 F.3d 649 (7th Cir., 2001).

Ployhart, R. E., & Holz, B. C. (2008). The diversity-validity dilemma: Strategies for reducing racioethnic and sex subgroup differences and adverse impact in selection. *Personnel Psychology, 61,* 153–172.

Pyburn, K. M., Jr., Ployhart, R. E., & Kravitz, D. A. (2008). The diversity-validity dilemma: Overview and legal context. *Personnel Psychology, 61,* 143–151.

Sackett, P., & Lievens, F. (2008). Personnel selection. *Annual Review of Psychology, 59,* 419–450.

11

Cut Scores and Adverse Impact

Jerard F. Kehoe

Introduction

The purpose of this chapter is to describe and evaluate the relationships between adverse impact and the various methods by which cut scores can be selected. Adverse impact is a decision made by enforcement agencies and by courts. This is the meaning of adverse impact from an organization's perspective. Although the "four-fifths rule" is a defined evidence threshold, the *Uniform Guidelines on Employment Selection Procedures* (1978) expressly allows that other evidence may also inform the decision about adverse impact. In Section 4D, the *Guidelines* establish that statistical and practical considerations as well as employer actions having an impact on minority applicant pools, such as recruiting programs, also be taken into consideration by agencies and courts. Nevertheless, the main focus of this chapter is on the four-fifths rule because the design and operation of selection decision processes, such as cut scores, are likely to influence adverse impact primarily through their effects on group selection rates.

The Role of Professional and Managerial Judgments

Inevitably, the degree of adverse impact of the operational selection system will be influenced by the organizational context as well as technical decisions made by the selection system designer. The organizational context includes (a) the organization's desires and values with respect to selection diversity; (b) the nature of the organization needs that are addressed by the selection process; (c) the organization's desires with respect to selection utility, including, specifically, the desired initial level of proficiency; (d) tolerance for costs; (e) the organization's sensitivity to the legal risk associated with adverse impact; and (f) the recruiting and sourcing practices used to create the applicant pools. These contextual factors can manifest themselves in a variety of ways, including specific requests/requirements from business or human resources (HR) managers, prevailing HR policies or strategies, corporate values and goals/objectives specific to diversity, direct or indirect influence from the organization's diversity and equal employment opportunity (EEO) compliance managers, process requirements imposed or preferred by employment delivery managers, and so on. However they manifest themselves, these organization factors can have a critical impact on the design and technical decisions made or recommended by the selection program designer that may affect adverse impact, including the choice and design of selection assessment tools and the rules and methods used to make the selection decisions. Indeed, these context factors can easily constrain the range of plausible options available to the selection program designer. In my experience working with organizations on the design of selection programs, I have found that it is almost always the case that the professional selection program designer has the most relevant expertise and experience to help the organization's managers understand the relationships among the many organization contextual factors and selection outcomes, including adverse impact. However, the selection program designer's influence with regard to these issues is not always commensurate with the experience and expertise. In any case, my recommendation is that business managers such as business leaders or HR leaders, not the selection program designer, ultimately own the key decisions, such as specific cut scores and even types of selection procedures, that have the most direct impact on adverse impact and business value.

While this chapter focuses on the impact of cut score-setting methods on adverse impact, it is important to understand that cut scores are chosen as a decision method, and specific cut scores are selected for many reasons, only some of which are directly related to considerations of adverse impact. The reader should not assume that simply because the effects of cut scores on adverse impact are identified and described here that these effects are the primary drivers of the professional and managerial decisions about cut scores.

The general point is that decisions about cut scores virtually always have other effects in addition to adverse impact and may be made for other reasons, such as cost, speed, applicant perceptions/reactions, utility, and initial proficiency. As noted, perhaps the most effective role for the selection program designer in determining the ultimate combination of choices is to provide accurate information and strong recommendations on the pivotal questions. Once the assessment procedures have been chosen, the story of adverse impact is largely the story of managing four types of considerations. The first consideration is the organization's goals with respect to diversity. The second is the nature of the organization needs the selection process is being designed to address. The third is the organization's tolerance for uncertainty about the quality of employees and legal risk. Finally, some set of boundary conditions will constrain the design and methodology of the entire selection system.

Diversity

When the selection assessment tools yield group differences, it is inevitable that the final design of the selection system will depend, in part, on an understanding of the organization's goals with respect to diversity. In some cases, this understanding will be based on explicit, well-established principles, values, and objectives regarding diversity. These may even go so far as to clarify the organization's desire regarding the role of selection decisions as a vehicle for achieving workforce diversity. For example, some organizations may have affirmative action plans (AAPs) that establish specific goals regarding hiring diversity. Others may endorse even more specific strategies that identify recruiting and sourcing as the employment levers for diversity but explicitly acknowledge that skill standards should not be trumped by diversity considerations. At the other end of the spectrum, some organizations may have no discernible diversity strategy to guide decisions about selection programs. In that case, the selection designer may choose to engage the local business leader for whom the selection system is being developed to describe the manner in which diversity considerations should affect decisions about the selection system. Every decision about the design of a selection system that affects the diversity of those selected depends in some fashion on this organization-level consideration. This can be a major consideration in the design of selection systems. This chapter about adverse impact and cut scores describes the methods by which diversity values can influence the establishment of cut scores.

Needs

Each selection system is designed for some intended use. Certainly, this intended use is the foundation for any eventual validation effort. Also, the intended use determines the choice/design of the specific assessment constructs and tools to be included in the selection system. These early decisions about intended use can make all the difference with respect to the eventual adverse impact of the operational selection process. For example, selection systems designed to improve task proficiency and accuracy are likely to create more adverse impact than selection systems designed to reduce turnover or counterproductive behavior. The reason, as described in this chapter, is that the performance factors associated with task proficiency are more likely to involve cognitive ability than are the personality-oriented performance factors contributing to turnover or counterproductive behavior. Group differences tend to be much larger on cognitive ability measures than on personality measures.

Since the 1990s, at least three meta-analyses have examined group differences in measures of work performance (Ford, Kraiger, & Schechtman, 1986; McKay & McDaniel, 2006; Roth, Huffcutt, & Bobko, 2003). All focused on race/ethnic differences, primarily black–white differences because those have been studied far more than other group differences. Certain consistent trends emerged, particularly in the Roth et al. (2003) and McKay and McDaniel (2006) studies, which analyzed differences in the common metric of corrected, standardized differences. Black–white performance differences are largest, in the .54 to .60 range, on work sample and job knowledge measures of performance. While it is unlikely that a business leader would describe the organization need in terms of performance on a work sample or job knowledge test, it is more plausible that an organization need would be described in terms of job expertise or job judgment, both of which might be assessed by work sample or job knowledge assessments. In contrast, black–white differences on nonproficiency performance factors such as absenteeism, accidents, applied social skills, and contextual behavior were much lower, in the −.09 to .22 range. As might be expected then, measures of overall performance resulted in intermediate black–white differences in the .35 to .46 range. In general, performance components loading on cognitive ability demands of work show higher black–white differences than components loading on motivation and disposition-temperament demands of work.

Both Roth et al. (2003) and McKay and McDaniel (2006) reported somewhat smaller differences, .18 and .25, respectively, for indicators of "on-the-job training." In contrast, McKay and McDaniel reported a much larger difference, .72, in classroom training performance, which they labeled "academy training performance." Classroom training measures included classroom mastery assessments such as final class grade, whereas on-the-job training included measures of training effectiveness gathered on the job in the context of work behavior rather than classroom behavior. As McKay and McDaniel noted, by the operational definitions of classroom training and on-the-job training, classroom training is more heavily cognitively loaded than on-the-job training.

The clear implication is that organization needs centering on learning and cognitive work behavior are more likely to result in selection procedures producing adverse impact than needs focusing on work behaviors that are less cognitively loaded, such as contextual behavior, absenteeism, and in many cases, turnover. It is important to note that this point about the relationship between business needs and likelihood of adverse impact is based primarily on a consideration of group differences in work performance, not group differences on predictor measures. The fundamental research conclusion underlying this point is that group differences appear to be larger on performance factors that depend more heavily on cognitive ability than on performance factors that depend more heavily on noncognitive factors. The implication of this point is that predictor measures designed to address performance issues that depend relatively more on cognitive ability are likely, themselves, to assess cognitive ability. It is well known that the format and design of cognitive measures can reduce the degree of group differences to some extent. However, to the extent such design and format tactics reduce the cognitive loading of the predictor, their validity with respect to cognitively driven performance factors is likely to be reduced.

Uncertainty

The role of uncertainty is often obscured by methods for setting cut scores or other selection decision standards. There are three primary certainty considerations. The first is the certainty that a selected applicant will be a successful employee. The second is the certainty that applicants who would be successful employees will be selected. The third is the degree of legal risk associated with a particular selection strategy. In the case of employment selection, the unfortunate reality for organizations is that, once the selection procedures have been chosen, steps to improve the certainty that selected applicants will be successful employees such as increased cut scores or reweighted predictor composites virtually always increase the degree of adverse impact and reduce the certainty that applicants who will be successful employees will be selected. For that reason, it is important to recognize the role of uncertainty as a factor that influences the degree of adverse impact. The framework used in this chapter for analyzing and setting cut scores explicitly distinguishes considerations of uncertainty from other considerations.

Boundary Conditions

Organizations always have boundary conditions that limit HR programs and systems, including selection. Chief among these are cost and time. Other boundary conditions specific to selection may include recruiting practices, hiring manager roles, technology, union contracts, external factors such as the threat of or impact of employment litigation, and so on. It is not uncommon for the limits imposed by boundary conditions relating directly to business operations (e.g., cost, speed, technology, hiring manager roles) to trump everything else in the design of methods for making selection decisions.

The Impact of Cut Scores on Adverse Impact: The Basics

One's choice of cut score affects adverse impact only if the majority and minority groups have different distributions of selection scores. The reason for this volume is that groups have been shown consistently to have different average scores on a variety of different types of selection procedures. Potosky, Bobko, and Roth's (2005) summary of this research estimated the majority-minority standardized group mean differences to be .72 for cognitive ability (CA), .57 for biodata, .31 for structured interviews, and .06 for conscientiousness. There is little evidence that the standard deviations (SD) of group score distributions are substantially different. The Civil Rights Act of 1991 effectively requires that cut scores used to make employment decisions apply to all applicants in the same way, regardless of group membership. The result is that any one cut score is a more extreme score value for the lower-scoring group than for the higher-scoring group.

For example, assume minority and majority applicants have average scores of 54.3 and 60.0, respectively, on a particular biodata inventory with $SD = 10$. This corresponds to a standardized group mean difference of .57, as reported by Potosky et al. (2005). In this case, a cut score of, say, 58 would be below the average majority group score and above the average minority group score. This cut score would be a more extreme score in the minority score distribution in that it is .37 SD above the minority group mean but .20 SD below the majority group mean. Assuming these biodata scores are normally distributed, it would be expected that approximately 36% of the minority applicants would "pass" this cut score requirement, whereas approximately 58% of the majority applicants would pass. In this case, the adverse impact ratio (AIR) would be approximately .62 (.36/.58), failing the four-fifths rule.

Table 11.1 shows expected AIR values for several combinations of group differences and selection ratios. (Note that in Table 11.1 and elsewhere, selection ratios are used as surrogates for cut scores, so that the results presented in the table apply regardless of the means and SD of the selection procedure.) The results depicted across the rows in Table 11.1 show that, for any given level of group difference, AIR improves as the selection ratio increases. Comparing AIR levels within a column, the results show the typical pattern that AIR decreases with increases in the mean difference between groups. It is instructive to note that the legal threshold value for AIR, .80, is satisfied by the combinations of selection ratios and group

TABLE 11.1

Effects of Group Mean Difference and Selection Ratio on an Adverse Impact Ratio (AIR) and Group Passing Percentages

Standardized group mean difference[a]	Selection ratio					
	.05	.10	.30	.50	.70	.90
.06 (conscientiousness)						
Adverse impact ratio	.88	.90	.93	.95	.97	.98
Minority pass %	4.5	9.2	28.1	48.0	68.4	89.1
Majority pass %	5.2	10.2	30.1	50.4	70.5	90.7
.31 (structured interview)						
Adverse impact ratio	.51	.56	.68	.76	.84	.93
Minority pass %	2.8	6.1	21.2	39.4	60.2	84.4
Majority pass %	5.5	10.8	31.2	51.6	71.6	90.7
.57 (biodata)						
Adverse impact ratio	.28	.34	.47	.58	.71	.86
Minority pass %	1.6	3.8	15.2	30.8	51.2	78.2
Majority pass %	5.8	11.3	32.3	52.8	72.6	91.2
.72 (cognitive ability)						
Adverse impact ratio	.20	.23	.37	.49	.63	.81
Minority pass %	1.2	2.8	12.1	26.4	46.0	74.2
Majority pass %	6.1	11.7	33.0	53.6	73.2	91.5
1.00 (large comparison value)						
Adverse impact ratio	.09	.13	.23	.34	.49	.71
Minority pass %	0.6	1.6	7.9	18.9	36.3	65.5
Majority pass %	6.4	12.3	34.1	54.8	74.2	91.9

[a] Assumes that the proportions of minority and majority applicants is .119 and .881, respectively, as reported in Potosky et al. (2005).

differences in the upper right-hand corner of Table 11.1. These results show that, among selection procedures on which group means differ by more than 0.30 SD, the .80 threshold is satisfied only at high selection ratios. While the *Uniform Guidelines* (1978) does not prohibit adverse impact, organizations have an interest in knowing the trade-offs required to substantially improve adverse impact. Table 11.1 depicts the empirical results relating to cut scores and AIR that have driven the extensive search in the personnel selection research literature for methods to improve AIR.

In addition to the basic results shown in Table 11.1, it is instructive to consider other results showing the impact of the same combinations of selection ratios and group differences on the characteristics of those applicants selected by a particular cut score required to produce a given selection ratio. Table 11.2 shows the effects of the selection ratio and applicant group mean difference on the average predictor scores of applicants who meet or exceed the cut score required of the target selection ratio. The

TABLE 11.2

Effects of Group Mean Difference and Selection Ratio on Average Predictor Scores Among Selected Applicants

Standardized group mean difference[a]	Selection ratio					
	.05	.10	.30	.50	.70	.90
.06 (conscientiousness)						
Adverse impact ratio	.88	.90	.93	.95	.97	.98
Average predictor score among selected minority applicants	2.05	1.74	1.15	0.78	0.47	0.16
Average predictor score among selected majority applicants	2.06	1.76	1.17	0.80	0.50	0.20
Standardized group mean difference among selected applicants[b]	.01	.02	.02	.02	.03	.04
.31 (structured interview)						
Adverse impact ratio	.51	.56	.68	.76	.84	.93
Average predictor score among selected minority applicants	2.02	1.71	1.10	0.71	0.37	0.01
Average predictor score among selected majority applicants	2.06	1.76	1.17	0.81	0.51	0.22
Standardized mean group difference among selected applicants[b]	.04	.05	.07	.10	.14	.21
.57 (biodata)						
Adverse impact ratio	.28	.34	.47	.58	.71	.86
Average predictor score among selected minority applicants	1.99	1.68	1.05	0.64	0.28	−0.12
Average predictor score among selected majority applicants	2.07	1.77	1.18	0.82	0.53	0.25
Standardized mean group difference among selected applicants[b]	.08	.09	.13	.18	.25	.37
.72 (cognitive ability)						
Adverse impact ratio	.20	.23	.37	.49	.63	.81
Average predictor score among selected minority applicants	1.98	1.66	1.03	0.61	0.23	−0.19
Average predictor score among selected majority applicants	2.07	1.77	1.19	0.83	0.54	0.26
Standardized mean group difference among selected applicants[b]	.09	.11	.16	.22	.31	.45
1.00 (large comparison value)						
Adverse impact ratio	.09	.13	.23	.34	.49	.71
Average predictor score among selected minority applicants	1.90	1.61	0.98	0.55	0.15	−0.32

TABLE 11.2 (*Continued*)

Effects of Group Mean Difference and Selection Ratio on Average Predictor Scores Among Selected Applicants

Standardized group mean difference[a]	Selection ratio					
	.05	.10	.30	.50	.70	.90
Average predictor score among selected majority applicants	2.07	1.78	1.20	0.84	0.56	0.28
Standardized mean group difference among selected applicants[b]	.17	.17	.22	.29	.41	.60

[a] Assumes the proportions of minority and majority applicants are .119 and .881, respectively, as in Potosky et al. (2005).
[b] Standardized based on applicant population SD of 1.00, not on range-restricted SD of selected population.

results in this table are known but have received relatively little attention in personnel selection research. First, for both majority and minority groups, results across rows show that the average predictor score of selected applicants decreases with increases in the selection ratio. Indeed, this decrease can be dramatic across the range of practically useful selection ratios ranging from .30 to .70. Typically, the average predictor score of applicants selected at a .70 ratio is 0.6 to 0.8 SD lower than the average predictor scores produced by a selection ratio of .30. Perhaps the most compelling result shown in Table 11.2 is that, among selected applicants, the mean difference between the minority and majority groups is much smaller than in the unselected applicant population. As shown in the rows reporting standardized mean group differences among selected applicants, the effect size at a high selection ratio of .90 is typically one third smaller than in the unselected population. Even a modest amount of selection substantially reduces group differences on the predictor.

The explanation for this reduction of effect sizes is well understood. When minority applicant population scores have a lower mean than the majority applicant population, any particular cut score represents a more extreme value in the minority score distribution than in the majority score distribution. For example, typically the minority biodata average score is 0.57 SD lower than the majority average. As a result, a cut score located at, say, the majority average score corresponds to a z value in the majority score distribution of 0.00 SD and a z value of 0.57 SD in the minority score distribution. The same cut score is a more extreme value in the minority distribution than in the majority distribution. By the shape of the assumed normal distribution, a higher proportion of majority scores are at or just above the majority z value of 0.00 compared to the proportion of minority scores at or just above the minority z value of 0.57. Assuming group scores are normally distributed, the estimated average predictor score of the (selected) majority candidates who are at or above a cut score of 0.00 is 0.80 *SD* above the majority mean, whereas the estimated average score of the (selected) minority candidates who are at or above the same cut score is 1.19 *SD* above the minority mean. As a result, even though members of both groups were required to satisfy exactly the same cut score, the mean difference between the selected and population majority groups is smaller than the mean difference between the selected and population minority groups. Selection based on cut scores produces a smaller group effect size among selected applicants than among the unselected applicant population. Further, the lower the selection ratio and the lower the AIR, the greater the reduction in group differences. In other words, adverse impact tends to reduce group mean differences on the predictor among employees compared to applicants. One important implication of this point is that research studies should not assume that group differences on predictor scores among selected employees are representative of group differences on those same predictors among unselected applicants. Also, it is worth noting that this effect is not related to the validity of the predictor in question because this effect is on the predictor scores of employees compared to applicants. A separate but related point is that group differences on performance factors, as noted, are impacted to the extent selection is based on a valid predictor.

A final set of basic information about cut scores and adverse impact is shown in Table 11.3. Tables 11.1 and 11.2 are based on the assumption that minority candidates represent .119 of the unselected applicant population, which is the overall empirical proportion reported by Potosky et al. (2005). This assumption was made in Tables 11.1 and 11.2 so that results in those tables would be comparable to adverse impact analyses reported in Potosky et al. (2005) and in De Corte, Lievens, and Sackett (2008). However, it is not unusual for the proportion of minority applicants to be different from .119 within certain job families, geographies, and organizations. Table 11.3 shows AIR values that result from different minority proportions at representative combinations of predictor group differences and selection ratios. The purpose of Table 11.3 is to assess the extent to which AIR results presented in Tables 11.1 and 11.2 apply across different minority proportions. The clear result is that the proportion of minorities in an applicant population has a small or modest effect on AIR when predictor group differences are moderate or small. In comparison to other factors, the effect of minority proportion on AIR across the likely range of minority proportions is much less than the effects of selection ratios or predictor mean differences across their typical ranges. Notably, there was only one combination of selection ratio and predictor group differences, Selection ratio = .90 and Predictor group differences = 1.00, where the effect of minority proportion shifted the level of AIR from one side of the four-fifths threshold to the other.

TABLE 11.3

The Basics: The Effects on AIR of Population Minority
Proportion, Selection Ratio, and Applicant Population
Standardized Mean Group Differences

	Minority proportion			
	.119[a]	.25	.50	.75
Selection ratio = .10				
Standardized mean group difference				
.06	.90	.90	.90	.90
.31	.56	.57	.57	.59
.57	.34	.34	.37	.37
.72	.24	.25	.28	.31
1.00	.13	.14	.17	.21
Selection ratio = .50				
Standardized mean group difference				
.06	.95	.95	.95	.95
.31	.76	.77	.77	.79
.57	.58	.60	.64	.67
.72	.49	.52	.56	.61
1.00	.34	.38	.45	.52
Selection ratio = .90				
Standardized mean group difference				
.06	.98	.99	.99	.99
.31	.93	.93	.94	.95
.57	.86	.87	.89	.91
.72	.81	.83	.86	.90
1.00	.71	.76	.81	.87

[a] Estimated minority proportion reported in Potosky et al. (2005).

Effects on AIR of Methods for Choosing Cut Scores

For selection processes that rely on cut scores, Tables 11.1–11.3 describe
basic relationships between AIR and three sets of considerations: group
mean differences on the predictor, the proportion of minorities, and the
selection ratio itself. The first of these considerations has received considerable research attention, most recently by Sackett and Ellingson (1997),
De Corte et al. (2008), and by Sackett et al. (Chapter 17, this volume). To a
great extent, that research has investigated the impact on AIR of strategies
for forming predictor composites to reduce group differences. The second
consideration, the effect of minority proportion, has received virtually
no research attention. The remainder of this chapter addresses the third
consideration. In particular, this chapter evaluates differences between

cut score-setting methods that may systematically lead to higher or lower cut scores, which will have an impact on AIR. This evaluation begins by acknowledging three limitations to this effort.

The first limitation is that any systematic effect of cut score methodology can be easily trumped by other considerations independent of the method itself. For example, a cut score derived from, say, the judgments of subject matter experts (SMEs) using an Angoff method is often adjusted to accommodate any of several organizational considerations, such as an employment budget or an organizational goal with respect to workforce diversity. Nevertheless, it improves our understanding of the rationale underlying various cut score-setting methods to examine the methodological features that systematically affect AIR.

The second point is that, without exception, all cut score-setting methods rely on judgment. This judgment can take many forms, such as judgments about the minimum level of work behavior considered acceptable, judgments about which employees are successful and which are not, judgments about the importance of selection mistakes, judgments about the acceptability of particular levels of AIR, and so on. The implication is that the outcomes of many cut score-setting methods cannot be completely known merely from a description of the prescribed procedural steps. In other words, for many cut score-setting methods there is no basis for concluding that there is any systematic tendency to result in higher or lower AIR.

A third limitation is that many methods vary considerably in the extent to which their procedures are closely prescribed. It is better to think of the name of a cut score-setting method as a general label for a class of methods that have certain key elements in common. A component of this point is that it is often unclear how far into the cut score-setting process a particular method extends before local adjustments are imposed on the output of the prescribed methodology. For example, Biddle (1993) described a modified Angoff method for setting cut scores for credentialing purposes that includes trade-off adjustments to the initial cut score derived from SME judgments. But, there is nothing unique to the Angoff methodology about the manner in which such adjustments might be made.

This evaluation examines the impact on AIR of two specific procedural facets of commonly used cut score methods. The first of these procedural facets is the manner in which the cut score is linked to a criterion threshold representing some desired level of performance or work behavior. This facet of the methodology addresses the manner in which a cut score is understood to predict or represent a particular threshold on the criterion. The second procedural facet is the manner in which initially derived cut scores are adjusted to accommodate the organization's interest in the likelihood of selecting successful performers. This facet of cut score methods is related to the consideration of certainty.

Cut Score-Setting Methods

Kehoe and Olson (2005) introduced a general framework for describing and evaluating cut score methods. This framework identifies three separate considerations: (a) thresholds, (b) certainty, and (c) trade-offs. Threshold considerations include the specification of a desired job behavior threshold and the determination of a test score threshold linked to the job threshold by some rationale. Certainty considerations address the organization's desires with respect to the probability that selected candidates will succeed on the job, $P(Succeed \mid Selected)$. Certainty considerations may also address the probability that candidates who would be successful will be selected, $P(Selected \mid Succeed)$. It is worth noting that the organization's values for either of these probabilities will be moderated by a variety of considerations. The point of this framework is not to specify what an organization's values for certainty are but rather to recognize formally the importance of these certainty considerations in establishing cut scores that reflect the organization's interests.

Trade-off considerations include any adjustment to cut scores that accommodate the organization's additional interest in factors such as cost, employment market, organization policies, and adverse impact. This framework does not imply that all cut score methods actually address each of these three considerations. In fact, many ignore one or more of these considerations. Rather, the purpose of the framework was to provide a set of criteria by which any cut score method could be evaluated and compared to other methods. To that end, this framework is used here to evaluate the two procedural facets of cut score methods that may have a systematic effect on AIR. The first procedural facet evaluated, the link between test scores and criterion thresholds, is relevant to the threshold considerations. The second procedural facet evaluated is related to considerations of certainty.

Criterion Thresholds and AIR

Cut score methods may have a systematic impact on AIR by the manner in which the method defines the relationship between the predictor score selected as the cut score and the criterion threshold targeted by the organization. The criterion threshold might be a desired minimum level of performance, a desired reduction in turnover, or any other desired outcome that is expressed in terms of a criterion score. Several methods can be clustered into two classes, prediction and representation, with respect to the relationship between the cut score and the criterion threshold. The first class of methods defines the relationship between the cut score and the criterion threshold in terms of *prediction*. A cut score is chosen based on some feature of that score's prediction with respect to the criterion threshold. The second class defines the relationship in terms of *representation*. The cut score is a score that represents some characteristic of those people who perform at the criterion threshold.

The following chart lists common cut score methods associated with each of these two classes.

Prediction	Representation
Forward regression	Reverse regression
Expectancy charts	Angoff methods
Contrasting groups	Borderline group
	Nedelsky
	Ebel

The prediction methods all rely on evidence of the ability of the predictor to predict (i.e., discriminate between) different levels of the criterion of interest. The methodology of forward regression and contrasting groups and the recommended use of expectancy charts, such as the Taylor-Russell (1939) tables, all choose a cut score based on the predictive information the cut score yields about performance at the target criterion threshold. The cut score is regarded by these methods as a predictor score that predicts future performance at some threshold level of work behavior. This feature of the cut score manifests itself somewhat differently in these three methods. Cut scores set using forward regression are chosen explicitly based on their regression prediction characteristics. Similarly, cut scores chosen based on the analysis of an expectancy table are based on predicted outcomes. Expectancy tables summarize criterion outcomes—either predicted or observed—associated with various predictor scores. In the contrasting groups methods, the selected cut score is the one that best discriminates successful performers from unsuccessful performers. This is a prediction standard in the sense that the cut score is chosen based on its ability to distinguish between outcomes of interest.

In contrast, representation methods share the common feature that the cut score is set equal to the predictor score obtained by the people who perform at the criterion threshold level. In more statistical terms, the cut score is the expected predictor score value among people who perform at the criterion threshold level. Cut scores chosen in this fashion are not chosen because of prediction properties. Rather, they are chosen on the basis that they represent some feature of the people who perform at a particular level on the criterion of interest. They are not chosen on the basis of a predicted criterion level because it is not meaningful to consider criterion values to be predictive of predictor values.

When empirical predictor and criterion data are available, this representation value can be derived arithmetically from reverse regression analysis in which the predictor scores are regressed on the criterion scores. This regression analysis is just the reverse of the validity regression analyses in which criterion scores are regressed onto predictor scores. The Angoff, borderline group, Nedelsky, and Ebel methods are all judgment methods for deriving cut score with exactly the same conceptual meaning as reverse regression. Each of these methods, which were developed for education achievement applications, represents a set of procedures by which SMEs estimate the predictor scores that would be obtained by examinees who had the "just-acceptable" level of skill or knowledge assessed by the test. The Angoff method, in a modified form, is quite commonly used for licensure, credentialing, and job knowledge selection tests. In effect, these four methods replace the arithmetic of reverse regression with judgments and estimates by SMEs to produce the same result, namely, the test score expected of applicants who would perform at the criterion threshold level. An operational advantage (disadvantage?) of the four judgment methods compared to reverse regression is that the four judgment methods do not require any empirical data for either the predictor or criterion. At the same time, variations of these methods have been adapted to circumstances in which predictor data, primarily, are available.

The distinction between these two classes is perhaps best captured by comparing forward and reverse regression methods. The forward regression method is based on the regression of the criterion scores onto the predictor scores. This is the same regression as would be used in an analysis of the validity of the predictor with respect to the criterion. In this method, the cut score is set equal to the predictor score that predicts a criterion value equal to the preidentified criterion threshold score associated with just-acceptable performance. For example, suppose a predictor has a validity of .40 and is used to select new employees into a job for which a just-acceptable threshold of performance has been established by SMEs at a criterion value equal to a z value of $-.50$. In this case, the regression formula in which both the predictor and criterion are expressed in standardized units is

$$\text{Criterion} = 0 + .40 \ (\text{Predictor})$$

Based on this forward regression formula, the predictor score (in z-score units) that predicts a criterion value of $-.50$ is

$$\text{Predictor score} = -.50/.40 = -1.25$$

The cut score would then be set equal to this predictor score, -1.25 (z units). (Of course, subsequent considerations may result in adjustments this initial cut score.)

Cut scores set by the method of forward regression have three clear properties. First, they have a meaning consistent with the predictive nature of
selection. They are the predictor scores that predict the target criterion
thresholds. Applicants who achieve these cut scores are expected, in a
statistical sense, to perform at the criterion threshold level. Second, and
closely related to the first, applicants who achieve these cut scores have a
probability of .50 of succeeding on the job. In other words, the organization has a 50% certainty that applicants scoring at the cut score will be
successful. This is true regardless of the errorfulness of the prediction.
Prediction systems with large standard errors of estimate yield the same
50% certainty as systems with small standard errors of estimate. The difference is in the range of prediction errors.

The third feature is more problematic. Forward regression cut scores
can easily be impractically extreme. In the case for which the criterion
threshold, −.50, is at the 31st percentile of performance [i.e., $P(z > -.50) =$
.69], the cut score, −1.25, is at the 11th percentile of predictor scores, which
yields an .89 pass rate. From a utility standpoint, a selection process with
a pass rate of .89 is likely to have marginal value. Consider the different
case in which the criterion threshold is somewhat lower and is set at −1.0
(z units) on the criterion. This would be the threshold for an organization that was satisfied with the performance of the top 84% of its workers.
This is not an extreme performance threshold. Yet, for a predictor with the
same validity of .40, forward regression would produce a cut score value
of −2.50 (−1.0/.40), which would yield a passing rate of .99. Such a passing
rate is impractical because it eliminates all value of the selection procedure. Because of regression toward the mean, criterion threshold values
that are not near the mean criterion value are likely to result in relatively
extreme cut scores. Such extreme cut scores can have large consequences
for adverse impact, in both directions, as is reviewed in this chapter.

Much can be said about the organizational and legal issues associated with choosing a particular just-acceptable score on the criterion.
While this is not the focus of this chapter, the primary issue is whether
any legal, regulatory, or professional standards compel this threshold
to be low, moderate, or high. Professional standards are clear. Both the
Principles for the Validation and Use of Personnel Selection Procedures (Society
for Industrial and Organizational Psychology, 2003) and the *Standards
for Educational and Psychological Testing* (American Educational Research
Association, American Psychological Association, & National Council
on Measurement in Education, 1999) allow organizations to choose criterion thresholds at any level that addresses the organization's needs.
These professional standards are clear in the sense that they both establish that there is no technical definition of what a cut score "ought" to be.
On the other hand, regulations are ambiguous. The *Uniform Guidelines for
Employee Selection Procedures* (1978) expects cut scores "to be reasonable

and consistent with normal expectations of acceptable proficiency" (Sec. 5H, p. 24). This language implies that cut scores should have some link to acceptable proficiency, but the link is not clearly described. Courts are mixed. Some have accepted cut scores that are higher than the scores achieved by satisfactory performers (e.g., *Bew v. City of Chicago*, 2001) whereas others have expressed the view that cut scores should be associated with minimum proficiency standards (e.g., *Lanning v. Southeastern Pennsylvania Transportation Authority*, 1999).

The primary exception to this diversity of views about criterion thresholds is in the case of cut scores for licensure and credentialing. The consensus view for such cut scores is that they should be associated with the minimum level of proficiency necessary to avoid harm to the public, whose interest is being protected by licensure. While there is consensus about this view, the typical procedure for establishing such cut scores relies on expert judgment and a highly structured process, which may not lead to an unambiguous definition of the target level of proficiency.

Because forward regression can yield impractically extreme cut scores, Jeanneret and Stelly (2003) evaluated an alternative regression-based method, reverse regression. Cascio, Alexander, and Barrett (1988) had briefly speculated about such a method in their review of cut score methods. The forward regression example in which validity is .40 and the criterion threshold is −.50 can be converted to its reverse regression counterpart in which the predictor is regressed onto the criterion. (Note, in this discussion of reverse regression, the labels *criterion* and *predictor* continue to be used as introduced here, with *criterion* referring to the outcome variable of interest such as job performance and *predictor* referring to the selection procedure.) The reverse regression analysis of this example is

$$\text{Predictor} = 0 + .40 \,(\text{Criterion})$$

Based on this reverse regression formula, the average predictor score achieved by the people who performed at the criterion threshold value, −.50, is estimated to be

$$\text{Predictor score} = -.50(.40) = -0.20$$

The cut score would then be set equal to this estimated average predictor score, −.20 (z units). The meaning of this reverse regression cut score is quite different from the meaning of its forward regression counterpart. First, the meaning of the score is that it is the test score expected of people who perform at the criterion threshold level. It is not the test score that predicts performance at the threshold level, as is true of the forward regression cut score. Second, in an actuarial sense, people who perform at the threshold level have a .50 probability of scoring above the cut score

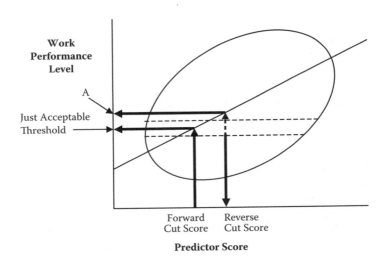

FIGURE 11.1
Comparison of forward and reverse regression methods: moderate-threshold case.

(passing). The applicants who achieve this cut score do not, in general, have a .50 probability of succeeding on the job, as is true of the forward regression cut score. Third, reverse regression virtually always yields less-extreme cut scores than does forward regression. This is because, when the arithmetic of regression analysis is used to "predict" a test score from a criterion score, regression toward the mean causes the predicted "predictor" scores to be less extreme than the "criterion" scores, which are being used as predictors in reverse regression.

Figure 11.1 and Figure 11.2 provide a visual display of the distinctions between forward and reverse regression methods. Both figures present the two regression methods as they would appear in a plot of the forward regression analysis. Figure 11.1 compares these methods in which the criterion threshold is moderately low at approximately the 25th percentile of the criterion distribution; that is, 75% of performers are successful. Figure 11.2 compares them in the case when the criterion threshold is very low at approximately the 5th percentile of performance; that is, 95% of performers are successful. In each figure, the group of applicants whose work performance is/would be at the threshold level is depicted by the horizontal dashed lines slightly above and below the threshold level. (These two dashed lines are separated purely for heuristic reasons so that the set of predictor scores achieved by just-acceptable performers can be more easily visualized.) Given the criterion threshold level, forward regression would choose as the cut score the predictor score that predicts the threshold score, which can be seen as the predictor score intersecting the forward regression line at the point of the threshold value. In contrast,

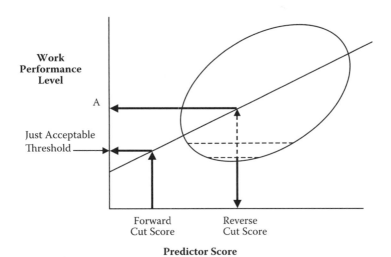

FIGURE 11.2
Comparison of forward and reverse regression methods: low-threshold case.

the cut score chosen by reverse regression can be described by considering the predictor scores achieved by people performing at the threshold level, depicted as the narrow range of criterion scores between the dashed lines. Reverse regression defines the cut score as the average predictor score among people who perform at the threshold. This is depicted in the figures as the average of the set of predictor scores between the dashed lines. Both figures show a downward arrow at this point identifying the predictor value chosen as the reverse regression cut score. These figures show the same result as the examples above that reverse regression cut scores are less extreme than forward regression cut scores.

One other feature of reverse regression cut scores can be seen in Figures 11.1 and 11.2. Having defined the reverse regression cut score as the average predictor score among people who perform just acceptably, one can then determine what criterion score would be predicted by that cut score in a forward regression sense, even though that cut score was not chosen for its prediction properties. This is of interest because this provides an estimate of the performance level expected—in a prediction sense—of the people who achieve the cut score. Figures 11.1 and 11.2 demonstrate the result that people whose predictor score is equal to the reverse regression cut scores are not predicted to perform at the just-acceptable threshold. In each figure, the level of work performance predicted by the reverse regression cut score is shown at Point A on the work performance axis. In both cases, this level of expected work performance is higher than the threshold level predicted by the forward regression method. The general conclusion is that where the just-acceptable performance threshold is below the performance mean, reverse regression cut scores select applicants who are expected to perform above the threshold and expected to perform, on average, above applicants selected by the forward regression method. The opposite holds when the just-acceptable threshold is above the performance mean. In that case, reverse regression cut scores select lower-performing applicants than forward regression cut scores.

These systematic differences between forward and reverse regression will have an impact on adverse impact in a predictable way. Table 11.4 and Table 11.5 show the levels of AIR produced by forward and reverse regression cut scores in each of several selection scenarios. Table 11.4 provides results for which validity is .60; for Table 11.5, validity is .30. Several pieces of information must be specified to derive AIR values based on cut scores. It is necessary to know the validity of the predictor, the size of the minority-majority group mean difference on the predictor, the proportion of minorities in the applicant population, and the just-acceptable threshold value on the criterion measure. Both tables report results for three levels of group mean difference reported in Potosky et al. (2005) associated with structured interviews, .31; biodata, .57; and cognitive ability, .72. Also, both tables report results at four levels of just-acceptable threshold (expressed in z-score units): .68, .00, −.68, and −1.65. Both tables assume minorities comprise .119 of the applicant population, as reported in Potosky et al. (2005). For each combination of threshold, group mean difference, and validity, the tables report the resulting overall passing percentage, the passing percentages for minority and majority applicants, and AIR.

The consistent pattern of results is that when the just-acceptable threshold is above the performance mean, reverse regression cut scores result in higher AIR compared to forward regression. Just the opposite occurs when the threshold is below the performance mean. When the threshold is at the performance mean, the methods are equivalent because they result in the same cut score. However, these results should be tempered with the understanding that forward regression achieves higher AIR values when the threshold is below the performance mean by establishing impractically low cut scores producing passing rates that defeat the value of the selection process. This effect is more pronounced at lower levels of validity. The lower the level of validity, the more extreme are the forward regression cut scores and the less extreme are the reverse regression cut scores.

Tables 11.4 and 11.5 demonstrate a dilemma for selection practitioners. The naturally appealing meaning of forward selection cut scores—that applicants who score at the cut score are expected to perform at the threshold level—results in unusable cut scores in many common selection situations. If the performance threshold is even moderately below the mean level of performance, which is common, unadjusted forward

TABLE 11.4

Effects of Forward Regression and Reverse Regression Cut Score-Setting Strategies on Group Passing Percentages and Adverse Impact Ratio When Validity = .60 and the Minority Proportion = .119

	Standardized group difference											
	.31				.57				.72			
Target work threshold (z score)	.68	.00	-.68	-1.65	.68	.00	-.68	-1.65	.68	.00	-.68	-1.65
Base rate of job success, %	25	50	75	95	25	50	75	95	25	50	75	95
Forward regression cut score (z value)	1.13	0.00	-1.13	-2.75	1.13	0.00	-1.13	-2.75	1.13	0.00	-1.13	-2.75
Overall pass, %	12.9	50.0	87.1	99.7	12.9	50.0	87.1	99.7	12.9	50.0	87.1	99.7
Minority pass, %	8.1	39.4	80.5	99.3	5.2	30.8	73.6	98.8	3.9	26.4	69.2	98.3
Majority pass, %	13.8	51.6	87.9	99.8	14.5	52.8	88.5	99.8	14.9	53.6	88.9	99.8
Adverse impact ratio	.59	.76	.92	.99	.36	.58	.83	.99	.26	.49	.78	.98
Reverse regression cut score (z value)	0.41	0.00	-0.41	-0.99	0.41	0.00	-0.41	-0.99	0.41	0.00	-0.41	-0.99
Overall pass, %	34.1	50.0	65.9	83.9	34.1	50.0	65.9	83.9	34.1	50.0	65.9	83.9
Minority pass, %	24.8	39.4	55.6	76.4	18.1	30.8	46.4	68.8	14.9	26.4	40.9	64.1
Majority pass, %	35.6	51.6	67.4	84.8	36.7	52.8	68.4	85.5	37.5	53.6	69.2	86.0
Adverse impact ratio	.70	.76	.82	.90	.49	.58	.68	.80	.40	.49	.59	.75

TABLE 11.5

Effects of Forward Regression and Reverse Regression Cut Score-Setting Strategies on Group Passing Percentages and Adverse Impact Ratio When Validity = .30 and the Minority Proportion = .119

| | Standardized group mean difference | | | | | | | | | | | |
	.31				.57				.72			
Target work threshold (z score)	.68	.00	-.68	-1.65	.68	.00	-.68	-1.65	.68	.00	-.68	-1.65
Base rate of job success, %	25	50	75	95	25	50	75	95	25	50	75	95
Forward regression cut score (z value)	2.27	0.00	-2.27	-5.50	2.27	0.00	-2.27	-5.50	2.27	0.00	-2.27	-5.50
Overall pass %	1.2	50.0	98.8	99.9	1.2	50.0	98.8	99.9	1.2	50.0	98.8	99.9
Minority pass %	0.5	39.4	97.7	99.9	0.3	30.8	96.8	99.9	0.2	26.4	94.9	99.9
Majority pass %	1.3	51.6	99.0	99.9	1.4	52.8	99.0	99.9	1.5	53.6	99.1	99.9
Adverse impact ratio	.38	.76	.99	1.00	.21	.58	.98	1.00	.13	.49	.96	1.00
Reverse regression cut score (z value)	.20	0.00	-.20	-.49	.20	0.00	-.20	-.49	.20	0.00	-.20	-.49
Overall pass %	42.1	50.0	57.9	68.8	42.1	50.0	57.9	68.8	42.1	50.0	57.9	68.8
Minority pass %	31.9	39.4	47.2	58.7	24.2	30.8	38.2	49.6	20.3	26.4	33.4	44.4
Majority pass %	43.6	51.6	59.5	70.2	44.2	52.8	60.6	71.2	45.6	53.6	61.4	71.9
Adverse impact ratio	.73	.76	.79	.84	.49	.58	.63	.70	.45	.49	.54	.62

regression cut scores will yield passing rates too high to be useful. Their AIR benefit becomes moot. This is the consequence of imperfect prediction and regression toward the mean, which is fundamental to the regression framework for prediction. In contrast, reverse regression produces cut scores that are not as meaningful for the prediction context of selection and produces higher adverse impact if thresholds are low. But, they produce cut scores yielding more useful passing rates. The implication of these results is that it is quite likely organizations will have an interest in adjusting cut scores produced by either regression method. Such adjustments are evaluated below.

This comparison of forward and reverse regression methods has implications beyond these two methods. This comparison has direct implications for the commonly used Angoff method as well as the conceptually similar but less commonly used Nedelsky, Ebel, and borderline group methods. These methods share the common feature that they are designed to estimate the expected test scores of applicants who have the level of knowledge and skills assessed by the test at the just-acceptable threshold. In effect, they are nearly conceptually identical to reverse regression but substitute expert judgment about just-acceptable applicants' test scores for the arithmetic and empiricism of reverse regression. Because these are judgment-based approaches to reverse regression, the specific analytic results in Tables 11.4 and 11.5 cannot be generalized to these methods with any confidence. On the other hand, to the extent that the SMEs made accurate judgments about examinees' test scores, Tables 11.4 and 11.5 would accurately reflect their score properties, including their impact on AIR.

A primary limitation of these judgment-based methods is that the resulting cut scores do not enable users to know the probability that applicants who score at the cut score will be successful on the job. As Kehoe and Olson (2005) demonstrated, the probability of job success for applicants scoring at the cut score could range from very high levels above .90 to very low levels below .10 depending on, among other things, the level of the just-acceptable threshold and the validity of the predictor. These methods tell us little about the applicants who score at the cut score except their judgmentally expected test score. A further limitation of these methods is that, often, the experts are job experts, not testing experts. As a result, the accuracy of their estimates of applicants' test scores is not directly relevant to the nature of their (job) expertise. Nevertheless, courts have demonstrated a willingness to rely on such expert judgments if the procedures followed are well specified and experts are trained in the specific cut score-setting process.

Beyond the uncertainty about the work performance levels of applicants scoring at cut scores produced by these judgmental methods, it is also important to consider whether representation methods are consistent with the prediction context of personnel selection. All the judgment-based methods included in the list of representation methods were developed for use in educational measurement. For the most part, the intended application of the resulting cut scores was to make decisions about examinees' mastery of the knowledge and skills assessed by the test for which the cut score was being established (e.g., Angoff, 1984; Nedelsky, 1954; Zieky & Perie, 2006). In these applications, the test scores are understood to be measures of the very underlying attributes—knowledge and skills—to which the just-acceptable threshold is applied. In this context, test scores are measures of the underlying attributes of interest, not predictors of a conceptually distinct consequence of the assessed attributes. In contrast, the use of cut scores for personnel selection attaches meaning to cut scores in terms of their prediction of separate work behavior. These methods were designed to fit a measurement context, not a prediction context. It is not surprising then to note the apparent popularity of the Angoff method and variations of it (it is procedurally the simplest of the four listed here) for setting cut scores on licensing and certification tests and on content-oriented employment exams. In both of these selection contexts, the concepts measured by the test have a close substantive connection to the more remote criteria of work performance. This is evidenced by the fact that, in personnel selection, job knowledge tests have been used as predictors and criteria alike. Similarly, licensing and credentialing exams are routinely designed to sample behaviors, situations, and conditions representative of "real-world" performance.

There are at least three implications of this analysis of Angoff-like methods for setting cut scores.

1. One implication of this measurement orientation of Angoff-like methods is that they would be suitable methods for systematically determining the just-acceptable threshold on criterion measures used in prediction-oriented methods for setting cut scores.

2. A second implication is that if these methods are used with tests designed to predict conceptually distinct criteria, it would be informative for users to estimate the probability of job success, the likely overall passing rate, and the AIR associated with the established cut score. Even if the additional pieces of information necessary to make these estimates—such as the predictive validity of the test, the size of group mean differences, and the relative level of the just-acceptable threshold with respect to the criterion distribution—were based on inferences from other research sources, users would be better informed about the meaning and consequences of the resulting cut scores.

3. A third implication is that a potentially significant improvement in these methods could be developed by modifying the methods

to reverse the predictive direction of the judgments made by SMEs to be consistent with the predictive direction of selection. The current forms of these methods require experts to estimate test scores given a level of work performance. A reversed judgment consistent with the direction of selection prediction would require experts to predict work performance given some level of test score. This might take the form, for example, of experts estimating, for each item, the probability that, for people who answered the item correctly, work performance would be above or below the just-acceptable threshold. A score would be formed for each item equal to the average estimated probability across judges that those who answer correctly would be above-threshold performers. Once this item-level information is obtained, the premise for choosing a cut score would rely on two considerations. The first consideration is the desired probability that an applicant who scores at the cut score would succeed on the job. (Forward regression fixes this probability at .50, whereas reverse regression allows this probability to vary considerably as a function of validity and the level of the threshold.) The second consideration would be to define a method for deriving the total test score most likely to be achieved by people who have just the level of ability to answer correctly those items that are associated with the desired probability of successful performance. One possible approach would be to treat the estimated successful performance probability for each item as a measure of that item's difficulty. The cut score could be defined as the score achieved by answering correctly all items that are equal or less difficult than the items with the desired probability of success. The primary advantage of this approach is that the meaning that could be attached to the cut score is consistent with the predictive direction of personnel selection. A secondary, but possibly important, advantage is that experts are required to have job expertise and relatively little test expertise. This has been a significant criticism of Angoff-like methods: They require job experts also to be test experts (National Academy of Education, 1993).

Certainty and AIR

A second major way in which the cut score method can predictably affect AIR is the manner in which the initial derived cut score is subsequently adjusted to increase or decrease the organization's certainty about its selection decisions. The difficulty in systematically evaluating this adjustment factor for its effect on AIR is that there are countless specific methods/rationales for making such adjustments. At the same time, in one sense, this is a trivial question. Regardless of the method by which a cut score is adjusted, if there are group mean differences on the predictor, any increase in a cut score will reduce AIR, and any decrease will improve AIR. The degree of reduction or improvement in AIR for any given amount of adjustment can be estimated by knowing or estimating the selection ratio, the group mean difference, and the minority proportion in the applicant population. Table 11.2 shows the various levels of AIR produced by representative combinations of these factors. In this sense, the effects on AIR of adjustments to cut scores are no different from the effects on AIR of any differences in cut score levels.

Nevertheless, there is one method of adjustment that appears to be used frequently for the purpose of changing the organization's certainty about their selection decisions. This method is simply to subtract or, in some cases, add one or two standard errors of measurement (*SEM*) to the initially derived cut score (Biddle, 1993). Because the *SEM* is an index of the amount of test score variance attributable to measurement error, the general rationale for adding or subtracting is to minimize the impact of measurement error on a selection decision. In my experience, the rationale is often no more specific or precise than that. If one's purpose in making the adjustment is to *increase* the certainty that just-qualified applicants will be hired, that is, reduce the likelihood that test score error would prevent a successful applicant from being hired, then one or more *SEM* may be subtracted from the initial cut score. An organization might have this interest if it has difficulty keeping positions filled and has a need for full workforces. On the other hand, if an organization's purpose is to increase the certainty that new employees will succeed on the job, then one or more *SEM* could be added to the initial cut score. Clearly, the opposite effects of adding and subtracting *SEM* adjustments underscore the fact that the two certainties discussed here, *P*(*Select* | *Success*) and *P*(*Success* | *Select*) are impacted in the opposite direction by cut score adjustments.

The effect on AIR of adding or subtracting some number of *SEM* can be analytically derived by specifying the level of the unadjusted cut score, the reliability of the test, the group mean difference, and the proportion of minorities in the applicant population. Table 11.6 and Table 11.7 show the effects on AIR of various levels of *SEM*-based adjustment in a representative set of conditions. Both tables assume the minority proportion is .119 and the group mean difference is .57. This value was chosen because it is an intermediate level of group difference and is similar to the level of group mean difference likely to be found with composite predictors that combine cognitive ability with one or two other predictors with lower group mean differences (De Corte et al., 2008). Both tables show the impact on AIR of *SEM*-based adjustments across several sizes of adjustment and several levels of the initial unadjusted cut score. Table 11.6 shows results where test reliability is .90, which is a relatively high level of reliability.

TABLE 11.6

Effects of *SEM*-Based Cut Score Adjustments on Passing Rate and AIR When Predictor Reliability Is High, .90[a]

| | Cut score adjustment in *SEM* units (*SEM* = .316) | | | | | | | | |
Unadjusted cut score pass %	−2.0	−1.5	−1.0	−0.5	Unadjusted cut score	+0.5	+1.0	+1.5	+2.0
10%									
Cut score (z value)	0.65	0.81	0.96	1.12	1.28	1.44	1.60	1.75	1.91
Overall pass %	26	21	17	13	10	7	5	4	3
Adverse impact ratio	.44	.41	.38	.36	.34	.31	.29	.26	.24
30%									
Cut score (z value)	−0.10	0.06	0.21	0.37	0.53	0.69	0.85	1.00	1.16
Overall pass %	54	48	42	36	30	25	20	16	12
Adverse impact ratio	.61	.57	.54	.50	.47	.44	.40	.38	.35
50%									
Cut score (z value)	−0.63	−0.47	−0.32	−0.16	0.00	0.16	0.32	0.47	0.63
Overall pass %	74	68	62	56	50	44	38	32	26
Adverse impact ratio	.73	.69	.66	.62	.58	.55	.51	.48	.45
70%									
Cut score (z value)	−1.16	−1.00	−0.85	−0.69	−0.53	−0.37	−0.21	−0.06	0.10
Overall pass %	88	84	80	75	70	64	58	52	46
Adverse impact ratio	.84	.81	.78	.74	.71	.66	.63	.60	.56
90%									
Cut score (z value)	−1.91	−1.75	−1.60	−1.44	−1.28	−1.12	−0.96	−0.81	−0.65
Overall pass %	97	96	95	93	90	87	83	79	74$
Adverse impact ratio	.94	.93	.91	.88	.86	.83	.80	.77	.73

Note: Assumes predictor scores are standardized with mean = 0 and *SD* = 1.0, group mean difference = .57, and minority proportion = .119.

[a] $SEM = .316 * SD_{Predictor}$

TABLE 11.7

Effects of *SEM*-Based Cut Score Adjustments on Passing Rate and AIR When Predictor Reliability Is Moderate, .70[a]

Unadjusted cut score pass %	Cut score adjustment in *SEM* units (*SEM* = .548)								
	−2.0	−1.5	−1.0	−0.5	Unadjusted cut score	+0.5	+1.0	+1.5	+2.0
10%									
Cut score (z value)	0.18	0.46	0.73	1.01	1.28	1.55	1.83	2.10	2.38
Overall pass %	43	32	23	16	10	6	3	2	1
Adverse impact ratio	.54	.48	.43	.37	.34	.29	.26	.24	.20
30%									
Cut score (z value)	−0.57	−0.29	−0.02	0.26	0.53	0.80	1.08	1.35	1.63
Overall pass %	72	61	51	40	30	21	14	9	5
Adverse impact ratio	.71	.65	.59	.53	.47	.42	.36	.32	.29
50%									
Cut score (z value)	−1.10	−0.82	−0.55	−0.27	0.00	0.27	0.55	0.82	1.10
Overall pass %	86	79	71	61	50	39	29	21	14
Adverse impact ratio	.77	.69	.61	.53	.45	.37	.31	.25	.20
70%									
Cut score (z value)	−1.63	−1.35	−1.08	−0.80	−0.53	−0.26	0.02	0.29	0.57
Overall pass %	95	91	86	79	70	60	49	39	28
Adverse impact ratio	.91	.87	.84	.76	.71	.64	.58	.52	.46
90%									
Cut score (z value)	−2.38	−2.10	−1.83	−1.55	−1.28	−1.01	−0.73	−0.46	−0.18
Overall pass %	99	98	97	94	90	86	77	68	57
Adverse impact ratio	.98	.96	.93	.90	.86	.81	.75	.69	.63

Note: Assumes predictor scores are standardized with mean = 0 and *SD* = 1.0, group mean difference = .57, and minority proportion = .119.

[a] $SEM = .548 * SD_{Predictor}$.

Table 11.7 shows results where reliability is .70, which is at the lower end of the acceptable range for scored selection tests.

Both tables show that *SEM*-based adjustments ranging from –2.0 *SEM* to 2.0 *SEM* will have notable effects on AIR as well as on the overall pass rate. Subtracting some number of *SEM* increases passing rates and AIR values. Adding some number of *SEM* decreases passing rates and AIR. Adding or subtracting 0.5 *SEM* does not change the AIR more than .08 points from that of the unadjusted cut score. Adding or subtracting 1.0 *SEM* has approximately twice the potential impact on AIR as .5 *SEM*. Of course, the lower the test reliability, the greater the impact on AIR of any given amount of *SEM*-based adjustment.

Because the purpose of this chapter is to evaluate the impact of cut score methods on AIR, Tables 11.6 and 11.7 are presented to show the impact of *SEM*-based adjustments on AIR. When organizations adjust an initial cut score by adding or subtracting some number of *SEM*, it is often for the purpose of improving some aspect of the organization's certainty about its selection decision. In most cases, the certainty of greatest interest to the organization is the probability that it is hiring applicants who will succeed on the job. Table 11.8 shows the impact on this certainty of the adjustments shown in Tables 11.6 and 11.7. For several levels of adjustment, several levels of initial unadjusted cut score, and for two levels of test reliability, Table 11.8 shows the probability that certain categories of "well-qualified" or "not qualified" applicants will satisfy the adjusted cut score and be selected. A *not qualified applicant* is defined here as an applicant whose "true" test score is lower than the initial unadjusted cut score by either 0.5 or 1.0 *SD*. Similarly, a *well-qualified applicant* is one whose true test score is either 0.5 or 1.0 *SD* above the initial unadjusted cut score. *Just-qualified applicants* are defined as applicants whose true test score is equal to the initial unadjusted cut score.

It is important to note that, strictly, Tables 11.6, 11.7, and 11.8 are about the effects of errorful predictor scores on selection rates when cut scores are adjusted up or down. However, the value of the results reported in Table 11.8 is the implications that they have for selecting applicants who will perform above or below the just-acceptable criterion threshold. By defining the initial unadjusted cut score as a forward regression cut score, just-qualified applicants whose true predictor score is equal to this initial unadjusted cut score are also expected, if selected, to perform at the just-acceptable threshold. Not qualified applicants are expected to perform below the just-acceptable threshold if selected; well-qualified applicants are expected to perform above the just-acceptable threshold if selected. Table 11.8 is about the probability of selecting these different categories of candidates.

Table 11.8 shows that adjustments based on the magnitude of the predictor's *SEM* can have a large effect on the probability that applicants in

certain qualification categories will be selected. For example, consider those applicants in the just-acceptable category who are expected to perform at the just-acceptable level if selected. They have a .50 probability of being selected by the initial unadjusted cut score. That probability changes dramatically by adding or subtracting even 0.5 *SEM*. For applicants who are not qualified or well-qualified, the effect of *SEM*-based adjustments is quite variable. The effect can be large or small. For example, reducing an initial cut score by 1.0 *SEM* has a negligible effect at either level of reliability on the probability of selecting applicants who are "well-qualified" by 1.0 $SD_{Predictor}$. The reason is that they are virtually certain to be selected by the unadjusted cut score, so lowering the cut score cannot increase their probability of being selected. In contrast, a 1.0 *SEM* decrease in the cut score will increase by seven-fold, from 3% to 21%, the passing percentage of applicants who are underqualified by 1.0 $SD_{Predictor}$. Table 11.8 also demonstrates clearly that cut scores reduced downward to improve the chances of selecting qualified applicants will also increase the likelihood of selecting unqualified applicants. Indeed, the increase in probability of selecting unqualified candidates increases more rapidly than does the probability of selecting qualified applicants. The converse pattern holds for cut scores that are increased to protect against the selection of unqualified applicants. Such adjustments decrease the probabilities of selecting qualified applicants more than they decrease the probabilities of selecting unqualified applicants.

The value of Table 11.8 is that, in combination with Tables 11.6 and 11.7, one can evaluate *SEM*-based score adjustments by examining the trade-offs that result from such adjustments between gains (losses) in AIR and gains (losses) in selection certainty. For example, adding 1.0 *SEM* to an unadjusted cut score when predictor reliability is .70 and group mean difference is .57 (third column from the right in Table 11.7), typically reduces (harms) AIR by approximately .10 to .03 and the probability of selecting moderately unqualified applicants from .18 to .03, while also reducing the probability of selecting moderately well-qualified applicants from .82 to .46. In this case, the adjustment made to avoid unqualified applicants who are already moderately unlikely to be selected, .18, comes at a cost of reduced AIR and reduced probability of selecting available qualified applicants. Of course, such an increase in cut score also increases the overall utility of the selection process. These tables demonstrate that if cut scores are adjusted in the *SEM*-based manner that is often used to improve selection certainty of one type of another, there are likely to be other countervailing consequences important to the organization, including changes in AIR.

Summary

This chapter investigated certain relationships between methods for setting cut scores and levels of AIR as well as other related outcomes, such as passing rates and expected levels of performance. The distinction between prediction-oriented methods characterized by forward regression and representation-oriented methods typified by reverse regression and Angoff-like methods received particularly close attention. Similarly, *SEM*-based methods for adjusting the certainty of selection decisions also received close attention. These methodological issues received attention because one can directly link features of the method to AIR outcomes.

Much relevant research has received little or no attention in this chapter. In particular, a significant amount of research in the education assessment literature has evaluated differences between Angoff methods, borderline group methods, Nedelsky methods, and Ebel methods, to name a few. This research often shows that a particular method results in higher or lower cut scores (e.g., Mills, 1983). All else the same, such differences in cut score levels will have an impact on AIR when the methods are applied to predictors on which groups differ. However, those results often are not clearly understood and may depend on the nature of a particular type of test or application. Such results are difficult to link to a particular feature of the methodology. For these reasons, this chapter does not summarize the education assessment research. Also, we must acknowledge that, in many cases, personnel selection cut scores are set by hybrid or myriad methods or rationales that may be very specific to the conditions of the local situation. This is not a criticism. No one method produces universally accepted cut scores. This is one reason that this chapter attempted to focus on two key methodological issues that are common to many specific procedures—the prediction-orientation of the approach and *SEM*-based adjustments for selection certainty—because those methodological elements may be present in many different processes used to set cut scores.

Although this chapter is about cut score methods and AIR, the most important conclusions of this chapter are about the meaningfulness of the cut scores selected or adjusted by various methods. One clear example came out of the comparison of prediction-oriented methods and representation-oriented methods. Cut scores established by forward regression have a clear prediction meaning. They are the predictor scores that predict the target level of performance. This meaning is consistent with the prediction direction of personnel selection and is likely to be relevant to organizations. Unfortunately, by the nature of regression-based prediction, forward regression scores can easily be extreme and of little practical use to an organization, even if their prediction properties are understood and desirable. In contrast, cut scores chosen by reverse regression are the average test scores of applicants who would perform at the target threshold level. In general, these predictor scores do *not* predict the target level of performance. They overpredict low target levels and underpredict high target levels. This meaning is less likely to be of interest to organizations. Furthermore, representation methods do not, themselves, provide a description of their predictive properties in which organizations may be most interested. And yet, in some cases such methods produce cut scores that are more pragmatically acceptable or with more favorable AIR values, even if their meaning is more ambiguous than prediction methods. In many situations, for the same, more favorable AIR value to be achieved by a forward regression methodology, the initial cut score must be adjusted and thereby lose its prediction property that it predicts the target criterion threshold.

A similar point can be made about *SEM*-based adjustments. They do affect AIR, but it is not always clear what other consequences they have. The simple rationale that they are added or subtracted to reduce the impact of measurement error does not reveal the consequences of these adjustments. Any cut score adjustment will reduce or increase the impact of measurement error on some category of applicants whose predictor score is within a standard deviation, or so, of the cut score. It is unlikely that an organization will be satisfied with a cut score adjusted by +1 *SEM* without having any understanding of the effects of that adjustment on the likelihood of selecting qualified (unqualified) applicants or on AIR, among other effects.

The information provided in this chapter is intended to inform organizations better not only about the impact on AIR of various cut score-setting tactics but also about the underlying meaning of methods for choosing cut scores and adjustments for modifying them.

References

American Educational Research Association, American Psychological Association, & National Council on Measurement in Education. (1999). *Standards for educational and psychological testing.* Washington, DC: American Education Research Association.

Angoff, W. H. (1984). *Scales, norms and equivalent scores.* Princeton, NJ: Educational Testing Service.

Bew v. City of Chicago, 252 F.3d 891 (7th Cir. 2001).

Biddle, R. E. (1993). How to set cutoff scores for knowledge tests used in promotion, training, certification and licensing. *Public Personnel Management, 22,* 63–79.

Cascio, W. F., Alexander, R. A., & Barrett, G. V. (1988). Setting cutoff scores: Legal, psychometric, and professional issues and guidelines. *Personnel Psychology, 41,* 1–24.

De Corte, W., Lievens, F., & Sackett, P. (2008). Validity and adverse impact potential of predictor composite formation. *International Journal of Selection and Assessment, 36,* 183–194.

Ford, J. K., Kraiger, K., & Schechtman, S. L. (1986). Study of race effects in objective indices and subjective evaluations of performance: A meta-analysis of performance criteria. *Psychological Bulletin, 99,* 330–337.

Jeanneret, P. R., & Stelly, D. J. (2003, April). *Setting cutting scores using regression: Would you do it backwards?* Master tutorial presented at the annual conference at the Society for Industrial and Organizational Psychology, Orlando, FL.

Kehoe, J. F., & Olson, A. (2005). *Cut scores and employment discrimination litigation.* In F. J. Landy (Ed.), *Employment discrimination litigation: Behavioral, quantitative, and legal perspectives* (pp. 410–449). San Francisco: Jossey-Bass.

Lanning v. Southeastern Pennsylvania Transportation Authority, 181 F.3d 478 (3d Cir. 1999).

McKay, P. F., & McDaniel, M. A. (2006). A reexamination of black-white differences in work performance: More data, more moderators. *Journal of Applied Psychology, 91,* 538–554.

Mills, C. N. (1983). A comparison of three methods of establishing cut-off scores on criterion-referenced tests. *Journal of Educational Measurement, 20,* 283–290.

National Academy of Education. (1993). *Setting performance standards for student achievement.* Washington, DC: Author.

Nedelsky, L. (1954). Absolute grading methods for objective tests. *Educational and Psychological Measurement, 14,* 3–19.

Potosky, D., Bobko, P., & Roth, P. L. (2005). Forming composites of cognitive ability and alternative measures to predict job performance and reduce adverse impact: Corrected estimates and realistic expectations. *International Journal of Selection and Assessment, 13,* 304–315.

Roth, P. L., Huffcutt, A. I., & Bobko, P. (2003). Ethnic group differences in measures of job performance: A new meta-analysis. *Journal of Applied Psychology, 88,* 694–706.

Sackett, P., & Ellingson, J. E. (1997). The effects of forming multi-predictor composites on group differences and adverse impact. *Personnel Psychology, 50,* 707–721.

Society for Industrial and Organizational Psychology. (2003). *Principles for the validation and use of personnel selection procedures* (4th ed.). Bowling Green, OH: Author.

Taylor, H. C., & Russell, J. T. (1939). The relationship of validity coefficients to the practical effectiveness of tests in selection: Discussion and tables. *Journal of Applied Psychology, 23,* 565–578.

Uniform Guidelines on Employee Selection Procedures, 29 C.F.R. § 1607 et seq. (1978).

Zieky, M., & Perie, M., (2006). *A primer on setting cut scores on tests of educational achievement.* Princeton, NJ: Educational Testing Service.

12

Subgroup Differences on Cognitive Tests in Contexts Other Than Personnel Selection

Paul R. Sackett and Winny Shen

Introduction

This chapter focuses on racial and ethnic group differences on cognitive tests of developed abilities. This includes measures of ability in the math and verbal domains, composite measures viewed as measures of g or of general intelligence, and measures viewed by their designers as tests of achievement in a specific domain (e.g., math, verbal, science) in contexts other than personnel selection. While industrial and organizational (I/O) psychologists are quite familiar with the common pattern of findings regarding subgroup differences on cognitive tests of developed ability and achievement in the employment context, we believe there is considerable value in putting these findings in a broader context. It is important to understand whether there is something about the employment context that contributes to the magnitude of subgroup differences or whether differences of comparable magnitude are found in other contexts, such as educational admissions or broad national samples tested for research purposes. It is useful to know whether subgroup differences are a phenomenon specific to individuals of working age or whether similar differences are found much earlier in life. It is of considerable interest to understand whether there are trends over time in the magnitude of subgroup differences: Are current differences larger, smaller, or comparable to those found, say, 10 or 20 years ago?

The focus of this chapter is limited. We focus on white–black and white–Hispanic differences on cognitive tests. We focus on these two comparisons as they represent the largest and most studied racial and ethnic subgroups in the United States. We focus on cognitively loaded tests, given the well-established finding that such measures are among the most valid predictors of job performance, particularly of task performance (as opposed to other components of job performance such as organizational citizenship or counterproductive work behavior). Schmidt and Hunter's (1998) meta-analytic review showed that even if other predictors (e.g., work samples, structured interviews) produce similarly high levels of validity, a composite of those predictors and cognitive ability measures produces higher validity than using the other predictors alone. The combination of favorable validity evidence and the generally consistent finding of substantial white–black and white–Hispanic mean differences make the pairing of these types of tests and these racial and ethnic groups the focus of considerable attention and study. We also focus on the cognitive domain because tests in this domain are widely used for various purposes from early childhood through adulthood. Many other predictors used in the employment setting do not have a clear counterpart throughout the age spectrum (e.g., interviews, assessment centers). While a number of predictors do have some cognitive loading (i.e., positive correlation with cognitive ability), those correlations are relatively small, indicating that those predictors constitute far more than simply measures of cognitive ability. In other words, these cognitively loaded predictors are more than simply a cognitive test in a different format from the traditional paper-and-pencil multiple-choice tests prototypic of ability tests. For example, the mean interview-ability r is 0.27 (Berry, Sackett, & Landers, 2007), and the mean ability-situational judgment test (SJT) r is 0.37 for SJTs with knowledge instructions (McDaniel, Hartman, Whetzel, & Grubb, 2007).

We also do not focus systematically on gender in this chapter. Because gender differences tend to be small in the cognitive domain, we do not devote space to extensive documentation of the comparability of findings outside the employment domain. The general finding is differences around 0.10 to 0.25 standard deviations (*SD*) favoring women on measures of verbal ability and differences of similar magnitude favoring men in quantitative ability; these tend to cancel out in composite measures combining the verbal and math domains. However, there is variability across studies and among subtests and item types within the verbal and quantitative domains. For summaries and meta-analyses, see the work of Hedges and Nowell (1995), Hyde and Linn (1988), Hyde, Fennema, and Lamon (1990), and Willingham and Cole (1997).

Issues in the Cognitive Measures Used

Our focus was on tests in the cognitive domain. This included measures of ability in the math and verbal domains, composite measures viewed as measures of *g* or of general intelligence, and measures viewed by their designers as tests of achievement in a specific domain (e.g., math, verbal, science). We viewed all of these as measures of developed ability; thus, education is a contributor for the developed ability. We acknowledge that we lacked the data needed for a detailed comparison of similarities and differences among measures as in most cases there were no data presenting correlations between the various measures examined. Our strategy was to group measures loosely by domains (e.g., math, verbal, composite) and then present results. We would not be surprised to see modest differences in the standardized mean difference, *d* values, across measures aimed at comparable populations due to differences in specific features of test content and format. We were more interested in "big picture" differences: If the white–black applicant *d* in employment settings averages about a standard deviation, are roughly similar differences found outside the employment context? Thus, we focused on commonly used cognitive ability measures, typically paper-and-pencil tests with multiple-choice format. Whether alternate testing modalities or item types produce differing findings is not a question we are able to address with our current focus on large national databases.

Issues in Estimating *d*

We used the standardized mean difference *d* as the index of group differences. This is the majority mean minus the minority mean divided by the pooled within-group standard deviation. This index expresses the group difference in standard deviation units, with zero indicating no difference, a positive value indicating a higher mean for the majority group, and a negative value indicating a higher mean for the minority group. However, in certain instances the pooled within-group standard deviation was not available, and the overall standard deviation across groups was used.

In the employment setting, adverse impact is a local issue; of interest is the impact of a given predictor in a given applicant sample. The applicant pool of a given job with a given employer may differ from the broader applicant population for a wide range of reasons (e.g., firm reputation, firm visibility, the nature of the firm's recruiting activities). Thus, while data on subgroup differences in various population samples can aid in estimating the likely adverse impact in a given situation, it must be realized that the local situation can differ. Nonetheless, there is interest in understanding the factors that influence the magnitude of *d* in various settings.

Useful insight comes from the largest meta-analysis to date of white–black and white–Hispanic differences on cognitive tests in employment settings, conducted by Roth, Bevier, Bobko, Switzer, and Tyler (2001). First, they reported smaller *d*s for incumbent samples than for applicant samples, which would be expected in a setting in which a given cutoff excludes a higher proportion of a lower-scoring group. Second, they reported smaller *d*s for applicants for a single job than for applicants pooled across jobs. The broader the set of jobs across which applicants were pooled, the closer the pooled sample came to an estimate of the workforce population value. Applicant pools for a single job tended to show restricted range on cognitive measures relative to broad workforce samples (Sackett & Ostgaard, 1994). These issues highlight the importance of the characteristics of the sample on which *d* is estimated.

As a result, we attend to characteristics of the sample as we review various studies in nonemployment contexts. We review research in five categories: (a) studies of nationally representative samples of young adults; (b) studies of nationally representative samples of enrolled high school students, with particular attention paid to seniors as they are on the verge of workplace entry; (c) studies of the population of students taking the two major college entrance exams, namely, the Scholastic Aptitude Test (SAT) and ACT (formerly the American College Testing Program); (d) studies of the norming samples for widely used intelligence tests (e.g., Wechsler Adult Intelligence Scale [WAIS], Stanford-Binet); and (e) studies of nationally representative samples of children (preschool through grade school students).

Note that we focus our investigation on studies intended as nationally representative of the population of interest (e.g., high school seniors). There are additional studies that focused on a more limited setting, such as studies of students in a single school district, but they are outside the purview of this summary. We also note that all studies included here were large-sample studies. While *N* did vary substantially (e.g., a few thousand for the typical study up to over 1 million), the large sample sizes are such that sampling error plays a minor role in effect size estimation. Thus, we did not use sample size weighting when averaging effect size estimates.

Nationally Representative Samples of Young Adults

The U.S. military has long used the Armed Services Vocational Aptitude Battery (ASVAB) to screen recruits and to qualify them for various military occupational specialties. A composite of verbal and quantitative subtests makes up the Armed Forces Qualification Test (AFQT), which is used for initial entry decisions. As there are restrictions on military entry (e.g., a score above the 10th percentile in the national population is required), there is a need for accurate population norm data. This has resulted in two large norming efforts in 1980 and in 1997. In both cases, attempts were made to draw nationally representative samples of youths aged 18–22, with careful attention to oversampling by race to ensure stable estimates of minority test performance. Individuals were recruited to take the test for research purposes, and it is important to note that this was a nationally representative sample of young adults and not a sample of military recruits. The white–black comparison was based on about 7,800 individuals in 1980 and 4,000 in 1997. While full details of the 1997 study results are not yet public, some initial findings focusing solely on the white–black comparison have been presented by Dickens and Flynn (2006). They converted AFQT scores to an IQ metric, from which we computed d values. The result was a white–black d of 1.23 in 1980 and 0.99 in 1997.

Note that these are the only young adult studies representative of the population. Other studies involved college-bound populations, which are range restricted as students self-select regarding whether to take the SAT and ACT, or high school senior populations, which are restricted because the high school dropouts are not included. Sackett and Mavor (2003) documented that the white high school graduation rate has remained relatively constant, rising from 86% to 88% between the late 1970s and 2000. The black rate has risen from 65% in 1972 to over 85% by 1995. The Hispanic rate has risen from 58% in 1976 to 63% in 2000. Thus, high school dropout rates are not inconsequential and vary by race/ethnicity. As a result, school-based assessments may differ from estimates based on representative sampling for youth population. A school-based sample will miss a substantial proportion of the Hispanic population. However, while these studies are not representative, they do involve samples for which level of educational attainment is constant, thus permitting a determination of whether group differences are comparable in samples with similar or dissimilar levels of educational attainment.

Representative Samples of High School Students, With Particular Attention to Seniors

In this section, we present the results of five nationally representative studies of high school students. Four of the studies included samples of 12th graders; we view these as of particular interest as these samples represent youths at the point of transition to the world of work. Table 12.1 presents white–black and white–Hispanic effect sizes for each of these studies, separately for the math and verbal domains. The table also includes the year of the study. We present an overview of each of the studies next and then discuss our findings.

TABLE 12.1

White–Black and White–Hispanic Score Gap in High School Age Students

	Pre-1970	1975	1978	1980	1982	1984	1986	1987	1988	1990	1992	1994	1996	1998	2004
Black–white differences															
Math															
EEO Math, Grade 9	0.98														
LSAY Math, Grade 10								0.75							
NELS Math, Grade 12										0.77					
HS&B Math, Grade 12				0.87											
NAEP Math, Grade 12			1.16		1.05		1.01			0.72	0.92	0.95	0.97	1.12	1.05
EEO Math, Grade 12	1.12														
NELS Math, Grade 12											0.80				
HS&B Math, Grade 12				0.86											
Reading															
EEO Reading, Grade 9	0.96														
NELS Reading, Grade 10										0.66					
HS&B Reading, Grade 10				0.77											

	C1	C2	C3	C4	C5	C6	C7	C8	C9	C10
NAEP Reading, Grade 12	1.30	1.30	0.84	0.56	0.74	0.92	0.70	0.72	0.77	0.70
EEO Reading, Grade 12	1.04									
NELS Reading, Grade 12						0.69				
HS&B Reading, Grade 12		0.83								
Vocabulary										
EEO Vocab, Grade 9	1.18									
HS&B Vocab, Grade 10		0.94								
EEO Vocab, Grade 12	1.24									
HS&B Vocab, Grade 12		0.82								
Hispanic–white differences										
Math										
NAEP Math, Grade 12	0.92	0.89	0.84		0.88	0.70	0.75	0.76	0.78	0.88
Reading										
NAEP Math, Grade 12	1.02	0.83	0.71	0.66	0.55	0.65	0.77	0.73	0.59	0.70

We note that Hedges and Nowell (1998) also presented an analysis of these same sets of data. Our analyses differed in several respects. First, Hedges and Nowell focused solely on white–black comparisons, while we also included white–Hispanic comparisons. Second, Hedges and Nowell included data through 1994. We were able to add more recent data, through 2004.

Equality of Educational Opportunity Math and Reading, 1965

Equality of Educational Opportunity (EEO) was a study undertaken in part due to societal concerns at the time, including the passage of the Civil Rights Act of 1964. EEO utilized a national sample of students in several grades between the 1st and 12th grades for assessments of math and reading ability. One of the primary concerns of EEO was to assess the educational opportunities for children of different backgrounds and circumstances. The results of EEO are reported in a document often known as the Coleman report (Coleman, 1966).

High School and Beyond Math, Reading, and Vocabulary, 1980 and 1982

High School and Beyond (HS&B) assessed a national sample of 10th and 12th graders on math, reading, and vocabulary, which is what is reported here (Phillips, Crouse, & Ralph, 1998). However, both cohorts were resurveyed two or three times and followed to assess the relationship between high school characteristics and educational and vocational outcomes (National Center for Education Statistics, n.d.-a).

Longitudinal Study of American Youth Math, 1987

The Longitudinal Study of American Youth (LSAY) followed a nationally representative sample of 12,686 youths (aged 14–22) beginning in 1979 to observe their employment-related outcomes (Bureau of Labor Statistics, 2001).

National Assessment of Educational Progress Math and Reading Long Term Trend, Ages 9, 13, and 17 (1975–2004)

The National Assessment of Educational Progress (NAEP) included periodic assessments of representative samples of school-enrolled youths at the ages of 9, 13, and 17 (Grades 4, 8, and 12) since the early 1970s in the areas of math, reading, and science. Our primary focus here is on the assessment at age 17; we return to the age 9 and age 13 assessments. As a school-based assessment, the age 17 assessment excluded youths who had dropped out of high school; this constitutes a sizable proportion of the population for some subgroups. The NAEP program includes both measures that change with each administration, thus reflecting changes in school curricula, and a fixed set of measures, referred to as the *long-term trend assessment*. The NAEP long-term trend utilizes the same procedures and types of questions every time it is administered for comparability across years; therefore, changes in curriculum and instruction are not reflected in this assessment (National Center for Educational Statistics, n.d.-b). Our focus here is solely on the long-term trend data. In recent years, the NAEP assesses approximately 3,000–4,000 white/Caucasian students, 500–1,000 African American/black students, and 400–800 Hispanic students.

National Education Longitudinal Study Math and Reading, 1988, 1990, and 1992

The National Education Longitudinal Study (NELS), like HS&B, was a longitudinal survey undertaken by the National Center for Educational Statistics (n.d.-c). NELS followed a national sample of eighth graders beginning in 1988 and then surveyed these students biennially.

Results

Table 12.1 presents white–black and white–Hispanic d values from these studies. For the white–black comparisons, there are 16 math ds (mean = 0.94, SD = 0.14), 16 reading ds (mean = 0.84, SD = 0.21), and 4 vocabulary ds (mean = 1.05, SD = 0.20). For the white–Hispanic comparisons, there are 9 math ds (mean = 0.82, SD = 0.08), and 10 reading ds (mean = 0.72, SD = 0.13).

Of particular interest are the NAEP findings as they include assessments in multiple years from 1975 to 2004. In the math domain, the two earliest assessments (1978 and 1982) showed white–black ds comparable to the two most recent assessments (1998 and 2004). In the reading domain, the more recent assessment (d = 0.70) was substantially smaller than the earlier assessments (d = 1.30). A similar pattern is seen for the white–Hispanic comparison: little consistent change in the math domain but a reduction in d in the reading domain.

College Applicants

Table 12.2 presents white–black and white–Hispanic ds for the two major college admissions tests (SAT and ACT) by year. We briefly overview these two testing programs and then discuss the findings.

TABLE 12.2

White–Black and White–Hispanic Score Gap in College Admissions Tests

	1987	1988	1989	1990	1991	1992	1993	1994	1995	1996	1997	1998	1999	2000	2001	2002	2003	2004	2005	2006	2007
White–black differences																					
ACT English											0.89	0.89	0.89	0.89	0.91	0.86	0.88	0.86	0.90		0.95
ACT Math											0.86	0.88	0.88	0.90	0.90	0.92	0.90	0.90	0.94		0.92
ACT Reading											0.84	0.82	0.83	0.85	0.88	0.87	0.85	0.87	0.88		0.89
ACT Science											0.94	0.98	0.98	0.98	1.00	0.98	0.96	0.91	0.96		0.96
ACT Composite											0.98	0.98	0.98	1.02	1.04	1.02	1.00	0.98	1.00		1.02
SAT Verbal	0.96	0.94	0.95	0.91	0.91	0.91	0.90	0.91	0.91	0.91	0.91	0.91	0.92	0.94	0.96	0.97	0.98	0.98	0.98	0.92	
SAT Math	1.01	0.97	0.94	0.96	0.94	0.96	0.94	0.97	0.96	0.98	1.01	1.00	1.03	1.02	1.03	1.04	1.05	1.02	1.03	1.04	
SAT Writing										0.83	0.83	0.82	0.85	0.86	0.88	0.90	0.88	0.89	0.93		
White–Hispanic differences																					
ACT English											0.60	0.61	0.61	0.62	0.62	0.66	0.66	0.66	0.67		0.70
ACT Math											0.44	0.48	0.47	0.47	0.48	0.55	0.55	0.55	0.55		0.53
ACT Reading											0.52	0.50	0.50	0.51	0.55	0.58	0.57	0.60	0.60		0.61
ACT Science											0.57	0.59	0.58	0.58	0.61	0.65	0.64	0.62	0.64		0.63
ACT Composite											0.59	0.60	0.60	0.63	0.65	0.69	0.66	0.68	0.68		0.68
SAT Verbal						0.67	0.66	0.67	0.67	0.67	0.68	0.69	0.69	0.71	0.74	0.75	0.76	0.72	0.73	0.69	
SAT Math						0.58	0.58	0.60	0.60	0.61	0.64	0.66	0.67	0.67	0.69	0.72	0.72	0.70	0.71	0.71	
SAT Writing										0.84	0.83	0.89	0.88	0.93	0.96	1.03	1.04	1.06	1.06		

ACT English, Math, Reading, Science, Verbal, and Composite (1997–2005, 2007)

The ACT is a standardized college admissions test taken by graduating high school seniors. Annually, approximately 1 million students take the ACT; the data presented represent the white–black and white–Hispanic data across all test takers for that particular year or the annual population of ACT test takers for three subgroups studied here (ACT, 2008). The ACT is made up of several subsections (e.g., English, Math, Reading, Science, and Verbal), which form an overall composite score. The ACT only represents potentially college-bound students.

SAT Verbal, Math, and Writing (White–Black 1987–2006, White–Hispanic 1992–2006)

The SAT is also a standardized college admissions test taken by graduating high school seniors. Annually, approximately 1.5 million students take the SAT, and the data presented represent the SAT test-taking population (Kobrin, Sathy, & Shaw, 2007). The SAT reports separate verbal, math, and writing scores. Like the ACT, the SAT only represents potentially college-bound students.

Results

The Table 12.2 findings show a grand mean white–black d of 0.93 (SD = 0.06) and white–Hispanic d of 0.66 (SD = 0.13) across SAT and ACT subtests. The white–black data do not show evidence of a time trend, with the possible exception of the SAT Writing subtest, for which d was 0.83 in 1995 and 0.93 in 2005. In contrast, there is a pattern of increasing d values over time for all SAT and ACT subtests for the white–Hispanic comparison. The largest change is seen for the SAT Writing subtest, for which d was 0.84 in 1995 and 1.06 in 2005. It is important to note that the population of test takers can change from year to year, and thus a change in d is difficult to interpret.

Norming Samples for Intelligence Tests

Dickens and Flynn (2006) obtained unpublished information from test publishers about white–black ds from norming samples for various IQ tests. We summarize their findings here. Comparable data about white–Hispanic differences are not available in the published literature; hence, this section focuses solely on white–black differences. We note that Dickens and Flynn focused solely on the total IQ score rather than on individual subtests.

Adult Samples: Wechsler Adult Intelligence Scale (WAIS Revised, WAIS Third Edition), 1978 and 1995

Both samples were standardization samples for a new version of the WAIS test. The standardization samples for the WAIS Revised (WAIS-R) in 1978 included both non-Hispanic white and Hispanic as white (Dickens & Flynn, 2006). The WAIS-R standardization sample consisted of 1,880 individuals aged 16–74 and the WAIS Third Edition (WAIS-III) standardization sample consisted of 1,250 individuals aged 16–89 (Kane, 2000). Both samples were representative by age group of the U.S. population at the time.

Dickens and Flynn (2006) reported white–black ds of 1.01 and 0.92 for the 1978 and 1995 norming samples, respectively. They reported a separate analysis for individuals aged 25 and under to determine whether young adult samples differed from the full sample; in this subsample, ds of 1.00 and 0.89 were obtained for the two norming samples, respectively.

Full Age Range, Adult and Child: Stanford-Binet (1985, 2001)

The Stanford-Binet is designed and normed for use from ages 2 through 85+. The data here are based on two standardization samples, which match the breakdown of the census at the time. There are some slight differences between the 1985 (SB-4) and the 2001 (SB-5) standardization samples and versions of the tests, such that the test in 2001 was more highly g loaded (+12%; Jensen, 1992), and special education and limited English proficiency students, in which blacks were more highly represented, were included (Dickens & Flynn, 2006). The Stanford-Binet uses adaptive testing through a routing subtest that allows a better estimate of appropriate starting points on other subtests and can be used with young children to the elderly (DiStefano & Dombrowski, 2006). The SB-5 standardization sample consisted of 4,800 individuals selected to match the U.S. census. Dickens and Flynn (2006) reported white–black ds of 0.90 and 0.77 for the 1985 and 2001 norming samples, respectively.

Child Samples: Wechsler Intelligence Scale for Children (WISC Revised, WISC Third Edition, WISC Fourth Edition), 1972, 1989, and 2002

Each of the samples was a standardization sample for a new version of the Wechsler Intelligence Scale for Children (WISC). The fourth edition (WISC-IV) norming sample was based on 2,200 children from 11 age groups (each covering 1 year, from ages 6 to 16), with an equal number of males and females in each group, and an ethnic, parental education, and geographic breakdown that matched the 2000 U.S. census. The standardization samples for the revised edition (WISC-R) in 1972 included both non-Hispanic white and Hispanic in the white group. Every version of the WISC is designed to be appropriate for assessing children from approximately ages 6 to 16 (Kaufman, Flanagan, Alfonso, & Mascolo, 2006); however, the specific sub-scales are not necessarily the same across different versions of the WISC. Dickens and Flynn (2006) reported white–black ds decreasing from a high of 1.15 in the 1972 norming sample to 0.78 in the 2002 norming sample.

Wide Range Achievement Test (WRAT), Pre-1970

The Wide Range Achievement Test (WRAT) sample included 7,028 students (6,049 white, 979 black) who were part of the National Health Examination Survey–Cycle II (Svanum & Bringle, 1982). This survey assessed a nationally representative sample of 6- to 11-year-olds from 1963 to 1965 on a number of physical, physiological, and psychological characteristics. These students were assessed on the reading and arithmetic subtests of the WRAT. The white–black d was 0.90.

Results

The findings are summarized in Table 12.3. The d values from the young adult norming samples for the AFQT are also reported here as Dickens and Flynn (2006) combined the AFQT data with the IQ norming samples for their analysis of time trends in white–black ds. As Table 12.3 shows, all samples showed a decrease in white–black d over time.

Differences in Preschool and Grade School Samples

Here, we turn to white–black and white–Hispanic differences in preschool and grade school children. We discussed the NAEP age 17 sample in the context of differences among high school-aged youths; here, we include findings from the age 9 and age 13 assessments. We briefly outline the additional nationally representative studies from which we extracted d values and then present findings.

National Longitudinal Study of Youth–Child Supplement, 1988 (Average)

The National Longitudinal Study of Youth–Child Supplement (NLSY-CS) is the supplemental assessment of the children of women in the National

TABLE 12.3

White–Black Score Gap in Norming Samples

	Pre-1970	1972	1978	1980	1985	1989	1995	1997	2001	2002
WISC (R, III, IV)	1.13	1.15				1.09				0.78
WAIS (<25, R & III)			1.00				0.89			
WAIS (All ages, R & III)			1.01				0.92			
Stanford-Binet					0.90				0.77	
WRAT	0.90									
AFQT					1.23			0.99		

Longitudinal Study of Youth, a panel study of a nationally representative sample of 14- to 21-year-olds. These data came from the 1986, 1988, and 1992 assessments of two groups of children, those who were 3–4 or 5–6 at the time of the assessments. The children assessed were not themselves a nationally representative sample because they represent children of younger women (Brooks-Gunn, Klebanov, Smith, Duncan, & Lee, 2003). The final 3- to 4-year-old sample consisted of 1,354 children, and the final 5- to 6-year-old sample consisted of 2,220 children. Children were tested on the Peabody Picture Vocabulary Test–Revised (PPVT-R), a measure of spoken word understanding (Dunn & Dunn, 1981). The same data from the NLSY-CS were also presented in the work of Phillips, Brooks-Gunn, Duncan, Klebanov, and Crane (1998).

Early Childhood Longitudinal Study–Kindergarten Cohort Math and Reading, 1998

The Early Childhood Longitudinal Study–Kindergarten Cohort (ECLS-K) began in 1998 to assess a nationally representative sample of 13,000 kindergarteners and will continue to track and assess this cohort until the eighth grade. The data here are for students in the kindergarten cohort in kindergarten (for white–black and white–Hispanic) and the third grade (for white–black differences) on both reading and mathematics reported by Magnuson and Duncan (2006). Items for the reading and mathematics assessments were adapted from national and state standards and other similar assessments (e.g., NAEP; National Center for Education Statistics, n.d.-b).

Panel Study of Income Dynamics–Child Development Supplement Math and Reading, 1997 and 2002

The Panel Study of Income Dynamics (PSID) is a longitudinal study that began in the 1960s of representative samples of men, women, children, and families in the United States. The Panel Study of Income Dynamics–Child Development Supplement (PSID-CDS) is a supplemental data collection effort that focuses on young children. In the first wave of data collection in 1997, information on 3,563 children between 0 and 12 years old was gathered. In 2002, follow-up data collection was conducted on 2,907 children between 5 and 18 years old. Children were assessed using the Woodcock-Johnson Psych-Educational Battery–Revised (WJ-R), an intellectual ability test designed for use on individuals between 2 and 90 years of age, either in English or Spanish. Children under 6 were assessed on two subtests, Letter-Word and Applied Problem Sets, and children over 6 were given an additional subtest, Passage Comprehension (Mainieri, 2006). The data reported here are based on calculations reported by Magnuson and Duncan (2006).

Iowa Test of Basic Skills–Science, 1993

The Iowa Test of Basic Skills–Science (ITBS-Science) was administered as part of a study examining the score gap between white and minority students on performance-based science assessments (Klein et al., 1997). Further information on the ITBS-Science can be found in Hoover, Hieronymus, Frisbie, and Dunbar (1994). Students in fifth and sixth grade were given the corresponding level of the ITBS-Science according to their grade in 1993. In total, the study assessed over 2,021 fifth- and sixth-grade students. The white–black and white–Hispanic difference scores reported here are in z-score units and not standardized mean differences (*d* scores) per se. However, research evidence suggested that variances were relatively equal between different racial groups (Hedges & Nowell, 1998), such that this z-score difference should approximate a standardized mean difference.

Prospects Math and Reading, 1991

Prospects (PROS) was also known as the congressionally mandated study of educational growth and opportunity. PROS was a 6-year longitudinal study following several cohorts of national samples of public school students (Puma, Jones, Rock, & Fernandez, 1993). PROS primary goals involved examining the impact of Chapter 1/Title I programs and the differential effects of poverty in schools or students.

Equality of Educational Opportunity Math and Reading, 1965

The EEO utilized a national sample of students in several grades between the 1st and 12th grades. One of the primary concerns of EEO was to assess the educational opportunities for children of different backgrounds and circumstances.

Results

Table 12.4 presents the white–black and white–Hispanic *d* values from these studies. For the white–black comparisons, there are 30 math *d*s (mean = 0.87, *SD* = 0.14), 29 reading *d*s (mean = 0.78, *SD* = 0.15), and 5 vocabulary *d*s (mean = 0.84, *SD* = 0.19). For the white–Hispanic comparisons, there are 19 math *d*s (mean = 0.77, *SD* = 0.12) and 21 reading *d*s (mean = 0.73, *SD* = 0.12).

Of particular interest are the NAEP findings as these involved samples over an extended period of time. For both the white–black and the white–Hispanic comparisons, at both Grade 4 and Grade 8 the pattern is for considerable fluctuation in the math *d*, making it hard to discern any time trend. However, the reading *d*s show a consistent trend of decrease over time.

Summary and Conclusions

Table 12.5 presents mean white–black and white–Hispanic *d*s across the different categories of studies discussed. When *d* values for math and verbal were available but scores on a composite of the two were not reported, we estimated *d* on a composite of the two using the formula provided by Sackett and Ellingson (1997). That formula requires the correlation between the two tests; we used $r = 0.65$ as the correlation between math and verbal tests as this is a typical value for the correlation between the two domains in large unrestricted samples. For example, the correlation between math and verbal composites in the large-scale AFQT norming sample is 0.64; the correlation between the math and verbal subsets of the SAT is about 0.70.

This table gives a clear answer to the question, Is there something specific about the employment context that causes or contributes to subgroup differences? The answer is, No: Differences in the employment context are very similar to differences found in young adult and adult samples in other contexts. Roth et al. (2001) reported mean white–black *d* values in job applicant samples of 1.00 for overall *g* measures, with smaller values for specific ability measures (*d* = 0.83 for verbal and 0.74 for math). The value of 1.00 for *g* measures is very close to the values obtained for composites of verbal and math for the national norming of the AFQT (*d* = 1.11), for college admissions test composites (*d* =1.06 for SAT and 1.00 for ACT), for representative samples of high school students (*d* = 0.98), and for norming samples for IQ tests (*d* = 0.90).

Moving to white–Hispanic comparisons, Roth et al. (2001) reported mean white–Hispanic *d* values of 0.84 for *g* measures in the employment setting. This is very similar to the values obtained here for composites for college admissions ($d = 0.75$ for SAT and 0.65 for ACT) and for representative samples of high school students ($d = 0.88$).

Note that these data include a mix of tests taken in high-stakes settings (e.g., employment and college admissions) and tests taken in low-stakes research settings (e.g., AFQT norming, IQ norming, and studies of high school students). Thus, the pressures of a high-stakes setting do not appear to affect minority student performance differentially as d values are similar in high-stakes and low-stakes settings.

A second question of interest is whether subgroup differences vary by age. Table 12.5 also contains data on white–black differences on g measures for preschool ($d = 0.92$) and elementary school ($d = 0.90$) samples. As an alternate approach to this question, we estimated regression models for math and verbal tests with examinee age and study year as predictors. There were 75 math and 105 verbal effect sizes available for this analysis. Note that these analyses excluded d values obtained from samples varying in age (e.g., IQ norming samples). Table 12.6 presents the results. These analyses produced statistically significant coefficients of 0.014 and 0.020 for age for math and verbal, respectively, net of the effects of study year. Thus, d is estimated to increase by 0.014 for math and 0.020 per year from age 4 to age 18.

For the white–Hispanic comparison, Table 12.5 shows white–Hispanic differences on g measures for elementary school samples ($d = 0.81$), very similar to the d value of 0.84 obtained in the employment setting by Roth et al. (2001). Table 12.6 shows regression analyses using age and study year to predict d values for math ($k = 55$) and verbal ($k = 78$) tests. Unlike the white–black analyses, for which age was related to d, for the white–Hispanic data there was no systematic relationship between age and d.

These data showed that subgroup differences measured in early childhood were similar to those obtained in young adulthood. While age was related to d in the white–black comparisons, it is nonetheless the case that d values in early childhood were nearly as large as values obtained in young adulthood. These findings do not identify the causes of group differences, but the fact that differences are observed in early childhood does make clear that it is not something about the employment context or about the transition from adolescence to young adulthood that is a primary determinant of these differences

A third question of interest is whether subgroup differences are changing over time. Our sense is that the preponderance of evidence is that there is some narrowing of the subgroup differences. Dickens and Flynn (2006) concluded that the IQ norming sample data reported here supported a narrowing of the white–black gap; Hedges and Nowell (1995) reached a similar conclusion about the set of nationally representative studies of high school students that they examined and that we also report here. Our Table 12.6 regression analysis also supported this conclusion regarding

TABLE 12.4

White–Black and White–Hispanic Test Score Gap in Children

	Pre-1970	1975	1978	1980	1982	1983	1984	1986	1987	1988	1990	1991	1992	1993	1994	1996	1997	1998	1999	2002	2004
White–black differences																					
Intelligence Tests																					
NLSY-CS-PPVT-R, Preschool										1.25											
NLSY-CS-PPVT-R, Kindergarten										10.09											
Math																					
PSID-CDS Math, Preschool																	0.79				
ECLS-K Math, Kindergarten																		0.65			
PROS Math, Grade 1												0.87									
EEO Math, Grade 3		0.86																			
ECLS-K Math, Grade 3																			0.89		
PSID-CDS Math, Grade 3 & 4																			0.99		
PROS Math, Grade 4												0.67									
NAEP Math, Grade 4			0.93		0.88			0.78			0.86		0.79	0.87	0.78	0.80			0.87		0.72
EEO Math, Grade 6	1.10																				
LSAY Math, Grade 7									0.74												
PROS Math, Grade 8												0.62									
NAEP Math, Grade 8			1.18		1.10			0.83			0.94		1.00		0.97	1.01			1.07		0.88
NELS Math, Grade 8										0.78											
Verbal/Reading																					
PSID-CDS Verbal, Preschool																	0.43				
ECLS-K Reading, Kindergarten																		0.40			

PROS Reading, Grade 1						0.74				
EEO Reading, Grade 3	0.87									
ECLS-K Reading, Grade 3									0.78	
PSID-CDS Verbal, Grades 3 & 4									0.68	
PROS Reading, Grade 4						0.67				
NAEP Reading, Grade 4	0.98	0.90	0.83	0.74	0.82	0.88	0.86	0.78	0.98	.75
EEO Reading, Grade 6	0.90									
PROS Reading, Grade 8						0.56				
NAEP Reading, Grade 8	1.09	0.97	0.78	0.55	0.60	0.77	0.82	0.88	0.78	0.61
NELS Reading, Grade 8					0.70					
Vocabulary										
PROS Vocab, Grade 1						0.70				
EEO Vocab, Grade 3	0.88									
PROS Vocab, Grade 4						0.70				
EEO Vocab, Grade 6	1.15									
PROS Vocab, Grade 8						0.77				
White–Hispanic differences										
Math										
ECLS-K Math, kindergarten									0.75	
NAEP Math, Grade 4	0.62	0.61	0.66	0.69	0.75	0.86	0.70	0.82		
NAEP Math, Grade 8	0.94	0.71	0.66	0.75	0.69	0.83	0.88	0.79		
Verbal/Reading										
ECLS-K Reading, kindergarten									0.41	
NAEP Reading, Grade 4	0.94	0.88	0.79	0.61	0.65	0.69	0.85	0.68	0.78	0.62
NAEP Reading, Grade 8	0.90	0.83	0.68	0.62	0.71	0.74	0.80	0.75	0.63	0.67

TABLE 12.5

Mean *d* Values and Standard Variances for White–Black and White–Hispanic Differences

Type of sample	No. of samples (*k*)	Average *d* value	SD
White–Black differences			
Job applicants (from Roth et al., 2001)		1.00	
Nationally representative sample of 18- to 22-year-olds (AFQT norming)	2	1.11	0.17
SAT Math	20	0.93	0.03
SAT Verbal	20	1.00	0.04
SAT Math + Verbal (estimated by formula)		1.06	
SAT Writing	10	0.87	0.04
ACT Math	10	0.90	0.02
ACT Verbal (English & Reading)	20	0.88	0.03
ACT Science	10	0.97	0.03
ACT Composite	10	1.00	0.02
High school math samples	16	0.94	0.14
High school reading samples	16	0.84	0.21
High school math + reading (estimated by formula)		0.98	
High school vocab samples	4	1.05	0.20
Adult norming	4	0.90	0.10
Child norming	5	1.01	0.16
Elementary school math samples	30	0.87	0.14
Elementary school verbal/reading samples	29	0.78	0.15
Elementary school math + verbal (estimated by formula)		0.91	
Elementary school vocabulary samples	5	0.84	0.19
Pre-elementary samples	3	0.92	0.43
White–Hispanic differences			
Industrial samples (from Roth et al., 2001)		0.83	
SAT Math	15	0.70	0.03
SAT Verbal	15	0.66	0.05
SAT Math + Verbal (estimated by formula)		0.75	
SAT Writing	10	0.95	0.09
ACT Math	10	0.51	0.04
ACT Verbal (Reading & Verbal)	20	0.60	0.06
ACT Science	10	0.61	0.03
ACT Composite	10	0.65	0.04
High school math samples	9	0.82	0.08
High school reading samples	10	0.72	0.13

TABLE 12.5 (*Continued*)

Mean *d* Values and Standard Variances for White–Black and White–Hispanic Differences

Type of sample	No. of samples (*k*)	Average *d* value	SD
High school math + reading (estimated by formula)		0.85	
Elementary school math samples	19	0.74	0.10
Elementary school reading samples	21	0.73	0.12
Elementary school math + reading (estimated by formula)		0.81	

Note: Average *d* values are not *n* weighted. Adult norming: WAIS overall sample and Stanford-Binet. Child norming: WRAT and WISC. Many samples here represent the same group of individuals' scores on different subtests.

white–black differences, finding a small, but significant study year coefficient of −0.002 for math and −0.007 for verbal. This suggests that the white–black gap has narrowed by about 0.04 in the math domain and 0.14 in the verbal domain in the last 20 years. Table 12.6 data show a similar study year effect for the white–Hispanic comparison, with coefficients of −0.006 for math and −0.005 for verbal. Thus, there is some narrowing of the white–black and white–Hispanic score gap.

We note that the data reviewed here are descriptive and do not offer a basis for determining the causes of the narrowing of the score gaps. Over the time period reviewed here, there have been changes in a variety of factors that might be posited as contributing to a reduction in the score gaps, such as improvement in quality of education, in health care, and in occupational status for minority group members. We do note that both Hedges and Nowell (1995) and Dickens and Flynn (2006) investigated whether the narrowing of the score gap occurred throughout the score distribution. Hedges and Nowell observed that changes were concentrated in the lower tail of the distribution, with little narrowing of the gap in the upper tail. The data presented by Dickens and Flynn also

TABLE 12.6

Regression Results Predicting *d* Values

	White–Black: Math (*K* = 75)	White–Black: Verbal (*K* = 105)	White–Hispanic: Math (*K* = 55)	White–Hispanic: Verbal (*K* = 78)
Study year	−0.002 (0.001)	−0.007* (0.001)	−0.006* (0.002)	−0.005* (0.002)
Age	0.014* (0.003)	0.020* (0.003)	−0.002 (0.005)	0.005 (0.006)
R^2	0.201	0.338	0.128	0.034

Note: Table *d* values are unstandardized regression coefficients; standard errors are in parentheses. *K* is the number of effect size values in each regression.

* $p < 0.05$.

supported this conclusion: They reported markedly smaller score gains at scores that would fall above the white mean than for the range below the mean.

In conclusion, findings regarding subgroup differences on cognitive measures in the employment context parallel those in other contexts. Differences measured in early childhood were quite similar to those measured in young adulthood. While there is evidence that the gap is narrowing to a modest degree over time, mean differences remained substantial. We believe these findings help put data from the employment setting in a broader context. We encourage continued research into the causes of the differences described here, into intervention strategies aimed at reducing these differences, and into the place of cognitive predictors along with the full range of other individual difference attributes as predictors of the full range of workplace criteria.

References

ACT. (2008). *ACT national and state scores*. Retrieved January 3, 2008, from http://www.act.org/news/data.html

Berry, C. M., Sackett, P. R., & Landers, R. (2007). Revisiting interview-cognitive ability relationships: Attending to specific range restriction mechanisms in meta-analysis. *Personnel Psychology, 60*, 837–874.

Brooks-Gunn, J., Klebanov, P. K., Smith, J., Duncan, G. J., & Lee, K. (2003). The black-white test score gap in young children: Contributions of test and family characteristics. *Applied Developmental Science, 7*, 239–252.

Bureau of Labor Statistics. (2001). *NLSY79 overview*. Retrieved December 2, 2007, from http://www.bls.gov/nls/nlsyouth.htm

Coleman, J. S. (1966). *Equality of Educational Opportunity (Coleman) Study (EEOS)*. Washington, DC: U.S. Department of Health, Education, and Welfare.

Dickens, W. T., & Flynn, J. R. (2006). Black Americans reduce the racial IQ gap: Evidence from standardization samples. *Psychological Science, 17*, 913–920.

DiStefano, C., & Dombrowski, S. C. (2006). Investigating the theoretical structure of the Stanford-Binet-fifth edition. *Journal of Psychoeducational Assessment, 24*, 123–136.

Dunn, L. M., & Dunn, L. M. (1981). *Peabody Picture Vocabulary Test–Revised*. Circle Pines, MN: American Guidance Service.

Hedges, L. V., & Nowell, A. (1995). Sex difference in mental test scores, variability, and number of high scoring individuals. *Science, 269*, 41–45.

Hedges, L. V., & A. Nowell, A. (1998). Are black-white differences in test scores narrowing? In C. Jencks & M. Phillips (Eds.), *The black white test score gap* (pp. 254–281). Washington, DC: Brookings Institution.

Hoover, H. D., Hieronymus, A. N., Frisbie, D. A., & Dunbar, S. B. (1994). *Iowa Test of Basic Skills: Interpretive guide for school administrators*. Chicago: Riverside.

Hyde, J. S., & Linn, M. C. (1988). Gender differences in verbal ability. *Psychological Bulletin, 104,* 53–69.

Hyde, J. S., Fennema, E., & Lamon, S. J. (1990). Gender differences in mathematics performance: A meta analysis. *Psychological Bulletin, 107,* 139–155.

Jensen, A. R. (1992). Spearman's hypothesis: Methodology and evidence. *Multivariate Behavioral Research, 27,* 225–233.

Kane, H. D. (2000). A secular decline in Spearman's *g*: Evidence from the WAIS, WAIS-R and WAIS III. *Personality and Individual Differences, 29,* 561–566.

Kaufman, A. S., Flanagan, D. P., Alfonso, V. C., & Mascolo, J. T. (2006). Test review: Wechsler Intelligence Scale for Children, Fourth Edition (WISC-IV). *Journal of Psychoeducational Assessment, 24,* 278–295.

Klein, S. P., Jovanovic, J., Stecher, B. M., McCaffey, D., Shavelson, R. J., Haertel, E., et al. (1997). Gender and racial/ethnic differences on performance assessments in science. *Educational Evaluation and Policy Analysis, 19,* 83–97.

Kobrin, J. L., Sathy, V., & Shaw, E. J. (2007). *A historical view of subgroup differences on the SAT Reasoning Test* (Rep. Research Report 2006-5). New York: College Board.

Magnuson, K. A., & Duncan, G. J. (2006). The role of family socioeconomic resources in the black-white test score gap among young children. *Developmental Review, 26,* 365–399.

Mainieri, T. (2006). *The panel study of income dynamics child development supplement: User guide for CDS-II.* Retrieved December 18, 2007, from http://psidonline. isr.umich.edu/CDS/cdsii_userGd.pdf

McDaniel, M. A., Hartman, N. S., Whetzel, D. L., & Grubb, W. L. (2007). Situational judgment tests, response instructions, and validity: A meta-analysis, *Personnel Psychology, 60,* 63–91.

National Center for Education Statistics. (n.d.-a). *High school and beyond overview.* Retrieved December 12, 2007, from http://nces.ed.gov/surveys/hsb/

National Center for Educational Statistics. (n.d.-b). *NAEP-long term trend.* Retrieved December 12, 2007, from http://nces.ed.gov/nationsreportcard/ltt/

National Center for Educational Statistics. (n.d.-c). *National education longitudinal study of 1988.* Retrieved December 14, 2007, from http://nces.ed.gov/surveys/nels88/

Phillips, M., Brooks-Gunn, J., Duncan, G., Klebanov, K., & Crane, J. (1998). Family background, parenting practices and the black-white test score gap. In C. Jencks & M. Phillips (Eds.), *The black-white test score gap* (pp. 103–145). Washington, DC: Brookings Institution Press.

Phillips, M., Crouse, J., & Ralph, J. (1998). Does the black-white test score gap widen after children enter school? In C. Jencks & M. Phillips (Eds.), *The black-white test score gap* (pp. 229–272). Washington, DC: Brookings Institution Press.

Puma, M. J., Jones, C. C., Rock, D., & Fernandez, R. (1993). *Prospects: The congressionally mandated study of educational growth and opportunity. The interim report.* Washington, DC: U.S. Department of Education, Planning, and Evaluation Service.

Roth, P. L., Bevier, C. A., Bobko, P, Switzer, F. S., III, & Tyler, P. (2001). Ethnic group differences in cognitive ability in employment and educational settings: A meta-analysis. *Personnel Psychology, 54,* 297–330.

Sackett, P. R., & Ellingson, J. E. (1997). On the effects of forming multi-predictor composites on group differences and adverse impact. *Personnel Psychology, 50,* 708–721.

Sackett, P. R., & Mavor, A. (Eds.). (2003). *Attitudes, aptitudes, and aspirations of American youth: Implications for military recruiting.* Washington, DC: National Academy Press.

Sackett P. R., & Ostgaard, D. J. (1994). Job-specific applicant pools and national norms for cognitive ability tests: Implications for range restriction corrections in validation research. *Journal of Applied Psychology, 79,* 680–684.

Schmidt, F. L., & Hunter, J. E. (1998). The validity and utility of selection methods in personnel psychology: Practical and theoretical implications of 85 years of research findings. *Psychological Bulletin, 124,* 262–274.

Svanum, S., & Bringle, R. G. (1982). Race, social class, and predictive bias: An evaluation using the WISC, WRAT, and teacher ratings. *Intelligence, 6,* 275–286.

Willingham, W.W., & Cole, N. S. (1997). *Gender and fair assessment.* Mahwah, NJ: Erlbaum.

Section V

Adverse Impact From an International Perspective

13

International Perspectives on Adverse Impact: Europe and Beyond

Paul J. Hanges and Emily G. Feinberg

Introduction

As discussed throughout this book, adverse impact occurs when organizational policies, practices, or procedures disproportionately affect members of one or more subgroups. In the United States, these subgroups have been a priori defined as a result of historical inequities in the United States. Specifically, these identifying subgroup characteristics include race, national origin, color, sex, religion, age, or disability status (Heneman & Heneman, 1994; Hough, Oswald, & Ployhart, 2001; Hunter & Hunter, 1984). While other subgroups (e.g., sexual orientation, obese individuals) can be harmed by organizational policies, practices, and procedures, these subgroups are currently not protected under the law.

There is a substantial body of legislative, legal, and scientific literature in the United States devoted to defining, measuring, and documenting adverse impact. In this chapter, we contribute to this literature by reviewing the growing European literature on adverse impact and discrimination (e.g., Aramburu-Zabala Higuera, 2001; Carrington & DeLima, 1996; Goldston, 2008; Helms-Lorenz, & van de Vijver, 1995; Kende & Nemenyi, 2006; te Nijenhuis & van der Flier, 1999; van de Vijver, Helms-Lorenz, & Feltzer, 1999). That is, we seek to highlight the facets of adverse impact important from a European perspective. Specifically, how is adverse impact defined in the European Union? What subgroups are protected in the European Union? What kinds of strategies have they started to use to combat adverse impact?

We believe that taking this international perspective could be informative for the development of a broader conceptualization of adverse impact.

Cross-cultural researchers are fond of pointing out that culture not only identifies what issues are important or problematic (e.g., adverse impact) in a particular society but also that culture affects the kinds of strategies used to address these problems (Hanges, Lord, & Dickson, 2000; Hofstede, 1980; House, Hanges, Javidan, Dorfman, & Gupta, 2004). Thus, an international review of the adverse impact literature holds the promise of yielding new insights regarding the cause of adverse impact as well as identifying different strategies for reducing it.

The cross-cultural and research methodology literatures both suggest that the causal mechanisms of interventions/manipulations on outcome variables are ambiguous when data are collected from only one group (or country). This is due to the presence of other factors that are confounded with the occurrence of the intervention/manipulation (Cook & Campbell, 1979; Shadish, Cook, & Campbell, 2002). It is possible that exploring adverse impact across nations might change the way we think about the causes of adverse impact. At the very least, this is the promise of international research. The extent to which the non-U.S. literature on adverse impact is currently fulfilling this promise is one of the issues that we assess in this chapter. We begin the review by exploring the history of the adverse impact construct in the European Union.

History of Adverse Impact in the European Union

Similar to the credo that "all men are created equal" expressed in the U.S. Declaration of Independence, the founding documents creating the European Union have explicit statements regarding the value of equality. For example, the European Convention for the Protection of Human Rights and Fundamental Freedoms (Council of Europe, 1950), states:

> The enjoyment of the rights and freedoms set forth in this convention shall be secured without discrimination on any ground such as sex, race, colour, language, religion, political or other opinion, national or social origin, association with a national minority, property, birth or other status. (Article 14)

Further, the Treaty Establishing the European Economic Community (popularly known as the Treaty of Rome) explicitly focused on gender discrimination and equal pay. It is explicitly stated in this article that countries signing this document shall "ensure and subsequently maintain the application of the principle that men and women should receive equal pay for equal work" (Article 119).

With the ratification of the European Convention on Human Rights in 1950 (Council of Europe, 1950), it is not surprising that subsequent treaties (i.e., the 1992 Treaty on the European Union and the 1997 Treaty of Amsterdam of the European Communities), whose objectives were to formally establish the European Union, also carried this spirit of equality. However, the wording of these treaties emphasized economic factors as the main reason for founding the European Union. Thus, these founding documents conveyed the belief and, indeed, explicitly stated that equal integration of all employees into the marketplace and the freedom of movement of workers were necessary preconditions for the development of a successful European common market. This can be directly seen in the Treaty of Amsterdam (European Communities, 1997), which explicitly stated that gender equality is a goal for the European Union as is the goal of eliminating inequalities and promoting equality in all aspects of E.U. life (Ellis, 2005). In other words, unequal treatment of individuals is conceptualized as a violation of the European Union's founding principles because it limits economic growth and prosperity (Aramburu-Zabala Higuera, 2001).

However, despite this initial progress, the European Union has actually lagged behind the United States in establishing antidiscrimination employment litigation (Laczko, 2002). While adverse impact was defined by the 1970s in the United States, this concept was first introduced in Europe in the early to mid-1980s as a result of the *Jenkins v. Kingsgate (Clothing Production) Inc.* (1981) court case and its extension, *Bilka-Kaufhaus GmbH v. Karin Weber von Hartz* (1986). In this case, a female employee worked for a German department store for 15 years, the last 4 years as a part-time worker. The German store refused to pay her a pension because the store's policy stated that the supplementary pension plan was only available to employees who worked full time for at minimum of 15 years. The former female employee charged that the department store violated the equal-pay for equal-work article (i.e., Article 119) of the Treaty of Rome. The Court of Justice of the European Communities concluded that:

> Article 119 of the EEC treaty is infringed by a department store company which excludes part-time employees from its occupational pension scheme, where that exclusion affects a far greater number of women than men, unless the undertaking shows that the exclusion is based on objectively justified factors unrelated to any discrimination on grounds of sex. (ECR 1607, 1986)

This decision from the E.U. court documents that, similar to the United States, adverse impact can be established by evaluating quantitative information. Indeed, Europeans commonly refer to adverse impact evidence as indirect discrimination.

The definition of indirect discrimination continued to be refined over the years. Currently, two points are the base for discriminatory results. These are:

- Any procedure or test that produces in a selection process an adverse impact against women and other groups of applicants is potentially discriminatory and goes against the fundamental rights of those persons;
- Measures meant to be formally neutral (for instance, a test, an interview, or a biodata questionnaire) which produce an unfavorable effect against any given subgroup have to be screened against criteria of technical validity and according to their value to measure "intrinsically necessary requisites" for that position. (Arambura-Zabala Hiquera, 2001, p. 105)

This shows that, over the years, the European Union extended the concept of indirect discrimination to protected groups other than gender. Finally, this quotation also documents that, similar to the shifting burden-of-proof model established in the *Griggs v. Duke Power Company* (1971) U.S. Supreme Court decision, demonstration of adverse impact by a plaintiff can be refuted by validity evidence for the organization practice in question.

Further, the European Communities adopted two directives in 2000. The first, Council Directive 2000/43/EC (European Communities, 2000a), implements the principle of equal treatment between persons irrespective of racial or ethnic origins (hereafter referred to as the E.C. Racial Equality Directive). The second, Council Directive 2000/78/EC (European Communities, 2000b), establishes a general framework for equal treatment in employment and occupation (hereafter referred to as the E.C. Employment Framework Directive) and outlines that while it is the plaintiff's burden to demonstrate adverse impact, it is the defendant's burden to demonstrate validity for the procedure. Specifically, the E.C. Racial Equality Directive (2000a) states:

> When persons who consider themselves wronged because the principle of equal treatment has not been applied to them establish, before a court or other competent authority, facts from which it may be presumed that there has been direct or indirect discrimination, it shall be for the respondent to prove that there has been no breach of the principle of equal treatment. (Article 8)

While there are many similarities between the United States and the European Union in terms of the conceptualization of adverse impact, one major difference is that the European Union does not specify a particular rule for assessing adverse impact. Both the E.C. Racial Equality Directive

(2000a) and E.C. Employment Framework Directive (2000b) state that indirect discrimination can be established by any means, including statistical evidence. In other words, nations are allowed, but not required, to use statistical data as evidence for discrimination.

Given the flexibility in how adverse impact can be demonstrated, it would be reasonable for one to expect that there would be little consistency among the E.U. nations. Fortunately, the majority of the member states have agreed with the European Union's stance on human rights (Laczko, 2002; Makkonen, 2007; Zegers de Beijl, 2000), and as of September 2005, of the 25 E.U. nations 17 had fully or partially incorporated the racial and employment directives into their national law. For example, in Belgium, the law explicitly says that "statistical data" and "situation tests"[1] are examples of the kind of evidence that leads to the shifting of burden to the defendant (Cormack & Bell, 2005). This focus on statistical evidence for establishing adverse impact is consistent with the long history of equality legislation in Belgium (e.g., the Belgian Constitution of 1994 [Article 10, 11, 191], antidiscrimination law of 2003). Indeed, all Belgian employers are covered under these laws, and most employment practices (e.g., selection and appointment, promotions, employment opportunities, labor conditions, dismissal, and wages) are included. With a long-standing focus on discrimination, it is unsurprising that Belgium has rigorous antidiscrimination policies.

Italy has also established antidiscrimination practices similar to those of Belgium, with the specific mention of the use of statistical data in their antidiscrimination law with regard to the selection and termination of employees (Cormack & Bell, 2005; Makkonen, 2007). This legislation covers sex, race, language, religion, and political opinions for citizens and noncitizens. This focus on antidiscrimination based on background goes back to the Italian Constitution of 1948 and more recently the Anti-Discrimination Rules in the 1998 Immigration Act, in which race was explicitly protected for equal treatment under law (Simoni, 2003). Despite this law, the effectiveness of this framework may be limited by the lack of awareness by immigrants and other subgroups that would benefit from its use and by the limited availability of relevant statistical information to identify adverse impact in organizational practices (Ferrari, Corbetta, & Parolin, 2002).

France also has many laws pertaining to employee discrimination and has agreed to many international conventions focused on equality for workers (e.g., French Constitution of 1958; the International Convention of the International Labor Organization, 1981). Furthermore, according to Viprey (2002), the French National Assembly passed antidiscrimination laws in the workplace in 2001 that not only included the E.C. directives (2000a, 2000b) and French case law but also included amendments to shift the burden of proof onto the employer (i.e., instead of the employee) and expanded these laws to age and physical appearance discrimination.

However, not all nations have chosen to adopt these policies. As of September 2005, the Czech Republic, Estonia, Latvia, Malta, and Poland had not fully incorporated either the E.C. Racial Equality Directive (2000a) or the E.C. Employment Framework Directive (2000b) into their national legislation. In these countries, statistical evidence may not be accepted or may not be considered sufficient evidence to establish indirect discrimination (Makkonen, 2007). This has resulted in several incidents of adverse impact that have been brought to court and unsuccessfully rectified based on problems in a particular nation's discrimination legislation (Cormak & Bell, 2005; European Roma Rights Center [ERRC], 2004; Laczko, 2002).

For example, in the Czech Republic there was a court case (i.e., *D.H. and Others v. the Czech Republic*, 2007) in which the complaint that Romani children were sent to schools for children with learning disabilities at a significantly higher rate than non-Romani children (ERRC, 2004; Smith, 1997). It was acknowledged in this court case that these schools are largely inferior to normal schools. Despite careful data collection and analysis that demonstrated that Romani children were 27 times more likely to end up in a special school than non-Romani children, local and state courts both dismissed the evidence, citing "no jurisdiction to consider statistical evidence" (ERRC, 2004, p. 82). This decision was eventually overturned by the Grand Chamber in 2007. In their decision, the Grand Chamber explicitly stated that it is completely appropriate to consider statistical evidence when establishing adverse impact.

In Latvia, there have also been problems based on the sparse antidiscrimination legislation. For example, the protection of sexual orientation has been deleted from drafts of antidiscrimination laws in the Latvian parliament, and the term has been replaced with a "nonexhaustive" list (Cormak & Bell, 2005). This is a serious problem for Latvia with respect to its status as a member of the European Union because Latvia was admitted in 2004 on the condition that it would agree to the E.C. Equal Rights Directives of 2000 (2000a, 2000b). This issue persists, as is evidenced by the Latvia government refusing in 2006 to introduce a law banning discrimination at work on sexual orientation grounds. Indeed, the majority political party in Latvia, the Christian Democratic Party, described homosexuality as a sin and homosexual people as "degenerate" and discouraged the inclusion of sexual orientation on the proposed the antidiscrimination bill (Sheeter, 2006). The Latvian president agreed with this belief and thus did not sign this amendment to the labor law. Thus, Latvia is the only E.U. nation that does not explicitly protect sexual orientation as grounds for discrimination (Lavrikovs, 2006).

In summary, there is substantial overlap in the definition of adverse impact and the evidence needed to establish adverse impact in the European Union and the United States. In addition, both the United States and the European

Union seem to have a similar shifting burden-of-proof model in that once adverse impact is established, the defendant has the responsibility to demonstrate the validity of the questioned organizational procedure.

However, despite these similarities, there are substantial differences between the European Union and the United States. First, the majority of the E.U. nations cover more subgroups than does the United States. This is particularly evident with regard to the protection of individuals with regard to sexual orientation. Second, the United States has established guidelines (i.e., four-fifths rule or statistical analysis) that apply to all states with regard to the magnitude of subgroup differences demonstrating adverse impact. The European Union does not. Indeed, the European Union is a relatively loose confederation of nations; thus, each nation has the power to uniquely define the critical magnitude of subgroup differences that constitute adverse impact. As discussed, the subgroups that are considered protected under discrimination laws varies across the E.U. nations (e.g., sexual orientation is protected in France but not in Latvia). Given these differences, it would not be surprising that organizations operating across multiple E.U. nations will find that the same policies, practices, and procedures that are considered nondiscriminatory in one E.U. nation will get the organization into trouble in another E.U. nation. This variability and the confusion that it may cause will probably impede the functioning of the European Union's common market.

It is interesting to contrast the "equality yields economic prosperity" belief explicitly stated in the E.U. founding documents with the "inequality yields economic prosperity" belief of some of the U.S. founding fathers. While an explication of the cultural and historic differences between pre–Civil War United States and Europe in the late 20th century is beyond the scope of this chapter, it is noteworthy that it took cataclysmic events to move both the United States and Europe toward the equality belief. In the United States, the adoption of the 14th Amendment to the American Constitution occurred after the Civil War, and the European Convention on Human Rights was ratified only 5 years after the defeat of Nazi Germany, whose society embodied the inequality yields economic prosperity belief. Consistent with the attitude change research (e.g., Hanges, Braverman, & Rentsch, 1991; Hanges, Lord, Godfrey, & Raver, 2002), extreme events are required to move dynamic systems from entrenched beliefs.

In the next section of this chapter, we examine which subgroups are considered disadvantaged in the European Union. As indicated, the United States has identified several population characteristics that should be independent of organizational procedures. These characteristics include race, gender, religion, age, and disability. Of these subgroups, racial discrimination has received the majority of the court's attention, with African Americans and Latinos repeatedly reporting unfair practices (Hunter &

Hunter, 1984; Ployhart & Holtz, 2008). Interestingly, these subgroups are relatively small in the United States, with African Americans making up 12.8% and Latinos comprising 14.8% of the population (United States Census Bureau, 2008).

Which Subgroups Are Disadvantaged in the European Union?

The concern regarding discrimination in the European Union has increased since the mid-1980s as a result of cultural and economic changes (Ambrosini & Barone, 2007; Laczko, 2002). The primary focus in the European discrimination literature is immigration issues and the extent to which immigrants are permitted access to jobs and education. This focus is quite logical as immigration of nonnationals has increased in the European Union since the late twentieth century by 20.2% (between 1995 and 2004, data from the Organization for Economic Cooperation and Development (OCED, 2006). This sharp increase is even more apparent when looking at the more recent data; from 2000 to 2004, immigration increased 26.1%. It is important to keep in mind that these data are based on legal immigration numbers, and actual figures are likely higher (Ambrosini & Barone, 2007).

With regard to the various immigrant subgroups, the Romani people, or Roma, have historically received the brunt of negative biases in the European Union (ERRC, 2004; Smith, 1997). The Roma were originally from many parts of the world, but mostly from south-central and eastern Europe (Smith, 1997). They are largely poor, uneducated, and stigmatized throughout Europe and North America, where they currently reside (Smith, 1997). Studies have repeatedly documented a strong negative bias against Roma, and this bias is believed to affect this population early in their lives. For example, Kende and Nemenyi (2006) documented that there is a relatively large percentage of Roma in Hungarian special schools. These special schools were originally developed for children with mental disabilities. When Kende and Nemenyi examined the selection tools used to determine school placement in Hungary, they found that the tools (primarily cognitive ability tests) did not actually predict school placement for Roma children. Rather, the primary factor determining the readiness of the Roma children for school and their school placement appeared to be a subjective decision by a school counselor. Even after controlling for ethnicity, Kende and Nemenyi found substantial and unexplained numbers of Roma children in these special schools compared to members of other subgroups with similar socioeconomic status levels.

Clearly, the Romani are not the only subgroup that has been disadvantaged in Europe. In Belgium, non-Western immigrants from Morocco and Turkey are disadvantaged (Okkerse & Termote, 2004). Studies have shown that migrant workers from these two subgroups have less job stability than native workers. Further, the unemployment rate in both of these subgroups is high (General Board Employment and Labor Market, 2006), with the majority of immigrants from these two subgroups working in unskilled and low-paying fields (Ambrosini, & Barone, 2007).

In France, 7.4% of the population is from several immigrant groups originating from European countries as well as North Africa, other parts of Africa, and Asia (Myors et al., 2008). In Germany, there is a very large Turkish population (3.7%) as well as reimmigrants (Volga-Germans). A large number of these immigrants came to the country in the 1960s when Germany was looking to increase its workforce, especially in the industrial sector. Since the decline of this field, many immigrants have lost their jobs and remain in the country in unskilled and low-paying jobs (Ambrosini & Barone, 2007).

Greece's disadvantaged immigrant population is also large (7%) with Albanians, Bulgarians, Georgians, and Romanians. With low levels of job satisfaction throughout the country, immigrants hold a particularly weak segment of the working population. Studies have shown that immigrants in Greece hold largely unprotected jobs (Ambrosini & Barone, 2007). Italy has the Roma group along with immigrants from Albania, Rumania, Morocco, Ukraine, and China. More than 10% of the population of the Netherlands is disadvantaged immigrants. These non-Western immigrants mainly come from Turkey, Morocco, Surinam, and the Antilles/Aruba. Spain also has a large immigrant population, with 9.5% of its population from mainly Morocco, Ecuador, Romania, Colombia, Argentina, Bolivia, China, and Peru. Spain has actually benefited from this influx of new workers; since the mid-1990s, there has been an increase in gross domestic product (GDP) and population growth. Despite these positive outcomes, immigrant workers are still subjected to poor working conditions (e.g., low pay, unskilled jobs, long working hours). Switzerland classifies 21.9% of its population as immigrants, mainly from the former Yugoslavia, Italy, Portugal, and Germany (Myors et al., 2008).

The United Kingdom also has a significant disadvantaged immigrant community. These groups are mainly Indian, Pakistani, black Caribbean, black African, Bangladeshi, and Chinese. Court cases have indicated the presence of adverse impact against these groups in the United Kingdom. For example, in *Panesar v. Nestle Corporation* (1980), a question was raised whether the rule prohibiting employees from having beards created indirect discrimination. It was concluded that individuals with Pakistani origins were more likely than others to have beards, so this rule was found to be discriminatory. A similar decision was made regarding rules against wearing turbans. In *Mandla v. Lee* (1983) and *Singh v. British Rail Engineering*

(1986), evidence was presented demonstrating that the ban on turbans created indirect discrimination toward Sikhs (Makkonen, 2007). Despite these instances, new laws that allow for more immigration have given nonnational workers the opportunity to spread into skilled professions.

In summary, there are multiple disadvantaged subgroups in the European Union. Unlike in the United States, these disadvantaged subgroups are primarily a function of recent changes in European immigration patterns. Further, classification of particular immigrant groups as disadvantaged varies across Europe and appears to be a function of whether the immigrant group is a cultural outsider in these nations. In the next section, we focus on these disadvantaged subgroups and ask whether these subgroups show significantly lower scores on standardized tests.

Manifestation of Average Subgroup Differences on Tests in the European Union

As discussed, subgroup differences are accepted in court as evidence of indirect discrimination. European researchers have found that immigrant minorities perform significantly worse than native majority group members on standardized tests, and that these differences are extremely easy to find on cognitive ability tests (e.g., Helms-Lorenz & van de Vijver, 1995; Roth, Beviert, Bobko, Switzer, & Tyler, 2001). For example, Mackintosh and Mascie-Taylor (1985) reported that there was approximately one standard deviation difference between native-born white English and West Indian children on cognitive ability tests. Interestingly, immigrant East Indian children initially scored approximately the same as the West Indian immigrant children, but the East Indian children's cognitive scores improved after a few years in British schools, and their test scores were soon equivalent to native English.

Studies in the Netherlands have found mean differences on cognitive ability tests between immigrants and native Dutch (te Nijenhuis, 1997; te Nijenhuis, Evers, & Mur, 2000; te Nijenhuis, Tolboom, Resing, & Bleichrodt, 2004; te Nijenhuis & van der Flier, 1997; 1999). Overall, the average cognitive ability score differences of immigrants in the Netherlands were approximately one standard deviation lower than native Dutch residents (te Nijenhuis & van der Flier, 2001, 2003).

Kahn (2004) found significant differences between immigrants and Swiss natives in cognitive ability scores. Further, Kvist and Gotfredsson (2007) found that Swiss natives outperformed both European and non-European immigrants on cognitive ability tests. In general, the immigrants from non-European countries scored the lowest on these tests.

What accounts for these subgroup differences? Not surprisingly, there is no definitive answer to this question, and the entire discussion of causes for these differences is quite controversial. Some researchers have argued that these subgroup differences are attributable to environmental factors. For example, Barber (2005) argued that mean differences in cognitive ability across nations are largely attributable to such environmental factors as enrollment rate differences in secondary education, illiteracy rates, and the proportion of agricultural workers in a nation. Similarly, Ceci (1991) argued that subgroup differences are explainable by differences in the quantity of formal education. Martorell (1998) and Wachs et al. (1996) pointed to nutritional explanations for these subgroup differences. Finally, many researchers (e.g., Helms-Lorenz, 2001; Helms-Lorenz & van de Vijver et al., 2003; Lopez, 1997; Pennock-Roman, 1992; Sandoval & Duran, 1998; van de Vijver et al., 1999) pointed to cultural or language issues on tests as the explanation for mean differences between immigrants and native citizens. For example, Kvist and Gotfredsson (2007) reported that native Swedish individuals outperformed both European and non-European immigrants on measures of crystallized as opposed to fluid intelligence. The differentiation of intelligence into crystallized and fluid components was first proposed by Cattell in the 1970s (Cattell, 1971). According to Cattell, crystallized intelligence is a function of skills and knowledge based on experiences and long-term memory. This type of intelligence is shaped by culture and cultural experiences. Fluid intelligence is categorized as problem-solving ability for confusing and new tasks; thus, fluid intelligence is unchanged by environmental factors (Carroll, 1993; Cattell, 1971; Ferrer & McArdle, 2004).

In contrast to these environmental explanations, other researchers have argued that subgroup mean differences are stable. In other words, these researchers have argued that subgroup mean differences would be larger on fluid intelligence measures. Consistent with this perspective, Rushton, Cvorovic, and Bons (2007) found that the Roma population of Serbia had significantly lower average scores on a supposed fluid intelligence measure compared to native Serbians. These authors argued that these subgroup mean differences could not be accounted for by culture. Similar subgroup mean differences on fluid intelligence have also been found in the Netherlands (te Nijenhuis, 1997; te Nijenhuis & Evers et al., 2000; te Nijenhuis & van der Flier, 1997) and other countries (Ja-Song & Lynn, 1992; Jensen & Whang, 1993; Lynn & Holmshaw, 1990; Nagoshi, Johnson, DeFries, Wilson, & Vandenberg, 1984).

The difficulty in interpreting the cause for the subgroup differences can be illustrated by research done by te Nijenhuis, de Jong, Evers, and van der Flier (2004). In this study, the authors found significant differences in school performance, work proficiency, and cognitive ability among various immigrant subgroups in the Netherlands (i.e., Turks, Moroccans,

Surinamese, Netherlands Antilleans, and Indonesians from the Moluccas) and Dutch natives. However, these discrepancies disappeared when children of these immigrants were examined. At first blush, it would appear that these results could be interpreted as demonstrating the effect of environmental explanations. That is, immigrant children were exposed to the same type of schools and to the same type of cultural environment and nutritional resources as the native Dutch children. However, the authors interpreted their results in terms of self-selection of immigrants. They argued that many of the immigrants to the Netherlands were poor and uneducated, and they specifically migrated to work in unskilled labor jobs. In other words, immigration was a nonrandom sampling process, and it is possible that the first-generation immigrants truly had lower cognitive skills than their compatriots who stayed in their original countries. In other words, the self-selection of individuals may have caused the immigrants to be a nonrepresentative sample of the average cognitive ability in their national country of origin. If that is true, then the subsequent rise in cognitive ability for the immigrant children could be interpreted as simply regression to the cognitive ability mean of the native country of origin. Which is the correct interpretation of these results? It is impossible to determine with only the information collected and provided by the researchers.

The bottom line with regard to the literature reviewed in this section is that the European literature shows that the previously identified disadvantaged groups exhibited significantly lower average scores on standardized tests compared to native subgroups. Indeed, the differences for the European immigrant versus native subgroups are similar in magnitude to the subgroup mean differences reported in the United States.

Unfortunately, while subgroup differences are easy to document, identifying the reason for these differences is difficult, and the European literature discussing this phenomenon is as contentious as it is in the U.S. literature. A great deal of this controversy is probably due to the polarized approach that the various researchers have taken with regard to this issue. That is, researchers are either in the "genetic-only" explanation camp or in the "culture/environment-only" explanation camp. There are signs that this polarization may be diminishing (Rushton & Jensen, 2005). However, what is disappointing about this literature is that very strong conclusions are stated even though the causal factors (i.e., cultural or genetic factors) are never directly measured in these studies.

We believe that the inconsistency in this literature and the lack of direct measurement of the supposed antecedent variables provide an opportunity for a substantial contribution to this literature. Clearly, conducting international studies dramatically reduces any range restriction in cultural or environmental factors typically encountered when research is done in a single country. Further, society-level cultural measures have been developed and refined since the 1970s. Thus, international research has an opportunity to assess cultural explanations of subgroup differences directly. In the final section of this chapter, we start this kind of work by combining the cultural measures from the GLOBE study (House et al., 2004) with some of the existing international adverse impact literature.

Is Culture Related to Adoption of Antidiscrimination Practices and Adverse Impact Around the World?

To what extent are national policies regarding who is protected from discrimination related to societal culture? Some of the literature reviewed in this chapter suggests that there should be a relationship. As discussed, Latvia does not recognize sexual orientation as a characteristic of a protected group, which is in contrast to the rest of the European Union. To what extent are subgroup mean differences on tests attributable to societal culture? Again, as discussed, there are researchers who have argued that culture should be related to subgroup test score differences. Unfortunately, to date there has been no direct attempt to correlate subgroup mean differences with actual measures of societal culture. In this final section, we attempt to bridge these two gaps by combining cultural information from a recent international study on culture and leadership (House et al., 2004) with two published data sets regarding characteristics of protected groups and societal mean differences on cognitive ability tests. These data sets contain information regarding non-E.U. nations. Thus, this section provides truly international information regarding adverse impact and cultural antecedents. We begin with a discussion of the culture measures used.

Societal Culture

The majority of our societal culture measures come from the GLOBE study by House et al. (2004). The GLOBE project was designed to explore issues surrounding leadership and culture. Specifically, the project was designed to address questions such as the following:

- Are there universally accepted and effective leader behaviors/ attributes?
  - Which leader behaviors/attributes are universal, and which are culturally specific?

- Can societal-level differences in leader behaviors/attributes be explained by culture?
  - Does societal-level culture affect desired leader behaviors/attributes?
- Does organizational-level culture affect desired leader behaviors/attributes?

Over 170 researchers from 62 societies were coinvestigators in this project. All coinvestigators participated in survey development, quantitative/qualitative data collection, assessment, and interpretation of the data. The GLOBE data were collected from over 17,000 middle managers in over 1,000 organizations located in 1 of 62 societies (House et al., 2004).

A total of 18 different societal culture scales were developed (Hanges & Dickson, 2004). Nine of these scales captured participants' perceptions of their societal culture as it is now (i.e., societal cultural practices), and the remaining nine scales assessed respondents' perceptions of their societal culture as it should be (i.e., societal cultural values). Table 13.1 shows

TABLE 13.1

Definitions of the GLOBE Cultural Scales

GLOBE culture dimension	Definition
Assertiveness	The degree to which individuals are assertive, confrontational, and aggressive in their relationship with others
Collectivism 1 (institutional collectivism)	The degree to which organizational and societal institutional practices encourage and reward collective distribution of resources and collective action
Collectivism 2 (ingroup collectivism)	The degree to which individuals express pride, loyalty, and cohesiveness in their organizations or families
Future Orientation	The extent to which individuals engage in future-oriented behaviors such as delaying gratification, planning, and investing in the future
Gender Egalitarianism	The degree to which a collective minimizes gender inequality
Humane Orientation	The degree to which a collective encourages and rewards individuals for being fair, altruistic, generous, caring, and kind to others
Performance Orientation	The degree to which a collective encourages and rewards group members for performance improvement and excellence
Power Distance	The degree to which members of a collective expect power to be distributed unequally
Uncertainty Avoidance	The extent to which a society, organization, or group relies on social norms, rules, and procedures to alleviate unpredictability of future events

the nine GLOBE cultural value dimensions and their definitions. For each dimension, a societal cultural practice and a societal cultural value were developed. The procedure used to develop these scales, their psychometric properties, and evidence concerning their construct validity is discussed in the work of Hanges and Dickson (2004, 2006).

In addition to the GLOBE cultural value scales, we accessed Gelfand, Nishii, and Raver's (2006) measure of cultural tightness-looseness. Cultural tightness-looseness is a function of the specificity and prevalence of social norms (i.e., strength of norms) as well as the severity of consequences for violating these norms (Gelfand et al., 2006). A new six-item measure of this construct was developed by Gelfand, Nishii, and Raver in 2008, and they reported that this scale has excellent psychometric properties.

We explore the relationship between societal culture and the types of legislation protecting discrimination against various subgroup characteristics next.

Societal Culture and Characteristics of Protected Groups

Myors et al. (2008) reviewed the antidiscrimination policies and procedures of 22 countries. These countries consisted of 10 E.U. nations (i.e., Belgium, France, Germany, Greece, Italy, Netherlands, Spain, Switzerland, Turkey, United Kingdom); 3 additional Anglo nations (i.e., Australia, Canada, New Zealand); 3 Asian countries (i.e., Japan, Korea, Taiwan); 2 African countries (i.e., Kenya, South Africa); along with Chile, India, and Israel. Table 3 of Myors et al. (2008) provides a listing of the most common characteristics for protected subgroups in each of these countries. Specifically, this table lists whether each country has legislation that protects race, color, religion, gender, national origin, age, disability status, political opinion, sexual orientation, and marital/family status.

A total of 20 countries were in common between the Myors et al. (2008) and the GLOBE (House et al., 2004) databases. The three countries excluded were Belgium, Chile, and Kenya. It should be noted that GLOBE included two South African and German samples. For purposes of our analyses, we used the GLOBE white South African and the GLOBE West German data. A total of 16 countries were in common between the Myors et al. and the Gelfand et al. (2008) databases. The six countries excluded were Canada, Chile, Kenya, South Africa, Switzerland, and Taiwan. We correlated the Myors et al. binary variables with each of the culture scales.

These analyses revealed several significant findings. For example, legislation protecting race was less likely in "tighter" nations ($r = -0.55$, $p < 0.05$) and nations with assertive cultural values ($r = -0.75$, $p < 0.01$). Nations with assertive cultural practices, however, were more likely to have legislation protecting race ($r = 0.56$, $p < 0.01$). Legislation against gender discrimination was more likely in nations with performance-oriented cultural practices ($r = 0.61$, $p < 0.01$) and institutional collectivistic practices ($r = 0.51$, $p < 0.01$). Legislation protecting against discrimination on the basis of national origin was less likely in cultures with future-oriented cultural values ($r = -0.48$, $p < 0.05$). Legislation protecting against discrimination on the basis of sexual orientation was less likely in tighter nations ($r = -0.57$, $p < 0.05$). Legislation protecting against discrimination on the basis of color was less likely in nations with institutional collectivistic cultural values ($r = -0.47$, $p < 0.05$). Legislation protecting against discrimination on the basis of disability was more likely in nations with uncertainty avoidance cultural practices. Finally, legislation protecting against discrimination on the basis of age was less likely in tighter nations ($r = -0.53$, $p < 0.05$), nations with institutional collectivistic cultural values ($r = -0.44$, $p < 0.05$), and nations with ingroup collectivistic cultural practices ($r = -0.47$, $p < 0.05$).

In summary, we found some evidence for the kinds of legislation passed by nations to be related to culture. While some readers may be disappointed by the number of significant correlations, it should be noted that the statistical power associated with the conventional α of 0.05 and 20 data points is only 37%. Thus, the present results should be interpreted as promising but tentative. We found evidence that culture affects the nature of legislative actions taken by nations. However, more data are needed to enable firmer statements regarding both the nature of the legislation that is susceptible to culture and the magnitude of these relationships.

Relationship Between Societal Culture and Cognitive Ability Test Scores

In this section, we examine the relationship between environmental factors, such as culture, national productivity, and adverse impact. The ideal database to understand the effect of the environment on adverse impact would consist of estimates of subgroup mean differences along with multiple measures of these environmental factors. Unfortunately, we did not have access to such a database. However, we did come across another database that we thought might provide some suggestive information regarding our primary question. Specifically, Lynn and Vanhanen (2002) created an international database consisting of national GDP information and average cognitive ability scores for 185 nations. These authors were interested in whether national IQ and national productivity (i.e., GDP) were related. They found a strong correlation between national IQ and GDP ($r = 0.62$, $p < 0.001$).

Templer and Arikawa (2006) extended this work by developing a measure of "preponderant" skin color for most of the nations in the Lynn and Vanhanen (2002) database. They developed their skin color measure in the following manner:

> A physical anthropology source was used to obtain data on skin color (Biasutti, 1967). ... The source contains a map of the world with eight categories of skin color ranging from 1 (very light) to 8 (very dark). Because the map does not delineate the various countries of the world, three graduate students who were unaware of the purpose of our study independently determined skin color for each of the 129 countries. The product-moment correlation coefficients between raters were 0.95, 0.95, and 0.93, suggesting very little subjectivity. (p. 122)

Using this measure, the authors reported that skin color had a significant negative correlation with average national IQ ($r = -0.92$, $p < 0.001$).

We are confident that any reader of this chapter will not be surprised to learn that the Templer and Arikawa (2006) article is quite controversial. Indeed, strong objections to the skin color measure in particular, and to the entire study in general, were immediately published by Hunt and Sternberg (2006). We completely agree that there are problems with the Templer and Arikawa study. Our issues with this study surround questions of statistical conclusion validity, construct validity, and internal validity problems. For example, several questions about levels of analysis (e.g., is there evidence that skin color aggregates to the national level?), construct validity of the study's measures (e.g., is there evidence that the 1967 anthropological map of skin color is still meaningful in 2006?), and research design can be easily raised. We tend to agree with Hunt and Sternberg's critique of the Templer and Arikawa study. However, despite these limitations, we used this database primarily because of the ridiculously large negative correlation between skin color and cognitive ability.

The GLOBE database (House et al., 2004) and the Templer and Arikawa (2006) database had 34 nations in common.[2] In addition to national skin color and cognitive ability scores, we also had access to another environmental variable, GDP. However, because of the dramatic range in GDP across nations, we followed the suggestion by Hunt and Wittmann (2008) and transformed GDP by taking the logarithm to the base 10 of this variable for our analyses.

We conducted a hierarchical regression predicting national IQ with three blocks of variables. The first block consisted of the GLOBE culture variables. We did not have any hypotheses regarding specific cultural dimensions and national IQ. We therefore entered the culture variables in this block in a stepwise regression fashion. The second block of variables consisted of GDP. The final block entered into the regression consisted of Templer and Arikawa's (2006) skin color variable.

The stepwise regression analysis only selected three societal culture variables in the first block of our analysis. Specifically, future-oriented societal values, institutional collective societal practices, and assertive societal practices accounted for a remarkable 49% of the variance in national IQ (incremental $F(3, 28) = 8.77$, $p < 0.01$). The next block, which consisted of the log of GDP, added an additional 15.8% of the variance in the prediction of national IQ (incremental $F(1, 27) = 11.92$, $p < 0.01$). Finally, the last block consisting of skin color still added a significant amount of variance to the prediction of national IQ (incremental $F(1, 26) = 9.39$, $p < 0.01$); it only accounted for an additional 9.5% of the variance in national IQ.

In summary, both the previous analysis that examined the subgroup characteristics protected by law in various nations and the present analysis that explored national IQ demonstrated that societal culture is an important factor. Indeed, in the national IQ analysis, just three dimensions of societal culture accounted for almost half of the variance in national IQ. Once GDP was entered into the equation, the environmental factors accounted for the majority (i.e., 64.2%) of the variance in national IQ. This remarkable level of explained variance was obtained by only testing for main effects of the environmental factors. The contribution of interactions among these variables will have to wait until a larger database is found.

Conclusion

In this chapter, we examined how E.U. nations conceptualized adverse impact. We started by arguing that a review of the international literature might broaden our understanding of this construct, identify unique strategies for reducing it, and yield new insights into its cause. After reviewing this literature, we believe that the E.U. literature has delivered on only some of these promises. Specifically, it appears that only the middle promise (i.e., yielding new insights into its cause) may have been kept.

The first promise (i.e., broadening our understanding of the construct) has not appeared to bear fruit. Indeed, there the conceptualization of adverse impact in the European Union and the United States appears to be almost completely identical. Similar to the United States, the European Union has defined adverse impact as an organizational policy or procedure that has substantially more negative consequences for one or more minority subgroups compared to the majority/native subgroup. Similar to the United States, statistical information can be used to establish adverse impact. Similar to the United States, demonstration of adverse impact shifts the burden of proof to the defendant, who is required to demonstrate validity for the questioned organizational policy or procedure. Thus, it appears that this international review has accomplished the first goal; namely, extending the conceptualization of this construct. It should be noted that we did find a minor difference between how the European Union and the United States conceptualizes adverse impact.

While the United States has a uniform standard (four-fifths rule or sta-tistical demonstration of differential consequences), Europe lacks such a uniform standard. It is up to each E.U. nation to determine the critical magnitude of subgroup differences that can be labeled adverse impact. This lack of uniformity is not surprising given that the European Union is a relatively new bonding of nations. Indeed, the first elected E.U. parlia-ment was formed only in 1979. It would be extremely surprising if the E.U. nations had completely worked out their differences on this topic in only 30 years.

With regard to the second promise of cross-cultural literature (i.e., identify new strategies for reducing it), we failed to find anything dif-ferent from how adverse impact issues are resolved in the United States. However, we believe that some fulfillment of the third promise (i.e., yield new insights into its cause) has been made. As we discussed, the E.U. nations have identified a number of subgroups as disadvantaged (e.g., Albanians, Georgians, Roma, Turks). What is important to note is that the particular subgroup labeled disadvantaged varies across the E.U. nations. The one characteristic that might cut across all of these subgroups is that they are of lower social status than the majority group. This social status differential is probably linked to differential educational opportunities (as documented in the *D.H. and Others v. the Czech Republic* (2007) court case), illiteracy rates, language difficulties, and the ability to obtain desir-able resources. The magnitude of these adverse impact differences do appear to disappear by the second or third generation. Thus, in the E.U. nations, it does appear that adverse impact is substantially diminished once immigrant children have become acculturated into their new nation. Given that the magnitude of adverse impact for the E.U. immigrant sub-groups is approximately equal to the U.S. black–white differences, one can reasonably ask what is unique about the American society that the magni-tude of adverse impact has not dissipated over the years?

In the United States, social status is determined largely by wealth. Wealthy individuals live in environments with more opportunities for education and jobs, while the lower class has fewer educational and job opportunities. In the United States, race and social status are highly con-founded, and the direction of this confound has been fairly consistent, on average, over the last 100 years. Perhaps the lesson from the international literature is that social status and the stability of status differentials over the generations play a big role in the relative stability of adverse impact on various standardized tests.

The statistical analyses performed in this chapter help to bolster this argument. The finding that societal culture accounts for nearly 50% of the variance in national IQ differences and that another environmental factor (i.e., GDP) accounts for an additional 15.8% suggests that environmental factors can have a large influence on adverse impact. While promising, it needs repeating that these analyses can only be considered tentative. A more substantial follow-up is needed.

Finally, we believe that continued exploration of adverse impact across different countries will yield additional insights. However, the benefit of this approach can only be realized when future adverse impact research is designed to test hypotheses cross-culturally.

Acknowledgment

We thank Juliet Aiken and Andrew Schmidt for their helpful comments on an earlier version of this chapter.

Notes

1. A *situation test* refers to an evaluation by a nonpartisan third party who assesses whether the organizational procedures and outcomes are discriminatory (Makkonen, 2007).
2. While the original Lynn and Vanhanen (2002) database contained 185 countries, Templer and Arikawa (2006) only used the 129 countries for which the average IQ score could be attributed to the indigenous population.

References

Ambrosini, M., & Barone, C. (2007). *Employment and working conditions of migrant workers*. Dublin, Ireland: European Foundation for the Improvement of Living and Working Conditions.

Aramburu-Zabala Higuera, L. (2001). Adverse impact in personnel selection: The legal framework and test bias. *European Psychologist, 6*, 103–111.

Barber, N. (2005). Educational and ecological correlates of IQ: A cross-national investigation. *Intelligence, 33*, 273–284.

Belgium Anti-Discrimination Act of 2003.

Biasutti, R. (1967). *Le Razze e I Popoli Della Terra*. Torino, Italy: Unione pipografiza-Editrice Torinese.

Bilka-Kaufhaus GmbH v. Karin Weber von Hartz (Case 170/84) ECR 1607 (1986).

Bureau of Labor Statistics. (2008). U.S unemployment rate. Retrieved May 18, 2008, from http://www.bls.gov/

Carrington, W. J., & DeLima, P. J. F. (1996). The impact of 1970s repatriates from Africa on the Portuguese labor market. *Industrial and Labor Relations Review, 49*, 330–347.

Carroll, J. B. (1993). *Human cognitive abilities: A survey of factor-analytic studies.* Cambridge: Cambridge University Press.

Cattell, R. B. (1971). *Abilities: Their structure, growth, and action.* New York: Houghton-Mifflin.

Ceci, S. J. (1991). How much does schooling influence general intelligence and its cognitive components? A reassessment of the evidence. *Developmental Psychology, 27*, 703–723.

Constitution of the United Kingdom of Belgium, Art. 10, 11, 191 (1994).

Cook, T. D., & Campbell, D. T. (1979). *Quasi-experimentation: Design and analysis for field settings.* Chicago: Rand McNally.

Cormack, J., & Bell, M. (2005). *Developing anti-discrimination law in Europe.* Brussels: Human European Consultancy and Migration Policy Group.

Council of Europe. (1950). *European convention for the protection of human rights and fundamental freedoms.* ETS 5, Article 14.

D.H. and Others v. the Czech Republic, Case 57325/00 [2007] ECHR.

Ellis, E. (2005). *EU anti-discrimination law.* Oxford: Oxford University Press.

European Commission. (1996). *Annual report of the commission: Equal opportunities between women and men at the European Union.* Brussels: COM(96) 650 final.

European Communities. (1992) *Treaty on European Union.* Maastricht, The Netherlands.

European Communities. (1997). Treaty *of Amsterdam amending the Treaty on European Union, the treaties establishing the European Communities and certain related acts.* Amsterdam, The Netherlands.

European Communities. (2000a). *Council Directive 2000/43/EC implementing the principle of equal treatment between persons irrespective of racial or ethnic origin.*

European Communities. (2000b). *Council Directive 2000/78/EC establishing a general framework for equal treatment in employment and occupation.*

European Economic Community. (1957). *The treaty establishing the European economic community.* Rome, Italy.

European Roma Rights Center. (2004). *Interights. Migration policy group. Strategic litigation in Europe: From principles to practice.* Nottingham, U.K.: Russell Press.

Ferrari, S., Corbetta, F., & Parolin, G. (2002). The situation of Muslims in Italy. In *Monitoring the EU accession process: Minority protection volume II* (Case Studies in Selected Member States by Open Society Institute). Budapest: Open Society Institute.

Ferrer, E., & McArdle, J. J. (2004). An experimental analysis of dynamic hypotheses about cognitive abilities and achievement from childhood to early adulthood. *Developmental Psychology, 40*, 935–952.

French Constitution of 1958.

Gelfand, M. J., Nishii, L., & Raver, J. (2006). On the nature and importance of cultural tightness-looseness. *Journal of Applied Psychology, 91*, 1225–1244.

Gelfand, M. J., Nishii, L., & Raver, J. (2008, April). Unpublished data presented at the 23rd Annual Conference of the Society for Industrial and Organizational Psychology, San Francisco, CA.

General Board Employment and Labor Market. (2006).

Goldston, J. A. (2008). *The European Union race directive.* Retrieved May 8, 2008, from http://www.justiceinitiative.org/activities/ec/ec_russia/moscow_workshop/ goldston_moscow

Griggs vs. Duke Power Company, 401 U.S. 424 (1971).

Hanges, P. J., Braverman, E. P., & Rentsch, J. R. (1991). Changes in raters' impressions of subordinates: A catastrophe model. *Journal of Applied Psychology, 76,* 878–888.

Hanges, P. J., & Dickson, M. W. (2004). The development and validation of the GLOBE culture and leadership scales. In R. J. House, P. J. Hanges, M. Javidan, P. W. Dorfman, & V. Gupta (Eds.), *Leadership, culture, and organizations: The GLOBE study of 62 societies* (pp. 122–151). Thousand Oaks, CA: Sage.

Hanges, P. J., Lord, R. G., & Dickson, M. W. (2000). An information processing perspective on leadership and culture: A case for connectionist architecture. *Applied Psychology: An International Review, 49,* 133–161.

Hanges, P. J., Lord, R. G., Godfrey, E. G., & Raver, J. L. (2002). Modeling nonlinear relationships: Neural networks and catastrophe analysis. In S. Rogelberg (Ed.), *Handbook of research methods in industrial and organizational psychology* (pp. 431–455). Malden, MA: Blackwell.

Helms-Lorenz, M. (2001). *Assessing cultural influences on cognitive test performance: A study with migrant children in the Netherlands.* Tilburg, Germany: Tilburg University.

Helms-Lorenz, M., & van de Vijver, F. (1995). Cognitive assessment in education in a multicultural society. *European Journal of Psychological Assessment, 11,* 158–169.

Helms-Lorenz, M., van de Vijver, F. J. R., & Poortinga, Y. H. (2003). Cross-cultural differences in cognitive performance and Spearsman's hypothesis: g or c? *Intelligence, 31,* 9–29.

Heneman, G. H., & Heneman, R. L. (1994). *Staffing organizations.* Middleton, WI: Mendota House.

Hofstede, G. (1980). *Culture's consequences: International differences in work-related values.* Newbury Park, CA: Sage.

Hough, L. M., Oswald, F. L., & Ployhart, R. E. (2001). Determinants, detection, and amelioration of adverse impact in personnel selection procedures: Issues, evidence, and lessons learned. *International Journal of Selection and Assessment, 9,* 152–194.

House, R. J., Hanges, P. J., Javidan, M., Dorfman, P. W., & Gupta, V. (2004). *Culture, leadership, and organizations: The GLOBE study of 62 societies.* Thousand Oaks, CA: Sage.

Hunt, E., & Sternberg, R. J. (2006), Sorry, wrong numbers: An analysis of a study of a correlation between skin color and IQ. *Intelligence, 34,* 131–137.

Hunt, E., & Wittmann, W. (2008). National intelligence and national prosperity. *Intelligence, 36,* 1–9.

Hunter, J., & Hunter, R. (1984). Validity and utility of alternative predictors of job performance. *Psychological Bulletin, 96,* 72–98.

International Labor Organization. (1981, June). International Convention of the International Labor Organization, Geneva, Switzerland.

Ja-Song, M., & Lynn, R. (1992). Reaction times and intelligence in Korean children. *Journal of Psychology, 126*, 421–428.

Jenkins v. Kingsgate (Clothing Production) Inc., Case 96/80 ECR 911 (1981).

Jensen, A. R., & Whang, P. A. (1993). Reaction times and intelligence. A comparison of Chinese-American and Anglo-American children. *Journal of Biosocial Science 25*, 397–410.

Kahn, L. M. (2004). Immigration, skills, and the labor market: International evidence. *Journal of Population Economics, 17*, 501–534.

Kende, A., & Nemenyi, M. (2006). Selection in education: The case of Roma children in Hungary. *Equal Opportunities International, 25*, 506–522.

Kvist, A. V., & Gotfredsson, J. E. (2007). *The relation between fluid intelligence and the general factor as a function of cultural background: A test of Cattell's investment theory.* Uppsala, Sweden: Institute for Labour Market Policy Evaluation.

Laczko, F. (2002). New directions for migration policy in Europe. *Philosophical Transactions: Biological Sciences, 357*, 599–608.

Lavrikovs, J. (2006). Latvia desperately wants to keep title of the homophobic bastion of the European Union. Equality for lesbian, gay, bisexual, and transgender people in Europe. Retrieved May 18, 2008, from http://www. ilga-europe.org/europe/media/latvia_desperately_wants_to_keep_title_ of_the_homophobic_ bastion_of_ the european_union

Lopez, E. C. (1997). The cognitive assessment of limited English proficient and bilingual children. In D. P. Flanagan, J. L. Genshaft, & P. L. Harrison (Eds.), *Contemporary intellectual assessment: Theories, tests, and issues* (pp. 503–516). New York: Guilford Press.

Lynn, R., & Holmshaw, 1990. Black-white differences in reaction times and intelligence. *Social Behavior and Personality, 18*, 299–308.

Lynn, R., & Vanhanen, R. (2002). *IQ and the wealth of nations.* Westport, CT: Praeger.

Mackintosh, N. J., & Mascie-Taylor, C. G. N. (1985). The IQ question. In *Report of a Committee of Inquiry into the education of children from ethnic minorities* (pp. 126–163). London: Her Majesty's Stationery Office.

Makkonen, T. (2007). *Measuring discrimination: Data collection and EU equality law.* Luxembourg: European Commission.

Mandla vs. Dowell Lee, IRLR 209 (HL) (1983).

Martorell, R. (1998). Nutrition and the worldwide rise in IQ scores. In U. Neisser (Ed.), *The rising curve: Long-term gains in IQ and related measures* (pp. 183–206). Washington, DC: American Psychological Association.

Myors, B., Lievens, F., Schollaert, E., Van Hoye, G., Cronshaw, S. F., Mladinic, A., et al. (2008). International perspective on the legal environment for selection. *Industrial and Organizational Psychology: Perspectives on Science and Practice, 1*, 266–270.

Nagoshi, C. T., Johnson, R. C., DeFries, J. C., Wilson H. R., & Vandenberg, S. G. (1984). Group differences and principal-component loadings in the Hawaii family study of cognition: A test of the generality of "spearman's hypothesis." *Personality and Individual Differences, 5*, 751–753.

Okkerse, L., & Termote, A. (2004). How alien is alien in the labor market? *Statistische Studiën*, nr. 111, tevens verschenen in het Frans in de reeks. *Etudes statistiques*, NIS.

Panesar vs. Nestle Corporation, IRLR 64 CA (1980).

Pennock-Roman, M. (1992). Interpreting test performance in selective admissions for Hispanic students. In K. F. Geisinger (Ed.), *Psychological testing of Hispanics* (pp. 95–135). Washington, DC: American Psychological Association.

Ployhart, R. E., & Holtz, B. C. (2008). The diversity-validity dilemma: Strategies for reducing racio-ethnic and sex subgroup differences and adverse impact in selection. *Personnel Psychology, 61*, 153–172.

Roth, P. L., Beviert, C. A., Bobko, P., Switzer, F. S., & Tyler, P. (2001). Ethnic group difference in cognitive ability in employment and educational settings: A meta-analysis. *Personnel Psychology, 54*, 297–330.

Rushton, J. P., Cvorovic, J., & Bons, T. A. (2007). General mental ability in South Asians: Data from three Roma (gypsy) communities in Serbia. *Intelligence, 35*, 1–12.

Rushton, J. P., & Jensen, A. R. (2005). Wanted: More race realism, less moralistic fallacy. *Psychology Public Policy and Law, 11*, 328–336.

Sandoval, J., & Duran, R. P. (1998). Language. In J. H. Sandoval, C. L. Frisby, K. F. Geisinger, J. D. Scheuneman, & J. R. Grenier (Eds.), *Test interpretation and diversity: Achieving equity in assessment* (pp. 181–211). Washington, DC: American Psychological Association.

Shadish, W. R., Cook, T. D., & Campbell, D. T. (2002). *Experimental and quasi-experimental designs for generalized causal inference*. Boston: Houghton-Mifflin.

Sheeter, L. (2006). Lativia defies EU over gay rights. BBC News Online. Retrieved May 15, 2008, from http://news.bbc.co.uk/1/hi/world/europe/5084832.stm

Simoni, A. (2003). Executive summary on race equality directive. Retrieved May 19, 2008, from http://ec.europa.eu/employment_social/ fundamental_rights/ pdf/aneval/italy.pdf

Singh v. British Rail Engineering Ltd., ICR 22 (1986).

Smith, T. (1997). Recognizing difference: The Romani "gypsy" child socialization and education process. *British Journal of Sociology of Education, 18*, 243–256.

Templer, D. I., & Arikawa, H. (2006). Temperature, skin color, per capita income, and IQ: An international perspective. *Intelligence, 34*, 121–139.

te Nijenhuis, J. (1997). *Comparability of test scores for immigrants and majority group members in the Netherlands*. Unpublished doctoral dissertation, Vrije Universteit, Amsterdam, The Netherlands.

te Nijenhuis, J., de Jong, M. J., Evers, A., & van der Flier, H. (2004). Are cognitive differences between immigrant and majority groups diminishing? *European Journal of Personality, 18*, 405–434.

te Nijenhuis, J., Evers, A., & Mur, J. P. (2000). Validity of the differential aptitude test for immigrant children. *Educational Psychology, 20*, 99–115.

te Nijenhuis, J., Tolboom, E. A., Resing, W. C., & Bleichrodt, N. (2004). Does cultural background influence the intellectual performance of children from immigrant groups?: Validity of the RAKIT intelligence test for immigrant children. *European Journal of Psychological Assessment, 20*, 10–26.

te Nijenhuis, J., & van der Flier, H. (1997). Comparability of GATB scores for immigrants and majority group members: Some Dutch findings. *Journal of Applied Psychology, 82*, 675–687.

te Nijenhuis, J., & van der Flier, H. (1999). Bias research in the Netherlands: Review and implications. *European Journal of Psychological Assessment, 15*, 165–175.

te Nijenhuis, J., & van der Flier, H. (2001). Group differences in mean intelligence for the Dutch and third world immigrants. *Journal of Biosocial Science, 33,* 469–475.

te Nijenhuis, J., & van der Flier, H. (2003). Immigrant-majority group differences in cognitive performance: Jensen effects, cultural effects, or both? *Intelligence, 31,* 443–459.

United States Census Bureau. (2008). State and County QuickFacts. Retrieved May 18, 2008, from http://quickfacts.census.gov/qfd/states/00000.html

van de Vijver, F., Helms-Lorenz, M., & Feltzer, M. J. A. (1999). Acculturation and cognitive performance of migrant children in the Netherlands. *International Journal of Psychology, 34,* 149–162.

Viprey, M. (2002). New anti-discrimination law adopted. European Industrial Relations Observatory online. Retrieved May 19, 2008, from http://www.eurofound.europa.eu/eiro/2001/12/feature/fr0112152f.htm

Wachs, T. D., McCabe, G., Mousa, W., Yunis, F., Kirksey, A., Galal, O., et al. (1996). Cognitive performance of Egyptian adults as a function of nutritional intake and sociodemographic factors. *Intelligence, 22,* 129–154.

Zegers de Beijl, R. (2000). *Documenting discrimination against migrant workers in the labour market: A comparative study of four European countries.* Geneva: International Labor Organization.

14

Adverse Impact in South Africa

Hennie Kriek and Kim Dowdeswell

Introduction

South Africa is a multicultural population, encompassing more than 47 million people of diverse origins, including four major ethnic groups and 11 official languages. The country has had a long history of segregation and racial strife between the different racial groups, culminating in the segregationist laws collectively known as apartheid, which were instituted in 1948 by the National Party. During the late 1980s and early 1990s, the laws of apartheid were progressively relaxed, leading to the first free and fair democratic elections held in 1994.

Although apartheid has been demolished, the legacy of apartheid still remains in South Africa. One of the most apparent areas in which this legacy manifests is the income distribution in the country, which is one of the most unequal income distribution patterns in the world. In 2004, it was reported that approximately 60% of the population earned less than R. 42,000 (about U.S. $7,000) per annum, while 2.2% of the population had an income exceeding R. 360,000 (about U.S. $50,000) per annum (World Socialist Web site, 2004).

During the apartheid regime, blacks were forced to go to "Bantu" schools where the educational level was very poor, and the white government reserved skilled work for the whites. The policy of the black schools was aimed to direct the black youth to the unskilled labor market, preparing blacks for lives as a laboring class (Rebirth Africa, 2000). The whites were and still are referred to as the advantaged minority, and the blacks (encompassing Africans, coloreds, and Indians as per the definition in the Employment Equity Act No. 55 of 1998) as the disadvantaged majority. The 2007 midyear estimated figures for these racial categories were 79.6% African, 9.1% white, 8.9% colored, and 2.5% Indian (Statistics

South Africa, 2007b). This racial distribution—the disadvantaged being the majority and the advantaged being the minority—contrasts with much of the rest of the developed world, where the disadvantaged group is usually in the minority.

The National Party began abolishing the laws that defined apartheid in 1990, following a long and sometimes violent struggle as well as economic sanctions from the international community. The first democratic election in the history of South Africa took place in 1994, marking the beginning of a societywide transformation as the country moved peacefully from minority white to majority black rule. The African National Congress emerged with a majority victory, and South Africa embarked on a program to promote reconstruction and development for the previously disadvantaged in an attempt to integrate the country into a rapidly changing global environment (Government Communication and Information Systems, 2007). Affirmative action was introduced into the labor market to redress the mistakes of the past.

Promoting and achieving equality in the workplace—termed *equity* in South Africa—became a legal and social imperative for organizations. However, the demand for achieving transformation and diversity in the workplace has in some respects led to a shift in focus: Organizations' goals in recruitment and selection have tended to shift from getting the "best" people to getting the "right" people, with right defined in terms of employment equity requirements. This challenges the organization's desire to maximize utility when selecting on the basis of instruments with strong predictive validity, which has resulted in an ongoing debate regarding the place of preemployment testing and psychological assessment in the country.

Not surprisingly, political dispensations have historically influenced and shaped psychological assessment and test development in South Africa. Foxcroft (1997) described how, in such a deeply segregated society, it was almost inevitable that psychological tests were developed in line with the segregation of the races. This has resulted in psychometric practice and psychological assessment in particular having a poor track record in the country as the practice is considered a tool of the politics and policies of apartheid. Possibly the most damaging to public perception of assessments was "the misuse of test results to reach conclusions about differences between groups without considering the impact of *inter alia* cultural, socio-economic, environmental, and educational factors on test performance" (Foxcroft & Roodt, 2005, p. 16).

The following sections explore the legal context within which employment practices are conducted in South Africa, together with how organizations are using preemployment tests and assessment instruments to effect transformation and achieve an equitable distribution of jobs across South Africa's rainbow nation.

The Legislative Context in South Africa

Subsequent to the 1994 democratic elections, the context has shifted away from job reservation and preferential treatment of whites to the prohibition of unfair discrimination for all, barring actions taken to further affirmative action and employment equity.

On May 26, 1994, South Africa was readmitted as a member of the International Labor Organization (ILO), following a period of 30 years of isolation from international labor forums after the country withdrew due to political pressures. The ILO criticized South Africa's previous Labour Relations Act (No. 28 of 1956), as it did not cover all situations and had material defects, which led to the promulgation of the new Labour Relations Act (No. 66 of 1995). This act, together with the Constitution of South Africa (No. 108 of 1996) and the Employment Equity Act (No. 55 of 1998), form the basis of South African legislation governing the employment relationship.

In short, the Bill of Rights (Chapter 2 of the Constitution of South Africa, 1996) enshrines each South African's right to fair labor practices. The Labour Relations Act (1995) protects employees' rights not to be unfairly dismissed or subjected to unfair labor practices, and the aim of the Employment Equity Act (1998) is to promote fairness and equality in the workplace. These laws cover all employers in South Africa, with the only exceptions being the National Defense Force, National Intelligence Agency, and the South African Secret Service. The laws cover all aspects of employment practices, which include but are not limited to (a) recruitment procedures, advertising, and selection criteria; (b) appointments and the appointment process; (c) job classification and grading; (d) remuneration, employment benefits, and terms and conditions of employment; (e) job assignments; (f) the working environment and facilities; (g) training and development; (h) performance evaluation systems; (i) promotion; (j) transfer; (k) demotion; (l) disciplinary measures other than dismissal; and (m) dismissal.

The changes brought about in South Africa's labor legislation by these acts have caused some degree of concern and uncertainty among employers, specifically among test users, regarding the legal and fair usage of preemployment tests. The present government in South Africa has taken a firm stance against the misuse of assessment in the workplace, especially on matters covered in the Employment Equity Act.

The Employment Equity Act (No. 55 of 1998)

The Employment Equity Act (1998) was introduced to promote fairness and equality in the workplace. The ways in which the act proposes to achieve equity (Section 2) are twofold, by (a) eliminating unfair discrimination in employment practices and procedures (occupational assessment procedures are subsumed under this term) and (b) implementing affirmative action measures to redress the imbalances and inequities in employment encountered by members of previously disadvantaged groups. While the Employment Equity Act per se does not provide a formal definition of what is meant by "affirmative action," summaries of key topics in South African labor legislation have been published in a series of basic guidelines. Therein, affirmative action is described as the process that "makes sure that qualified designated groups (black people, women and people with disabilities) have equal opportunities to get a job" (South African Department of Labor, 2004).

In the *Basic Guide to Affirmative Action* (South African Department of Labor, 2004), employers are tasked to "find and remove things that badly affect designated groups; support diversity through equal dignity and respect to all people; make changes to ensure designated groups have equal chances; ensure equal representation of designated groups in all job categories and levels in the workplace; and retain and develop designated groups." This is supported by Section 5 of the Employment Equity Act, which addresses the elimination of unfair discrimination in employment practices:

> Every employer must take steps to promote equal opportunity in the workplace by eliminating unfair discrimination in any employment policy or practice. (p. 14)

Section 6 of the act deals with the prohibition of unfair discrimination based on arbitrary grounds. According to this section, no person may unfairly discriminate, directly or indirectly, against any employee in any employment policy or practice, on one or more arbitrary grounds, including race, gender, and other protected categories (which include pregnancy, marital status, family responsibility, ethnic or social origin, color, sexual orientation, age, disability, religion, HIV status, conscience, belief, political opinion, culture, language, and birth). While the act does not provide definitions for all the categories listed, family responsibility, for example, is viewed as "the responsibility of employees in relation to their spouse or partner, their dependant children or other members of their immediate family who need their care or support" (p. 10).

However, it is not considered unfair discrimination to take affirmative action measures consistent with the purpose of the Employment Equity Act or distinguish, exclude, or prefer any person on the basis of an inherent requirement of a job. The Employment Equity Act therefore allows for legal discrimination against white males, and to a lesser extent white females, if it is based on a clearly defined affirmative action policy within the organization. A South African trade union, Solidarity, reports on figures that reflect the effect of such policies: From 2001 to 2006, there was a 55.99% increase in African males alone in top management positions, while during the same time period the number of white males in these positions decreased by 22.85% (Herman, Du Plooy, & Calldo, 2007).

The decline of whites in South Africa is not only observed in top management positions. In an article, "Where Have All the Whites Gone?" by Sharon Dell and published in the *Weekend Witness* (January 9, 2006), a decline in the white population in South Africa was investigated. According to the South African Institute of Race Relations, the white population of the country dropped by almost a million (841,000) from 1995 to 2005. Among a number of issues Dell explored regarding why such a decline took place, including HIV infections and birth rate, the conclusion reached was that the only likely explanation for the decline in numbers was emigration. The argument was made that there are both pull factors, such as a demand for skills in industrial countries overseas, and push factors, such as affirmative action, that are influencing the emigration of the white population.

Concerning preemployment testing and assessment, the first draft of the Employment Equity Act (1998) unilaterally banned psychological assessment in industry. The wording of the act was only amended to its present form after Parliament considered submissions made by psychologists from the Professional Board, the Psychological Society of South Africa, the Psychological Assessment Initiative, and others working in industry. Section 8 of the act, also falling under the chapter relating to the prohibition of unfair discrimination, now makes specific provision for both psychological testing and other similar assessments:

> Psychological testing and other similar assessments of an employee are prohibited unless the test or assessment being used:
>
> 1. has been scientifically shown to be valid and reliable;
> 2. can be applied fairly to all employees; and
> 3. is not biased against any employee or group. (p. 16)

With the promulgation of the act in 1998, users of preemployment testing and assessments and organizations braced themselves for a deluge of court cases. However, there is very little to no case law relating specifically to employment testing. Bam (2007) could not find any cases to date in the South African Labour Court dealing with Section 8 of the Employment Equity Act. The closest he found were two arbitration cases for which testing had been used. One concerned promotion and the other restructuring and the reappointment of staff to the new posts. In both cases, however, the issue under arbitration was the process followed by the organizations. The tests themselves were not challenged in terms of Section 8 of the Employment Equity Act.

Possibly a reason for the lack of case law in the South African context is that the provisions of the Employment Equity Act have increased the awareness of employers with regard to the employment practices and procedures they implement.

There has been a surge of interest in occupational assessment procedures and how best to utilize them to the benefit of organizations and individuals alike. A number of best practice guidelines for organizations are available in this regard, ranging from the *Guidelines for the Validation and Use of Assessment Procedures for the Workplace,* published in 2005 by the Society for Industrial and Organizational Psychology of South Africa (SIOPSA), to the *Code of Practice for Psychological and Other Similar Assessment in the Workplace* (People Assessment in Industry, 2006). From the individual's perspective, the dominant body of reference for the provisions of all labor legislation would probably be the various labor unions, which make it their business to advise their members on all labor matters. Throughout South Africa's history, the trade unions have played an influential role in determining labor market and industrial relations policies in the country.

The Broad-Based Black Economic Empowerment Act (No. 53 of 2003)

During 2003, the president of South Africa assented to the Broad-Based Black Economic Empowerment Act (No. 53 of 2003) to establish a legislative framework for the promotion of black economic empowerment (BEE). BEE itself is geared at redressing the inequities of apartheid by giving previously disadvantaged groups economic opportunities not previously available to them. The aims of this act are described as:

- promoting economic transformation in order to enable meaningful participation of black people in the economy;
- achieving a substantial change in the racial composition of ownership and management structures and in the skilled occupations of existing and new enterprises;
- increasing the extent to which communities, workers, cooperatives and other collective enterprises own and manage existing and new enterprises and increasing their access to economic activities, infrastructure and skills training;
- increasing the extent to which black women own and manage existing and new enterprises, and increasing their access to economic activities, infrastructure and skills training;
- promoting investment programmes that lead to broad-based and meaningful participation in the economy by black people in order to achieve sustainable development and general prosperity;

- empowering rural and local communities by enabling access to economic activities, land, infrastructure, ownership and skills; and

- promoting access to finance for black economic empowerment. (pp. 4–5)

Based on these objectives, broad-based black economic empowerment (BBBEE) codes were approved by the cabinet in December 2006. The main aim of these codes is to standardize requirements of all entities operating in South Africa. Based on a balanced scorecard method, the codes provide the framework to determine the BEE status of a company. Every organ of state or public entities must develop and implement a preferential procurement policy. While this is to provide all companies in the supply chain with incentives, in turn, to implement BBBEE, it places additional pressure on companies to achieve transformation or transition from white to black empowerment and ownership.

Following the introduction of the Employment Equity Act and BEE legislation, organizations in South Africa have had to ensure that the demographics of their employers reflect the demographics of the country as far as possible. The cascading impact of the Broad-Based Black Economic Empowerment Act (2003) places economic pressure on organizations to ensure racial and cultural diversity. For example, organizations that do not have a sufficient BEE rating cannot undertake government contracts. Often, such organizations also cannot work with other corporate companies implementing BEE since the companies' preferential procurement policies require them to use BEE compliant suppliers.

The South African National Accreditation System (SANAS) was appointed to develop, maintain, and enforce the accreditation of BEE verification agencies on behalf of the South African Department of Trade and Industry, although the first verification agencies will only be accredited during April 2008. However, there currently appears to be confusion around who may undertake and submit these ratings; an article appearing in *The Business Report* on March 13, 2008, reported that, according to BEE verification agencies, self-ratings are not permissible. Conversely, according to the Department of Trade and Industry, business owners may still conduct their own ratings, and according to a recent survey, over 30% of companies produced scorecards by self-assessment (Timm, 2008).

South African Legislation in the Global Context

We find that South African antidiscrimination legislation, to large extent, has followed global but especially U.S. legislation trends. Over the years, there has also been a strong U.S. academic influence in industrial and organizational (I/O) psychology in South Africa. Thus, it should be no surprise that South African I/O psychologists, facing very similar challenges to those faced by U.S. psychologists regarding fairness in the workplace, decided to develop South African best practices in line with those developed by U.S. I/O psychologists.

We have seen typical U.S. and international best practice in terms of ensuring fairness in the workplace implemented in South Africa. Job analysis and the need to be able to demonstrate job relatedness in decision criteria meant that U.S. best practice in the design of selection and decision-making systems had a major influence in the practice of South African I/O psychologists. The principle of job analysis has also been adopted in the Codes of Best Practice as issued by the minister of labor. The adoption of the American SIOP *Principles for the Validation and Use of Personnel Selection Procedures* by SIOPSA, with minor changes, is another indication of the strong influence of the United States on South African thinking around fairness in the workplace. To date the U.S. Uniform Guidelines on Employment Selection Procedures played a less-obvious role in South Africa, and the more detailed guidelines, like the four-fifths rule as it relates to adverse impact, have not been accepted in any South African published best practice guidelines. The reason for this is unclear. While this is still a developing proposition in South Africa, we might very well see some aspects of the U.S. Uniform Guidelines on Employment Selection Procedures adopted in the future.

However, possibly the most important difference from U.S. legislation could be the fact that South African law allows organizations to use methods of achieving equity—and addressing adverse impact—that are prohibited in the United States. For example, racial quotas are legal and practiced by most of the bigger organizations in South Africa. Due to BEE, companies are required to meet certain racial targets and requirements to be rated as a black-empowered organization.

While within-group norming and separate rank lists can be used for selection decisions in South Africa, the U.S. Civil Rights Act of 1991 deemed such actions to be unlawful employment practices. Section 106 of this act specifically states:

> It shall be an unlawful employment practice for a respondent, in connection with the selection or referral of applicants or candidates for employment or promotion, to adjust the scores of, use different cutoff scores for, or otherwise alter the results of, employment related tests on the basis of race, color, religion, sex, or national origin.

Group differences on tests can have dramatic effects on the selection rates from different groups, with the lower-scoring group having a far lower selection rate compared to the higher-scoring group (Sackett & Wilk, 1994). The organization's subsequent dilemma—achieving productivity gains using a selection instrument while reducing or eliminating adverse impact—leads to possible score adjustments based on group membership.

Sackett and Wilk (1994) discussed several different methods of test development or use that utilize information about group membership for score adjustments and minority preference:

- Bonus points: Involves adding a constant number of points to the scores of all individuals belonging to a particular group before making selection decisions.

- Within-group norming: Individual scores are converted to either standard or percentile scores within one's group. Decisions based on test scores then take into account the individual's relative standing within his or her group.

- Separate cutoffs for different groups: In practice, identical to using bonus points; using separate cutoffs for different groups makes it very clear, and transparent, that a lower standard is being used for one group than for another.

- Top-down selection from separate lists: Candidates are ranked separately within groups and then selected top down within each group in accordance with a preset rule regarding the number of individuals to be appointed from each group.

- Banding: Individuals within a specific score range, or band, are regarded as having equivalent scores. All individuals within a band are seen as of equivalent standing in the construct of interest, and the order of selection of candidates within a band could be either random or on the basis of additional selection criteria (e.g., minority preference).

- Empirical keying by group: The relationship between individual test items and a criterion of interest (e.g., job performance) is examined, and items are selected for inclusion based on their relationship with the criterion. This can mean that different sets of items are used for different groups, chosen to provide optimal prediction for each group.

- Item elimination based on group performance: Potentially problematic items are removed either during the development and trialing of a new test or after a test has been administered. In the latter case, problematic items are typically identified through differential item functioning, where the question asked is "Is this item harder for members of Group X with true score Z than it is for members of Group Y with true score Z?"

Minority preference is permissible under U.S. law in certain circumstances, including a finding of discrimination, a court-monitored plan to
remedy an imbalance, or a voluntary plan undertaken to remedy an existing imbalance (Sackett & Wilk, 1994). Barring these exceptions to the rule,
however, U.S. law prohibits the adjustment of test scores in an employment context.

In contrast to the legislative context in the United States, South African
organizations can apply any and all of these methods of test use. The pro-
viso in the South African context is that the application thereof must be
consistent with an approved affirmative action policy the organization
has implemented in line with the goals of the Employment Equity Act.
This affirmative action policy can be applied in practice through any of
the strategies discussed by Sackett and Wilk (1994) or even through placing a moratorium on the appointment of any white or advantaged individuals. While it is difficult to determine the extent to which some or all
of these techniques have been utilized in the South African context, the
next section discusses some examples of positive discrimination and the
current use of preemployment testing in the country as well as the likely
impact of it.

The Current Use of Preemployment Testing in South Africa

In the new South Africa, with organizations facing the challenge of transformation and achieving a diverse workforce, a criticism has often been
leveled at objective and psychological assessments that the use thereof
acts as a barrier to change. The antitesting view is that tests available in
South Africa are biased and lead to unfair discriminatory practices, so
they should consequently be banned (Foxcroft, 1997). However, 10 senior
academics teaching psychological assessment at various South African
universities all answered in the affirmative when asked whether there
was a need for psychological tests in present-day South Africa (Plug, 1996,
as cited in Foxcroft, 1997).

While the debate over whether testing is useful in a multicultural environment continues, it is known that disadvantaged groups do tend to score
lower on certain types of assessment instruments, particularly on cognitive
ability tests (Kriek & Dowdeswell, 2007; van Eeden, de Beer, & Coetzee,
2001). Depending on how assessment instruments are used, the occurrence
of these group differences can then potentially lead to indirect discrimination and adverse impact against the previously disadvantaged groups.

To understand the implications this has for practice, the current status of group differences in South Africa is explored for ability tests and

personality questionnaires, followed by a view of what organizations are currently doing to achieve transformation within the legal framework governing the use of tests and assessments.

Group Differences in the South African Context

Group differences occur if the average performance on an assessment instrument differs significantly between different ethnic groups, or men and women, or any of the protected groups, for that matter. In the absence of validation evidence, there is likely to be a presumption that the group with the lower average performance was indirectly discriminated against. That is, if the same entry standard were demanded of all applicants, the lower-scoring group would find it more difficult to comply with the requirement, and adverse impact would occur.

When looking at cognitive ability tests—according to Schmidt and Hunter (1998) the most valid predictor of future performance and learning (discounting previous experience)—international literature generally reflects group differences between racial groups, with whites on average scoring one standard deviation higher than blacks (Hunter & Hunter, 1984; Roth, BeVier, Bobko, Switzer, & Tyler, 2001; Sackett & Wilk, 1994). In the South African context, a similar pattern of differences is observed (Kriek & Dowdeswell, 2007; van Eeden et al., 2001). However, the mean score differences between black and white groups are normally larger than what is seen in international studies, ranging from one to one and a half standard deviations where the whites obtain the higher mean scores.

To give an example of typical group differences observed using real data, attention is turned to a validation study conducted in 2005 for a South African financial services organization. The study involved various business advisory services in which verbal, numerical, and diagrammatical ability tests were used. Group differences found between the racial groups favored the whites, with d statistics of $d = 0.99$ for the verbal ability, $d = 1.03$ for the numerical ability, and $d = 1.14$ for the diagrammatic ability test being observed (SHL South Africa, 2005).

These differences are largely ascribed to differences in the level of education between the racial groups. In the 2001 census, it was determined that 22.3% of Africans, 8.3% of coloreds, 5.3% of Indians, and 1.4% of whites had no formal schooling (Statistics South Africa, 2003). Table 14.1 provides detailed information on the population's level of education.

While language also plays a role in the group differences found in South Africa, the language issue is closely related to the educational level of the candidate. For most of the cognitive ability tests as well as personality questionnaires used in the selection process, it is recommended that the candidate have a minimum educational level of Grade 12. Further, English is the business language of most companies in South Africa. To use the

TABLE 14.1

South African Population's Level of Education (%)

Level of schooling	African	Colored	Indian	White	Total
No schooling	22.3	8.3	5.3	1.4	17.9
Some primary	18.5	18.4	7.7	1.2	16.0
Complete primary	6.9	9.8	4.2	0.8	6.4
Some secondary	30.4	40.1	33.0	25.9	30.8
Grade 12	16.8	18.5	34.9	40.9	20.4
Higher education	5.2	4.9	14.9	29.8	8.4

Note: From *Primary Tables South Africa: Census '96 and 2001 Compared*, Statistics South Africa, 2003, Pretoria: Author.

English versions of an instrument, a company must prove that fluency in English is an inherent requirement of the job. It is, therefore, always recommended that the required level and complexity of a candidate's ability to speak, read, and write English be determined through job analysis. A test "simulating" the position for which it is used, both in content and in language, would give a clear picture of a person's ability to cope on the job.

Experts suggested that the adverse impact of measures such as cognitive ability tests may be lessened when combined with measures showing less adverse impact, such as personality questionnaires, but that it can still increase the overall predictive validity of the assessment. Research in South Africa also suggested that tests, used in combination with information gathered from other sources, enhances decision making (Foxcroft, 1997).

If we turn our attention to personality questionnaires, we find that internationally differences between races on mean scores for personality measures are negligible (Bobko, Roth, & Potosky, 1999; Schmitt, Clause, & Pulakos, 1996). In South Africa, the research evidence mirrors this trend, with differences found to be considerably smaller between different racial and language groups. For example, SHL South Africa conducted a study with the Occupational Personality Questionnaire 32i (OPQ32i) and a sample of approximately 21,000 candidates, examining mean group differences between blacks and whites as well as between the four ethnic groups (i.e., African, colored, Indian, and White). The largest differences between the means of the four ethnic groups were found between the African and white groups (Kriek, 2006). These differences were, however, typically not larger than half a standard deviation. The largest difference observed was a moderate effect size ($d = 0.56$ on the scale of Decisiveness, followed by $d = 0.53$ on Forward Thinking). For the remaining 30 scales of the OPQ32i, 10 showed a d statistic greater than 0.30 but smaller than 0.50; 10 fell between 0.10 and 0.30, and the d statistics for the last 10 scales were smaller than 0.10.

These group differences on personality scores seem to be slightly higher than in the U.S. population but are very similar to the typical effect size found in the U.K. population. The South African effect size differences, however, should be seen within the South African environment where the cultural context of the various ethnic groups differs greatly. In most cases, these effect sizes reflect real differences between groups. For example, it is important to note that for certain personality scales—for example, Rule Following—the black population in South Africa tended to get higher mean scores than the white population. To determine the adverse impact caused by a personality questionnaire would therefore depend on the relative importance of certain personality scales for the job. Should certain personality traits—such as rule following—be essential for the job, reverse adverse impact against the whites is a possibility.

An argument sometimes heard in South Africa against testing, and based on the presence of ethnic group differences on scores, is that assessments cannot be used to predict job performance for black candidates. In the first few years during the postapartheid era, calls for the abolition of psychological assessments sprang from a wide variety of sources and throughout various industries. Counter to this argument is a trend observed in validation data over the years: The predictive validity of assessment is typically higher for blacks than for whites (Kriek & Dowdeswell, 2007). This is largely due to data sets showing a greater range of performance (from low to very high) for the black groups, in both the predictor (assessments) and criterion (performance) data, than we tend to see in the white groups, for whom it is more often that we see restriction of range.

Typical Strategies Followed to Achieve Transformation in Organizations

Given that we know group differences exist between the previously disadvantaged majority and the advantaged minority in South Africa, the question comes to mind of what organizations are doing to achieve the transformation that is a legal, economic, social, and ethical obligation.

Keep in mind the practical implications of South Africa's employment legislation: It is legal to use race-specific norm groups, or within-group top-down selection strategies, to address the affirmative action needs of organizations. During the apartheid era, the black population was not given the same educational and work opportunities as the white population, so selection based on meritocracy only would not have addressed employment equity since the white group historically had access to better schools and universities. Therefore, to ensure that previously disadvantaged individuals achieved greater representation in the workplace it was necessary for the South African government to enforce selection via affirmative action policies and the use of race-specific methods to address equity. According to Muchinsky, Kriek, and Schreuder (2003), the original intent of affirmative action was aimed at the recruitment of new employees. This implies that employers should take action to appoint employees from the previously disadvantaged groups. Muchinsky et al. (2003) also described the different interpretations of affirmative action. It ranges from the most passive interpretation by which it only pertains to procedures related to recruiting, to preferential selection by which organizations will select previously disadvantaged group members from an applicant pool if they are judged to have the same qualifications as white applicants.

The Employment Equity Act requires designated employers—employers employing more than 50 employees or whose annual turnover exceeds a certain level—to design and implement equity plans that specify, among other details, year-by-year objectives to be reached. Although these objectives are set by individual organizations, we find that bigger organizations will enforce racial and other quotas to change the demographics of their workforce. But, how are these targets achieved? The following sections explore four methods commonly observed in South African organizations.

Strategy 1: Top-Down Selection From Separate Lists

The top-down selection from separate lists approach to considering group membership in test use involves ranking candidates separately within groups (e.g., ethnic groups or gender) and then selecting top-down from within each group (Sackett & Wilk, 1994). The organization typically specifies the number of positions available to each group (a quota) and will select the specified number of candidates from the previously disadvantaged list before starting to look at the previously advantaged list.

Since 1994, however, the demographics of the workforce and in particular the graduate applicant pool has been changing rapidly, with increasing participation of previously disadvantaged individuals. This begs a question to be explored: Given the changing demographics of the workforce, what is the impact of using a single rank list without quotas?

To answer this question, the graduate recruitment data gathered over 4 years by a large financial institution in South Africa were examined (Kriek & Dowdeswell, 2007). The initial process followed by the organization in its recruitment is threefold:

1. Applicants apply online through the organization's Web site and complete a standard application blank, which allows for screening based on gross negative disqualifiers.

2. Applicants meeting the basic qualifications then complete online competency-based behavioral questionnaires.

3. Applicants meeting the cutoff on the behavioral questionnaire are invited to complete cognitive ability tests and a personality

TABLE 14.2

Racial Distribution of Graduate Applicants, 2004–2007

Year	African	Colored	Indian	White	Other
2004	1,959 (58%)	183 (5%)	567 (17%)	559 (17%)	116 (3%)
2005	1,813 (63%)	163 (6%)	540 (19%)	352 (12%)	24 (1%)
2006	744 (63%)	92 (8%)	171 (14%)	160 (14%)	18 (1%)
2007	1,699 (73%)	130 (6%)	283 (12%)	189 (8%)	24 (1%)

questionnaire online. The results of these measures are combined and matched against the requirements of the position to provide an indication of each applicant's potential to succeed in the position.

In its selection process, the organization only applies quotas in terms of previously disadvantaged individuals at the third stage, when short-listing the applicants based on the applicants' potential to succeed in the position (as reflected by the applicants' person-job match scores).

Table 14.2 reflects how the percentage of previously disadvantaged applicants to the graduate program has increased over the years, with the umbrella category of "blacks" rising from 80% in 2004 to 91% in 2007. Over the 4 years, group differences on the ability tests are observed between the racial groups, in favor of the whites and ranging from half a standard deviation to just over one standard deviation. However, looking at the racial distribution of the top 50 applicants per year, rank listed on cognitive ability alone, an interesting trend emerges (refer to Table 14.3). Despite the group differences remaining throughout the years, the number of previously disadvantaged (black) individuals in the top 50 applicants increased, from 34% in 2004 to 62% in 2007. This trend is even more

TABLE 14.3

Racial Distribution of the Top-Ranking Applicants Based on Ability

Year	African	Colored	Indian	White	Other
The top 50 applicants based on cognitive ability alone					
2004	4 (8%)	2 (4%)	11 (22%)	32 (64%)	1 (2%)
2005	2 (4%)	1 (2%)	15 (30%)	32 (64%)	0 (0%)
2006	5 (10%)	1 (2%)	15 (30%)	26 (52%)	3 (6%)
2007	19 (38%)	1 (2%)	11 (22%)	19 (38%)	0 (0%)
The top 100 applicants based on cognitive ability alone					
2004	10 (10%)	4 (4%)	25 (25%)	58 (58%)	3 (3%)
2005	14 (14%)	3 (3%)	37 (37%)	46 (46%)	0 (0%)
2006	14 (14%)	9 (9%)	28 (28%)	42 (42%)	7 (7%)
2007	35 (35%)	4 (4%)	29 (29%)	30 (30%)	2 (2%)

clearly observable when increasing the number of applicants considered to 100—the number of positions the organization typically fills each year—with the number of previously disadvantaged individuals increasing from 39% in 2004 to 68% in 2007.

As mentioned, accumulated literature highlights how including assessments less likely to cause adverse impact can minimize the impact of group differences observed on cognitive ability tests. This is reflected when applied to the graduate recruitment data, for which the ability results are combined with personality data and job requirements to produce a person–job match score, which in turn is used to rank list the applicants. To calculate this score, the assessment results are combined to form a number of competencies, with differential weightings assigned to the ability and personality scores depending on the nature of each competency. These competencies are then combined to form the person–job match score, with the competencies identified through job analysis as essential to the job given more weight than the competencies identified as less relevant. Table 14.4 illustrates how the racial distribution of the top 50 applicants, in terms of the combined person–job match data, shifted from roughly equal in 2004 to 78% previously disadvantaged individuals in 2007. Extending the rank list to the top 100 applicants reflects a similar distribution as for the top 50 applicants.

In this particular organization, top-down selection was supplemented with other information based on the organization's operational needs (e.g., particular degree specialty of the graduates), together with the organization's racial and gender targets (i.e., 70% black candidates) and a minimum level of performance on the ability tests. The applicants short-listed in this

TABLE 14.4

Racial Distribution of the Top-Ranking Applicants Based on Combined Ability and Personality Data

Year	African	Colored	Indian	White	Other
The top 50 applicants based on combined ability and personality in view of job requirements					
2004	12 (24%)	3 (6%)	9 (18%)	25 (50%)	1 (2%)
2005	12 (24%)	3 (6%)	10 (20%)	25 (50%)	0 (0%)
2006	19 (38%)	3 (6%)	12 (24%)	15 (30%)	1 (2%)
2007	25 (50%)	3 (6%)	11 (22%)	11 (22%)	0 (0%)
The top 100 applicants based on combined ability and personality in view of job requirements					
2004	32 (32%)	6 (6%)	20 (20%)	39 (39%)	3 (3%)
2005	35 (35%)	5 (5%)	21 (21%)	39 (39%)	0 (0%)
2006	40 (40%)	6 (6%)	25 (25%)	25 (25%)	4 (4%)
2007	55 (55%)	5 (5%)	19 (19%)	21 (21%)	0 (0%)

manner subsequently completed a group exercise and interview before the final selection decision was made. In 2007, for example, the organization made a final offer to 70 of the short-listed applicants, 70% of whom were black. Had the organization followed a strict top-down approach, selecting the top 70 applicants based on person–job match score alone, 79% of these candidates would have been from a previously disadvantaged group.

Strategy 2: Separate (Lower) Cutoffs for Previously Disadvantaged Groups

Due to the legal, social, and economic pressures to achieve transformation, management is often under pressure to accelerate the employment of previously disadvantaged individuals. One strategy that can be utilized by organizations to do so is to set lower cutoffs for the previously disadvantaged group, making it easier for previously disadvantaged individuals to meet requirements for entry.

However, this approach may act as a double-edged sword. While on the one hand lowering the cutoffs for previously disadvantaged groups makes it easier for such individuals to be employed, it could have negative utility implications. This subsequently leads to higher failure rates and higher incidents of unsuccessful candidates being appointed.

For example, lower-scoring blacks admitted on the basis of a quota are more likely to fail than the higher-scoring whites rejected on the basis of the quota. Beyond the impact on productivity for the organization, another important implication the organization needs to take into account is the potentially harmful psychological impact the employee's failure can have on the individual and his or her self-esteem (Huysamen, 1995; Nunns & Ortlepp, 1994).

A practical example of when lowering cutoff scores to increase selection of previously disadvantaged candidates had an adverse effect is that of a large South African organization in the telecommunications industry some years ago. The organization utilized a series of ability tests to determine admission into software training courses but found that fewer previously disadvantaged candidates were able to meet the requirements to enter the course. To address this, the organization lowered the cutoff scores required for the previously disadvantaged candidates, thereby increasing the number coming into the training. Subsequently, however, the organization experienced an increase in students failing the training course. An investigation established that the ability tests themselves were indeed good predictors of training success (SHL South Africa, 2000); candidates with lower ability test scores were far more likely to fail the training course than were candidates with higher ability test scores. Based on these findings, the organization then decided to raise the cutoff scores required and revisit their attraction-and-recruitment model. The organization then sought to narrow the range of candidates attracted by targeting previously disadvantaged individuals satisfying certain criteria (e.g., Grade 12 English with a minimum of a C symbol, or a pass mark between 60% and 69%). This would typically be achieved through advertising in different newspapers and targeting schools or universities. The organization subsequently saw an improvement in students' success on the training course.

A South African organization in the aviation industry experienced a similar situation brought about through abolishing cutoffs when recruiting applicants. Under pressure from management to place more previously disadvantaged individuals into the organization's in-house training courses, the recruitment department continued testing applicants as they applied but appointed individuals despite their test scores being well below the desirable cutoff scores. The organization consequently experienced a rising level of failures on the training courses, with severe financial loss in training expenses and creating a shortage of qualified individuals reentering the workplace after successfully completing the training. The organization was forced to review its recruitment practices, increasing the applicant pool and taking the decision to once more implement cutoff scores for the tests in the selection process. Anecdotal evidence at this stage is that managers in the organization have commented that the level of applicants selected into the organization has improved.

Strategy 3: Discontinuing All Preemployment Testing

An example of the possible implications of not using preemployment testing occurred in one of the business units of a large organization in the insurance industry in South Africa. The business unit decided to discontinue all testing in the selection process due to the adverse impact on previously disadvantaged candidates, although testing was used companywide. About 2 years later, the unit was underperforming; the overall productivity of the unit had dropped, and turnover was up when compared to other business units in the organization. The line managers of the underperforming unit singled out the (lower) quality of candidates coming into the unit as the cause for the drop in performance, and objective preemployment testing was subsequently reintroduced into the selection process. Due to the diversity in the applicant pool, the organization is still in the position to comply with equity legislation and continues to use preemployment testing.

Strategy 4: Moratorium on Employment of Advantaged Individuals

Some organizations only consider previously disadvantaged individuals for selection and promotion decisions, placing a moratorium on the employment or promotion of whites. At one of South Africa's largest banking institutions, for example, the recruitment and selection policy stipulates that only previously disadvantaged individuals may be appointed. The appointment of white individuals is prohibited unless the recruiting manager can demonstrate with sufficient proof that there are no suitably qualified previously disadvantaged candidates for the position. This particular organization also placed a ban on all objective pre-employment testing, and only uses interviews as part of their personnel decision-making process.

The effectiveness of strategies of this kind currently rely on anecdotal evidence, with the verdict still out. Apart from the company-specific results in terms of the overall loss of utility, it is also important to consider the possible impact on the wider society and perceptions of equal employment opportunities that policies like this create.

Implications of South African Employment Practice for I/O Psychology, Principles, and Theory

Given the complexities in the socioeconomic development over the years, I/O psychologists have been challenged to continue their positive contribution to society. The South African context in practice both legally, in terms of our employment law, and demographically, with the disadvantaged "minority" being the majority population groups and the advantaged "majority" the minority population group, holds certain implications for I/O psychology principles and theory.

Hunter and Schmidt (1976) discussed three ethical positions concerning the fairness of testing to minority groups: (a) unqualified individualism, by which an organization should use whatever information it possesses to select those with the highest predicted performance; (b) quotas, by which organizations implement selection procedures that admit a defined ratio of blacks and whites (or any other desired groups), usually representative of the population ratio; and (c) qualified individualism, by which even if race (or another protected group) is a valid predictor of success, it may not be used in predicting likely performance.

In South Africa, we have seen a pendulum shifting from one view to another. In the days of apartheid and work reservation, the racial group to which individuals belonged determined the jobs for which they could apply. This was effectively a quota system for whites only. The Interim Constitution of 1993, stating that discrimination based on race was not allowed on any grounds, shifted the prevailing view at the time to one of qualified individualism, by which differential treatment of different groups based on race was rejected even if this would result in poorer prediction for some groups. While Section 8(2) of the Interim Constitution specifically states, "No person shall be unfairly discriminated against, directly or indirectly," and Section 8(3)(a) qualifies this with, "This section shall not preclude measures designed to achieve the adequate protection and advancement of persons or groups or categories of persons disadvantaged by unfair discrimination, in order to enable their full and equal enjoyment of all rights and freedoms," differential treatment in favor of blacks has been used in the postapartheid era supported by the view that past injustices be rectified through affirmative action policies until such time that designated groups are equally represented in the workplace. Affirmative action was, however, voluntary and not forced by legislation in any way. Under the leadership of Nelson Mandela, as the first democratic elected president in South Africa, this was a period of reconciliation and a true desire to strive toward a nonracial society.

With the promulgation of the Employment Equity Act in 1998 and the official introduction of affirmative action policies, supported by BEE legislation in 2006, the view shifted once more to a quota system. Although the quotas are determined as self-imposed targets by organizations, the net effect is that of a quota system.

Another area of I/O psychology the South African context holds implications for is the use of statistical models in determining fairness of test use. Selection fairness in preemployment testing is subject to different definitions in different social and political circumstances (Cascio & Aguinis, 2005), and a number of statistical models have been put forward over the years in an effort to define selection fairness. Internationally, there has been a strong focus on the use of fairness models such as Cleary's regression model, Thorndike's constant ratio model, and Darlington's conditional probability model (Cascio & Aguinis, 2005; Hunter & Schmidt, 1976; Muchinsky et al., 2003).

Cleary's model of test fairness posits that a test may be considered fair if there are no differences between the regression lines estimated in predicting between groups (Muchinsky et al., 2003). This approach is based on the fact that different groups may score significantly differently on certain selection tests but perform equally well in the job.

Following on from Cleary's model of test fairness, Thorndike's view is that, if differences in regression lines occur, the use of regression lines to set cutoffs for selection is likely to be to the disadvantage of the previously disadvantaged group (Muchinsky et al., 2003). Thorndike's constant ratio model therefore proposes that different cutoff scores should be identified so that a representative proportion of the previously disadvantaged group is selected. In other words, selection procedures are fair when the selection ratio is proportional to the success ratio between blacks and whites.

Finally, the basic principle of Darlington's conditional probability model is that for both previously disadvantaged and white groups whose members can achieve a satisfactory score, there should be the same probability of selection regardless of group membership (Muchinsky et al., 2003). When applying the conditional probability model in practice, candidates are divided into the different groups of interest (usually on the basis of race) and ranked according to their test scores. Each group then has a set cutoff point above which candidates are selected; alternatively, a top-down approach may be adopted by which the top candidates of each group are selected.

These statistical fairness models have also been advocated in South Africa (Huysamen, 1995; Owen & Taljaard, 1996), with Huysamen (1995) providing a discussion of the applicability of the models in the South African context. In his examination of the applicability of these fairness models, Huysamen (1995) acknowledged that in the South African context the majority group is the disadvantaged, as opposed to the situation in the United States, where the minority group is the disadvantaged. However, he argued that the number and relative sizes of the groups involved have no bearing on the principles involved. Further, Huysamen (1995) argued that these fairness models are suited to accommodating the demands of affirmative action as well as allowing the implementation of such a program to be done in a transparent manner.

In 2005, SIOPSA recommended in their *Guidelines for the Validation and Use of Assessment Procedures for the Workplace* that "only fairness models based models based on the regression model" be used in studies investigating the fairness of assessment procedures. However, they also stated that "no agreement has been reached with regard to which is the correct or best model, as each research and test user will identify the model that best suits their objectives, and which fits their definitions of fairness in assessment and in the use of psychological assessment" (p. 29).

The practical usefulness of these fairness models, although theoretically applicable in the South African context, has very little bearing on what is happening in reality. Since some South African organizations place a moratorium on the appointment of advantaged individuals and are still in compliance with the country's equal opportunities legislation, the theoretical question of statistical fairness becomes less and less relevant in the practical use of preemployment testing in personnel decision making.

Conclusion

The situation in South Africa, while very different from that found in the United States, is not static but evolving over time. For example, while group differences exist between black and white groups on cognitive ability measures, although less so on personality measures, as the demographics of applicant pools shift increasingly more in favor of the previously disadvantaged, we see the impact of those group differences lessening when using a top-down selection approach. While it is true that more whites are leaving the country, the demographic shift cannot necessarily be ascribed to only fewer white people participating in application procedures. We know of no research that has been conducted on this subject, but with the government focusing on improving the education system and with more previously disadvantaged individuals attending universities, this demographic shift is more likely to be a combination of various factors. With better education and opportunities, slowly more and more previously disadvantaged individuals are now becoming advantaged individuals, and race can no longer be used as the only criterion for being disadvantaged.

Currently, affirmative action policies have been in existence in South Africa for less than two decades. Although the face of organizations and their demographic composition changed during this period, change is a lengthy and ongoing process, and it is potentially premature to draw conclusions at this stage regarding how effective particular strategies ultimately are. Going forward, we need to understand and study how organizations cope with the socioeconomic challenges and how their actions succeed or fail to meet both economic and social needs of the country. I/O psychology in South Africa is faced with several challenges unique to the context.

The official unemployment rate in South Africa, expressed as a percentage of the labor force, was 25.5% in March 2007 (Statistics South Africa, 2007a). With such a large unemployment figure, South African organizations can and do receive large numbers of applications, often from individuals without the minimum level of qualification or education required for the job. Given that larger proportions of South Africa's previously disadvantaged race groups have no formal schooling (e.g., 22.3% of Africans vs. 1.4% of whites), organizations are faced with greater difficulties in obtaining appropriately qualified applicants from designated groups.

Another consideration not directly addressed in this chapter relates to the diversity of languages spoken in South Africa. While there are 11 official languages, the 2001 census reported that only 8.2% of South Africans spoke English at home. While English is the accepted language most widely used in business, non-first-language-speaking individuals may find it harder to comply with such job requirements. Given that the majority of preemployment tests available are conducted in English, this would mean that over 90% of the population would be tested in their second or even third language. This raises the question of whether it can be considered fair to assess individuals in a language other than their home language. There is a case for testing in English if it is an inherent requirement of the job, but if English is not an inherent requirement of the job, alternative measures should be considered.

In terms of the role testing plays in achieving the balance between economic and social needs, perhaps too much emphasis has been placed on the presence of group differences at the cost of how assessment results can be used in fair decision-making processes. Organizations need to consider the total picture of using valid instruments, the requirements of the positions to be filled, the composition of their applicant pools and the impact of adjusting selection cutoff scores, all within the context created by the employment legislation of the day.

Perhaps a final question to be addressed concerns what kind of assessment practice organizations in South Africa will be facing in the future. Currently, there appear to be two likely scenarios: a continuation of current affirmative action practices in pursuit of employment equity or a shift in focus toward greater emphasis on business informing policy. As in the past, the deciding factor for which way the pendulum will swing will most likely be the disposition of the political dispensation at the time. Should the political view remain oriented around a socialistic perspective, it is likely that the emphasis of current employment equity practices (e.g., racial quotas and preferential treatment of previously disadvantaged individuals) will either remain or even increase. On the other hand, if the political view moves toward a predominantly capitalistic perspective that is more favorable toward business, the scenario in South Africa will likely shift from a quota-based system to a meritocracy in which the best individual for the position is appointed or promoted regardless of being previously advantaged or disadvantaged. Given the history of South African capitalism and the fact that the employment system in South Africa has never been based on a meritocracy, it will most probably be a challenge for any South African government in the near future to convince the majority of the population to embrace the latter proposition. The challenge for IO psychology is, however, to demonstrate the value we can add to society and business irrespective of the direction the pendulum may swing.

References

Bam, P. G. (2007, October 19). *The latest case law relating to assessment testing in South Africa.* Paper presented at People Assessment in Industry's symposium, Fair Assessment in Organisations, Centurion Lake Hotel, Pretoria.

Bobko, P., Roth, P. L. & Potosky, D. (1999). Derivation and implications of a meta-analytic matrix incorporating cognitive ability, alternative predictors, and job performance: The effectiveness of strategies. *Personnel Psychology, 52,* 561–589.

Broad-Based Black Empowerment Act, Act 53 of 2003, Republic of South Africa.

Cascio, W. F., & Aguinis, H. (2005). *Applied psychology in human resource management* (6th ed.). Upper Saddle River, NJ: Pearson Prentice-Hall.

Civil Rights Act, Pub. L. 102-166, 1991.

Constitution of the Republic of South Africa, Act 108 of 1996, Republic of South Africa.

Dell, S. (2006, January 9). Where have all the whites gone? *Weekend Witness.* Retrieved February 29, 2008 from http://www.solidaritysa.co.za/home/wmview.php?ArtID=548

Employment Equity Act, Act 55 of 1998, Republic of South Africa.

Foxcroft, C. D. (1997). Psychological testing in South Africa: Perspectives regarding ethical and fair practices. *European Journal of Psychological Assessment, 13,* 229–235.

Foxcroft, C. D., & Roodt, G. (2005). *An introduction to psychological assessment in the South African context* (2nd ed.). Cape Town: Oxford University Press Southern Africa.

Government Communication and Information Systems. (2007). *South African yearbook 2006/2007.* Retrieved March 12, 2008, from http://www.gcis.gov.za/docs/publications/yearbook

Herman, D., Du Plooy, T., & Calldo, F. (2007). *The truth about employment equity in South Africa.* Retrieved February 29, 2008 from http://www.solidaritysa.co.za/news/latest reports

Hunter, J. E., & Hunter, R. E. (1984). Validity and utility of alternative predictors of job performance. *Psychological Bulletin, 96,* 72–98.

Hunter, J. E., & Schmidt, F. L. (1976). Critical analysis of the statistical and ethical implications of various definitions of test bias. *Psychological Bulletin, 83,* 1053–1071.

Huysamen, G. K. (1995). The applicability of fair selection models in the South African context. *Journal of Industrial Psychology, 21*(3), 1–6.

Kriek, H. J. (2006, May). *Personality assessment: Group differences, language proficiency and fairness.* Paper presented at the SIOP Symposium, Dallas, TX.

Kriek, H. J., & Dowdeswell, K. E. (2007, October 19). *Adverse impact and validity evidence in South Africa: 12 years of data trends.* Paper presented at People Assessment in Industry's symposium, Fair Assessment in Organisations, Centurion Lake Hotel, Pretoria.

Labour Relations Act, Act 28 of 1956, Republic of South Africa.

Labour Relations Act, Act 66 of 1995, Republic of South Africa.

Muchinsky, P. M., Kriek, H. J., & Schreuder, D. (2003). *Personnel psychology* (3rd ed.). Oxford: Oxford University Press.

Nunns, C., & Ortlepp, K. (1994). Exploring predictors of academic success in Psychology I at WITS university as an important component of fair student selection. *South African Journal of Psychology, 24*(4), 201–207.

Owen, K., & Taljaard, J. J. (1996). *Handbook of the use of psychological and scholastic tests of the HSRC* (Rev. ed.). Pretoria, South Africa: Human Sciences Research Council.

People Assessment in Industry. (2006). *Code of practice for psychological and other similar assessment in the workplace.* Pretoria: SIOPSA.

Rebirth Africa. (2000). *Apartheid South Africa: Bantu education.* Retrieved April 17, 2007, from http://www.rebirth.co.za/apartheid_segregation_bantu_education3.htm

Roth, P. L., BeVier, C. A., Bobko, P., Switzer, F. S., III, & Tyler, P. (2001). Ethnic group differences in cognitive ability in employment and educational settings: A meta-analysis. *Personnel Psychology, 54,* 297–330.

Sackett, P. R., & Wilk, S. L. (1994). Within-group norming and other forms of score adjustment in preemployment testing. *American Psychologist, 49*, 929–954.

Schmidt, F. L., & Hunter, J. E. (1998). The validity and utility of selection methods in personnel psychology: Practical and theoretical implications of 85 years of research findings. *Psychological Bulletin, 124*, 262–274.

Schmitt, N., Clause, C. S., & Pulakos, E. (1996). Subgroup differences associated with different measures of some common job-relevant constructs. In C. L. Cooper & I. T. Robertson (Eds.), *International review of industrial and organizational psychology* (Vol. 11, pp. 115–140). New York: Wiley.

SHL South Africa. (2000). *Validation Study V018*. Retrieved November 9, 2007 from http://www.research.shl.co.za

SHL South Africa. (2005). *Validation Study V036*. Retrieved November 9, 2007 from http://www.research.shl.co.za

Society for Industrial and Organizational Psychology. (2003). *Principles for the validation and use of personnel selection procedures* (4th ed.).

Society for Industrial and Organizational Psychology of South Africa. (2005). *Guidelines for the validation and use of assessment instruments in the workplace.* Pretoria: SIOPSA.

South African Department of Labor. (2004). *Basic guide to affirmative action.* Retrieved March 12, 2008, from http://www.labour.gov.za/basic_guides/bguide_display.jsp?id=5848&programme_id=2670

Statistics South Africa. (2003). *Primary tables South Africa: Census '96 and 2001 compared.* Pretoria: Statistics South Africa.

Statistics South Africa. (2007a). *Labour force survey: March 2007.* Statistical release P0210, September 26, 2007. Retrieved December 19, 2007, from http://www.statssa.gov.za/keyindicators/lfs.asp

Statistics South Africa. (2007b). *Mid-year population estimates 2007.* Statistical release P0302, July 3, 2007. Retrieved November 20, 2007, from http://www.statssa.gov.za/publications/P0302/P03022007.pdf

Timm, S. (2008, March 13). Agencies "wrong to deny self-rating." *The Business Report.* Retrieved from http://www.busrep.co.za/index.php?fSectionId=561&fArticleId=4300977

Uniform guidelines on employee selection procedures. (1978). *Federal Register, 43*, 38290–38315.

Van Eeden, R., de Beer, M., & Coetzee, C. H. (2001). Cognitive ability, learning potential, and personality traits as predictors of academic achievement by engineering and other science and technology students. *South African Journal of Higher Education, 15*, 171–179.

World Socialist Web site. (2004). *United Nations report highlights growing inequality in South Africa.* May 21, 2004. Retrieved November 9, 2007, from http://www.wsws.org/articles/2004/may2004/safr-m21.shtml

Section VI

Methods of Reducing Adverse Impact

15

Balancing Adverse Impact, Selection Errors, and Employee Performance in the Presence of Test Bias

Herman Aguinis and Marlene A. Smith

Introduction

Adverse impact (AI) is a central issue in organizational staffing and high-stakes selection. Although this concept has a long history (Zedeck, 2009), it is usually operationalized as a ratio of two selection ratios (SRs) (Biddle, 2005; Bobko & Roth, 2004). $AI = SR_1/SR_2$, where SR_1 and SR_2 are the number of applicants selected divided by the total number of applicants for the minority and majority groups of applicants, respectively.

It is desirable for AI to be as close to 1.0 as possible because $AI = 1.0$ means that the selection ratios are identical across groups (e.g., ethnic majority and ethnic minority groups). However, the 80% AI benchmark (i.e., $AI = 0.80$) has been institutionalized as a desirable target since the publication of the *Uniform Guidelines on Employee Selection Procedures* in 1978. Specifically, Section A notes that "a selection rate for any race, sex, or ethnic group which is less than 4/5ths (or 80%) of the rate for the group with the highest rate will generally be regarded by the Federal enforcement agencies as evidence of adverse impact" (p. 38297). Federal agencies use the 80% benchmark when judging compliance with federal guidelines. For example, Roth, Bobko, and Switzer (2006) noted that the typical first step in compliance proceedings includes checking the 80% benchmark and continuing with the process only if this benchmark is not met. Violating the 80% benchmark has important and often very costly implications for organizations, and in most situations, organizations will be better off avoiding or at least mitigating AI. In practice, this means that personnel selection decision makers try to achieve an AI ratio of at least 0.80.

Achieving an acceptable AI ratio (i.e., AI $\geq$ 0.80) is often difficult when measuring constructs such as general mental abilities (GMAs), which are known to result in mean score differences across ethnicity-based groups (Aguinis, 2004b). Accordingly, personnel selection decision makers are often faced with a paradoxical situation: Using GMA and other predictors that maximize individual performance and resulting economic utility, as is typically conceptualized in human resources management and indus-trial and organizational psychology (Cascio & Aguinis, 2005, Chapter 3), often leads to the exclusion of members of ethnic minorities (Aguinis, Cortina, & Goldberg, 1998; Murphy, 2004).

Test bias exists when the same test score leads to different predicted performance scores for members of groups based on protected class sta-tus (e.g., race, sex). The presence of test bias is usually assessed using a multiple regression framework in which race, sex, and other categori-cal variables related to protected class status are entered as moderators (Aguinis, 2004a; American Educational Research Association, American Psychological Association, and National Council on Measurement in Education [AERA, APA, & NCME], 1999, Standard 7.6; Cleary, 1968; Hough, Oswald, & Ployhart, 2001). Assessing test bias often leads to the incorrect conclusion that there is no bias because of low statistical power (Aguinis, Beaty, Boik, & Pierce, 2005; Aguinis, Boik, & Pierce, 2001; Aguinis & Stone-Romero, 1997). In other words, in many situations in which there is test bias, the test bias assessment procedures lead to the incorrect conclusion that bias is not present.

In this chapter, we offer an expanded way of thinking about AI in organi-zational staffing and high-stakes selection. As we noted, extensive simula-tion studies have demonstrated that test bias often exists in spite of results that moderating effects by group are statistically nonsignificant (Aguinis et al., 2001, 2005; Aguinis & Stone-Romero, 1997; see Aguinis, 1995, 2004a, for reviews). As a result, the decision to mitigate AI by lowering selection cut scores leaves an important issue out of the picture (see Kehoe, 2009, for a detailed treatment of the relationship between cut scores and AI). What has been left out in previous treatments of the cut score-AI relationship is that lowering cut scores to reach more acceptable levels of AI must be weighed against the collateral damage due to test bias that often exists unbeknown to test developers and users: unexpected performance levels of individuals selected and unexpected bias-based selection errors (both false positives and false negatives). In this chapter, we use the Aguinis and Smith (2007) decision-making model and Web-based calculator to demonstrate why information about possible test bias should be brought *explicitly* into the decision-making process. By doing so, selection deci-sion makers will have a more comprehensive picture of how changing cut scores to mitigate AI can also influence the organization regarding other important outcomes: the performance of those individuals hired and bias-based false positive and false negative errors.

Basics Concepts and Terminology

In selection decision making, a test score random variable X and a job performance random variable Y are presumed to follow a joint probability distribution. Y is related to X via a regression line as shown in Figure 15.1. For simplicity, this figure includes two groups only; Group 1 represents the minority group (e.g., ethnic minority) and Group 2 the majority group (e.g., ethnic majority), but the model can be extended to multiple groups. Group 1 and Group 2 may follow a *common regression line* $E(Y|X) = \alpha + \beta X$. This common regression line represents an unbiased test because, at any given test score (x^* in Figure 15.1), it predicts identical performance levels y^* for both groups (AERA, APA, & NCME, 1999). This, of course, would be the ideal situation because no test bias exists. In other situations, however, and unbeknown to selection decision makers due to the low statistical power of the bias assessment procedures, each group may follow its unique *group-specific regression line*, which are also shown in Figure 15.1. If a test is biased, it will predict average performance $y_1^* = E(Y_1|x^*)$ for Group 1 and $y_2^* =$

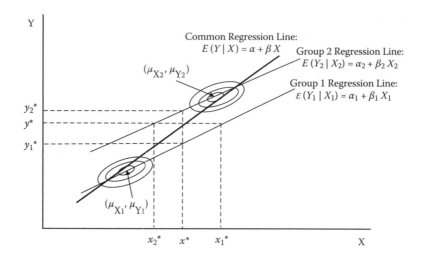

FIGURE 15.1
Common and group-specific regression lines and cut scores (Group 1 is the ethnic minority group).

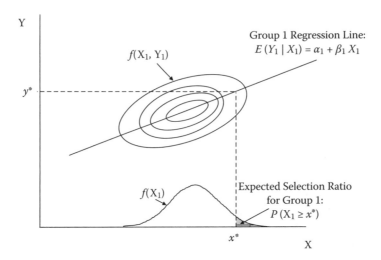

FIGURE 15.2
Expected selection ratio for Group 1 (i.e., ethnic minority group).

$E(Y_2|x^*)$ for Group 2 at test score x^*. The group-specific regression lines in Figure 15.1 depict a fairly common finding regarding the use of cognitive ability tests in human resource selection: Differences between groups are detected regarding intercepts (but not slopes) for the group-based regression lines (Hunter & Schmidt, 1976; Reilly, 1973; Rotundo & Sackett, 1999).

In many selection situations, decision makers stipulate a desired performance level (i.e., y^*, the minimum value for Y needed to perform the job satisfactorily) and then use the regression relationship to determine the associated expected selection cut (i.e., x^* in Figure 15.2). Given the expected selection cut, Aguinis and Smith (2007) defined the *expected selection ratio* to be the upper-tail area under the test score (X) marginal probability distribution at the expected selection cut. Aguinis and Smith (2007) also introduced the terms *expected AI* and *bias-based expected selection errors*. The use of the word *expected* was intentional and explicit. Expected AI differs from observed AI in the same way as the expected value of a random variable differs from a sample mean; the former uses assumed probability models to weigh outcomes according to probability mass. To illustrate, Figure 15.2 depicts the expected selection ratio for Group 1 as the area under $f(X_1)$ to the right of x^* (i.e., the percentage of the Group 1 population under consideration for employment). Similarly, expected AI is the ratio of the minority expected selection ratio to the majority expected selection ratio at the expected selection cut.

Although it may be small in magnitude, test bias exists every time that the group-specific lines do not overlap perfectly. When test bias exists, there are three possible cut scores associated with performance level y^*

(see Figure 15.1): (a) one to be used for both groups based on the common regression line (i.e., x^*), (b) one to be used for Group 1 based on its group-specific line (i.e., x_1^*), and (c) one to be used for Group 2 based on its group-specific line (i.e., x_2^*). Since the passing of the Civil Rights Act of 1991, the use of group-specific lines and cut scores in selection decision making is generally unlawful. So, either because bias is not detected due to low statistical power or because it is generally unlawful to use differential cut scores, the common regression line is often used for both groups even when bias exists. In such situations, selection errors (i.e., bias-based expected selection errors) are inevitably introduced because using group-specific lines and cut scores would maximize decision-making accuracy. Therefore, considering test bias provides a more comprehensive picture and increases the complexity of the cut score–AI relationship in that different forms and the degree of bias will lead to different types of bias-based selection errors. Next, we discuss three ranges of test scores and conditions under which selection decision makers are likely to be surprised (in some cases quite unpleasantly) in terms of selection outcomes other than the AI they are attempting to mitigate by lowering cut scores.

Three Relevant Regions of Test Scores

Figure 15.3 includes a graphic display of what we identify as three important ranges of test scores using as illustration a fairly commonly observed situation in selection contexts (i.e., differences in intercepts but not slopes across groups in which only two groups are under consideration). We identify these three ranges, which we refer to as *regions*, because several unanticipated selection outcomes will depend on the location of the cut scores in one or another region:

I. Region I encompasses low-performance and low selection cutoff values. In the illustrative selection scenario depicted in Figure 15.3, Region I will specifically be defined as the area to the left of the intersection of the common and Group 1 regression lines. Note in Figure 15.3 that for a given y^* value, $x_2^* < x_1^* < x^*$ in this region. In other words, the group-specific cut scores are lower than that of the common regression line in this region given y^*.

II. Region II includes the middle range of performance and selection cutoffs. For a situation such as the one in Figure 15.3, this region includes the area between the intersection of the common and Group 1 regression lines and the intersection of the common and

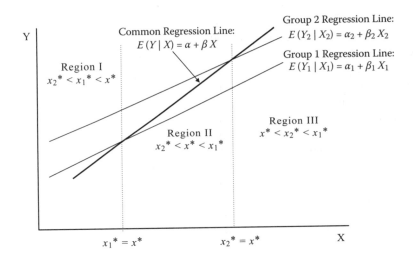

FIGURE 15.3
Three regions of test scores in the presence of intercept-based test bias.

Group 2 regression lines. In Figure 15.3, note that $x_2^* < x^* < x_1^*$ for any given performance level in this region; the common regression cut score lies between the group-specific cut scores.

III. Region III encompasses the high-performance, high selection cut score range. Referring again to Figure 15.3, this region is the area to the right of the intersection of the common and Group 2 regression lines so that $x^* < x_2^* < x_1^*$ for a given value of y^* (i.e., the common regression cut score is lower than that of the group-specific cut scores).

Understanding the Relationship Among Test Score Regions, Cut Scores, Expected Performance, Bias-Based Expected Selection Errors, and Expected Selection Ratios

In this section, we provide a discussion of what happens when test bias is present (albeit small in magnitude) and cut scores are lowered along the test score continuum to mitigate AI. We refer to the three regions identified and discuss implications in terms of (a) differentials between anticipated and actual performance of those individuals who are selected, (b) selectivity and utility of the selection system, and (c) bias-based selection errors (i.e., expected false positives and false negatives). To make our presentation more user friendly, we first keep our discussion general and use

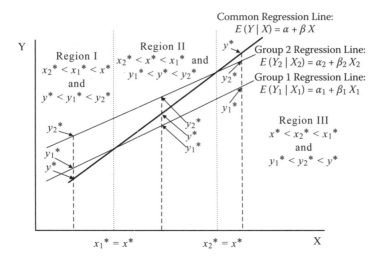

FIGURE 15.4
Performance differentials by test score region for intercept-based test bias.

graphs. We discuss two realistic numerical cases, including actual data, later in the chapter.

Consider again the illustrative and yet fairly typical situation in which there is bias based on intercept differences, but not slope differences, across two groups. Let us discuss first the issue of how those selected would perform relative to their anticipated performance level, as displayed in Figure 15.4. The severity and form of discrepancy between anticipated and actual performance depend on the region in which the cut scores are located. In Region I, selection decision makers would be pleasantly surprised because both groups would perform better than expected. That is because in Region I, decision makers, using the common regression line as mandated by law, expect performance level y^* for both groups. However, actual performance will be y_1^* for Group 1 and y_2^* for Group 2 because the test is biased and produces different performance levels for different groups. In Region II, results regarding performance are mixed. The majority group (Group 2) would perform better than expected on average, but the minority group would perform worse on average because for any given cut score in Region II, $y_1^* < y^* < y_2^*$. Finally, in Region III, unanticipated performance outcomes would be unpleasant all around: Both groups would perform worse than expected on average. Of course, results regarding each of the three regions would be accentuated to the extent that bias is more severe.

Consider now the implications of changing cut scores to mitigate AI in terms of the degree of selectivity of the system. As depicted in Figure 15.5, expected selection ratios in Region I will be larger than expected selection

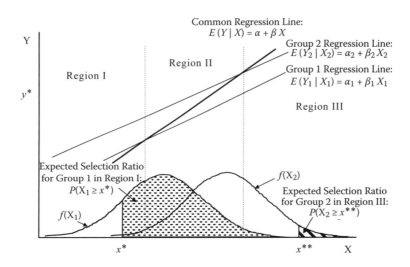

FIGURE 15.5
Expected selection ratios by test score region for intercept-based test bias.

ratios in the other two regions. For example, the largest shaded area in Figure 15.5 coincides with the expected selection ratio for Group 1 at the selection cutoff x^* in Region I. As depicted, that shaded area is about two thirds of the total area under the distribution of test scores for minority Group 1, $f(X_1)$; thus, at cutoff x^* in Region I a large percentage of applicants from Group 1 is expected to be selected. Also at x^* in Region I, note that virtually all candidates from the majority Group 2 are expected to be selected because the area under $f(X_2)$ to the right of x^* (an area that is not shaded in Figure 15.5) captures almost all of the Group 2 test score probability mass. Figure 15.5 can be used to visualize clearly what happens to expected selection ratios when selection cutoffs are increased: The expected selection ratios for both groups become increasingly small with larger cutoffs. See, for example, the smaller shaded area in Figure 15.5 depicting the expected selection ratio for Group 2 in Region III at x^{**}. Thus, large percentages of applicants are expected to be selected in Region I and smaller percentages in Region III.

Taken together, Figures 15.4 and 15.5 illustrate the kinds of trade-offs that decision makers face when using selection systems as if they were unbiased in the presence of actual test bias. Considering performance differentials only, Region I is desirable because both groups are expected to exceed performance expectations (Figure 15.4). However, this would mean that the expected selection ratios are very large (i.e., large proportions of applicants are expected to be selected from each group (Figure 15.5), which may seriously compromise the economic utility of using the test as is usually conceptualized in terms of individual performance in industrial and organizational psychology (Cascio & Aguinis, 2005, Chapter 3). Conversely, minimizing expected selection ratios to enhance test utility, which occurs when cuts fall within Region III, would lead to the most disadvantageous results in terms of expected performance.

Now, let us discuss implications of lowering cut scores in terms of bias-based selection errors. There are two types of bias-based errors that can occur: (a) expected false positives (i.e., individuals selected do not meet standards) and (b) expected false negatives (i.e., individuals not selected who could have met the standards). We turn first to bias-based expected false positives. Expected false positives that arise from test bias occur whenever, at any given performance level, y^*, a group-specific selection cutoff, exceeds the common line selection cutoff (Aguinis & Smith, 2007). Careful scrutiny of Figure 15.3 reveals that there will be no expected false positives in Region I because, everywhere in this region, the common line cutoff x^* exceeds the group-specific cutoffs x_1^* and x_2^*. In Region II, there are expected false positives for Group 1 only. Both groups will have expected false positives in Region III.

We can ascertain the magnitude of expected false positives by using probability calculations analogous to those applied to expected selection ratios. Consider Figure 15.6 and suppose, for example, that the desired performance level is y^*. At y^*, all individuals with test scores exceeding x^* are under consideration for employment. However, over the range of test scores x^* and x_1^*, individuals from Group 1 will actually perform worse than the expected performance level y^* because the values for Y over this range are lower than y^* along the Group 1 regression line. These are

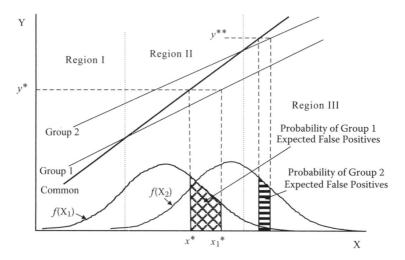

FIGURE 15.6
Expected false positives by test score region for intercept-based test bias.

expected false positives. The *probability* of expected false positives will be the area under the Group 1 test score distribution $f(X_1)$ between x^* and x_1^* as shown in Figure 15.6. Probabilities of expected false positives for Group 1 in Region II will generally be larger than those in Region III because Region III coincides with smaller probability mass regions (i.e., the tails) of $f(X_1)$. Figure 15.6 also shows how to identify probabilities of expected false positives for Group 2 in Region III, where a different performance level y^{**} exceeds the performance level predicted by the Group 2 regression line over the relevant range of test scores.

Bias-based expected false negatives occur whenever, for a given performance level, the common line cutoff exceeds a group-specific cutoff (Aguinis & Smith, 2007). Referring to Figure 15.3, we see that bias-based expected false negatives will not occur in Region III. Region II will have expected false negatives but for Group 2 only. Both groups will have expected false negatives in Region I.

Now, please refer to Figure 15.7 to consider probabilities of expected false negatives. At performance level y^*, only those applicants whose test scores exceed x^* are under consideration; those with test scores less than x^* are not. Note, however, that over the range x_2^* to x^*, performance levels at the Group 2 regression line exceed y^*; in other words, Group 2 individuals in this range exceed the expected performance level but are not being considered for employment. This is an expected false negative. Probabilities of expected false negatives are areas under group-specific test score distributions, as shown in Figure 15.7. Although Group 2 will have expected false positives in Regions I and II, they will typically be larger in Region II, where there is more probability mass.

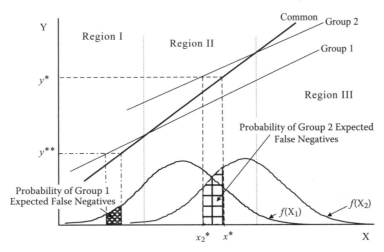

FIGURE 15.7
Expected false negatives by test score region for intercept-based test bias.

Finally, the expected AI ratio will be more severe at high selection cutoffs than at low ones for the scenarios such as those in Figures 15.3 through 15.7, in which test bias is characterized by intercept differences by group. Therefore, Region I is the most desirable, and Region III the least, as regards expected AI.

To summarize our discussion thus far, Table 15.1 shows what happens when intercept-based test bias is taken into account when cut scores are changed in an attempt to mitigate AI. This table makes the various trade-offs explicit and demonstrates that a decision to vary cut scores to address AI is more complex than has been discussed thus far in the literature. For example, if cut scores fall within Region III, the test will be highly selective

TABLE 15.1

Summary of Trade-Offs Among Expected Adverse Impact, Expected Selection Ratios, and Expected False Positives and False Negatives by Test Score Region in the Presence of Intercept-Based Test Bias

	Region I: Low selection cut scores	**Region II: Moderate selection cut scores**	**Region III: High selection cut scores**
Expected adverse impact (EAI)	*Desirable*: Large numerical values for EAI (i.e., more likely to meet the 80% heuristic)	*Moderate*	*Undesirable*: Small numerical values for EAI (i.e., more severe adverse impact)
Expected selection ratios	*Undesirable*: Larger (i.e., minimizes test utility)	*Moderate*	*Desirable*: Smaller (i.e., maximizes test utility)
Performance differentials	*Desirable*: Both groups would perform better than expected	*Mixed*: Group 1 would perform worse than expected, and Group 2 would perform better than expected	*Undesirable*: Both groups would perform worse than expected
Expected false negatives	*Undesirable* but not as severe as Region II: Both groups would have expected false negatives but tend to be small	*Mixed*: Group 2 only—can be large; *undesirable* if the primary goal is to minimize expected false negatives	*Desirable*: No expected false negatives
Expected false positives	*Desirable*: No expected false positives	*Mixed*: Group 1 only—can be large; *undesirable* if the primary goal is to minimize expected false positives	*Undesirable*, but not as severe as Region II: Both groups would have expected false positives, but tend to be small

(in the sense that selection cutoffs are large and expected selection ratios are low), and test utility will be maximized. Also on the positive side, there will be no bias-based expected false-negative errors, which would be a highly desirable outcome in a tight labor market (i.e., all applicants who are likely to succeed on the job are given a job offer). However, expected AI will be severe (likely violating the 80% heuristic) and observed performance will be worse than anticipated for both groups. In addition, there will be false positives (yet small in magnitude) for both groups.

What happens if we are faced with a Region III situation and decided to lower the cut score to reach a more acceptable level of AI? If we go from Region III to Region II, there would be expected false negatives for Group 2 (possibly large in magnitude) as well as expected false-positive errors for Group 1 (also possibly large). If AI is still not acceptable, we could decide to lower the cut scores even more and move into Region I. If this happened, Table 15.1 shows that the test would decrease its selectivity (and utility), perhaps to a level that is just unacceptable (i.e., almost all applicants would have to be selected), and there would be expected false negatives in both groups.

In closing, we have known for some time that higher cut scores are associated with more severe AI and greater test utility, whereas lower cut scores are associated with less-severe AI and less test utility (Aguinis, 2004b). Our discussion shows that the relationship between cut scores and AI is more complex, and there are several additional unanticipated consequences of changing cut scores to yield a more acceptable AI ratio. When test bias exists (even if it is small), changing cut scores leads to important consequences in terms of expected employee performance as well as expected selection errors (both false negatives and false positives) that have not been considered thus far.

To this point, we intentionally limited our discussion to the use of graphs to illustrate our points. Next, we offer two numerical cases to demonstrate the complexity of the cut score–AI relationship when test bias exists. By changing cut scores to mitigate AI, there can be unanticipated outcomes that are beneficial in terms of selection decision making (i.e., better performance than anticipated), but in other cases the unanticipated outcomes can be quite negative (i.e., larger expected false positives and negatives than anticipated).

Case 1: Intercept-Based Differences

In this first numerical example, we use the same parameters from Scenario B in Aguinis and Smith (2007). Specifically, in this situation the minority

TABLE 15.2

Summary of Trade-Offs Among Expected Adverse Impact, Expected Selection Ratios, and Expected False Positives and False Negatives by Test Score Region in the Presence of Intercept-Based Test Bias (Case 1)

	Region I: Low selection cut scores[a]	Region II: Moderate selection cutoffs	Region III: High selection cutoffs
Expected adverse impact (EAI)	N/A	Ranges from 100% at cutoff (x^*) < 54 to 17% at $x^* = 117$ EAI = 80% at $x^* = 87$	EAI is 17% to 4%
Expected selection ratios	N/A	*Group 1* ranges from 100% at $x^* = 23$ to 0.7% at $x^* = 117.4$ *Group 2* ranges from 100% at $x^* = 23$ to 4% at $x^* = 117.4$	*Group 1*: 0.7% or less *Group 2*: 4% or less
Performance differentials	N/A	Negligible; within ± 0.4 points of expected performance for both groups	*Group 1*: Underperforms by as much as 0.5 points *Group 2*: Negligible
Expected false negatives	N/A	*Group 2* ranges from zero to 6% (the latter at $x^* = 96$)	
Expected false positives	N/A	*Group 1* ranges from zero to 22% (the latter at $x^* = 91$)	Negligible; 0.6% or less for Group 1 and 0.1% or less for Group 2

Note: N/A, not applicable.
[a] Region I is out of the applicable range for this particular case.

group (i.e., Group 1) comprises 20% of the total number of applicants, has a mean score on the test of $\mu_{X1} = 92.8$, and mean performance score of $\mu_{Y1} = 2.75$ (on a 5-point scale of supervisory ratings). For the majority group (i.e., Group 2), $\mu_{X2} = 100$ and $\mu_{Y2} = 3.5$. Also, $\sigma_{X1} = \sigma_{X2} = 10$, $\sigma_{Y1} = \sigma_{Y2} = 1$, and $\rho_1 = \rho_2 = 0.5$, which, as noted by Aguinis and Smith (2007) is consistent with evidence generated by several meta-analytic reviews. Also, when the entire population is considered without breaking it down into groups, $\mu_X = 98.56$, $\sigma_X = 10.41$, $\mu_Y = 3.35$, $\sigma_Y = 1.04$, and $\rho = 0.54$.

We used the Aguinis and Smith (2007) calculator available online at http://mypage.iu.edu/~haguinis/selection/, which presumes bivariate normality of test scores and performance, to generate the values shown in Table 15.2 for each of the three relevant regions. Sample-based statistics can be used in lieu of population parameters in obtaining numerical results for actual selection situations. For the purposes of discussion, we set the lower bounds for Region I at performance level $Y = -1.25$ and test score $X = 52.8$ and the upper bounds for Region III at $Y = 7.5$ and $X = 140$.

These values are four standard deviations beyond the closest group-specific means. For this particular case, the transition from Region I to Region II occurs at X = 23.4 and Y = −0.7. Therefore, for all practical purposes of users of a test such as this one, Region I will never be encountered as it is beyond the relevant range of test scores.

Using the Web-based calculator to obtain precise numerical results based on realistic data showed that the decision to lower cut scores to mitigate AI leads to several unanticipated outcomes. As expected, using a cut score in Region III, the one with the highest degree of selectivity, leads to severe expected AI (i.e., around 17% or smaller), which obviously violates the 80% heuristic. So, selection decision makers would consider lowering the cut scores to Region II. In this region, expected AI may now fall between the 80% and 100%, which is an acceptable range. However, selectivity (and test utility) is lowered. One set of surprising results relate to performance differentials because there would be an unanticipated observed mean performance decrease of up to 0.4 points (on a 5-point scale of supervisory ratings) for the minority group and an unanticipated observed increase of up to 0.4 points for the majority group. Expected false negatives could be as high as 6% for the majority group. In terms of expected false positives, the minority group could reach as much as 22%, a potentially substantial number of workers who will not meet performance expectations. In short, for this realistic case, lowering the cut score would lead to the benefit of reaching an acceptable level of expected AI and would need to be weighed against the cost of a decrease in selectivity, a decrease in performance for the minority group (albeit small), and an increase in expected false positives for the minority group. Using the online calculator allows decision makers to obtain precise numerical results that make the trade-offs involved explicit. Consequently, the decision to lower the cut score can be made within a broader context of outcomes beyond AI.

Case 2: Intercept- and Slope-Based Differences

In this second numerical example, we use parameter values that are similar to those in Case 1, but we changed them slightly so that differences across groups are based on both intercepts and slopes. In this scenario in which the group-based regression lines are not parallel, $\mu_{X2} = 100$, $\mu_{X1} = 85$, $\sigma_{X1} = \sigma_{X2} = 20$, $\sigma_{Y1} = 1.2$, $\sigma_{Y2} = 0.8$, $\rho_1 = 0.58$, $\rho_2 = 0.49$, $\mu_{Y2} = 5$, $\mu_{Y1} = 4$, $\mu_X = 92.5$, $\sigma_X = 21.36$, $\mu_Y = 4.5$, $\sigma_Y = 1.1358$, $\rho = 0.603$, and half of the population is in Group 1 (the other half is in Group 2). Again, these parameter values are quite realistic (cf. Hunter, Schmidt, & Hunter, 1979). The group-specific

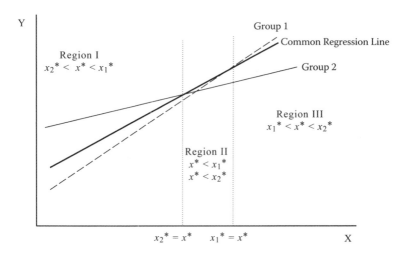

FIGURE 15.8
The three regions of test scores in the presence of intercept- and slope-based test bias (Case 2).

and common regression lines that result from these parameter values are displayed in Figure 15.8.

As we did throughout, Region I is defined as including the low cut scores, Region III includes the high cut scores, and Region II includes the intermediate range. However, given the configuration of the lines shown in Figure 15.8, the boundary between Regions I and II is now the intersection of the Group 2 and common regression lines, and the boundary separating Region II from Region III is now the intersection of the Group 1 and common regression lines. And, because the group-specific regression lines are no longer parallel, they intersect in Region II (as displayed in Figure 15.8).

Like Case 1, expected selection ratios are largest in Region I and decline with increasing cut scores. Also like Case 1, expected AI ratios are acceptable in Region I but become smaller (i.e., more severe expected AI) with increasing cut scores, so that expected AI is most severe in Region III. However, that is where the similarity between Case 1 and Case 2 ends. Specifically, as depicted Figure 15.8, we observe the following outcomes by region:

- Region I: The majority Group 2 performs better than expectations and includes expected false negatives. The minority Group 1 underperforms relative to expectations and exhibits expected false positives.
- Region II: Both the minority and majority groups are expected to underperform relative to expectations, minority Group 1 more so

at low cut scores and majority Group 2 more so at high cut scores. Both groups experience expected false positives.

- Region III: Minority Group 1 performs better than expected, but with expected false negatives. Majority Group 2 underperforms and exhibits expected false positives.

Again, we used the Aguinis and Smith (2007) online calculator available at http://mypage.iu.edu/~haguinis/selection/ to obtain precise numerical results and understand what happens when we lower cut scores in an effort to mitigate AI. Table 15.3 summarizes these results. For purposes of discussion, we set the lower bound for Region I at $X = 5$ and $Y = -0.8$ and the upper bound for Region III at $X = 200$ and $Y = 8.8$. In Figure 15.3,

TABLE 15.3

Summary of Trade-Offs Among Expected Adverse Impact, Expected Selection Ratios, and Expected False Positives and False Negatives by Test Score Region in the Presence of Intercept- and Slope-Based Test Bias (Case 2)

	Region I: Low cut scores	Region II: Moderate cut scores	Region III: High cut scores
Expected adverse Impact (EAI)	Ranges from 100% at $x^* < 7.3$ to 25% at $x^* = 120.8$ EAI = 80% at $x^* = 72.7$	25% to 3%	Under 3%
Expected selection ratios	*Group 1:* Ranges from 100% at x^*, 7.2 to 4% at $x^* = 120.8$ *Group 2:* Ranges from 100% at $x^* < 22.1$ to 15% at $x^* = 120.8$	*Group 1:* 4% or less *Group 2:* 15% or less	Virtually no one is selected in Region III; Region III is not relevant for this scenario
Performance differentials	*Group 1:* Underperforms by 0.5 points at $x^* = 5$ and by 0.2 points at $x^* = 120.8$ *Group 2:* Performs better than expected by up to 1.4 points at $x^* = 5$	*Group 1:* Underperforms by up to 0.2 points at $x^* = 120.89$ *Group 2:* Underperforms by up to 0.7 points at $x^* = 170.9$	
Expected false negatives	*Group 2:* Up to 26% at $x^* = 96$		*Group 1:* Negligible
Expected false positives	*Group 1:* Up to 16% at $x^* = 77$	Negligible: No more than 1.5% for Group 1 and 3% for Group 2	*Group 2:* Negligible

Region I is separated from Region 2 at X = 120.8 and Region II from Region III at X = 179.9.

Table 15.3 shows that if we lowered cut scores from Region III to Region II, we would improve AI from under 3% to up to 25%. Note, however, that this figure is still quite far from the 80% target. So, we may wish to move to Region I because we would be able to achieve an expected AI of 80% (by using a cut score of 72.7). This move from Region III to I comes at a cost, though. First, the selectivity (and utility) of the test is compromised. Specifically, by using a cut score of 72.7, which is associated with an AI of 80%, selection ratios are 73% for the minority group and 91% for the majority group. So, virtually every single applicant in the majority group would have to be offered employment. This would obviously render the test virtually useless, and errors would be about 15% false positives for the minority group and about 8% false negatives for the majority group.

Discussion

This chapter's main contribution is to demonstrate the complex issues involved in changing cut scores in an attempt to mitigate AI in the presence of test bias. Specifically, depending on the degree and form of test bias, lowering cut scores can help mitigate AI. However, this lowering of cut scores can also degrade the selectivity of a test, decrease a test's economic utility, and increase bias-based false positives and false-negative errors. Also depending on the situation in hand, lowering cut scores may actually lead to beneficial outcomes such as a decrease in bias-based false positives or false negatives. The Aguinis and Smith (2007) decision-making framework and online calculator can be used to understand what are the expected outcomes of a particular decision (i.e., decrease the cut score by a given amount given a particular situation, specific mean test and criterion scores for each of the groups, group-based validity coefficients, and so forth). Next, we discuss some implications for theory and research as well as practice.

Implications for Theory and Research

The scholarly literature relating cut scores and AI has thus far focused on the implications of lowering cut scores in terms of a system's selectivity and test utility. Our chapter offers an expanded and more comprehensive view of the cut score–AI relationship that includes a consideration of the presence of test bias. It would be difficult to argue that regression lines across groups are always precisely identical. Likely, albeit small in some cases, differences across lines exist. The fact that such differences are sometimes reported (i.e., Hunter & Schmidt, 1976; Reilly, 1973; Rotundo & Sackett, 1999) in spite of the lack of statistical power for the moderating effect suggests that test bias may be more pervasive than thought (Aguinis et al., 2005). Thus, there is a need for further theory work, as well as empirical research, on the reasons why test bias exists, how to detect it, and how to mitigate it. Some efforts in this regard are quite promising (e.g., Cronshaw, Hamilton, Onyura, & Winston, 2006), but much work remains to be done.

A second implication for theory and research is that understanding where expected selection errors will occur (i.e., under which region) and the severity of such errors (i.e., percentages of false positives and negatives in each group) is not a simple process. Rather, such outcomes are understood by engaging in an inductive and interactive process in which a researcher enters values in a sort of trial-and-error fashion in the online calculator to obtain results for each scenario. Although Tables 15.2–15.3 include summary information regarding the trade-offs involved by region in two typical cases, these numerical values change based on the degree of bias that may be present. Future research could investigate thresholds for test bias that may lead to undesirable results. For example, given intercept-based test bias, how different can the regression lines be until there is a noticeable impact on, for example, expected performance for the minority group? Future research can address similar questions regarding a maximum test bias threshold that would allow for acceptable selection outcomes (e.g., false positives and false negatives).

Implications for Practice

One important implication for practice is that test bias should no longer be excluded from selection decision making in organizational staffing and high-stakes testing. Given the availability of the Aguinis and Smith (2007) online calculator, there is no reason not to use it to anticipate the impact of lowering cut scores on such crucial selection outcomes as AI, differences between anticipated and observed performance in those hired, and selection errors, including bias-based false positives and false negatives. If test bias does not have an important effect on these outcomes given a specific situation, then the online calculator will show that. On the other hand, if bias is present (even if it is small in magnitude), the online calculator will consider its effects when computing the anticipated outcomes. Practitioners have the professional mandate to make the best possible decision in terms of selection, particularly when high-stakes testing is involved. Using the online calculator allows for the consideration of possible test bias and its effects on important selection outcomes explicitly. In many cases, and depending on the particular situation, using the online calculator may show that the cure (i.e., lowering cut scores) may actually be worse than the disease (i.e., AI). In fact, our analyses showed that there is no cut score region in which some kind of unpleasant outcome does not occur when test bias is present.

Another implication of our analyses is that, given typical test characteristics that we discussed, it is virtually impossible to use a GMA test and reach the 80% AI heuristic without hiring such a large proportion of applicants that the utility of the test is compromised. Stated differently, how many GMA tests can be used with cut scores in Region III and yet lead to minimum, or even acceptable, AI? This is a challenge for practitioners but obviously is linked to a need for further research to solve this problem.

In closing, the possibility of test bias must be taken into account before deciding to lower a cut score to mitigate AI. The Aguinis and Smith (2007) online calculator allows researchers and practitioners to consider specific numerical characteristics of a testing situation and compute anticipated selection outcomes, including AI, differences in expected versus observed performance for those who will be hired, and false-positive and false-negative selection errors. Obtaining these numbers and considering them explicitly before a test is put to use will help improve organizational staffing and high-stakes selection decisions.

Acknowledgment

This research was conducted, in part, while Herman Aguinis held the Mehalchin Term Professorship in Management at the University of Colorado at Denver and visiting appointments at the University of Salamanca (Spain) and University of Puerto Rico.

References

Aguinis, H. (1995). Statistical power problems with moderated multiple regression in management research. *Journal of Management, 21,* 1141–1158.

Aguinis, H. (2004a). *Regression analysis for categorical moderators.* New York: Guilford.

Aguinis, H. (Ed.). (2004b). *Test-score banding in human resource selection: Legal, technical, and societal issues.* Westport, CT: Praeger.

Aguinis, H., Beaty, J. C., Boik, R. J., & Pierce, C. A. (2005). Effect size and power in assessing moderating effects of categorical variables using multiple regression: A 30-year review. *Journal of Applied Psychology, 90,* 94–107.

Aguinis, H., Boik, R. J., & Pierce, C. A. (2001). A generalized solution for approximating the power to detect effects of categorical moderator variables using multiple regression. *Organizational Research Methods, 4,* 291–323.

Aguinis, H., Cortina, J. M., & Goldberg, E. (1998). A new procedure for computing equivalence bands in personnel selection. *Human Performance, 11,* 351–365.

Aguinis, H., & Smith, M. A. (2007). Understanding the impact of test validity and bias on selection errors and adverse impact in human resource selection. *Personnel Psychology, 60,* 165–199.

Aguinis, H., & Stone-Romero, E. F. (1997). Methodological artifacts in moderated multiple regression and their effects on statistical power. *Journal of Applied Psychology, 82,* 192–206.

American Educational Research Association, American Psychological Association, & National Council on Measurement in Education. (1999). *Standards for educational and psychological testing.* Washington, DC: American Educational Research Association.

Biddle, D. (2005). *Adverse impact and test validation: A practitioner's guide to valid and defensible employment testing.* Burlington, VT: Gower.

Bobko, P., & Roth, P. L. (2004). The four-fifths rule for assessing adverse impact: An arithmetic, intuitive, and logical analysis of the rule and implications for future research and practice. In J. Martocchio (Ed.), *Research in personnel and human resources management* (Vol. 19, pp. 177–197). New York: Elsevier.

Cascio, W. F., & Aguinis, H. (2005). *Applied psychology in human resource management* (6th ed.). Upper Saddle River, NJ: Pearson Prentice Hall.

Civil Rights Act of 1991, 42 U.S.C. §§ 1981, 2000e *et seq.* (1991)

Cleary, T. A. (1968). Test bias: Prediction of grades of Negro and white students in integrated colleges. *Journal of Educational Measurement, 5,* 115–124.

Cronshaw, S. F., Hamilton, L. K., Onyura, B. R., & Winston, A. S. (2006). The case for non-biased intelligence testing against Black Africans has not been made: A comment on Rushton, Skuy, and Bons (2004). *International Journal of Selection and Assessment, 14,* 278–287.

Hough, L. M., Oswald, F. L., & Ployhart, R. E. (2001). Determinants, detection and amelioration of adverse impact in personnel selection procedures: Issues, evidence and lessons learned. *International Journal of Selection and Assessment, 9,* 152–194.

Hunter, J. E., & Schmidt, F. L. (1976). Critical analysis of the statistical and ethical implications of various definitions of test bias. *Psychological Bulletin, 83,* 1053–1071.

Hunter, J. E., Schmidt, F. L., & Hunter, R. (1979). Differential validity of employment tests by race: A comprehensive review an analysis. *Psychological Bulletin, 86,* 721–735.

Kehoe, J. (2009). Cut scores and adverse impact. In J. L. Outtz (Ed.), *Adverse impact: Implications for organizational staffing and high stakes selection* (pp. 293–328). New York: Routledge.

Murphy, K. R. (2004). Conflicting values and interests in banding research and practice. In H. Aguinis (Ed.), *Test-score banding in human resource selection: Legal, technical, and societal issues* (pp. 175–192). Westport, CT: Praeger.

Reilly, R. R. (1973). A note on minority group test bias studies. *Psychological Bulletin, 80,* 130–132.

Roth, P. L., Bobko, P., & Switzer, F. S. (2006). Modeling the behavior of the 4/5ths rule for determining adverse impact: Reasons for caution. *Journal of Applied Psychology, 91,* 507–522.

Rotundo, M., & Sackett, P. R. (1999). Effect of rater race on conclusions regarding differential prediction in cognitive ability tests. *Journal of Applied Psychology, 84,* 815–822.

Schmidt, F. L., & Hunter, J. E. (2004). SED banding as a test of scientific values in I/O psychology. In H. Aguinis (Ed.), *Test-score banding in human resource selection: Legal, technical, and societal issues* (pp. 151–174). Westport, CT: Praeger.

Uniform Guidelines on Employee Selection Procedures. 43 Fed. Reg. 38290–38315 (1978).

Zedeck, S. (2009). Adverse impact: History and evolution. In J. L. Outtz (Ed.), *Adverse impact: Implications for organizational staffing and high stakes selection* (pp. 3–28). New York: Routledge.

16

Reductions in Measured Subgroup Mean Differences: What Is Possible?

Neal Schmitt and Abigail Quinn

Introduction

Certainly one of the most perplexing concerns for those involved in assessing human talent for the purpose of making selection decisions regarding employment, admission to academic institutions, or other high-stakes decisions is the fact that cognitive ability tests typically show substantial differences between racial or ethnic subgroups. The magnitude of these differences is such that the use of cognitive ability tests in these situations almost always produces differences in the proportion of members of different racial groups who receive a desired outcome in these high-stakes situations. These proportional differences are the subject of this book.

Mean black–white differences tend to be about one standard deviation in magnitude; Hispanic–white differences are usually two thirds of a standard deviation, and Asians usually score higher than white groups on measures of quantitative ability and lower on verbal ability measures (e.g., Bobko, Roth, & Potosky, 1999; Neisser et al., 1996; Roth, Bevier, Bobko, Switzer, & Tyler, 2001). Some (Dickens & Flynn, 2006) alleged that these differences, particularly black–white differences, are decreasing. While others (Rushton & Jensen, 2006) disputed these claims, both parties agree that a substantial racial difference in mean test scores remains. Moreover, there is an extensive body of research conducted in employment and educational arenas that indicates that cognitive ability tests do not underpredict the performance of minority group members (American Educational Research Association, American Psychological Association, & National Council of Measurement in Education, 1999; Neisser et al., 1996; Sackett & Wilk, 1994). Finally, there is evidence that the level of validity typically displayed by cognitive ability tests is such that there will be practically significant losses in expected performance if scores on these measures are ignored (Schmidt, Mack, & Hunter, 1984). However, it is possible that the use of other predictors such as personality measures or interviews can result in maintaining or increasing validity while reducing subgroup differences. The likelihood that this is the case is explored in this chapter as one option available to personnel selection researchers. Whether cognitive ability measures are replaced or used in combination with these other predictors should be based on what is known of the criterion domain of interest.

The dilemma, then, is how best to balance organizational concerns with the maximization of expected levels of performance against the individual, social, and organizational desire for a diverse workforce/student body and equitable treatment of members of different racial/ethnic groups. In many situations, a diverse workforce may be an economic or competitive necessity. Selecting the highest-scoring individuals and a small proportion of applicants for a particular treatment will virtually eliminate members of lower-scoring subgroups (see Sackett & Wilk, 1994, for various scenarios). One solution is to provide some form of minority group preference. However, federal legislation (Civil Rights Act of 1991, see http://www.eeoc.gov/laws/cra91.html) and case law have prohibited the use of set-aside programs for minority-owned businesses and the use of race in college admissions. State statutes in California, Washington, and Michigan have prohibited the use of race in academic admissions and public sector employment.

Given these scientific results and the legal situation, Sackett, Schmitt, Ellingson, and Kabin (2001) explored various strategies that have been proposed to minimize the mean difference in the measured capabilities of different racial subgroups as well as maintaining or enhancing the validity of the selection process. These methods included (a) the use of measures of constructs on which there are small or no subgroup difference in combination with cognitive ability measures, (b) the inclusion and consideration of additional criterion constructs against which the validity of different measures is evaluated, (c) the identification and removal of culturally biased items, (d) the use of alternate modes of presenting test stimuli, (e) attempts to change the motivational set of examinees, (f) the use of coaching or special preparation programs, and (g) the use of more generous time limits for the completion of tests. Based on their qualitative review of the literature on these various strategies, they recommended that selection materials include assessments of the full range of relevant attributes, that measures be as face valid as possible, and test preparation methods be introduced whenever possible. However, they also stated that available strategies will not allow for the joint maximization of expected employee performance and equal hiring rates for members of various racial groups, although we conclude at the end of this chapter that progress has been made.

In this chapter, we explore the various ways in which researchers have sought to produce valid measures of employee or student potential that minimize subgroup mean differences. We start with the solutions described by Sackett et al. (2001). The literature reviewed in that article and any subsequent research studies are examined to provide estimates of the reduction in standardized subgroup mean differences (*d*) that are possible with each proposed solution. We then make an estimate based on this literature regarding what might be possible if these various solutions were used in combination while considering organizational demands that a maximally competent and motivated workforce be hired.

Identification and Removal of Biased Items

In Table 16.1, we present the results of articles in which items that were biased for or against particular groups of individuals were identified and removed from the test. *Bias* was defined in these studies as the existence of an item for which the responses of equally able (as defined by the total score on the test or the latent trait measured by the test) members of different groups of individuals exhibit different responses. As can be seen in Table 16.1, both gender and race differences have been examined, and the results indicated that some items are biased both for and against protected groups in all studies. In most cases, the number of items favoring a group is almost the same as the number biased against that group.

Removing such items from a test would be one approach to the removal of bias and hopefully a decrease in the magnitude of subgroup test score differences. Not all studies reported data that allowed the computation of differences on the total test resulting from such removal of items. Predictably, in those cases for which data exist, the impact on overall test mean differences when these biased items are removed is minimal. The largest change (*d* = −0.14) was reported by Whitney and Schmitt (1997) for a biodata exam. All other comparisons were done using ability measures, and change in *d* resulting from the removal of biased items was typically very small (−0.04 or less). Clearly, the removal of biased items alone will not make much difference in overall test score means either at the observed score or latent variable score levels.

Weighting Criterion Components

That job performance is multidimensional is a consistent theme in the literature of the past 25 years (e.g., Borman & Motowidlo, 1993; Campbell,

TABLE 16.1

Identification (and Removal) of "Biased" Items

Reference	Test	Total item N	Reference	N favoring R	Focal	N favoring F	Difference in d[a] (After − Before)
Donlon, Hicks, & Wallmark (1980)	GREAT–Vocabulary	55	Male	2	Female	3	
Donlon, Hicks, & Wallmark (1980)	GREAT–Reading Comprehension	40	Male	3	Female	3	
Donlon, Hicks, & Wallmark (1980)	GREAT–Mathematics	55	Male	4	Female	5	
Doudin & Al-Darabee (2003)	Math test for Jordanian 10th graders	50	Male	8	Female	9	
Dragow (1987)	Mathematics Usage Test	40	White male	5	White female	4	
Dragow (1987)	Mathematics Usage Test	40	White male	8	Black male	2	
Dragow (1987)	Mathematics Usage Test	40	White male	8	Black female	8	
Dragow (1987)	Mathematics Usage Test	40	White male	2	Hispanic male	2	
Dragow (1987)	Mathematics Usage Test	40	White male	11	Hispanic female	4	
Dragow (1987)	English Usage Test	75	White male	2	White female	5	
Dragow (1987)	English Usage Test	75	White male	5	Black male	5	

Drasgow (1987)	English Usage Test	75	White male	12	Black female	10	
Drasgow (1987)	English Usage Test	75	White male	2	Hispanic male	2	
Drasgow (1987)	English Usage Test	75	White male	10	Hispanic female	3	
Garner & Engelhard (1999)	1994 Georgia high school graduation test	60	Male	15	Female	16	
Kim et al. (unpublished)	Life Events Assessment and Development (SJT)	39	White	3	Black	1	−0.04
Lane, Wang, & Magone (1996)	QUASAR Cognitive Assessment Instrument (sixth/seventh grade)	42	Male	2	Female	4	
Scheunemann & Gerritz (1990)	SAT (Reading items)	150	Male	26	Female	21	
Scheunemann & Gerritz (1990)	GRE General Test (Reading items)	132	Male	20	Female	20	
A. Schmitt (1988)	SAT–Verbal (Form 1)	85	White	5	Mexican American	3	
A. Schmitt (1988)	SAT–Verbal (Form 1)	85	White	7	Puerto Rican	5	
A. Schmitt (1988)	SAT–Verbal (Form 2)	85	White	10	Mexican American	4	
A. Schmitt (1988)	SAT–Verbal (Form 2)	85	White	9	Puerto Rican	7	
Stark, Chernyshenko, & Drasgow (2004)	Professional licensing exam	79	White		Asian		−0.03
Stark, Chernyshenko, & Drasgow (2004)	Professional licensing exam	79	White		Black		−0.08

Continued

TABLE 16.1 (*Continued*)

Identification (and Removal) of "Biased" Items

Reference	Test	Total item N	Reference	N favoring R	Focal	N favoring F	Difference in d[a] (After – Before)
Stark, Chernyshenko, & Drasgow (2004)	Professional licensing exam	79	White	4	Hispanic	9	–0.04
Stark, Chernyshenko, & Drasgow (2004)	ACT (English subtest)	75	White		Asian		–0.02
Stark, Chernyshenko, & Drasgow (2004)	ACT (English subtest)	75	White		Black		0.01
Stark, Chernyshenko, & Drasgow (2004)	ACT (English subtest)	75	White		Hispanic		0.00
Wang & Lane (1996)	QUASAR Cognitive Assessment Instrument (sixth/seventh grade)	33	Male	5	Female	2	
Whitney & Schmitt (1997)	Biodata items	107	White	14	Black	8	–0.14

[a] In Stark et al. (2004), *d* was assessed using latent variables (i.e., DTF). For Kim et al. (unpublished) and Whitney & Schmitt (1997), it was assessed using observed variables.

DTF = differential test functioning; GREAT = Graduate Record Examination Aptitude Test.

McCloy, Oppler, & Sager, 1993; Motowidlo, 2003). The number of such dimensions that have been identified by these authors ranges from two to eight, but probably the most popular view is that performance is represented by two broad domains called task and contextual performance. *Task performance* includes behaviors that contribute to the transformation of goods into services or to the maintenance of the organization's technical core. *Contextual performance* usually includes behaviors that support the organization's climate and culture (Borman & Motowidlo, 1997).

As might be expected if these dimensions are relatively independent, empirical research has indicated that the two performance dimensions are best predicted by different individual difference constructs. McHenry, Hough, Toquam, Hanson, and Ashworth (1990) showed that technical proficiency and general soldiering proficiency were best predicted by cognitive ability, while measures of contextual performance were best predicted by personality or temperament. Similar results have been reported by others (e.g., Barrick & Mount, 1991; Motowidlo & Van Scooter, 1994). Given these differential relationships, the appropriate weight placed on a predictor based on its relationship with criteria will be a function of the weighting of criterion elements.

Using this research as support and cumulated correlations between variables as input, two simulation studies (DeCorte, 1999; Hattrup, Rock, & Scalia, 1997) explored the impact of different weights placed on criterion elements on expected job performance and the proportion of members of minority and majority groups hired given different selection ratios. Weights applied to these two criterion dimensions in Hattrup et al. were 0, 1, 3, and 5 to 1. Hattrup et al. did not compute mean differences between majority and minority individuals in the predictors but did produce percentages of increase in minorities hired as the weight on the two criterion dimensions varied. Relative to a situation in which contextual performance was not considered at all to a situation in which contextual and task performance were equally weighted, the percentage fewer minorities hired went from −0.4% to −4% as the selection ratio went from 0.05 to 0.80. When task performance was not considered, the percentage increase in minorities hired went from 1.6 to 11.1 as the selection ratio went from 0.05 to 0.80. Intermediate increases or decreases in minority hiring were observed when the weightings of the two criterion dimensions were less extreme than zero and one. The analysis by DeCorte (1999) yielded similar results, but DeCorte was interested in examining the performance loss that occurred when the simulation was constrained so that adverse impact was controlled. In both these studies and others that estimated expected performance or utility (e.g., Schmidt et al., 1984), the assumption was that changes in individuals' performance are additive when estimating organizational performance. This may not be the case when work is performed in teams, for example, and does not appear to be supported when studies of the utility of human resource efforts, including selection, are evaluated at the organizational level (e.g., Huselid, 1995).

A study by Dubois, Sackett, Zedeck, and Fogli (1993) involved a comparison of the typical and maximum performance of black and white grocery checkout personnel. While typical and maximum performance measures were relatively uncorrelated and different predictors were related to each dimension, the subgroup differences favoring white employees were larger for typical than maximum performance. In this case, considering motivational predictors that are likely to relate to typical performance would likely have overpredicted the performance of black applicants, while cognitive predictors would have underpredicted maximum performance of blacks. The authors cautioned against generalizations from this sample, and they did not provide data that would allow us to compare subgroup predictor performance for batteries that might have been selected based on their validity in the prediction of typical and maximum performance.

As was true in the case of item bias studies, using predictor weights based on the incorporation of relevant criteria can have an impact on minority selection in a positive way, but the changes will not be dramatic. The values reported from Hattrup et al. (1997) are the maximum changes reported in Table 16.2; most differences under realistic weighting schemes and selection ratios are smaller.

Use of Alternative Modes of Presenting Stimuli

An additional approach to reducing subgroup differences has been to change the way in which test material is presented to examinees. There have been two main theories underlying the attempts to manipulate test format. One theory has focused on changing the cultural context of test items, with the assumption that racial minorities do not perform as well as racial majorities because traditional cognitive tests are written with a majority culture bias. The other theory has focused on changing the format of the tests (often to some sort of job simulation), with the goal of keeping the content constant (or at least similar). The main assumption of this tactic is that traditional tests measure constructs that lead to subgroup differences in addition to the constructs they are intended to measure. If the constructs that lead to subgroup differences are job irrelevant, it should be possible to eliminate them from the measures without lowering predictive validity.

Research findings have not supported the idea that changing the cultural bias of a test will reduce subgroup differences. Schmeiser and Ferguson (1978) sought to test this theory by giving both white and

TABLE 16.2

Use of Alternative Modes of Presenting Test Stimuli

Authors	Method 1	Method 2	Reduction in d
Chan & Schmitt (1997)	Paper-and-pencil SJT	Video-based SJT	0.74
O'Neil & Brown (1997)	Multiple-choice math	Open-ended math	0.66 (Hispanic)[a]
Pulakos & Schmitt (1996)	Verbal ability measure	Munitions simulation	0.58 (Black) 0.41 (Hispanic)
Pulakos & Schmitt (1996)	Verbal ability measure	Health fraud simulation	0.12 (Black) 0.26 (Hispanic)
Sackett (1998)	Multistate bar examination	Video-based trial practice test	0.00
Schmeiser & Ferguson (1978)	English test with white content	English test with black content	−0.12
Schmeiser & Ferguson (1978)	Social studies test with white content	Social Studies test with black content	0.01 (black content V1) 0.12 (black content V2)
Schmitt & Mills (2001)	Paper-and-pencil test	Telephone simulation	0.31

[a] The d-values for the O'Neil and Brown (1997) and Schmeiser and Ferguson (1978) articles were estimated from the means and standard deviations presented in the articles. Positive d values reflect the fact that the difference between minority and white groups was smaller as a function of changes in items, whereas negative d values reflect the fact that differences were greater when item content was changed.

black ACT (formerly the American College Testing Program) examinees English and Social Studies test sections that were specifically developed to contain "white" or "black" content. Their implicit hypothesis was that white examinees would outperform black examinees on the tests of white content, but that black examinees would outperform white examinees on the tests of black content. Contrary to this hypothesis, the white examinees outperformed the black examinees on both the white and black content area tests, and changing the cultural framing of the test items actually increased the difference between groups (see Table 16.2).

In an early study of the impact of culture on test performance, Medley and Quirk (1974) examined test scores on the National Teacher Examination in the areas of social studies, literature, and the arts. They found large differences (approximately 18 points on a 65-item test) between forms that contained items that were related to "black" culture versus items that assessed "traditional" culture. The study is not included in Table 16.2 because data were not reported that would allow computation of an effect size, although the effects were obviously large and practically meaningful. The size of the difference in this case was impacted by the fact that the test content itself should be related to culture. Ignoring the cultural experience of one group in this examination should produce differences because culture is the target construct. However, our position would be that items addressing the cultures of various groups that represent the heterogeneous American society should be part of this examination.

DeShon, Smith, Chan, and Schmitt (1998) conducted two studies based on a similar premise. They suggested that, because abstract, "culture-free" measures of cognitive ability yield some of the highest performance differences between white and black examinees, racial differences should decrease when traditional cognitive ability items are rewritten in a social context. They found, however, that although both white and black examinees performed better on the test items placed in a social context, placing the items in a social context did not decrease the racial subgroup differences. Their results were reported in terms of odds ratios of correct responses on the part of white and black examinees and are not included in Table 16.2. These odds ratios indicated nearly identical subgroup differences in scores across item types. DeShon et al. suggested that perhaps researchers have overemphasized the theoretical cultural differences between white and black groups, citing research that suggests that values may not differ greatly between the communities.

An alternative tactic to changing the cultural context of tests has been to change test format from traditional cognitive ability measures to alternative formats that may yield lower subgroup differences. Pulakos and Schmitt (1996) gave job applicants a typical verbal ability measure (three subtests of the Air Force Officer Qualification Test) and two alternative measures of verbal ability (a Munitions Simulation and a Health Fraud Simulation), which involved writing essays in response to stimulus material. The latter were then rated regarding the accuracy of the information conveyed and their grammatical and spelling correctness. There was a considerable reduction in d (see Table 16.2) between the traditional verbal ability measure and the Munitions Simulation but very little reduction with the Health Fraud Simulation. Pulakos and Schmitt found that all three measures were equally reliable, but that the Munitions Simulation was less valid than the other two measures. They concluded that, although it is possible to reduce adverse impact by changing the format of a measure, it may occur at the loss of some predictive validity. It should also be noted that while both types of tests may address aspects of verbal ability, they may also measure different constructs as well.

O'Neil and Brown (1997) measured the effects of a much simpler change in test item format. They compared the performance of eighth-grade students on multiple-choice math questions and open-ended math questions. They found that, although there was a substantial subgroup difference between white and Latino students on the multiple-choice items, there was no significant difference between the students on the open-ended items. O'Neil and Brown were unable to explain these findings.

Chan and Schmitt (1997) compared subgroup differences in performance on a video-based situational judgment test (SJT) of interpersonal skills and work habits with performance on a written version of the same scenarios. The written and video versions of the test were comprised of identical verbal content and multiple-choice formats. They found a very substantial reduction in white–black differences from the written test to the video-based test in a laboratory study with student participants. They originally hypothesized that increased face validity of the video-based test might account for some of the reduction in *d*, but it did not. The reduction in subgroup differences between the video and paper-and-pencil SJT was almost totally explained by individual differences on the Nelson-Denny Reading Test.

Sackett (1998) examined another case in which multiple formats were used to measure similar test content. Millman, Mehrens, and Sackett (1993) found a white–black *d* of 0.89 for the Multistate Bar Examination (MBE). Klein (1983) gave a video-based alternative to the MBE. Sackett estimated that the white–black *d* for the video-based version would also have been 0.89, such that the video-based alternative led to no reduction in *d* for the MBE. While questions asked in the video-based alternative were objective in nature, it is not clear whether they were multiple choice in format as was the MBE.

Schmitt and Mills (2001) conducted a field study in which they examined performance on a paper-and-pencil test battery versus performance on a high-fidelity computerized telephone job simulation. They found a significant reduction in *d* (although much smaller than that of Chan and Schmitt, 1997) for white and black examinees in the simulation. Schmitt and Mills concluded, similar to Pulakos and Schmitt (1996), that the simulation was a valid predictor, but that predictive validity would be reduced by eliminating the paper-and-pencil tests. Again, there may have been construct differences in the two batteries compared, so that the effect of format may have been confounded with the constructs measured, as was the case with the Pulakos and Schmitt (1996) effort.

Finally, Gallagher, Bridgeman, and Calahan (2002) examined differences in subgroup performance for paper-based versus computer-based testing programs. They compared quantitative and verbal scores on the Graduate Record Examination (GRE), SAT (Scholastic Aptitude Test), Praxis, and GMAT (Graduate Management Admission Test) for racial and gender subgroups. The effect sizes that they found were extremely small but suggest that computer-based tests may slightly favor black (reductions in *d* ranged from 0.01 to 0.14) and Hispanic groups (0.01 to 0.12) as well as males (0.01 to 0.09). The largest effect was seen for the writing section of the Praxis exam. Although still a very small effect, the reduction in *d* related to a switch to computer-based testing was 0.14 for blacks and 0.12 for Hispanics as compared to the white reference group.

So, the question remains regarding why some researchers are able to reduce subgroup differences by manipulating test format whereas others are not. Sackett et al. (2001) suggested that the success of this method of reducing adverse impact lies in examining the focal construct measured. In the Sackett (1998) study (which found no reduction in d), scores on the written test and the video-based alternative were highly correlated, indicating that the tests were measuring the same constructs. Those constructs probably have inherent subgroup differences. Presumably, although the format of the tests changes in the conversion to computer-adaptive testing, the standardized exams in the Gallagher et al. (2002) study also measured the same constructs as the paper-based versions.

Alternatively, the Pulakos and Schmitt (1996), O'Neil and Brown (1997), Chan and Schmitt (1997), and Schmitt and Mills (2001) studies all found moderate-to-substantial reductions in d related to a change in test format. Although the alternative test measures in all of these studies were designed to measure the same focal constructs as the original measures, the alternative measures probably eliminated aspects of these constructs that were causing adverse impact. The alternative measure in the Pulakos and Schmitt and Schmitt and Mills studies were job simulations that were more face valid than the original measures. The alternative measure in the O'Neil and Brown study used open-ended item formats as opposed to a multiple-choice format. The Chan and Schmitt manipulation, which kept the test content fairly identical, appeared to eliminate the reading comprehension component of the measure. Rather than firm conclusions, what this set of results illustrates is the difficulty that all researchers have had in disentangling format and construct effects.

Manipulating test format can reduce subgroup differences if it is done carefully. There is no evidence to suggest that manipulating cultural content will help to reduce differences. Creating alternative test formats that measure the same focal constructs but eliminate job-irrelevant constructs that have inherent subgroup differences appears to be a useful method for reducing adverse impact. In conclusion, it is important to remember that alternative test measures must only eliminate constructs if they are job irrelevant; otherwise, there is a potential to lose predictive validity.

Use of Combination of Measures of Relevant Constructs

Cognitive ability tests usually display the largest subgroup differences; personality, motivational, or interpersonal skills and other noncognitive measures typically display small or no differences in scores between subgroups. If these constructs are relevant in the workplace or academic situations for which people apply, then these measures should be used along with cognitive ability measures assuming they also are relevant. It should not be surprising, then, that selection researchers have seen the use of a combination of cognitive and noncognitive measures as one means of decreasing the measured difference between members of high- and low-scoring subgroups. What is surprising, though, are analyses by Sackett and Ellingson (1997) that showed that composites of measures on which there are large subgroup differences (one standard deviation) and measures with no subgroup difference showed subgroup differences of 0.71 standard deviation units.

Combinations of measures with differing levels of subgroup difference (d) were examined analytically by Schmitt, Rogers, Chan, Sheppard, and Jennings (1997). Even when conditions were ideal for reduction of subgroup differences (d for added predictors was 0.00, and their intercorrelations with cognitive ability and each other were zero), the reduction in composite d was not as much as might be expected, and in some realistic situations with moderate predictor intercorrelation and levels of d, the composite d actually increased. Given realistic values of the validity of most predictors, the removal of a cognitive ability measure would result in substantial losses in composite validity. While the Schmitt et al. results were based on a relatively realistic set of validity and intercorrelation values, it is certainly the case that the role of cognitive ability would be less important in those instances when task performance (and presumably cognitive ability) was a relatively minor component of the criterion space. One illustrative example is the case in which a single alternative predictor is added to cognitive ability. The two predictors are uncorrelated. As validity of the alternative varies from 0.10 to 0.30, d varies from 0.94 to 0.67. The reduction in d varies as a complex function of the validity of the predictors, their intercorrelations with each other, and the levels of d of the alternative predictors.

These analytic results are supplemented by empirical studies (Pulakos & Schmitt, 1996; Ryan, Ployhart, & Friedel, 1998) and by an analysis (Bobko et al., 1999) based on meta-analytic estimates of the key variables used in the Schmitt et al. (1997) article. The results of these three analyses and the Schmitt et al. values are summarized in Table 16.3. Given the estimates based on reviews of the empirical literature on various types of tests, both Schmitt et al. and Bobko et al. (1999) estimated the d of an optimally weighted composite of cognitive ability and a number of alternatives as 0.76 compared to 1.00 for cognitive ability only. A larger decrease in d (i.e., 0.40 or 1.03 − 0.63) was observed by Pulakos and Schmitt (1996) when comparing a composite of verbal ability plus three alternative predictors versus the verbal ability test only considering black and white applicants. In

TABLE 16.3

Use of Multipredictor Composites

Authors	Reference group	Focal group	Cognitive ability (d)	Alternate predictor A (d)	Alternate predictor B (d)	Alternate predictor C (d)	Composite (d)	Composite wo cognitive ability (d)
Bobko et al. (1999)	White	Black	1.00	Structured interviews (0.23)	Conscientiousness (0.09)	Biodata (0.33)	0.76	0.36
Schmitt et al. (1997)	White	Black	1.00	Structured interviews (0.09)	Conscientiousness (0.09)	Biodata (0.2)	0.76	0.19
Pulakos & Schmitt (1996)	White	Black	Verbal ability (1.03)	Structured interview (0.12)	Situational judgment (0.41)	Biodata (−0.05)	Verbal ability plus (0.63)	Without verbal ability (0.23)
Pulakos & Schmitt (1996)	White	Hispanic	Verbal ability (0.78)	Structured interview (0.22)	Situational judgment (0.02)	Biodata (0.05)	Verbal ability plus (0.48)	Without verbal ability (0.16)
Ryan, Ployhart & Friedel (1998)	White	Black	0.90	Service orient. (0.15)	Stress tolerance (0.27)	Reliability (0.06)		
Ryan, Ployhart & Friedel (1998)	White	Hispanic	0.31	Service orient. (0.05)	Stress tolerance (0.09)	Reliability (0.01)		
Ryan, Ployhart & Friedel (1998)	White	Black	0.69	Service orient. (0.20)	Stress tolerance (0.06)	Intellectance (0.47)		
Ryan, Ployhart & Friedel (1998)	White	Hispanic	0.21	Service orient. (0.09)	Stress tolerance (0.16)	Intellectance (0.20)		
Ryan, Ployhart & Friedel (1998)	Male	Female	0.01	Service orient. (0.24)	Stress tolerance (0.18)	Intellectance (0.52)		

the case of Hispanic applicants, the reduction in d was 0.30 (i.e., 0.78 – 0.48). Similar differences between racial subgroups were observed by Ryan, Ployhart, and Friedel (1998). Unfortunately, they did not provide data that would allow the computation of d for different predictor composites.

Motivational and Instructional Sets

How a test is presented or framed to examinees and the impact that framing has on the performance of subgroups of examinees has been the subject of intense examination since the mid-1990s. Steele and his colleagues (Steele, 1997; Steele & Aronson, 1995) have hypothesized that cognitive ability tests constitute a stereotype threat when confronted by minority groups for whom a cultural stereotype exists that suggests that they are not as able on the construct measured by the test. Stereotype threat theory is based on the hypothesis that when a person enters a situation in which a stereotype of his or her group is salient, the person's performance is inhibited because of concerns about being evaluated against the stereotype. The impact of stereotype threat is greatest when the person's group membership is salient to them and when the domain being measured or evaluated is one that is important to the individual's self-concept. Stereotype threat has generated many dozens of laboratory research studies, most of which confirm the existence of a stereotype threat.

Nguyen (2006) has provided a meta-analytic estimate of the size of effects produced by stereotype threat. For the 38 studies in which minority group members were explicitly reminded that their group performed lower on average than members of other groups, their scores were 0.30 standard deviations lower than members of control groups that did not receive such a message. Similar comparisons when male and female groups' performance (N of studies = 73) was compared yielded mean differences of 0.21 standard deviation units. The effect sizes were largest for minority group comparisons when the stereotype threat manipulations were explicit (N of studies = 7, d = 0.64). Similar comparisons of the stereotype threat messages for male–female comparisons did not differ greatly. The effect sizes were slightly greater than those reported in the preceding discussion when corrected for unreliability in the test performance measure.

Nguyen (2006) also meta-analyzed studies in which messages to test takers were directed to the removal or deactivation of a stereotype threat. In these studies, the mean effect size comparing control and experimental groups for minority groups was 0.42 standard deviation units (N of studies = 30), while the same effect for females was 0.23 (N of studies = 61). When the stereotype threat removal attempt was explicitly stated as part of the experimental manipulation, then the effect was much larger (0.8 standard deviations for minority individuals), but approximately the same for studies in which women were the target of the manipulation (0.34 standard deviation units). The average effect size in both types of stereotype threat studies seems to be at least moderate in size; the 90% credibility interval in all cases included zero. Given the relatively large variability in effect sizes, much remains unknown about the conditions in which this manipulation has an effect on the test scores of stereotyped groups.

One thing that does seem relatively certain is that this manipulation would be relatively difficult to produce or evaluate in a field or actual testing context. The types of manipulations involved would likely be considered unethical even when possible. This limitation has led Cullen and his colleagues (Cullen, Hardison, & Sackett, 2004; Cullen, Waters, & Sackett, 2006) to attempt to evaluate the possibility that a stereotype threat mechanism is operating in field situations. Using archival data regarding SAT–academic performance and Armed Services Vocational Aptitude Battery–military performance relationships for groups that were and were not expected to be affected by stereotype threat, they failed to find evidence for the effect. They concluded that any generalizations of the laboratory research on stereotype threat to actual real-world testing situations should be made with caution.

Chan and his colleagues (Chan, 1997; Chan & Schmitt, 1997; Chan, Schmitt, DeShon, Clause, & Delbridge, 1997) have investigated the impact of examinees' perceptions of the face validity and predictive validity of a test on test scores. Presumably, these perceptions had motivating impact on the performance of examinees. Chan et al. (1997) found that the relationship between race and test performance was partially mediated by test motivation, although the mediating effect was very small. Face and predictive validity effects, when they were found, seemed to operate similarly for racial subgroups. These studies, however, did not involve manipulations of instructional or response formats, so there may be explanations other than the motivational one offered by the researchers.

Nguyen and McDaniel (2003) reported a study in which examinees were asked either to indicate the "best" and "worst" answers or to indicate what they would be "most (least)" likely to do. Both response formats produced racial group differences, but the cognitive or knowledge frame produced a difference of 0.46 standard deviation units, whereas the behavioral tendency (least and most likely) frame produced a black–white difference of 0.34 standard deviation units. So, the response frame in this study contributed 0.12 in observed-score differences between the racial groups and 0.21 when mean differences were corrected for measurement error.

In combination, these studies indicated that, in laboratory studies at least, the instructional frame or motivational set of examinees does have an impact on their test scores. That these results generalize to field situations or that such manipulations are ethically justifiable, both remain unresolved questions.

Coaching

Another method that has been proposed for reducing subgroup differences is to coach test takers prior to their examination. There are two hypotheses for why coaching would help to reduce subgroup differences. The first hypothesis is that providing coaching to all students would reduce subgroup differences because coaching will differentially affect minority students, improving their scores to a greater degree. The second hypothesis is that coaching in general leads to improved scores. Thus, to reduce subgroup differences, it would be necessary to coach minority students to help them reach the level of performance of majority students. Neither of these hypotheses has been widely supported by empirical research. It appears that coaching can and often does improve subsequent performance but not necessarily at a practically significant level. It also appears that coaching is not differentially effective for different subgroups.

Frierson (1986) reported what seem to be moderate coaching effect sizes in four studies, although he did not report means and standard deviations, so it was not possible to calculate the standard mean differences. In his first study, he reported that 79% of students who received coaching for Part I of the National Board of Medical Examiners (NBME) Examination passed the test as compared to 52% of the comparison group. In his second study, Frierson reported that a coached group had a mean score that was 80 points higher than a comparison group on a subtest of the NBME Exam. In his third study, Frierson found that coached students had an average gain of 91 points on the science subtest of the Medical College Admission Test (MCAT). In his fourth study, Frierson reported that an experimental group that received test-taking skills instruction and participated in learning teams scored 105 points higher than a comparison group on the Nursing State Board (NSB) Examination, and that a second experimental group that received only the test-taking skills instruction scored 62 points higher than the comparison group. Frierson concluded that coaching has a positive effect on performance. Unfortunately, it was not possible to calculate the effect sizes of his findings to determine the magnitude of the gains (d) due to coaching.

Powers (1987) conducted a two-factor experimental design in which he had five treatment levels for test preparation materials for the GRE and then sent the materials either with an accompanying note of encouragement or with a neutral form letter without encouragement. For the white and black participants who received no test preparation materials and no encouragement (both control conditions), the standardized mean difference in performance was 1.51. For white and black participants who received the highest level of test preparation materials and were encouraged, the standardized mean difference in performance was 1.41. Thus, there was a decrease in d of 0.10, which is very small. Although providing test materials and encouragement did lead to improvements in performance, there was not a differential effect across different subgroups. Interestingly, in this study, black examinees reported spending more time preparing for the test than did white examinees.

Ryan, Ployhart, Greguras, and Schmit (1998) examined the effects of an optional test preparation program for applicants for firefighter positions. They found that black and female applicants were more likely to attend the preparation program than white and male applicants, but that attendance at the program did not explain any variance in test performance, anxiety, or motivation. To determine whether test preparation differentially benefited different subgroups, Ryan, Ployhart, Greguras, and Schmit conducted hierarchical regression analyses predicting test performance. The interactions of sex and race with attendance were not found to be significant predictors, which led them to conclude that there was no differential benefit of test preparation for racial and gender subgroups.

Two studies have attempted to summarize across multiple studies to determine the overall effect of coaching programs on test performance. Messick and Jungeblut (1981) specifically examined studies of test preparation programs for the SAT. They determined that, although coaching programs do tend to lead to increases in test performance, the amount of coaching required (in hours) to increase test scores more than 20–30 points (on the scale from 200 to 800 and with standard deviations equal to roughly 100, this would equal d of 0.2 to 0.3) is so large that it would approximate full-time schooling. Thus, their conclusions imply that attending a coaching program will not help students to improve their scores in any meaningful way.

Bangert-Drowns, Kulik, and Kulik (1983) examined 30 studies of coaching programs of various types. They found an average effect size of 0.25, which is fairly small, but positive. Only 9 of the 30 studies had a significant effect, although all significant effects were in the positive direction. Bangert-Drowns et al. found that amount of coaching time was positively related to performance, such that more coaching time would lead to higher performance. However, they did not address the issue that Messick and Jungeblut (1981) suggested—that the increase in coaching time required for a meaningful increase in test scores would be infeasible.

Hausknecht, Halpert, Di Paolo, and Gerrard (2007) meta-analyzed data from 107 samples in which practice effects on scores on cognitive ability tests were estimated. Overall, the effect size d was 0.26 corrected for measurement error; when combined with coaching, the effect size was 0.70. The number of studies with retesting plus coaching ($k = 23$) and the number of study participants ($N = 2,323$) was relatively small, and the 95% credibility interval did include 0.00. Unfortunately, the meta-analysis did not include any assessment of the differential impact of coaching or retesting on racial or gender subgroups because those data were provided in very few studies. The authors also indicated that very few studies reported the impact of retesting or coaching on validity.

In conclusion, although coaching does appear to have a generally positive effect on test performance, it remains unclear whether that effect is meaningful enough to pursue coaching as a viable method for reducing subgroup differences. What little information we have suggests that coaching does not appear to differentially assist minority subgroups and, according to the findings of Ryan, Ployhart, Greguras, and Schmit (1998), does not reduce test anxiety or improve motivation.

Time Limits

Yet another strategy that has been explored for reducing subgroup differences is to increase the amount of time that examinees are given to complete tests. The rationale for this strategy is that certain tests may be more "speeded" for members of certain racial subgroups than others. A test that is speeded presumes that most examinees could complete all of the answers correctly if they were given unlimited time. Depending on one's definition of ability or proficiency, it may be possible that members of different subgroups who are equally able may need different amounts of time to demonstrate their ability. By extending the time for all test takers, the "speededness" could potentially be reduced. In general, this strategy has not been shown to be effective at reducing group differences.

Evans and Reilly (1972) sought to examine whether reducing the amount of speededness on the reading comprehension section of the LSAT (Law School Admission Test) would have a differential effect on examinees from predominantly black colleges relative to examinees from other locations. Examinees were given either a speeded measure of 35 questions to complete in 40 minutes or an unspeeded measure of 27 items to complete in the same time limit. The reduction in d was only 0.08, indicating that the experimental manipulation had little effect in reducing subgroup differences. This study is typically cited as a demonstration that reducing time limits is not effective in reducing adverse impact; however, there are several limitations with this study that should be considered. The sample of students who took the measure at predominantly black colleges was offered the test free of charge, whereas the sample who took the measure elsewhere paid the testing fee. Evans and Reilly did not address the actual makeup of their samples in their article. It is not possible to determine how representative their "black" sample is of black test takers in general. In addition, it seems plausible that the black test takers who chose to take the test on the day that the test was offered free might not be as highly motivated as test takers who paid the fee.

Wild, Durso, and Rubin (1982) examined an experimental section of the GRE. They had four conditions: an unspeeded and a speeded version of the verbal and quantitative sections. They concluded that the average effects of the manipulation did not differ across male–female and white–black subgroups. When we calculated the d values, however, we found slightly different results. For the verbal tests, the reductions in ds were 0.13 for white–black groups and 0.08 for male–female groups, consistent with the researchers' conclusions. For the quantitative tests, however, the reductions in ds were 0.32 for white–black comparisons and 0.26 for male–female comparisons, indicating a modest effect of increasing the time limit.

Munger and Lloyd (1991) examined whether reducing the speededness of testing would differentially assist handicapped students. They gave all participants one timed and one untimed section of the Iowa Test of Basic Skills (ITBS). Their handicapped pool mainly consisted of learning disabled students, and their reference pool consisted of nonhandicapped elementary school children. All participants had tested in the normal range of intellectual functioning. Similar to Evans and Reilly (1972), Munger and Lloyd found no meaningful effect of eliminating the time limit. The reduction in d for the Language Usage test was −0.14, and the reduction for the Mathematical Concepts test was 0.04.

Powers and Fowles (1996) examined the effect of extending time limits on essay writing for the GRE. They gave volunteers two essays to complete, one in 40 minutes and the other in 60. They did not examine racial or gender subgroup differences but instead looked at self-reported test-taking style (fast vs. slow). They found that test takers who described their style as slow did not benefit any more or less from extended time limits than did those who described their style as fast. They also found that self-described speed was unrelated to gender, age, or ethnicity. Powers and Fowles did not report means and standard deviations that would be necessary to calculate reductions in d values.

Finally, Bridgeman, Cline, and Hessinger (2004) examined an optional experimental section of the GRE. Similar to Wild et al. (1982), they had four groups: a speeded and a less-speeded version of a verbal and a quantitative section. They did not report d values or the means and standard deviations necessary to calculate d values, but they reported that the effects of extra time appeared to be relatively constant across ethnic groups for both verbal and quantitative sections.

It is difficult to conclude how effective the strategy of extending time limits is in reducing group differences. The empirical evidence suggests that the strategy is largely unsuccessful, but the studies have similar flaws in methodology that limit our ability to state any conclusions with much confidence. In most of the studies, the experimental sections were administered outside normal testing conditions. In general, they were offered as optional to test takers, many of whom presumably refused to take the test (Bridgeman et al., 2004). In addition, none of the researchers calculated d values in their results. From those studies in which we were able to use their data to calculate ds, it appears that some researchers may have based their conclusion that their findings were nonsignificant on tests of significance rather than an examination of effect sizes. Extending time limits may have a very small effect on reducing subgroup differences in certain contexts, perhaps more on quantitative measures than verbal measures (Wild et al., 1982).

Summary and Conclusions

Our primary objectives in this chapter were to update the Sackett et al. (2001) qualitative review of various efforts to reduce the subgroup differences that appear to occur whenever one compares minority performance on cognitive ability tests and to provide a quantitative estimate of the impact of these methods individually and in combination. Not a great deal of research has addressed this question in the years since the Sackett et al. article. Moreover, we found it difficult to extract the data from various articles that would allow us to put a quantitative estimate on the efficacy of these various efforts. Even more difficult to estimate is the cumulative effect of the various methods discussed. The latter would require evidence regarding the manner in which such methods are related or interact, and those studies are nonexistent. However, the following several paragraphs represent our attempt to make an informed guess. We conclude with our sense of what would be "best practice" when one is examining members of different minority groups and one hopes to minimize differences irrelevant to the purpose of testing, that is, assessment of individual capacity to perform in some work or academic context.

Certainly, the largest number of quantifiable estimates of the impact of measures proposed and explored are those for item bias (see Table 16.1). The reduction in differences that accrues from the removal of items that appear to show psychometric bias is probably less than 0.05 on cognitive ability tests. The one study that showed a larger reduction was a study of a biodata measure. Biased items should be removed from tests, but we can state with relative confidence that such efforts are unlikely to have any practical effect on the reduction of subgroup differences in test scores.

The question of what to measure or how to supplement cognitive ability test scores in high-stakes testing is really addressed by two of the methods we discussed. Differential weighting of criterion dimensions in research that is conducted as a basis for weighting the most relevant and valid predictors (e.g., Hattrup et al., 1997) and research that examines test batteries comprised of various predictor types (e.g., Bobko et al., 1999) are similar in approach, and both lead to the conclusion that subgroup differences can be reduced by approximately 0.25 under optimal conditions. The conditions under which these approaches will be helpful will be those in which there is justification (they are relevant and valid) for the use of alternate criterion or predictor dimensions, alternative predictors are not highly correlated with cognitive ability and each other, and the selection ratio is relatively low.

The literature on alternative modes of presenting test stimuli produces the largest variability in changes in differences between racial subgroups (−0.12 to 0.74). There are several problems with this research, and the most intractable is probably the difficulty of separating the impact of the construct being measured and the method by which it is measured. This particular problem has been addressed in several of the studies summarized in Table 16.2, but with varying degrees of success. In addition, some of the change in subgroup differences may be due to the differential reliability of modes of measurement. Perhaps the strongest conclusion that we can draw from this literature is that researchers should take care to address only the constructs relevant to the outcome that they wish to predict. This may be an obvious conclusion, and one that could have been posited without this research, but it is also very subtle and demands attention. Unnecessary reading requirements or levels of judgment or reasoning in a test of interpersonal skills are often difficult to assess and minimize.

Research on motivational or instructional sets has been dominated by work on stereotype threat. Nguyen (2006) demonstrated that the effect of stereotype threat is generalizable and probably of a magnitude of 0.3 to 0.4 standard deviation units when considering black–white differences. However, the major problem with this body of research is that there have been no demonstrations that intentionally producing the effect is ethically acceptable in an actual testing situation, and that the effect generalizes to such situations. Indirect evidence suggests that the effect is not generalizable (Cullen et al., 2004, 2006). Evidence of the impact of perceptions of face validity is also indirect (Chan, 1997; Chan & Schmitt, 1997), and the effect on measured test performance seems small or nonexistent (DeShon et al., 1998).

In many high-stakes testing situations, examinees are allowed to retest, and in many instances, the organization or independent organizations such as Kaplan provide coaching on how to take a test along with practice tests. Examinees do appear to benefit from retesting (*d* approximately equal to 0.25) and probably more from coaching, although the amount of coaching required may be excessive. However, we uncovered no evidence that practice or coaching was differentially effective across subgroups. If opportunities for coaching are not equally accessible, however, this could certainly result in greater impact on those groups for which coaching opportunities are unavailable.

Finally, investigations of the impact of the amount of time available to examinees suggests that differences between racial subgroup scores are less under liberal time limits (*d* approximately 0.10). There is also some evidence that this change is greater for tests of quantitative ability than verbal ability (Wild et al., 1982). The number of studies investigating this question is small, and most such studies were conducted two or more decades ago.

If we add optimistic estimates of the reduction in subgroup differences across these methods, we can probably reduce the black–white subgroup difference by one half. We make this estimate in the following manner: < 0.05 for removal of biased items; < 0.25 for including measures of relevant alternative constructs; < 0.10 for altering the mode of presenting test stimuli in relevant ways; < 0.05 by attending to motivational issues; < 0.05 for reduction or elimination of time limits; and little or nothing for coaching effects, assuming all have equal opportunities to avail themselves of such opportunities. The overall estimate is also based on the assumption that all of these efforts are cumulative; that is, they are not correlated with each other. If we examine these suggestions, they all represent good testing practices as outlined in various texts on personnel selection (Guion, 1998; Ployhart, Schneider, & Schmitt, 2006). We should measure what is relevant, remove the influence of irrelevant constructs (e.g., culturally unique content or unnecessary reading requirements), provide equal opportunity or standardized testing conditions to all examinees, attend to motivational issues, and if time is not an academically or job-relevant construct, provide sufficient time for all to complete the measures. We expect that others will challenge the estimates provided, but we hope that in doing so they will be motivated to conduct additional research on the reduction of measured subgroup differences while maintaining or increasing validity. Such research should also include work on the reduction of educational or opportunity differences responsible for these measured differences, a topic not addressed in this chapter.

References

American Educational Research Association, American Psychological Association, & National Council on Measurement in Education. (1999). *Standards for educational and psychological testing.* Washington, DC: American Psychological Association.

Bangert-Drowns, R. L., Kulik, J. A., & Kulik, C. C. (1983). Effects of coaching programs on achievement test performance. *Review of Educational Research, 53,* 571–585.

Barrick, M. R., & Mount, M. K. (1991). The Big 5 personality dimensions and job performance. *Personnel Psychology, 44,* 1–25.

Bobko, P., Roth, P. L., & Potosky, D. (1999). Derivation and implications of a meta-analytic matrix incorporating cognitive ability, alternative predictors, and job performance. *Personnel Psychology, 52,* 561–590.

Borman, W. C., & Motowidlo, S. J. (1993). Expanding the criterion domain to include elements of contextual performance. In N. Schmitt & W. C. Borman (Eds.), *Personnel selection in organizations* (pp. 71–98). San Francisco: Jossey-Bass.

Borman, W. C., & Motowidlo, S. J. (1997). Task performance and contextual performance: The meaning for personnel selection research. *Human Performance, 10,* 99–110.

Bridgeman, B., Cline, F., & Hessinger, J. (2004). Effect of extra time on verbal and quantitative GRE scores. *Applied Measurement in Education, 17,* 25–37.

Campbell, J. P., McCloy, R. A., Oppler, S. H., & Sager, C. E. (1993). A theory of performance. In N. Schmitt & W. C. Borman (Eds.), *Personnel selection in organizations* (pp. 35–70). San Francisco: Jossey-Bass.

Chan, D. (1997). Racial subgroup differences in predictive validity perceptions on personality and cognitive ability tests. *Journal of Applied Psychology, 82,* 311–320.

Chan, D., & Schmitt, N. (1997). Video-based versus paper-and-pencil method of assessment in situational judgment tests: Subgroup differences in test performance and face validity perceptions. *Journal of Applied Psychology, 82,* 143–159.

Chan, D., Schmitt, N., DeShon, R. P., Clause, C., & Delbridge, K. (1997). Reactions to cognitive ability tests: The relationships between race, test performance, face validity perceptions, and test-taking motivation. *Journal of Applied Psychology, 82,* 302–310.

Cullen, M. J., Hardison, C. M., & Sackett, P. R. (2004). Using SAT-grade and ability-job performance relationships to test predictions from stereotype threat theory. *Journal of Applied Psychology, 89,* 220–230.

Cullen, M. J., Waters, S. D., & Sackett, P. R. (2006). Testing stereotype threat theory predictions for math-identified and non-math-identified students by gender. *Human Performance, 19I,* 421–440.

DeCorte, W. (1999). Weighing job performance predictors to both maximize the quality of the selected workforce and control the level of adverse impact. *Journal of Applied Psychology, 84,* 695–702.

DeShon, R. P., Smith, M. R., Chan, D., & Schmitt, N. (1998). Can racial differences in cognitive test performance be reduced by presenting problems in a social context? *Journal of Applied Psychology, 8,* 438–451.

Dickens, W. T., & Flynn, J. R. (2006). Black Americans reduce the racial IQ gap. *Psychological Science, 17,* 913–920.

Donlon, T. F., Hicks, M. M., & Wallmark, M. M. (1980). Sex differences in item responses on the Graduate Record Examination. *Applied Psychological Measurement, 4*(1), 9–20.

Doudin, H., & Al-Darabee, M. (2003). Gender-related differential item functioning on mathematics performance. *Dirasat, Educational Sciences, 30*(2), 414–419.

Drasgow, F. (1987). Study of the measurement bias of two standardized psychological tests. *Journal of Applied Psychology, 72,* 19–29.

Dubois, C. L. Z., Sackett, P. R., Zedeck, S., & Fogli, L. (1993). Further exploration of typical and maximum performance criteria: Definitional issues, prediction, and white-black differences. *Journal of Applied Psychology, 78,* 205–211.

Evans, F. R., & Reilly, R. R. (1972). A study of speededness as a source of test bias. *Journal of Educational Measurement, 9,* 123–131.

Frierson, H. T. (1986). Enhancing minority college students' performance on educational tests. *Journal of Negro Education, 55,* 38–45.

Gallagher, A., Bridgeman, B., & Calahan, C. (2002). The effect of computer-based tests on racial-ethnic and gender groups. *Journal of Educational Measurement, 39,* 133–147.

Garner, M., & Engelhard, G. (1999). Gender differences in performance on multiple-choice and constructed response mathematical items. *Applied Measurement in Education, 12*(1), 29–51.

Guion, R. M. (1998). *Assessment, measurement, and prediction for personnel decisions.* Mahwah, NJ: Erlbaum.

Hattrup, K., Rock, J., & Scalia, C. (1997). The effects of varying conceptualizations of job performance on adverse impact, minority hiring, and predicted performance. *Journal of Applied Psychology, 82,* 656–664.

Hausknecht, J. P., Halpert, J. A., Di Paolo, N. T., & Gerrard, M. O. M. (2007). Retesting in selection: A meta-analysis of coaching and practice effects for tests of cognitive ability. *Journal of Applied Psychology, 92,* 373–385.

Huselid, M. A. (1995). The impact of human resource management practices on turnover, productivity, and corporate financial performance. *Academy of Management Journal, 38,* 635–672.

Kim, B. H., Schmitt, N., Imus, A. L., Oswald, F. L., Drzakowski, S. M., Friede, A. J. et al. Interpreting differential item functioning in a situational judgment test: A matter of differential access to opportunities? Unpublished manuscript.

Klein, S. P. (1983). *An analysis of the relationship between trial practice skills and bar examination results.* Unpublished manuscript.

Lane, S., Wang, N., & Magone, M. (1996). Gender-related differential item functioning on a middle-school mathematics performance assessment. *Educational Measurement: Issues and Practice, 15*(4), 21–27, 31.

McHenry, J. J., Hough, L. M., Toquam, J. L., Hanson, M. A., & Ashworth, S. (1990). Project A validity results: The relationship between predictor and criterion domains. *Personnel Psychology, 43,* 335–354.

Medley, D. M., & Quirk, T. J. (1974). The application of a factorial design to the study of cultural bias in general culture items on the National Teacher Examination. *Journal of Educational Measurement, 11,* 235–245.

Messick, S., & Jungeblut, A. (1981). Time and method in coaching for the SAT. *Psychological Bulletin, 89,* 191–216.

Millman, J., Mehrens, W. A., & Sackett, P. R. (1993). *An evaluation of the New York State Bar Examination.* Unpublished manuscript.

Motowidlo, S. J. (2003). Job performance. In W. C. Borman, D. R. Ilgen, & R. J. Klimoski (Eds.), *Handbook of psychology* (Vol. 12, pp. 39–54). Hoboken, NJ: Wiley.

Motowidlo, S. J., & Van Scooter, J. R. (1994). Evidence that task performance should be distinguished from contextual performance. *Journal of Applied Psychology, 79,* 475–480.

Munger, G. F., & Lloyd, B. H. (1991). Effect of speededness on test performance of handicapped and nonhandicapped examinees. *Journal of Educational Research, 85,* 53–57.

Neisser, U., Boodoo, G., Bouchard, T. J., Jr., Boykin, A. W., Brody, N., Ceci, S. J., et al. (1996). Intelligence: Knowns and unknowns. *American Psychologist, 51,* 77–101.

Nguyen, H. D. (2006). *Does stereotype threat differentially affect cognitive ability test performance of minorities and women? A meta-analytic review of experimental evidence.* Unpublished doctoral dissertation, Michigan State University, East Lansing.

Nguyen, N. T., & McDaniel, M. A. (2003). Response instructions and racial differences in a situational judgment test. *Applied Human Resource Management Research, 8,* 33–44.

O'Neil, H. F., & Brown, R. S. (1997). *Differential effects of question formats in math assessment on metacognition and effect* (Tech. Rep. No. 449). Los Angeles: University of California, National Center for Research on Evaluation, Standards, and Student Testing.

Ployhart, R. E., Schneider, B., & Schmitt, N. (2006). *Staffing organizations: Contemporary practice and theory.* Mahwah, NJ: Erlbaum.

Powers, D. E. (1987). Who benefits most from preparing for a "coachable" admissions test? *Journal of Educational Measurement, 24,* 247–262.

Powers, D. E., & Fowles, M. E. (1996). Effects of applying different time limits to a proposed GRE writing test. *Journal of Educational Measurement, 33,* 433–452.

Pulakos, E. D., & Schmitt, N. (1996). An evaluation of two strategies for reducing adverse impact and their effects on criterion-related validity. *Human Performance, 9,* 241–258.

Roth, P. L., Bevier, C. A., Bobko, P., Switzer, F. S., III, & Tyler, P. (2001). Ethnic group differences in cognitive ability in employment and educational settings. *Personnel Psychology, 54,* 297–330.

Rushton, J. P., & Jensen, A. R. (2006). The totality of available evidence shows the race IQ gap still remains. *Psychological Science, 17,* 921–922.

Ryan, A. M., Ployhart, R. E., & Friedel, L. (1998). Using personality testing to reduce adverse impact: A cautionary note. *Journal of Applied Psychology, 83,* 298–307.

Ryan, A. M., Ployhart, R. E., Greguras, G. J., & Schmit, M. J. (1998). Test preparation programs in selection contexts: Self-selection and program effectiveness. *Personnel Psychology, 51,* 599–621.

Sackett, P. R. (1998). Performance assessment in education and professional certification: Lessons for personnel selection. In M. D. Hakel (Ed.), *Beyond multiple choice: Evaluating alternatives to traditional testing for selection* (pp. 113–129). Mahwah, NJ: Erlbaum.

Sackett, P. R., & Ellingson, J. E. (1997). The effects of forming multi-predictor composites on group differences and adverse impact. *Personnel Psychology, 50,* 707–721.

Sackett, P. R., Schmitt, N., Ellingson, J. E., & Kabin, M. B. (2001). High-stakes testing in employment, credentialing, and higher education. *American Psychologist, 56,* 302–318.

Sackett, P. R., & Wilk, S. L. (1994). Within-group norming and other forms of score adjustment in preemployment testing. *American Psychologist, 49,* 929–954.

Scheunemann, J. D., & Gerritz, K. (1990). Using differential item functioning procedures to explore sources of item difficulty and group performance characteristics. *Journal of Educational Measurement, 27*(2), 109–131.

Schmeiser, C. B., & Ferguson, R. L. (1978). Performance of black and white students on test materials containing content based on black and white cultures. *Journal of Educational Measurement, 15,* 193–200.

Schmidt, F. L., Mack, M. J., & Hunter, J. E. (1984). Selection utility in the occupation of U.S. park ranger for three modes of test use. *Journal of Applied Psychology, 69,* 490–497.

Schmitt, A. P. (1988). Language and cultural characteristics that explain differential item functioning for Hispanic examinees on the Scholastic Aptitude Test. *Journal of Educational Measurement, 25*(1), 1–13.

Schmitt, N., & Mills, A. E. (2001). Traditional tests and job simulations: Minority and majority performance and test validities. *Journal of Applied Psychology, 86,* 451–458.

Schmitt, N., Rogers, W., Chan, D., Sheppard, L., & Jennings, D. (1997). Adverse impact and predictive efficiency of various predictor combinations. *Journal of Applied Psychology, 82,* 719–730.

Stark, S., Chernyshenko, O. S., & Drasgow, F. (2004). Examining the effects of differential item functioning and differential test functioning on selection decisions: When are statistically significant effects practically important? *Journal of Applied Psychology, 89*(3), 497–508.

Steele, C. M. (1997). A threat in the air: How stereotypes shape intellectual identity and performance. *American Psychologist, 52,* 613–629.

Steele, C. M., & Aronson, J. (1995). Stereotype threat and the intellectual performance of African Americans. *Journal of Personality and Social Psychology, 77,* 1213–1227.

Wang, N., & Lane, S. (1996). Detection of gender-related differential item functioning in a mathematics performance assessment. *Applied Measurement in Education, 9*(2), 175–144.

Whitney, D. J., & Schmitt, N. (1997). Relationship between culture and responses to biodata employment items. *Journal of Applied Psychology, 82,* 113–129.

Wild, C. L., Durso, R., & Rubin, D. B. (1982). Effect of increased test-taking time on test scores by ethnic group, years out of school, and sex. *Journal of Educational Measurement, 19,* 19–28.

17

Decision Aids for Addressing the Validity–Adverse Impact Trade-Off

Paul R. Sackett, Wilfried De Corte, and Filip Lievens

Introduction

Typically, adverse impact (AI) is an after-the-fact analysis: Once predictor scores for a pool of applicants are available, AI is evaluated. Sometimes the analysis is made in real time, as predictor scores are obtained on a set of applicants, and AI calculations are done on a "what if" basis as input to decisions about features such as where to set a cutoff score. The focus of this chapter, however, is on attempts to estimate in advance the likely impact of a given selection system. Here, estimates are made based on available information about the features such as the expected magnitude of subgroup differences, expected interpredictor correlations, and expected predictor-criterion correlations. Such information may be local (e.g., group differences observed the last time a predictor was used) or based on a more general research literature (e.g., group differences reported in publisher manuals or in the published literature for a given predictor type and a given job category).

These projections of AI and other outcomes are generally made in one of two ways. The first is via simulation, in which multiple samples of data are generated from populations with specified parameters (e.g., means, standard deviations [SDs], interpredictor rs, subgroup differences). Indices of interest (e.g., AI ratios [AIRs], proportion of positions filled by minority group members) are computed for each sample, and the distributions of these indices are tallied and examined. The second is via analytic solution, in which the outcomes of interest can be determined precisely via equation. For example, while one can determine the expected value of an

AIR obtained if a selection device with a d of 1.0 SD is used with a selection ratio (SR) of 10% by drawing repeated random samples from a normal distribution, one can determine this more directly via the equation for the area under a normal curve. Simulations are more useful in settings for which an analytic solution is not available.

We use the standardized mean difference d as the index of group differences. This is the majority mean minus the minority mean divided by the pooled within-group standard deviation. This index expresses the group difference in standard deviation units, with zero indicating no difference, a positive value indicating a higher mean for the majority group, and a negative value indicating a higher mean for the minority group.

In this chapter, we summarize a number of decision aids for AI planning. These design tools address a range of applied questions. They fall into two major categories. The first involves those that focus solely on AI as an outcome. While these are useful for understanding the likely AI in a specific selection setting, they are silent regarding the consequences for other outcomes of attempts to reduce AI. The second involves those that focus on both AI and other outcomes, with the mean criterion performance of those selected as the most common additional outcome. Studies in this second category permit examining trade-offs between AI and mean criterion performance (e.g., documenting the performance consequences of setting a low cutoff score). In the remainder, we examine each category in turn.

Category 1: Approaches That Focus Solely on Adverse Impact

AI as a Function of d and SR

A basic starting point for insight into AI is a clear understanding of the major components that contribute to it. If top-down selection on a given score distribution (which may be a single predictor or a composite of multiple predictors) is used, and if normality assumptions are met, the expected value of the AIR is a function of the standardized mean difference d between the two groups of interest and the SR. The relationship among d, SR, and AI can then be derived from properties of the normal distribution. Tables showing this relationship were presented by Sackett and Wilk (1994) and expanded to a broader range of SRs by Sackett, Schmitt, Ellingson, and Kabin (2001). They presented separate tables for the effects of d and majority group SR on two outcomes: the minority group SR and the AIR. Table 17.1 integrates this information into a single table.

TABLE 17.1

Minority Group Selection Ratios and Four-Fifths Ratios When the Majority Group Selection Ratio Is 1%, 5%, 10%, 25%, 50%, 75%, 90%, 95%, or 99%

Standardized group difference (d)	Majority group selection ratio[a]								
	1%	5%	10%	25%	50%	75%	90%	95%	99%
0.0	.010	.050	.100	.250	.500	.750	.900	.950	.990
	1.00	**1.00**	**1.00**	**1.00**	**1.00**	**1.00**	**1.00**	**1.00**	**1.00**
0.1	.008	.041	.084	.221	.460	.716	.881	.938	.987
	.80	**.82**	**.84**	**.88**	**.92**	**.95**	**.98**	**.99**	**.99**
0.2	.006	.033	.069	.192	.421	.681	.860	.925	.983
	.60	**.66**	**.69**	**.77**	**.84**	**.91**	**.96**	**.97**	**.99**
0.3	.004	.026	.057	.166	.382	.644	.837	.910	.978
	.40	**.52**	**.57**	**.66**	**.76**	**.86**	**.93**	**.96**	**.99**
0.4	.003	.021	.046	.142	.345	.606	.811	.893	.973
	.30	**.42**	**.46**	**.57**	**.69**	**.81**	**.90**	**.94**	**.98**
0.5	.002	.016	.038	.121	.309	.568	.782	.873	.966
	.20	**.32**	**.38**	**.48**	**.62**	**.76**	**.87**	**.92**	**.98**
0.6	.002	.013	.030	.102	.274	.528	.752	.851	.957
	.20	**.26**	**.30**	**.41**	**.55**	**.70**	**.84**	**.90**	**.97**
0.7	.001	.010	.024	.085	.242	.488	.719	.826	.947
	.10	**.20**	**.24**	**.34**	**.48**	**.65**	**.80**	**.87**	**.96**
0.8	.001	.007	.019	.071	.212	.448	.684	.800	.936
	.10	**.14**	**.19**	**.28**	**.42**	**.60**	**.76**	**.84**	**.95**
0.9	.001	.006	.015	.058	.184	.409	.648	.770	.922
	.10	**.12**	**.15**	**.23**	**.37**	**.54**	**.72**	**.81**	**.93**
1.0	.000	.004	.011	.047	.159	.371	.610	.739	.907
	.00	**.08**	**.11**	**.19**	**.32**	**.49**	**.68**	**.78**	**.92**
1.1	.000	.003	.009	.038	.136	.334	.571	.705	.889
	.00	**.06**	**.09**	**.15**	**.27**	**.45**	**.63**	**.74**	**.90**
1.2	.000	.002	.007	.031	.115	.298	.532	.670	.869
	.00	**.04**	**.07**	**.12**	**.23**	**.40**	**.59**	**.71**	**.88**
1.3	.000	.002	.005	.024	.097	.264	.492	.633	.846
	.00	**.04**	**.05**	**.10**	**.19**	**.35**	**.55**	**.67**	**.85**
1.4	.000	.001	.004	.019	.081	.233	.452	.595	.821
	.00	**.02**	**.04**	**.08**	**.16**	**.31**	**.50**	**.63**	**.83**
1.5	.000	.001	.003	.015	.067	.203	.413	.556	.794
	.00	**.02**	**.03**	**.06**	**.13**	**.27**	**.46**	**.59**	**.80**

[a] Selection ratio = number of applicants hired/number of applicants applied. Per cell, two values are given. The first value refers to the minority group selection ratio. The second value in bold represents the four-fifths ratio (i.e., the minority group selection ratio/ majority group selection ratio). Tabled values in bold less than .80 represent scenarios that violate the four-fifths rule.

This table illustrates a variety of useful general principles. First, at a given d, the AIR increases as SR increases. This is certainly a well-known result, but the table is useful in making clear the magnitude of this effect. For example, with $d = 0.5$, the AIR ranges from 0.20 at a majority SR of 1% to 0.62 at a majority SR of 50% to 0.98 at a majority SR of 99%. Of course, as SR approaches 100%, subgroup SRs must converge, and the AIR must approach 1.0. Second, at a given SR, the AIR increases as d increases. This is also a well-known result; again, the table is useful in making clear the magnitude of the relationship. Third, the table illustrates the combination of SRs and d values that results in a violation of the four-fifths rule. For small d values (e.g., 0.1 to 0.2), the four-fifths rule is violated only when SR is less than 50%. For d values larger than 0.5, the four-fifths rule will be violated unless SR is very large, typically 90% or higher.

This decision aid can help project the likely effects of using a particular predictor with a particular SR. It permits addressing questions such as, If d could be reduced by adding additional valid predictors with lower d, how much change from the current d would be needed to avoid violating the four-fifths rule? or How large a change from a planned SR would be needed to avoid violating the four-fifths rule? Other similar questions might focus on target levels other than the four-fifths rule, such as, How much of a change from the current d would be needed to improve the AIR by a specified magnitude?

The discussion to this point has dealt with expected values of the AIR. However, given the small-to-modest sizes of applicant pools in many settings, it is certainly possible for a given sample to deviate from the population value. The AIR, like any sample statistic, has a sampling distribution, and De Corte and Lievens (2005) extended the work with an explicit treatment of this sampling distribution. They presented the relevant equations and offered illustrative examples. Table 17.2 shows the distribution of AIRs for various d values for the situation in which there are 300 applicants, a 10% SR, and 20% of the applicant pool is from the minority group. The table shows each possible AIR value as well as the likelihood of obtaining an AIR value of that magnitude or lower. For example, it shows that even if d were 0.00, such that we would expect no AI, the AIR would drop below 80% for 24.2% of samples. Note that large deviations from the expected value are more likely when a small minority applicant pool is paired with a small SR. Further exploration of the sampling variability in AI can be found in the work of Roth, Bobko, and Switzer (2006).

While the discussion to this point has focused on the AIR as the outcome of interest, AI is sometimes operationalized as a finding that the difference in selection rates for the two groups of interest is statistically significant. De Corte and Lievens (2005) also extended prior work by examining the probability with which a planned selection using a predictor with a given effect size d will result in a selection outcome that reflects AI according

TABLE 17.2

Sampling Distribution Function of the AI Ratio When Selecting 30 Candidates From a Total of 300 Applicants (60 Minority and 240 Majority Candidates) Using a Selection Test With Population Mean Difference Equal to 0, 0.2, 0.5, and 1.0

			Population mean difference			
J	K	AI ratio	$\delta = 0.0$	$\delta = 0.2$	$\delta = 0.5$	$\delta = 1.0$
0	30	0.000	0.001	0.007	0.058	0.394
1	29	0.138	0.008	0.044	0.237	0.770
2	28	0.286	0.037	0.146	0.495	0.940
3	27	0.444	0.110	0.321	0.732	0.988
4	26	0.615	0.242	0.532	0.885	0.998
5	25	0.800	0.420	0.725	0.960	1.000
6	24	1.000	0.609	0.862	0.988	1.000
7	23	1.217	0.770	0.942	0.997	1.000
8	22	1.455	0.883	0.979	0.999	1.000
9	21	1.714	0.949	0.994	1.000	1.000
10	20	2.000	0.981	0.998	1.000	1.000
11	19	2.316	0.994	1.000	1.000	1.000
12	18	2.667	0.998	1.000	1.000	1.000
13	17	3.059	1.000	1.000	1.000	1.000

Note: *J* indicates the number of selected minority applicants. *K* indicates the number of selected majority applicants.

to Fisher's exact test. They referred to this probability as the risk of AI. For both extensions (examining the sampling distribution of the AIR and assessing the risk of AI), De Corte and Lievens offered the needed equations and illustrative examples as well as a flexible computer program permitting the user to input values of specific interest. The program can be downloaded from the Internet at http://users.ugent.be/~wdecorte/software.html. This site also offers access to most of the other programs that are mentioned in this chapter.

Prospects for Reducing *d* by Adding Additional Low-*d* Predictors

One potential strategy for reducing AI is to supplement a high-*d* predictor with one or more additional predictors with lower *d*. Sackett and Ellingson (1997) offered a set of formulas that permit an estimation of the expected effect of supplementing an existing predictor with additional predictors. They offered the following formula for determining the degree of group differences present when two or more predictors are combined to form an equally weighted composite:

$$d = \frac{\sum_{i=1}^{k} d_i}{\sqrt{k + k(k-1)r_{ii}}}$$

where d_i indicates the d value for each predictor included in the composite, k indicates the number of predictors combined to form the composite, and r_{ii} indicates the average correlation between the predictors included in the composite. The equation for d reduces to the following when only two predictors are combined to form a composite:

$$d = \frac{d_1 + d_2}{\sqrt{2 + 2r_{12}}}$$

where d_1 indicates the d value of the first predictor, d_2 indicates the d value of the second predictor, and r_{12} indicates the correlation between the two predictors. Table 17.3 presents the d values that would be observed when two predictors are combined to form a composite. The two factors that influence composite d (i.e., the summation of standardized difference

TABLE 17.3

Standardized Group Differences (*d*) for Two Predictors Combined to Form a Composite

Sum of *ds*	Correlation between the two predictors										
	0.00	0.10	0.20	0.30	0.40	0.50	0.60	0.70	0.80	0.90	10.0
0.0	0.00	0.00	0.00	0.00	0.00	0.00	0.00	0.00	0.00	0.00	0.00
0.2	0.14	0.13	0.13	0.12	0.12	0.12	0.11	0.11	0.11	0.10	0.10
0.4	0.28	0.27	0.26	0.25	0.24	0.23	0.22	0.22	0.21	0.21	0.20
0.6	0.42	0.40	0.39	0.37	0.36	0.35	0.34	0.33	0.32	0.31	0.30
0.8	0.57	0.54	0.52	0.50	0.48	0.46	0.45	0.43	0.42	0.41	0.40
1.0	0.71	0.67	0.65	0.62	0.60	0.58	0.56	0.54	0.53	0.51	0.50
1.2	0.85	0.81	0.77	0.74	0.72	0.69	0.67	0.65	0.63	0.62	0.60
1.4	0.99	0.94	0.90	0.87	0.84	0.81	0.78	0.76	0.74	0.72	0.70
1.6	1.13	1.08	1.03	0.99	0.96	0.92	0.89	0.87	0.84	0.82	0.80
1.8	1.27	1.21	1.16	1.12	1.08	1.04	1.01	0.98	0.95	0.92	0.90
2.0	1.41	1.35	1.29	1.24	1.20	1.15	1.12	1.08	1.05	1.03	10.00
2.2	1.56	1.48	1.42	1.36	1.31	1.27	1.23	1.19	1.16	1.13	10.10
2.4	1.70	1.62	1.55	1.49	1.43	1.39	1.34	1.30	1.26	1.23	10.20
2.6	1.84	1.75	1.68	1.61	1.55	1.50	1.45	1.41	1.37	1.33	10.30
2.8	1.98	1.89	1.81	1.74	1.67	1.62	1.57	1.52	1.48	1.44	10.40
3.0	2.12	2.02	1.94	1.86	1.79	1.73	1.68	1.63	1.58	1.54	10.50

Note: Sum of *d* = the *d* value for one predictor + the *d* value for the second predictor.

scores for each predictor and the correlation between the two predictors) are systematically varied.

A review of Table 17.3 reveals a number of trends. First, holding sum of d constant, as the correlation between the two predictors increases, the level of composite d decreases. When two predictors become more highly correlated, they share increasing amounts of common variance. Combining two such predictors in a composite creates additional common variance, which produces decreased group differences. Second, Table 17.3 demonstrates that, in certain contexts, supplementing a predictor with a large d with another predictor with a smaller d actually produces a composite with a larger d than either of the individual predictors. Third, in discussions about this issue we find that the intuition of many of our colleagues is that the d for a composite of two predictors will be approximated by "splitting the difference" between the d values for the two predictors (e.g., a composite of a predictor with a d of 1.0 and another with a d of 0.0 will have a d of 0.5). Particularly when the correlation between the predictors is low, this intuition will severely underestimate the composite d (e.g., in the example, with two uncorrelated predictors, the composite d will actually be 0.71). Thus, the degree to which group differences, and subsequently AI, can be reduced by supplementing a predictor with a large d with a second predictor with a small d may be commonly overestimated.

Sackett and Ellingson (1997) also showed that adding additional supplemental measures has diminishing returns. For example, when $d_1 = 1.0$ and each additional measure is uncorrelated with the original measure and has $d = 0.0$, the composite d values when adding a second, third, fourth, and fifth measure are 0.71, 0.58, 0.50, and 0.45, respectively. Finally, they also offered an expanded equation for composite d when differing weights are applied to the predictors.

While the approaches discussed thus far shed light on the features driving AI, they are silent regarding the effects of modifying a selection system to reduce AI on mean criterion performance. We turn now to a set of decision aids that do attend to both AI and performance.

Category 2: Focus on Both AI and Criterion Performance as Outcome

Estimating AI and Other Selection Outcomes for Single-Stage and Multistage Selection

De Corte and Lievens (2003) and De Corte, Lievens, and Sackett (2006) described analytic procedures that enable selection researchers and practitioners to explore the consequences in terms of several key outcomes of single- and multistage selection decisions. These procedures extend earlier related work by Cronbach and Gleser (1965) to the case for which applicants belong to several subpopulations with different mean predictor and performance structures. The procedures build on and generalize from earlier work by Tallis (1961) and Muthen (1990). They focused on the prototypic scenario that the *Standards for Educational and Psychological Testing* (American Educational Research Association, American Psychological Association, & National Council on Measurement in Education [AERA, APA, & NCME], 1999) labeled as "fixed applicant pool." In this scenario, the organization has information on the size and makeup of the applicant pool and considers using several predictors with known effect sizes, validities, and intercorrelation values to select the required number of applicants. Because single-stage selection is a special case of the more general multistage selection decisions, only the latter type of decisions are henceforth considered.

When planning a fixed-pool multistage selection system in which the applicants belong to different populations, a variety of decisions are to be made, each of which affects the selection cost, the mean performance of those selected, and the minority hiring rate. The first is determining which predictors to administer at an initial stage and which to administer at subsequent stages. The second relates to the proportion of the pool that will advance to subsequent stages in the selection procedure. The third is determining how final selection decisions should be made. Here, the key decision is whether the predictors used in initial screening also play a part in the final selection decision (i.e., if A is administered at Stage 1 and B at Stage 2, is the final selection done on the basis of B only or on A + B?).

The analytical procedure described by De Corte et al. (2006) is designed to assist the selection practitioner in making these decisions. Compared to the simulation approach proposed by Doverspike, Winter, Healy, and Barrett (1996), which may serve the same purpose, the analytical procedure is more flexible and permits dealing with the common situation in which only approximate values for some or most of the decision parameters (e.g., the predictor validities, effect sizes, and intercorrelations) are available. Also, whereas the results of the simulation method vary over repeated applications on the same input data, the analytical method always results in the same point estimate.

To illustrate the potential of the analytical procedure, we consider a situation in which the applicant population is a mixture of white and black candidate populations (with mixture proportions of 0.80 and 0.20, respectively) and four predictors are available (i.e., biodata [BI], a cognitive ability test [CA], a measure of conscientiousness [CO], and a structured interview [SI]). Table 17.4 displays the input parameter data for the predictor and criterion (i.e., task performance) mean subgroup differences, the predictor

TABLE 17.4

Standardized Mean Differences, Validities, and Intercorrelations for a Planned Selection System

Predictors	d	Validity	Intercorrelation matrix		
1. Cognitive ability (CA)	0.72	0.51			
2. Structured interview (SI)	0.31	0.48	0.31		
3. Conscientiousness (CO)	0.06	0.22	0.03	0.26	
4. Biodata (BI)	0.57	0.32	0.37	0.17	0.31

validities, and the predictor intercorrelation values. The reported data correspond to the meta-analytic values provided by Potosky, Bobko, and Roth (2005) and to estimates obtained from Cortina, Goldstein, Payne, Davison, and Gilliland (2000); Ployhart, Weekley, Holtz, and Kemp (2003); and Dalessio and Silverhart (1994).

With these input parameter data in hand, the selection practitioner may now explore the likely consequences of alternative courses of action. For example, the practitioner may contrast, for a planned two-stage selection with equal selection rates of 0.5 in the stages, (a) the usage of the unit-weighted composite of the low-impact predictors (i.e., SI and CO) in the first stage followed by the unit-weighted composite of the high-impact predictors (i.e., CA and BI) in the second stage (Scenario 1) with (b) the reverse approach in which the initial selection is based on the unit weighted high-impact predictor composite, and the unit-weighted low-impact composite is used in the second stage (Scenario 2). Other possibilities, such as giving zero weight to one or more predictors, can also be explored. The expected effect of using regression-weighted composites instead of unit-weighted composites in Scenarios 1 and 2, leading to the Scenarios 3 and 4, respectively, as well as the expected merits of a single-stage approach in which either the unit-weighted or the regression-based composite of all four predictors is used with a selection rate of 0.25 (i.e., Scenarios 5 and 6), may also be of interest.

Table 17.5 summarizes the results in terms of AI and average criterion performance of the six previously described scenarios. As expected, these results reveal that scenarios in which regression-based composites are used result in a higher average quality of the selected candidates and in a somewhat less-favorable AIR than comparable scenarios with unit-weighted composites (cf. Scenario 1 vs. 3 and Scenario 2 vs. 4). Also, comparing the results of Scenarios 1 and 2 to those of Scenario 5 and the results of Scenarios 3 and 4 to those of Scenario 6, it is again quite natural to find that the single-stage Scenarios 5 and 6, which use all the available predictor information at once, show a higher expected criterion score for the selected applicants than their two-stage counterparts. Alternatively, the comparison of Scenario 1 with Scenario 2 and the comparison of Scenario

TABLE 17.5

Projected Selection Quality (i.e., Average Criterion Score of the Selected Applicants) and AI Ratio for Several Planned Selection Scenarios

Scenario	Selection rate		Predictor composite		Average criterion score	AI ratio
	Stage 1	Stage 2	Stage 1	Stage 2		
1	0.50	0.50	1.00 SI + 1.00 CO	1.00 CA + 1.00 BI	0.70	0.39
2	0.50	0.50	1.00 CA + 1.00 BI	1.00 SI + 1.00 CO	0.69	0.45
3	0.50	0.50	0.45 SI + 0.10 CO	0.45 CA + 0.15 BI	0.75	0.38
4	0.50	0.50	0.45 CA + 0.15 BI	0.45 SI + 0.10 CO	0.74	0.42
5	0.25	/	1.00 CA + 1.00 SI + 1.00 CO + 1.00 BI		0.75	0.40
6	0.25	/	0.37 CA + 0.32 SI + 0.09 CO + 0.10 BI		0.80	0.37
7	0.25	/	0.00 CA + 0.00 SI + 1.00 CO + 0.00 BI		0.28	0.93

3 with 4 suggest the less-intuitive finding that it may be better, in terms of AI, to sequence the high-impact predictors (i.e., CA and BI) before the low-impact predictors (i.e., SI and CO), without incurring any substantial loss of selection quality. However, Sackett and Roth (1996) and De Corte et al. (2006) obtained a similar result, and we refer to the latter authors for a tentative explanation of the phenomenon.

On the basis of the Table 17.5 results and those presented by De Corte et al. (2006), one might be tempted to pursue the quest for a set of rules or guidelines for the design of multistage selection scenarios that optimize the AI and the average quality of the selection. However, both De Corte et al. and Sackett and Roth (1996) warned against such a quest by observing that "there are no simple rules that can be offered about which approach to hurdle based selection is preferred" (Sackett & Roth, 1996, p. 569). Instead, these authors recognized that informative design principles are typically contingent on both generic and specific characteristics of the situation (such as, for example, the set of available predictors and the makeup of the applicant pool).

So, although the analytic approach can be used to investigate the expected consequences of different selection designs, its merit as a decision aid remains limited to the exploration of alternative what if approaches. Within such an exploratory perspective, and provided that the boundary conditions for its application are reasonably fulfilled, the procedure is quite versatile. So, provided that the joint distribution of the predictor and criterion variables is approximately multivariate normal in the different subpopulations and that reasonably accurate data on the effect sizes, validities, and intercorrelations of the predictors are available, the procedure is applicable and produces fairly accurate results for a broad class of planned selection designs. As discussed by De Corte et al. (2006), the method can under these boundary conditions be applied to study general single- and multistage selection schemes either with or without a probationary period and involving an arbitrary number of protected applicant groups besides the majority group. Selection systems with multidimensional job performance criteria are handled within the same framework. Doing so requires the correlation between performance dimensions and the specification of the relative weights to be assigned to each dimension in creating an overall performance measure.

De Corte et al. (2006) also provided a computer program to apply their procedure. The program output provides detailed information on the expected applicant flow through the stages by calculating for each selection stage the proportion retained and the stage-specific AIR of each applicant group. In addition, the program computes how the initial group differences on the predictors evolve through the subsequent selection stages. Finally, the program enables integrating the analytic procedure within a Monte Carlo approach to handle uncertainty in the selection parameters related to the predictor effect sizes, validities, and intercorrelations as well as to the makeup of the applicant pool.

As emphasized by De Corte et al. (2006), their analytical procedure has, compared to using simulation, the major advantage that it can be integrated within a straightforward approach to the design of selection scenarios that aim to achieve a given set of goals in terms of workforce quality and desired levels of workforce diversity. To highlight the importance of such an integration, we return to Table 17.5 and, in particular, to the results reported there for Scenario 7. This scenario, in which candidates are selected in a single stage on the basis of only the CO predictor scores, corresponds to the best-possible design when only the goal of reducing the expected AI of the selection is of importance, whereas Scenario 6 is the optimal design when only the average criterion score of the selected applicants is valued. The expected outcomes of these two scenarios show a wide range of possible values for the AIR (i.e., between 0.37 and 0.93) and the average criterion score of the selected applicants (i.e., between 0.28 and 0.80).

Such substantial ranges of possible values for the AI ratio and selection quality are common, and if both workforce quality and workforce diversity are valued, only scenarios that offer an optimal trade-off between these often-conflicting goals will be of interest. To identify these optimal trade-off scenarios, the computational procedure of De Corte et al. (2006) could be used many times, each time inserting different values for the predictor weights and the stage-specific retention weights, but it is obvious that this "trial-and-error" approach is far from practical. Instead, a more direct procedure is to be preferred. Such a procedure, which integrates the De Corte et al. computational method within a multicriteria optimization approach, is discussed next.

Pareto-Optimal Trade-Offs

To assist selection practitioners in planning future selection systems to optimize both AI and selection quality, De Corte, Lievens, and Sackett (2007) presented a decision tool. This decision tool focuses on the common scenario in which employers have to make decisions on forming a composite of a set of predictors (e.g., cognitive tests, personality tests, interviews, work samples; Sackett & Ellingson, 1997; Schmitt, Rogers, Chan, Sheppard, & Jennings, 1997). In this scenario, how to maximize the mean criterion score of selected applicants is well known, namely, by inputting all predictors into a regression equation and using the resulting weights. However, employers often ask whether there exists an alternative way of using the predictors that comes close to this optimal solution in terms of the level of criterion performance achieved but does so with less AI.

Prior approaches tried to answer this question by using a trial-and-error strategy for determining various predictor weights to find a composite alternative that comes closest to meeting the two objectives (Hattrup, Rock, & Scalia, 1997; Pulakos & Schmitt, 1996; Sackett & Ellingson, 1997; Schmitt et al., 1997). Such ad hoc trial-and-error strategies are also exemplified by technical reports that typically present a series of alternative models that use varying combinations of available predictors, weighted in differing ways.

De Corte et al. (2007) developed an analytical and formal procedure to determine in advance whether there is an alternative way of using the predictors that comes close to the regression-based weighting in terms of predictive efficiency but does so with less AI. Thus, this procedure enables the determination of values for the predictor weights such that the resulting predictor composites provide an optimal balance or trade-off between productivity (i.e., high-validity) and diversity (i.e., low-AI) objectives. To this end, the notion of Pareto-optimal trade-offs between the two outcomes was presented. Given a set of predictors, there are an infinite number of possible weighting schemes that could be applied in forming predictor composites. A Pareto-optimal trade-off corresponds to a weighting scheme for which one outcome cannot be improved without harm to the other outcome given the details of the intended selection scenario (e.g., SR) and the available selection predictors. For example, there may be multiple weighting schemes that would result in a given correlation between the predictor composite and the criterion; of these schemes, the Pareto-optimal one is the set of weights that result in the highest AIR. Similarly, there may be multiple weighting schemes that would result in a given AIR; the Pareto-optimal one is the set of weights that result in the highest level of validity. So, Pareto-optimal composites offer optimal trade-offs between the AI and the validity objective, and the entire collection of these Pareto-optimal trade-offs is usually referred

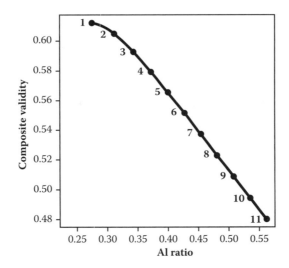

FIGURE 17.1
Pareto-optimal validity-adverse impact ratio trade-off curve for a selection with selection rate of 0.10 using a composite of cognitive ability and a structured interview as based on values from Potosky et al. (2005; cf. Table 1 of Potosky et al.).

to as the Pareto-optimal trade-off curve or function (Keeney & Raiffa, 1993; Pareto, 1906).

De Corte et al. (2007) wrote a computer program to implement the multicriteria optimization procedure for identifying the set of Pareto-optimal composites. As input for the program, a set of predictors with given validity, intercorrelations, and subgroup differences and the specification of an SR are needed. Both probationary and nonprobationary selection as well as situations in which the applicants come from several different minority populations can be addressed.

The results of the procedure are expressed in tabular or graphical form. Figure 17.1 illustrates the graphical outcome of the technique; it presents the Pareto-optimal trade-off curve for a composite of cognitive ability and a structured interview, based on values from Table 1 of Potosky et al. (2005) (cf. the present Table 17.4 values). The figure shows the optimal levels of AIR achievable at each level of validity or, equivalently, the optimal level of validity achievable at each level of AIR. Table 17.6 shows the tabular presentation as it further details a selected number of optimal trade-offs. For each selected trade-off (the numbered trade-off points on Figure 17.1), the table summarizes the validity and AIR value as well as the weighting (with weights scaled to have unit sum) of the predictors that characterize the corresponding optimal composite.

The definition of the set of Pareto-optimal composites implies that the regression-based composite is one particular element of the set. As

TABLE 17.6

Selected Pareto-Optimal Trade-Off
Composites of Cognitive Ability (CA) and
Structured Interview (SI)

			Predictor weights	
Point	Validity	AI ratio	CA	SI
1	0.61	0.27	0.53	0.47
2	0.61	0.31	0.42	0.58
3	0.59	0.34	0.35	0.65
4	0.58	0.37	0.30	0.70
5	0.57	0.40	0.25	0.75
6	0.55	0.43	0.20	0.80
7	0.54	0.45	0.16	0.84
8	0.52	0.48	0.12	0.88
9	0.51	0.51	0.08	0.92
10	0.49	0.53	0.04	0.96
11	0.48	0.56	0.00	1.00

regression-based weights maximize the validity of the resulting composite, no other weighing of the predictors can outperform this composite in terms of the validity criterion. In the figure, the regression-based composite refers to Point 1, with a mean quality of 0.61 and an AIR of 0.27. The minimal impact composite, defined as the composite with the highest possible AIR value (0.56), is another example of the set (see Point 11 in Figure 17.1). Under the common condition of all positive predictor effect sizes, the regression-based and the minimum impact composite are the boundary points of the Pareto-optimal set, with all the other Pareto-optimal composites showing more balanced trade-offs between validity and AI. More specifically, these intermediate composites are all characterized by a smaller validity than the regression-based composite, and they all show a smaller value for the AIR than the minimum impact composite. Table 17.6 also illustrates how this technique can be used to answer whether there exists a different weighting of predictors that will come close (i.e., within a specified distance) to the maximum mean quality attainable, but with less adverse impact. To address this, the definition of *close* must be specified; once a given decision maker defines it (e.g., anything within 95% of the maximum mean quality attainable), then Figure 17.1 permits this question to be answered. As noted, the maximum mean quality attainable with these predictors at this SR is 0.61. Thus, we can move down the optimal trade-off curve to the point at which mean quality (as gauged by the validity coefficient) is 0.58 (i.e., 95% of 0.61); we find that the Pareto-optimal weighting of predictors at this point produces an AIR of 0.37 compared to the value of 0.27 for the weighting that maximizes quality. The table also presents the predictor weights that would be used to obtain this result. Finally, it can be determined that the gain in AI from 0.27 to 0.37 corresponds to a 32% improvement of minority hiring.

Alternately, suppose another decision maker is willing to accept 10% reduction in validity (rather than the 5% in the example). Here, we can move down the optimal trade-off curve to the point at which mean quality is 0.55 (i.e., 90% of 0.61) and find that the Pareto-optimal weighting of predictors at this point produces an AIR of 0.43 compared to the value of 0.27 for the weighting that maximizes quality.

Possible reactions to the Pareto-optimal approach might include questions about whether it is permissible to deviate from a validity maximization strategy and whether the Civil Rights Act of 1991 precludes any selection strategy that takes AI into account when weighting predictors. Regarding the first issue, there is no general requirement to maximize validity; in fact, the use of methods that depart from validity maximization is routine. Unit weights are often used for administrative ease; score bands (e.g., "green-yellow-red" or "pass-fail") are commonly used to simplify decision making; shorter forms of tests are commonly used to reduce costs and testing time. What is restricted by the U.S. Civil Rights Act of 1991 is treating scores differently by subgroup. The key point is that the Pareto-optimal approach does not involve such differential treatment. All candidates are treated the same: Any decision about the predictor weights applies to all of the candidates. The procedure simply includes workforce diversity as an additional objective to be met by the selection system. Note that the Pareto-optimal approach does not tell the selection system designer which weights should be used. Instead, it serves essentially as a method of choosing among differing weighting schemes given a set of predictors, providing information regarding relative gains and losses in terms of validity and AI if differing weights are chosen. It is a matter of values about whether an employer is willing to accept a given reduction in validity (i.e., 1% or 5%) for a given reduction in AI. The phrase "willing to accept" is important because the approach does not specify a particular trade-off that one should accept. Finally, it is important to emphasize that investigating weighting schemes a priori may be legally more defensible than waiting until after predictor data have been gathered. In some settings, organizations are even required by statute or policy to reveal the weights given to the components of a selection system to applicants prior to testing.

Aguinis and Smith (2007)

Aguinis and Smith (2007) offered a decision aid that is quite different in nature from those discussed. They presented an approach that integrates four variables: (a) magnitude of the predictor-criterion relationship, (b) AI,

(c) selection errors (false positives and false negatives), and (d) test bias. Their approach incorporates the specification of a desired level of criterion performance; that specification permits the determination of false positives and false negatives at a given SR. It also incorporates the Cleary model of test bias, in which a test is viewed as unbiased if the regression line relating predictor and criterion scores is identical for the subgroups compared. If the regression lines are not identical (i.e., they differ in slopes, intercepts, or both), the test is viewed as biased, and the use of a common regression line would result in systematic errors of prediction being made. The Aguinis and Smith approach distinguishes between prediction errors due to imperfect validity and error made due to treating a biased test as if it were unbiased (e.g., using a common regression line when, in fact, the regression lines for the groups under consideration differ).

Aguinis and Smith (2007) developed an analytical approach that integrates all four of these features and offered a computer program that permits users to enter values for the predictor and criterion of interest to them and to examine the resulting AI, mean criterion performance, and false-positive and false-negative rates by subgroup. One important way in which their approach differs from others discussed is in the information needed as input to the program. While the other approaches focus on correlations, the Aguinis and Smith formulation focuses on regression analysis. It requires as input means and standard deviations for predictors and criteria for each subgroup as well as predictor-criterion correlations. As such, it requires more concrete and detailed information than the approaches described. For example, the other approaches permit addressing a question such as, What would we expect to happen if we added a conscientiousness measure to a cognitive ability measure? The approaches discussed would require an estimate of subgroup differences on both predictors, predictor-criterion correlation estimates for both predictors, and the correlation between the two predictors. The Aguinis and Smith approach requires predictor and criterion means and standard deviations as well and thus seems to focus on specific measures in specific situations rather than on general planning strategy prior to selecting specific measures. Nonetheless, in settings in which these specific details are available, the approach does incorporate issues of rates of false positives and false negatives as well as information about test bias.

Discussion

One crucial point is that all of the approaches are descriptive: They outline the consequences of various courses of action (e.g., What would we expect to happen if we lower a cutoff score? What would we expect to happen if we add a structured interview to our selection system?). These decision aids do not tell the user what they *should* do as that is a matter of values. This is perhaps made most explicit in the work on Pareto-optimal selection by De Corte, Lievens, and Sackett (2007). That approach specifies the amount of improvement in AI that would be expected to result from any given reduction in the mean criterion performance of those selected (i.e., a reduction in validity). Whether a given validity loss for a given AI gain is seen as acceptable is a value judgment, not a technical issue. A trade-off that seems reasonable to some will be seen as inappropriate by others. We anticipate that some readers will take the stance that validity is the only outcome of interest, and that it is inappropriate to even consider AI–validity trade-offs. Our response is that it is our experience that many organizations do value both diversity and performance and are willing to consider trade-offs between the outcomes. Our stance is that one is best served by as clear an understanding as possible of the implications of any choices made regarding trade-offs between these outcomes, and thus we have pursued the series of investigations and developed the series of decision aids described in this chapter.

A second issue worthy of discussion is the fact that some of the values required as input for the approaches described in this chapter may not be known with certainty. For example, what does one do if one is considering adding a new predictor to a selection system that already includes a predictor with known validity and known *d*, but the correlation between the new predictor and the existing predictor is unknown? Here, we advocate a sensitivity analysis, in which a range of possible values are input into the decision aid. In some cases, the emergent finding is that variation on the unknown parameter has little effect on the outcomes of interest, in which case one can proceed without concern. In other cases, the finding may be that the outcomes of interest do indeed hinge on this parameter. Here, one option is to work harder to locate an estimate of the parameter, perhaps conducting a local study to obtain the needed value. Another option is to "prepare for the worst" by identifying the worst-case scenario and estimating its effect. Yet another is to note that one truly is uncertain about the expected outcome and thus shy away from offering a priori statements about the likely degree of AI. In short, in some cases one may conclude that one does have a pretty good idea about likely outcomes prior to actual data collection; in other cases, one is best off admitting to a high degree of uncertainty.

A third issue concerns the limitations of the present decision aids. Some of these limitations are tied to the assumption underlying these methods, whereas others point to aspects of the decision situation that still need to be addressed. Thus, several of the presented methods are based on the assumption that the predictor-criterion space is multivariate normal, or that the within-group regressions of the criterion on the predictors is linear. Features of the decision situation that require further elaboration include job refusal and a focus on classification rather than selection decisions. The extension to multiple-hurdle selection situations of the multicriteria optimization approach to uncover Pareto-optimal trade-offs is another example. All these extensions should provide the selection practitioner with a set of more realistic and generally applicable tools when planning selection decisions to achieve given valuable goals in terms of workforce quality and diversity.

Fourth, we note that work on trade-offs has focused on AI and mean performance among those selected as outcomes. A broader range of outcomes are certainly of interest to organizations. These range from narrow outcomes, such as costs of implementing the selection system (e.g., De Corte et al., 2006) or administrative ease in administering a selection system, to much broader outcomes, such as organizational effectiveness and firm reputation. These broader outcomes are more difficult to measure and model. Nonetheless, we do note that there are additional trade-offs of potential interest that are worthy of investigation.

Fifth, we acknowledge that adding low-impact predictors and predictor weighting are only some routes to workforce diversity (Ployhart & Holtz, 2008). Apart from these routes, there exist other routes to workforce diversity, such as banding and the development of innovative test presentation (e.g., video; see Chan & Schmitt, 1997) and response (e.g., constructed responses; see Edwards & Arthur, 2007). Clearly, these strategies also have important merits. While prior research has typically used these strategies in isolation, we need studies that examine the combination of various strategies for reducing AI.

References

Aguinis, H., & Smith, M. A. (2007). Understanding the impact of test validity and bias on selection errors and adverse impact in human resource selection. *Personnel Psychology, 60*, 165–199.

American Educational Research Association, American Psychological Association, & National Council on Measurement in Education. (1999). *Standards for educational and psychological testing*. Washington, DC: American Educational Research Association.

Chan, D. & Schmitt, N. (1997). Video-based versus paper-and-pencil method of assessment in situational judgment tests: Subgroup differences in test performance and face validity perceptions. *Journal of Applied Psychology, 82*, 143–159.

Civil Rights Act of 1991, Pub. L. No. 102-166, 7 U.S.C. §701, 702, 703, 705, 706, 717 (1991).

Cortina, J. M., Goldstein, N. B., Payne, S. C., Davison, H. K., & Gilliland, S. W. (2000). The incremental validity of interview scores over and above cognitive ability and conscientiousness scores. *Personnel Psychology, 53,* 325–351.

Cronbach, L. R., and Gleser, G. C. (1965). *Psychological tests and personnel decisions.* Urbana: University of Illinois Press.

Dalessio, A., & Silverhart, T. (1994). Combining biodata test and interview information: Predicting decisions and performance criteria. *Personnel Psychology, 47,* 303–315.

De Corte, W., & Lievens, F. (2003). A practical procedure to estimate the quality and the adverse impact of single-stage selection decisions. *International Journal of Selection and Assessment, 11,* 89–97.

De Corte, W., & Lievens, F. (2005). The risk of adverse impact in selections based on a test with known effect size. *Educational and Psychological Measurement, 65,* 737–758.

De Corte, W., Lievens, F., and Sackett, P. R. (2006). Predicting adverse impact and mean criterion performance in multi-stage selection. *Journal of Applied Psychology, 91,* 523–537.

De Corte, W., Lievens, F., and Sackett, P. R. (2007). Combining predictors to achieve optimal trade-offs between selection quality and adverse impact. *Journal of Applied Psychology, 92,* 1380–1393.

Doverspike, D., Winter, J., Healy, M., & Barrett, G. (1996). Simulation as a method of illustrating the impact of differential weights on personnel selection outcomes. *Human Performance, 9,* 259–273.

Edwards, B. D., & Arthur, W., Jr. (2007). An examination of factors contributing to a reduction in subgroup differences on a constructed-response paper-and-pencil test of scholastic achievement. *Journal of Applied Psychology, 92,* 794–801.

Hattrup, K., Rock, J., & Scalia C. (1997). The effects of varying conceptualizations of job performance on adverse impact, minority hiring, and predicted performance. *Journal of Applied Psychology, 82,* 656–664.

Keeney, R. L., & Raiffa, H. (1993). *Decisions with multiple objectives: Preferences and value tradeoffs.* Cambridge: Cambridge University Press.

Muthen, B. (1990). Moments of the censored and truncated bivariate normal distribution. *British Journal of Mathematical and Statistical Psychology, 43,* 131–143.

Pareto, V. (1906). *Manuale di economica polittica* [Manual of political economy]. Milan, Italy: Societa Editrice Libraia.

Ployhart, R. E., & Holtz, B.C. (2008). The diversity-validity dilemma: strategies for reducing racioethnic and sex subgroup differences and adverse impact in selection. *Personnel Psychology, 61,* 153–172

Ployhart, R. E., Weekley, J. A., Holtz, B. C., & Kemp, C. (2003). Web-based and paper-and-pencil testing of applicants in a proctored setting: Are personality, biodata, and situational judgment tests comparable? *Personnel Psychology, 56,* 733–752.

Potosky, D., Bobko, P., & Roth, P. L. (2005). Forming composites of cognitive ability and alternative measures to predict job performance and reduce adverse impact: Corrected estimates and realistic expectations. *International Journal of Assessment and Selection, 13,* 304–315.

Pulakos, E. D., & Schmitt, N. (1996). An evaluation of two strategies for reducing adverse impact and their effects on criterion-related validity. *Human Performance, 9,* 241–258.

Roth, P. L., Bobko, P., & Switzer, F. S. (2006). Modeling behavior of the 4/5ths rule for determining adverse impact: Reasons for caution. *Journal of Applied Psychology, 91,* 507–522.

Sackett, P. R., & Ellingson, J. E. (1997). On the effects of forming multi-predictor composites on group differences and adverse impact. *Personnel Psychology, 50,* 708–721.

Sackett, P. R., & Roth, L. (1996). Multistage selection strategies: A Monte Carlo investigation of effects on performance and minority hiring. *Personnel Psychology, 49,* 549–572.

Sackett, P. R., Schmitt, N., Ellingson, J. E., & Kabin, M. B. (2001). High stakes testing in employment, credentialing, and higher education: Prospects in a post-affirmative action world. *American Psychologist, 56,* 302–318.

Sackett, P. R., & Wilk, S. L. (1994) Within-group norming and other forms of score adjustment in pre-employment testing. *American Psychologist, 49,* 929–954.

Schmitt, N., Rogers W., Chan, D., Sheppard L., & Jennings, D. (1997). Adverse impact and predictive efficiency of various predictor combinations. *Journal of Applied Psychology, 82,* 719–730.

Tallis, G. M. (1961). The moment generating function of the truncated multi-normal distribution. *Journal of the Royal Statistical Society, Series B 23,* 223–229.

18

A Five-Year Journey With Coca-Cola

Irwin L. Goldstein and Kathleen K. Lundquist

Introduction

This chapter describes our 5-year journey of program implementation and research with the Coca-Cola Company. Following an employment discrimination lawsuit brought by African American employees,[1] the Coca-Cola Company entered into a settlement agreement that created our roles as joint experts assisting an external task force to review and revise virtually all human resource (HR) processes within the company. The agreement was originally established for 4 years but at the request of the company at the end of the fourth year, the agreement was extended to 5 years to further achieve the goals.

In the settlement agreement, the company committed to evaluate and, if appropriate, implement specific changes to HR programs for its non-hourly U.S.-based employees. The agreement defined the objective of these changes in the statement of principle:

> The Coca-Cola Company commits to excel among Fortune 500 Companies in promoting and fostering equal opportunity in compensation, promotion, and career advancement for all employees in all levels and areas of the business, regardless of race, color, gender, religion, age, national origin, or disability, and to promote and foster an environment of inclusion, respect and freedom from retaliation. The Company recognizes that diversity is a fundamental and indispensable value and that the Company, its shareholders and all of its employees will benefit by *striving to be a premier "gold standard" company on diversity* [italics added]. The Company will set measurable and lawful business goals to achieve these objectives during the next four years. (From the transcript of May 29, 2001. Fairness Hearing, p. 214.)

The concept of gold standard was not defined in the agreement but was central to its purpose. We defined it in terms of implementing best practices for each HR process as well as integrating data across processes to manage the interventions as a comprehensive framework for change.

Given the gold standard goal of the agreement, this case study concerns an examination of adverse impact in the broadest sense. Much has been written about adverse impact specific to such HR processes as selection, promotion, retention, performance appraisal, compensation, training, and career development opportunities. This study examines not only those types of issues but also interventions that affect the organization as a whole. In other words, what can an organization do to develop a climate in which adverse impact is less likely to occur and employees view the organization as fair and transparent? It involves multiple interventions, including the development of model HR systems and people support systems. The project also involves a commitment by the organization that diversity as part of business is a positive asset, and that sustaining that commitment is an important aspect of how the company is viewed by its employees.

As the court recognized in approving the agreement, the company's commitment to the agreement and its statement of principle is "historic … [and] … the possibilities for change and for improving the lot of all employees at Coca-Cola are tremendous."[2]

A Brief History of the Project

In addition to specific reporting requirements and monetary relief for the class members, the settlement agreement provided a structure and a mission for the 5 years.

- An outside, seven-member task force was appointed by the court to provide independent oversight of the Coca-Cola Company's compliance with the terms of the agreement. Former Secretary of Labor Alexis Herman was chosen to chair the task force. The other distinguished members of the task force included M. Anthony Burns, retired chair of the board of Ryder; Gilbert Casellas, former chair of the U.S. Equal Opportunity Commission; Ed Cooke, an attorney and former counsel to the Commission on Education and Labor of the U.S. House of Representatives; Marjorie Fine Knowles, former dean of the Georgia State University College of Law; Bill Lann Lee, former assistant attorney general for civil rights; and Rene Redwood, former executive director for the federal Glass Ceiling Commission.

- As two joint experts, we were appointed by the court to work with the company and the task force to ensure the task force was guided by best practices concerning HR program development and assessment.

- The task force, with the advice of the joint experts, was empowered to evaluate the company's human resources policies and practices, recommend any necessary improvements to those policies and practices, monitor Coca-Cola's practices for the duration of the agreement, investigate complaints, and provide periodic written reports at least annually to the court on the company's progress toward fulfilling the terms of the agreement.

As a first step, the various HR processes were organized into nine HR process areas. The HR processes that were the focus of the task force's work are shown in Figure 18.1 and defined in Table 18.1.

In the first year of the agreement, the focus was on evaluating the existing HR practices in these areas and on designing new and improved processes for all Coca-Cola employees. We, based on experience, a review of relevant literature and a comparison of Coca-Cola and its peer organizations, made recommendations to the task force concerning best practices (Coca-Cola Task Force Report, 2002). In conjunction with the company, the task force evaluated, recommended changes to, and ultimately approved various new or revised HR systems.

During the second year, the emphasis focused on monitoring the implementation and effectiveness of these systems to ensure that they were working as designed and that progress was being made. Although considerable

FIGURE 18.1
The nine human resource process areas.

TABLE 18.1

Defining the Nine Human Resource Processes

Performance management covers the annual appraisal of employee job performance as well as the procedures used to communicate expectations and provide feedback on performance throughout the year and at year end.

Staffing covers the identification of internal and external candidates for employment positions (through job posting and recruitment, respectively), the assessment of candidates' qualifications (primarily through structured interviews), and the process for selecting candidates.

Compensation includes the process for classifying jobs into pay grades; making base pay, bonus, and stock option decisions; and evaluating the fairness of resulting compensation decisions.

Diversity learning and strategy includes diversity awareness education programs and related strategies to promote diversity and reinforcement of diversity concepts over time through company policies, programs, and practices.

EEO covers compliance with federal and state laws and regulations related to equal opportunity and affirmative action as well as monitoring the fairness of ongoing human resources systems through adverse impact analyses, exit interviews, and diversity goal-setting.

Problem resolution covers the methods for internally surfacing, investigating, and resolving employee complaints, including the Employee Reporting Service (i.e., hotline), Ombuds Office, and Office of Ethics and Compliance.

Career development covers programs designed to assist employees at all levels in the organization to define their career objectives, assess existing skills, and develop additional skills needed for a desired career path.

Succession planning relates to the identification, assessment, and development of internal candidates for senior management positions, including the defining of candidate slates and planning for organizational continuity.

Mentoring covers both one-on-one and self-study programs in which a coach other than an employee's supervisor assists the employee to identify and develop the experience and expertise necessary for their desired professional development.

progress was made in the implementation of some HR systems, the company was not able to implement several key programs because personnel and resources were focused on a massive restructuring effort involving significant layoffs and other matters. As noted in this chapter, the restructuring effort negatively affected many indicators, including perceptions by employees about the diversity climate and organizational climate of the company. When the task force expressed its concerns about areas in which the company's efforts had fallen short, executive leadership responded by developing a detailed plan to provide the necessary resources, monitoring, and management accountability to achieve the results required.

At the end of the third year, the company was assessed concerning the renewed commitment by measuring the company's progress on initiatives that were delayed as well as the extent to which all of the newly designed HR programs were implemented effectively.

At the completion of the fourth year, the joint experts and the task force assessed whether programs were being effectively implemented and evaluated whether the company's efforts were sustainable. It was generally concluded that most of the revised HR systems (e.g., performance management, compensation, staffing, mentoring, equal employment opportunity [EEO], problem resolution) were working as planned, while others that had been implemented or revised more recently (such as career development and succession planning) were showing promise in their early stages. Also, the company made progress in developing a comprehensive diversity strategy linking diversity to business goals.

During the fifth and final year, the joint experts and task force assessed the degree to which the company had instilled the commitment shown by senior management to the principles embodied in the settlement agreement throughout the company.

Need for an Integrated HR System Committed to People Progress

Successful companies require greater cooperation among business units and increased reliance on integrated information when managing talent within and across the organization. Unfortunately, many organizations maintain independent silos within business units and often between such HR processes as performance evaluation, career development, mentoring, succession planning, and other related HR processes, thus losing the potential for data integration and synergy.

As Coca-Cola faced the challenge of transforming isolated HR programs and processes into a comprehensive framework in support of its HR strategy, it attempted to integrate HR information across structures, connect processes, and incorporate all of the elements into a common framework. This new framework (see Figure 18.2) gave the organization the ability to manage HR programs and processes in a more meaningful way.

To provide the specific job-related content necessary for these systems, the Joint Experts designed a comprehensive work analysis methodology. The company used this methodology to identify the key responsibility areas (KRAs) and required competencies (i.e., knowledge, skills, and abilities) for each particular job throughout the organization. Because the new HR initiatives are linked, the company can analyze integrated data centrally and use accurate information for critical real-time employee decisions. For example, when tapping into the talent pipeline for the best-available job candidates, managers can access data on both internal

FIGURE 18.2
Putting it all together.

and external sources while considering career development and mentoring systems for sources of talent. The company can also determine the strengths of its employees in various parts of the organization and translate those needs into staffing, succession planning, and training practices that complement each other.

Also, as a result of HR data integration, it was possible to link all systems and obtain reports and data that provide accountability information in a time-sensitive manner. To ensure full utilization of the integrated HR system by managers and employees, the company built in training programs and online aides for each HR system. In addition, processes to ensure the equitable use of programs, such as a comprehensive problem resolution process, were constructed as a part of the integrated HR effort. Many of these efforts are discussed in this chapter, but first we discuss the methodology and data collection systems that provided information to ensure accountability.

Methodology and Data Collection

Overview of the Procedures Used to Implement and Conduct the Project

1. The task force and joint experts met with the company at least bimonthly over the 5-year period to review all aspects of company performance regarding the settlement agreement and the

development and implementation of all HR systems. Over each annual period, this included meetings with the leadership, such as their chair and chief executive officer, president of Coca-Cola North America, senior vice president and general counsel, senior vice president for HR, and various senior managers. The leadership of the task force also met at least annually with the public issues committee of the board of directors and the full board of directors.

2. Initially, the group in the company that had responsibility for the HR system (the process owners) worked with the joint experts to develop and implement each HR system and develop data systems to provide accountability concerning outcomes. At least monthly, there were briefings between the company and the joint experts concerning the development of various HR systems.

3. On a monthly basis, the joint experts briefed the task force on the development, implementation, and accountability for the HR systems.

4. At least annually, each process owner presented information to the task force concerning the development, implementation, and evaluation for each HR system.

5. On an annual basis, a report to the court was provided with an analysis of each HR program, including development and implementation information, qualitative and quantitative assessment results, and recommendations for future work.

Overview of the Time Period for Data Collection

The data set began with baseline information covering the period from July 2001 through June 2002. It included baseline data against which progress could be measured over the remainder of the agreement. New data sets were presented throughout the 5-year period of the agreement, concluding September 30, 2006.

Information Reviewed to Track Progress

An extensive data collection system was designed to assess progress accomplished over the 5 years of the settlement agreement and in considering future actions to sustain these accomplishments. This included the following:

1. Annual data comparing the demographics of the workforce in the company at that time to the baseline demographics and to each successive year of the agreement

2. Employee survey results collected annually covering attitudes and perceptions about diversity, fairness, and the various HR processes introduced. In a few instances when a program was introduced more recently, comparative analyses covered only the most recent years; however, there are considerable data, which permitted the comparison of results over the entire 5-year period.

3. Both qualitative and quantitative data from a wide variety of sources, including data provided by the company (e.g., training completion rates, trend data on complaints, and statistical analyses of adverse impact)

4. Information provided by the company that was independently audited and verified by the joint experts (e.g., audits of performance management, posting, and staffing, and slating data)

5. Information independently developed by the joint experts and task force (e.g., employee survey data)

6. Information obtained from focus groups conducted by the joint experts and the task force

Goals of the Project

Above and beyond the specific requirements of the settlement agreement, a set of goals evolved that both Coca-Cola and the task force wished to achieve in its efforts together. These goals speak to the broader commitment of the company to both the letter and the spirit of developing a diverse and inclusive culture. The goals are:

1. The development of best-in-class HR systems as a part of a commitment to people progress in the organization

2. Inclusion of minorities and women as an organizational goal

3. The reduction of adverse impact when utilizing HR systems

4. Utilization of all systems in a manner perceived by employees as fair and equitable

5. Use of database systems as an accountability indicator for progress

6. Organizational commitment to diversity as a part of the company's business strategy

Before discussing particular changes in the HR systems to help achieve these goals, we first present some of the global indicators used to assess change over the 5-year period.

Inclusion and Representation: Workforce Demographics

Overall Workforce

The Coca-Cola Company's nonhourly U.S. workforce (i.e., those employees covered by the agreement) as of September 30, 2006, consisted of a total of 6,557 employees. Over the entire course of the settlement agreement, the relative percentage of minorities in the workforce increased by a fifth, from approximately 29% in December 2000 to 35% as of September 2006. Net percentage increases or decreases in representation of various groups from December 31, 2000 to September 2006 are shown in the last column of Table 18.2.

Senior Leadership

The company also made substantial progress in diversifying senior leadership after January 2000. Table 18.2 shows the participation of women and minorities at the senior levels of the organization. Minorities, who constituted 35% of the employee workforce and slightly over 20% of the senior levels of the workforce (Salary Grade 13 and above), constituted slightly over 20% of elected and appointed officers in September 2006. Women, who represented 50% of the workforce and 30% of the workforce at Salary Grade 13 and above, were roughly 27% of elected and appointed officers at the company. The trend since 2000 shows a substantial net increase and

TABLE 18.2

Percentage Representation of Nonhourly Workforce by Gender and Ethnicity

	2000	2001	2002	2003	2004	2005	2006	% ± since 2000
Total	**6,628**	**6,728**	**6,876**	**6,151**	**5,878**	**6,155**	**6,557**	**2000**
Male	50.5	50.5	50.6	51.4	51.4	50.9	50.8	+0.3
White male	39.1	38.2	38.1	38.5	38.0	36.7	35.9	−3.2
Minority male	11.4	12.3	12.5	12.9	13.2	14.1	14.6	+3.2
Female	49.5	49.5	49.4	48.6	48.6	49.1	49.2	−0.3
White female	32.2	32.0	31.8	31.0	30.4	29.9	28.7	−3.5
Minority female	17.2	17.5	17.7	17.6	18.0	19.1	20.3	+3.1
Minorities	28.7	29.8	30.2	30.3	31.2	33.2	34.9	+6.2
African American	19.7	20.8	20.5	20.5	21.0	21.8	23.0	+3.3
Hispanic	5.5	5.4	5.7	5.7	5.9	6.2	6.4	+0.9
Asian/Pacific Islander	3.2	3.4	3.6	3.7	4.0	4.7	5.0	+1.8
Native American	0.2	0.3	0.4	0.4	0.4	0.4	0.4	+0.2

TABLE 18.3

Percentage Representation in Senior Leadership

	2000		2002		2003		2004		2005		2006		% ± since 2000
	N	%	N	%	N	%	N	%	N	%	N	%	
Executive committee													
Total	6		10		11		13		16		14		
Female	0		1	10.0	1	9.0	1	7.7	3	18.7	3	21.4	+21.4
Minorities	1	17.0	3	30.0	3	27.3	3	23.1	2	12.5	3	21.4	+4.4
Elected and appointed officers													
Total	107		152		173		190		182		199		
Female	17	16.0	37	24.0	42	24.3	47	24.7	49	26.9	54	27.1	+11.1
Minorities	9	8.0	33	22.0	36	20.8	42	22.1	38	20.9	42	21.1	+13.1

a consistent improvement in minority and female representation among elected and appointed officers.

Senior Leadership Pipeline

Table 18.3 shows a promising trend in minority and female representation in the pipeline jobs to senior leadership, those in entry-level senior management jobs (Salary Grades 14 and above), and those in the feeder pool jobs for senior management (Salary Grades 10 through 13). Since the end of 2002, representation for minorities in the feeder pool jobs and entry-level senior management jobs increased roughly 20% to 25% (a net gain of 7% and 4%, respectively). Gains in net representation were made by all ethnic groups and by women in both job-level groups during this period.

These gains in representation for women and minorities reflect the company's commitment not only to meeting the requirements of the settlement agreement but also to increasing diversity as a strategic business goal. The increasing diversity of the marketplace for consumer products and the changing demographics of the applicant pool are imperatives that not only Coca-Cola but also the vast majority of U.S. companies must recognize and address as they evaluate the diversity of their workforces.

Task Force Survey Results

In 2002, 2004, and 2006, the Coca-Cola Company commissioned an outside firm to conduct an anonymous electronic survey of all employees for the corporate and North American groups. In 2003, the survey was administered to persons participating in focus groups, with approximately 700 employees participating who were chosen through a stratified random-sampling process. In 2005, a stratified random-sampling process was used that resulted in a sample size of approximately 3,500. Response rates for all surveys were at least 70%.

The survey included questions developed by the task force and joint experts; these questions were used in 2002, 2003, 2004, 2005, and 2006 surveys on diversity climate, company climate, and fairness of the HR processes. These results are discussed next. In addition, questions specific to HR processes were included; these items are discussed when specific HR changes are discussed.

Survey Sample

In 2006, which was the last year of this project, the entire work population for Coca-Cola corporate and North America were sampled. Approximately 4,700 employees responded to the survey. This represented a 74% response rate, resulting in a robust sample. Of the respondents, 65% were Caucasian, 23% African American, 5% Hispanic, and 5% Asian/Pacific Islander. The sample was representative of the ethnic and gender population of the company. The sample was also of sufficient size to assess group differences by ethnicity and gender.

Diversity Climate

To measure employee perceptions and attitudes regarding the diversity climate at the company, the task force and the joint experts drafted specific questions to include in the annual surveys to track changes in the company's diversity climate over time. The diversity climate questions covered employees' perceptions of whether the company is committed to diversity and equal opportunity, the visibility of senior management in demonstrating that commitment and in making the business case for diversity, and perceptions of whether employees are treated fairly and consistently.

For interpretation purposes, it is important to note the events that occurred between 2002 and 2003 that resulted in significant declines on all perception measures. The company decided that it needed to streamline the organization to be more responsive to both customers and consumers. It performed a detailed analysis of the jobs needed for a restructuring and an assessment of its current employees and their skill levels for the new jobs. This resulted in a loss of 800 jobs, which was fully a tenth of the U.S. workforce. For an organization that had only once previously had a reduction in force, these reductions resulted in the workforce forming very critical perceptions of the company and presented a significant challenge. These changes were also featured prominently in the local press

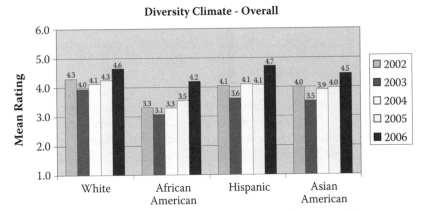

Note that the scale points are as follows: 1= strongly disagree, 2=disagree, 3=slightly disagree, 4=slightly agree, 5=agree, 6=strongly agree

FIGURE 18.3
Comparison of diversity climate ratings over time.

and the national financial press. These concerns are clearly reflected in the survey result changes between 2002 and 2003.

As shown in Figure 18.3, after the dip in diversity climate perceptions in 2003 across all groups, there was a general trend of increasing perceptions of the diversity climate over time. By 2006, this improvement in diversity climate scores was such that all groups achieved higher mean scores than at any time since the task force surveying began in 2002. African Americans, Hispanics, and Asian Americans all improved from 2005 by approximately one half of a scale point on a 6-point scale (the scale values are shown below Figure 18.3). Whites improved, and there were essentially no differences between Hispanics, Asian Americans, and whites. While African American scores were still somewhat below those of whites and the other groups, those differences narrowed significantly from past years.

The scores were especially positive on questions related to senior management's commitment to diversity as part of the company's business success and the commitment to a work environment that respects diversity and fosters workplace equity. Gender differences were minimal, with males having a slightly more positive perception.

During several focus groups conducted by the task force and joint experts during 2003 and 2004, it became apparent that minorities who had been employed for many years by the company were more skeptical about the new changes being implemented. From these focus groups, it was apparent that African American employees felt that over the years Coca-Cola did not have a commitment to retain, promote, and develop opportunities for them. Indeed, that was a focus of the original lawsuit.

During the time of the lawsuit and for several years following, the media in Atlanta were very critical of Coca-Cola on these issues. An analysis of the diversity climate data from the 2005 survey indicated that African Americans who were hired in the preceding 3 years had a much more favorable view of the diversity climate than African Americans hired into the company more than 3 years prior to the survey. By this time, Coca Cola was instituting many practices to promote diversity, and many of these new employees did not have the negative experiences of more long-term employees. In 2006, the last year of the project, that trend continued, with more recent hires having a more positive perception (by one half of a scale point) as compared to longer-tenure employees. However, in 2006, both recent hires and long-term hires had much more positive views as compared to 2005, again by about half a scale point. Indeed, the perception of longer-term hires in 2006 improved enough that they were equivalent to the positive perceptions of the shorter-term hires in 2005. It is hoped that the overall pattern showing positive increases for both short- and long-term tenure supports the impact of the company's efforts in establishing diversity as part of the business case.

Company Climate

The employee survey included questions regarding employees' perceptions about the company, including their pride in the company, their willingness to say good things about the company to others, and their commitment to staying employed by the company.

Again, after the decline in 2003 associated with the downsizing, there were significant increases in company climate for all groups (most notably in the 2006 survey) indicating an increasingly positive perception of the company (Figure 18.4). Also, the company climate perceptions in 2006 for whites, African Americans, and Asian Americans were essentially identical, with Hispanics slighter higher. There were no gender differences on company climate. Again, all ethnic groups (except whites) rated company climate higher than diversity climate year over year, indicating that employees viewed the brand and the company somewhat more favorably than the diversity climate. However, it is important to view that result in the context of significant improvements in perceptions for both diversity climate and company climate for all groups.

Also, consistent with prior survey results, company climate ratings were quite similar across ethnic groups. It is also important to note that the patterns of higher scores and minimal differences between ethnic groups also occurred for a company climate item that stated "the Company's policies and procedures create a positive work environment for me." Thus, perceptions of improvements in company climate extended to the effect of policies on employees themselves.

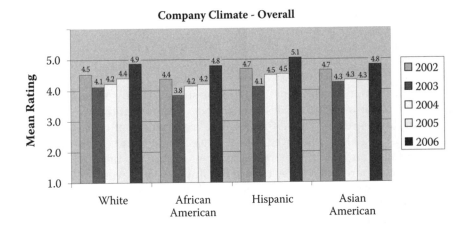

FIGURE 18.4
Comparison of company climate ratings over time.

Another consistent finding for all groups across all of the time periods was that company climate measures were always more positive than diversity climate measures. In our opinion, part of this, as noted, results from the concerns about the company's commitment to diversity that led to the lawsuit. But, in addition, employees in focus groups continually referred to Coca-Cola as having one of the strongest brands nationally and internationally, as well as its longtime stature as a company. It was our opinion from these conversations that if Coca-Cola was able to accomplish goals related to fairness and commitment to diversity that its employees would embrace these efforts.

The patterns on company climate for African Americans hired in the last 3 years as compared to employees at the company more than 3 years are the same as the results found for diversity climate. That is, shorter-tenure employees had a more positive perception of the organization than longer-tenure employees. In the last year of the project, 2006, both the shorter- and longer-term employees had significantly more positive perceptions than those found with the same groups in 2005.

Company Interventions and Their Impact

The data on representation presented showing significant changes in the representation of minorities and women stemmed from a number of HR efforts involving staffing, succession planning, and other efforts. We describe a number of these interventions.

Staffing

In designing its approach to selection, the company chose to design and implement new staffing processes for both internal and external candidates, even though the requirements of the agreement covered only internal candidates. The principal selection device used is a structured interview. The company's purpose here was to extend all of its work to embrace best practices and develop validated systems for all employees to ensure the best possible workforce who also viewed the HR practices as fair and equitable.

The company utilizes an automated, internal job-posting process. All vacant positions below the senior management level must be posted on the system for a minimum of 15 calendar days prior to an offer being made, and the job-posting process specifies that a candidate pool must consist of three or more qualified candidates, at least one of whom must be a woman or a minority. It should also be noted that this was a requirement of the consent decree.

The settlement agreement further provides that any nondiverse candidate slates may be considered only on approval or modification by the senior vice president of HR. The task force received quarterly reports to monitor whether a diverse pool of candidates had been routinely considered for each such position. In addition, the company incorporated a review of all slates for open positions to ensure diversity as part of regular senior management review. For 2006, of the 1,199 postings examined by the joint experts across Salary Grades 1 through 13, only 49 (4%) did not meet these requirements, most typically for having fewer than three candidates. Approximately 90% of the postings had both gender and ethnic diversity in the candidate pool. In 14 cases (approximately 1%), the slates had no diverse candidates. A review of the candidate and interview pools provided further indication of the company's success in diversifying the pools of candidates considered for jobs. For most ethnic groups and women, selection rates were similar to or slightly higher than representation in the candidate pool and the interview pool.

Adverse impact analyses were conducted to evaluate the results of the staffing process. Analyses were conducted for two comparisons: candidate pool to interview pool and interview pool to final selection decision. Candidates selected for hire did not differ significantly by ethnicity or gender. The company's efforts to cast a broader net and significantly "enhance the diversity of slates" appeared to be contributing to some adverse impact in the candidate pool to interview stage, although this result did not carry over into the critical selection decision.

Additional incentives for hiring managers especially at the more senior levels are provided by the diversity goals program, tying executive compensation to the increase in representation of women and minorities in those jobs in the levels that serve as feeder pools to senior management.

Under the diversity goals program, all senior managers based in North America had a portion of their incentive tied to the achievement of the company's diversity goals. This program tracked progress on an annual basis. In its first year, the program tied executive and senior manager compensation to a 2% net increase in representation of women and minorities at or above middle management. Net increase compared the percentage representation of women or minorities at the beginning and end of the review period, regardless of whether representation decreased due to turnover, restructuring, or other legitimate factors out of the control of the employer. Moreover, for this program, lateral moves were excluded. Since the focus was on net representation instead of accountability for the results of decisions under the manager's control, such as hiring and promotion decisions, these were judged as ambitious goals for the first year of this program. At the conclusion of the first year of the diversity goals program, two of four goals were completely met, and two were partially met. The company continued the diversity goals program but adjusted the manner in which goals were set to be a reflection of opportunities to make decisions. The effect of these diversity goals is reflected in the representation data presented in the previous discussion.

While not strictly a part of staffing, it should be noted that the company invested significant resources in training to build the organizational capability in the EEO area. The company provided extensive training for its HR department, including all HR generalists and talent acquisition staff. Also, the company developed an innovative, CD-based course on "civil treatment" that was required training for managers and a voluntary training program available to employees. As of September 2006, 83% of managers and 79% of employees had completed the program, reflecting the company's commitment to train new hires and new managers continuously on these topics.

Surveys previously administered to managers completing training indicated that 90% of managers felt the program "gave me a better understanding of my responsibilities in managing a civil workplace," and 82% indicated "I know more about my company's EEO-related policies and procedures because of the program."

Succession Planning

Succession planning relates to the identification, assessment, and development of internal candidates for senior management positions. Succession planning also includes defining candidate slates for senior-level jobs and planning for organizational continuity in the event of turnover or retirement.

The strategic resource review (SRR) is the company's process for talent review and succession management. In the "talent review" process, an employee's potential for movement within the organization is assessed. Managers compare the talent needs identified in the business-planning process with the capabilities of current senior-level employees. Through the talent review process, regular discussions occur among the highest-level managers regarding talent and talent gaps. The company anticipates this process will result in the development of existing internal talent and, when appropriate, the recruitment of external talent.

The SRR process begins when an employee is asked to complete a profile summarizing his or her performance, strengths, developmental areas, career aspirations, educational background, and career history. This information is then discussed with the employee's manager, who completes a talent assessment. The managers' assessments are then reviewed by successive levels of management and combined at the business unit level, at which they are summarized and eventually presented to the executive committee. These presentations include the strategy and vision of the business unit, its organizational structure, a summary of potential ratings for the business unit, a diversity review, a succession plan, and an action plan for the upcoming year to develop talent.

Also, as a part of this process, the company has continued to build managers' skills in assessing the capability of employees and providing regular, candid feedback. Calibration discussions among senior managers and individual coaching have increased the consistency and impact of the SRR process.

The SRR assessment information is used to identify potential candidates for openings at the senior management level in a process known as *slating*. As is consistent with most organizations, jobs at the senior management level are not subject to posting. By drawing on the comprehensive SRR information, the company believes that a broader range of candidates can be identified for open positions. This is an important feature that permits the organization to manage its talent and develop the skill sets necessary for future opportunities.

The SRR process assesses approximately 1,000 U.S.-based employees annually. It involves significant time from the most senior levels of management. For example, in 2002 the executive committee committed 9 days to its review of talent, with additional time for review of midyear results against action plans developed in the SRR assessments. Individual feedback letters were prepared for each business unit leader, and overall SRR outcomes were shared and discussed at the division presidents meeting. The diversity of women and minorities in pipeline jobs was also examined as part of SRR and is encouraging for the future diversification of senior management.

A number of significant steps have been taken over the past few years to implement senior management's commitment to improve the identification and development of a diverse talent pool for senior-level jobs. This effort goes beyond ensuring the diversity of slates to monitoring the diversity of the pool in pipeline jobs. It includes implementing an executive-mentoring

TABLE 18.4

Percentage Representation in Senior Leadership Pipeline Jobs

	2002		2006			
	Entry-level leader SG 14+	Feeder pool jobs SG 10–13	Entry-level leader SG 14+	% ± since 2002	Feeder pool jobs SG 10–13	% ± since 2002
Male	75.5	58.5	72.4	−3.1	56.2	−2.3
White male	62.0	47.3	55.6	−6.4	42.1	−5.2
Minority male	13.5	11.2	16.8	+3.3	14.1	+2.9
Female	24.3	41.4	27.6	+3.3	43.8	+2.4
White female	19.4	31.3	21.8	+2.4	29.4	−1.9
Minority female	4.9	10.1	5.8	+0.9	14.4	+4.3
Minorities	18.4	21.3	22.1	+3.7	27.9	+6.6
African American	9.9	12.0	10.5	+0.6	15.5	+3.5
Hispanic	5.5	4.9	6.0	+0.5	5.9	+1.0
Asian/Pacific Islander	3.0	4.1	5.5	+2.5	6.0	+1.9
Native American	0.0	0.3	0.2	+0.2	0.5	+0.2

program and instituting a formal training curriculum for executives and those considered to be in the immediate pipeline. Strong reporting tools and routines were instituted to make data and actions visible to leaders and the HR team supporting senior-level selections, including incorporating a review of the diversity of slates as part of regular business routines.

As with the discussion of job posting, the slating process is subject to diversity representation on each slate. The settlement agreement requires that the senior vice president of HRs shall first review and approve or modify any nondiverse candidate slate. In 2006, almost two thirds of the slates had both ethnic and gender diversity in the candidates considered.

Moreover, of the 112 positions at the senior management level filled in 2006, 32% were filled by minorities and 32% by women. Adverse impact analyses conducted by the joint experts indicated that no adverse impact was found in filling jobs at this level, either in referring candidates for interview or in making final selection decisions. These findings continue the progress toward greater diversity in filling positions at this level and reflect the substantial commitment of senior management to communicate and support the diversity of selection into jobs at this level.

Also, as noted in the tables in the section on representation, the company made overall progress in increasing minority and female representation in the pipeline jobs to senior leadership (see Table 18.4).

Data were also provided by the company about the ethnic and gender makeup of the individuals assessed as "high potential," "promotable," and "well placed," as well as those deemed to be too new in a role or evidencing difficulty in their positions due to learning or performance issues. Among those assessed as high potential, minorities and women were at or above their representation in the population of employees at that level, with approximately 15% of minorities and 20% of females identified as high potential. In 2006, over 40% of women and minorities were considered to be promotable, a dramatic jump when compared to 24% and 13%, respectively, in 2005. In addition, the company has also assessed individuals at lower salary grades to provide accelerated development to increase the diversity of pipeline talent.

The responses of management employees who participated in the employee survey also indicated that perceptions are beginning to change about the succession-planning process. Regardless of ethnicity, managers believed that the way people are identified for advancement in the company is fair, a noticeable improvement from previous years in both level and consistency across the various ethnic groups.

Career Development

Many companies have career development programs. However, Coca-Cola's approach to career development is a totally integrated online system that makes available all the tools for each employee to use in devising a personal career path.

The career development system also includes an online career coaching guide, training sessions, and workshops to enable managers to support employees in realizing their career plans. In addition, the company has integrated this program with other HR initiatives, such as performance management and succession planning.

The company has designed a career development model for employees, incorporating career information, assessment tools, and educational resources to help employees compare their skills and competencies with those needed by the company. The company developed mentoring programs as a part of the career development process for employees at higher grade levels who were identified as having potential through the succession planning process.

In designing and implementing the career development program, the company utilized work analysis data to provide the competency and skill information both for the career development process and for job profiles and job posting. In addition, consistent with best practices, the roles of managers, employees, and the company have been clarified and communicated, with monitoring of career development reinforced within the performance management process.

In addition, as noted in the next section, the company implemented a mentoring program focused on career development for persons identified

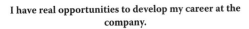

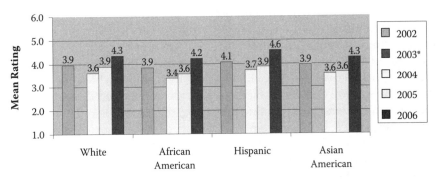

FIGURE 18.5
Comparison of career development perceptions over time.

through the succession planning process and has piloted workshops on career planning for both managers and employees.

Data concerning the use of the online career development system are promising. From October 2004 to October 2005, the tool was utilized by 2,603 persons, which represents 36% of the U.S. employee population. These data also indicate that minorities' use tended to exceed their representation in the workforce. For example, African Americans represented 24% of the users of the system. In addition, 73% of the mentees who participated in the mentoring program from September 2005 to September 2006 utilized the online tool, and 48% of the mentors used the tool. The company mentoring program is discussed next. In addition, 65% of the users were in job Grades 10 to 13, which is the feeder population for higher level jobs.

As noted in Figure 18.5, responses from the 2006 survey concerning the opportunities for developing a career, gaining skills, and using the online career development tools developed by the company were more positive for all employees and improved from previous years' surveys for all groups, including African Americans.

The career development system was one of the last HR efforts to be implemented. Thus, it is encouraging to see that employees were responding positively to its impact on their ability to understand what career development opportunities exist.

Mentoring

Organizations universally acknowledge that mentoring is an effective tool for developing and retaining talent, but many companies find it difficult to deliver effective programs (Allen, Eby, & Lentz, 2006; Allen, Eby, Poteet, Lentz, & Lima, 2004; Brown, Zablah, & Bellenger, 2008; Eby, Butts,

Lockwood, & Simon, 2004). Of top executives, 75% cite the experience of having been mentored as a key factor in their success. However, traditional mentoring programs are often informal efforts with minimal training for participants. They are also challenged by having too many candidates who want to be mentored and too few employees with the experience and resources to be mentors.

Coca-Cola has been innovative in developing a menu of different types of mentoring experiences that provide a variety of opportunities. These include a formal companywide one-on-one mentoring process, a group-mentoring process, and a self-study guide for those who do not wish or are not able to participate in the formal programs.

Each of these programs includes a number of important best practices, as identified in the meta-analytic review of the research literature on mentoring conducted by Allen et al. (2006) and their related research. Thus, the one-on-one mentoring program is characterized by significant senior management sponsorship and communication; active recruitment of both mentors and mentees; a formal application-and-matching process; training for both mentors and mentees in their responsibilities; and an ongoing evaluation of the program's effectiveness. In addition, the program includes a one-on-one mentoring program with high-level executive mentors working with mentees who are either identified through the succession planning process or are directly in the pipeline for leadership positions. Because of the limited number of mentors available for the large number of potential mentees in the one-on-one program, the company has also used an innovative group-mentoring program in which a single mentor facilitates sessions with a group of mentees. The company has also developed a mentoring program driven by a self-study guide. These efforts have also been combined with more informal mentoring experiences, including, for example, a "networking for success" course.

A sign of the success of the program is that mentees typically fill up mentoring opportunities within an hour of their announcement. The mentoring program has incorporated routine interim evaluations of effectiveness through a 90-day survey of participants and focus groups conducted after 6 months. Analyses indicated the vast majority of mentees viewed the program as useful in assisting their development. Key benefits included sharing of knowledge and experiences, giving and receiving coaching, and learning something new about the company.

At the request of the joint experts and the task force, the company has also provided data tracking work outcomes for employees who participated in the mentoring process as mentees. Approximately 78% or 348 of 448 mentees remained with the company, with 32% of those remaining mentees African Americans, 9% Hispanics, and 4% Asian Americans. Thus, for the 348 persons still remaining with the company, only 20% were in the same position, while 80% experienced position changes. These data clearly indicate that mentees who participated in the program were experiencing positive outcomes in terms of position changes. This means that for the 348 mentees who remained with the organization, 42% of them were promoted, and 38% experienced positive lateral moves in the sense that they involved new career opportunities. Of the mentee promotions, 33% have gone to African Americans, 11% to Hispanics, and 3% to Asian Americans. These data indicate that nearly half of the mentee promotions were for minorities. In addition, 65% of the promotions were for females. For lateral moves, 36% have gone to African Americans, 13% to Hispanics, 4% to Asian Americans, and 61% to females.

Problem Resolution

Transparency concerning financial matters is required in today's regulatory environment. However, when considering employee issues, less attention has been given to a similar need for transparency and safe avenues to voice concerns. Failure to listen and act in a timely manner to employee concerns can seriously impact shareholder value, reputation, employee morale, and engagement. Providing employees with a clear, risk-free mechanism to raise issues, offer suggestions, and resolve problems reduces the perception of unfairness, lowers prospects for negative publicity, and avoids costly litigation.

In our experiences, despite some companies' attempts to deal with internal conflicts and ethical issues, employees in general remain silent about their concerns. This was also supported by focus groups, whose members indicated that employees do not understand the process itself; they believe that no action will be taken; they fear confidentiality will be breached; and they suspect they will suffer retribution for speaking out. Coca-Cola's response to this problem was to provide employees with a series of options for problem resolution focused on early identification and negotiation of unresolved employee concerns rather than litigation. Continuous and ongoing communications reinforce the availability of these numerous options and emphasize the company's commitment to a fair and equitable workplace.

This company process, known as the "solutions program," consists of a five-step progression:

1. Open Door: The open door process allows for conversations with up to three levels of the employee's management structure and includes HR.
2. Facilitation: If the employee is not satisfied with the results of the open door process, the next step is working with a program manager from the ethics and compliance office to attempt a resolution to the issue.

3. Written appeal: If the issue is not resolved through the facilitation process, the employee can appeal to the senior management panel for a final internal decision.

4. Mediation: If the senior management panel decision is unacceptable to the employee, mediation is the next option available to the employee.

5. Arbitration: If mediation fails to resolve the legal dispute, an arbitrator will then make a decision, which is binding on the company but not the employee, thus preserving the good faith option of the employee to retain the right to litigate or seek external resolution.

In addition, an employee may contact the ombuds office, a confidential, informal, and neutral resource for employees seeking assistance in resolving a work-related problem. The ombuds office reports directly to the chief executive officer.

Also available is the Employee Reporting Service (ERS), an independent and anonymous toll-free phone service by which employees can report problems and concerns to the company for appropriate handling within 24 hours. In addition, the company utilizes an employee assistance program to provide an effective avenue for resolving employee issues more appropriate for professional counseling.

By 2006, virtually all employees indicated on the employee survey that they were aware of the ethics and compliance office, and employees generally felt more positively about the company's implementation of an effective problem resolution program. The responses were positive for all groups with minimal differences based on ethnicity.

As noted in Figure 18.6, responses regarding whether the company makes it clear that discrimination is unacceptable in the workplace were positive for whites, Hispanics, and Asian Americans, with African Americans less certain but still positive about this issue. Between 2005 and 2006, the responses for all groups improved significantly. Note that the scores for all groups were at least a 5 on a 6-point scale, where a score of 5 corresponds to "agree" and a score 6 corresponds to "strongly agree." However, as noted, even though the responses for all groups were high, African Americans were still less positive than all other groups about this issue. Given the large sample size, those differences are statistically significant. On the other hand, perceptions of African Americans improved the most for any group between 2005 and 2006, so we believe progress has been made by the company in ensuring that the messages concerning discrimination in the workplace are being heard. The results of analyses involving many of the HR systems support this view. For example, as noted, there were virtually no differences in 2006 between African

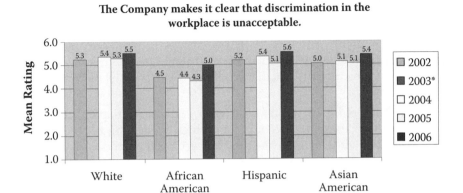

FIGURE 18.6
Comparison of EEO (equal employment opportunity) over time.

Americans and whites on whether they had real opportunities to develop their careers in the company.

In sum, it appears that the company made progress in ensuring that the workforce knows of the services that are available and in assuring the workforce that they will be treated fairly.

Communications and Diversity Strategy

Too often, communications is the final thought in the diversity strategy. Clearly, it is important for the diversity strategy to be grounded in the business strategy. Beyond that, however, communication and visible senior management support of diversity are essential in reinforcing the company's commitment, fostering engagement, and most of all, ensuring the sustainability of the effort. In our experience, a proactive, well-thought-out internal diversity communications plan, linked to an organization's business strategy, can be a powerful tool to make clear to employees the importance of diversity to success in the workplace, the marketplace, and the business. The ongoing commitment and involvement of the leaders is critical to this process. To be effective, the message must be grounded in the business and driven from the top.

In spring 2005, the company launched the Manifesto for Growth initiative that focused the global company's vision and plan. A stated goal of this effort was for the Coca-Cola Company to "be a great place to work where people are inspired to be the best they can." The manifesto was designed to provide clarity of direction, increase engagement and personal ownership, align efforts and system energy, and create momentum. Practically, the manifesto put a focus on the development of the workforce, including extensive career development strategies and training as a critical element to capture and expand markets. The company worked with the task force to integrate diversity into the overall corporate strategies, with emphasis on establishing diversity as part of the company's business plan.

The company presented to the task force a comprehensive plan for developing diversity as part of the business plan. The plan consisted of the following components:

- Development and communication of the "four Cs" strategy, with company efforts focused on commitment, communications, culture, and consumption

- Affirmation of a diversity strategy that also focuses on workplace, marketplace, community, and suppliers using a balanced approach with specific actions

- Establishment of corporate ownership and accountability for the process
  - Utilization of the president and chief operating officer of the North American group as key drivers in "diversity as business" as a core component of the 2006 business-planning process
  - Development of a plan to translate the chief executive officer's commitment to diversity into an actionable strategy

- Development and implementation of diversity as business training for managers, including development of a diversity as business learning module to be included as part of the midlevel leadership program

- Description and outline of the institutionalized slating process for filling positions for North America and for corporate

- Development and activation of a communication plan with detailed actions to be incorporated in the task force report to the court

- Development of a communications strategy to acknowledge compliance efforts and show progress building on foundational work

- Activation of the diversity advisory councils and employee forums as part of employee engagement

- Development of a recognition and rewards program

The plans to achieve these goals included cascading diversity plans across the organization, rewarding and recognizing success, expanding progress with supplier diversity, supporting the development of initiatives with global key customers, global employee branding campaigns, and supporting linkages to all HR strategies. Especially notable is the company's multicultural marketing plan, which provides critical market-place position on the importance of diversity as business.

The 2006 initiatives also included the following:

- Development and leveraging of diversity advisory councils
- Engagement of employees through forums in the workplace
- Periodic employee roundtables
- Development and implementation of diversity as business education components
- Assignment of senior management to leadership roles with employee forums
- Increase of supplier diversity program spending
- Creation of supplier diversity field champions for eight regions

Before the development of these plans, the company had a supplier diversity plan with a commitment of spending $800 million over the 5-year period from 2001 to 2005. By the end of 2005, total spending reached $1 billion, with yearly spending increasing from $66 million in 2000 to $256 million in 2005.

In general, the data from the employee survey indicated that the diversity education effort was viewed positively by all employees regardless of race or gender. A specific survey item stated, "The diversity education program has helped me understand and respect the differences of others." However, focus group data in 2003 and 2004 indicated that employees did not believe that the company had made clear the business case for diversity. However, the efforts described changed the view of employees, as demonstrated in Figure 18.7. The absolute response level was quite high, and the differences between minority groups was minimal, except for

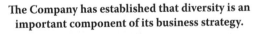

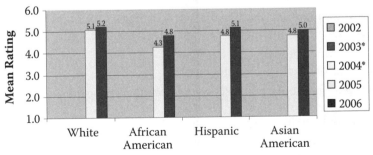

FIGURE 18.7
Perceptions concerning diversity as a component of business strategy.

African Americans, who were slightly less positive, although the response level improved from 2005 to 2006.

Since this is a major goal of the company, these positive results along with the positive diversity climate results clearly reflect that these efforts have been communicated and supported by the workforce. As was noted in a number of focus groups in 2005 and 2006, the employees appreciated the importance of diversity as part of the company's strategic plan rather than it only being a compliance effort.

A Few Final Thoughts

The joint experts, the task force, and the company went through many learning periods. From our perspective as the joint experts, here are a few thoughts about the process:

1. We needed to have effective HR systems that gave employees a fair opportunity to achieve in the workplace. When we entered the organization, employees indicated the importance of being able to compete for jobs, to be mentored, and to have career development opportunities.

2. Accountability was critical to help the organization move forward. It was only by collecting data, both quantitative and qualitative, that the organization understood where they were in the process and what they needed to do next. Another part of the accountability system was having court-appointed joint experts and a task force that met regularly, worked with the company to achieve joint goals, and reported regularly on the progress. The value of the external task force cannot be overstated; both the independent perspective it afforded the company in "rethinking" its HR processes and the momentum for change it presented were instrumental in bringing about the level of significant and comprehensive change achieved by this project.

3. Despite everyone's best intentions, we all learned that there were events that took over and sometimes made progress difficult. A good example was a business decision that resulted in the elimination of 10% of the company's positions in the second year of our 5-year tenure. It is clear from all of our quantitative and qualitative data that this event had a very negative effect on what we were trying to accomplish. It took years to regain the momentum and reach a point at which goals were being accomplished.

4. Our final point in achieving these goals was all about leadership. Unless the executive leadership of the organization is really committed, nothing happens. Leadership on diversity, as with other key business decisions, requires foresight, tenacity, courage, and skill:

- Foresight to understand changing demographics and the link between the workplace and the marketplace
- Tenacity in executing a vision of diversity as a business imperative and in holding managers accountable and motivating them to act
- Courage to look at the data and to act accordingly
- Skill in communicating—and reinforcing—the importance of leading inclusively, acting consistently, and creating a culture of fairness

We believe that leaders who are willing to do this hard work will be best positioned to lead their organizations in a very demographically complex domestic and international world where competition will be an ongoing part of life. The leaders at Coca-Cola took this opportunity not only to meet the requirements of a court-approved settlement agreement but also to go beyond minimum compliance and to use this experience as an opportunity for learning. As a result, they have been recognized externally as one of the most successful companies in the area of diversity (Coca-Cola ranked number 4 on the 2007 *DiversityInc* Top 50 Companies for Diversity).

For us, after 5 years with Coca-Cola, we left with the feeling that the organization has a real commitment to "walking the talk." We also left with a real understanding of how difficult it is to achieve the goals of diversity as part of business. It was clear how much depended on the leadership of the organization.

We hope this case study is useful to others who might have the grand opportunity to spend 5 years working with an organization going through this type of change process.

Notes

1. *Ingram et al. v. The Coca-Cola Company* (Case No. 1-98-CV-3679 (RWS)), brought in the United States District Court for the Northern District of Georgia.
2. *Ingram et al v. The Coca-Cola Company*. From the transcript of May 29, 2001, Fairness Hearing at p. 214.

References

Allen, T. D., Eby, L. T., & Lentz, E. (2006). The relationship between formal mentoring program characteristics and perceived program effectiveness. *Personnel Psychology, 59,* 125–153.

Allen, T. D., Eby, L. T., Poteet, M. L., Lentz, E., & Lima, L. (2004). Career benefits associated with mentoring for proteges: A meta-analysis. *Journal of Applied Psychology, 89,* 127–136.

Brown, B. P., Zablah, A. R., & Bellenger, D. N. (2008). The role of mentoring in promoting organizational commitment among black managers: An evaluation of the indirect effects of racial similarity and shared racial perspectives. *Journal of Business Research, 61,* 732–738.

Coca-Cola Task Force. (2002). *First annual report of the Task Force to the United States District Court (Northern District of Georgia) in* Ingram et al. v. The Coca-Cola Company *(Case No. 1–98-CV-3679 (RWS)).* Retrieved from http://www.the coca-colacompany.com/ourcompany/taskforce_report.html

Coca-Cola Task Force. (2006). *Fifth annual report of the Task Force to the United States District Court (Northern District of Georgia) in* Ingram et al. v. The Coca-Cola Company *(Case No. 1–98-CV-3679 (RWS)).* Retrieved from http://www.the coca-colacompany.com/ourcompany/taskforce_report.html

Eby, L., Butts, M., Lockwood, A., & Simon, S. (2004). Proteges' negative mentoring experiences: Construct development and nomological validation. *Personnel Psychology, 57,* 411–447.

19

Conclusions

James L. Outtz

The origin of the concept of adverse impact can be traced to the mid-1960s (see Chapter 1). It was developed within the context of Title VII of the 1964 Civil Rights Act, which prohibits discrimination in employment. Indeed, adverse impact is the bedrock for myriad social, legal, and scientific debates that have evolved, and even seem to expand, from year to year.

The criticality of the concept of adverse impact stems from the fact that it is considered, from a legal and federal regulatory perspective, to be a sign of possible illegal discrimination by an organization. As Zedeck explained in Chapter 1, the significance of a finding of adverse impact is that, at a minimum, it triggers a legal obligation on the part of the organization to address it. This is not to say that organizations may not feel a moral/social imperative to address adverse impact regardless of any legal responsibilities (see Chapter 18).

The unlawful activity that is linked to adverse impact is the denial of a positive outcome, such as employment, promotion, or college admission, on the basis of a factor such as race rather than merit. Clearly, this connection places the concept of adverse impact within the realm of "social issues." Thus, industrial and organizational (I/O) psychologists have been forced, from the outset, to grapple with an issue that cannot properly be addressed solely via scientific study. This has proven to be somewhat vexing, if not outright frustrating, to I/O psychologists, as evident by the apparent overreliance on the four-fifths rule in the academic literature, despite the accepted scientific practice of relying on statistical inference in academic research. Bobko and Roth (Chapter 2) made the case that both the four-fifths rule and significance testing are appropriate methods of assessing adverse impact, with each having strengths and weaknesses in any given situation.

Why does adverse impact occur? The question of why adverse impact occurs is no doubt on the minds of all those who are affected by it, be they managers, admissions officers, judges, or psychologists. This question has been raised most with regard to subgroup differences on cognitive ability tests. Sackett and Shen (Chapter 12) showed that the problem extends far beyond the employment context, and they suspected that there is little evidence that the employment context contributes to the problem.

There has been surprisingly little written in I/O literature about why adverse impact occurs. The reason may be because no one has attempted to address adverse impact from a theoretical, rather than descriptive, perspective. Outtz and Newman (Chapter 3) attempted to fill this vacuum by suggesting a theoretical model from which to study adverse impact. It is interesting to note that several of the components of their model, such as socioeconomic status, cognitive exercise, early childhood care, educational opportunity, and exposure to test content, fit nicely with the data presented by Sackett and Shen (Chapter 12). It is certainly evident that the foundations of adverse impact, particularly with regard to cognitive ability tests, begin early in life, long before an applicant sits down to take an employment test or a student applies to college. It is also evident that there is little that I/O psychologists can do to correct historical differences in educational and economic opportunity. The problem for I/O psychology is not so much that subgroup differences exist on predictors such as cognitive ability tests. The problem is that the differences are much larger than differences in actual job performance (see, e.g., Chapter 5). This poses myriad challenges for practitioners, such as organizational consultants, who advise organizations on personnel selection issues (see Chapter 7).

Adverse Impact and Performance

Everything in selection focuses on performance. Employers seek to hire the best applicants, promote the best employees, or retain the best employees in times of downsizing. Colleges seek to admit the best students. The operative term, however, is *best*. Who are the best performers?

Murphy (Chapter 5) argued, quite correctly, that the way in which performance is defined significantly affects the validity coefficient produced by a given predictor. Unfortunately, this point seems to be lost in typical discussions of validation and the utility of selection procedures. In general, statements such as "such and such predictor has an average validity of x" do not make sense unless one identifies the aspect of job performance being predicted. We know most, for example, about the validity coefficients produced by cognitive ability tests. However, we also know that job performance is multidimensional; therefore, a cognitive ability test may be a better predictor for one aspect of performance (e.g., task performance) than another. Unless we can establish the relative importance of that aspect of performance to organization effectiveness, we cannot determine, with sufficient certainty, exactly how useful a predictor the test is or its relative importance among several predictors. Hattrup and Roberts (Chapter 6) noted that we have devoted very little research to finding out who, within an organization, is best qualified to establish the relative importance of various dimensions of job performance and the values that underlie such judgments.

Another significant problem, with regard to performance, is whether performance measures are themselves biased. Landy (Chapter 8) followed up on his initial examination of the literature on supervisors' ratings conducted over 30 years ago. He concluded that, with regard to race, (a) there are often significant differences between white and black mean ratings to the disadvantage of black ratees; (b) all things considered, the variance associated with race is small; and (c) there seems to be nothing fundamental in the performance evaluation process to suggest discriminatory stereotypes. He based this last conclusion in large part on his assessment that the proper research designs needed to determine the existence of bias (e.g., ratings of the same ratees by raters from different racial groups) are few and far between. Landy's conclusion that supervisor ratings tend to be lower for blacks than whites is, nevertheless, quite troubling.

If employers can expect to find that their performance appraisal systems have adverse impact, they will be required, under the *Uniform Guidelines on Employee Selection Procedures* (1978), to demonstrate that they are valid or attempt to reduce the adverse impact. Taking the position that they cannot determine whether the differences are real or due to rater bias will, standing alone, be of little consequence as a defense. Clearly, more research focused on within-subject designs is desperately needed. McKay (Chapter 9) revealed the enormous complexity of the problem by showing that there are several moderators of subgroup differences in performance, such that they appear, at this time, to be situation specific.

Reducing Adverse Impact

There have been significant advances in our understanding of strategies to reduce adverse impact. These strategies fall into two categories: adverse impact forecasting and design of alternatives. Sackett, De Corte, and Lievens (Chapter 17) described several aids that can be used to forecast the outcome of balancing various trade-offs in designing a selection process. This allows one at least to establish a range of outcomes associated with a selection system prior to implementing it. Aids such as these were not available a decade ago. Aguinis and Smith (Chapter 15) advanced the strategy of forecasting, arguing that test bias must be explicitly considered when attempting to balance the trade-off between diversity and work-force quality. This also is a novel approach that expands the boundaries of our thinking. The significance of this growing literature on forecasting, however, is that it advances and refines the definition of a "search for alternatives." To the extent that these alternative strategies are effective, they place greater responsibility on practitioners to be aware of them and to be able to demonstrate that they were considered in the design of a selection system. This is particularly true with regard to setting cut scores. Kehoe (Chapter 11) pointed out that cut scores are typically set on the basis of many considerations, not just adverse impact. In essence, this means balancing trade-offs. Therefore, making use of evolving methods of forecasting will become an indispensable tool in setting cut scores.

Regardless of the forecasted outcome of a selection system, adverse impact is ultimately determined by actual outcomes. Schmitt and Quinn (Chapter 16) provided an assessment of results that are possible based on data in the psychological literature. Their work, in essence, provides a barometer of our progress in developing alternatives that minimize adverse impact and maintain validity. They concluded that black–white subgroup differences can be reduced by 50% using a combination of strategies that includes:

- Removing biased items
- Including measures of alternative relevant constructs
- Altering the mode of presenting test stimuli in relevant ways
- Paying attention to the motivation of examiners
- Reducing or eliminating time limits

Schmitt and Quinn's conclusions were based on research conducted since the 1980s. Of this research, however, 80% was conducted since 1995. Clearly, much progress has been made in a short period of time. There remains much to be done. It will be interesting to see whether these conclusions hold up in countries outside the United States, such as those in the European Union (see Chapter 13) or in a country such as South Africa (see Chapter 14).

Reference

Uniform Guidelines on Employee Selection Procedures. (1978). 43 Fed. Reg. 38, 290–338, 315.

Author Index

Subject Index

A

AAP. *see* Affirmative action plans (AAP)

Academia
   achievement, 138
   literature, 17, 38, 42–43, 229–230
   performance, 138
   performance prediction, 125

Access-and-legitimacy perspective, 185

ACT. *see* American College Testing Program (ACT)

ADA. *see* Americans With Disabilities Act (ADA)

Adaptive behaviors in workplace environment, 169

Adaptive performance, 169–170

Adolescents, 125

Adults
   AFQT, 335
   cognitive tests, 326–327
   divergent thinking format, 82
   environmental effects on cognitive ability, 68
   norming, 342–343
   pro-diversity contexts, 259
   WAIS, 99, 326, 334

Adverse impact
   academic literature, 17, 42–43
   after-the-fact analysis, 453
   Aguinis and Smith approach, 467–468
   alternative models of presenting stimuli, 432–436
   alternative selection procedure investigation, 213
   applied psychology literature, 38
   assessing, 41–42
   average predictor scores, 296–297
   battery of tests, 214
   black selection rate, 7
   calculation, 203–208, 209, 211
   categorization, 78–80
   causes, 350
   changing cut scores, 409
   coaching, 441–443
   coaching programs, 442
   cognitive ability, 58–59
   cognitive subtests, 65
   cognitive tests, 55, 138
   cognitive test scores, 66
   communities, 140
   concepts, 405–407
   contextual performance, 147
   convergent thinking, 82
   courts, 15–17
   criteria definition, 161–187
   criterion domain, 139–143
   criterion performance, 459–468
   criterion space expansion, 148–150
   culture relationship, 361–366
   cutoff scores, 214
   cut scores, 289–321, 419
   cut scores impact, 294–299
   decision aids, 469
   definition, 3, 18, 24, 31, 137–158, 161, 201, 366
   detection approaches, 39–41
   determination, 7
   determination issues, 36
   divergent thinking, 82
   diverse multicultural contexts, 170
   diversity, 164, 167, 177, 182–183, 291
   diversity-validity dilemma, 161
   educational opportunity, 74–75
   elimination, 281
   employee performance, 403–421
   employee selection procedures, 201–222